Sharon D. Nelson ▪ Bruce A. Olson ▪ John W. Simek

# The
# Electronic
# Evidence and
# Discovery
# Handbook

## Forms, Checklists, and Guidelines

**ABA LawPracticeManagementSection**

MARKETING • MANAGEMENT • TECHNOLOGY • FINANCE

**Commitment to Quality:** The Law Practice Management Section is committed to quality in our publications. Our authors are experienced practitioners in their fields. Prior to publication, the contents of all our books are rigorously reviewed by experts to ensure the highest quality product and presentation. Because we are committed to serving our readers' needs, we welcome your feedback on how we can improve future editions of this book.

Cover design by Andrew Alcala, ABA Publishing.

### Library of Congress Cataloging-in-Publication Data

The Electronic Evidence and Discovery Handbook: Forms, Checklists, and Guidelines. Sharon D. Nelson, Bruce A. Olson, and John W. Simek. Library of Congress Cataloging-in-Publication Data is on file.

ISBN 1-59031-670-3

09 08 07 06   5 4 3

Discounts are available for books ordered in bulk. Special consideration is given to state bars, CLE programs, and other bar-related organizations. Inquire at Book Publishing, American Bar Association, 321 N. Clark Street, Chicago, Illinois 60610.

# Dedication

The authors dedicate this book, with love and gratitude, to their parents:

Gull and Shirley Nelson
Ed and Mickey Simek
Edwin and Lois Olson

Author Bruce Olson also dedicates this book, with love and gratitude, to his wife Eileen.

# Contents

# Acknowledgments

It takes a lot of help to develop a book like this one. The authors are grateful to their friends at CaseShare Systems, Inc., the Association of Records Managers and Administrators (ARMA), Jurinnov Ltd., Kroll OnTrack, Inc., Ken Withers of the Federal Judicial Center, Richard Braman of the Sedona Conference and the editors of www.discoveryresources.org for their contributions to this book. Thanks for sharing!

Also, we are grateful for the encouragement and hard work of the ABA's Law Practice Management (LPM) Publishing staff (Bev Loder, Neal Cox and Tim Johnson), the inspiration provided by the chair of the LPM Publications Board, Reid Trautz, and the enthusiasm and insights of our Project Director, Jeff Flax.

Thanks everyone!

# Introduction:
# Welcome to the Labyrinth

It was only six years ago that the three of us began lecturing on the subject of electronic evidence. At the time, Bruce Olson was one of the first lawyers in Wisconsin to teach the perils and pitfalls of electronic discovery (ED). John Simek and Sharon Nelson ran one of a handful of computer forensics/ED companies in the nation. When they warned audiences that *all* lawyers would have to become familiar with e-discovery over the next few years, they were greeted with cavalier disregard. A common remark was, "I don't think so—folks will pretty much go on practicing law the way they always have."

It was only three years ago that John and Sharon lectured to a group of Circuit Court judges in Southwestern Virginia. Although their hosts were uniformly gracious, they were also uniformly adamant about electronic evidence and courtroom technology. "Not in my courtroom!" several of them said firmly. Indeed, they chuckled at the very idea!

At the same time, Bruce was lecturing to a group of Circuit Court judges in eastern Wisconsin—and found a very similar response!

My, how times change.

Most federal court litigators have come to accept ED as a daily fact of life. Though the use of e-evidence has seeped more slowly into state courts, virtually all state litigators have now, however reluctantly, begun the process of educating themselves about electronic evidence.

Is it a labyrinth? Certainly. Can it be navigated? Sure, but cautiously, and step by step for novices. We hope that, by providing templates, this book will help lawyers get a handle on the e-discovery juggernaut as they stick a timid toe into the churning waters.

# The Fulbright Jaworski Study: ED Grows Up

The recent release of the second annual *2005 Litigation Trends Survey*, conducted by the international law firm Fulbright & Jaworski L.L.P., has made it eminently clear that electronic discovery has come of age. Some things haven't changed—to no one's surprise, we are an intensely litigious society.

The survey included 354 corporate counsel and chief executive officers (CEOs), 50 from the United Kingdom, the rest from the United States. These were not small businesses, to be sure. The median company reported annual gross revenues of $484 million. Still, it is startling to read that the average company in the survey juggles thirty-seven lawsuits at a time. For $1 billion-plus companies, that number grows to a staggering 147. Keep sending Jack and Jill to law school!

Here's the ED kicker: for corporations with more than $100 million in revenues, the greatest concern of the responding general counsels and CEOs was ED. For those under that mark, the greatest worry was compliance issues. If you think about it a moment, failure to comply will almost invariably involve electronic evidence in the ensuing compliance actions or litigation. Taken as a whole, ED has, in its own fashion, painted the town red—in this case, the color of panic.

What a departure from the good old days the study reveals. Eighty percent of the respondents now have document retention policies and 75 percent have litigation-hold policies. Nevertheless, the respondents worry about the quality of their policies, the enormous costs of electronic discovery and the sanctions that may accompany a failure to live up to statutory, regulatory, and case law requirements.

# What Does All This Mean to Smaller Companies and Their Law Firms?

The big boys felt the impact of ED while most lawyers slumbered on, practicing law without a thought to electronic evidence. Only a fool would suppose that ED will stay in the stratosphere with the large firms and their clients. Inevitably, ED will drift downward and seep into more and more small cases.

Sharon & John's current caseload of forensics/ED cases may be instructive. Currently, about a quarter of their cases are divorce cases. If you're surprised, think about how often people e-mail, instant message (IM), or text message their lovers. It's where the evidence is. Next time you see someone using two thumbs on a BlackBerry, you might justifiably wonder if they are telling a special someone what kind of new erotic treats they have planned for their next rendezvous. Trust them when they tell you that people will write *anything and everything* to their paramours. Their eyebrows are permanently singed from reading such missives.

Criminal cases comprise the next 25 percent. Child pornography cases account for a depressingly large chunk of that, followed by everything from stalking to embezzlement to murder. Business litigation constitutes about 25 percent—software that doesn't work as advertised, employees who are funneling company data elsewhere, competitors that have pilfered proprietary data, etc. The final 25 percent is a hodgepodge of everything from terrorist cases to defamation to people who have forged wills. Perhaps three or four of all these cases involve significant amounts of money. The rest are really the everyday cases that comprise the law practice of the solo and small firm practitioner—with one notable difference. ED is now a critical component. No doubt this is the tip of an immensely large iceberg. Sensei Enterprises is now seeing the beginning of seepage of ED into everyone's law practice.

Make no mistake about it. Most cases still go from A to Z without anyone thinking about e-evidence. But the times, they are a-changing.

## Fear Is a Great Motivator

Lawyers have not precisely embraced electronic evidence, but their trepidation about dealing with e-evidence has gradually abated. Their newfound willingness to deal with e-evidence seems to stem largely from fear—that they will be guilty of ineffective assistance of counsel if they ignore it, or that the other side will find a "smoking gun" unbeknownst to them. If you want to be a good lawyer, and serve your client well and competently, there is no longer any way to evade the fact that e-evidence is a factor in a growing number of cases. Mind you, the authors have heard stories from litigator friends of deals between opposing counsel in which both sides agree that they will not ask for electronic evidence. One has to wonder about the ethical implications of such deals when, often, that is where the evidence is to be found!

## More Statistics

Statistics, as they say, lie. They can be manipulated to prove anything, and often are. Nevertheless, no matter whose statistics you believe, all of the recent studies show that somewhere between 93 and 97 percent of all information is now created electronically. It is commonly accepted that less (some would say *much* less) than 3 percent of that information will ever be converted to paper. That being the case, what lawyer worth his or her salt can afford to ignore at least the possibility of electronic evidence being relevant every time a new case is opened?

According to the Radicati Group, we are now sending more than 35 billion e-mail messages daily in the United States. More than 80 percent of corporate communications are sent via e-mail. Worldwide, we are sending more than 141 billion e-mails and producing 1-2 exabytes of information per year. If you're scratching your head wondering what an exabyte is, it is equal to roughly a trillion books.

The *National Law Journal* reported in September 2005 on figures that keep counsel awake at night, drawn from a variety of sources, including Socha Consulting, MetalNCS, Microsoft, and the ABA Digital Evidence Project:

- $4.6 billion—the amount of money that U.S. companies spent internally in 2005 to analyze e-mails.
- More than 50 percent—the portion of evidence that is e-mail.
- 25-30 million—the number of outside e-mails that Microsoft receives daily.
- $1.2 billion—the amount that U.S. firms spent on outside e-discovery services in 2005, projected to be $1.9 billion for 2006.
- 62 percent—the percentage of companies that doubt they can show their e-records are reliable and accurate.
- 10 percent—the share of corporate lawyers reporting that they settled a case rather than incur the costs of e-discovery.
- 18 months—the sentence given to ex-banker Frank Quattrone for sending an e-mail telling Credit Suisse First Boston employees to "clean up" their files during a criminal inquiry of the bank. He is appealing the verdict.

According to a February 2005 survey by the ABA, more than 80 percent of Corporate Counsel members were not aware of or familiar with the proposed e-discovery related changes to the Federal Rules of Civil Procedure, expected to go into force in December of 2006. Ouch.

The American Management Association and the ePolicy Institute conducted a survey of 840 businesses in their 2004 Workplace E-mail and Instant Messaging Survey. They found that 21 percent of the business had had employee e-mail and IMs subpoenaed in the course of a lawsuit or regulatory investigation. Thirteen percent have had to contend with workplace lawsuits triggered by employee e-mail. Only 6 percent of the respondents retained and archived business IMs, and only 35 percent had an e-mail-retention policy in place. Although 79 percent had a written e-mail policy, only 20 percent had a policy governing IM use and content. Only 11 percent of the respondents employed IM gateway/management software to monitor, purge, retain, and otherwise control IM risks and use. And yet, 90 percent of the respondents said they were spending as many as 90 minutes per workday on IM. Ten percent of employees reported spending more than half the workday on e-mail. The average employee spent about a quarter of the workday on e-mail. What a change a decade has wrought!

## The States and the Feds

In case you thought you might get away with ignoring electronic evidence, federal and state governments have made sure you can't. Even if you and your clients are not subject to the Health Insurance Portability and Accountability Act (HIPAA), the Sarbanes-Oxley Act (SOX), or various other federal and states laws, federal and state agencies have been issuing regulations with respect to electronic data at a ferocious rate. There was a day when the authors lectured that there were more than 200 laws and regulations involving electronic data. These days, the authors wouldn't even hazard a guess as to how many laws and regulations there might be, though they wouldn't hesitate to say it now numbers in the thousands. Agencies such as the Federal Trade Commission and the Securities and Exchange Commission have been at the forefront of regulating electronic data—in the case of the SEC, even regulating the preservation of IMs under given circumstances.

## Your Client's Data Management

Although companies are far more likely to have a document retention policy (DRP) these days, not many of them have faith in their consistent enforcement. Often, they grow stale and inattentive to changes in the law or technology. Enforcement is frequently erratic at best. Hence, lawyers must worry about data that has been retained in spite of the corporate DRP. One extraordinary statistic is that 10 percent of employees will ignore compliance orders and fail to delete data. No doubt their intent is generally not malicious—they are overwhelmed with work at the moment, they think they may genuinely need the data one day—there are many possible reasons. The irrefutable fact, however, is that data that should have been destroyed under the policy is not. It may or may not come back to "bite you." Then there is every lawyer's nightmare—the backup media. In most organizations, backups are not cleansed of data that is removed from the active system. Therefore, for better or worse, the data survives to be unearthed during the discovery process.

Remember the statistics from the Fulbright Jaworski study—the part about 80 percent of the corporations having document retention policies and 75 percent having litigation-hold policies? If you represent smaller companies, you will find such numbers only wishful thinking. Although reliable data does not appear to currently exist, it is eminently clear to anyone working in the e-evidence arena that only a fraction of smaller companies have DRPs or litigation-hold policies. Many of them would not even recognize the terms. Much needs to be done in the way of education—this is where their lawyers can be very helpful.

## You Can Run, But You Can't Hide

Electronic discovery's rite of passage is ongoing. As the Fulbright Jaworski study makes clear, however, ED has arrived in force, striking first at the largest law firms and corporations.

Perhaps the best thing for solo and small firm practitioners to do is heed carefully the various disasters that have befallen their larger counterparts as they became the first to encounter the full breadth and depth of ED's impact. On a smaller scale, the very same thing is likely to happen to anyone not prepared for ED. You can wish it away, will it away, even pray it away, but ED is here to stay. Just look at all the ED companies that have sprung up faster than chickweed. Many of them fail rapidly in this volatile new market, but for each one that fails two seem to take its place.

We all wish that ED were more settled, that laws and regulations were more uniform, that case law wasn't all over the map, but ED is like an unruly toddler, just learning its full strength, wildly unpredictable, and leaving a trail of destruction in its wake.

## Electronic Evidence Forms: Forging a Trail

The very first thing you discover when you set out to compile a book of electronic evidence forms is that the forms in use today are extraordinarily erratic. There is precious little consistency. In the absence of long-standing traditions and readily available resources, lawyers are often flying by the seat of their pants and composing original forms of wildly varying quality and substance. Judges, most of them new themselves to the constructs of e-evidence, have not yet been much of a force in developing standards. A "Motion to Acquire and Analyze a Computer" may go by hundreds of different names and the contents may scarcely bear any resemblance to one another.

Because e-evidence is barely out of its infancy, the authors offer these forms with a great deal of humility, knowing that such forms must constantly be honed and updated in light of statutory and rule changes, as well as with experience and court decisions. Forms for e-evidence matters will continue to morph dramatically for some time, until all of us are veterans in this arena. In the meantime, we all need to start somewhere. Here, at least, is a beginning.

# Gathering the Evidence

*Even if you are on the right track,*
*you will get run over if you just sit there.*
—Will Rogers

**B**egin at the beginning. My goodness, that sounds simple. In real life, it isn't how it happens. The beginning of litigation tends to happen amid much sound, fury, and gnashing of teeth. Having a plan would be a good thing, right? Having information at hand with which to devise a plan also sounds like a practical thought, doesn't it?

For whatever reason, most of the cases that come our way tend to arrive in disarray. No one has figured out what electronic evidence may be in issue, where it might be located, and who might have custody and control of it. No one knows the first thing about the backup systems or computing infrastructure.

It doesn't matter whether you are plaintiff or defendant—it is important to know the size and nature of the elephant at the first possible moment. For one thing, if you are David fighting Goliath, you are going to need comprehensive information so that you stand a chance of winning with your slingshot. If you are David fighting another David, neither of you may have much money—and if the electronic evidence is massive, the arbitration table may look more and more appealing.

Without question, you must understand the server(s), for it is the brain of the operation. You can't grasp the nature of the mob until you know the boss. Not quite an Elliot Ness quote, but close. Remember that the workstations and laptops connected to the server are largely drones—it is the server that commands them and the server on which the vast majority of the data resides.

But don't be complacent. Most firms intend that data should indeed reside on their servers, but it doesn't always happen that way. Someone who is doing something "they shoudn't oughta be doing" is very likely to store what they are doing on their local hard disk or on removable media of some kind. Local hard drives are frequently a gold mine of information overlooked while everyone chases down the server data. Likewise, folks forget about those thumb drives, CD-ROMs, and disks. Remember, data on servers is generally purged on a regular basis—much detritus remains behind, though, in other places.

Think outside the box. The company's data is unlikely to be entirely within the company's infrastructure. Who among us does not take work home? So what's on the home machine—or the loose media there? Does the company use an online or third party backup system? Are archived tapes stored off-site? Do affiliate companies have data? Do branch offices have relevant information? The prudent lawyer will follow the ones and zeroes to all of their possible destinations.

The forms in this section are only guideposts. Every situation differs. Sometimes, you may simply care about a single workstation or laptop—in other cases, a massive number of servers may be involved. Because there must be a starting point, consider the preliminary questions for your client, so you'll have some sense of what is involved overall. Narrow the scope as best you can, following our checklists. The desktop and server information forms will allow you to build a file that's easy to refer to. You're going to need to contact key information technology personnel—better to have that information easily at hand as soon as possible.

It is imperative to pay attention to chain of custody, a remarkably simple step that is often ignored. Mind you, we have yet to see—though maybe it's happened—a case which falls by the wayside because of faulty chain of custody involving electronic evidence. The judicial mantra is "I'm letting it in anyway, and you can argue its weight." But clearly, sloppy procedure is a risk, and it's all too simple to keep the procedure intact by executing point to point chain of custody forms. And yes, you can FedEx evidence and use the tracking numbers to maintain chain of custody!

In the best of all possible worlds, you and your opponent will get together early in the case and establish an electronic evidence protocol. In the real world, this document will emerge only after major and minor skirmishes in court and frequently only when an irate judge has told both sides to come up with a protocol. The new Federal Rules of Civil Procedure (see chapter 4) may alleviate that problem in federal courts, but the fracas in the state courts is likely to continue until the states adopt similar procedures ensuring that e-evidence is taken into consideration early on. No matter when you construct your protocol, the checklist in this chapter will help you ensure that you do not overlook something that may come back to bite you later.

# Form 1.1
## General Preliminary Electronic Evidence Questions for Your Client

1. Provide detailed description of computer systems used by the company, including hardware systems, primary operating systems, and major software systems, including any customized software.
2. Provide a detailed description of how those computers are networked or connected to others outside of the company (with a graphical representation if one is available).
3. Provide a detailed description of how your employees can network with your computers from outside of the company.
4. Provide a detailed description of the computer systems used by your employees outside of the corporate system (e.g., from home desktops or laptops, personal digital assistants [PDAs]).
5. Provide a detailed description of the backup processes and schedules, document retention and destruction schedules, organized by type of data. Identify the responsible persons for each process, with contact data. Identify storage locations for all backup data.
6. Provide the company's document retention policy, e-mail, and Internet-usage policies and litigation-hold policy, to the extent they exist.
7. Describe any monitoring or logging of employees' computer usage.
8. If any third parties hold or have access to the company's data, identify those third parties with full contact information.

## Form 1.2
## Checklist to Define the Scope of Electronic Discovery

To facilitate the collection, analysis, and preservation of electronic evidence (and to keep costs down), the following elements should be identified:

- The architecture and elements of the technology infrastructure, including, but not limited to, the amount and types of computers, operating systems, and software applications, including customized applications, with graphical representations if available.
- The topology of the network environment, including, but not limited to, the physical placement of computers and their connectivity within the intranet and Internet, with graphical representations if available.
- The architecture of the electronic mail system, including, but not limited to, server and workstation software and version, lists of users, and location of e-mail files.
- Enterprise user information applications, including, but not limited to, contact lists, calendars, to-do lists, word processing, project management, and accounting.
- Internal and external personnel responsible for the management and maintenance of the technology infrastructure and all of its components, with contact information.
- Information about any business activity of employees that is not backed up by the company, including the use of home machines, laptops, PDAs, etc.
- The names of all key players in any actual or potential lawsuit or investigation.
- The names, addresses, and contact info for any third party that holds or has access to company data.
- Backup policies and procedures, including, but not limited to, hardware and software used to back up and archive information, documentation of what data is backed up, backup schedules, and locations of all backup media devices.
- Computer-use policies and procedures, including, but not limited to, employee guidelines, password use, system logging, security controls, data retention, litigation holds, information sharing, and acceptable Internet and electronic message usage.
- The location and contents of any relevant system and event logs.

## Form 1.3
## Checklist for Electronic Media Device Evaluations

Although the exact methodology for the evaluation and analysis of electronic media devices is sophisticated, this general checklist conveys the major components in the identification, isolation, evaluation, and preservation of electronic evidence in a standardized way that will be admissible in court.

- ◆ Record each media device with a unique identifying number.
- ◆ Write protect each media device.
- ◆ Forensically duplicate each media device to create a true mirror image (note that this does *not* mean copying or "Ghosting").[1]
- ◆ Mathematically verify and validate that the mirror image is identical to the original by using hashing algorithms (MD5, SHA1, SHA2).
- ◆ Scan media devices for viruses and spyware—document the results.
- ◆ Produce directory structure for each media device.
- ◆ Analyze the electronic media and extract relevant information.
- ◆ Secure each media device.

---

[1] Norton Ghost is a software application by Symantec.

## Form 1.4
## Checklist of Sources for Electronic Evidence

Electronic evidence may reside in numerous different locations throughout an organization's technology infrastructure, so it is important to ensure that all possibly relevant sources for electronic information are identified. The following is a sample list of common sources for electronic evidence:

### *Electronic Information*

- ◆ Servers
- ◆ Mainframes
- ◆ Network file systems
- ◆ Workstations
- ◆ Laptop computers
- ◆ Personal digital assistants (PDAs)
- ◆ Personal home computers
- ◆ Private branch exchange (PBX)[1]
- ◆ Voice mail
- ◆ Digital printers or copiers
- ◆ Cell phones

### *Backup Media*

- ◆ Monthly systemwide backups
- ◆ Weekly systemwide backups
- ◆ Incremental systemwide backups
- ◆ Unscheduled backups
- ◆ Personal backups

### *Additional Media Devices*

- ◆ CD-ROMs
- ◆ DVDs
- ◆ Floppy diskettes
- ◆ Zip disks
- ◆ Tape archives
- ◆ Removable hard drives
- ◆ Thumb drives[2]
- ◆ Digital camera media

---

[1] Company telephone systems are typically called PBXs.

[2] Also known as Flash Memory, USB Memory Stick, Jump Drive, etc.

**Form 1.5**
**Desktop Information Form**

*Sensei Enterprises, Inc.*

## Computer Forensics Lab

3975 *University Drive*
*Suite 225*
*Fairfax, Virginia 22030*
*703-359-0700—phone*
*703-359-8434—fax*

**Desktop Information Form**

Date _____

Sensei Case Number _____

Case Client Name _____

<u>Computer User</u>

Name        _____

Address     _____

City         _____   State _____   Zip _____

Phone       _____

E-Mail       _____

User Name   _____

Password    _____

              _____

<u>Computer Description</u>

Manufacturer: _____

Model: _____

Serial Number: _____

Location: _____

❑ 3-$1/_2$" Floppy

❑ 5-$1/_4$" Floppy

❑ 100 MB Zip

- ❏ 250 MB Zip
- ❏ CD-ROM
- ❏ CD/RW
- ❏ DVD
- ❏ Modem _____
- ❏ Firewire _____
- ❏ USB _____
- ❏ Sound _____
- ❏ NIC _____
- ❏ Tape Unit _____
- ❏ SCSI _____

❏ Hard Disk        Evidence Number _____

- ■ Mfg: _____
- ■ Model: _____
- ■ S/N _____
- ■ Size: _____
- ■ Interface: _____

❏ Hard Disk        Evidence Number _____

- ■ Mfg: _____
- ■ Model: _____
- ■ S/N _____
- ■ Size: _____
- ■ Interface: _____

BIOS Information

Access Method: _____

BIOS Date/Time: _____     Actual Date/Time: _____

Boot sequence: _____

Hard Disk 1 Geometry: _____

Hard Disk 2 Geometry: _____

Hard Disk 3 Geometry: _____

Hard Disk 4 Geometry: _____

Power Saving Features: _____

Comments:

_____

_____

_____

_____

_____

_____

**Form 1.6**
**Server Information Form**

*3975 University Drive*
*Suite 225*
*Fairfax, Virginia 22030*
*703-359-0700—phone*
*703-359-8434—fax*

## Computer Forensics Lab

**Server Information Form**

Date _____

Sensei Case Number _____

Case Client Name _____

<u>On-Site Contact</u>

Name _____

Address _____

City _____ State _____ Zip _____

Phone _____

E-Mail _____

Administrator ID _____

Password _____

_____

<u>Server Description</u>

Manufacturer: _____

Model: _____

Serial Number: _____

Application: _____

Location: _____

❏ 3-$\frac{1}{2}$" Floppy

❏ 100 MB Zip

❑ 250 MB Zip

❑ CD-ROM

❑ CD/RW

❑ DVD

❑ Modem  _____

❑ Firewire  _____

❑ USB  _____

❑ Sound  _____

❑ NIC  _____

❑ Tape Unit  _____

❑ SCSI  _____

  ❑ Hard Disks

  ■ Number:  _____

  ■ RAID Level:  _____

  ■ Stripe Size:  _____

  ■ Size:  _____

  ■ Interface:  _____

  ■ Containers:  _____

  ❑ Hard Disks

  ■ Number:  _____

  ■ RAID Level:  _____

  ■ Stripe Size:  _____

  ■ Size:  _____

  ■ Interface:  _____

  ■ Containers:  _____

<u>OS Configuration</u>

Operating System Version and Service Pack  _____

Domain Name  _____

Machine Name  _____

E-Mail Version and Service Pack _____

Site Name _____

Organization Name _____

Backup Software Manufacture and Version _____


BIOS Information

Access Method: _____


BIOS Date/Time: _____    Actual Date/Time: _____

Boot sequence: _____


Comments:

_____

_____

_____

_____

_____

_____

## Form 1.7
## Identification of Key IT Personnel

| Title | Name and Department | Phone and e-mail |
|---|---|---|
| Chief Information Officer | | |
| IT Manager | | |
| E-mail | | |
| Network | | |
| Desktop/Server | | |
| Applications/ Database Manager | | |
| Information Security | | |
| Records Management | | |
| Help Desk | | |
| Telecom | | |
| | | |
| | | |

## Form 1.8
## Evidence Custody Form

**Computer Forensics Lab**

*3975 University Drive*
*Suite 225*
*Fairfax, Virginia 22030*
*703-359-0700—phone*
*703-359-8434—fax*

### Evidence Custody Form

Case No.: _____ Date: _____ Time: _____

Evidence received by:

Name: _____ Firm: _____

Phone (w): _____ Phone (cell) _____

Address: _____

_____

Signature: _____

Evidence received from:

Name: _____ Firm: _____

Phone (w): _____ Phone (cell) _____

Address: _____

_____

Signature: _____

Evidence received: Computers

1.) Manufacturer: _____     Model: _____

    Serial No.: _____

2.) Manufacturer: _____     Model: _____

    Serial No.: _____

Other evidence received:

Description/Serial #/Notes:

## Form 1.9
## Electronic Database Management Checklist

Case Name:

Case Number:

Attorney:

Office:

File:


Date Assigned

Date Completed

Assigned to:


Original Data Source:

_____ E-mail only

_____ E-mail and files

_____ Files only

_____ Nonstandard data _____

_____ Other _____


Formatting Details:

Excel Options

Reformat Excel: _____ (yes) _____ (no)


Automated Options:

_____ Replace auto codes

_____ Row and column headings

_____ Force gridlines

_____ Black and white (remove colors)

_____ Unhide rows, columns and sheets

_____ Print comments

_____ Clear workbook print area

_____ Scale all documents to ____%

_____ Remove blank rows and columns

Manual Options:

\_\_\_\_\_ Include data outside set print area

\_\_\_\_\_ Autofit (remove spaces)

\_\_\_\_\_ Rolling titles

\_\_\_\_\_ Remove filters

\_\_\_\_\_ Other: _____

\_\_\_\_\_ Use Excel text extraction tool

Word Options:

\_\_\_\_\_ Replace auto codes

\_\_\_\_\_ Print comments

\_\_\_\_\_ Print hidden text

\_\_\_\_\_ Print revisions (track changes)

\_\_\_\_\_ Print drawing objects

Deliverables:

\_\_\_\_\_ TIFFs \_\_\_\_\_ Single page \_\_\_\_\_ Multipage

\_\_\_\_\_ PDFs

\_\_\_\_\_ Paper copies

\_\_\_\_\_ Other: _____

Objective Database Fields to Code:

\_\_\_\_\_ Date created

\_\_\_\_\_ Date saved

\_\_\_\_\_ Author

\_\_\_\_\_ Application

\_\_\_\_\_ File name(full path)

\_\_\_\_\_ Full text @ OCR

\_\_\_\_\_ Full text @ fielded

\_\_\_\_\_ Other: _____

Subjective Database Fields to Code:

\_\_\_\_\_ Identify _____

Load Files:

    \_\_\_\_\_ Summation

    \_\_\_\_\_ iConnect

    \_\_\_\_\_ CaseMap

    \_\_\_\_\_ Concordance/opticon

    \_\_\_\_\_ Other: _____

On-Line Review and Export:

    \_\_\_\_\_ Identify format of data being sent (i.e., backup tapes, copied data):

    \_\_\_\_\_ Estimate quantity of data being sent:

    \_\_\_\_\_ Identify filter or date restrictions to be applied prior to review:

    \_\_\_\_\_ Establish de-duplicating criteria:

    \_\_\_\_\_ Identify output format:

    \_\_\_\_\_ Identify who will be receiving data and in what format:

## Form 1.10
## Guidelines for an Electronic Evidence Protocol

- **Names, addresses, phone numbers and e-mail addresses of parties.** After all of this information is stated, make sure it is clear how the parties are to communicate with one another under the protocol.
- **Who is to perform the forensic acquisition?** (Note: from a cost and efficiency standpoint, it is clearly better to have one forensic technologist.) Will both sides have their own experts? If not, is the forensic technologist forbidden to have ex parte communications?
- **Confidentiality Agreement:** Designate and attach a confidentiality agreement to be signed by anyone who is to have substantive access to the data—the forensic technologist, the electronic discovery vendor, the Internet-hosting company, etc. Make sure it is made clear that the disclosure of confidential data has no adequate remedy at law in case a temporary restraining order or preliminary injunction may be in order.
- **Acquisitions schedule:** Make sure the time period is reasonable and allow for an extension if unexpected problems develop. Have the computers or media delivered to the expert's lab for acquisition where possible—this will be more efficient and reduce costs. In a lab setting, the expert can set up the case, kick off the acquisition(s) and go do other billable work while the acquisition(s) proceed. In the event there is some sort of complication, the expert has all his or her hardware, software, and reference materials close at hand to solve the problem.
- **On-site acquisitions:** Sometimes, the acquisition will have to be done on site, either to minimize business impact or because the other side will not agree to any other kind of acquisition. This can be economically painful because the expert must "babysit" the acquisition irrespective of time consumed. As an example, it may take twelve to thirty-six hours to acquire a single server. It is possible to run multiple acquisitions simultaneously, which will help cut costs, but often the scenario is that it is only a single server that needs to be acquired. Clients tend to be very impatient with the costs of on-site acquisition, but it simply takes as long as it takes—there is no acceleration process. Be sure to specify if the work is to be done after hours or on weekends, extending the time period for acquisition as needed to accommodate the slower pace. Overtime (after hours and weekends) hours also increase the cost.

From the point of view of security, here are a couple of tips: the best time to acquire a server is often on Saturday morning. That way, a full backup can be run on Friday night. On the off chance that anything may go amiss with the acquisition, restoration of your data is complete. Also, of course, businesses tend to be closed (or at least slower) on a weekend, and acquisitions can be completed quickly and efficiently in a quiet environment. Finally, if Saturday presents an unexpected challenge, the technologist has Sunday to rebound.

◆ **Full backup prior to acquisitions:** This an all-important point, in case (and yes, it has happened) the forensic technologist makes some sort of blunder (unlikely, but possible) or the drive magically decides to fail for no reason at the same time as the acquisition (improbable, but it has happened). You must make absolutely sure that whatever is being acquired has been fully backed up. Recriminations and finger pointing will not bring your data back.

◆ **Scope of acquisition:** It is imperative to define the scope of the acquisition. Each workstation or server to be acquired should be specifically identified. Likewise, if backup media are to be restored, generally a more time-consuming and costly process, identify which media are in issue. Likewise, if there are digital cameras, digital printers, PDAs, or other peripherals to be acquired, enumerate them. If the case involves loose media (CD-ROMS, DVDs, floppy disks, Zip disks, Flash drives, etc.), they too must be specified. Sometimes, the parties can agree to acquire certain obvious workstations and/or servers and then determine whether any further forensic acquisition and analysis are required after evaluating the results from the initial acquisition and analysis.

◆ **Security consideration:** Each device must be separately considered with respect to the data it holds so that the law firm considers what proprietary or confidential information may be present that must be protected. This can be particularly distressing when the target to be acquired is an employee's home computer or even a workstation at the office when the law firm may have no idea what is on them. Without meaning to engage in spoliation, many folks who are the target of an imaging request inadvertently stomp all over the evidence, changing access dates and similar information because they want to find out what is there and how much trouble they may be in.

◆ **Previews of the Evidence:** If the parties do not agree to a full-scale acquisition, they can sometimes agree to a preview of the evidence. In fact, courts seem increasingly amenable to previews in cases where one side adamantly insists there is no relevant evidence on their computers. What is a forensic preview? A preview allows you to look at the evidence in a "read-only" mode without the need to acquire it. The expert can generate a report of this examination, but it is not repeatable because it represents a "point in time" and there is no frozen image of the data. The best part of previews, from the point of view of many clients, is that it limits access to the data. If the preview shows no relevant evidence, the remainder of the data will never be seen by the other side. Previews can be a throw of the dice—if you're lucky, it will work out to your advantage. If not, the court is much more likely to order full-blown acquisition and analysis.

- **Software/hardware to be used in acquisition/analysis:** Commonly, private experts will use FastBloc (hardware write blocker) and EnCase (forensic software), which have more than 12,000 licensed users and have been successfully admitted into evidence in thousands of criminal and civil court cases. There are no known instances of sustained objections to EnCase-based computer evidence on authentication grounds relating to the program itself. Be mindful, however, that any program is only as good as the expert who is using it, and the expert may be subject to attack for a lack of expertise. Although the acquisitions of any subject media will generally be done using FastBloc write-blocking hardware and EnCase software, there are other forensically sound methods that could be employed in unusual situations and may be referenced in the protocol. The acquisitions will result in a complete bit-by-bit image of the media. Analysis will be done on the imaged evidence—the original media will not be affected in any way. EnCase acquires the data and saves it into a proprietary evidence format, which is constantly hashed and verified for errors and compared against the original at the conclusion of the acquisition to verify that an exact forensic bit-by-bit image has been obtained.

- **Data security and chain of custody:** Once the evidence is acquired, the protocol should state that the evidence will be kept under lock and key in a secure environment, specifying those who will have access to the evidence. The degree of care to be followed varies somewhat by the case. Where a law firm's data may be involved, you want to make very sure that it is in reputable hands and that careful security procedures will be followed. Of course, chain of custody should be maintained in writing throughout the course of the acquisition and analysis.

- **Forensic report:** In general, the protocol will state that all work on the imaged drive will be documented and included within a forensic report. The protocol may also state specific items that are to be included within the report.

- ◆ **Scope of analysis:** To target relevant evidence narrowly, both sides may agree upon a period of time that is in issue, a list of names or e-mail addresses to search for, or other keywords designed to produce the relevant evidence. Make sure the protocol gives a time limit for both sides to agree upon the search parameters, a time at which the expert is required to turn over the evidence for screening, and a time at which the screening party must produce the evidence to other side. The search criteria must be relevant, must not cross the line into a fishing expedition, and must be as narrow as possible. The burden on the producing party must be reasonable.

- ◆ **Timeline for analysis:** Analysis timelines must also be established. Beware, though, because no expert will be able to precisely predict the amount of time needed for analysis before he or she has seen the "size of the elephant," and that will not happen until analysis has begun. It is a good idea to include a clause that indicates that the timetable will be adjusted as agreed by the parties if the volume of evidence so requires.

- ◆ **Screening for privilege:** Once the expert has completed the analysis, the protocol will generally provide that documents and data will be extracted and forwarded to defendant's counsel, who will review them for privilege and proprietary information prior to producing all non-privileged documents to opposing counsel. As part of that process, the party creates a privilege log identifying the documents that will not be turned over and the privilege claimed. Any data or documents that are claimed to be privileged will be available to the judge for an *in camera* inspection upon the appropriate motion by the moving party. The protocol will provide that all data and documents the judge deems are not confidential or privileged are to be released to opposing counsel, pending the resolution of any and all objections and/or motions from parties. If there is proprietary information that needs protection, a protective order may be issued, or other measures taken by the court to ensure that certain data is locked down during the litigation process.

- ◆ **Agreement to seek protective order or to seal certain documents or the entire case:** This is the moment, if the parties can agree, to jointly commit to the protection of proprietary or confidential information.

- ◆ **Costs:** Typically, the electronic evidence protocol will address the issue of costs. The normal rule of thumb is that the producing party must bear the costs of evidence production. It is sometimes smarter, however, for the other side to pick up the costs, especially where it is fairly certain that damning evidence exists. If the proposed discovery is not overbroad and designed to unearth relevant evidence with a minimum of business impact, a judge is not likely to look with favor upon the other side's claims of hardship where the party requesting discovery agrees to pick up the expenses. If money is a major issue, it may not be feasible to offer to assume expenses. In accordance with the *Zubulake v. UBS Warburg* line of cases, though, it may be possible to achieve cost shifting depending upon the following (in order of priority):

- The extent to which the request is tailored to discover relevant information:
  - Whether the information is available from other sources;
  - The cost of production compared to the amount in controversy;
  - The cost of production compared to each party's resources;
  - The ability and incentive of each party to control costs;
  - The importance of the issues at stake; and
  - The relative benefits to the parties of obtaining the information requested.

- **What happens to the data when the case ends?** From a security standpoint, the protocol may also provide that, at the conclusion of the case, the expert will destroy the evidence files upon receipt of written, signed instructions from the parties. Alternatively, the protocol may decree that the evidence is to be returned to the originating party. Frequently, any order entered with the court will require that the expert, at the conclusion of the case, submit an affidavit to the court certifying that the court's orders have been complied with.

# Form 1.11
# Nonwaiver of Privilege Agreement[1]

The parties hereto, _____ and _____, are engaged in the production and exchange of documents, including electronic data, pursuant to various discovery requests propounded by each party. Both parties acknowledge that, while each party is making effort to identify and withhold from production any document which that party believes is privileged, given the volume and nature of material being exchanged, there is a possibility that certain privileged material may be produced inadvertently. Accordingly, the parties have agreed to the following nonwaiver agreement. A party who produces any privileged document without intending to waive the claim of privilege associated with such document may, within ten days after the producing party actually discovers that such inadvertent production occurred, amend its discovery response and notify the other party that such document was inadvertently produced and should have been withheld as privileged. Once the producing party provides such notice to the requesting party, the requesting party must promptly return the specified document and any copies thereof. By complying with this obligation, the requesting party does not waive any right it has to challenge the assertion of privilege and request on order of the court denying such privilege.

_____

[DATE]

_____

[SIGNATURE]

_____

[SIGNATURE]

---

[1] The essence of this form is part of the Amendments to the Federal Rules of Civil Procedure, expected to become effective in December 2006.

# *Third-Party Experts* 2

*There is nothing as deceptive as an obvious fact.*
—Arthur Conan Doyle's Sherlock Holmes

**M**ost of us tend to believe what our eyes see. If we read it in a well-respected newspaper, it's truth. If we hear Katie Couric tell us a story, we believe her. If we see electronic evidence (e.g., an e-mail), we tend to think it's real. Maybe, but maybe not.

Sometimes, altered and fabricated evidence is as obvious as a tarantula on a bowl of butterscotch pudding. Other times, it is as subtle as a blond hair in a very large haystack. So how good is your computer forensic technologist?

The way electronic evidence acquisition often works is this: It drizzles, then it rains, then you're in the middle of monsoon season. Drowning may seem inevitable. So how good is your e-discovery expert and your data-hosting expert? Can they keep your head above water?

You're a very good lawyer, right? Maybe you even know something about technology, at least enough to be dangerous. But let's face it, most lawyers know very little about technology, and even those who are technically adept are adrift at sea when the fog of complicated and/or voluminous e-evidence rolls in.

Enter the third-party experts. They all have a role to play, and sometimes the roles will overlap, but they are essential for the proper and efficient handling of electronic evidence. The overlapping roles make for confusion, but here are the essential distinctions.

The forensics technologist is a scientist—someone highly skilled in technology generally, and hopefully, someone with a distinguished certification in forensic technology. Beware the folks who have simply taken a course and now proclaim themselves "certified." Today, the most respected certifications in the private sector are the EnCE (EnCase Certified Examiner) and CIFI (Certified Information Forensics Investigator), but undoubtedly more will follow in time. The law enforcement technologists have their own certifications, unavailable to the private sector.

If your computer forensic technologist is to be a testifying or consulting expert, pay close attention to his or her CV—the sample CV included in this chapter will give you a good idea of what you're looking for.

More often than you might imagine, the winning difference in cases involving electronic evidence is the skill level of the computer forensic expert. Whose expert will the jury or judge find more credible? Scarcer than rubies are talented computer forensics experts who are also skilled at writing expert reports and giving court testimony. So how do you find a good expert when you have electronic evidence in issue? This can be a daunting task, and the right selection may depend upon a number of factors, including what's at issue in the case, the budget, the geographic location of the expert, and balancing the relative credentials of the experts under consideration.

The electronic evidence expert generally helps to manage the evidence after it has been acquired and extracted by the forensic technologist. This expert will make sure the data is in a format in which you can review the evidence and will assist you in making all decisions relating to e-evidence management.

The data-hosting company will set up a "case vault" online, containing all the documents and electronic evidence in the case. Among some of the concerns here are:

1. How quickly are documents placed online?
2. How is security provisioned?
3. What kind of technical support is offered?
4. What is the response time if there are problems?
5. How is the cost determined, and how can it be allocated among multiple parties?
6. What kind of audit trail is maintained?

Before your headache reaches epidemic proportions, carefully review the checklists and guidelines in this chapter, which are specialized to help you select the best possible forensic technologist, electronic evidence company, and data-hosting firm. Remember that some of the largest firms may do all three—but, then again, the price tag may be very high and the quality of service may vary among the three functions.

Identify your primary needs: Are you going to need a testifying witness? Are computer forensics likely to be an issue? Is your major problem simply managing the sheer volume of data? Do you need to get the data converted into a format that can be imported into Concordance or Summation? Are you going to be working with lawyers around the country, all of whom will need access to case documents and electronic evidence?

For many of you, your customary cases are small. You really want a small computer forensics firm that can extract the relevant evidence for you. You will do your own review of the evidence and won't be working with other lawyers. In cases like this, your bill for your third-party expert may well be no more than $5,000–$10,000.

At the other end of the spectrum, if you are working on a multimillion-dollar case with several firms involved and terabytes of data, you probably want one of the largest e-evidence companies, which at the very least can handle all of the computer forensics and management of the electronic evidence. Some will also have data-hosting capacity—if they don't, they will undoubtedly be able to refer you to a good data-hosting firm. Remember that security of your data must be a paramount concern—if you are going to take your evidence and place it on the Internet, you certainly want to assure yourself that it will remain confidential! If you are playing in the stratosphere, you already know that the price tag will be steep, often hundreds of thousands of dollars.

After reviewing the checklists and guidelines in this chapter, look at the sample contracts to get an idea of how contracts may differ from specialist to specialist. No matter what kind of third-party expert you need, make sure that there is a confidentiality agreement in place. A sample is included in this chapter.

Selecting the appropriate experts to work with is one of the most critical decisions you will make as you embark upon an e-evidence case. One of the most common errors in litigation is choosing such experts poorly. With thought and care, this most important decision can reap great rewards, including victory with the able assistance of those skilled in the provision of expert services related to electronic evidence.

# E-Discovery Vendors

## Form 2.1
## Electronic Discovery Vendor Checklist

SCOPE-OF-WORK ASSUMPTIONS

Define Tasks: _____

For example, vendor will review e-mail data and user files received from law firm, which will be received, indexed and, hosted by vendor using (identify hosting provider and software). Vendor will receive hard drive containing e-mail data in the form of user .PST and user files. Vendor will restore data from hard drive, remove duplicates, and host resultant message sets for review using hosting provider/software such that no special software is needed by the client.

Define Timelines: _____

    Define Data Types and Volume of Data:

       ❑ Data is from _____ custodians, each with _____ megabytes of data

       ❑ Estimate of total data size to be processed _____

       ❑ Estimate of _____ items/pages per gigabyte

       ❑ Estimate total items processed _____

Define Pricing: _____

       ❑ State task-based and/or time-based price for specified work

    Note all extra charges:

       ❑ Recovery of data from defective media or corrupt data files

       ❑ Breaking passwords or access control

       ❑ Translating or migrating data

       ❑ Developing customized hardware or software environments to restore or read data

       ❑ Processing of foreign-language information.

Confirm price based on work with standard office suite files (word processing, spreadsheet, presentation, in Corel or Microsoft formats, or plain text format; not compressed, encoded or encrypted). Identify any additional charges for processing nonstandard formats.

Define Responsibilities Of Vendor:

- ❏ Project management
- ❏ Expert consulting
- ❏ Receipt of and data restoration
- ❏ Data analysis and reporting
- ❏ E-mail processing
- ❏ Provisioning of hosting software
- ❏ Loading data to hosting software
- ❏ Hosting data
- ❏ Data production in Summation or Concordance format
- ❏ Software training
- ❏ End-user support
- ❏ Extraction of compressed files and association with parent files
- ❏ Virus scanning of all files
- ❏ Identification of nonsearchable files
- ❏ De-duplication
- ❏ Data integrity checking
- ❏ Indexing of data
- ❏ Creation and configuration of database
- ❏ Allocation of storage space
- ❏ Creation of user IDs and passwords,
- ❏ Establish connectivity and remote workstations
- ❏ Configure software at attorney-specified locations
- ❏ Logging of data access
- ❏ Data conversion from native format

**Form 2.2**
**Electronic Discovery Vendor Contract**

This Agreement is made by and between AAA Enterprises, Inc., an independent contractor (hereafter "AAA"), whose address is _____, and _____ (hereafter "CLIENT"), whose address is _____.

SCOPE OF WORK AND COSTS. AAA agrees to perform such electronic evidence management and analysis services as may be requested by CLIENT in conformity with the attached Statement of Work (SOW)[1] for the costs stated therein and payment of all reasonable documented out-of-pocket costs incurred, including travel costs. Travel time is billed at the rate of $_____ per hour from the point of leaving AAA's office until the point of return. Payment is due within 30 days of monthly invoicing. An interest charge of 1.5% monthly ($_____ minimum) shall be applied to all unpaid balances. A $ _____ nonrefundable deposit is required upon execution of this contract. Services will be billed against this deposit in accordance with the SOW.

ASSUMPTIONS. AAA has agreed upon the costs stated in the SOW based upon assumptions provided by CLIENT and set forth in the SOW. In the event that these assumptions should be changed and the costs therefore increased, AAA will provide written notice to CLIENT prior to incurring such additional costs.

THIRD-PARTY SERVICES. CLIENT shall be responsible for payment of all costs incurred for all third-party services necessary to the fulfillment of this Agreement. AAA agrees to notify CLIENT in advance if such services are reasonably necessary to fulfill its obligations under this contract.

CONFIDENTIALITY. To the extent that AAA is granted access to trade secrets or other confidential information and materials of CLIENT, AAA agrees to hold such secrets, information and materials in confidence. To the extent that CLIENT is granted access to trade secrets or other confidential information and materials of AAA, CLIENT agrees to hold such secrets, information, and materials in confidence.

MODIFICATION OF AGREEMENT. No modification or waiver of any of the terms of this Agreement shall be valid unless in writing and signed by all parties.

_____

[1] Use form 2.1 to develop your SOW.

GOVERNING LAW. This Agreement shall be construed and interpreted in accordance with the laws of _____.

INVALIDITY OF PROVISIONS. If any of the provisions of this Agreement are held by a court of competent jurisdiction to be invalid or unenforceable, all other provisions shall nonetheless continue in full force and effect.

SUCCESSORS AND ASSIGNS. All of the provisions herein shall be binding on and inure to the benefit of the successors, heirs, and assigns of the parties.

ENTIRE AGREEMENT. This Agreement (along with any Attachments hereto, which are referenced in this Agreement) constitutes the entire understanding between the parties, superseding all prior or contemporaneous understandings or agreements, written or oral.

NOTICES. Any notices or other communications required under this Agreement will be sent to the addresses the parties have set forth above.

ENFORCEMENT. The parties agree that any expenses, including but not limited to counsel fees, court costs, and travel, reasonably incurred by a party in the successful enforcement of any of the provisions of this Agreement shall be borne by the defaulting party as determined by a court of competent jurisdiction. All parties agree that any litigation involving this Agreement shall be sited in _____.

IN WITNESS WHEREOF, the parties have signed this Agreement on the date set forth below.

DATED: _____

AAA ENTERPRISES, INC.

BY:

_____

CLIENT NAME:

BY:

_____

# Computer Forensic Experts

## Form 2.3
## Guidelines for Hiring an Electronic Discovery or
## Computer Forensic Expert

1. *Which kind of expert do you need?* Many computer forensic technologists do electronic discovery, but few electronic discovery experts do true computer forensics. In a nutshell, computer forensics means performing a forensic acquisition of a hard drive or other media and extracting and documenting the data. For the most part, electronic discovery is the analysis and manipulation of the data once it has been logically extracted. It doesn't help that folks often use these terms interchangeably.

2. *Forensics certifications.* Currently, the most prestigious certification available to private firms is the EnCE (EnCase Certified Examiner) issued by Guidance Software. Another certification rapidly gaining respect is the Certified Information Forensics Investigator (CIFI) issued by the International Information Systems Forensics Association (IISFA), a nonprofit organization. More certifications are emerging and will gain credibility over time, but in the private sector, the EnCE and the CIFI are the certifications to look for. A caveat: many unscrupulous people will claim certifications on their CV when the truth is that they took classes or had training courses—no real meaningful certification was granted, just a "certification of attendance." If you see a certification you don't recognize, find out whether a written exam was required. Did the applicant have to prove some minimum time that he or she had been involved in computer forensics? Was the expert certified in computer forensics or merely in the use of a particular forensics tool? What organization issued the certification? Who was on the faculty? Was a practical hands-on component part of the testing? Is there a recertification component?

3. *Technical certifications.* A good forensic technologist will have a lot of letters after his or her name, indicating a broad range of certifications with a number of different technologies. If you see no certifications, or a "base-level" certification (such as A+), you do not have an individual with a wealth of experience. If the expert is (just by way of example—there are many, many valuable certifications) a Certified Novell Engineer, Certified Cisco Network Administrator, Microsoft Certified Professional + Internet, Microsoft Certified Systems Engineer, NT Certified Independent Professional, and a Certified Internetwork Professional, you've got someone with an expansive technical background.

4. *The CV.* Get the expert's CV early on and study it. Don't be afraid to ask questions. Does it show that the expert has spoken at a lot of seminars

and/or written a lot of articles? Those who present or teach frequently and have to answer questions on the fly tend to be excellent testifying experts. Also, teaching and authorship frequently add credibility with a judge or jury. What is the expert's educational and professional background? Is this a broad-based technologist or someone who is a new college grad and wet behind the ears or with just a sliver of technical knowledge?

5. *The Jack of all trades.* Beware the individual who claims multiple disciplines. Whether a private detective, computer repairman, or software engineer, or some combination of many things, a forensic technologist worth having is generally billed as a forensic technologist and does not offer a Chinese buffet of services.

6. *Court qualifications.* The last thing you need as an lawyer is an expert who hasn't qualified as an expert. Good experts have qualified in multiple courts and they are all listed on the CV. Mind you, most cases of any kind tend to settle, so even the best of experts may only appear in court several times a year. It is wise, however, to be wary of someone who has only qualified in one court—or none at all. You don't need a greenhorn cutting his teeth on your case.

7. *Confidentiality.* Remember the line from the gossip columnist in the movie *L.A. Confidential*? "Off the record, on the QT, and very hush-hush." Not all cases are shrouded in secrecy, but a fair proportion of them are. There are well-known figures getting divorced, major companies with proprietary information at issue, public figures in the headlines, and people charged with felonies. Make sure the expert you pick has a confidentiality clause in the retainer agreement, and don't hesitate to ask the expert to sign your own confidentiality agreement. Remember as well that the expert may be working on your case with others and that the entire firm should have an impeccable reputation for keeping client secrets. During the course of a major case where the expert has been identified, the press will undoubtedly come sniffing around the expert probing for information. A good expert knows the standard answer, "I'm sorry, I have no comment," and is as immoveable as the Great Wall of China.

8. *Geography may not matter.* How often lawyers forget that this is the electronic era! You can maintain chain of custody perfectly well by shipping a computer from California to New York if that's where the best expert is located. Although it is true enough that local experts are often preferred where monies are tight and travel expenses may be in issue, many lawyers lose sight of the value of having the best possible expert, regardless of location. If the case has a significant amount at stake and/or may well end up in trial, it is a disservice to clients to restrict them to local experts. Those experts who are well known in the field have clients across the nation and beyond because their expertise is so often sought.

9. *English 101 and 201.* An expert *must* speak the English language. We have many wonderful and brilliant friends who are of foreign descent, but their English will not pass muster with an ethnically mixed jury. If an accent is too pronounced for many people to comprehend, especially for those who may have learned English as a second language, that expert is not a good choice. That's English 101, being able to speak the language clearly. English 201 is being able to speak about highly technical matters in lay terms, with analogies that a judge or jury can understand. Geek-speak is worse than useless in a courtroom situation. You will come to revere an expert who easily makes analogies in terms of TV, cars, sports, and other things that represent part of Joe Q. Public's everyday life.

10. *The price tag.* Computer forensics is not cheap. Small cases may run in the $5,000–$10,000 range, but larger cases can hit six figures with astonishing rapidity. It is almost never possible to quote a probable final figure at the outset of a case, because the technologist has not yet seen the "size of the elephant." It will generally require some time into the case before it is possible to let a client know how much work will ultimately be involved. It is, as we all know, often the same predicament lawyers face when trying to give clients a rational estimate. As a general rule, the larger the forensics firm, the larger the bill. It is not uncommon to pay as much as $500/hour in the largest firms. In high-quality but smaller firms, $250–$350/hour may be a more common charge. If the firm you're looking at charges less than $200/hour, you probably want to raise your eyebrows and seriously investigate the firm credentials, references, number of courts qualified in and standing in the industry. Heed this advice well: some technologists bill fairly. They turn their clocks off while a process is running and go work on someone else's case. They account for their time accurately and precisely. On the other hand, there are those (often with lower rates), who charge you for every moment they are at work—and sometimes beyond. We have seen countless invoices for nine or ten hours a day at work, with no time removed for going to lunch, bathroom breaks, chatting with colleagues, meetings, etc. Frequently, we have found that those with lower rates compensate by billing for more hours. A conundrum for a client. Is the lower rate really going to mean a lower bill? Or will the higher rate, accurately applied, result in a smaller total? In the end, getting references is your best bet here. Caveat emptor!

11. *References, references, references.* There is no better way to secure a good expert. Ask your potential expert for references and then make sure you follow up with those references. Did the expert do a thorough, professional job? Was the expert responsive when contacted? Was the work completed on time? What was the quality of the expert's report? Did the expert make a credible witness? Was this an expert amenable to being "spun?" Experts who are "experts for hire" are a nightmare in court. If your candidate has the attitude

that "the truth is the truth," you may not want that truth in court, but at least you will know the realities of your case, its strengths and weaknesses. Did the expert stay within budget (not always possible) or at least alert the client to additional costs before incurring them? Perhaps the number one complaint heard about experts involved in electronic evidence is that costs spiraled out of control without notification to the law firm, resulting in a client highly perturbed with its bill—and its law firm.

12. *Evidence format.* What format do you want/need the evidence in? Is it to be placed on CDs? DVDs? A hard drive? Can you read the evidence in its native format or do you need it converted? Should it be ready for importing into Concordance or Summation?

13. *Vetting the expert and getting vetted.* You should be peppering your expert with questions and having the warm, fuzzy feeling that you are dealing with a true pro. Likewise, true professionals will ask many questions of you to get a feel for the case—and for you. You're both going to need to work together, so you need to have some sense of rapport. If something doesn't feel right, trust your instincts.

14. *Did you read the expert's contract?* All that law school training and it is amazing how many lawyers fail to read the contracts of those they hire. Make sure the contract contains a confidentiality provision. Make sure the billing terms and fees are clearly spelled out. If there are "caps" or "do not exceed without written authorization" provisions, make sure they are adequately expressed. You need to know what your expert must do if they run into child pornography. Who is to sign the contract? Frequently, especially in the cases of a nontestifying expert, the lawyer will wish to sign the contract in order to invoke the work-product doctrine where applicable.

**Form 2.4**

**Guidelines for Working with a Computer Forensic or Electronic Discovery Expert**

1. *Be careful to ascertain what electronic scope each expert can accomplish.* The lines between computer forensics and electronic discovery are blurred, so it is helpful to inquire whether the computer forensics or electronic discovery expert (for instance) is qualified to help draft pleadings or provide support (or ask the technical questions) at depositions or has legal counsel on staff to ascertain the legal relevance of unearthed data.

2. *Do not go stomping all over the evidence yourself (or let your client do it).* When computer forensics specialists get together and swap war stories, one recurrent theme is the unbelievable number of times that clients have fouled themselves up by trampling electronic evidence. Typically, as soon as a potential legal matter is recognized, a law firm or corporation authorizes someone from its IT department to "look through" the evidence. Unbeknownst to them, while their IT staff is busy finding golden nuggets of evidence, they are also changing the dates and times of the files they are accessing and possibly altering information that indicates which user ID did what. Although it may not entirely discredit the case, you have now given fodder to opposing counsel at the very least—and you will have to spend more money on the forensic examination because unraveling dates and times and explaining "the stomping" effect is now part of the examiner's job. It is a very foolish client that contaminates evidence by having in-house folks look at it—from a judge's or jury's point of view, the client has a vested interest in that evidence. Far more credible is an initial, independent forensic examination by a certified third party. As an ex-New York City police detective frequently laments at seminars, many of his cases went "in the hopper" because of trampled evidence. He jokes that the first two officers on the scene are always named "I Don't Know" and "Not Me" because when he asks who stomped all over the evidence, those are always the first two answers he gets.

3. *For heaven's sake, give your expert copies of the original pleadings, or (prelitigation) a statement of case facts.* How do lawyers expect their experts to function well in a vacuum? Yet it is astonishing how often lawyers will leave their experts with only a minimal understanding of case facts and simply give them a set of instructions. Experts worth their salt will carefully review any pleadings or case facts so they know what they are looking for. Often, lawyers produce keywords that make no sense (any idea how many "hits" you'll get on the search term "system"?) or they give their experts wonderfully vague instructions, such as "poke around and see what you can find." Even a little knowledge goes a long way toward helping an expert do a good job, thereby reducing the time and cost of analysis.

4. *Use your expert for litigation support.* Good lawyers are smart enough to know what they do not know. If you are not a technologist, how are you going to draft proper complaints, motions, discovery pleadings, and so forth that relate specifically to technology? It may well be that your expert is only needed to help you with slices of the documents, but it behooves the lawyer to make full use of the expert to make sure those slices are appropriately drafted. If you don't understand technology, your attempt to depose an IT administrator is likely to be a disaster. You may have the list of questions prepared by your expert, but in all likelihood, you'll ask some preliminary question about system authentications, and the answer you receive will sound to you like "Blah blah blah blah blah." Only if your expert is present or asking the questions can appropriate follow-up questions be addressed. In addition, your expert can screen for the nonsense factor, which is likely to completely elude someone without a technical background. Experts can be an enormous help in trial preparation and can often see the technical questions that may be raised on the other side and help construct answers.

5. *Treat your expert professionally.* There is nothing more frustrating than having a pivotal question for an lawyer, and having the lawyer be completely unresponsive. No wonder clients get so frustrated. The expert should promptly return a lawyer's calls and the lawyer should do likewise. Procrastination by a lawyer should not constitute an emergency on the part of the expert. Good experts, like good lawyers, are always handling multiple cases. It simply isn't fair to procrastinate until the last minute and then demand that the expert work all weekend or all night because something the lawyer knew about long ago is due on Monday or, worse yet, tomorrow. On the other hand, good experts who have been treated courteously and professionally by lawyers will break their backs to deliver for that lawyer even when notice is unavoidably short or the amount of work vast and the time frame constricted.

6. *Avoid misunderstandings by drawing lines of demarcation.* If you want your computer forensics technology to simply acquire evidence and then turn that evidence over to you or to an EDD (electronic data discovery) firm, let them know. If either one is supposed to convert evidence to particular formats and then turn the evidence over to you for analysis, make sure they know. If you want a preliminary report after a few hours of work, to ascertain "the size of the elephant" and the costs, make sure your expert knows that. If money is an issue, and you'd like your expert to tell you when charges reach a specified sum, make that clear—in writing.

7. *What would you like in writing?* As many commentators have noted, that which is not written is not discoverable. For the most part, we are instructed by lawyers not to write anything until we have instructions to do so. Bear in mind that there will always be, depending on the particular computer

forensics/analysis software used, some sort of report and documentation. This report, however, will constitute a simple explanation of what was done and what was found—expert opinions are another creature entirely. Remember that even drafts of expert opinions have been found to be discoverable. This is problematic, because there are many sound reasons why drafts will change—nonetheless, the alterations may provide fodder for the other side.

8. *Covet only the truth, not the smoking gun.* As the country music lyrics tell us, "Sometimes you're the windshield and sometimes you're the bug." There is nothing more gratifying than finding a digital smoking gun—it can be so exhilarating that we have been known to break into an enthusiastic, if woefully off-key, rendition of "We Are the Champions." Those are good days, but not all days are good days. Sometimes, after hours or days of searching and analyzing, it becomes painfully evident that what the client hoped to find is simply not there. On those days, we are the bugs. Sometimes lawyers or their clients become agitated and even fixated on the notion that what they are looking for must be there. If you have a competent, certified forensic examiner, or electronic discovery expert, believe her if she says she has followed all appropriate procedures and the evidence you are looking for is not there. Perhaps the evidence never existed at all, or it may have been overwritten (and therefore unrecoverable), or the drive/specific files may have been wiped, sometimes with a special utility, or it resides on a different computer or system.

9. *Don't ask your expert to bear false witness.* Amazingly, this seems to be very hard for lawyers. They want to write the expert opinion themselves and require nothing more than an obliging John Hancock. There are certainly "experts for hire" who will indeed oblige. Heaven help the expert or the lawyer if those documents end up as part of a court proceeding. If your expert is going to be on the stand, he or she had better be completely comfortable that anything they've signed is the truth. It is far better to let the expert write the opinion and explain in their own way, with lawyer input where desirable to clarify or stress particular points. Let's face it, in many instances what your expert may find is, to put in mildly, not helpful. In fact, the expert may find a digital smoking gun that is pointed directly at your client. In that case, be thankful you know the truth, can construct your strategies accordingly, and keep your expert out of court.

10. *Get used to working with electronic evidence.* Killing trees seems to be a great preoccupation of lawyers. In an electronic world, they constantly insist on paper. It is astonishing how often we hear a lawyer ask, "May I have my electronic discovery in paper please?" Other than the obvious violation of "green" practices, electronic evidence is uniquely designed to stay that way so that it may be catalogued, indexed, cross referenced, and searched. For the

moment, if a case actually goes to trial, paper may be required in court, though even courts are increasingly accepting and encouraging electronic evidence. During the analysis stage, there are so many helpful tools to organize data that it is inconceivable that anyone would want to go back to the old paper ways. If this is a hurdle for you, it is probably time to invest some hours in training so that you are comfortable with analyzing and manipulating electronic evidence.

11. *Be fiscally prudent, but not cheap.* Forensic acquisition and data analysis are slow, painstaking functions that, done correctly, are part of a scientific process punctuated by constant documentation of work done. Nonetheless, lawyers (and clients) frequently seem to think that "Filene's Basement" prices should apply. It is wise to get your expert's "best guess" up front and then to reevaluate after the expert has had a chance to immerse himself or herself in the case facts and the data. Keeping the client in the loop is always helpful. It should be possible for client, lawyer, and expert, working together, to come up with a rational set of numbers before the case has progressed too far. Remember that on-site work is always more expensive than work experts can do in their labs. A lab has the fastest equipment and the expert is surrounded by the entire forensic toolkit at his or her command.

12. *Think out of the box.* This is a brand-new world, and even the experts have much to learn as this world evolves so quickly. Think like your kids. It was our teenage interns who pointed out to their computer forensics bosses that music-swapping services could be used just as easily to swap pornographic images of children. Duh. It was the younger generation who glommed onto steganography (hiding files within files). As an example, you can be looking at a beautiful sunset on your computer monitor but with the right decryption code, you could uncover a formula for manufacturing a fertilizer bomb. In today's world, a driver who killed a pedestrian said he was going the speed limit, but his car's computer recorded his actual, highly excessive speed and the electronic evidence resulted in the driver's conviction. If you think you know it all today, rest assured that there will be more to learn tomorrow. Use your legal skills and your expert's skills in combination, to push the envelope of what electronic evidence can reveal.

In sum, working with your expert can be a joy or a disaster. If you've picked a good expert and follow some of the pointers above, you can maximize your chances of having a good experience. Above all, treat your expert with the same professional courtesy you would like to be accorded yourself, and you will almost invariably find your expert ready to go the extra mile to help you. As the old saying goes, "Nice begets nice," and sometimes it begets a better-quality work product as a fringe benefit!

# Form 2.5
## Confidentiality Agreement

This Confidentiality Agreement ("Agreement") is made and entered into as of this _____ day of _____, _____, by and between Sensei Enterprises, Inc., a Virginia corporation (hereafter "Sensei") and _____ (hereafter "Company").

Sensei has been engaged by Company to perform certain computer forensics examination work that may involve having access to confidential and proprietary commercial information. Sensei agrees to examine a computer __[describe computer]__ provided by Company and to disclose to Company only the information described below. The parties agree as follows.

1. Sensei agrees to disclose to Company the following:

2. Sensei agrees that the computer and any forensic image thereof in its possession shall be held under lock and key and shall be accessible only to Sharon D. Nelson, Esq., and John W. Simek. A strict chain of custody of the evidence shall be maintained.

3. Sensei acknowledges that substance/contents of any file or portion thereof on the computer shall be considered proprietary trade secrets and matters of strict confidentiality. Sensei also stipulates that the unauthorized use or disclosure of any confidential data will cause irreparable harm to the owner of the information. As a result, Sensei agrees that Company or any third-party owner of proprietary information located on the computer shall have the right to seek immediate injunctive relief in the event of any breach of this Agreement, in addition to any other remedies available to Company at law or equity.

4. In the event that Sensei is requested or required (by law or regulation, interrogatories, requests for information or documents, subpoenas, civil investigative demand, or other legal process) to disclose any confidential information on the computer, Sensei agrees to provide the Company or any third-party owner of proprietary information located on the computer (if such third-party owner has been identified to Sensei) with prompt notice of such request prior to compliance so that the Company or third-party owner may seek an appropriate protective order or such other remedy as may be appropriate. If Sensei is legally compelled to disclose such information, Sensei will incur no liability under this Agreement.

5. Sensei agrees to destroy all evidence and images of evidence containing information derived from the computer in its possession upon receipt of written instructions to do so by Company.

6. This Agreement shall be governed by, interpreted, and construed in accordance with the laws of the Commonwealth of Virginia and shall benefit and be binding upon the parties and their respective successors and assigns. The parties consent to jurisdiction and venue in Fairfax County, Virginia, for all disputes arising from or relating to this Agreement.

IN WITNESS WHEREOF, the parties have executed this Agreement as of the day and year written above.

SENSEI ENTERPRISES, INC.

_____

CLIENT

_____

## Form 2.6
## Computer Forensics Services Agreement

This agreement is made by and between SENSEI ENTERPRISES, INC., an independent contractor (hereafter "SENSEI"), whose address is 3975 University Dr., Suite 225, Fairfax, VA. 22030 and _____ (hereafter "CLIENT"), whose address is _____.

SENSEI agrees to perform such computer forensics, data recovery, electronic evidence, or expert testimony services as may be requested by CLIENT in consideration for the payment of an hourly rate of $_____ (except that each hard drive forensically acquired is billed at a flat rate of $_____ plus the cost of the hard drive upon which it is imaged), and payment of all reasonable documented out-of-pocket costs incurred. This hourly rate applies to courtroom or office waiting time as well as actual time testifying or performing forensic services. Travel time is billed at the rate of $_____ per hour from the point of leaving SENSEI's office until the point of return. Each full day away from the Washington, D.C., metropolitan area is billed on the basis of an eight-hour day $_____. Where more than eight hours of work or travel is performed in one day, the actual time is billed. Payment is due within 30 days of monthly invoicing. An interest charge of 1.5% monthly ($_____ minimum) shall be applied to all unpaid balances. A $_____ nonrefundable deposit is required upon execution of this contract.

THIRD-PARTY SERVICES. CLIENT shall be responsible for payment of all costs incurred for all third-party services necessary to the fulfillment of this Agreement. SENSEI agrees to notify CLIENT in advance if such services are reasonably necessary to fulfill its obligations under this contract.

CONFIDENTIALITY. To the extent that SENSEI is granted access to trade secrets or other confidential information and materials of CLIENT, SENSEI agrees to hold such secrets, information, and materials in confidence.

CHILD PORNOGRAPHY. To the event that a forensics examination reveals the existence of possible child pornography on the examined media, SENSEI will immediately cease its examination and advise CLIENT and appropriate law enforcement authorities of the nature of the materials found. Before proceeding with further forensic examination, CLIENT will secure a court order or take such other legal action as may be necessary to prevent both SENSEI and CLIENT from being subject to any legal charges regarding the possession or distribution of child pornography.

MODIFICATION OF AGREEMENT. No modification or waiver of any of the terms of this Agreement shall be valid unless in writing and signed by all parties.

GOVERNING LAW. This Agreement shall be construed and interpreted in accordance with the laws of the commonwealth of Virginia.

INVALIDITY OF PROVISIONS. If any of the provisions of this Agreement are held by a court of competent jurisdiction to be invalid or unenforceable, all other provisions shall nonetheless continue in full force and effect.

SUCCESSORS AND ASSIGNS. All of the provisions herein shall be binding on and inure to the benefit of the successors, heirs, and assigns of the parties.

ENTIRE AGREEMENT. This Agreement (along with any Attachments hereto, which are referenced in this Agreement) constitutes the entire understanding between the parties, superseding all prior or contemporaneous understandings or agreements, written or oral.

NOTICES. Any notices or other communications required under this Agreement will be sent to the addresses the parties have set forth above.

ENFORCEMENT. The parties agree that any expenses, including but not limited to counsel fees, court costs, and travel, reasonably incurred by a party in the successful enforcement of any of the provisions of this Agreement shall be borne by the defaulting party as determined by a court of competent jurisdiction. All parties agree that any litigation involving this Agreement shall be sited in Virginia.

IN WITNESS WHEREOF, the parties have signed this Agreement on the date set forth below.

DATED: _____

SENSEI ENTERPRISES, INC.

BY: _____

SHARON D. NELSON, PRESIDENT     or     JOHN W. SIMEK, VICE PRESIDENT

CLIENT NAME:

BY: _____

## Form 2.7
## Computer Forensics Expert CV

*John W. Simek*
**Vice President**
**Sensei Enterprises, Inc.**
3975 University Drive
Suite 225
Fairfax, VA 22030
(703) 359-0700 (O)
(703) 359-8434 (F)
jsimek@senseient.com (e-mail)

---

**Certifications/Credentials: EnCase Certified Examiner (EnCE), Certified Novell Engineer, Microsoft Certified Professional + Internet, Microsoft Certified Systems Engineer, NT Certified Independent Professional and a Certified Internetwork Professional. Member, High Tech Crime Network, American Bar Association, ABA TECHSHOW 2006 Planning Board and International Information Systems Forensics Association**

---

For over 25 years, Mr. Simek has been involved with commercial distribution and sales processes in addition to the implementation of computer systems to support the manufacture and distribution of goods and design of integrated systems. In his tenure with Mobil Oil Corporation, he was part of the Operations organization, which has responsibility for the refining, distribution, accounting, agency reporting, inventory management and delivery of lubricant and fuel products. Additional assignments in the Engineering and Financial Planning organizations addressed multi-million dollar projects and financial reporting requirements. Later in his career, his involvement included analysis, design, implementation, and troubleshooting of computer applications (concentrating in client/server and networks) to automate and facilitate the previously mentioned responsibilities. Following his Mobil career, he became the Vice President of Sensei Enterprises, Inc. in 1997, where he concentrates in legal technology, expert witnessing, computer forensics, electronic evidence and data recovery. Mr. Simek is a co-author of the following books: *Information Security for Lawyers & Law Firms* (2006, ABA Publishing) and *Electronic Evidence and Discovery Handbook: Forms, Checklists & Guidelines* (2006, ABA Publishing).

**Qualified as an expert or appointed by the court as an expert in the following courts:**

Fairfax County Circuit Court (VA)
Fairfax County General District Court (VA)

Fairfax County Juvenile and Domestic Relations Court (VA)
County of Albemarle Juvenile and Domestic Relations Court (VA)
Arlington County Circuit Court (VA)
Loudoun County Circuit Court (VA)
Prince William Circuit Court (VA)
Prince William Juvenile and Domestic Relations Court (VA)
Venango County Court of Common Pleas (PA)
State of Connecticut Superior Court
Superior Court of California—County of Los Angeles
U.S. District Court, Eastern District of Virginia
U.S. District Court, Western District of Virginia
United States District Court for the District of Columbia
U.S. Bankruptcy Court, Maryland
U.S. Air Force Trial Judiciary, Eastern Circuit
U.S. Marine Corps, Atlantic Judicial Circuit

**Representative recent work**:

♦ Testified as an expert (in computer forensics) in a sealed case involving a juvenile. (2006, Charlottesville, VA)

♦ Testified as an expert (computer forensics) in *U.S. v. Nunes* (2006, Quantico, VA). Case involving child pornography and solicitation of a minor.

♦ Telephone testimony as an expert (computer forensics) in *Commonwealth v. Hewston*. (2006, Venango County, PA) Case involving child pornography and real versus artificial images.

♦ Expert witness (computer forensics) in *Bulletin News Network, Inc. v. Briefings, Inc., et al.* (2006, Fairfax, VA). Case involving alleged theft of proprietary information. Forensic analysis was performed and deposition taken. Case settled.

♦ Testified as an expert (computer forensics) in *Jackson et al. v. ComputerXpress* et al. (2006, Superior Court, Los Angeles, California). Case involving fraud and defamation. Testified on behalf of plaintiff. No objections or cross examination by defense. Ruling pending.

♦ Expert witness (computer forensics) in *American LaFrance Corporation, et al. v. Elite Power Products Corp., et al.* (2005, Shawano, WI). Case involving alleged theft of proprietary information and falsification of evidence. Forensic analysis was performed and deposition taken. The case settled the following week.

♦ Requested by judge in *Gerner et al. v. Applied Industrial Materials Corporation et al.* (2004, Superior Court, Stamford, Connecticut) to participate in bench conference rather than taking the stand as an expert. Explained the process of computer forensic acquisition and performing a "preview" of the evidence. Court determined that a "sampling" of evidence should be performed, pending a determination of whether a full scale forensic acquisition was required. The sampling revealed more than 900 instances of proprietary information on Defendants computers. Testified as an expert (computer forensics) in subsequent trial. Jury awarded damages to plaintiff.

♦ Testified as an expert (computer forensics) in *Hart v. Hart* (2004, Loudon County Circuit Court) a divorce proceeding. Case involving the posting of nude images on the Internet and usage of Internet anonymizers.

♦ Testified as an expert (computer forensics) in *United States v. A1C Kevin Mead* (2004, United States Air Force Trial Judiciary, Eastern Circuit), a matter involving possession of child pornography. Defendant found guilty.

♦ Testified as an expert (computer and networking) in *Commonwealth of Virginia v. Jeremy Jaynes, Richard Rutkowski & Jessica Degroot* (2004, Loudon County Circuit Court, VA) in preliminary hearing. The case was the first test of Virginia's Anti-Spam law. Testimony included explaining how the Internet operates, specifically as it relates to e-mail communication. Two defendants found guilty (one verdict later overturned by the trial judge) and one acquitted. Appeal is pending.

♦ Testified as an expert (electronic evidence/e-mail origination analysis) in *Miller v. Miller* (Prince William Juvenile and Domestic Relations Court, 2004), a stalking/harassment case.

♦ Testified as an expert (computer forensics) in the U.S. District Court for the District of Columbia (2004) in *U.S. v. Perry*, in which the defendant allegedly gained unauthorized access to the computer network of the EPA and caused damages. Analysis showed remote access consistent with network logs. Defendant found guilty.

♦ Retained by the United States Senate to perform internal computer forensics acquisition and analysis in connection with litigation by former Senate employees against the Senate (2003).

♦ Testified as an expert witness (computer forensics) in a jury trial in *Commonwealth v. Helem* (Fairfax County Circuit Court, 2003), a murder case in which the defendant was charged with strangling a woman, but all evidence was circumstantial. Sensei was provided with an image of the victim's computer for forensic analysis. Findings indicated a cursory analysis of the victim's machine by law enforcement and failure to identify relevant peripheral equipment, including a scanner and a digital camera. Supplemental information was turned over to defense counsel. The first trial resulted in a hung jury. The second trial resulted in a mistrial. Testified in the third trial as to Internet activity on the night of death. Jury found defendant guilty in third trial.

◆ Testified as a fact witness (attorney neglected to make timely designation of expert) in *Human Resources Institute v. Federal Training Academy* (Fairfax County Circuit Court, 2003), a case involving the alleged use of spyware to gain access to proprietary data of HRI. Deposition taken. Testified to the existence of spyware on a home machine belonging to an HRI executive.

◆ Testified as an expert witness (computer forensics) in the Circuit Court for Prince William County (2003) in *Coolbaugh v. Coolbaugh* to search a hard drive for evidence of adultery. Judge found that adultery had been committed.

◆ Testified as an expert witness (computer forensics) in *Manley v. Wislocki* (Fairfax Juvenile and Domestic Relations Court, 2003), a case in which the husband's alcoholism and obsessive visiting of extreme pornographic sites, was in issue. The court ordered the husband to participate in a parenting program, to get an alcoholism evaluation, to cooperate with a therapist and to have limited visitation subject to the court's further review over time.

◆ Appointed by the U.S. Bankruptcy Court, Maryland (2003) to do the computer forensics in the involuntary bankruptcy proceeding of First-Pay, Inc., a payroll service company which allegedly failed to pay millions of dollars in taxes to the IRS on behalf of its clients.

◆ Testified as an expert witness (computer forensics) in Arlington County Circuit Court in *Heining v. Heining*, a divorce case in which forensic analysis of the evidence indicated possible spoliation (2003).

◆ Retained by defense counsel in *U.S. v. Ebersole* (E.D.V.A. 2003), a case in which the government charged the defendant with multiple counts of fraud, one of which involved the alleged en masse falsification of electronic records evidencing the certification of drug/bomb-sniffing dogs. Forensic analysis revealed that the electronic evidence as to this one count was consistent with defendant's claim that he copied records from an old computer to a new one and worked off a template. This aspect of the evidence was not challenged by the government at court. The defendant was found guilty on multiple counts and the case is on appeal. Defendant was convicted of 25 counts of wire fraud and two counts of presenting false claims to the government. The circuit court affirmed the convictions and remanded the case to district court for resentencing.

◆ Performed the initial computer forensics (acquisition and analysis) in the Washington Teachers' Union (WTU) case (2002). The evidence indicated that top union officials had misappropriated more than $5 million dollars in union funds. The American Federation of Teachers (the parent union) has taken over the WTU. Several of the identified participants entered into plea agreements.

- Expert witness (networking) against the FBI expert's in *U.S. v. Gray* (the issue was whether the FBI's search of a hard drive was consistent with its warrant or exceeded its scope). This case (E.D.V.A., 1999) is now taught at the FBI Academy.
- Expert witness (computer forensics) in *Praisner v. Daigler* (2003, Fairfax County Circuit Court), a child custody case involving alleged e-mail forgery. Indicia of forgery sufficient to warrant seizure and examination of computer. The findings indicated that the father had forged e-mail to himself purporting to be from the wife. Full custody was transferred from the husband to the wife.
- Expert witness (systems integration/networking) in *Caudill Seed v. Prophet 21* (2001, breach of contract by a major software developer involving the adequacy of their distribution industry software). Expert report filed and video deposition taken, after which the case settled.
- Non-testifying expert (software evaluation) in *Impact Imaging, Inc. v. eCom eCom.com, Inc.* (2002, breach of contract case involving a determination of whether the graphic compression software provided by Impact met business standards of being an acceptable alpha product).
- Forensic consulting for Prudential Securities, Inc. (2002) in a case involving allegations that three stockbrokers violated their employment contracts by removing proprietary information from Prudential's information sources and by contacting Prudential's clients in an attempt to transfer their business to the stockbrokers' new firm. Three laptops and three Palm Pilots were acquired and analyzed. After submission of the electronic evidence, the case settled.
- Court appointed expert in *Belanger v. Outlaw* (Fairfax County Circuit Court, 2001) in which the issue was the economic circumstances of one party. Recovered all economic data responsive to search terms and submitted to Special Master. Case settled.
- Expert witness, by federal court appointment, in *Sy Technologies v. S3* (U.S. District Court, EDVA, 2001). Recovered deleted data and e-mail, which led to settlement in case involving alleged misappropriation of proprietary information.

### Professional Experience

**Sensei Enterprises, Inc.**                                    1997–Present
Fairfax, Virginia

*Vice President. Computer forensics, expert testimony, data recovery, computer consulting, network design and configuration, systems integration, software application development, web site design, representing over 150 Northern Virginia law firms and corporations.*

**Mobil Business Resources Corporation/** 1996–1999
**Global Information Services**
Fairfax, Virginia

*Engineering & Design Consultant. Responsible for support and implementation of all infrastructure components for a North and South American common computing system. Concentrations in telecommunications and integrated systems implementations.*

**Mobil Oil Corporation/USF&IS Technical Services** 1992–1996
Fairfax, Virginia

*Telecommunications Consultant. Recommended, designed and implemented communications technologies and strategies for voice and data requirements. Concentration in client/server infrastructure including LAN/WAN, micro/mini-computers, hubs, routers, switching technology and end-to-end management.*

**Mobil Oil Corporation/USM&R SCS** 1988–1992
Fairfax, Virgini

*Core Systems Manager/Systems Consultant. Managed 9 professionals in the core systems organization. Responsible for support and implementation of mainframe operational system for distribution and invoicing of petroleum products. Voice response, process control and linear programming techniques utilized in the core systems.*

**Mobil Oil Corporation** 1979–1988
VA, PA, NY, MA, NJ

*Various staff and field positions to include Financial Analyst, Light Product System Supervisor/Capital Analyst, Facilities Analyst/Supply Analyst, Field Engineer/Maintenance Supervisor, Terminal Supervisor, Terminal Foreman, Operating Analyst.*

## Publications

Co-Author, *Information Security for Lawyers & Law Firms* (2006, ABA Publishing) and *Electronic Evidence and Discovery Handbook: Forms, Checklists & Guidelines* (2006, ABA Publishing)

Co-Editor, *Bytes in Brief*, 1997-present (an electronic law and technology newsletter)

Co-Author, *Hot Buttons* column, published monthly in the ABA Magazine: *Law Practice*

Co-author of various articles published in *ABA Family Advocate*, *The Academy of Florida Trial Lawyers Journal*, *The Advocate: Arizona Trial Lawyers Association*, *The American Car Association/TIPS Civil Procedure*, *Arkansas Trial Lawyers' Association Docket*, *Atlantic Coast In-House*, *The Colorado Lawyer*, *Consumer Attorneys of California*, *The Corporate Lawyer*, *The Docket*, *Environmental Systems Update*, *eTECHnews*, *Evidence Committee Newsletter*, *The Fairfax Bar Journal*, *The Fee Simple: The Newsletter of the Virginia State Bar Real Property Section*, *The General Counsel Roundtable*, *Glasser's Electronic Filing Newsletter*, *GP/SOLO*, *In-House Counsel*, *The Internet Lawyer*, *Law Office Computing*, *Law Practice Today (American Bar Association)*, *Legal Assistant Today*, *Louisiana Advocate*, *Michigan Bar Journal*, *The Michigan Defense Quarterly*, *Michigan Lawyers Weekly*, *The Nebraska Lawyer*, *The Nevada Lawyer*, *The New Hampshire Bar News*, *The New Jersey Lawyer*, *New Mexico Trial Lawyers Journal*, *The Newsletter of the Virginia State Bar Real Property Section*, *The Promulgator*, *The Ohio Association of Civil Trial Attorneys Newsletter*, *The Ohio Lawyer*, *Ohio Trial*, *Ohio Lawyers Weekly*, *Oregon State Bar Bulletin*, *The Pennsylvania Lawyer Magazine*, *The Promulgator and Tort Trends*, *The Tennessee Bar Journal*, *Texas Bar Journal*, *Texas Criminal Defense Lawyers Association*, *Trial Bar News*, *Trial News: Washington State Trial Lawyers Association*, *Trial Talk: Colorado Trial Lawyers Association*, *The Vermont Bar Journal*, *The Virginia Lawyer*, *Virginia Lawyers Weekly*, *The Wisconsin Lawyer*, *The Wisconsin Law Journal*, *Wyoming Lawyer*

Articles published in the last ten years include the following:

♦ *Electronic Discovery Comes of Age: The Fulbright Jaworski Study*
♦ *Metadata: What You Can't See Can Hurt You*
♦ *Unified Threat Management: To Dream the Impossible Dream?*
♦ *Disaster Preparedness: What's Reasonable*
♦ *Finding Wyatt Earp: Your Computer Forensic Expert*
♦ *Three Strikes and You're Out: Judges Talk About Courtroom Technology*
♦ *Spyware: When You Look at Your Computer, Is It Looking Back at You?*
♦ *Drafting Electronic Evidence Protocols: Staying Out of the Briar Patch*
♦ *Battening Down the Hatches: Security for Small and Mid-size Law Firms*
♦ *Computer Forensics for Legal Support Staff*
♦ *Status Report: Electronic Filing in the Federal Courts: 2004*
♦ *Electronic Evidence: Is it Better to Give or Receive?*
♦ *Document Retention Policies*
♦ *Lawyers Inch Their Way Toward a Paperless Practice: May I Have My Electronic Discovery in Paper, Please?*
♦ *Wireless Security for Law Firms*
♦ *Electronic Evidence: The Ten Commandments*
♦ *Canning Spam: Unclogging Law Firm Mailboxes*

- *Shackled to Microsoft: What It Means to the Legal Profession*
- *Bringing the Bench and Bar Online*
- *Status Report: Electronic Filing in the Federal Courts—2002*
- *Law Office Security: Building the Castle Moat*
- *Takedowns: Legendary Successes in Computer Forensics*
- *Disgruntled Employees in Your Law Firm: The Enemy Within*
- *The Bailiwick Inn: Everything But a Ghost*
- *Finding and Securing Electronic Evidence*
- *Mel Gibson Proves You Should be Wary of Electronic Evidence*
- *Big Brother is Watching: Monitoring and Filtering Employees' E-Mail Use*
- *The Scourge of NIMDA*
- *ASPs: Why Lawyers Should Beware Their Bite*
- *House of Horrors: Moving Your Law Firm*
- *The Internet at Warp Speed*
- *Floods, Fires and Firebombs: Can Your Law Office Recover From Disaster?*
- *Golden Geese That Lay Brown Eggs: The Importance of Electronic Marketing*
- *Attorney Disciplinary Records Online*
- *Judicial Evaluations Online: Nuts and Bolts*
- *Legal Road Warriors Come of Age: Remote Access Solutions*
- *Electronic Filing: Using Technology to Balance the Competing Rights of Public Access and Privacy*
- *Special Report: The Seventh Annual Court Technology Conference*
- *Electronic Filing in the Federal Courts: 2001*
- *The State of Electronic Filing in the States: 2001*
- *E-Filing Primer*
- *Hacked: Court Web Sites Under Assault*
- *Electronic Discovery: What Dangers Lurk in the Virtual Abyss?"*
- *Law Firm Y2K Problems: A Quick Thumbnail View*

### Seminars and Presentations

Mr. Simek, in conjunction with Ms. Nelson, Sensei's President, is a frequent speaker for such groups as the American Bar Association, American Lawyer Media, American Records Management Association, the Air Force Defense Counsel, the Alaska State Bar Association, the Community Associations Institute, the Fairfax Bar Association, the Fourth Circuit Judicial Conference, George Mason University, the Georgia Institute of Continuing Legal Education, Girl Scouts of the Nation's Capitol, the International Judiciary Academy, the National Capital Area Paralegal Association, the National Association of Bar Related Insurance Companies, the National Association of Regulatory Utility Commissioners, North Carolina Bar Association, the Oklahoma State Bar, the Private Investigators Association of Virginia, the Pennsylvania Bar Institute, the South Carolina Bar Association, the University of Rhode Island, the Virginia Bar Association, the Virginia Circuit Court Clerk's Association, Virginia CLE, the Virginia Coalition for Open Government, the Virginia Electronic Commerce Technology Center, the Virginia Local Government Management Association, the Virginia State Bar, Virginia Tech, the Virginia Trial Lawyers Association and the West Virginia Bar Association.

- *Cool Technology for Lawyers*
- *Cool Technology for Bar Presidents*
- *Threat and Response: Real Security and Practice Protection Stories*
- *Paranoia Justified: Unified Threat Management for Your Law Practice and Fact and Fiction*
- *Electronic Discovery in Everyday Cases*
- *Spy v. Spy: Spyware in Divorce Cases*
- *Electronic Evidence: Sherlock Holmes Goes Digital*
- *Document Retention: Limiting Client Risk Today in E-Discovery Tomorrow*
- *The Sky Has Fallen! Disaster Recovery*
- *Advanced Networking: Advancing Cautiously Through the Labyrinth*
- *Where Worlds Collide: Computer Security and Ethics*
- *Computer Forensics For Paralegals*
- *Electronic Discovery Toolkit*
- *Canning Spam and E-mail Triage*
- *SANs, NAS and Other High-end Networking & Storage Solutions*
- *Computer Forensics: A Primer for Lawyers*
- *Security Demons and How to Exorcise Them*
- *The Smoking Guns of Electronic Evidence: Wielding the Guns and Dodging the Bullets*
- *The Secrets Your Computer Can Tell: Electronic Data Discovery*
- *Computer Forensics: A Guide for Lawyers*
- *Cyberterrorism*
- *The Fabrication/Alteration of Electronic Evidence: Mel Gibson Demonstrates*
- *Electronic Filing in Courts and Agencies: Wins, Losses and Draws*
- *Virus Writing and Web Site Hacking*
- *E-filing: Balancing Privacy Rights and Public Access Rights*
- *30 Fun Legal Sites in 30 Minutes*
- *Digital Signatures and Encryption*
- *Electronic Evidence: Getting It and Using It*
- *Network Security*
- *Electronic Briefs*
- *Microsoft Word for Lawyers*
- *Electronic Marketing for Lawyers*
- *Legal Research on the Net*

- *Students on the Net: Protecting Them and Prosecuting Them*
- *Net Law 2002: Current Developments*
- *E-Commerce: Legal Pitfalls for the Unwary*
- *Office Management for Small Law Firms: Technology Issues*
- *Hot Issues in Law Office Technology: High Speed Internet Access and Re-mote Access*
- *Electronic Commerce: Legal Fundamentals*
- *A Lawyer's Guide to the Tech Side of the Net*
- *Technology in the Law Office: Making Logical Transitions: The Process and the Nuts and Bolts*
- *Legal and Business Web Sites: A Primer*
- *Disgruntled Employees in the Electronic Workplace: The Enemy Within*

## Education

**Courtroom 21**                                                2005
Fairfax, VA
*Certified Trial Technologist*

**Guidance Software**                                    2002, 2004
Pasadena, California
*Encase Certified Examiner (EnCE)*

**Lanop**                                                          2000
Jeffersonville, New York
*NT Certified Independent Professional*

**Learning Tree International**                              1996
Reston, VA
*Certified Internetwork Professional*

**Novell, Incorporated**                              1994–2000
Provo, Utah
*Certified Netware Engineer*

**Microsoft**                                                      1998
Redmond, Washington
*Microsoft Certified Professional + Internet*
*Microsoft Certified Systems Engineer*

**Saint Joseph's University**                           1985–1987
Philadelphia, Pennsylvania
*Master of Business Administration, Finance.*

**United Sates Merchant Marine Academy**      1973–1977
Kings Point, New York
*Bachelor of Science, Marine Engineering with honors.*

# Data Hosting

## Form 2.8
## Internet Hosting Services Checklist[1]

1. Physical Facility
   a. Data center site location(s)
   b. Sole-site or co-locations
   c. Security, including guards, biometric scanners, keycards, cameras, windows, doors, etc.
   d. Fire/water/earthquake protections
   e. Electric power including redundancy, battery and/or generator backup
   f. Access rights to facility
   g. Prior security audit results
   h. Facilities tour
2. Communications Backbone
   a. Description and connection type
   b. Redundancy
   c. Historic availability and contractual availability
   d. Internet latency, transmission speeds
   e. Internet hardware and software used
3. Network Security
   a. Evaluate topology including firewalls, servers, routers, etc.
   b. Established protocols for denial of service attacks, viruses, etc.
   c. Alternative methods for user authentication
   d. Password policies
   e. Warranties and guarantees: Packet security, Internet latency, Availability
   f. Prior network security audit results
4. Server and Data Integrity and Reliability
   a. Redundancy options such as mirroring
   b. Backup procedures and frequency
   c. Disaster recovery
   d. Scalability for data storage and rack space
   e. Server hardware configuration such as processors, ram and hard drive size
   f. Data storage configuration
   g. Facility resources
   h. Application level security measures

---

[1] From Jurinnov, Ltd. Reprinted with permission.

5. Company, Staffing, and Support
   a. Staff description
   b. Experience and resources
   c. Software, database, and networking certifications held by staff
   d. Description of applications currently hosted
   e. Options for technical support coverage
   f. Response times or service standards
   g. Technical support problem escalation procedures
   h. Notification for service interruptions
   i. Relationship manager
   j. Flexibility
   k. Reputation
   l. Sophistication and presence
   m. Confidentiality
   n. Financial stability
   o. Use of subcontractors
6. Costs
   a. Pricing Structure
   b. Payment terms
   c. Term of contract
   d. Hidden costs
   e. Termination fees
   f. Discounts
   g. Taxes
7. Contract Issues
   a. Disclaimers
   b. Warranties
   c. Limitation of liability
   d. Indemnification
   e. Intellectual property or other proprietary rights
   f. Limitations on use
   g. Dispute resolution
   h. Conflicts resolution

## Form 2.9
## Master Hosting and Services Agreement

## Master Hosting and Services Agreement[1]

This Master Hosting and Services Agreement ("Agreement") is made and entered into by and between CaseShare Systems, Inc. ("CaseShare" or "We") and _____ ("Customer" or "You"). It will be supplemented by one or more Schedules to be agreed upon and signed by us separately.

## 1. Definitions

**"Applications"** mean our software systems relating to electronic document exchange, communication, collaboration and case/claim or workflow management, to which you are granted a limited right and license to use pursuant to one or more Schedules.

**"End Users"** means those third parties who have been granted permission to access your Extranet Site(s) pursuant to the terms and conditions of the Case-Share End-User Agreement. Such third parties shall include your employees, contractors and agents as well as those of any third party to whom such access has been granted by you.

**"Extranet Site"** means a private network Hosted by us that uses standard Internet protocols (e.g., http, https, ftp, www, SMTP, etc.) and the public telecommunication system for the provision of the Services. An Extranet Site may, among other things, provide the Customer with a repository by which your authorized End Users may process, store and communicate electronic documents, and information using Applications developed by us for a specific transaction or project identified by you.

**"Host" or "Hosted"** means to make Extranet Sites and/or Applications available to you and End Users via the Internet and to provide electronic storage for data or electronic files relating to those Applications.

**"Other Services"** means any services other than the Services that may be provided by us at your request, including scanning, OCR conversion, coding, printing, custom programming, creation of CD-ROMs, etc. Any Other Services

---

[1] Reprinted with permission from CaseShare Systems, Inc.

we provide and the prices related to such Other Services will be set forth in an exhibit to the appropriate Schedule.

**"Schedule"** means each separate document setting forth the specific Applications, Extranet Site(s), Services, and Other services to be provided by us to you. Each Schedule will specifically reference this Agreement and be executed by each of us.

**"Services"** means the secure online document exchange, communication, and collaboration environment and related services, provided by us through our Applications and Extranet Site(s), to which you are granted a limited right and license to use pursuant to one or more Schedules. The Services do not include (a) data transmitted through the Services by you or End Users; (b) any hardware or software used by you or End Users to access our Extranet Site(s); or (c) Other Services.

**"System"** means those of our Applications, Extranet Site(s) and Services, collectively, provided to you by us under this Agreement.

## 2. Limited License; Services

**License.** Subject to the terms of this Agreement and any related Schedules, we hereby grant to you during the term of this Agreement a nonexclusive, nonsublicensable, nontransferable limited right and license to access and use the System for the purposes specified by you in one or more Schedules. You will only use the System for the purpose set forth in the Schedule for which the System was created and for no other use or purpose. This Agreement, without a Schedule executed by both parties, does not give you any right or license to use any portion of the System.

**Training.** We will provide you with an electronic copy of a User manual for the Extranet Site and any Applications we provide. You are licensed to make as many copies of the manual as you need and to distribute them to whomever you choose so long as they have a need for this information in conjunction with using the Applications. At your request, we will provide on-site or telephone-based training at our then-prevailing fees for those services.

## 3. Fees

**Fees.** You will pay us for Services provided pursuant to each Schedule on the terms and rates, and at the times, set forth in such Schedule. All charges payable pursuant to a Schedule hereto will begin to accrue on the Commencement Date for such Schedule unless otherwise specified, and are payable in United States Dollars.

**Taxes.** You agree to pay or reimburse CaseShare for all taxes based upon the charges in this Agreement or the services or materials provided under this Agreement, including state and local sales, privilege, or excise taxes but excluding our federal, state and local income taxes or other taxes levied against CaseShare based on its income, property or work force. Should applicable taxes be assessed against CaseShare after a billing cycle or after this Agreement has been terminated, you agree to reimburse CaseShare for those taxes upon receipt of a subsequent billing. You have the right to audit any tax billing assessed by CaseShare to determine its nature and amount.

**Change in Fees.** We may change the terms and rates contained in any Schedule upon the commencement of any renewal term of such Schedule provide we have provided you with at least ninety (90) days prior written notice of such change.

**Past-Due Amounts.** Unless otherwise agreed in a Schedule, you agree to pay interest at the rate of 1% per month, compounded annually, on amounts more than 60 days past due (i.e., from the date of invoice).

## 4. Term and Termination

**Term.** The term of this Agreement will commence on the Effective Date and end upon the earlier of (a) the termination or expiration of all Schedules to this Agreement; or (b) the termination of this Agreement in accordance with the termination rights set forth herein. The term of each Schedule will be as set forth in such Schedule, unless earlier terminated in accordance with the terms of such Schedule or this Agreement.

**Right to Terminate.** Either party may terminate this Agreement and/or all Schedules 30 days following the receipt the other party of written notice of a breach of a material term of this Agreement or a Schedule in the event that such breach remains uncured. If the breach (a) cannot be cured within such period; (b) the breaching party has made good faith efforts to cure the breach; and (c) such efforts were commenced promptly during such cure period, such cure period shall be extended as long as the cure is being diligently prosecuted to completion to a maximum extension period of 15 calendar days.

**Termination.** Upon termination of this Agreement, unless otherwise specified in a Schedule, you will immediately cease using, and we may terminate your access to the System. Notwithstanding the foregoing, in the event that such termination is due to your breach of a material term of this Agreement, you will immediately cease using, and we may terminate your access to, the System regardless of anything set forth in a Schedule. In the event of a termination, we will provide copies of your data and images in an industry-standard format on one or more DVDs or CD-ROMs or other appropriate magnetic media at your request at our then prevailing charge for this service.

**Denial of Access.** We retain the right to immediately deny you access and/or any of your End Users access to the System if (a) you or such End User is using our Services in violation of any applicable law or governmental regulation; or (b) you have failed to pay any overdue invoice after receipt of written or electronic notice of such delinquency and a 14-calendar-day opportunity to cure.

## 5. Service Availability Commitment

**Scope.** Our goal is to limit server unavailability due to causes within our control (and excepting Scheduled Maintenance) to less than one consecutive hour in any calendar month. An Extranet Site server shall be deemed to be unavailable if the Extranet Site is not responding to HTTP requests.

**Scheduled Maintenance.** Scheduled Maintenance means any maintenance in our data center at which your Extranet Site is located (a) of which you are notified 48 hours in advance: and (b) that is performed during a standard maintenance window on Monday through Friday from 12 A.M. to 6 A.M. Mountain Time or during weekends. Notice of Scheduled Maintenance will be provided to your designated point of contact by e-mail.

**Service Availability Commitment Process.** If you notify our Customer Support within 5 days of a failure to access your Extranet Site and we determine in our reasonable commercial judgment that the Extranet Site was unavailable due to a server outage caused by the items of the service managed by us, such outage will be used to calculate Extranet Site unavailability. Unavailability of your Extranet Site due to your web content or application programming, your acts or acts of End Users, network unavailability outside of our server network and firewall, or events of *force majeure* shall not be deemed unavailability.

**Service Availability Commitment Remedy.** If an Extranet Site is unavailable for one or more (but fewer than four) consecutive hours during a calendar month, we will credit your account for such month the pro-rated charges for one day's service for that Extranet Site. If an Extranet Site is unavailable for four (4) or more consecutive hours during any calendar month, we will credit your account for such month for the pro-rated charges for one week's service for that Extranet Site.

## 6. Security

**Passwords.** Each Extranet Site will be protected by passwords or other technological means so that access to such Extranet Site can be restricted to you and your End Users. End Users will select their personal passwords and may change them passwords as they deem appropriate. Controls on password length, complexity, etc., are defined within the CaseShare Information Security Policy, a copy of which is attached as Annex A.

**Security Audits.** You have the right to conduct security audits or to have security audits performed by third parties at any time upon reasonable notice at your expense, provided that you and any such third parties may not take any action during such audit that might reasonably be expected to adversely affect the performance by us of our business. This right shall extend to our network devices, servers, and other relevant systems.

## 7. Confidentiality

**Definition of Confidential Information.** We each acknowledge that information provided by either of us in connection with this Agreement will contain confidential and proprietary data, and disclosure of such information may be damaging to the disclosing party. The term "Confidential Information" means any and all technical and business information disclosed in any manner or form, including, but not limited to, our Applications and Services, the System, terms and pricing set forth in this Agreement and the Schedules, financial plans and records, litigation data, marketing plans, business strategies, trade secrets, present and proposed products, computer software programs, source code, relationships with third parties, customer lists, information regarding customers and suppliers and "privileged information." Privileged information shall mean written or oral information created or possessed by you or your representatives that would be subject to a claim of privilege (e.g., attorney-client, work product, etc.) before a court or other tribunal.

**Nondisclosure.** Neither party will disclose the other party's Confidential Information to anyone other than the directors, officers, employees, agents, and contractors of the receiving party who have a need to have access to such Confidential Information to perform obligations under this Agreement. Each party will use the same degree of care to protect Confidential Information of the other party as it uses to protect its own Confidential Information of like importance, but no less than a reasonable degree of care. No license to either parties' Confidential Information is either granted or implied by the disclosure of Confidential Information. The duties and obligations to protect Confidential Information will survive termination of this Agreement for any reason.

**Exceptions.** The receiving party will not have any obligation with respect to any Confidential Information of the disclosing party which the receiving party can establish (a) is or becomes publicly available through no wrongful act of the receiving party; (b) was lawfully obtained by the receiving party from a third party without any obligation to maintain the Confidential Information as proprietary or confidential; (c) was previously known to the receiving party without any obligation to keep it confidential; (d) was independently developed by the receiving party; (e) is required to be disclosed pursuant to the law, court order, or duly authorized subpoena, provided that the recipient promptly notifies the other party prior to disclosure, and provided further that the recipient makes diligent efforts to limit such disclosure to that which is reasonably required; or (f) is required to be disclosed pursuant to a regulatory agency or for audit purposes, provided that the recipient is notified of the confidential nature of the Information.

**Injunctive Relief.** The parties recognize and acknowledge that the Confidential Information may have competitive value and that irreparable damage might result to the disclosing party if Confidential Information is improperly disclosed by the receiving party to any nonauthorized third party. The parties agree that legal proceedings at law or in equity, including injunctive relief, may be appropriate in the event of a breach hereof, and that the arbitration procedures provided for herein shall not prevent the parties hereto from seeking such relief under this Section 7 in an appropriate court or other tribunal.

## 8. Rights in the System

**Our Rights.** We own all computer code and other materials developed or provided by us, or our suppliers, and any trade secrets, know-how, methodologies, and processes related to our products or services, including without limitation all copyrights, trademarks, patents, trade secrets, and other proprietary rights. You agree not to reverse engineer the Services or any portion thereof, and, except as permitted hereunder, agree that you will not use, disclose or divulge to others any data or information relating to our Services and Applications, the System and/or the technology, ideas, concepts, know-how and techniques embodied therein without our express prior written permission to do so.

**Customer Rights.** You own all your data and materials provided to us and/or stored in an Extranet Site ("Customer Materials"). Customer Materials are and shall remain your sole and exclusive property, including all applicable rights to patents, copyrights, trademarks, trade secrets or other proprietary or intellectual property rights inherent therein or appurtenant thereto.

## 9. Warranties

**Limited Warranty.** CaseShare warrants that (a) it is the lawful owner of or has the right to license or sublicense the Services, Extranet Site(s) and Applications; and (b) the System will perform substantially in accordance with the current documentation provided by us in conjunction with any Schedule, including, without limitation, any updates thereof. In the event that the System fails to perform in accordance with this warranty, you agree to promptly inform us of such fact, and, as your sole and exclusive remedy, we will either (a) repair or replace the System to correct any defects in performance without any additional charge to you, or (b) in the event that such repair or replacement cannot be done within a reasonable time, terminate the Agreement and provide you with a pro rata refund of the fees paid to us for the System hereunder with respect to such calendar year.

The foregoing warranties will not apply to the extent that (a) the System is used for any purpose other than those set forth in this Agreement regardless of whether we have terminated this Agreement because of such misuse; (b) the cause of a breach of warranty is due to a malfunction in your hardware, software or communications network though which the System is accessed; or (c) the cause of a breach of warranty is due to any other cause outside of our sole and reasonable control.

**DISCLAIMER OF WARRANTY.** THE FOREGOING CONSTITUTE OUR ONLY WARRANTIES WITH RESPECT TO THE PERFORMANCE OR NONPERFORMANCE OF THE SERVICES AND APPLICATIONS AND/OR THE SYSTEM WHICH ARE OTHERWISE PROVIDED ON AN "AS IS" AND "AS AVAILABLE" BASIS. THE FOREGOING LIMITED WARRANTIES ARE IN LIEU OF, AND WE HEREBY EXPRESSLY DISCLAIM, ALL OTHER WARRANTIES, EXPRESS OR IMPLIED, INCLUDING, WITHOUT LIMITATION, WARRANTIES OF MERCHANTABILITY AND FITNESS FOR A PARTICULAR PURPOSE.

**LIMITATION OF LIABILITY.** EXCEPT FOR OUR WILLFULL MISCONDUCT OR GROSS NEGLIGENCE, YOU AGREE THAT UNDER NO CIRCUMSTANCES ARE WE LIABLE TO YOU FOR ANY INDIRECT, INCIDENTAL, SPECIAL, PUNITIVE OR CONSEQUENTIAL DAMAGES OR LOST PROFITS ARISING OUT OF THE SYSTEM OR OUR SERVICES OR OBLIGATIONS UNDER THIS AGREEMENT EVEN IF WE HAVE BEEN ADVISED OF THE POSSIBILITY OF SUCH DAMAGES. IN ANY EVENT, YOUR EXCLUSIVE REMEDY AND OUR ENTIRE LIABILITY TO YOU FOR ANY REASON UPON ANY CAUSE OF ACTION ARISING OUT OF THE SYSTEM OR OUR SERVICES UNDER THIS AGREEMENT SHALL BE THE AMOUNT ACTUALLY PAID BY YOU TO US WITH RESPECT TO THOSE DEFICIENT SERVICES. THE LIMITATION OF LIABILITY PROVIDED BY THIS SECTION IS LIMITED TO OUR DUTIES AND LIABILITIES BY REASON OF THIS AGREEMENT ONLY, AND DOES NOT AFFECT ANY OTHER RELATIONSHIP WE MAY HAVE WITH YOU.

THE FOREGOING LIMITATION IS A FUNDAMENTAL PART OF THE BASIS OF THE BARGAIN HEREUNDER AND IS INTENDED TO APPLY WITHOUT REGARD TO WHETHER OTHER PROVISIONS OF THIS AGREEMENT HAVE BEEN BREACHED OR HAVE BEEN HELD TO BE INVALID OR INEFFECTIVE.

NO ACTION, REGARDLESS OF FORM, ARISING OUT OF OR RELATED TO THE USE OF THE SERVICES PURSUANT TO THIS AGREEMENT MAY BE BROUGHT BY YOU MORE THAN 12 MONTHS AFTER THE CAUSE OF ACTION FIRST AROSE.

## 10. Indemnification

Each party agrees to indemnify, defend, and hold harmless the other party, its affiliates, and their current and former employees and agents, and defend any action brought against same with respect to any claim, demand, cause of action, debt or liability (including reasonable attorneys' fees) brought by a third party arising out of, or in connection with a breach of the other party's representations, warranties, covenants and agreements set forth in this Agreement or to the extent attributable to such party's gross negligence or willful misconduct.

In claiming any indemnification hereunder, the indemnified party shall promptly provide the indemnifying party with written notice of any claim which the indemnified party believes falls within the scope of the foregoing paragraphs. The indemnified party may, at its own expense, assist in the defense if it so chooses, provided that the indemnifying party shall control such defense and all negotiations relative to the settlement of any such claim and further provided that any settlement intended to bind the indemnified party shall not be final without the indemnified party's written consent, which shall not be unreasonably withheld.

The terms of these provisions shall survive the expiration or termination of this Agreement.

## 11. Arbitration

In the event any disputes or controversies arise between the parties (including a claim of uncured or continuing default), the aggrieved party shall advise the other party of the dispute in writing within ten (10) business days. Within ten (10) business days after written notice is received, an authorized representative of each company shall meet and attempt to resolve the dispute. Any agreement reached relating to the dispute shall be committed to writing and signed by both authorized representatives. Disputes arising hereunder which cannot be resolved between the parties shall be submitted to binding arbitration under the rules then prevailing of the American Arbitration Association.

If we initiate the arbitration, it will be held in your home city. If you initiate the arbitration, it will be held in Denver, Colorado. The judgment upon any award rendered in the arbitral proceeding may be entered in any court having jurisdiction. In addition to any amounts awarded, the arbitrator shall be directed to also award costs, expenses and reasonable attorneys' fees to the prevailing party. The arbitrators shall have no authority to order punitive or exemplary damages, may not ignore or vary controlling terms of this Agreement, and shall be required to apply controlling law.

## 12. Conflict of Interest

It is considered to be in conflict with our interests for our employees or any member of their immediate family to accept gifts, payment, extravagant entertainment, services, loans or material beneficial ownership interests in any form from anyone soliciting business, or who may already have established business relations with us. Gifts of nominal value and entertainment, meals, and social invitations that are customary and proper under the circumstances and do not place the recipient under obligation are acceptable. If any employee of ours has received or should otherwise solicit a gift or gratuity from you, you hereby agree to notify our Chief Executive Officer of such event or act. We agree to hold such notification in confidence. It is further understood that failure by you to comply with our policies regarding gifts and gratuities may, at our option, result in the termination of this Agreement and may further preclude any dealings between us.

## 13. Miscellaneous

**Entire Agreement.** This Agreement and the related Schedules constitute our entire agreement between us and supersedes any other existing agreements between us, whether oral or written, with respect to the subject matter hereof. There are no oral understandings or undertakings of any kind with respect hereto not expressly set forth and contained herein. No agent of either party shall have any authority to change or modify any of the terms of this Agreement and no amendment of this Agreement shall be of any effect unless in writing and signed by a duly authorized officer of each party.

**Subcontractors.** The use of subcontractors by us to develop Services, Extranet Sites, and Applications, shall not relieve us of our responsibility for the performance of our obligations under this Agreement, and we will be responsible for any services performed by any permitted subcontractor as if we had performed such services ourself.

**Force Majeure.** WE DO NOT AND CANNOT CONTROL THE FLOW OF DATA TO OR FROM THE SERVICES, AS SUCH FLOW DEPENDS IN LARGE PART ON THE PERFORMANCE OF INTERNET SERVICES AND SOFTWARE PROVIDED OR CONTROLLED BY THIRD PARTIES AND ON THE PUBLIC INTERNET INFRASTRUCTURE, AS WELL AS ON OTHER EVENTS BEYOND OUR CONTROL ("FORCE MAJEURE EVENTS"). AT TIMES, ACTION OR INACTION OF PARTIES OTHER THAN US AND/OR FORCE MAJEURE EVENTS CAN IMPAIR OR DISRUPT OUR ABILITY

TO PROVIDE THE SERVICES AND/OR YOUR ABILITY TO ACCESS THE SERVICES. NOTWITHSTANDING ANYTHING TO THE CONTRARY IN THIS AGREEMENT, WE DISCLAIM, AND YOU SHALL NOT HOLD US RESPONSIBLE FOR, ANY AND ALL LIABILITY RESULTING FROM OR RELATED TO SUCH ACTIONS AND/OR EVENTS.

**Permitted Successors and Assigns.** All of the terms and provisions of this Agreement shall be binding upon, inure to the benefit of, and be enforceable by the parties and their respective legal representatives, successors and permitted assigns, whether so expressed or not.

**Nonexclusivity.** Nothing in this Agreement shall limit or restrict either party from entering into or continuing any agreement or other arrangement with any other party, whether similar to this Agreement in nature or scope. Moreover, each party shall remain free to provide products and services to any customer or prospective customer so long as the terms of this Agreement are not violated.

**Independent Contractors.** We are acting as independent contractors with respect to the services to be performed under this Agreement and not as your employees or agents.

**Governing Law.** This Agreement shall be governed by the laws of the State of Colorado. Consistent with the above arbitration provisions, any judicial action or proceeding between the parties relating to this Agreement must be brought in the state or federal courts of the State of Colorado. Each party consents to the jurisdiction of such courts, agrees to accept service of process by mail, and hereby waives all jurisdictional and venue defenses otherwise available to it.

**Notice.** All notices hereunder shall be in writing. All such notices may be given personally, by certified or registered mail, by overnight courier using a delivery receipt of record, by facsimile transmission, or as expressly permitted in this Agreement, by e-mail. All such notices shall be deemed to be received as follows: (a) if delivered personally, when received; (b) if mailed, three days after being mailed; (c) if sent by overnight courier, when signed for; and (d) if sent by facsimile, when the telefax has been transmitted over the telephone lines, as evidenced by a facsimile confirmation report generated by the transmitting machine. Notices shall be sent to the parties at the addresses listed below or to such other address as one party may, from time to time, designate by notice to the other party.

**Assignment.** Neither party shall assign, sublicense or otherwise transfer (voluntarily, by operation of law or otherwise) this Agreement or any right, interest or benefit under this Agreement without the prior written consent of the other Party.

**Severability.** If any provision of this Agreement is determined to be invalid or unenforceable under any applicable statute or rule of law, such provision shall be reformed to the minimum extent necessary to cause such provision to be valid and enforceable, provided the reformed provision shall not have a material adverse effect on the substantive rights of either party. If no such reformation is possible, then such provision shall be deemed omitted, and the balance of the Agreement shall remain valid and enforceable, unaffected by such provision.

**Remedies.** To the extent permitted by applicable law, the rights and remedies of the parties provided under this Agreement are cumulative, and in addition to any other rights and remedies of the parties at law or equity. Without limitation of the foregoing, Customer shall be entitled to the remedy of specific performance of CaseShare's obligations hereunder.

**Survival.** All provisions of this Agreement relating to confidentiality, proprietary rights, indemnification and limitations of liability shall survive the termination or nonrenewal of this Agreement.

**Counterparts; Signatures.** This Agreement may be executed in counterparts by each party, each copy of which will have the force and effect of fully executed original. A copy or facsimile of a signature will be binding upon the signatory as if it were an original signature.

This Agreement is executed by the duly authorized representatives of CaseShare and Customer as of April 1, 2005 (the "Effective Date").

**Customer:**                          **CaseShare Systems, Inc.**

                                       1860 Blake Street, Suite 700,
                                       Denver CO 80202

_____            _____
Name                                   Name


_____            _____
Title                                  Title

# *Preservation and Spoliation*

**3**

"What we've got here . . . is failure to communicate"
   —Prison Captain, *Cool Hand Luke*

After six years of dealing with evidence that should have been preserved and wasn't, and evidence that was destroyed when it should have been kept, we have come to one rock solid conclusion. Most of the time, "What we've got here . . . is failure to communicate." Though we have indeed seen deliberate acts, an astonishing percentage of the time, people seem to have no idea what they are supposed to preserve and why, nor do they understand that the routine destruction of data in their company may well be regarded as spoliation.

On a regular basis, we see folks who have stomped all over the evidence, not with any intent to destroy, but because they were simply curious or wanted to determine "how much trouble we're in." A remarkable number believe that their document retention policies will act as a shield from spoliation charges—and they have never heard of the term "litigation hold." To be sure, a document retention policy may indeed provide a defense (and there are samples in this chapter), but only if it is reasonable, not adopted in response to the threat of litigation, and was appropriately modified when a "litigation hold" should have been in place. When is that? When litigation or an official investigation has begun or is reasonably anticipated. But we are ahead of ourselves.

Let us go backward in time.

Ancient mariners navigated by maps that sometimes depicted dragons in uncharted waters, occasionally even bearing the legend "This way be dragons." Within the legal profession, spoliation of electronic evidence has constituted murky, dangerous, and uncharted waters, and it is no exaggeration at all to say, "This way be dragons."

Then came *Zubulake V,* and the waters became clearer—but more fearsome. The fifth decision in *Zubulake v. UBS Warburg LLC et al.* (2004 WL 1620866 S.D.N.Y.) came down on July 20, 2004, and its effects have rippled throughout the legal profession. In an otherwise routine employment discrimination case, plaintiff Laura Zubulake moved to sanction UBS Warburg for its failure to produce relevant information and for its tardy production of evidence.

Warburg's counsel had issued a litigation hold after Zubulake filed EEOC charges and had orally transmitted preservation of evidence instructions but failed to mention backup tapes. A visibly disgruntled Judge Scheindlin noted that some employees deleted e-mails in spite of the instructions and others did not produce relevant information to counsel. The judge acknowledged that this was not the fault of the defense lawyers; however, she chided the lawyers for failure to request retained information from one key employee and failure to give litigation-hold instructions to another. She admonished the lawyers for failure to talk with another employee about how she maintained her computer files. Judge Scheindlin was clearly irked by counsel's failure to safeguard backup tapes that might have contained some of the deleted e-mail, thereby mitigating the damage done by the client's e-mail deletions. Her decision provides a detailed list of the client's and lawyer's shortcomings. Worse yet, evidence eventually recovered from the backup tapes (and some had inexplicably "gone missing") clearly showed that relevant evidence favorable to the plaintiff had been destroyed.

As the judge noted wryly, the famous line from *Cool Hand Luke* was right on target: "What we've got here is failure to communicate." The result? UBS Warburg was ordered to pay the costs of plaintiff's motion including attorney's fees, as well as to pay the costs of any other depositions required by the late production of the e-mails. Most distressing was the imposition of the dreaded "adverse inference instruction," which Judge Scheindlin announced she would give to the jury. The judge considered but declined to award sanctions against the lawyers, citing the specific set of facts and the dearth of judicial direction in this area; however, she laid out a list of counsel responsibilities intended to give future guidance and made it clear that lawyers might be subject to sanction if they did not abide by them. The guidelines say that counsel must

1. Actively monitor compliance so that all sources of discoverable information are identified and searched, noting that it is *not* sufficient to

advise the client of a litigation hold and then expect the client to retain, identify and produce the relevant evidence;

2. Become familiar with the client's document retention policies and
   computing infrastructure, speaking with the client's key IT personnel
   to do so;
3. Communicate with all key players involved in litigation, inquiring as
   to how and where they store their information, and advising them of
   their preservation of evidence obligations;
4. Ensure that a "litigation hold" is implemented whenever litigation is
   reasonably anticipated and periodically reissue the notice;
5. Communicate directly with key players; and
6. Instruct all employees to produce responsive electronic files and ensure that relevant backup tapes or other archival media are safely
   stored.

If some of this seems onerous, the judge was careful to point out that the
actions of counsel must be reasonable, noting that counsel cannot be obligated to monitor their client like a parent watching a child. Nevertheless,
Judge Scheindlin observed that counsel is more aware of the legal duties surrounding evidence preservation and production and therefore held to a high
standard of involvement and monitoring.

Will Zubulake's clear reasoning and explicit standards be heeded? Commentators, the authors included, believe it will. Judges are showing increasing intolerance for spoliation, whether it is the open mockery of the system
displayed by Arthur Andersen and Enron or the more subtle spoliation that
comes from lassitude and failure to energetically get (and keep) a handle on
the preservation of electronic evidence. Hefty fines have become the norm
(fines exceeding $1,000,000 are no longer rare), and the issuance of adverse
inference instructions is also on the rise.

*Zubulake* continues to spawn precedent-setting opinions with which all
lawyers should be familiar. *Zubulake V* represents the first time that a court
has set forth such explicit guidelines for lawyers managing the preservation
and production of electronic evidence. The betting money is that courts will
largely fall in line behind the principles of *Zubulake* with only minor modifications.

In support of that premise, note the recent *Morgan Stanley* decision
(*Coleman (Parent) Holdings, Inc. v. Morgan Stanley & Co., Inc.*, 2005 WL 679071
(Fla. Cir. Ct. Mar. 1, 2005)). The high-stakes fraud trial pitted New York finan-
cier Ronald Perelman against investment banking firm Morgan Stanley. The
two sides had sparred endlessly over Morgan Stanley's repeated failure to
hand over e-mail messages connected to a $1.5 billion merger in 1998 between
Coleman Inc., a camping gear maker majority-owned by Perelman, and Sun-

beam Corp., the Wall Street firm's client. Perelman wanted to review e-mails to find evidence that Morgan Stanley knew or should have known of accounting fraud at Sunbeam before he struck a deal with the company. Ultimately, Morgan Stanley was found by the Court to be in noncompliance with the Court's Agreed Order. Although Morgan Stanley did order the preservation of related paper documents, it continued to overwrite e-mail after 12 months despite an SEC regulation requiring that it be preserved for two years. Moreover, Morgan Stanley falsely certified that it had complied with the Court's Agreed Order. Late in the game, it corrected the false certification and said that more responsive material had been discovered. The company, however, continued to frustrate the court by a series of further e-discovery missteps and what the court called a "lack of candor" by the company's counsel. Ultimately, the Court found "a willful and gross abuse of discovery obligations" many of which "were done knowingly, deliberately and in bad faith." Consequently, the Court found that Morgan Stanley spoiled evidence justifying sanctions based on its failure to maintain e-mail in readily accessible form as required by SEC regulations and with knowledge that legal action was threatened. Sanctions were also justified based on willful disobedience of the Agreed Order. The Court granted plaintiff's motion for an adverse inference instruction, which essentially told the jury it could infer that Sunbeam had defrauded investors like Perelman. This was undoubtedly a major factor leading to the jury's $1.5 billion verdict in favor of the plaintiff.

To say that judges are impatient with spoliation is a little like saying that it is breezy during a hurricane. Judges are downright irate and frequently lose their composure in the face of clear misconduct by clients, sometimes abetted by counsel. As heftier fines—as well as adverse inference instructions—have become par for the course, it is imperative that all lawyers ensure that they have full knowledge of what may constitute spoliation and take all reasonable measures to make sure that they and their clients do not, even unknowingly, engage in spoliation. On the other hand, spoliation on the other side may well pave the road to victory in court, if it can be manifested to the court convincingly.

The documents included in this chapter will assist counsel in preparing preservation of evidence letters to clients, opposing counsel and third parties. Do not fear to brandish the sword of spoliation—if you are not crystal clear as to what constitutes spoliation and what its possible consequences may be, you will not get the attention of your client, your opponent, or a third party. This way you will be sure there is no "failure to communicate."

# Client Preservation of Evidence Letter

## Form 3.1
## Preservation of Evidence Letter to Client

October 29, 2005

RE: [Case Name]—Data Preservation

Dear:

Please be advised that the Office of General Counsel requires your assistance with respect to preserving corporate information in the above-referenced matter.

Electronically stored data is an important and irreplaceable source of discovery and/or evidence in this matter.

The lawsuit requires preservation of all information from [Corporation's] computer systems, removable electronic media, and other locations relating to [description of event, transaction, business unit, product, etc.]. This includes, but is not limited to, e-mail and other electronic communication, word processing documents, spreadsheets, databases, calendars, telephone logs, contact manager information, Internet usage files, and network access information.

Employees must take every reasonable step to preserve this information until further notice from the Office of General Counsel. *Failure to do so could result in extreme penalties against [Corporation].*

If this correspondence is in any respect unclear, please contact [designated coordinator] at [phone number].

Sincerely,

## Form 3.2
## Preservation of Evidence Letter to Client Post-*Zubulake*

CLIENT ADDRESS BLOCK

Re: Preservation of Electronic Data
     Your File No.
     Our File No.

Dear _____:

As I am sure you are aware, the advent of e-discovery has brought with it a new dimension to litigation with potentially serious consequences for the unwary. Not long ago a $1.45 billion judgment ($604 million compensatory, $850 million punitive), plus ongoing interest charges in excess of $200 million, was entered against Morgan Stanley. In that case, the judge took the unusual step of instructing the jury that it should assume Morgan Stanley had participated in a scheme to mislead and cover up information because it and its lawyers had consistently and deliberately violated the judge's electronic discovery orders by failing to produce internal e-mails. In another well known case, a $29.3 million judgment was entered against UBS Warburg in favor of a former employee in the context of a sex-discrimination claim. Because of UBS's failure to preserve and produce e-mails, the court instructed the jury it could assume that any e-mails discarded by the bank after the plaintiff filed her EEOC complaint would have hurt its case. This instruction had obvious consequences given the jury's verdict. In light of these concerns, it is imperative at the outset of this litigation that you understand your obligations with respect to the preservation of electronic data and information in all its forms.

The series of reported decisions arising from the employment discrimination suit of Laura Zubulake against UBS Warburg, LLC, in the U.S. District Court, Southern District of New York, has created a set of guiding principles concerning electronic discovery that must be followed in this case. In *Zubulake v. UBS Warburg, LLC*, 217 F.R.D. 309, 312 (S.D.N.Y. 2003) (referred to generally as "*Zubulake I*"), Judge Scheindlin addressed the issues of both the scope of electronic discovery and who should pay for its production. At this time there is no question, subject to any limitations set forth in the applicable procedural rules on discovery, that essentially all electronic data is potentially discoverable. This includes e-mail sent or received by any employee, other "active" information stored on servers, or information stored on backup tapes or other media that are capable of restoration, even if the information was deleted at some prior time. In the appropriate case the court will consider whether the cost of producing such information should be shifted from the party possessing the information to the party requesting the information. That determination, however, does not affect the basic obligation of every party, including business entities and all of their employees, to preserve all electronic data once the reasonable likelihood of litigation becomes apparent.

The failure to properly preserve such information can result in serious adverse consequences. In *Zubulake v. UBS Warburg, LLC*, 220 F.R.D. 212 (S.D.N.Y. 2003) (*Zubulake IV*) the court addressed the obligations of the litigants. Once a party reasonably anticipates litigation, it must suspend its routine document retention/destruction policy and put in place a "litigation hold" to ensure the preservation of relevant documents. As a general rule, that litigation hold does not apply to inaccessible backup tapes (e.g., those typically maintained solely for the purpose of disaster recovery), which may continue to be recycled on the schedule set forth in the company's policy. On the other hand, if backup tapes are accessible (i.e., actively used for information retrieval), such tapes would likely be subject to the litigation hold. If a company can identify where particular employee documents are stored on backup tapes, then the tapes storing the documents of "key players" to the existing or threatened litigation should be preserved if the information contained on those tapes is not otherwise available.

A party's obligations do not end with the implementation of a litigation hold. Counsel must oversee compliance with the litigation hold, and monitor the party's efforts to retain and produce the relevant documents. Proper communication between the lawyer and the client must ensure that all relevant information, or at least all sources of relevant information, is discovered and retained on a continuing basis, and that relevant nonprivileged material is produced to the opposing party.

In *Zubulake v. UBS Warburg, LLC*, 2004 WL 1620866 (S.D.N.Y.) ("*Zubulake V*") the court discussed the obligation of lawyers, both in-house and outside counsel, to communicate to their clients clearly and effectively the client's obligation to preserve and timely produce all relevant electronic information, and to heed counsel's instructions on preservation on an ongoing basis. In addition, independent of the client's obligations, legal counsel have an obligation to take steps to safeguard backup tapes, request retained information from key employees, and give litigation-hold instructions to the client's key employees. Failure to follow these admonitions could result in the court finding there has been spoliation of evidence that will result in the imposition of sanctions.

Although the issues in *Zubulake V* were not in front of the court in *Hagemeyer North America, Inc. v. Gateway Data Sciences Corporation*, 222 F.R.D. 594 (2004), in that case Judge Randa, the Chief Judge for the United States District

Court, Eastern District of Wisconsin, found the reasoning of *Zubulake I* persuasive. He specifically adopted the seven-factor test of *Zubulake I* in addressing a dispute on the scope of requested discovery and the issue of cost shifting. Barring the development of any case law to the contrary, I believe for any case venued in the Eastern District of Wisconsin, everyone should operate under the assumption that the court's reasoning in all of the *Zubulake* cases will ultimately apply to this action.

To comply with counsel's obligations, once a litigation hold is in place, a party and counsel must make certain that all sources of potentially relevant information are identified and placed on hold. To do that counsel must become fully familiar with the client's document retention policies as well as the client's data retention architecture. This will invariably involve speaking with information technology personnel, who can explain system-wide backup procedures and the actual (as opposed to theoretical) implementation of the firm's recycling policy. It will also involve communicating with the "key players" in the litigation in order to understand how they stored information. In *Zubulake*, for example, some of the UBS employees created separate computer files pertaining to the plaintiff, while others printed out relevant e-mails and retained them in hard copy only. Unless counsel interviews each employee, it is impossible to determine whether all potential sources of information have been inspected. It is not necessary that counsel review the documents at that time, only that counsel ensures that they are retained. It is not sufficient to notify all employees of a litigation hold and expect that the party will then retain and produce all relevant information. Counsel must take affirmative steps to monitor compliance so that all sources of discoverable information are identified and searched.

Once potentially relevant information is identified, there is a continuing duty to retain the information and to produce it if it is responsive to the opposing party's requests. The continuing duty to supplement discovery under the Federal Rules of Civil Procedure strongly suggests that parties also have a duty to make sure that discoverable information is not lost or destroyed. To meet this obligation, counsel should issue a litigation hold at the outset of litigation. The litigation hold must be periodically reissued so new employees are aware of it and it remains fresh in the mind of all employees. Counsel must meet with the key players, explain the preservation obligation, and periodically remind them the preservation duty is still in place. Finally, all employees should be instructed to produce electronic copies of their relevant active files. Counsel must also make sure that all backup media the party is required to retain is identified and stored in a safe place. In appropriate cases counsel should take possession of the backup tapes. Alternatively, counsel can take steps to ensure the backup tapes are segregated and placed in storage.

Failure to comply with these preservation obligations could result in severe sanctions being imposed by the court including monetary penalties, the giving of an adverse inference instruction to the jury at trial, or even dismissal of certain legal claims or defenses.

Based on the foregoing, I would ask that you issue a written notification to all affected employees to institute a litigation hold concerning any of the information related to this action. While I understand you have discussed this with some of your employees, it is imperative that you provide everyone with written notice. In addition, you should reissue the litigation-hold instructions periodically. Please make sure you have consulted with your IT department so they are aware of the litigation hold. I would also ask that you arrange for us to have an appropriate conference with your IT supervisor so we can discuss document retention policies, backup practices, and related items. Please remind all of the key players we met at our recent meeting of their obligations in this regard. Although we did discuss their individual responsibilities to both identify and preserve any information they may have in electronic form, they need to be reminded in written form of their obligation to preserve such information. If you have any questions about these issues please contact me, so we can discuss them in detail.

Very truly yours,

# Opposing Party Preservation of Evidence Letter

## Form 3.3
## Preservation of Evidence Letter to Opponent or Third Party

[Date]

RE: [Case Name]—Data Preservation

Dear:

Please be advised that [Plaintiffs/Defendants/Third Party] believe electronically stored information to be an important and irreplaceable source of discovery and/or evidence in the above-referenced matter.

The discovery requests served in this matter seek information from [Plaintiffs'/Defendants'] computer systems, removable electronic media and other locations. This includes, but is not limited to, e-mail and other electronic communications, word processing documents, spreadsheets, databases, calendars, telephone logs, contact manager information, Internet usage files, and network access information.

The laws and rules prohibiting destruction of evidence apply to electronically stored information in the same manner that they apply to other evidence. Because of its format, electronic information is easily deleted, modified, or corrupted. Accordingly, [Plaintiffs/Defendants/Third Party] must take every reasonable step to preserve this information until the final resolution of this matter. This includes, but is not limited to, an obligation to discontinue all relevant data destruction and backup tape recycling policies.

If this correspondence is in any respect unclear, please do not hesitate to call me.

Sincerely,

# Form 3.4
## Preservation of Evidence Letter to Opposing Counsel

[Date]

[Address]

re:  [matter, case number]

Dear: _____:

By this letter, you and your client(s) are hereby given notice, with respect to the above-referenced case, not to destroy, conceal, or alter any paper or electronic files and other data generated by and/or stored on your client's (clients') computers and storage media (e.g., hard disks, floppy disks, backup tapes), or any other electronic data, such as voice mail. As you know, your client's (clients') failure to comply with this notice can result in severe sanctions being imposed by the Court (and liability in tort) for spoliation of evidence or potential evidence.

Through discovery, we expect to obtain from you a number of documents and things, including files stored on your client's (clients') computers and your client's (clients') computer storage media. (As part of our initial discovery efforts, you [are hereby served with/will soon receive] [initial/supplemental] interrogatories and requests for documents and other information.)

In order to avoid spoliation, you will need to provide the data requested on the original media. Do not reuse any media to provide this data.

Although [we may bring/have brought] a motion for an order preserving documents and things from destruction or alteration, your client's [clients'] obligation to preserve documents and things for discovery in this case arises in law and equity independently from any order on such motion.

Electronic documents and the storage media on which they reside contain relevant, discoverable information beyond what may be found in printed documents. Therefore, even where a paper copy exists, we [seek/will seek] all documents in their electronic form along with information about those documents contained on the media. We also [seek/will seek] paper printouts of only those documents that contain unique information after they were printed out (such as paper documents containing handwriting, signatures, marginalia, drawings, annotations, highlighting and redactions) along with any paper documents for which no corresponding electronic files exist.

Our discovery requests [ask/will ask] for certain data on the hard disks, floppy disks and backup media used in your client's (clients') computers, some of which data are not readily available to an ordinary computer user, such as "deleted" files and "file fragments." As you may know, although a user may "erase" or "delete" a file, all that is really erased is a reference to that file in a table on the hard disk; unless overwritten with new data, a "deleted" file can be as intact on the disk as any "active" file you would see in a directory listing.

(Courts have made it clear that all information available on electronic storage media is discoverable, whether readily readable ["active"] or "deleted" but recoverable. See, e.g., *Easley, McCaleb & Assocs., Inc. v. Perry,* No. E-2663 [Ga. Super. Ct. July 13, 1994; "deleted" files on a party's computer hard drive held to be discoverable, and plaintiff's expert was allowed to retrieve all recoverable files]; *Santiago v. Miles,* 121 F.R.D. 636, 640 [W.D.N.Y. 1988; a request for "raw information in computer banks" was proper and obtainable under the discovery rules]; *Gates Rubber Co. v. Bando Chemical Indus., Ltd.,* 167 F.R.D. 90, 112 [D. Colo. 1996; mirror-image copy of everything on a hard drive "the method which would yield the most complete and accurate results," chastising a party's expert for failing to do so]; and *Northwest Airlines, Inc. v. Teamsters Local 2000, et al.,* 163 L.R.R.M. [BNA] 2460, [USDC Minn. 1999]; court ordered image-copying by Northwest's expert of home computer hard drives of employees suspected of orchestrating an illegal "sick-out" on the Internet.)

Accordingly, electronic data and storage media that may be subject to our discovery requests and that your client(s) are obligated to maintain and not alter or destroy, include but are not limited to the following:

### Introduction: Description of Files and File Types Sought

All digital or analog electronic files, including "deleted" files and file fragments, stored in machine-readable format on magnetic, optical, or other storage media, including the hard drives or floppy disks used by your client's (clients') computers and their backup media (e.g., other hard drives, backup tapes, floppies, Jaz cartridges, CD-ROMs) or otherwise, regardless of whether such files have been reduced to paper printouts. More specifically, your client(s) is (are) to preserve all of your e-mails, both sent and received, whether internally or externally; all word-processed files, including drafts and revisions; all spreadsheets, including drafts and revisions; all databases; all CAD (computer-aided design) files, including drafts and revisions; all presentation data or slide shows produced by presentation software (such as Microsoft PowerPoint); all graphs, charts, and other data produced by project management software (such as Microsoft Project); all data generated by calendaring, task management, and personal information management (PIM) software (such as Microsoft Outlook or Lotus Notes); all data created with the use of personal data assistants (PDAs), such as PalmPilot, iPAQ, or other Windows CE, Pocket PC, or Windows Mobile devices; all data created with the use of document-management software; all data created with the use of paper and electronic mail logging and routing software; all Internet and Web-browser-generated history files, caches, and "cookies" files generated at the workstation of each employee and/or agent in your client's (clients') employ and on any and all backup storage media; and any and all other files generated by users through the use of computers and/or telecommunications, including but not limited to voice mail. Further, you are to preserve any log or logs of network use by employees or otherwise, whether kept in paper or electronic form, and to preserve all copies of your backup tapes and the software necessary to reconstruct the data on those tapes, so there can be made a complete, bit-by-bit "mirror" evidentiary image copy of the storage media of each and every personal computer (and/or workstation) and network server in your control and custody, as well as image copies of all hard drives retained by you and no longer in service, but in use at any time from _____ to the present.

Your client(s) is (are) also not to pack, compress, purge or otherwise dispose of files and parts of files unless a true and correct copy of such files is made.

Your client(s) is (are) also to preserve and not destroy all passwords, decryption procedures (including, if necessary, the software to decrypt the files); network access codes, ID names, manuals, tutorials, written instructions, decompression or reconstruction software, and any and all other information and things necessary to access, view and (if necessary) reconstruct the electronic data we [are requesting/will request] through discovery.

1. **Business Records:** [All documents and information about documents containing backup and/or archive policy and/or procedure, document retention policy, names of backup and/or archive software, names and addresses of any offsite storage provider.]
   a. All e-mail and information about e-mail (including message contents, header information and logs of e-mail system usage) (sent or received) by the following persons:

      [list names, job titles]

   b. All other e-mail and information about e-mail (including message contents, header information and logs of e-mail system usage) containing information about or related to:

      [insert detail]

c. All databases (including all records and fields and structural information in such databases), containing any reference to and/or information about or related to:

[insert detail]

d. All logs of activity (both in paper and electronic formats) on computer systems and networks that have or may have been used to process or store electronic data containing information about or related to:

[insert detail]

e. All word processing files, including prior drafts, "deleted" files, and file fragments, containing information about or related to:

[insert detail]

f. With regard to electronic data created by application programs that process financial, accounting and billing information, all electronic data files, including prior drafts, "deleted" files, and file fragments, containing information about or related to:

[insert detail]

g. All files, including prior drafts, "deleted" files, and file fragments, containing information from electronic calendars and scheduling programs regarding or related to:

[insert detail]

h. All electronic data files, including prior drafts, "deleted," files and file fragments about or related to:

[insert detail]

2. **Online Data Storage on Mainframes and Minicomputers:** With regard to online storage and/or direct access storage devices attached to your client's (clients') mainframe computers and/or minicomputers: they are not to modify or delete any electronic data files, "deleted" files and file fragments existing at the time of this letter's de-

livery, which meet the definitions set forth in this letter, unless a true and correct copy of each such electronic data file has been made and steps have been taken to ensure that such a copy will be preserved and accessible for purposes of this litigation.

3. **Offline Data Storage, Backups and Archives, Floppy Diskettes, Tapes, and Other Removable Electronic Media:** With regard to all electronic media used for offline storage, including magnetic tapes and cartridges and other media that, at the time of this letter's delivery, contained any electronic data meeting the criteria listed in paragraph 1 above: Your client (clients) is (are) to stop any activity that may result in the loss of such electronic data, including rotation, destruction, overwriting and/or erasure of such media in whole or in part. This request is intended to cover all removable electronic media used for data storage in connection with their computer systems, including magnetic tapes and cartridges, magneto-optical disks, floppy diskettes, and all other media, whether used with personal computers, minicomputers, or mainframes or other computers, and whether containing backup and/or archive data sets and other electronic data, for all of their computer systems.

4. **Replacement of Data Storage Devices:** Your client (clients) is (are) not to dispose of any electronic data storage devices and/or media that may be replaced due to failure and/or upgrade and/or other reasons that may contain electronic data meeting the criteria listed in paragraph 1 above.

5. **Fixed Drives on Stand-Alone Personal Computers and Network Workstations:** With regard to electronic data meeting the criteria listed in paragraph 1 above, which existed on fixed drives attached to stand-alone microcomputers and/or network workstations at the time of this letter's delivery: Your client (clients) is (are) not to alter, erase, wipe or scrub such electronic data, and not to perform other procedures (such as data compression and disk defragmentation or optimization routines) that may impact such data, unless a true and correct copy has been made of such active files and of completely restored versions of such deleted electronic files and file fragments, copies have been made of all directory listings (including hidden files) for all directories and subdirectories containing such files, and arrangements have been made to preserve copies during the pendency of this litigation.

6. **Programs and Utilities:** Your client (clients) is (are) to preserve copies of all application programs and utilities, which may be used to process electronic data covered by this letter.

7. **Log of System Modifications:** Your client (clients) is (are) to maintain an activity log to document modifications made to any electronic data processing system that may affect the system's capability to process any electronic data meeting the criteria listed in paragraph 1 above, regardless of whether such modifications were made by employees, contractors, vendors and/or any other third parties.

8. **Personal Computers Used by Your Employees and/or Their Secretaries and Assistants:** The following steps should immediately be taken in regard to all personal computers used by your client's (clients') employees and/or their secretaries and assistants.

   a. As to fixed drives attached to such computers: (i) a true and correct copy is to be made of all electronic data on such fixed drives relating to this matter, including all active files and completely restored versions of all deleted electronic files and file fragments; (ii) full directory listings (including hidden files) for all directories and subdirectories (including hidden directories) on such fixed drives should be written; and (iii) such copies and listings are to be preserved until this matter reaches its final resolution.

   b. All floppy diskettes, magnetic tapes and cartridges, and other media used in connection with such computers prior to the date of delivery of this letter containing any electronic data relating to this matter are to be collected and put into storage for the duration of this lawsuit.

9. **Evidence Created Subsequent to This Letter:** With regard to electronic data created subsequent to the date of delivery of this letter, relevant evidence is not be destroyed and your client (clients) is (are) to take whatever steps are appropriate to avoid destruction of evidence.

To assure that your and your client's (clients') obligation to preserve documents and things will be met, please forward a copy of this letter to all persons and entities with custodial responsibility for the items referred to in this letter.

Sincerely, etc.

## Form 3.5
## Preservation of Evidence Letter

Re: [case name]

Dear Sir or Madam:

As you are aware, the scope of the above referenced litigation includes critical evidence in the form of electronic data contained in the computer systems of _____. This letter constitutes notice and demand that such evidence identified below in paragraphs 2 through 6 must be immediately preserved and retained by _____ until further written notice from the undersigned. This request is essential, as a paper printout of text contained in a computer file does not completely reflect all information contained within the electronic file. In addition, the continued operation of the computer systems identified herein will likely result in the destruction of relevant evidence because electronic evidence can be easily altered, deleted, or otherwise modified. The failure to preserve and retain the electronic data outlined in this notice constitutes spoliation of evidence and will subject _____ to legal claims for damages and/or evidentiary and monetary sanctions.

1. For purposes of this notice, "Electronic Data" shall include, but not be limited to, all text files (including word processing documents), spread sheets, e-mail, and information concerning e-mail (including logs of e-mail history and usage, header information, and "deleted" files), Internet history files and preferences, graphical image files (including, but not limited to ".JPG, .GIF, .BMP, and TIFF" files), databases, calendar and scheduling information, computer system activity logs, and all file fragments and backup files containing Electronic Data.
2. Please preserve and retain all Electronic Data generated or received by _____.
3. Please preserve and retain all Electronic Data containing any information about _____.
4. _____ must refrain from operating (or removing or altering fixed or external drives and media attached thereto) stand-alone personal computers, network workstations, notebook, and/or laptop computers operated by _____.
5. _____ must retain and preserve all backup tapes or other storage media, whether on-line or off-line, and refrain from overwriting or deleting information contained thereon, which may contain Electronic Data identified in paragraphs 2 through 4.

6. To alleviate any burden upon _____, the undersigned is prepared to immediately enlist the services of a computer forensic expert to image and examine all drives and media in the custody and control of _____, which may contain Electronic Data relevant to this matter. This can be accomplished in a manner outlined by the court in *Simon Property Group v. mySimon, Inc.* 194. F.R.D. 639 (S.D.Ind. 2000), to ensure retention of all privileges while properly processing computer evidence as mandated by the court in *Gates Rubber Co. v. Bando Chemical Indus., Ltd.*, 167 F.R.D. 90 (D.C.Col., 1996).

Please contact me if you have any questions regarding this request.

Sincerely,

## Form 3.6
## Preservation of Evidence Letter

Date:

Re:

Dear _____:

This letter is to notify you that potential litigation is contemplated against XYZ corporation involving alleged sexual harassment of Jane Doe by her supervisor, John Smith (the "Claim") and that, in connection with such Claim, you may have in your possession, custody, or control documents, information, and electronically or digitally stored information relevant to the Claim. In addition, you and/or your agents and employees may have knowledge of facts relevant to the Claim.

You are under a legal duty to preserve, retain, and protect all possibly relevant evidence, including electronic evidence, once litigation appears eminent or has commenced. The failure to preserve and retain the electronic data outlined in this notice constitutes spoliation of evidence and will subject you to legal claims for damages and/or evidentiary and monetary sanctions.

For purposes of this notice, "electronic data" or "electronic evidence" shall include, but not be limited to, all text files (including word processing documents), presentation files (such as PowerPoint), spread sheets, e-mail files and information concerning e-mail files (including logs of e-mail history and usage, header information, and deleted files), Internet history files and preferences, graphical files in any format, databases, calendar and scheduling information, task lists, telephone logs, contact managers, computer system activity logs, and all file fragments and backup files containing electronic data.

Specifically, you are instructed not to destroy, disable, erase, encrypt, alter, or otherwise make unavailable any electronic evidence relevant to the Claim, and you are further instructed to take reasonable efforts to preserve such data. To meet this burden, you are instructed by way of example and not limitation, to:

- ◆ Preserve all data storage backup files (i.e., not overwrite any previously existing backups);
- ◆ Preserve and retain all electronic data generated or received by employees who may have personal knowledge of the facts involved in the Claim, including but not limited to those of _____, _____, and _____;

- Refrain from operating (or removing or altering fixed or external drives and media attached thereto) any workstations or laptops that are reasonably thought to have data related to the Claim, including but not limited to the workstations and laptops of Linda Bate, Tim Jones, and Mary Green;

- Preserve and retain all data from servers and networking equipment logging network access activity and system authentication;

- Preserve and retain all electronic data in any format, media, or location relating to the Claim, including data on floppy disks, Zip disks, CD-ROMs, CD-RWs, tape, PDAs, cell phones, memory cards/sticks, or digital copiers;

- Prevent employees from deleting or overwriting any electronic data related to the Claim; and

- Take such other security measures, including, but not limited to, restricting physical and electronic access to all electronically stored data directly or indirectly related to the Claim.

To facilitate the preservation of data, this firm has engaged __[insert name of forensic company]__, to forensically acquire the hard drives and other media that may contain electronic data related to the Claim. Kindly call me upon receipt of this letter so that we may arrange the details of the acquisition.

Thank you for your cooperation.

Very truly yours,

_____

Address and Phone Number

## Form 3.7
## Preservation of Evidence Letter to
## Opposing Counsel Post-*Zubulake*

Dear Sir or Madam:

I am the attorney for _____, the plaintiff/defendant in the above-referenced matter. This letter constitutes my client's demand that you and your client immediately take all steps necessary to identify, retain and preserve all electronic media in your client's possession or control that contain data relevant to the claims and defenses in the matter within, and that your client avoid spoliation of all relevant data. Data includes not only information that can be perceived and read by your client's computer systems and programs installed thereon, but also all data resident on relevant electronic media that cannot be perceived by your client's computer system but that can be recovered and analyzed using computer forensic techniques. Data that cannot be perceived by your client's operating system includes deleted, hidden, and orphaned data as well as artifacts and residual data created in the normal course of using a computer system. It is essential that your client act quickly to protect this data because the continued operation of your client's relevant computer systems will overwrite data resident on the hard drive, including discoverable data that is invisible to the operating system. See, for example, *Antioch v. Scrapbook Borders, Inc.* 210 F.R.D. 645 (D. Minn. 2002). Finally, this letter is notice and demand that all relevant data be safeguarded from destruction from any cause whatsoever, including destruction caused by any of your client's policies related to retention of electronic data, including but not limited to backup, restoration, deletion, destruction, and tape recycling. Destruction of relevant data pursuant to a corporate document retention policy may be spoliation. *Ramabus, Inc. v. Infineon Technologies AG, et al.*, 220 F.R.D. 264 (E.D. Va. March 17, 2004).

I expect that relevant data will be resident on the computers or computer systems used to create, modify, access, store, archive, and/or delete any information related to the within litigation. Although I have not yet had an opportunity to identify with specificity the exact computers containing relevant data, I anticipate doing so during a deposition of your client pursuant to Rule 30(b). Please be advised that I have instructed my client to similarly preserve all relevant data that resides upon any electronic media within my client's possession or control. My client has suspended the application of its corporate retention policy as to relevant computers.

At this stage of the litigation, you and I have similar duties: identifying the computers used by our respective clients to process any data relevant to this matter. Because we both must assist our clients to preserve and identify relevant electronic data, I suggest that we both employ the services of a computer forensic company to create electronic images of all relevant computers using a protocol as set forth in *Simon Property Group v. mySimon, Inc.* 194 F.R.D. 639, 2000 U.S.Dist.LEXIS 8950 (S.D. Ind. 2000). Images of relevant computers can be created simultaneously, during nonworking hours, at night, or on weekends. They can be created on-site, off-site, at attorneys' offices, or wherever may be convenient, with no material disruption of our client's businesses.

The cost of creating these images is not burdensome. I expect the cost to not exceed _____, and my client will pay for the cost of imaging your client's computers. Alternatively, we can discuss whether there is ground for shifting the cost pursuant to the factors set forth in *Zubulake v. UBS Warburg LLC*, 2003 U.S. Dist. LEXIS 7939 (S.D.N.Y. May 13, 2003).

Please contact me to discuss the manner in which we can cooperate in identifying and accessing the respective relevant computers in this matter.

Sincerely,

_____

# Third-Party Preservation of Evidence Letter

## Form 3.8
## Preservation of Evidence Letter to Third Party

Re: Data Preservation—[Case Name]

Dear [Name],

Please be advised that [Plaintiff/Defendant] has reason to believe that electronic information in your company's control or possession may be relevant to the aforementioned legal matter.

Accordingly, discovery requests filed in this matter seek to collect and review electronic information within computer systems, removable electronic media, and other electronic devices owned and/or operated on behalf of [Company Name]. Sources of electronic information that must be preserved may include, but are not limited to, electronic documents, e-mail and electronic correspondence, images and graphics, deleted files, spreadsheets, presentations, databases, system usage logs, Internet history and cache files, as well as enterprise user information, such as contact lists, calendars, task lists, etc.

Because electronic evidence can be both fragile and vulnerable to inadvertent destruction, [Plaintiff/Defendant] has an obligation to take reasonable steps to ensure that electronic information is preserved until this matter has been resolved. Data preservation includes, but is not limited to, ceasing all data destruction activities, automatic e-mail deletion functions, backup tape recycling, hard drive reformatting or degragmenting, and cache-clearing processes.

Laws and regulations barring the destruction of evidence directly apply to electronic evidence and any information created or stored in digital form that is relevant to a case. Failure to take all reasonable steps toward preserving electronic information may cause irreparable harm in this case and could result in sanctions against your [Company Name].

I would be happy to speak with you regarding this matter and provide further guidance or answer any questions.

Thank you for your attention to this matter.

[Signature]

# Document Retention Policy

## Form 3.9
## Document Retention Policy

> Intended for small firms not subject to specific regulatory requirements, SOX, HIPAA, etc.

The corporate records of ACME, INC., and its subsidiaries (hereafter the "Company") are important assets. Corporate records include essentially all records you produce as an employee, whether paper or electronic. A record may be as obvious as a memorandum, an e-mail, a contract, or a case study or something not as obvious, such as a computerized desk calendar, an appointment book, or an expense record.

The law requires the Company to maintain certain types of corporate records, usually for a specified period of time. Failure to retain those records for those minimum periods could subject you and the Company to penalties and fines, cause the loss of rights, obstruct justice, spoil potential evidence in a lawsuit, place the Company in contempt of court, or seriously disadvantage the Company in litigation.

The Company expects all employees to fully comply with any published records-retention or -destruction policies and schedules, provided that all employees should note the following general exception to any stated destruction schedule: If you believe, or the Company informs you, that Company records are relevant to litigation, or potential litigation (i.e., a dispute that could result in litigation), you must preserve those records until the Legal Department determines the records are no longer needed. That exception supersedes any previously or subsequently established destruction schedule for those records. If you believe that exception may apply, or have any question regarding the possible applicability of that exception, please contact the Legal Department.

From time to time the Company establishes retention or destruction policies or schedules for specific categories of records in order to ensure legal compliance and also to accomplish other objectives, such as preserving intellectual property and cost management. Several categories of documents that bear special consideration are identified below. Although minimum retention periods are suggested, the retention of the documents identified below and of documents not included in the identified categories should be determined primarily by the application of the general guidelines affecting document retention identified above, as well as any other pertinent factors.

1. <u>Tax Records.</u> Tax records include, but may not be limited to, documents concerning payroll, expenses, proof of deductions, business costs, accounting procedures, and other documents concerning the Company's revenues. Tax records should be retained for at least six years from the date of filing the applicable return.

2. <u>Employment Records/Personnel Records.</u> State and federal statutes require the Company to keep certain recruitment, employment, and personnel information. The Company should also keep personnel files that reflect performance reviews and any complaints brought against the Company or individual employees under applicable state and federal statutes. The Company should also keep all final memoranda and correspondence reflecting performance reviews and actions taken by or against personnel in the employee's personnel file. Employment and personnel records should be retained for six years.

3. <u>Board and Board Committee Materials.</u> Meeting minutes should be retained in perpetuity in the Company's minute book. A clean copy of all Board and Board Committee materials should be kept for no less than three years by the Company.

4. <u>Press Releases/Public Filings.</u> The Company should retain permanent copies of all press releases and publicly filed documents under the theory that the Company should have its own copy to test the accuracy of any document a member of the public can theoretically produce against the Company.

5. <u>Legal Files.</u> Legal counsel should be consulted to determine the retention period of particular documents, but legal documents should generally be maintained for a period of ten years.

6. <u>Marketing and Sales Documents.</u> The Company should keep final copies of marketing and sales documents for the same period of time it keeps other corporate files, generally three years.

    An exception to the three-year policy may be sales invoices, contracts, leases, licenses, and other legal documentation. These documents should be kept for at least three years beyond the life of the agreement.

7. <u>Development/Intellectual Property and Trade Secrets.</u> Development documents are often subject to intellectual property protection in their final form (e.g., patents and copyrights). The documents detailing the development process are often also of value to the Company and are protected as a trade secret where the Company:

    (a) derives independent economic value from the secrecy of the information; and

    (b) the Company has taken affirmative steps to keep the information confidential.

The Company should keep all documents designated as containing trade secret information for at least the life of the trade secret.

8. <u>Contracts.</u> Finally, execution copies of all contracts entered into by the Company should be retained. The Company should retain copies of the final contracts for at least three years beyond the life of the agreement, and longer in the case of publicly filed contracts.

    (a) <u>Electronic Mail.</u> E-mail that needs to be saved should be either:

        (i) printed in hard copy and kept in the appropriate file; or

        (ii) downloaded to a computer file and kept electronically or on disk as a separate file.

The retention period depends upon the subject matter of the e-mail, as covered elsewhere in this policy.

Failure to comply with this Document Retention Policy may result in punitive action against the employee, including suspension or termination. Questions about this policy should be referred to [name] ([phone], [e-mail address]), who is in charge of administering, enforcing, and updating this policy.

READ, UNDERSTOOD, AND AGREED:

Employee's signature _____

_____
Date

## Form 3.10
## Records Management Policy Statement[1]

Policy Purpose: To provide guidelines for properly establishing a records and information management (RIM) program and assisting those departments that require long-term records retention and procedures for implementing an effective RIM program. Records and information management includes areas such as inactive records, vital records, microfilming, and records retention.

## *Policy*

1. Records and information management (RIM) is the systematic control of all records, regardless of media, from their creation or receipt, through their processing, distribution, organization, storage, and retrieval to their disposition. Information flows through the organization in the form of paper and electronic records such as word processing documents, spreadsheets, e-mail, graphical images, and voice or data transmissions. Information can be stored on a variety of storage media, such as microfilm, microfiche, diskette, optical disk, CD-ROM, videotape, and paper.

2. This policy details the requirements and responsibilities to initiate a well-defined RIM program. The RIM program applies to those departments that require a long-term records-retention, -storage, and -destruction program.

    a. Ensure only essential records of continuing value are preserved. Records should be retained in the active office areas as long as they serve the immediate administrative, legal, or fiscal purpose for which they were created.

    b. Establish safeguards against the illegal removal, loss, or destruction of records. Records either should be disposed of in accordance with an approved records-retention schedule or transferred to the records-retention center until the prescribed retention period has expired.

    c. Management of records is the responsibility of the owner, or creator, of the record. The department director or the director's designated representative should contact the records manager to discuss initiating a records-management program or reviewing an existing records-management program to handle records properly from their creation through their destruction. Departments can be provided guidance on how records should be organized and stored to ensure timely and efficient retrieval.

---

[1]Provided courtesy of the American Records Management Association (ARMA).

    d. The records-retention schedule is the key tool for departments to use to manage their records effectively. Information is a valuable asset; however, if records that contain information cannot be retrieved efficiently or are retained beyond their legal, regulatory, or administrative retention period, they lose their value and may impose a liability to the organization.

3. The benefits of an effective RIM program include:

    a. Greater assurance of legal compliance to minimize liability and discovery impacts;

    b. Improved customer service with higher quality of service and faster retrieval of documents;

    c. Improved staff productivity with effective records-management systems;

    d. Reduced storage costs through elimination of unnecessary and duplicate documents;

    e. Ensured safety of vital organizational records; and

    f. Efficient, cost-effective records-retention and -disposal system.

4. The components of an effective RIM program that may be activated by the records manager include:

    a. Records-retention program;

    b. Vital records program;

    c. Inactive records-management program;

    d. Electronic records-management program;

    e. Records-management handbook/records liaisons' training;

    f. Micrographics (microfilming) program;

    g. Forms-management program (corporate communications);

    h. Active records-management program; and

    i. Copy and reprography program (purchasing).

5. Significant recurring activities initiated by the records manager include:

    a. Annual inventory of the records center: The records manager will annually inventory all records in the records center to confirm information in the records-retention tracking system.

    b. Annual review of the records-retention schedule: The records manager will have the records-retention schedule reviewed and validated annually for accuracy.

    c. Annual files purge program: The records manager will advertise and initiate an annual files purge by all departments. The purpose is to have individuals review personal active file systems, as well as electronic document folders, and to purge documents that are no longer required. No original documents are to be destroyed.

## *Proponent*

1. The vice president for information systems or his designee is the proponent for the RIM program.
2. All questions concerning compliance with this policy should be directed to the records manager unless otherwise indicated.

## *Roles and Responsibilities*

1. The vice president of finance, vice president of legal affairs, and the chief information officer, as needed, will be requested to identify to the records manager the individual who can perform the following tasks:
   a. Review and provide functional approval of an updated or changed records-retention schedule, as required, for all departments.
   b. Become familiar with the purpose of the records-retention schedule.
2. Department directors who need to implement a records-management program should contact the records manager for guidance/assistance and will need to:
   a. Identify a records liaison and inform them of the duties of the records liaison;
   b. Review and update records-retention schedules annually;
   c. Review the records-management handbook, as needed; and
   d. Coordinate departmental activities that may impact records management with the records manager to include office consolidation, office closures, and approval of new or replacement, records storage, and file equipment as requested.
3. Departmental records liaisons are responsible for:
   a. Obtaining records liaisons' overview training from the records manager;
   b. Becoming familiar with and maintaining the records-management handbook;
   c. Assisting in developing and enforcing the records-retention schedule for their department;
   d. Managing the department's records; and
   e. Attending quarterly or as otherwise required records liaisons' meetings.
4. Records manager is responsible for:
   a. Assisting in the design, development, implementation, and/or review of records-management programs to include the programs listed in paragraph 2, Policy, above;
   b. Managing the records-retention center for all departments to ensure safe storage, quick retrieval, records confidentiality, and appropriate records disposition;

    c. Developing and maintaining the records-retention schedule;

    d. Managing the microfilming of records as required;

    e. Issuing and updating the records-management handbook;

    f. Educating and training records liaisons;

    g. Approving records storage and retrieval equipment for departmental purchase as requested;

    h. Participating actively as a member of the following committees:
       i. Records Committee on an as-needed basis for retention issues;
      ii. Forms Approval Committee as a member on an as-needed basis;

    i. Presenting records and information management issues, as required, to the Information Systems Steering Committee or other appropriate forum; and

    j. Chairing quarterly Records Management Committee meeting with records liaison.

## Procedures

Detailed procedures can be found in the records-management handbook. For the most frequent requirements, procedures are summarized below.

  1. Records-Retention Schedules

    a. Each department is responsible for determining retention periods for records created. A record may be kept beyond the legal or regulatory retention period if it satisfies an administrative need based on business necessity, which is stated on the records-retention schedule. To create or update a records retention schedule:
       i. Contact the records manager to assist you;
      ii. Inventory all current records maintained, including all media types;
     iii. Create a master list of data and record types and draft preliminary retention schedule;
     iv. Determine retention periods based on legal, administrative, and historical value;
      v. Obtain approval for retention schedule from IS, Finance, and Legal;
     vi. Publish and implement the retention schedule; and
    vii. Review annually.

    b. State, federal, and/or regulatory requirements prescribe minimum records-retention periods.

    c. Once the specific retention period for any paper or electronic record has been reached, the record will be destroyed consistent with appropriate procedures.

    d. Notwithstanding minimum retention periods, all records shall be maintained until all required audits are completed and shall be kept beyond the listed retention period if litigation is pending or in progress. Records manager must be notified of any litigation that would require retention of records beyond normal disposition.

    e. Destruction of records is permitted in accordance with the law only after expiration of the retention periods stated on the approved departmental retention schedules.

2. Files Transferred to Records Center

    a. Files will be accepted throughout the year once the department has coordinated set patterns for retention with the records manager.

    b. The departmental records liaison will contact records manager via e-mail of a files transfer requirement.

    c. Storage boxes and Records Center Control Card Form must be obtained from records management.

    d. Files must be packed in approved storage boxes.

    e. A Records Center Control Card Form must accompany the boxes.

    f. Records management will provide instructions for proper packing and labeling of boxes in the records-management handbook.

    g. Pickup will be coordinated with records manager.

3. Request for Retrieving Files or Records

    a. Office wishing to retrieve records will contact the records-retention center.

    b. The departmental records liaison will provide information for locating the file from the Records Center Control Card.

    c. Telephone request should not exceed five (5) records per call. For more than five records, a written request should be mailed or e-mailed to records management.

    d. Retrieved records will be tagged with a Records Center Reference Request form. This form *must* be returned to allow prompt and accurate refiling.

    e. Notify records management if file is to be reactivated.

4. Microfilming Records

    a. Medical records will be microfilmed in records management and stored in the information services department for reference and retrieval.

    b. Other departmental records meeting certain specifications will be microfilmed and stored within the department or in records management. This should be coordinated with the records manager.

5. Assistance in the Selection of Records Filing System Equipment
   a. All new records-management and filing equipment should be reviewed by the records manager, as requested, prior to purchase to ensure they are efficient and cost-effective in storage space.
   b. Existing file systems can be reviewed and recommendations provided for improvement.
6. Records-Retention Requirements for Automated Systems
   a. Systems and programming managers will contact the records manager who will assist the department that owns the data in determining records-retention requirements for the electronic data on new and existing systems.
   b. A valid retention schedule will be prepared for electronic records.
7. Vital Records Program

The implementation of a vital records program to protect and preserve records that contain information vital to the conduct of business in the event of a major disaster is crucial. These documents contain the information necessary to recreate the organization's legal and financial position. Vital records generally represent only a small portion of all records and information maintained by the organization. The records manager will review the vital records program annually. Areas of importance are financial records, employee records, insurance policy information, ownership records, major contracts and agreements, corporate records, and negotiable instruments.

## Electronic Records Policy Statement

Each organization's e-mail policy should reflect its own culture and the legal and regulatory framework within which it operates. Developers of the policy must consider factors such as legal issues, records-management retention policies, and information management administration of the e-mail system, along with financial and regulatory issues.

Sample 1: The electronic-mail system is owned by the company, and it is to be used for company business. Occasional use of the system for messages of a personal nature will be treated like any other message. The company desires to respect the right to privacy of its employees and does not monitor electronic mail messages as a routine matter. It does, however, reserve the right to access them, view their contents, and track traffic patterns.

Sample 2: When using e-mail, the message created or used may or may not be a record. When it is designated as a record, it is subject to the records-retention policies of the company. Within the company, each person is responsible for controlling records according to the records-management policies, and when an e-mail message is considered a record, it falls into this category.

Sample 3: Before selecting e-mail as a means for communication or document transmission, users should consider the need for immediacy, formality, accountability, access, security, and permanence. E-mail differs from other forms of communication. It is immediate and informal, similar to a telephone conversation, yet it is more permanent. It is as irrevocable as a hard-copy document, yet easy to duplicate, alter, and distribute.

The City (organization, company, etc.) reserves the right to monitor employee use of e-mail by systems administrators or departmental supervisors. Employees are reminded that e-mail use is provided *primarily* for business purposes and not for personal purposes and that employees cannot expect protection of their personal or business-related e-mail correspondence under privacy laws and regulations.

The City will not monitor e-mail messages as a routine matter. The City will, however, respond to legal processes and fulfill its obligations to third parties. The City will inspect the contents of e-mail messages in the course of an investigation triggered by indications of impropriety or as necessary to locate substantive information that is not more readily available by other means.

## Electronic Records Guideline

Retention periods are established for records according to departmental, fiscal, and legal requirements. Each record listed on a records-retention schedule specifies a specific period of time that the record is retained. *This retention applies whether the record is on paper or residing on magnetic or optical media (hard disk, floppy disk, tape, CD, etc.).* Once records have reached their designated time for destruction, they should be destroyed or eliminated from all storage media; that is, file cabinets, inactive storage, magnetic media, backups, etc.

Backup media should be stored in a different location than the computer equipment that is used to create them. Electronic records retained in a backup system follow the same retention as similar paper records listed on a retention schedule.

Drafts generally are not retained and should never be retained longer than the finalized version that becomes the record.

Databases are modified over time through the addition, deletion, or revision of information. Reports may be periodically generated to capture or record the information at a point in time. Records that are in databases may use a retention period until they are superseded. Once information has been superseded, it is generally lost unless provision is made to save it as a report. Historical data should be archived or deleted according to the department's retention schedule.

# Electronic Data Preservation Protocol

## Form 3.11
## Electronic Data Preservation Protocol

UNITED STATES DISTRICT COURT
FOR THE [Name District] OF [Name State]

| | | |
|---|---|---|
| [Name of Plaintiff], | ) | |
| | ) | |
| Plaintiff, | ) | |
| | ) | |
| v. | ) | Civil No. |
| | ) | |
| [Name of Defendant], | ) | |
| | ) | |
| Defendant. | ) | |

## Electronic Data Preservation Protocol

1. As used herein, the term "potentially discoverable electronic information" refers to Defendant's and Plaintiff's electronic "documents" that contain or potentially contain information relating to facts at issue in the litigation, where the term "documents" is used as it is defined in Fed. R. Civ. P. 34(a)

2. During the pendency of these actions, the Defendant and the Plaintiff shall securely maintain, to the extent that they currently exist and may contain potentially discoverable electronic information: (1) e-mail backup tapes and (2) network backup tapes (together, the "Backup Tapes") created in the ordinary course of business during the period from ___[start date]___ through ___[stop date]___. The Defendant and the Plaintiff shall be obligated to retain only one day's Backup Tapes among all Backup Tapes created in the ordinary course during a given month, provided that such day's Backup Tapes represent a complete backup of the data contained on the subject servers on that day (as opposed to merely an incremental backup of the subject servers). If only incremental backup tapes have been retained for a given month, then all such incremental tapes shall be retained. All Backup Tapes other than those specifically required to be preserved pursuant to this paragraph and para-

graph 3 below may be recycled, overwritten, or erased, as the case may be, pursuant to Defendant's and Plaintiff's otherwise applicable retention schedule.

3. All electronic information or data archived or backed up during the period from __[date range]__ as part of a special backup, i.e., a backup made other than in the ordinary course of business by Defendant or Plaintiff, whether due to system upgrade, transition planning, system migration, disaster recovery planning, or any other reason, that potentially contains potentially discoverable electronic information shall be securely retained, to the extent that they currently exist, for the remainder of the litigation.

4. All current or legacy software and hardware necessary to access, manipulate, print, etc., potentially discoverable electronic information that either is "live" or has been archived or backed up shall be securely retained, to the extent that they currently exist, for the remainder of the litigation.

5. Defendants and Plaintiff shall circulate retention notices designed to ensure the preservation of potentially discoverable electronic and other information to those employees potentially possessing such information. Thereafter, Defendant and Plaintiff shall quarterly renotify their employees of their continuing obligation to preserve such information.

6. Defendant and Plaintiff shall take the following measures to secure and retain, to the extent that it exists, the potentially discoverable electronic information that is on the desktop and laptop hard drives of their respective employees. Either (1) hard drives containing potentially discoverable electronic data shall be retained with all potentially discoverable electronic data contained therein retained intact; or, (2) employees shall be instructed to copy all potentially discoverable electronic information to a secure, backed-up network storage device or backup medium for the remainder of the litigation, making all reasonable efforts to retain all meta-data (file creation dates, modification dates, etc.) associated with the potentially discoverable electronic information at issue. The periodic retention notifications disseminated pursuant to paragraph 5 above shall advise employees potentially possessing potentially discoverable electronic information of their obligation to store discoverable electronic information on a secure, backed-up network storage device or backup medium to ensure its preservation and instruct such employees in the manner of doing so in accordance with this paragraph.

7. Plaintiff, within 15 days of receiving the list of business units referred to below, shall identify by name, title, or departmental category, em-

ployees of Defendant for which the Defendant shall be responsible for maintaining the hard drive, or a mirror-image copy (i.e., a bit-by-bit copy) of such hard drive, during the pendency of this litigation. Defendant, within 15 days of receiving the list of business units referred to below, shall identify by name, title, or departmental category, employees of Plaintiff for which the Plaintiff shall be responsible for maintaining the hard drive, or a mirror-image copy (i.e., a bit-by-bit copy) of such hard drive, during the pendency of this litigation. In no event shall the number of computers subject to the provisions of this paragraph be greater than __[insert number]__ for Defendant and Plaintiff. The hard drives or image copies of such hard drives preserved pursuant to this paragraph shall be labeled to identify the employee who primarily used the computer associated with that hard drive. To facilitate the identification of the appropriate employees, the parties will provide to each other identification by business unit and positions the employees they reasonably believe could have potentially discoverable electronic information. The parties will meet and confer in good faith and exchange additional information as may be necessary to facilitate the identification, and limit the number, of employees for whom the provisions of this paragraph shall be applicable.

8. To the extent that Defendant or Plaintiff have implemented a system for the purpose of preserving external e-mails (e-mails sent to or received by Defendant's or Plaintiff's employees) in an easily accessible form, other than an e-mail server or the Backup Tapes identified in paragraph 2 or 3 above, all e-mails that were created during the period from __[date range]__ that contain potentially discoverable electronic information, and that are stored on any such system as of the date hereof, shall be preserved during the pendency of this litigation.

9. Within 45 days, Defendant and Plaintiff will provide written answers to the best of their ability to the questions concerning information system and electronic document retention practices set forth in attached Schedule C [omitted]. Should any party believe it cannot in good faith answer any of the questions as posed, the parties will confer to resolve any disputes and, if necessary, seek Court intervention.

10. By agreeing to preserve potentially discoverable electronic information in accordance with the terms hereof, Defendant and Plaintiff are not waiving any objection to the ultimate discoverability of such information at such point when discovery is authorized in these actions.

11. Nothing herein shall be deemed to affect the Defendant's and Plaintiff's obligations to preserve hardcopy documents pursuant to the Court's Case Management Order. If counsel learn that potentially discoverable hardcopy documents were destroyed by a party subsequent to being named as a party in, and receiving a copy of, a complaint pertaining to that public offering, counsel for such party shall notify opposing counsel in writing of such destruction within two weeks of learning so.

# *Proposed Amendments to the Federal Rules of Civil Procedure*

**4**

**I**n January 2006, as this book was being prepared, the Report of the Judicial Conference Committee on Rules of Practice and Procedure had been submitted to the Chief Justice of the United States and Members of the Judicial Conference of the United States. It contained recommendations with respect to changes to the Federal Rules of Civil Procedure that specifically addressed issues related to the discovery of electronically stored information. The Advisory Committee on Civil Rules submitted proposed amendments to Rules 16, 26, 33, 34, 37, and 45 and revisions to Form 35 of the Federal Rules of Civil Procedure.[1] The authors have prepared this book with the assumption that these recommendations will be adopted as proposed in December 2006, which is currently expected by experts in the field.

The amendments recognize that the traditional discovery framework dealing with paper-based documents is no longer adequate. The proposed amendments to Rule 16, Rule 26(a) and (f), and Form 35 are intended to provide a better framework to address frequently recurring problems with preservation of evi-

---

[1]For a complete review of the proposed amendments along with the comments thereto please refer to Committee on Rules of Practice & Procedure, Report to the Judicial Conference, Agenda E-18, September 2005, http://www.uscourts.gov/rules/Reports/ST09-2005.pdf, Appendix C at Rules App.C-1—C-155.

dence and the assertion of privileges and work product at an early stage in the litigation process. In recognition of the significance of modern e-discovery, the court is encouraged to address disclosure and discovery of electronic information in its Rule 16 scheduling order. The court is given wide discretion to enter an order adopting any agreements the parties may reach with respect to the assertion of claims of privilege or the protection of trial preparation materials that may be inadvertently produced in discovery.

Rule 26(a) clarifies a party's duty to include disclosure of electronically stored information in its initial disclosures. Under Rule 26(f), the parties' conference is to include consideration of issues related to disclosure or discovery of electronically stored information, including the form of production of stored information, the identification of any distinctive and recurring problems resulting from the fact the information is stored electronically, issues related to preservation of electronically dynamic information, and inadvertent production of privileged information in discovery. Parties are encouraged to develop agreed-upon procedures and protocols to facilitate discovery that are faster and less expensive and can be included by the court in its case management order.

The proposed amendment to Rule 33 clarifies that a party may answer an interrogatory involving review of business records by providing access to the information if the interrogating party can find the answer as readily as the responding party can. Rule 34 explicitly recognizes electronically stored information as a category that is distinct from "documents" and "things." By recognizing the distinction between paper documents and electronically stored information, better discovery management is possible.

Rule 34 specifically authorizes the requesting party to specify the form of production and gives the responding party a means to object to the requested format. Absent a court order, party agreement, or a request for a specific form for production, a party may produce the electronically stored information in the form in which it is ordinarily maintained or in a reasonable usable form. Absent a court order, the information need only be produced in one form.

The proposed amendment to Rule 45 conforms to the provisions for subpoenas to changes in other rules related to discovery of electronically stored information. Form 35 is amended to add the parties' proposals regarding disclosure or discovery of electronically stored information to the list of topics to be included in the parties' report to the court.

Rule 26(b)(5)clarifies the procedure to apply when a responding party asserts a claim of privilege or work product after production. The producing party must notify the receiving party of its claim of inadvertent production. After notification, the receiving party must return, sequester, or destroy the information and cannot use or disclose it to third parties until the claim is resolved. If disclosed before receiving the claim, appropriate recall steps must be taken. The receiving party may submit the information to the court to decide whether it is privileged or protected as claimed and, if so, whether a waiver has occurred. The producing party must submit its claim on a timely basis and the court may consider any delay in notification in addressing the issue of waiver. This rule is procedural and is not intended to alter the substantive rules for determining whether waiver of the privilege or protection has occurred. It is intended to help the parties address the burden of privilege review.

Rule 26(b)(2) clarifies the obligation of a responding party to provide discovery of electronically stored information that is not reasonably accessible. A party need not produce information that is not reasonably accessible because of undue burden or cost. Examples include deleted information, information on backup systems for disaster-recovery purposes, and legacy data remaining from systems no longer in use. The responding party must identify the sources of potentially responsive information that it has not searched or produced because of the costs and burdens of accessing the information. If the requesting party moves for production, the responding party has the burden to show the information is not reasonably accessible. Even if the responding party makes this showing, a court may order discovery for good cause and may impose appropriate terms and conditions. This rule is not intended to undermine or reduce common-law or statutory preservation obligations. Information identified as not reasonably accessible must be difficult to access by the producing party for all purposes. A party may not make it inaccessible because it is likely to be discoverable in litigation. Such activity would be subject to sanctions.

Rule 37(f) addresses the fact that recycling, overwriting, and alteration of electronically stored information is a necessary feature of the normal routine operation of computer systems. Routine cessation or suspension of these features can result in the accumulation of duplicative and irrelevant data and make discovery more expensive and time consuming. The rule provides limited protection against sanctions for a party's failure to provide electronically stored information in discovery. Absent exceptional circumstances, sanctions may not be imposed if electronically stored information has been lost as a result of the routine operation of an electronic information system as long as the operation is done in good faith. The rule recognizes that all electronic information systems are designed to recycle, overwrite, and change information in routine operation. The rule also recognizes that suspending or interrupting these features can be prohibitively expensive and burdensome.

Sanctions cannot be avoided simply by showing the information was lost in the routine operation of the information system. It must also be shown that the operation was in good faith. The rule does not provide a shield for a party that intentionally destroys specific information because of its relationship to litigation or for a party that allows such information to be destroyed to make it unavailable in discovery by exploiting the routine operation of an information system. Good faith may require the party take steps to modify or suspend certain features of routine operation to prevent loss of information if the information is subject to preservation obligations. When the obligation arises is subject to the substantive law of each jurisdiction that is not affected by the proposed rule.

Finally, it should be noted that no effort is being made in this book to identify state specific issues or procedures. It is assumed that materials developed for federal court can be adapted by the reader to conform to any requirements of local state rules.

# *Electronic Discovery*

**5**

## Interrogatories

Interrogatories are particularly well suited to elicit basic information that can then be used with other discovery methods to obtain relevant discovery of electronic information systems. However, because of Rule 33(a)'s initial limitation on the number of interrogatories that can be propounded, and the fact this limitation applies to inquiries on case information across the board and not just to e-discovery issues, one of several approaches will need to be followed to make the use of interrogatories effective and worthwhile. At a minimum, the initial set of interrogatories must be used to identify the basics regarding the electronic information systems involved, including hardware, software, type of information stored, and the people who have the most knowledge of the systems. With that preliminary information, more targeted discovery methods can then be developed.

It is not really feasible to develop more detailed inquiries by interrogatory unless the parties stipulate to their use or leave is obtained from the court to file more extensive interrogatories. Thus, an immediate effort should be made to arrive at an agreement concerning the use of additional targeted sets of interrogatories. Examples that follow include sets designed to elicit information on IT staffing, Internet access and usage, software, backup systems, e-mail, telephony, remote access, and work-at-home issues.

By choosing appropriate supplemental sets of interrogatories by category and avoiding the use of one comprehensive set of interrogatories designed to cover all aspects of e-discovery, you are more likely to obtain cooperation from opposing counsel in obtaining a stipulation on the number of interrogatories they would be willing to answer. In the event a stipulation cannot be reached, you will need to file a motion for leave to file additional interrogatories with the court. By submitting different targeted sets of questions that are designed to obtain categories of information clearly relevant to your case, you are less likely to receive a ruling that simply limits you to a set number of additional interrogatories. If the judge sees the logic in your categorical inquiry, you are more likely to obtain the requested relief even if multiple sets of interrogatories might appear more burdensome at first blush.

# Interrogatories

## Form 5.1
## Initial Interrogatories Subject to Rule 33(a) Limitations

UNITED STATES DISTRICT COURT
FOR THE [Name District] OF [Name State]

| | | |
|---|---|---|
| [Name of Plaintiff], | ) | |
| | ) | |
| Plaintiff, | ) | |
| | ) | |
| v. | ) | Civil No. |
| | ) | |
| [Name of Defendant], | ) | |
| | ) | |
| Defendant. | ) | |

## Initial Interrogatories Subject to Rule 33(a) Limitations

1. Identify all employees employed by you during the period of [date] to the present time—providing name, title, job description, department, and location—who are or were responsible for managing and maintaining your technology infrastructure that includes, but is not limited to, servers or other network storage devices and related peripheral equipment, desktop computers, portable computers, laptop computers, personal digital assistants (PDAs), telephones, and other similar electronic devices, all used in your normal course of business.

2. Identify all nonemployee consultants, consulting firms, contractors, or similar entities who were retained by you during the period of [date] to the present time—providing individual and company names, job descriptions, addresses, and telephone numbers—who are or were responsible for installing, servicing, managing, or maintaining your technology infrastructure that includes, but is not limited to, servers or other network storage devices and related peripheral equipment, desktop computers, portable computers, laptop computers, personal digital assistants (PDAs), telephones, and other similar electronic devices all used in your normal course of business.

3. Describe all groups of connected computer systems used in your normal course of business that permit users to share information and transfer data, including, but not limited to, local area networks (LANs), wide area networks (WANs), client-server networks, virtual private networks (VPNs), and storage area networks (SANs); and identify all equipment, devices, components and network resources that establish and maintain the network environment, including, but not limited to, routers, switches, hubs, bridges, firewalls, proxies, etc.

4. Describe all available third-party connectivity between the computer systems and network environment identified in your answers to Interrogatory 3 above, including the type of information that is shared, the manner in which the information is transferred, and the identity of any individuals who have authorization to transfer information into or out of your network environment.

5. Identify each individual personal computer system that is or has been used by your employees for the period of __[date]__ to the present time, which includes, but is not limited to, desktop computers, portable computers, laptop computers, personal digital assistants (PDAs), telephones, and other similar electronic devices, including descriptions of equipment and any peripheral technology attached to the computer system.

6. Describe the Internet and intranet connectivity of each computer system identified in your answer to Interrogatory 5 above, including, but not limited to, client-server communications and client-client communications facilitated through modem, wireless, network, or direct connection.

7. Identify all hardware or software modifications made to the computer systems identified in your answers to Interrogatories 3 through 6 above from __[date]__ to the present time, including type and nature of each modification, dates of modification, software and hardware titles, version numbers, contact information of person(s) performing the modification, and location of data backups made prior to modification.

8. Identify all operating systems, including, but not limited to, Microsoft Windows, Linux, Unix, DOS, Solaris, etc., installed on each of your computer systems from __[date]__ to the present time.

9. Identify the title and version number of any and all software installed or executed on each of your computer systems from __[date]__ to the present time.

10. Describe your policies and procedures governing the use of removable media, such as CD-ROMs, Zip disks, floppy disks, tape drives, re-

movable hard drives, etc., associated with your computer systems or network from __[date]__ to the present time.

11. Describe your policies and procedures for performing backups on all computer systems, and identify any hardware or software used to perform such backup from __[date]__ to the present time.

12. Identify all employees employed by you—providing name, title, job description, department, and location—who were responsible for conducting backups or other archiving of electronic information from __[date]__ to the present time.

13. Identify all removable media that may contain information relevant to this legal matter.

14. Identify all server-based, workstation-based, and handheld-based software and hardware used to transmit or receive e-mail from [date]__ to the present time.

15. Identify all e-mail accounts (internal and/or external) used by you and your employees from __[date]__ to the present time.

16. Describe your policies and procedures for performing backups or for archiving e-mail messages and identify any hardware or software used to perform such backups or archiving from __[date]__ to the present time.

17. Describe any e-mail-based encryption used by you or your employees from __[date]__ to the present time.

18. Identify the components and design implementation or distribution of your telephone and voice messaging systems, including all hardware, software, and third-party service providers used from __[date]__ to the present time.

19. Describe your policies and procedures for performing backups or for archiving any and all voice messaging records and identify any hardware or software used to perform such backups or archiving from __[date]__ to the present time.

20. Describe your policies and procedures governing employee use of Internet newsgroups, chat rooms, or instant messaging on your computer systems from __[date]__ to the present time.

21. Identify any and all cell phones, PDAs, digital convergence devices, or other portable electronic devices, whether owned by you or by others, used by any of your employees in the performance of his or her employment from __[date]__ to the present time.

22. Describe your policies and procedures pertaining to data retention and destruction from __[date]__ to the present time.

23. Identify all hardware or software used to facilitate the deletion of data subject to the data retention and destruction policies and procedures identified in your answer to Interrogatory 22 above.

24. Identify any and all servers or other network storage devices, desktop computers, portable computers, laptop computers, personal digital assistants (PDAs), telephones, and other similar electronic devices that have had their hard drives reformatted, wiped, or replaced from __[date]__ to the present time.

25. Identify any and all information deleted, physically destroyed, corrupted, damaged, lost, or overwritten, whether pursuant to the data retention and destruction policies and procedures identified in your answer to Interrogatory 22 above or not, that was relevant to this legal matter.

## Form 5.2
## Interrogatories for Network Infrastructure

1. Identify any and all documents and things related to networks or groups of connected computers that allow people to share information and equipment, including but not limited to local area networks (LAN), wide area networks (WAN), metropolitan area networks (MAN), storage area networks (SAN), peer-to-peer networks (P2P), client-server networks, point-to-point networks, integrated services digital networks (ISDN), and virtual private networks (VPN).

2. Identify any and all devices related to networks, including but not limited to topology (e.g., Ethernet, token-ring, ATM), channel service unit/data service unit (CSU/DSU), traffic measurement, hubs, switches, network interface cards, cables, firewalls, routers, gateways, media converters, intrusion-detection devices, and intranet connections.

3. Identify any and all graphical representations of the components of your computer network, and the relationship of those components to each other, including but not limited to flow charts, videos, photos, or drawings?

4. Identify the manufacturer and version number for each network operating system in use.

5. Identify the person(s) responsible for the ongoing operation, maintenance, expansion, and upkeep of the network.

6. Describe in detail any direct interconnection of your company network to those networks of other parties.

7. Describe in detail all communications circuits, their termination points, and their configurations. This would include, but is not limited to, T-1 circuits (full and fractional), POTS (Plain Old Telephone Service) lines, Primary Rate Interface (PRI) circuits, Basic Rate Interface (BRI) circuits, Digital Subscriber Line (DSL) circuits, satellite links, microwave connections, and cable modem lines.

8. Describe any video surveillance system that may be in use and the location and retention period of any video records.

9. Describe any method for remote access to the company network.

10. Describe any logging of events or audit trail for any network devices. This includes, but is not limited to, syslogs for routers, activity logs for remote access devices, firewall logs, web server logs, and caller ID logs.

11. Identify any monitoring capability that may exist or existed during the period in question.

12. Describe any access control methods and activity records. This may include, but is not limited to, facility access (via badge, RFID, Biometrics, keypad entry, etc.), restricted room access, and remote access.

13. Identify any information that is needed to access network devices and the configuration of the devices such as user IDs, passwords, keys, etc.

14. Identify any and all documents related to bandwidth capacity, bandwidth delegation and usage.

15. Identify any assigned network configuration values. This would include, but is not limited to, IP network assignments, Network Address Translation (NAT) assignments, IPX network numbers, IGRP autonomous zones, DECnet, Systems Network Architecture (SNA) nodes, etc.

16. Describe in detail any wireless networks or connections, such as WiFi, cellular, satellite, Bluetooth, infrared, etc.

## Form 5.3
## Interrogatories for Internet Access and Usage

1. Describe in detail how Internet access is provisioned. This should include, but is not limited to, such items as the method of connection (e.g., DSL, T-1, dialup, etc.), connection speed (bandwidth), and the Internet Service Provider (ISP).
2. Identify all computers that have Internet access.
3. Describe in detail any logging of Internet activity that is done. Identify where the logging information is kept and the period of retention.
4. Are there specific computers designated for Internet access?
5. Describe the credentials (if any) that are needed to access the Internet. This can include such things as a user ID and password or security key fob.
6. Describe any Internet usage monitoring.
7. Is Internet usage restricted? If so, describe, in detail, the terms of restriction.
8. Are there specific times during the day where there is unrestricted Internet usage?
9. Is access to specific Web sites or domain names blocked? If so, how are the blocked destinations determined? Describe any hardware or software (manufacturer and version) that is used.
10. Is instant messaging allowed on the network? If so, are instant message conversations logged?
11. How much bandwidth is dedicated to Internet access?
12. Is there a central firewall for Internet access for the entire company?
13. Is there a software firewall on each computer that has Internet access?
14. Are employees allowed to clear their Internet history activity, cookies, and change the browser security settings?
15. Is anti-spyware software installed (and updated) on each computer that has Internet access? Identify the software and version.
16. Identify the person(s) responsible for the ongoing operation, maintenance, expansion, and upkeep of the Internet access.
17. Describe any Internet usage policy that exists or may have existed.

## Form 5.4
## Interrogatories for Computers/Servers

1. Describe in detail the computers and servers that comprise the company computer infrastructure, including, but not limited to, the number of servers and their functions, the number of desktop computers, and the number of laptops and portable devices.
2. Identify the following for each server:
   a. Technical hardware specification, to include, but not limited to, manufacturer, model, serial number, type, and quantity of hard drive storage system, memory, processor, network connectivity, externally attached devices, tape units, optical drives, alternate media drives (e.g., floppy, Zip, etc.);
   b. Operating system version and patch level;
   c. Function within the computing infrastructure (e.g., web server, e-mail server, data server, DNS server, domain controller, database server, etc.);
   d. Physical location.
3. Identify the following for each desktop computer, laptop, or portable device:
   a. Technical hardware specification, to include, but not limited to, manufacturer, model, serial number, type, and quantity of hard drive storage system, memory, processor, network connectivity, externally attached devices, tape units, optical drives, alternate media drives (e.g., floppy, Zip, etc.);
   b. Operating system version and patch level;
   c. Primary user of the computer;
   d. Physical location.
4. Identify the person(s) responsible for the ongoing operation, maintenance, expansion, and upkeep of the computers/servers.
5. Identify any power-on and/or BIOS (Basic Input/Output System) passwords for each computer/server.
6. Have any computers/servers been replaced or decommissioned from [date]__ to the present time? If so, identify them and describe how they were disposed of.
7. Are biometrics used to access any of the computers? If so, describe fully.

## Form 5.5
## Interrogatories for Software

1. Describe in detail the names of all software programs and versions used for such functions as, but not limited to, electronic mail, calendars, project management files, word processing, financial, and database management.
2. Identify the person(s) responsible for the ongoing operation, maintenance, replacement, and upkeep of the various software applications.
3. Have any software applications been replaced or decommissioned from __[date]__ to the present time?
4. Describe in detail the software and methods used for antivirus protection. The description should include, but not be limited to, the method for updating signature files, distribution of program updates, scheduled scan properties, file or folder exclusions, etc.
5. Describe any computer usage policies that exist or may have existed from __[date]__ to the present time.
6. Are users authorized to install their own software?
7. If not, what procedure must they follow to obtain authorization?
8. Are there restrictions on the types of software that can be installed?
9. Are all copies of software, including operating systems, properly licensed?
10. Is software installed on each computer from a "base" load, or is each application installed individually as needed?
11. Describe in detail the software and methods used for anti-spyware protection. The description should include, but not be limited to, the method for updating signature files, distribution of program updates, scheduled scan properties, file or application exclusions, etc.
12. Describe in detail any software that is used to monitor employees' computer activity. The description should include, but not be limited to, the software name and version, those employees that are monitored, the type of information that is logged and captured, the retention period and location for the logs, and when monitoring began.
13. Identify any encryption software that is installed or may have been installed from __[date]__ to the present date.
14. Describe in detail the installed locations for all software.
15. Describe in detail any software that is used to wipe or permanently delete information from the computers. Also, identify any logging or activity of said deletion utilities, to include, but not be limited to,

dates of usage, files/folders deleted, and targeted devices and areas for deletion.

16. Describe in detail any software that is used to monitor and maintain the computer systems. This would include, but not be limited to, web statistic software, intrusion-detection software, defragmentation utilities, indexing and searching utilities, and content-management software.

## Form 5.6
## Interrogatories for Backup Systems

1. Provide the following information concerning data backups performed on all computer systems in the organization:
   a. Descriptions of any and all procedures and/or devices used to backup the software and/or data, including, but not limited to, name(s) of backup software and version used, tape rotation schedule, type of tape backup drives (e.g., DDS4, DLT, SDLT, LTO, etc.), including name and version number.
   b. Are multiple generations of backups maintained? If so, describe how many and whether the backups are full, differential or incremental.
   c. Are backup storage media kept off-site? If so, where are such media kept? Describe the process for archiving and retrieving off-site media.
   d. Are backup storage media kept on-site? If so, where are such media kept? Describe the process for archiving and retrieving on-site media.
   e. Identify who conducts the backup, including name, title, office location, and telephone number.
   f. Describe, in detail, what information is backed up.
   g. Please provide a detailed list of all backup sets, regardless of the magnetic media on which they reside, showing current location, custodian, date of backup, and a description of backup content.
2. Identify the person(s) responsible for the ongoing operation, maintenance, and upgrade of the backup system(s).
3. Have any backup media been replaced or destroyed from __[date]__ to the present time? If so, identify the medium that was replaced or destroyed.
4. Have the backup procedures been modified as a result of the current legal action?
5. May users backup their own data and programs?
6. Describe any disaster recovery plans in place now and for the relevant time period.
7. Are the backed up data encrypted on the backup media? If so, identify the methods and software used to encrypt and any decryption keys or methods.
8. Describe any document retention plans in place now and for the relevant time period.
9. Are there any restrictions as to whether computer files can be copied to floppy disks, USB thumb drives, CDs, Zip disks, or any other removable media?

## Form 5.7
## Interrogatories for E-mail, Instant Messages, and Other Forms of Electronic Communication

1. Identify any and all methods related to the exchange of electronic communication, to include, but not limited to, e-mail, instant messaging, paging, or text messaging.
2. Identify any and all devices that are related to electronic communication, including but not limited to, e-mail servers, and gateway servers (e.g., BlackBerry Enterprise Server).
3. Describe any graphical representation of the components of your computer network, and the relationship of those components to each other, including, but not limited to, flow charts, videos, photos, or drawings that facilitate the flow of electronic communication.
4. Identify the manufacturer, model number, version number, and primary user for each portable electronic communication device (e.g., BlackBerry, convergent cellular telephone).
5. Identify the person(s) responsible for the ongoing operation, maintenance, and upgrade of the electronic messaging system(s).
6. Describe any logging of e-mail communication activity, the location of the log files, and the retention period.
7. Is instant messaging allowed by policy or technical ability? If so, are instant message conversations logged?
8. Describe any instant message logging ability, the location of any logs, and the retention period.
9. Describe in detail any Internet browser access to e-mail.
10. Identify all software clients (applications) that are used to access e-mail messages (e.g., Outlook, Outlook Express, Eudora, AOL, etc.)
11. Identify all software clients that are used for instant messaging (e.g., AIM, Yahoo! Messenger, etc.)
12. Identify all e-mail accounts in use during the period __[start date]__ to __[end date]__.
13. Is electronic communication using text messaging via cellular telephones utilized? If so, identify those individuals who text message and the manufacturers and model numbers of the cellular telephones used.
14. Is communication via a peer-to-peer (P2P) network an accepted form or communication for employees of the company? If so, identify all P2P software used (e.g., Limewire, Morpheus, eDonkey, KaZaa, etc.), the primary user, and the installed location.
15. Do any employees of [party name] subscribe to or participate in Internet newsgroups or chat groups in the course of their employ-

ment? If so, identify all users and the services that they subscribe to or participate in.

16. Describe in detail any e-mail-based encryption algorithms in place. This description should include, but is not limited to, the software used for encryption, the users of encryption, and the location of any passphrases, passwords, or tokens used for the encryption and decryption of messages.

## Form 5.8
## Interrogatories for Telephony

1. Identify any and all documents and things related to voice communication that allows people to communicate telephonically.

2. Describe in detail any telephone equipment (e.g., PBX, telephones, answering machines, etc.) used for voice communication. The description should include, but not be limited to, the manufacturer, model number, software version, and serial number.

3. Identify any and all graphical representations of the components of the telephone and voice messaging system of [party name], and the relationship of those components to each other, including, but not limited to, flow charts, videos, photos, or diagrams?

4. Identify the provider, account number and contact information of any cellular service in use from ___[date]___ until the present time.

5. Identify the person(s) responsible for the ongoing operation, maintenance, expansion, and upgrade of the voice communications systems.

6. Identify all cellular telephones in use from ___[date]___ until the present time, including, but not be limited to, manufacturer, model, serial number, user, and telephone number.

7  Identify the provider, account number, pager ID, user, and provider contact information of any pager service in use from ___[date]___ until the present time.

8. Describe in detail any logging of voice communications. The description should include, but not be limited to, caller ID logs, voice circuit usage, detailed call records, cellular phone records, and location of the documents.

9. Describe in detail any voice mail or answering system recording methods including, but not be limited to, equipment manufacturer, software name and version, storage capacity, and physical location.

10. State whether users have the capacity to store voice mail messages. If so, please provide the following information:
    a. Is storage optional or systematic?
    b. What is the retention period for messages?
    c. How many messages or amount of time may be stored by each user?
    d. Are voice mail messages are automatically purged? If so, describe in detail the purging schedule.
    e. Can each user change the default retention period and/or purge period?

    f. Are passwords required to access stored voice messages?

    g. Is there remote access to the voice mail system? Is so, describe in detail the procedure to remotely access the system.

    h. Are the voice mail messages backed up? If so, describe in detail, the schedule of backup, storage location of backups, currently available backup media, and retention period.

    i. Can users remotely accessing their mailbox gain access to a dial tone in order to make an external call?

11. Have any logging, data retention practices, backups, etc. been modified as a result of the current legal action?

12. Are there any security measures (e.g., user ID, password, locked cabinet, etc.) in place to restrict access to the configuration of the telephone system (PBX) or voice mail systems?

## Form 5.9
## Interrogatories for Remote Access/Home Issues

1. Describe in detail the means by which any employees may remotely access the company network or directly connect to devices that are connected to the company network.
2. Are employees allowed to work from home?
3. Do employees use their personal computers or company provided computers when working from home?
4. Identify the following for each desktop computer, laptop, or portable device used for company business at home:
    a. Technical hardware specification, to include, but not be limited to, manufacturer, model, serial number, type and quantity of hard drive storage system, memory, processor, network connectivity, externally attached devices, tape units, optical drives, alternate media drives (e.g., floppy, Zip, etc.);
    b. Operating system version and patch level;
    c. Primary user of the computer;
    d. Physical location.
5. Identify the person(s) responsible for the ongoing operation, maintenance, expansion, and upkeep of the remote access solutions and work-at-home environment.
6. Identify any power-on and/or BIOS (Basic Input/Output System) passwords for each computer/device.
7. Have any computers/devices been replaced or decommissioned from __[date]__ to the present time? If so, describe their disposition.
8. Are biometrics used to access any of the computers? If so, describe.
9. Describe in detail any security and authentication procedures for remotely accessing the company network.
10. Is the communication connection from the home an encrypted connection?
11. Are remote connections to the company network logged? If so, identify the information that is logged, physical location of the logged information, retention period of the logged information, and currently available information.
12. Have any logging, data retention practices, backups, etc. been modified as a result of the current legal action?
13. Describe in detail the methods employees use to transfer data from the office to a work-at-home environment. This description would in-

clude such items as USB thumb drives, floppy disks, Zip disks, CDs, e-mail to personal accounts, etc.

14. Identify any company policies and procedures regarding remote access or work-from-home issues.

15. Identify all company data that is currently in existence at the homes of employees.

## Form 5.10
# Plaintiff's Motion for Leave to File Supplemental Interrogatories under Fed. R. Civ. P. 33(a) and 26(b)(2)

UNITED STATES DISTRICT COURT
FOR THE [Name District] OF [Name State]

| | | |
|---|---|---|
| [Name of Plaintiff], | ) | |
| | ) | |
| Plaintiff, | ) | |
| | ) | |
| v. | ) | Civil No. |
| | ) | |
| [Name of Defendant], | ) | |
| | ) | |
| Defendant. | ) | |

## Plaintiff's Motion for Leave to File Supplemental Interrogatories under Fed. R. Civ. P. 33(a) and 26(b)(2)

To: [Counsel of Record]

## 1. Relief Sought.

Plaintiff moves this court pursuant to Rule 33(a) and Rule 26 (b)(2) Fed. R. Civ. P., for an order permitting it to propound the attached Supplemental Sets of Interrogatories inquiring into the Internet Usage (Exhibit A) and Backup Procedures (Exhibit B) of Defendant.

## 2. Date and Time of Hearing.

Date:      To Be Determined by the Court
Time:      To Be Determined by the Court
Judge:     Hon. [name]
Place:     United States District Court

## 3. Grounds for Relief.

Under Rule 33(a) of the Federal Rules of Civil Procedure, a party may serve no more than 25 interrogatories, including subparts, on any other party unless the court grants leave on the basis that additional interrogatories would be consistent with the principles of Rule 26(b)(2) of the Federal Rules of Civil

Procedure. Plaintiff has propounded an initial set of interrogatories directed toward ascertaining information relevant to electronic discovery. A copy of those interrogatories is attached as Exhibit C. These initial interrogatories sought comprehensive information of a general nature regarding the use of computer technology by defendant's employees and the computer technology infrastructure available to defendant's employees. The supplemental interrogatories that plaintiff is seeking leave to propound attempt to elicit more specific and detailed technical information relative to the Internet usage and backup procedures of defendant, which can only be understood within the context of the broader information sought by the initial set of interrogatories.

[Summarize factual nature of case, legal issues, and why detailed understanding of Internet usage and backup procedures are relevant]

In this case, the Internet usage of multiple employees of defendant is critical in addressing the factual and legal issues involved. The identification of employees who had access to the Internet, their history of Internet usage, their access to certain Web sites, and their adherence to usage policies, if any, put in place by defendant are all highly relevant to both liability and damage issues. Furthermore, because there is a concern that defendant's employees may have altered or deleted information, particularly after learning about the filing of this action, including their Internet history and temporary files and other log files maintained by the defendant to monitor employee Internet usage, the ability to understand and gain access to the requested backup information is critical. The use of additional interrogatories to make further specific inquiry into these issues would be the most efficient and expeditious manner for exploring these facts.

Interrogatories on the factual issues, exceeding 25 in number, would be consistent with the principles of rule 26(d)(2) of the Federal Rules of Civil Procedure because the discovery is not unreasonably cumulative or duplicative. To the contrary, the additional interrogatories seek factual information that will summarize the available information held by multiple employees in one spot, potentially eliminating the need for random and wide-ranging requests for production of documents or numerous depositions of multiple witnesses, which might themselves be unreasonably cumulative or duplicative. In contrast, answers to these proposed interrogatories would narrow future discovery regarding these issues. Plaintiff has no other opportunity to obtain this information by other means that are as efficient. There is no undue expense or burden in compelling defendant to answer the supplemental interrogatories. In contrast, if exploration of these issues by the proposed supplemental interrogatories is denied, the defense will be subject to the time and expense of multiple depositions and record requests, which will be just as burdensome, if not more so, than responding to the proposed supplemental interrogatories.

The affidavit of plaintiff's counsel attached to this motion shows that, in accordance with the local rule, prior to seeking relief from the court, plaintiff's counsel sent copies of the proposed interrogatories to defense counsel. He explained in that letter the reasons why the additional information was necessary and asked that defense counsel stipulate to answer the supplemental interrogatories or simply provide the information by letter in order to permit plaintiff counsel to determine whether certain persons should be deposed on computer technology–related issues. Counsel for the defense did not respond to plaintiff's counsel's letter of __[date]__. Subsequently, plaintiff's counsel personally contacted defense counsel by telephone on __[date]__ at __[time]__. Plaintiff's counsel attempted to reach a stipulation or other agreement from opposing counsel. Plaintiff's counsel made a sincere attempt to resolve their differences, but, because of the refusal of defense counsel to provide any of the requested information, whether informally or in any other manner, plaintiff's counsel was unable to reach an agreement to obtain a written stipulation as to the reasonable number of additional interrogatories that could be propounded. Despite these good-faith efforts by plaintiff's counsel, counsel for the defense refused to consent to be served more than 25 interrogatories in this matter.

This motion is based upon Fed. R. Civ. P. 33(a), on this document, on the attached affidavit of counsel, on the sets of supplemental interrogatories attached hereto as Exhibits A and B, on the original interrogatories attached hereto as Exhibit C, and on all of the pleadings and papers already on file in this action.

Date: __[date]__

[Name of Firm]

By: _____

[Attorney name]
Attorney for Defendant
[Street address]
[City, state, zip code]
[Telephone number]

## Form 5.11
## Proposed Order Permitting Plaintiff to Propound Additional Interrogatories

UNITED STATES DISTRICT COURT
FOR THE [Name District] OF [Name State]

| | | |
|---|---|---|
| [Name of Plaintiff], | ) | |
| | ) | |
| Plaintiff, | ) | |
| | ) | |
| v. | ) | Civil No. |
| | ) | |
| [Name of Defendant], | ) | |
| | ) | |
| Defendant. | ) | |

### Proposed Order Permitting Plaintiff to Propound Additional Interrogatories

On plaintiff's Motion for Leave to File Supplemental Interrogatories under Fed. R. Civ. P. 33(a) and 26 (b)(2), having reviewed and considered the motion and affidavit in support of the motion, the Court now orders as follows:

Plaintiff's Motion for an Order Permitting Plaintiff to Propound Additional Interrogatories is hereby granted on the following terms:

1. Plaintiff shall be permitted to propound the supplemental interrogatories regarding Defendant's Internet usage attached to Plaintiff's moving papers as Exhibit A and the supplemental interrogatories regarding Defendant's backup procedures attached to Plaintiff's moving papers as Exhibit B. Defendant shall have 30 days from the date of signing of this order to answer the supplemental interrogatories.

IT IS SO ORDERED.

Date: _____          _____
Honorable Judge [name]
United States District Court Judge

## Form 5.12
## Joint Stipulation to Permit Supplemental Interrogatories (Defined Interrogatories by Number)

UNITED STATES DISTRICT COURT
FOR THE [Name District] OF [Name State]

| | | |
|---|---|---|
| [Name of Plaintiff], | ) | |
| | ) | |
| Plaintiff, | ) | |
| | ) | |
| v. | ) | Civil No. |
| | ) | |
| [Name of Defendant], | ) | |
| | ) | |
| Defendant. | ) | |

### Joint Stipulation to Permit Supplemental Interrogatories (Defined Interrogatories by Number)

COME NOW the parties in the above-identified action who hereby stipulate that __[insert interrogating party name]__ shall be permitted to propound and serve upon __[insert recipient party name]__ __[insert the number of permitted questions]__ additional interrogatories exceeding the specified 25 interrogatories permitted under Rule 33(a) F.R.C.P.

[Name of Firm]

Date: __[date]__          By: _____
                              [Attorney Name]
                              Attorney for Plaintiff
                              [Street address]
                              [City, state, zip code]
                              [Telephone number]

[Name of Firm]

By:     _____

[Attorney name]
Attorney for Defendant
[Street address]
[City, state, zip code]
[Telephone number]

## Form 5.13
## Order to Permit Supplemental Interrogatories

UNITED STATES DISTRICT COURT
FOR THE [Name District] OF [Name State]

| | | |
|---|---|---|
| [Name of Plaintiff], | ) | |
| | ) | |
| Plaintiff, | ) | |
| | ) | |
| v. | ) | Civil No. |
| | ) | |
| [Name of Defendant], | ) | |
| | ) | |
| Defendant. | ) | |

## Order to Permit Supplemental Interrogatories

Upon the Stipulation of counsel for the plaintiff and defendant to permit __[insert interrogating party name]__ to propound __[insert the number of permitted questions]__ additional interrogatories that exceed the specified 25 interrogatories permitted under Rule 33(a) F.R.C.P.,

NOW, THEREFORE, IT IS HEREBY ORDERED:

That __[insert interrogating party name]__ is hereby permitted to propound upon __[insert recipient party name]__ __[insert the number of permitted questions]__ additional interrogatories.

IT IS SO ORDERED.

Date: _____          _____

Honorable Judge [name]
United States District Court Judge

## Form 5.14
## Joint Stipulation to Permit Supplemental Interrogatories (Defined Interrogatories by Attachment)

UNITED STATES DISTRICT COURT
FOR THE [Name District] OF [Name State]

| | | |
|---|---|---|
| [Name of Plaintiff], | ) | |
| | ) | |
| Plaintiff, | ) | |
| | ) | |
| v. | ) | Civil No. |
| | ) | |
| [Name of Defendant], | ) | |
| | ) | |
| Defendant. | ) | |

### Joint Stipulation to Permit Supplemental Interrogatories (Defined Interrogatories by Attachment)

COME NOW the parties in the above-identified action who hereby stipulate that __[insert interrogating party name]__ shall be permitted to propound and serve upon __[insert recipient party name]__ the attached additional interrogatories that exceed the specified 25 interrogatories permitted under Rule 33(a) F.R.C.P.

[Name of Firm]

Date: __[date]__     By: _____
[Attorney Name]
Attorney for Plaintiff
[Street address]
[City, state, zip code]
[Telephone number]

[Name of Firm]

By: _____
[Attorney name]
Attorney for Defendant
[Street address]
[City, state, zip code]
[Telephone number]

# Requests for Production

Once you have a general sense of your opponent's technological infrastructure, you should be in a position to draft appropriate requests for the production of electronically stored information. Typically, you will be looking for information in three basic areas: e-mail, electronic documents, and data compilations. Not every case will include the need for discovery in all three areas, but stopping to consider whether such information exists in all three areas is important as you frame your requests. As you draft your requests, it is also important to consider how broad you want the requests to be. The old standby of "produce any and all . . . relating to . . ." may well be problematic if you find yourself the recipient of terabytes worth of information that you need to pay large sums of money to process and analyze only to find out it is ultimately useless to your case.

One way to contain the expenses associated with e-discovery is to limit judiciously the scope of what you ask for. Why ask for too much when you can ask for what seems right in the first place, review the response, and then request additional information if appropriate? This is a judgment call that must be made early on, and it is probably more important now in dealing with e-discovery than it ever was in dealing with conventional paper-based discovery.

There are some general considerations that should be kept in mind that relate to requests for all types of electronic information. Do you want the information in native format? To get the most out of the requested information you would typically want the information produced in this fashion. If you do, is there certain metadata that you do not want included? If so, indicate that in your request, because it may expedite the process of producing the information and limit associated expenses that someone might try to shift to your client. If you do not want the information in native format, what format do you want used for the production? Do you simply want images, and if so, do you want TIFFs, PDFs, or something else?

The answer to these last questions may well be determined by the method you intend to use to work with the information. If you use some type of litigation-support software like Summation or Concordance, you will generally want the metadata included (or at least the metadata these programs are capable of displaying), and you will want the information produced in native format if it is in a common format that is supported by your litigation-support program. If it is in an unsupported format, however, you may want it processed and produced as an image file. You must recognize that, if you don't ask for it in native format and accept the initial production as an image file, you will lose the potential for uncovering available metadata. On the other hand, not every case hinges on issues for which the metadata will provide answers. In the vast majority of cases, you are simply looking for the electronic equivalent of a copy of the original document in a format that you can work with most successfully. If that is the case, there is no need to complicate the process by asking for information you will never use. Once again, this is a judgment call that must be made early in the course of discovery.

When dealing with requests for e-mail, you must be sure to request not only all related metadata, but also all attachment files. This is one area in particular where metadata is often very important, not only substantively for the case, but also in terms of using litigation-support technology to successfully manage the information. You need to know how to ask for the information in a way that will work successfully with the tools that are available to process it.

When dealing with cases involving large volumes of compiled data, a higher level of technical expertise is often required. If you request information in its native format, and it is produced in a proprietary format, you might find yourself in a position in which you think you need to purchase some extraordinarily expensive software just to work on the case. On the other hand, it may well be that if you make the right request, the information can be exported in a format that can be used by other programs you already have such as Microsoft Excel or Access. Alternatively, some inexpensive programs may be able to view the data in native format accurately, though you may not be able to process it in the same way you would with the native application. For example, in a construction case you might receive AutoCAD drawing files in native format. If deconstructing the design process is not an issue in the case, and you only need to be able to view the drawings and perhaps present them as graphical exhibits at trial, you may be able to import them into a much less expensive program like SmartDraw and then generate an image file that will meet your purposes. If something develops as the case progresses, you still have the native files and you can have them analyzed later by an expert using the original program if necessary. As with all dealings involving electronic data, you may need to protect the original files in a read-only format so as not to inadvertantly modify metadata or the file contents. Thus, it is important to seek technical advice early in the process of requesting electronic information if it is at all out of the ordinary.

Depending on the nature of the case, this is also an area where the services of an e-discovery vendor may well be worth considering for purposes of providing assistance in formulating your requests and planning on how to work with the information you anticipate receiving. It may even be appropriate to confer with a computer forensic expert if there are any suspicions of data or e-mail alteration or there are questions concerning the use of the Internet.

## Form 5.15
## Request for Production of Documents, Electronically Stored Information, and Things

UNITED STATES DISTRICT COURT
FOR THE [Name District] OF [Name State]

| | | |
|---|---|---|
| [Name of Plaintiff], | ) | |
| | ) | |
| Plaintiff, | ) | |
| | ) | |
| v. | ) | Civil No. |
| | ) | |
| [Name of Defendant], | ) | |
| | ) | |
| Defendant. | ) | |

## Request for Production of Documents, Electronically Stored Information, and Things

1. Produce all documents and electronically stored information that you referred to, relied upon, consulted, or used in any way in answering each interrogatory set forth in __[insert party name]__ Interrogatories dated __[insert date]__.
2. Produce organization charts for all of your Information Technology or Information Services departments or divisions during the period of __[date]__ to the present time.
3. Produce all written policies, procedures, guidelines, or records developed by or used by you for your computers, computer systems, electronic data, or electronic media, during the period of __[date]__ to the present time.
4. Produce all written policies, procedures, guidelines, or records developed by or used by you for backup or emergency restoration of electronic data, including backup tape rotation schedules, during the period of __[date]__ to the present time.
5. Produce all written policies, procedures, guidelines, or records developed by or used by you for electronic data retention, preservation, and destruction, including any schedules relating to those procedures, during the period of __[date]__ to the present time.

6. Produce all employee-use policies developed by or used by you for company computers, data, and other technology, during the period of __[date]__ to the present time.

7. Produce all written policies, procedures, guidelines, or records developed by or used by you for file naming conventions and standards, during the period of __[date]__ to the present time.

8. Produce all written policies, procedures, guidelines, or records developed by or used by you for password, encryption, or other security protocols, during the period of __[date]__ to the present time.

9. Produce all written policies, procedures, guidelines, or records developed by or used by you for labeling standards for Diskette, CD, DVD, or other removable media;

10. Produce all written policies, procedures, guidelines, or records developed by or used by you for e-mail storage conventions (e.g., limitations on mailbox sizes/storage locations; schedule and logs for storage) during the period of __[date]__ to the present time.

11. Produce all written policies, procedures, guidelines, or records developed by or used by you for electronic media deployment, allocation, and maintenance procedures for new employees, current employees, or departed employees, during the period of __[date]__ to the present time.

12. Produce all written policies, procedures, guidelines, or records developed by or used by you for software and hardware upgrades, including patches, during the period of __[date]__ to the present time.

13. Produce all written policies, procedures, guidelines, or records developed by or used by you for personal or home computer usage for work-related activities during the period of __[date]__ to the present time.

14. Produce all backup tapes containing e-mail and other electronically stored information related to this action during the period of __[date]__ to the present time.

15. Produce exact copies (i.e., bit-by-bit copies) of all hard drives on the desktop computers, laptop computers, notebook computers, personal digital assistant computers, servers, and other electronic media related to this action, used by __[name]__, during the period of __[date]__ to the present time.

16. Produce exact copies (i.e., bit-by-bit copies) of all relevant disks, CDs, DVDs, or other removable media containing electronically stored information created, reviewed, or received by __[name]__ related to this action during the period of __[date]__ to the present time.

17. Produce copies of all database files, e-mail, or other files maintained on servers or mainframe or minicomputers, containing electronically stored information created, reviewed, or received by __[name]__ related to this action during the period of __[date]__ to the present time.

18. Produce exact copies (i.e., bit-by-bit copies) of all data that was stored, retrieved, downloaded, restored, reconstructed, removed, deleted, salvaged, regenerated, and/or forensically extracted from the computer devices used by __[name]__ related to this action during the period of __[date]__ to the present time.

19. Produce all documents relating to costs and fees billed to you by any computer forensic examiner or other third-party technology provider with respect to the data that was stored, retrieved, downloaded, restored, reconstructed, removed, deleted, salvaged, regenerated, and/or forensically extracted from the computer devices used by __[name]__ related to this action during the period of __[date]__ to the present time.

20. Produce all documents relating to the terms of any agreement to provide services by any computer forensic examiner or other third-party technology provider with respect to the data that was stored, retrieved, downloaded, restored, reconstructed, removed, deleted, salvaged, regenerated, and/or forensically extracted from the computer devices used by __[name]__ related to this action during the period of __[date]__ to the present time.

21. Produce all documents relating to the hash of any drive image created by any computer forensic examiner or other third-party technology provider with respect to the data that was stored, retrieved, downloaded, restored, reconstructed, removed, deleted, salvaged, regenerated, and/or forensically extracted from the computer devices used by __[name]__ related to this action during the period of __[date]__ to the present time.

22. Produce all documents relating to the original drive hash with respect to any drive image created by any computer forensic examiner or other third-party technology provider with respect to the data that was stored, retrieved, downloaded, restored, reconstructed, removed, deleted, salvaged, regenerated, and/or forensically extracted from the computer devices used by __[name]__ related to this action during the period of __[date]__ to the present time.

23. Produce all documents relating to the chain of custody with respect to any computer drive examined or copied by any computer forensic examiner or other third-party technology provider with respect to the data that was stored, retrieved, downloaded, restored, reconstructed,

removed, deleted, salvaged, regenerated, and/or forensically extracted from the computer devices used by __[name]__ related to this action during the period of __[date]__ to the present time.

24. Produce all documents, reports, and conclusions relating to the forensic analysis of any computer drive examined or copied by any computer forensic examiner or other third-party technology provider with respect to the data that was stored, retrieved, downloaded, restored, reconstructed, removed, deleted, salvaged, regenerated, and/or forensically extracted from the computer devices used by __[name]__ related to this action during the period of __[date]__ to the present time.

Date: __[date]__

[Name of Firm]

By: _____

[Attorney name]
Attorney for __[name]__
[Street address]
[City, state, zip code]
[Telephone number]

## Form 5.16
## Request for Production of Documents, Electronically Stored Information, and Things Regarding Network Infrastructure

UNITED STATES DISTRICT COURT
FOR THE [Name District] OF [Name State]

| | |
|---|---|
| [Name of Plaintiff], | ) |
| | ) |
| Plaintiff, | ) |
| | ) |
| v. | ) Civil No. |
| | ) |
| [Name of Defendant], | ) |
| | ) |
| Defendant. | ) |

## Request for Production of Documents, Electronically Stored Information, and Things Regarding Network Infrastructure

1. Produce all documents and electronically stored information that you referred to, relied upon, consulted, or used in any way in answering each interrogatory set forth in __[insert party name]__ Interrogatories for Network Infrastructure dated __[insert date]__.

2. Produce all written policies, procedures, guidelines, or records developed by or used by you that relate to networks or groups of connected computers that allow people to share information and equipment, including, but not limited to, local area networks (LANs), wide area network (WANs), metropolitan area networks (MANs), storage area networks (SANs), peer-to-peer networks (P2Ps), client-server networks, point-to-point networks, integrated services digital networks (ISDNs), and virtual private networks (VPNs) during the period of __[date]__ to the present time.

3. Produce all written policies, procedures, guidelines, or records developed by or used by you that relate to your networks, including, but not limited to, topology (e.g., Ethernet, token-ring, ATM), channel service unit/data service unit (CSU/DSU), traffic measurement, hubs, switches, network interface cards, cables, firewalls, routers, gateways, media converters, intrusion-detection devices, and intranet connections, during the period of __[date]__ to the present time.

4. Produce all written policies, procedures, guidelines, or records developed by or used by you that relate to graphical representations of the components of your computer network and the relationship of those components to each other, including, but not limited to, flow charts, videos, photos, or drawings, during the period of __[date]__ to the present time.

5. Produce all written policies, procedures, guidelines or records, developed by or used by you that relate to the network operating systems in use during the period of __[date]__ to the present time.

6. Produce all written policies, procedures, guidelines, or records developed by or used by you that relate to the operation, maintenance, and upgrade of the computer network, during the period of __[date]__ to the present time.

7. Produce all written policies, procedures, guidelines, or records developed by or used by you that relate to any direct interconnection of your company network to networks of other parties, during the period of __[date]__ to the present time.

8. Produce all written policies, procedures, guidelines, or records developed by or used by you that relate to all communications clients, their termination points, and their configurations, including, but not limited to, T-1 circuits (full and fractional), POTS (Plain Old Telephone Service) lines, Primary Rate Interface (PRI) circuits, Basic Rate Interface (BRI) circuits, Digital Subscriber Line (DSL) circuits, satellite links, microwave connections, and cable modem lines, during the period of __[date]__ to the present time.

9. Produce all written policies, procedures, guidelines, or records developed by or used by you that relate to any video surveillance system in use, during the period of __[date]__ to the present time.

10. Produce all written policies, procedures, guidelines, or records developed by or used by you that relate to remote access to your network, during the period of __[date]__ to the present time.

11. Produce all written policies, procedures, guidelines, or records developed by or used by you that relate to any logging of events or audit trails for the network devices including, but not limited to, syslogs for routers, activity logs for remote access devices, firewall logs, web server logs, and caller ID logs, during the period of __[date]__ to the present time.

12. Produce all written policies, procedures, guidelines, or records developed by or used by you that relate to any employee monitoring software or devices in use, during the period of __[date]__ to the present time.

13. Produce all written policies, procedures, guidelines, or records developed by or used by you that relate to access control methods and activity records, including, but not limited to, badges, RFID, biometrics, keypad entry, restricted room access, and restricted remote access, during the period of __[date]__ to the present time.

14. Produce all written policies, procedures, guidelines, or records developed by or used by you that relate to bandwidth capacity and usage, during the period of __[date]__ to the present time.

15. Produce all written policies, procedures, guidelines, or records developed by or used by you that relate to any wireless networks such as WiFI, cellular, satellite, etc., during the period of __[date]__ to the present time.

16. Produce all written policies, procedures, guidelines, or records developed by or used by you that relate to information needed to access network devices and the configuration of the devices, such as user IDs, passwords, keys, etc., during the period of __[date]__ to the present time.

17. Produce all written policies, procedures, guidelines, or records developed by or used by you that relate to any assigned network configuration values, including, but not limited to, IP network assignments, Network Address Translation (NAT) assignments, IPX network numbers, IGRP autonomous zones, DECnet, systems Network Architecture (SNA) nodes, etc., during the period of __[date]__ to the present time.

Date: __[date]__

[Name of Firm]

By: _____
[Attorney name]
Attorney for __[name]__
[Street address]
[City, state, zip code]
[Telephone number]

## Form 5.17
## Request for Production of Documents, Electronically Stored Information, and Things Regarding Internet Access and Usage

UNITED STATES DISTRICT COURT
FOR THE [Name District] OF [Name State]

| | | |
|---|---|---|
| [Name of Plaintiff], | ) | |
| | ) | |
| Plaintiff, | ) | |
| | ) | |
| v. | ) | Civil No. |
| | ) | |
| [Name of Defendant], | ) | |
| | ) | |
| Defendant. | ) | |

## Request for Production of Documents, Electronically Stored Information, and Things Regarding Internet Access and Usage

1. Produce all documents and electronically stored information that you referred to, relied upon, consulted, or used in any way in answering each interrogatory set forth in __[insert party name]__ Interrogatories for Internet Access and Usage dated __[insert date]__.
2. Produce all written policies, procedures, guidelines, or records developed by or used by you for your company's or its employees' Internet access and usage, during the period of __[date]__ to the present time.
3. Produce all written policies, procedures, guidelines, or records developed by or used by you that relate to the provisioning of Internet access, including, but not limited to, such items as method of connection (e.g., DSL, T-1, dialup, etc.), connection speed (bandwidth), and Internet Service Provider (ISP), during the period of __[date]__ to the present time.
4. Produce all written policies, procedures, guidelines, or records developed by or used by you that relate to the logging of Internet activity, during the period of __[date]__ to the present time.
5. Produce all written policies, procedures, guidelines, or records developed by or used by you that relate to credentials that are needed to access the Internet, including, but not limited to, things such as

user IDs, passwords, security, or biometric devices, during the period of __[date]__ to the present time.

6. Produce all written policies, procedures, guidelines, or records developed by or used by you that relate to Internet monitoring, during the period of __[date]__ to the present time.

7. Produce all written policies, procedures, guidelines, or records developed by or used by you that relate to restrictions on Internet usage, during the period of __[date]__ to the present time.

8. Produce all written policies, procedures, guidelines, or records developed by or used by you that relate to specific blocked Web sites or domain names, during the period of __[date]__ to the present time.

9. Produce all written policies, procedures, guidelines, or records developed by or used by you that relate to usage or restrictions on usage of instant messaging, during the period of __[date]__ to the present time.

10. Produce all written policies, procedures, guidelines, or records developed by or used by you that relate to the use of a central firewall for Internet access for the entire company, during the period of __[date]__ to the present time.

11. Produce all written policies, procedures, guidelines, or records developed by or used by you that relate to the use of a software firewall for individual computers used at the company, during the period of __[date]__ to the present time.

12. Produce all written policies, procedures, guidelines, or records developed by or used by you that relate to employee access or ability to clear their Internet history activity, cookies or change browser security settings, during the period of __[date]__ to the present time.

13. Produce all written policies, procedures, guidelines, or records developed by or used by you that relate to the installation and/or update of anti-spyware software installed on each computer that has Internet access, during the period of __[date]__ to the present time.

Date: __[date]__

[Name of Firm]

By: _____
[Attorney name]
Attorney for __[name]__
[Street address]
[City, state, zip code]
[Telephone number]

## Form 5.18
## Request for Production of Documents, Electronically Stored Information, and Things Regarding Computers/Servers

UNITED STATES DISTRICT COURT
FOR THE [Name District] OF [Name State]

| | | |
|---|---|---|
| [Name of Plaintiff], | ) | |
| | ) | |
| Plaintiff, | ) | |
| | ) | |
| v. | ) | Civil No. |
| | ) | |
| [Name of Defendant], | ) | |
| | ) | |
| Defendant. | ) | |

### Request for Production of Documents, Electronically Stored Information, and Things Regarding Computers/Servers

1. Produce all documents and electronically stored information that you referred to, relied upon, consulted, or used in any way in answering each interrogatory set forth in __[insert party name]__ Interrogatories for Computers/Servers dated __[insert date]__.

2. Produce all written policies, procedures, guidelines, or records developed by or used by you related to your company's computer infrastructure, including, but not limited to, servers, computers, and peripheral devices, during the period of __[date]__ to the present time.

3. Produce all written policies, procedures, guidelines, or records developed by or used by you that relate to the specifications of your workstations, laptops, and servers during the period of __[date]__ to the present time.

4. Produce all written policies, procedures, guidelines, or records developed by or used by you that relate to maintenance, upkeep, and expansion of your computing environment, during the period of __[date]__ to the present time.

5. Produce all written policies, procedures, guidelines, or records developed by or used by you that relate to the use of passwords, biometrics, or other authentication procedures, during the period of __[date]__ to the present time.

6. Produce all written policies, procedures, guidelines, or records developed by or used by you that relate to the replacement or decommissioning of workstations, laptops, or servers, during the period of __[date]__ to the present time.

7. Produce all written policies, procedures, guidelines, or records developed by or used by you that relate to the logging of e-mail or other electronic communication activity, during the period of __[date]__ to the present time.

8. Produce all written policies, procedures, guidelines, or records developed by or used by you that relate to Internet browser access to e-mail, during the period of __[date]__ to the present time.

9. Produce all written policies, procedures, guidelines, or records developed by or used by you that relate to software clients that are used to access e-mail messages (e.g., Outlook, Outlook Express, Eudora, AOL, Lotus, etc.), during the period of __[date]__ to the present time.

10. Produce all written policies, procedures, guidelines, or records developed by or used by you that relate to all software clients used for instant messaging, during the period of __[date]__ to the present time.

11. Produce all written policies, procedures, guidelines, or records developed by or used by you that relate to the use of e-mail accounts (internal and external), during the period of __[date]__ to the present time.

12. Produce all written policies, procedures, guidelines, or records developed by or used by you that relate to text messaging via cellular telephones or pagers, during the period of __[date]__ to the present time.

13. Produce all written policies, procedures, guidelines, or records developed by or used by you that relate to the use of communication via a peer-to-peer (P2P) network, during the period of __[date]__ to the present time.

14. Produce all written policies, procedures, guidelines, or records developed by or used by you that relate to the use of communication via Internet newsgroups or chat rooms, during the period of __[date]__ to the present time.

15. Produce all written policies, procedures, guidelines, or records developed by or used by you that relate to the use of communications using encryption, during the period of __[date]__ to the present time.

Date: __[date]__

                         [Name of Firm]

By:       _____
           [Attorney name]
           Attorney for __[name]__
           [Street address]
           [City, state, zip code]
           [Telephone number]

## Form 5.19
## Request for Production of Documents, Electronically Stored Information, and Things Regarding Software

UNITED STATES DISTRICT COURT
FOR THE [Name District] OF [Name State]

| | | |
|---|---|---|
| [Name of Plaintiff], | ) | |
| | ) | |
| Plaintiff, | ) | |
| | ) | |
| v. | ) | Civil No. |
| | ) | |
| [Name of Defendant], | ) | |
| | ) | |
| Defendant. | ) | |

## Request for Production of Documents, Electronically Stored Information, and Things Regarding Software

1. Produce all documents and electronically stored information that you referred to, relied upon, consulted, or used in any way in answering each interrogatory set forth in __[insert party name]__ Interrogatories for Software __[insert date]__.

2. Produce all written policies, procedures, guidelines, or records developed by or used by you for your company's software applications during the period of __[date]__ to the present time.

3. Produce all written policies, procedures, guidelines, or records developed by or used by you that relate to the maintenance, licensing, and upgrading of software during the period of __[date]__ to the present time.

4. Produce all written policies, procedures, guidelines, or records developed by or used by you that relate the replacement or decommissioning of software applications, during the period of __[date]__ to the present time.

5. Produce all written policies, procedures, guidelines, or records developed by or used by you that relate to any software usage or installation (including employee installation) policies during the period of __[date]__ to the present time.

6. Produce all written policies, procedures, guidelines, or records developed by or used by you that relate to the use of anti-spyware, antivirus, and employee monitoring software, during the period of __[date]__ to the present time.

7. Produce all written policies, procedures, guidelines, or records or developed by or used by you that relate any encryption software used or installed, during the period of __[date]__ to the present time.

8. Produce all written policies, procedures, guidelines, or records, developed by or used by you that relate to any wiping software installed or used by the Company or its employees, during the period of __[date]__ to the present time.

9. Produce all written policies, procedures, guidelines, or records developed by or used by you that relate to software clients that are used to access e-mail messages (e.g., Outlook, Outlook Express, Eudora, AOL, Lotus, etc.), during the period of __[date]__ to the present time.

10. Produce all written policies, procedures, guidelines, or records developed by or used by you that relate to software used to monitor and maintain the computer system, including but limited to web statistic software, intrusion-detection software, defragmentation utilities, indexing and searching utilities, and content-management software, during the period of __[date]__ to the present time.

Date: __[date]__

[Name of Firm]

By: _____

[Attorney name]
Attorney for __[name]__
[Street address]
[City, state, zip code]
[Telephone number]

## Form 5.20
## Request for Production of Documents, Electronically Stored Information, and Things Regarding Backup Systems

UNITED STATES DISTRICT COURT
FOR THE [Name District] OF [Name State]

| | |
|---|---|
| [Name of Plaintiff], | ) |
| | ) |
| Plaintiff, | ) |
| | ) |
| v. | ) Civil No. |
| | ) |
| [Name of Defendant], | ) |
| | ) |
| Defendant. | ) |

## Request for Production of Documents, Electronically Stored Information, and Things Regarding Backup Systems

1. Produce all documents and electronically stored information that you referred to, relied upon, consulted, or used in any way in answering each interrogatory set forth in __[insert party name]__ Interrogatories for Backup Systems dated __[insert date]__.

2. Produce all written policies, procedures, guidelines, or records developed by or used by you related to your company's backup procedures, policies, and devices during the period of __[date]__ to the present time.

3. Produce all written policies, procedures, guidelines, or records developed by or used by you that relate to any off-site backup or online backup during the period of __[date]__ to the present time.

4. Produce all written policies, procedures, guidelines, or records developed by or used by you that relate to backup maintenance, testing and retention and the data to be backed up during the period of __[date]__ to the present time.

5. Produce all written policies, procedures, guidelines, or records developed by or used by you that relate to any backup media that may have been replaced or destroyed during the period of __[date]__ to the present time.

6. Produce all written policies, procedures, guidelines, or records developed by or used by you that relate to individual user backups of data during the period of __[date]__ to the present time.

7. Produce all written policies, procedures, guidelines, or records developed by or used by you that relate to disaster recovery, during the period of __[date]__ to the present time.

8. Produce all written policies, procedures, guidelines, or records developed by or used by you that relate to the backup of encrypted data and the means of decryption during the period of __[date]__ to the present time.

9. Produce all written policies, procedures, guidelines, or records developed by or used by you that relate to document retention during the period of __[date]__ to the present time.

10. Produce all written policies, procedures, guidelines, or records developed by or used by you that relate to the coping of files to removable media, during the period of __[date]__ to the present time.

Date: __[date]__

           [Name of Firm]

By: _____

[Attorney name]
Attorney for __[name]__
[Street address]
[City, state, zip code]
[Telephone number]

## Form 5.21
## Request for Production of Documents, Electronically Stored Information, and Things Regarding E-Mail, Instant Messaging, and Other Forms of Electronic Communication

UNITED STATES DISTRICT COURT
FOR THE [Name District] OF [Name State]

| | | |
|---|---|---|
| [Name of Plaintiff], | ) | |
| | ) | |
| Plaintiff, | ) | |
| | ) | |
| v. | ) | Civil No. |
| | ) | |
| [Name of Defendant], | ) | |
| | ) | |
| Defendant. | ) | |

## Request for Production of Documents, Electronically Stored Information, and Things Regarding E-Mail, Instant Messaging, and Other Forms of Electronic Communication

1. Produce all documents and electronically stored information that you referred to, relied upon, consulted, or used in any way in answering each interrogatory set forth in __[insert party name]__ Interrogatories for E-Mail, Instant Messaging, and Other Forms of Electronic Communication __[insert date]__.

2. Produce all written policies, procedures, guidelines, or records developed by or used by you for your company's or its employees' use of e-mail, instant messages, and other forms of electronic communication during the period of __[date]__ to the present time.

3. Produce all written policies, procedures, guidelines, or records developed by or used by you that relate to devices that are related to electronic communication, including, but not limited to, e-mail servers and gateway servers (e.g., BlackBerry Enterprise Server) during the period of __[date]__ to the present time.

4. Produce all written policies, procedures, guidelines, or records developed by or used by you that relate to graphical representations of the components of your computer network and the relationship of

those components to each other, including, but not limited to, flow charts, videos, photos, or drawings that facilitate the flow of electronic communication, during the period of __[date]__ to the present time.

5. Produce all written policies, procedures, guidelines, or records developed by or used by you that relate to the each portable electronic communication device (e.g., BlackBerry, convergent cellular telephone) during the period of __[date]__ to the present time.

6. Produce all written policies, procedures, guidelines, or records developed by or used by you that relate to the operation, maintenance, and upgrade of the electronic messaging system(s) during the period of __[date]__ to the present time.

7. Produce all written policies, procedures, guidelines, or records developed by or used by you that relate to the logging of e-mail or other electronic communication activity during the period of __[date]__ to the present time.

8. Produce all written policies, procedures, guidelines, or records developed by or used by you that relate to Internet browser access to e-mail during the period of __[date]__ to the present time.

9. Produce all written policies, procedures, guidelines, or records developed by or used by you that relate to software clients that are used to access e-mail messages (e.g., Outlook, Outlook Express, Eudora, AOL, Lotus, etc.) during the period of __[date]__ to the present time.

10. Produce all written policies, procedures, guidelines, or records developed by or used by you that relate to all software clients used for instant messaging, during the period of __[date]__ to the present time.

11. Produce all written policies, procedures, guidelines, or records developed by or used by you that relate to the use of e-mail accounts (internal and external) during the period of __[date]__ to the present time.

12. Produce all written policies, procedures, guidelines, or records developed by or used by you that relate to text messaging via cellular telephones or pagers during the period of __[date]__ to the present time.

13. Produce all written policies, procedures, guidelines, or records developed by or used by you that relate to the use of communication via a peer-to-peer (P2P) network during the period of __[date]__ to the present time.

14. Produce all written policies, procedures, guidelines, or records developed by or used by you that relate to the use of communication via Internet newsgroups or chat rooms during the period of __[date]__ to the present time.

15. Produce all written policies, procedures, guidelines, or records developed by or used by you that relate to the use of communications using encryption during the period of __[date]__ to the present time

Date: __[date]__

                                [Name of Firm]

By:   _____

                                  [Attorney name]
                                  Attorney for __[name]__
                                  [Street address]
                                  [City, state, zip code]
                                  [Telephone number]

## Form 5.22
## Request for Production of Documents, Electronically Stored Information, and Things Regarding Telephony

UNITED STATES DISTRICT COURT
FOR THE [Name District] OF [Name State]

| | | |
|---|---|---|
| [Name of Plaintiff], | ) | |
| | ) | |
| Plaintiff, | ) | |
| | ) | |
| v. | ) | Civil No. |
| | ) | |
| [Name of Defendant], | ) | |
| | ) | |
| Defendant. | ) | |

## Request for Production of Documents, Electronically Stored Information, and Things Regarding Telephony

1. Produce all documents and electronically stored information that you referred to, relied upon, consulted, or used in any way in answering each interrogatory set forth in __[insert party name]__ Interrogatories for Telephony dated __[insert date]__.

2. Produce all written policies, procedures, guidelines, or records developed by or used by you for your company's or its employees' use of telephonic or other voice communication devices during the period of __[date]__ to the present time.

3. Produce all written policies, procedures, guidelines, or records developed by or used by you that relate to devices that are related to telephonic equipment used by the company during the period of __[date]__ to the present time.

4. Produce all written policies, procedures, guidelines, or records developed by or used by you that relate to graphical representations of the components of your telecommunications components and the relationship of those components to each other and your computer network, including, but not limited to, flow charts, videos, photos, or drawings that facilitate the flow of telecommunications, during the period of __[date]__ to the present time.

5. Produce all written policies, procedures, guidelines, or records developed by or used by you that relate to the providers of telecommunications services during the period of __[date]__ to the present time.

6. Produce all written policies, procedures, guidelines, or records developed by or used by you that relate to the operation, maintenance, and upgrade of the company's telecommunications system(s) during the period of __[date]__ to the present time.

7. Produce all written policies, procedures, guidelines, or records developed by or used by you that relate to the specifications of and assignment of the company's telecommunications equipment, including, but not limited to, cell phones and pagers during the period of __[date]__ to the present time.

8. Produce all written policies, procedures, guidelines, or records developed by or used by you that relate to the logging of voice communications during the period of __[date]__ to the present time.

9. Produce all written policies, procedures, guidelines, or records developed by or used by you that relate to voicemail or answering systems and the retention of their data during the period of __[date]__ to the present time.

10. Produce all written policies, procedures, guidelines, or records developed by or used by you that relate to remote access to voicemail or answering systems, during the period of __[date]__ to the present time.

11. Produce all written policies, procedures, guidelines, or records developed by or used by you that relate to the modification of any voice communications policies and procedures during the period of __[date]__ to the present time.

Date: __[date]__

[Name of Firm]

By: _____
[Attorney name]
Attorney for __[name]__
[Street address]
[City, state, zip code]
[Telephone number]

## Form 5.23
## Request for Production of Documents, Electronically Stored Information, and Things Regarding Remote Access/Home Issues

UNITED STATES DISTRICT COURT
FOR THE [Name District] OF [Name State]

| | | |
|---|---|---|
| [Name of Plaintiff], | ) | |
| | ) | |
| Plaintiff, | ) | |
| | ) | |
| v. | ) | Civil No. |
| | ) | |
| [Name of Defendant], | ) | |
| | ) | |
| Defendant. | ) | |

## Request for Production of Documents, Electronically Stored Information, and Things Regarding Remote Access/Home Issues

1. Produce all documents and electronically stored information that you referred to, relied upon, consulted, or used in any way in answering each interrogatory set forth in __[insert party name]__ Interrogatories for Remote Access/Home Issues dated __[insert date]__.
2. Produce all written policies, procedures, guidelines, or records developed by or used by you for your company's or its employees' remote access to your network or work at home issues during the period of __[date]__ to the present time.
3. Produce all written policies, procedures, guidelines, or records developed by or used by you that relate to laptops or home computers issued to or in use by employees for business purposes during the period of __[date]__ to the present time.
4. Produce all written policies, procedures, guidelines, or records developed by or used by you that relate to authentication, security issues, encryption, and logging of remote access to your network during the period of __[date]__ to the present time.
5. Produce all written policies, procedures, guidelines, or records developed by or used by you that relate to the replacement or decommissioning of any laptops or home computers used for business purposes during the period of __[date]__ to the present time.

6. Produce all written policies, procedures, guidelines, or records developed by or used by you that relate to document retention policies affecting remote access or home computer use for business purposes during the period of __[date]__ to the present time.

7. Produce all written policies, procedures, guidelines, or records developed by or used by you that relate to the transfer of company data to laptops or removable media for use at home during the period of __[date]__ to the present time.

8. Produce all written policies, procedures, guidelines, or records developed by or used by you that relate to business data kept on employees' personal computers.

Date: __[date]__

[Name of Firm]

By: _____

[Attorney name]
Attorney for __[name]__
[Street address]
[City, state, zip code]
[Telephone number]

# Depositions

Depositions are an important part of any effort to engage in e-discovery. Typically, however, they do not occur until after sufficient preliminary information is gathered through other means. The sample interrogatories and requests for production of documents contained in other sections in this book provide examples of basic preliminary information that should be obtained before the planning process for depositions begins. The sample Rule 30(b)(6) Notice of Deposition also contains requests to produce information at the deposition that can be reviewed to help you plan your questions.

Because of the potentially open-ended nature of e-discovery, the examining attorney must make some initial determinations as to the nature and scope of the litigation and the amount in controversy before deciding who to depose or the depth or detail of the inquiry. You need to strike the right balance in terms of the level of detail you seek. Your ultimate goal is to learn enough about the specific computer systems and potentially available data to determine where the information that is relevant to the disputed issues in the case resides and how best to collect it. Depositions in particular are a useful tool to enable the examiner to develop a more targeted and, one hopes, more cost-effective means of obtaining case specific information once the initial background information is obtained.

Depositions will ordinarily be taken of persons with specific information technology backgrounds who play a day-to-day role in the management of a party's computer systems and electronic information. Depending on the size of the target, it may be necessary to depose several different people to get a complete understanding of the technology and data held, for example, by a large corporate entity. You may need to depose an IT director for basic information and then move to network administrators for general network information, records management personnel for backed-up and archived information, and other IT personnel for e-mail-related information. You should also consider whether to use the services of an appropriate computer consultant to help you plan your deposition questions. Whether you need computer technology experts, computer forensic experts, or the expertise of an e-discovery vendor will vary from case to case, depending on the complexity of the technological issues involved and the skill level of the lawyer.

Depositions are a useful way to develop a more detailed understanding of these systems and the available information to ultimately enable you to secure key evidence for use in the preparation and presentation of your case and to lay the foundation for any necessary e-discovery-related motions that may be required to acquire this evidence. The following topical checklist (Form 5.24) may be of assistance in formulating your deposition questions. Each case obviously has its own particular issues that must be addressed, and no checklist fits all circumstances. These suggestions are not intended to be inclusive but are intended to give you ideas to develop lines of inquiry in your own particular case.

## Form 5.24
## Electronic Discovery Deposition Checklist

### General Background

◆ Are the computer systems managed in-house, or is that function out-sourced?

◆ If outsourced, identify the outsourcing vendor(s) and qualifications.

◆ Identify the terms and conditions of the contractual relationships with the vendor.

◆ Identify what systems are supported by the vendor.

◆ Identify how vendor support is provided (on-site or remote access) and by whom.

◆ Identify whether the vendor performs system configuration, maintenance, and/or backup. Does the vendor perform any other services? If so, identify the details of each category of services provided.

◆ If managed in-house, describe the structure of the IT/IS department, its general organization, its reporting hierarchy, and its method of interaction and integration with other departments within the company.

◆ Identify key personnel.

◆ Identify whether there are formal policies or practices in place, written or otherwise, to manage the department.

◆ Identify whether there are different systems, policies, or practices used for different corporate subdivisions/departments, and, if so, identify what they are.

◆ Is there a help desk/support department? If so, how is support implemented?

◆ Is a database used to track inquiries and responses (e.g., trouble tickets)? What information is recorded in this database?

### Networks

◆ Identify the types of networks used—LANs, WANs, VPNs, SANs, etc.

◆ Identify locations and users connected through any of the above.

◆ Identify by name, version, manufacturer, date of purchase, and date of rollout of all network operating systems.

◆ Identify by name, version, manufacturer, date of purchase, and date of rollout all network hardware—servers, routers, switches, etc.

◆ Identify all network protocols in use during the relevant time period.

◆ Identify all communications circuits, their termination points, and their configurations.

◆ Identify any video surveillance system that may be in use and the location and retention period of any video records.

- Identify any method for remote access.
- Identify layout and design of network, including number, type, and function of all file servers, e-mail servers, fax servers, Web servers, or other similar equipment.
- Identify storage capacity and type for the network.
- Identify location of stored data on network.
- Identify organizational structure of data at the volume and folder level at a minimum and to a greater level of detail if necessary.
- Identify naming conventions for users, folders, files, volumes, and server(s).
- Identify any system performance logging and/or auditing functions.
- Identify any user activity logging and auditing functions.
- Identify any time-synchronization functions for servers, workstations, and other devices on network.
- Identify all software applications installed on network.
- Identify all software application installation and usage policies and practices.
- Identify all data retention policies, including time limitations on file storage and disk capacity limitations for users.
- Identify user directory management and procedures for establishing and removing accounts and assigning rights.
- Identify all policies and procedures relating to network usage of individual, departmental, and other public network shares.
- Identify all other network usage policies and practices.
- Identify all network system administration personnel.

## E-Mail/Instant Messaging

- Identify all e-mail/instant messaging applications by name, version and manufacturer.
- Identify history of upgrades and/or replacements of the e-mail/instant messaging applications.
- Identify servers and network operating systems for each e-mail/instant messaging application, including locations of e-mail servers, post offices, and/or databases and approximate quantity of data by size of database, number of messages, or both.
- Identify e-mail/instant messaging system architecture connectivity between servers, message transport, replication, and gateways to external systems.
- Identify e-mail/instant messaging distribution procedures.
- Identify whether local e-mail archives exist.
- Identify whether encryption of e-mail and/or other enhanced security is used.

- Identify any policies or practices regarding replication of e-mail to remote locations or local storage areas.
- Identify all legacy e-mail/instant messaging systems decommissioned during the relevant time period and, if they exist, determine whether any data from the decommissioned system(s) is maintained or otherwise preserved on a server or backup media and/or whether information was migrated to a newer system? If migration took place, what policies or procedures were followed and what relevant records exist regarding what information was or was not migrated?
- Identify setup and removal procedures for e-mail accounts.
- Identify how long e-mail is maintained when a user leaves, who had subsequent access to it, and what procedures were followed to preserve or dispose of the data.
- Identify e-mail account names by individual user, including multiple accounts for a single user, alias accounts, or functional users like "help desk" or "techsupport."
- Identify all methods for e-mail retrieval (e.g., POP, IMAP, Outlook, Web).
- Identify whether collection mailboxes for litigation or record-retention purposes have been used and, if so, where e-mail comes from, where it goes, and who has access to it.
- Identify any use of public folders by user, purpose, and location and describe any policies or procedures for setup or removal of public folders, maintaining data, and setting retention periods.
- Identify use of discussion databases/bulletin boards by user, purpose, and location and describe any policies or procedures for setup or removal, maintaining data, and setting retention periods.
- Identify whether instant messaging is available in the e-mail system, if it is used, and the location of any logs of IM activity.
- Identify whether voice mail functions are integrated with the e-mail system.
- Identify whether voice mail messages are stored and, if so, how they are identified in the system and how long they are maintained.
- Identify all e-mail client application software in use or installed.
- Identify whether there is an e-mail archiving system.
- Identify any policies or procedures for retrieval of archived e-mail.
- Identify whether there is bulk archiving of historical e-mail.
- Identify what archiving systems are used—by name, version, manufacturer—and how the system is configured.
- Identify whether all messages are archived or, if not, how and why some messages are selected for archiving.
- Identify the retention period of e-mail archives?

- Identify whether an automatic deletion function is used on e-mail and, if so, whether it applies to all folders, what the time limits are before deletion, and whether there is a process for excluding e-mail from deletion.
- Identify any disk space limitations for e-mail accounts, including the maximum allowed capacity.
- Identify what happens when maximum capacity is exceeded and whether there is a procedure for expanding capacity if requested.
- Identify any listserves or newsgroups that users subscribe to, by user and group.
- Identify any available tools for searching or retrieving e-mail messages.
- Identify any procedures for monitoring quantities and/or content of e-mail usage.
- Identify any content filtering that may exist. If used, identify the criteria for content filtering, how the criteria are maintained, the disposition and handling of filtered messages, individuals responsible for maintaining the content filtering system and retention period of filtered messages.
- Identify any spam or blocking for e-mail. If used, how is the system maintained? Is a third-party service used? What is the process and flow for e-mail moving through the spam-prevention system? Are tagged messages deleted or quarantined? How are the messages released and who screens the individual messages that are tagged?
- Identify all e-mail system administration personnel.
- Identify any outside services used for e-mail and/or for information transmission and retrieval, including the name of the service, and the time period during which the outside services were used.
- Identify any limitations on users accessing outside services.

## Web, FTP, and Intranet Servers

- Identify any web, FTP, or intranet server applications used by name, manufacturer and version.
- Identify the platform used for Web sites including the brand and model of server, and the name, manufacturer, and version of the operating system.
- Identify the logging of system and user information, including but not limited to: change logs, access logs, SSH logs, FTP logs, Telnet logs, and logs of system and user activities.
- Identify site names and aliases, IP addresses, and IP addresses of any DNS servers used.

♦ Identify whether the site is mirrored and, if so, the location of the mirror server(s) and how often it(they) is(are) updated.

## Backup and Archiving

♦ Identify all backup and archiving software, including name, version number, manufacturer, and date of purchase.

♦ Identify any third-party vendor that is or may have been used for backing up data.

♦ Identify all tape drives or other hardware devices used to store and retrieve backup and archival data, including type of device, manufacturer, model number, and date of purchase.

♦ Identify all media used for backup and archival storage, including types of media, manufacturer, brand, capacity, physical size, and other specifications.

♦ Identify platform(s) used for backup and archiving applications, including name, manufacturer, and version of platform operating systems and brand, manufacturer, and model of platform computer systems.

♦ Identify schedules for backup and archiving activity.

♦ Identify policies and procedures for retention, rotation and destruction of backup and archival data and storage media.

♦ Identify the format of backup and archival data, including specifications for all hardware and software encryption and data compression routines.

♦ Identify any records describing or providing a history of backup and data archiving activities.

♦ Identify any records that describe the existence, location, rotation, and custodianship of backup and archive tapes and other media.

♦ Identify media labeling conventions and all other codes and abbreviations used in connection with backup and archival data.

♦ Identify how often data was restored from backups during the past year, why it was restored, and what was restored.

## Desktop and Laptop Computers

♦ Identify the operating system(s) used on each desktop/laptop computer by name, version, and manufacturer.

♦ Identify any power-on or BIOS (Basic Input/Output System) passwords for each desktop/laptop.

♦ Identify the hardware configurations of each desktop/laptop.

♦ Identify the software installed on each desktop/laptop.

♦ Identify any policies or limitations regarding installation or usage of application software.

- Identify any hardware or biometric requirement to gain access to each desktop/laptop.
- Identify standard hard drive configurations, including number and size of physical drives and partitioning.
- Identify procedures for assignment and reassignment of desktop/laptop and for replacement or reimaging of hard disk drives.
- Identify any policies or limitations regarding the use of any peripheral data storage devices, including CDs, tape drives, removable disk cartridges, Flash drives, and floppy diskettes.
- Identify any backup procedures used for desktop/laptop computers, including a description of where the data is copied and the method and software used for backup purposes.
- Identify the assignment of rights to desktop/laptop computer users and administrators.
- Identify any policies or procedures to be followed regarding the organization of user data in directories and folders.
- Identify any policies or procedures to be followed regarding file, directory, folder, volume, and media labeling conventions.
- Identify any policies or procedures to be followed regarding the use of encryption and data compression.
- Identify any other policies and procedures relating to usage of such computers.

## Personal Digital Assistants

- Identify whether any personal digital assistants are provided or supported by the company. If so, what individuals or groups of employees are provided PDAs?
- Identify each PDA by user, manufacturer, model, serial number, and operating system.
- Identify any standard configuration?
- Identify any standard procedures for synchronizing PDA data to desktop and e-mail systems.
- Identify any policies and procedures relating to use of PDAs.

## Application Software

- Identify all pertinent information on the use of the following software applications:
  - Document management software
  - Office Suite
  - E-mail/instant messaging
  - Voice-activated dictation or other digital dictation

- Project/practice management
- Time and billing/accounting
- Projection, forecasting, and modeling relating to relevant issues/subjects
- Fax receipt, transmission
- Voice mail
- Graphical images
- Collaborative/group work space applications
- CAD and other design systems
- Contact management
- Data mining, searching, and retrieval
- Other relevant applications

## Form 5.25
## Notice of Taking Deposition Pursuant to Fed. R. Civ. P. 30(b)(6)

UNITED STATES DISTRICT COURT
FOR THE [Name District] OF [Name State]

| | |
|---|---|
| [Name of Plaintiff], | ) |
| | ) |
| Plaintiff, | ) |
| | ) |
| v. | ) Civil No. |
| | ) |
| [Name of Defendant], | ) |
| | ) |
| Defendant. | ) |

### Notice of Taking Deposition Pursuant to Fed. R. Civ. P. 30(b)(6)

TO:

PLEASE TAKE NOTICE that pursuant to Fed. R. Civ. P. 30(b)(6), the deposition of the __[insert party name]__ will be taken on __[insert date]__ at __[insert time]__ for the purposes of discovery or as evidence in this action at the offices of __[insert location]__ before a court reporter authorized to administer oaths. The deposition will be recorded by stenographic means.

The above-named corporation, pursuant to Fed. R. Civ. P. 30(b)(6), shall designate an individual or individuals with personal knowledge to appear and attend at the time and place specified for the purpose of testifying to:

1. The identity of all employees employed by __[insert party name]__ during the period of __[date]__ to the present time who are or were responsible for managing and maintaining its technology infrastructure that includes, but is not limited to, servers or other network storage devices and related peripheral equipment, desktop computers, portable computers, laptop computers, personal digital assistants (PDAs), telephones, and other similar electronic devices.

2. The identity of all nonemployee consultants, consulting firms, contractors, or similar entities retained by __[insert party name]__ during the period of __[date]__ to the present time who are or were responsible for installing, servicing, managing, or maintaining its technology infrastructure that includes, but is not limited to, servers

or other network storage devices and related peripheral equipment, desktop computers, portable computers, laptop computers, personal digital assistants (PDAs), telephones, and other similar electronic devices.

3. A description of and the operation of all groups of connected computer systems used by __[insert party name]__ that permit users to share information and transfer data, including, but not limited to, local area networks (LANs), wide area networks (WANs), client-server networks, virtual private networks (VPNs), and storage area networks (SANs); including all equipment, devices, components, and network resources that establish and maintain the network environment, including, but not limited to, routers, switches, hubs, bridges, firewalls, proxies, etc.

4. A description of and the operation of all available third-party connectivity between the computer systems and network environment used by __[insert party name]__, including the type of information that is shared, the manner in which the information is transferred, and the identity of any individuals who have authorization to transfer information into or out of the network environment.

5. A description of and the operation of each individual personal computer system that is or has been used by employees of __[insert party name]__ for the period of__[date]__ to the present time that includes, but is not limited to, desktop computers, portable computers, laptop computers, personal digital assistants (PDAs), telephones, and other similar electronic devices, including descriptions of equipment and any peripheral technology attached to the computer system.

6. A description of and the operation of the Internet and intranet connectivity of each computer system used by __[insert party name]__, including, but not limited to, client-server communications and client-client communications facilitated through modem, network, or direct connection.

7. A description of all hardware or software modifications made to the computer systems used by __[insert party name]__ from __[date]__ to the present time, including type and nature of each modification, dates of modification, software and hardware titles, version numbers, contact information of person(s) performing the modification, and location of data backups made prior to modification.

8. A description of all operating systems, including, but not limited to, Microsoft Windows, Linux, Unix, DOS, Solaris, etc., installed on each of __[insert party name]__ computer systems from __[date]__ to the present time.

9. A description of the title and version number of any and all software installed or executed on each of __[insert party name]__ computer systems from __[date]__ to the present time.

10. A description of policies and procedures governing the use of removable media, such as CD-ROMs, Zip disks, floppy disks, tape drives, removable hard drives, etc., associated with __[insert party name]__ computer systems or network from __[date]__ to the present time.

11. A description of policies and procedures used for performing backups on all computer systems and a description of any hardware or software used to perform such backup from __[date]__ to the present time.

12. A description of all e-mail accounts used by __[insert party name]__ and your employees from __[date]__ to the present time.

13. A description of policies and procedures used to perform backups or for archiving e-mail messages and a description of any hardware or software used to perform such backups or archiving from __[date]__ to the present time.

14. A description of any e-mail-based encryption used by __[insert party name]__ or your employees from __[date]__ to the present time.

15. A description of the components and design implementation or distribution of __[insert party name]__ telephone and voice messaging systems, including all hardware, software, and third-party service providers used from __[date]__ to the present time.

16. A description of policies and procedures used for performing backups or for archiving any and all voice messaging records and a description of any hardware or software used to perform such backups or archiving from __[date]__ to the present time.

17. A description of all policies and procedures governing employee use of Internet newsgroups, chat rooms, or instant messaging on your computer systems from __[date]__ to the present time.

18. A description of any and all cell phones, PDAs, digital convergence devices, or other portable electronic devices, whether owned by __[insert party name]__ or by others, used by any __[insert party name]__ employees in the performance of his or her employment from __[date]__ to the present time.

19. A description of all policies and procedures pertaining to data retention and destruction from __[date]__ to the present time and a description of all hardware or software used to facilitate the deletion of data subject to any data retention and destruction policies and procedures.

20. A description of any and all servers or other network storage devices, desktop computers, portable computers, laptop computers, personal digital assistants (PDAs), telephones, and other similar electronic devices that have had their hard drives reformatted, wiped, or replaced from __[date]__ to the present time.

21. A description of any and all information relevant to this legal matter that was deleted, physically destroyed, corrupted, damaged, lost, or overwritten, and whether this information was lost pursuant to the data retention and destruction policies and procedures.

[Name of Firm]

Date: __[date]__                    By: _____

[Attorney name]
Attorney for __[name]__
[Street address]
[City, state, zip code]
[Telephone number]

## Form 5.26
## Sample Subpoena to Internet Service Provider

SUBPOENA DUES TECUM (CIVIL)—Case No.:____C133333____

ATTORNEY ISSUED VA CODE §§ 8.01-413, 16.1-89, 16.1-265;

Commonwealth of Virginia     Supreme Court Rules 1:4,4:9

_____December 22, 2005, 10:00 A.M._____

HEARING DATE AND TIME

_____FAIRFAX COUNTY CIRCUIT COURT_____Court

_____4110 Chain Bridge Road, Fairfax, Virginia 22030_____

COURT ADDRESS

_____JANE DOE_____*v.In re:* _____JOHN DOE_____

TO THE PERSON AUTHORIZED BY LAW TO SERVE THIS PROCESS:

You are commanded to summon

Custodian of the records for Coxcom, Inc., SERVE: Registered Agent, Beverly
L. Crump

NAME

_____11 S. 12th Street_____

STREET ADDRESS

Richmond_____Virginia_____23219_____

CITY                    STATE              ZIP

TO the person summoned: You are commanded to make available the documents and tangible things designated and described below:

Confirmation on whose (name and address) broadband account was assigned the following IP address: 192.168.150.312 on November 15, 2005, 2:51 P.M. eastern standard time. (Fax is acceptable).

at <u>10605 Judicial Drive, #A3, Fairfax, VA 22030 (see fax)</u> at <u>12/2/05 at 9:50 A.M.</u>
LOCATION                                                                    DATE AND TIME

To permit such party or someone acting in his or her behalf to inspect and copy, test or sample such tangible things in your possession, custody or control.

This Subpoena Duces Tecum is issued by the attorney for and on behalf of

<u>JANE DOE</u>
PARTY NAME

<u>Phil Barrister</u>                        <u>1111</u>
NAME OF ATTORNEY          VIRGINIA STATE BAR NUMBER

<u>11111 Judicial Dr. Suite 1</u>          <u>703-111-1111</u>
OFFICE ADDRESS               TELEPHONE NUMBER OF ATTORNEY

<u>Fairfax, VA 22030</u>                    <u>703-222-2222</u>
OFFICE ADDRESS               FACSIMILE NUMBER OF ATTORNEY

<u>November 22, 2005</u>
DATE ISSUED                  SIGNATURE OF ATTORNEY

Notice to Recipient: See page 2 for further information.

RETURN OF SERVICE

TO the person summoned:

If you are served with this subpeona less than 14 days prior to the date that compliance with this subpeona is required, you may object by notifying the party who issued the subpeona of your objection in writing and describing the basis of your objection in that writing.

❏ This SUBPOENA DUCES TECUM is being served by a private process server who must provide proof of service in accordance with Va. Code § 8.01-325.

TO the person authorized to serve this process: Upon execution, the return of this process shall be made to the clerk of court.

---

NAME: _____

ADDRESS:_____

_____

❏ PERSONAL SERVICE Tel. No.

Being unable to make personal service, a copy was delivered in the following manner:
❏ Delivered to family member (not temporary sojoumer or guest) age 16 or older at usual place of abode of party named above after giving information of its purport. List name, age of recipient, and relation of recipient to party named above:

_____

_____

❏ Posted on front door or such other door as appear to be the main entrance of usual place of abode, address listed above. (Other authorized recipient not found.)

❏ not found _____, Sheriff

_____ by _____, Deputy Sheriff
    DATE

---

CERTIFICATE OF COUNSEL

I, _____Phil Barrister_____, counsel for _____Jane Doe, hereby certify that a copy of the foregoing subpoena duces tecum was <u>hand delivered</u>
                                         METHOD OF DELIVERY

to _____Albert Einstein, Esquire_____, counsel of record for _____John Doe_____,

on the _____16th_____ day of _____November_____, _____2005_____.

_____.

## Motions to Compel

Motions to compel discovery are probably more likely in the area of e-discovery than in any other area of discovery in modern litigation. This is due in part to the dynamic nature of information that exists in electronic form. There is potentially relevant information that exists electronically that would not be available with the paper copy of a document. In the past, a document would typically exist in final form. There might be a precursor draft available in some file, but more often than not any drafts were destroyed in the normal course of business. Furthermore, the preservation of the document would depend on the extent and capacity of the available filing system and any normal document retention practices. Thus, receipt of a simple photocopy of the document would suffice more often than not.

No one in the past would have dreamed that the type of information contained in the metadata of a computer-generated document about its creation and editing as it evolved toward final form would one day be available for scrutiny. No one would have anticipated a potentially unending electronic shelf life—depending on backup procedures—either. Of course, none of us used to trying cases using contracts, memos, and letters as evidence would have anticipated what e-mail would do to business communication as it exists today. Throw in access to the Internet and inappropriate web browsing and you have an explosion of potentially relevant information to discover.

Today, all of this information is potentially fair game. The real challenge is to determine what is available and whether it is worth pursuing. If it seems worth pursuing, a decision must be made about how to get it in the face of efforts to resist its production. An unspecified demand for too much, given the potentially vast amounts of electronic information available coupled with the expense to produce it, will meet with obvious resistance. On the other hand, the possibility of finding the smoking gun, particularly if there is an altered document or a deleted e-mail out there, is something no lawyer can ignore.

By now e-discovery has probably evolved to the point where it is no longer necessary to file a motion to compel to force a party to produce information electronically rather than as a paper printout or photocopy. However, it still may be necessary to file a motion to educate a judge on the need to produce a document in its native format so its metadata is included. It is also likely that the vast majority of judges lack access to computerized litigation-support tools and may be baffled when you try to explain that a party should be required to produce information in a particular electronic format so that it will work successfully with a particular litigation-support program. Motions to compel must educate the court on the underlying technology involved so issues like the method and mode of production, the scope of production, and the cost of production can be understood. Such motions are always case and fact specific, but the materials in the case digest and the exemplar materials below will provide useful examples of the kinds of issues that can be addressed with motions to compel discovery.

## Form 5.27

### Plaintiff's Motion to Permit Inspection and Copying of Computer Storage Devices or to Compel Production of Computer Equipment by Defendant[1]

UNITED STATES DISTRICT COURT
FOR THE [Name District] OF [Name State]

| | | |
|---|---|---|
| [Name of Plaintiff], | ) | |
| | ) | |
| Plaintiff, | ) | |
| | ) | |
| v. | ) | Civil No. |
| | ) | |
| [Name of Defendant], | ) | |
| | ) | |
| Defendant. | ) | |

### Plaintiff's Motion to Permit Inspection and Copying of Computer Storage Devices or to Compel Production of Computer Equipment by Defendant

Pursuant to Federal Rule of Civil Procedure 37 generally, and 37(a)(2)(B) specifically, and upon reasonable notice to Defendant, Plaintiff moves this Court to permit inspection and copying of computer storage devices in accordance with Plaintiff's Request for Production of Documents, Electronic Information and Things and/or to compel production of computer equipment, software and documents by Defendant for inspection and copying. Plaintiff respectfully requests that this Court enter an Order (Attachment A) [omitted] directing Defendant to produce for inspection and copying, within five (5) business days of the Order, certain computer equipment, computer storage devices, software, and documents used by Defendant during the time period relevant to the actions taken that constitute the basis for this lawsuit.

### BACKGROUND

On __[date]__, counsel for Plaintiff sent a letter to Defendant informing Defendant that Defendant's electronic data or compilations would be an impor-

---

[1]By Daniel Seymour, CoreFacts, LLC. Reprinted with permission from the ABA Section of Labor and Employment Law.

tant and irreplaceable source for discovery and/or evidence, and that Plaintiff intended to submit discovery requests to obtain documents and other information in electronic form and to access computer(s), computer network(s), and computer systems. (Attachment B) [omitted]

This letter reminded Defendant that his or her obligation to preserve electronic data is the same as for other forms of evidence. Counsel for Plaintiff requested that Defendant safeguard against the destruction of evidence until final resolution of the litigation and listed eight (8) categories of electronic data that should be preserved.

After receipt of this letter and after commencement of this lawsuit, Defendant has embarked on a course of conduct designed to hinder and delay and even destroy evidence that is relevant to this lawsuit. For example, Defendant's records-management program was not suspended and electronic documents have been deleted, or in the normal course of Defendant's ongoing disaster recovery program systems administrators have reused critical backup tapes and thereby overwritten discoverable information, or files have been deleted from the hard drives of critical desktop or laptop computers.

As part of the discovery in this lawsuit, Plaintiff served a set of Requests for Production of Computer Equipment, electronic documents, software, and other items upon Defendant. Each of the requests is narrow and directed to the issues relevant to this lawsuit, and none is overbroad or burdensome. Defendant has refused to produce responsive material on the grounds that the requests are vague, ambiguous, overly broad, and burdensome and because they seek confidential and proprietary documents, as well as documents protected by attorney-client and work-product privileges. Since the filing of this lawsuit, Defendant has knowingly permitted or contributed to the destruction of responsive evidence.

Counsel for Plaintiff sent a letter to opposing counsel proposing a procedure to access Defendant's computers and servers. The procedure incorporated the parties' agreed Confidentiality Order for protection of attorney-client and work-product privileges and protection of trade secrets and proprietary information. The procedure proposed by counsel provided:

1. Defendants and defense counsel will meet with plaintiff's counsel and their computer forensic experts and review each file on the computer. This review will be conducted in a manner that does not disrupt defendant's business.
2. If a file may lead to discovery of admissible evidence and is not protected from production by a privilege, it will be copied and produced.
3. A privilege log will be maintained of all documents withheld on basis of privilege.

4. If the parties conclude a file may not lead to discovery of admissible evidence, it will not be produced.
5. Plaintiffs will use and pay for their own expert for this process. If defendants want a neutral expert, costs for the neutral expert will be shared equally.

Counsel for Defendant rejected this proposal.

## ARGUMENT

Plaintiff put Defendant on notice at the outset of this lawsuit that discovery would include electronic versions of documents. A party's duty to preserve relevant documents arises when a party has notice of the relevance. *Applied Telematics, Inc. v. Sprint Communications Co.*, 1996 U.S. Dist. LEXIS 14053 (E.D.Pa. September 17, 1996); *Turner v. Hudson Transit Lines, Inc.*, 142 F.R.D. 68 (S.D.N.Y. 1991); see Civil Discovery Standards, ABA Section of Litigation, at part IV, page 17 (August 1999). Defendant has a duty to suspend its ongoing records management or the reuse of backup tapes once the duty to preserve documents arises. *Lewy v. Remington Arms Co.*, 836 F.2d 1104 (8th Cir. 1988); *Applied Telematics, Inc. v. Sprint Communications Co.*, 1996 U.S. Dist. LEXIS 14053 (E.D.Pa. September 17, 1996); Plaintiff has no means to obtain the full content of documents prepared with the use of computer equipment other than by inspection of the equipment itself.

Under Federal Rule of Civil Procedure 26(b)(2)(i)–(iii), the interests of Plaintiff outweigh those of Defendant. See *Fennell v. First Step Designs, Ltd.*, 83 F.3d 526 (1st Cir. 1996). Defendant will suffer no undue burden or prejudice from being required to comply with Plaintiff's document production request. On the other hand, absent compliance by Defendant with its discovery obligations, Plaintiff will be unable to effectively pursue its claims against Defendant because, due to the inexcusable conduct of Defendant, relevant material and nonprivileged information will have been withheld from Plaintiff.

Federal Rule of Civil Procedure 34(a) provides, in pertinent part, that "[a]ny party may serve on any other party a request (1) to produce and permit the party making the request, or someone acting on the requestor's behalf, to inspect and copy, any designated documents (including . . . data compilations)." *Bills v. Kennecott Corp.*, 108 F.R.D. 459 (D. Utah 1985). The obligation to produce electronic versions of documents and records is not new. Since 1970, Federal Rule of Civil Procedure 34 has authorized a party to request production of designated documents in electronic form and the electronic source itself. Advisory Committee Notes for the 1970 Amendments to Rule 34; *Illinois Tool Works, Inc. v. Metro Mark Products, Ltd.*, 43 F.Supp.2d 951 (N.D. Ill. 1999).

The electronic version of a document contains valuable information that the hard copy does not provide. In *Armstrong v. Executive Office of the President,* 1 F.3d 1274 (D.C. Cir. 1993), the court said that printing a hard copy of an e-mail message was not the same as preserving the electronic version because the hard copy does not contain directories, distribution lists, acknowledgment of receipts, or transmittal information. A printout of a document or its appearance on a computer monitor may not indicate any change or what existed before the change. *Does Discovery of Electronic Information Require Amendments to the Federal Rules of Civil Procedures?* Commercial & Federal 35 Litigation Section, Committee on Federal Procedure, New York State Bar Association Report (February 22, 2001). Numerous recent court decisions have ruled that Rule 34 permits a party to request production of a document in its electronic form and not merely rely on the hard copy of a document. In *Playboy Enterprises, Inc. v. Welles*, 60 F.Supp.2d 1050 (S.D. Cal. 1999), plaintiff requested access to defendant's hard drive to attempt to recover deleted files that may have been stored on the hard drive. The court determined that plaintiff's need for access outweighed the potential interruption to defendant's business and approved plaintiff's request. In *TY, Inc. v. Le Claire*, 2000 WL 1015934 (N.D. Ill. June 1, 2000), the court granted plaintiff's motion and authorized plaintiff, at its own expense, to inspect the hard drives of computers defendants used during the relevant time period. In *Simon Property Group v. mySimon, Inc.*, 194 F.R.D. 639 (S.D. Ind. 2000), the court granted plaintiff's motion to compel defendants to produce their computers so that plaintiffs could attempt to recover deleted computer files.

## RELIEF REQUESTED

For the reasons stated, Plaintiff respectfully requests that this Court enter an Order directing Defendant to permit inspection and copying of certain computer equipment, computer storage devices, software and documents used by Defendant during the time period relevant to the actions taken that constitute the basis for this lawsuit and directing Defendant to produce the designated computer equipment, software and documents within five (5) business days of this Order.

## Form 5.28
## Proposed Order

UNITED STATES DISTRICT COURT
FOR THE [Name District] OF [Name State]

| | |
|---|---|
| [Name of Plaintiff], | ) |
| | ) |
| Plaintiff, | ) |
| | ) |
| v. | ) Civil No. |
| | ) |
| [Name of Defendant], | ) |
| | ) |
| Defendant. | ) |

## Proposed Order

On Plaintiff's motion under Fed. R. Civ. P. 37(a)(2)(B) to permit inspection and copying of computer storage devices or to compel production of computer equipment, having reviewed and considered the motion and materials submitted in support of the motion, the Court now orders as follows:

Plaintiff's motion to permit inspection and copying of computer storage devices or to compel production of computer equipment is hereby granted on the following terms:

1. Defendant shall produce for inspection and copying, within five (5) business days of the Order, the following computer equipment, computer storage devices, software, and documents used by Defendant: [List equipment, devices, etc., that are subject of motion].
2. Plaintiff shall engage the services of __[Computer Forensic Imaging Service]__ to make a bit-by-bit copy of all electronic data identified in Paragraph 1, above.
3. All costs associated with the copying of the electronic data identified in Paragraph 1, above, including the fees of __[Computer Forensic Imaging Service]__, shall be paid by Defendant.

IT IS SO ORDERED.

Date: _____          _____
                                Honorable Judge [name]
                                United States District Court Judge

# Motions for Protective Orders

As counsel for the recipient of an e-discovery request, the possibility of a motion for a protective order is something that should always be at the forefront of your thinking. There is nothing more onerous in the litigation process than being the recipient of an extensive e-discovery request. The cost and operational disruption that accompanies the response to such a request can be overwhelming, particularly where historic data being sought is no longer active and readily accessible. When that is coupled with concerns regarding potential sanctions for spoliation of evidence, inadvertent or otherwise, it is no wonder that in-house corporate counsel and the corporate world in general see e-discovery as a huge problem, and that defense counsel see their own activities as fraught with the potential for malpractice. The *Zubulake* case has raised the bar of expected technical competency on the part of lawyers as it relates to e-discovery, and while its dictates may not end up being adopted in all jurisdictions it certainly sets a high level of understanding and involvement on the part of counsel that will be argued as applicable across the board. Consequently, this is an area where recourse to a motion for a protective order should be kept in mind at all times to benefit not only the client, but also the client's lawyers.

Early efforts should be made between the parties to agree upon the terms of e-discovery, and e-discovery issues should always be addressed as thoroughly as possible in any case management order. Not every issue, however, can be anticipated. The old adage of "He (or she) who lives by the sword shall die by the sword," should always be kept in mind. When issues cannot be dealt with by stipulation, you must seek appropriate protection from the court. This is not an area where it pays to delay. Furthermore, when you do seek the court's intervention, be sure you abide by the court's decisions. Failure to comply strictly with court orders regarding e-discovery can result in the type of multimillion dollar consequences seen in the *Morgan Stanley* case.

The need for a protective order and the specific grounds relating to that need will always be case specific. Thus, no particular forms can be generated for the motions, supporting papers, or resulting orders. The case law is always in a state of transition, and, with the new revisions to the Federal Rules of Civil Procedure, there may be changes in the substantive law that are as yet unanticipated. The case digest included with this book, however, is a resource for the substantive law. In addition, the exemplar motions, briefs, and resultant orders that are included in this book will give guidance as you address the issues of the scope of discovery, the cost of production, the methods and formats of production, and the possibility of cost shifting.

## Form 5.29
## Defendant's Rule 7.4 Expedited Nondispositive Motion for Protective Order under Fed. R. Civ. P. 26(c)

UNITED STATES DISTRICT COURT
FOR THE [Name District] OF [Name State]

| | | |
|---|---|---|
| [Name of Plaintiff], | ) | |
| | ) | |
| Plaintiff, | ) | |
| | ) | |
| v. | ) | Civil No. |
| | ) | |
| [Name of Defendant], | ) | |
| | ) | |
| Defendant. | ) | |

### Defendant's Rule 7.4 Expedited Nondispositive Motion for Protective Order under Fed. R. Civ. P. 26(c)

To: [COUNSEL OF RECORD]

### 1. Relief Sought.

Defendant requests that the court enter a protective order relieving Defendant of the obligation to maintain ongoing daily backup of its electronic data generated in the normal course of its business. All data pertinent to any claims in this matter, or any other matter relating to any of the co-defendants, is backed up on monthly backup tapes that are normally maintained for seven years. Currently, they are subject to a litigation-hold instruction from counsel. The maintenance of daily backup tapes in addition to the monthly backup tapes is redundant and a burdensome expense to Defendant.

### 2. Date and Time of Hearing.

Date:  To Be Determined by the Court
Time:  To Be Determined by the Court
Judge:  Hon. __[name]__
Place:  United States District Court

### 3. Grounds for Relief.

This action was filed by plaintiffs to seek payment of unpaid medical bills and expenses for medical treatment provided to Plaintiff in March of

2003. Plaintiff had health insurance through a self-insured health plan sponsored by Co-defendant for employees of __[Company]__ , her husband's employer. Defendant was a Contract Administrator hired by the Plan and the Plan Administrator to process any claims submitted by participants under the Plan. The employer failed to fund the Plan in early 2003 and as a result Plaitniff's medical expenses, though preauthorized, were not paid. Because of the failure to fund the Plan, Defendant terminated its contract as Contract Administrator retroactively, effective February 2003. Defendant was not a plan fiduciary.

Defendant maintains the vast majority of its operational data used for the processing and management of claims on a centralized mainframe computer system knows as the Data General or "DG." Normally, daily backup tapes are created for all information stored on the DG, and the system is also backed up on a monthly basis. Once the monthly backup has been created, the daily backup tapes are normally reused. All other electronic data such as e-mail, electronic faxes, plan forms and amendments, information on the internal and external Web sites used by Defendant, and other information used in day-to-day operations are maintained on Defendant's Exchange Server or on its Active Advice Server. Both of these servers are backed up daily and monthly, and when the monthly tapes are created the daily tapes are ordinarily reused.

Since the inception of this litigation Defendant has instituted a "litigation hold" and has been maintaining its daily backup tapes on an indefinite basis, along with the monthly backup tapes created in the normal course of business, in order to avoid any allegation of spoliation of evidence. To date, Defendant has spent more than $40,000.00 to purchase additional daily backup tapes that it would not have purchased but for this litigation.

Because all of the data regarding the Company's Plan and account is backed up on monthly backup tapes, and because there has been no activity regarding that Plan or account on the Defendant's system for several years, the preservation of daily backup tapes is unnecessary and constitutes a burdensome expense that Defendant should not be forced to incur. Defendant seeks a protective order relieving it of any obligation to maintain daily backup tapes indefinitely and limiting the time period that certain monthly backup tapes must be preserved. Defendant requests an order requiring it to preserve the first daily backup tapes created from its three servers after this litigation was commenced and a litigation hold was put in place, but relieving it of any obligation to maintain any other daily backup tapes. Defendant further requests that the preservation order provide that any monthly backup tapes created at the time the Company account was established at Defendant up through to the time there was no further activity on the account in the normal course of business be preserved indefinitely. Monthly backup tapes created thereafter would not be subject to a further litigation hold and could be maintained according to the normal seven-year retention policy Defendant ordinarily follows.

This motion is based upon Fed. R. Civ. P. 26(c), and upon the attached affidavit of defense counsel

[Name of Firm]

By: _____

[Attorney name]
Attorney for Defendant
[Street address]
[City, state, zip code]
[Telephone number]

## Form 5.30
## Affidavit of Defense Counsel in Support of Defendant's Rule 7.4 Expedited Nondispositive Motion for Protective Order under Fed. R. Civ. P. 26(c)

UNITED STATES DISTRICT COURT
FOR THE [Name District] OF [Name State]

| | |
|---|---|
| [Name of Plaintiff], | ) |
| | ) |
| Plaintiff, | ) |
| | ) |
| v. | ) Civil No. |
| | ) |
| [Name of Defendant], | ) |
| | ) |
| Defendant. | ) |

## Affidavit of Defense Counsel in Support of Defendant's Rule 7.4 Expedited Nondispositive Motion for Protective Order under Fed. R. Civ. P. 26(c)

State of __[name state]__

County of __[name county]__

Defense Counsel being sworn states:

1. I am the attorney for the defendant and make this affidavit on its behalf in support of the attached Rule 7.4 Expedited Nondispositive Motion for a Protective Order under Fed. R. Civ. P. 26(c).

2. Shortly after I was retained, after I had an opportunity to meet with my client and its representatives and employees and to make the necessary inquiries concerning the computer systems and backup used by Defendant in the normal course of its business, I instructed my client to institute a litigation hold on all electronic data and information potentially relevant to this case, including instructions not to destroy any backup tapes of any kind generated in the normal course of business.

3. In the course of my meetings with my client I learned that it maintains its electronic data on three different servers. Defendant follows a

backup procedure of backing up all active and historical data on each of its three servers on a daily basis. At the end of the month, a monthly backup is made. The monthly backup is normally maintained for seven years. After the monthly backup is created, the daily tapes are then reused.

4. To preserve the daily backup tapes as part of my litigation-hold instructions, it was necessary for Defendant to purchase additional tapes. To date they have spent more than $40,000.00 on the purchase and preservation of additional daily backup tapes. This is a significant expense that will be ongoing. In light of the monthly backup, the preservation of the daily backup is redundant and places an unreasonable and unnecessary financial burden on Defendant. This is particularly true as this case will not move forward at the normal speed because of the bankruptcy filings of several of the co-defendants.

5. All data that is relevant to the claims of the plaintiffs in this case, or to the claims of anyone else that was covered under the Company Plan, is inactive historical data that are backed up as part of the normal monthly backup procedures. The Company data has been inactive for several years, and no new data is being created that would require the preservation of any daily backup tapes.

6. Pursuant to the applicable Local Rule, I have conferred with Plaintiffs' Attorney and the Attorney for the Co-Defendants, advising them of Defendant's request for a protective order. They have each indicated they have no objection to the requested relief.

7. Defendant is willing to voluntarily and indefinitely preserve the daily backup tapes that were created on the first day after the litigation hold was instituted and the monthly backup tapes that were created for the time period between the inception of the Company Group Plan or Account through to the time of the last activity on the account that occurred in the normal course of business.

_____

[Defense Counsel]

Subscribed and sworn to before me
this __[day]__ day of __[month]__ , __[year]__

_____ [Insert Name]
Notary Public, State of __[state]__
My commission expires: _____ [Insert Date]

# Form 5.31
# Proposed Order

UNITED STATES DISTRICT COURT
FOR THE [Name District] OF [Name State]

| | | |
|---|---|---|
| [Name of Plaintiff], | ) | |
| | ) | |
| Plaintiff, | ) | |
| | ) | |
| v. | ) | Civil No. |
| | ) | |
| [Name of Defendant], | ) | |
| | ) | |
| Defendant. | ) | |

## Proposed Order

On Defendant's Rule 7.4 Expedited Nondispositive Motion for Protective Order under Fed. R. Civ. P. 26(c), having reviewed and considered the motion and affidavit in support of the motion, the Court now orders as follows:

Defendant's Motion for a Protective Order is hereby granted on the following terms:

1. Defendant shall preserve indefinitely, or until otherwise ordered by this court, the first set of daily backup tapes from its Data General, Exchange, and Active Advice file servers that were created and preserved after this lawsuit was commenced. All subsequent daily backup tapes may be reused in accordance with Defendant's normal retention practices.

2. Defendant shall preserve indefinitely, or until otherwise ordered by this court, all monthly backup tapes from its Data General, Exchange, and Active Advice file servers that were created on or after the first contact between Defendant and the Company concerning Defendant's contract for administrative services for the self-insured health plan sponsored by the Company. Any monthly backup tapes created after the last occurrence of any normal non-litigation related activity on the Company account need not be preserved indefinitely and may be preserved in accordance with Defendant's normal retention practices.

IT IS SO ORDERED


Date: _____          _____
                                Honorable Judge [name]
                                United States District Court Judge

## Form 5.32
## Proposed Protective Order Regarding Preservation of Home Computer

UNITED STATES DISTRICT COURT
FOR THE [Name District] OF [Name State]

| | | |
|---|---|---|
| [Name of Plaintiff], | ) | |
| | ) | |
| Plaintiff, | ) | |
| | ) | |
| v. | ) | Civil No. |
| | ) | |
| [Name of Defendant], | ) | |
| | ) | |
| Defendant. | ) | |

## Proposed Protective Order Regarding Preservation of Home Computer

On __[insert party name]__ Motion for Protective Order under Fed. R. Civ. P. 26(c), having reviewed and considered the motion and affidavit in support of the motion, the Court now orders as follows:

1. The Plaintiff is hereby ordered immediately to stop using, accessing, turning on, powering, copying, deleting, removing, or uninstalling any programs, files, and/or folders or booting up her personal laptop computer used at home.
2. The Plaintiff shall immediately deposit said laptop computer with [insert name] , Clerk of the Court, and said laptop computer shall be marked as a Court Exhibit in the above file and stored in the evidence vault at said Superior Court.
3. Said order shall extend to any and all floppy disks, CDs, Zip files, or any other similar type of computer storage device.
4. Neither party, counsel, nor anybody acting on behalf of either party or counsel, directly or indirectly, shall edit, access, or otherwise tamper with said laptop computer and/or any computer storage device marked as an exhibit.
5. The said laptop computer and said computer storage devices will only be accessed and read in open court when the said laptop com-

puter and said computer storage devices are accessed by a recognized computer expert under oath testifying from the witness stand. The hearing shall be open to the public.

6. In the event the plaintiff shall object at said hearing on the ground of privilege or any other grounds, the presiding judge may continue the computer expert's examination *in camera*.

7. Thereafter plaintiff's counsel will prepare a written privilege log of any items subject to any privilege and the written privilege log will be submitted to defendant's counsel. The written privilege log will be filed as a pleading.

8. In the event defendant's counsel wishes access to any document claimed in the privilege log, a hearing will be held in open court concerning the claim of privilege.

9. The parties shall pay equally all costs and expenses associated with the computer expert, unless otherwise ordered by the court.

10. The computer expert shall sign a confidentiality agreement that the results of the search of the said laptop computer, and said computer storage devices will be kept confidential and not disclosed to anyone, directly or indirectly. Both counsel shall prepare said agreement.

11. The parties shall mutually select the computer expert and, if the parties cannot agree, the parties shall each submit the names and addresses of two computer experts and the court will select the computer expert from among those four names.

12. The defendant shall purchase and deliver at his own cost and expense a new laptop computer containing power and programs similar to that of the Plaintiff's current laptop computer. The defendant shall purchase at his own cost and expense replacement computer storage devices. The defendant shall provide and pay for the installation and setup of said laptop computer and computer storage devices in the Plaintiff's home. This replacement laptop computer with replacement computer storage devices will be in operable condition and the replacement will occur simultaneously with the placement of the said laptop computer and computer storage devices into evidence in accordance with this Order.

13. At no time will any person access said laptop computer for the purpose of installing and activating the new laptop computer.

14. The Plaintiff, prior to the installation of the new laptop computer, will provide the defendant with a list of all programs, files and folders currently used in said laptop computer. In the event that said items are not readily available to the installer, the Plaintiff shall at her own cost and expense provide copies of said programs, files, and folders

for installation on the new laptop computer. Thereafter, the new laptop computer and the programs, files, folders, and computer storage devices will become the sole property of the Plaintiff.

IT IS SO ORDERED

Date:  _____        _____
                               Honorable Judge [name]
                               United States District Court Judge

## Motions for Sanctions

If the opposition fails to respond properly to your legitimate e-discovery requests, or fails to take appropriate steps to preserve electronic information when the possibility of litigation is apparent, you have a powerful weapon available to you in the form of a motion for sanctions. Spoliation of evidence can occur intentionally or inadvertently; but, depending on the circumstances, the absence of intent may be no defense. Whether the result is an adverse inference instruction to the jury, the dismissal of a claim for relief, the striking of a defense, a shifting of costs associated with electronic discovery, or the imposition of onerous financial penalties, the potential consequences of a failure to take e-discovery seriously can be disastrous. It is incumbent upon all lawyers to educate their clients early on about the risks inherent in e-discovery. If there is any lesson that can be gleaned from the recent cases dealing with the issue, it is that the courts are not afraid to fashion orders that can severely punish those parties who do not take the issue of e-discovery seriously.

Again, this is an area that is case and fact specific and subject to the evolving substantive and procedural law. No specific forms can be generated, but the exemplar materials on motions for sanctions and the reported decisions in the case digest will offer guidance as you assess the possibility of seeking sanctions for failure to live up to an e-discovery obligation.

## Form 5.33
## Defendant's Rule 7.4 Expedited Nondispositive Motion for Sanctions under Fed. R. Civ. P. 37

UNITED STATES DISTRICT COURT
FOR THE [Name District] OF [Name State]

| | | |
|---|---|---|
| [Name of Plaintiff], | ) | |
| | ) | |
| Plaintiff, | ) | |
| | ) | |
| v. | ) | Civil No. |
| | ) | |
| [Name of Defendant], | ) | |
| | ) | |
| Defendant. | ) | |

## Defendant's Rule 7.4 Expedited Nondispositive Motion for Sanctions under Fed. R. Civ. P. 37

To: COUNSEL OF RECORD

### 1. Relief Sought.

Defendant requests that the court enter an order imposing sanctions, to-wit, precluding the plaintiff from using or offering any evidence at trial relating to or referring to certain DNA test data and results at trial, together with its costs and actual attorneys' fees related to this motion, based upon multiple violations of this court's discovery orders.

### 2. Date and Time of Hearing.

Date: To Be Determined by the Court
Time: To Be Determined by the Court
Judge: Hon. __[name]__
Place: United States District Court

### 3. Grounds for Relief.

This motion is based on plaintiff's counsel's violation of discovery orders as follows:

1. Destruction of Evidence: Paragraph 1 of the Court's Discovery Order required the plaintiff to produce copies of computer "image files." These files are digital pictures of the "autorads" that show the DNA test results in this case. The Court's order covers image files that were created at the specific request of the defense when the autorads in this case were rescored.

In response to a Request for Production of Documents dated ___[date]___, plaintiff stated that these image files would be disclosed to the defense upon payment of a bill from the genetic testing company that covered the cost of rescoring the autorads. A motion to compel production of those images without requiring the defense to pay for this testing was filed by the defense. A hearing was held on ___[date]___. At the conclusion of that hearing, the Court ordered the plaintiff to produce those image files upon payment of the testing company's bill by the defense.

The defense paid the testing company's bill the day after the hearing. Thereafter, at his deposition, plaintiff's expert from the genetic testing company informed defense counsel that the image files had been <u>erased</u> from the hard drive of the testing company's computer where they had been stored. Thus, after demanding and receiving payment for creating the image files, the testing company announced that the files could not be delivered because they had been destroyed.

The intentional erasure of the image files is an egregious violation of the Court's orders and an act of extreme bad faith. Counsel for plaintiff knew that the image files were the subject of a request for production of documents filed on ___[date]___, and that the image files were the subject of this Court's orders. He had discussed with defense counsel on several occasions technical issues surrounding the transfer of the files from the hard drive to floppy disks for disclosure to the defense. All parties were aware that a major purpose of having the genetic testing company rescore the autorads was to provide defendant's experts copies of the <u>same</u> image files that were used in the rescoring. For the genetic testing company to subsequently destroy the image files under these circumstances is outrageous.

The image files provided a record of the appearance of the autorads at the time of the rescoring and thereby provided a check against subsequent alteration of the autorads. Destruction of these image files will make such alterations, if they occur (or have occurred), difficult to prove.

More important, the image files were crucial to defendant's effort to determine whether the testing company engaged in scientific misconduct by "fudging" its results when it rescored the autorads in this case. As noted in earlier motions, defendant's experts suspect that the genetic testing company "fudged" its results when it rescored the autorads in this case. "Fudging" could have been proved if defendant's experts found it impossible to reproduce the genetic testing company's scoring using the <u>same</u> image files. The destruction of those files undermines defendant's effort to prove (or disprove) the suspicions of its experts and thereby compromises his ability to mount an effective defense.[1]

2. Refusal to Comply with Court-Ordered Disclosure of Database Diskette: Paragraph 3 of the Court's prior Order required production of copies of "all data that the genetic testing company has sent to outside consultants for the purpose of Hardy-Weinberg/linkage studies" and specified that "[t]he data is to be provided in the same form that it was provided to outside consultants (i.e., on computer diskettes)." During the earlier motion hearing plaintiff's counsel asked the Court to modify this order to allow the plaintiff to provide the database in the form of a hard-copy (paper) printout. After hearing extensive argument on the issue, the Court denied the motion to modify the order and again ordered the production of the database in the form of a computer diskette.

Plaintiff's counsel has now informed defense counsel that the genetic testing company refuses to comply with the Court's order to produce the data-base diskette. Without access to the data-base diskette, defendant's experts will be unable to check the accuracy and appropriateness of the genetic testing company's statistical computations in this case.

In light of these serious violations of the Court's orders, defendant respectfully requests that plaintiff be precluded from presenting the results or any reference of any kind to any DNA testing done by the genetic testing company in this case. In addition, the defense asks that the plaintiff be required to reimburse the defense for all sums paid by it to the genetic testing company and that the costs incurred in bringing this motion and the prior motion to compel, including actual ss, be awarded.

This motion is based upon Fed. R. Civ. P. 37 and upon the attached affidavit of defense counsel.

---

[1] Although new image files can be created scoring the autorads a third time, the images may not be identical. Just as two photos of the same person, taken at different times, may look a bit different, two computer images of the same autorads, generated at different times, may vary slightly. Thus, the testing company can now attribute any inconsistency between its re-scoring of the autorads and defense experts' scorings to differences in the image files rather than "fudging" during the re-scoring.

Date: ___[date]___

[Name of Firm]

By: _____

[Attorney name]
Attorney for Defendant
[Street address]
[City, state, zip code]
[Telephone number]

# Form 5.34
## Proposed Order for Sanctions

UNITED STATES DISTRICT COURT
FOR THE [Name District] OF [Name State]

| | |
|---|---|
| [Name of Plaintiff], | ) |
| | ) |
| Plaintiff, | ) |
| | ) |
| v. | ) Civil No. |
| | ) |
| [Name of Defendant], | ) |
| | ) |
| Defendant. | ) |

## Proposed Order for Sanctions

On Defendant's Rule 7.4 Expedited Nondispositive Motion for Protective Order Under Fed. R. Civ. P. 37, having reviewed and considered the motion and affidavit in support of the motion, the Court now orders as follows:

Defendant's Motion for an Order For Sanctions is hereby granted on the following terms:

1. Plaintiff shall be precluded from using any DNA test results obtained from, or from making any reference at trial to any genetic testing performed by genetic testing company.
2. Plaintiff shall immediately reimburse defendant for any and all sums paid by defendant to genetic testing company.
3. Plaintiff shall pay to defendant the sum of $[dollar amount] as actual attorneys' fees incurred in the bringing of this motion and the prior motion to compel discovery.

IT IS SO ORDERED.

Date: __[date]__

_____
Honorable Judge [name]
United States District Court Judge

## Rule 16 Meet and Confer

Whether your case is in federal or state court, it always makes sense for the lawyers to meet and confer early in the process to address e-discovery concerns. Early involvement helps avoid the risks associated with spoliation of evidence. It encourages parties to establish proper procedures to preserve evidence and copy or image computer hard drives and other electronic storage media in an agreed-upon fashion satisfactory to all. It can help the parties come to a useful agreement on the deployment of technology to help manage all aspects of the case, not just e-discovery, and this can have a salutary effect in keeping litigation costs under control. Finally, it can help everyone know in advance how they will deal with the risk of inadvertent disclosure of privileged or work product–protected material. This last concern is one particularly affected by the way electronic information is disseminated. With the proposed revisions to the Federal Rules of Civil Procedure, early agreement among the parties is encouraged, and even without these revisions many courts have been adopting procedures to address e-discovery concerns in a comprehensive fashion early on. The exemplar orders included with these materials give a good overview of the issues that need to be addressed at the outset of every case where e-discovery is involved.

## Form 5.35
## A Rule 16(c) Pretrial Conference Agenda for Computer-Based Discovery[1]

The following checklist represents a maximalist approach. It should be scaled to fit the needs of the particular case, the resources of the parties, and the litigating styles of the lawyers involved.

## I.  When Is a Detailed Rule 16 Notice Most Appropriate?

- ◆ When the substantive allegations involve computer-generated records (e.g., software development, e-commerce, unlawful Internet trafficking, etc.)
- ◆ When the authenticity or completeness of computer records is likely to be contested
- ◆ When a substantial amount of disclosure or discovery will involve information or records in electronic form (e.g., e-mail, word processing, spreadsheets, and databases)
- ◆ When one or both parties is an organization that routinely used computers in its day-to-day business operations during the period relevant to the facts of the case
- ◆ When one or both parties have converted substantial numbers of potentially relevant records to digital form for management or archival purposes
- ◆ When expert witnesses will develop testimony based in large part on computer data and/or modeling or when either party plans to present a substantial amount of evidence in digital form at trial
- ◆ In any potential "big document" case in which cost associated with managing paper discovery could be avoided by encouraging exchange of digital or imaged documents (especially if multiple parties are involved)

The purpose of a detailed Rule 16 notice is to save the parties time and expense by anticipating the most common issues of computer-based discovery, developing a reasonable discovery plan, and avoiding unnecessary conflict. A detailed Rule 16 notice would not be appropriate if, in the opinion of the judge, the notice might serve to alarm the parties needlessly, raise unreasonable expectations or demands, or encourage the parties to engage in wasteful discovery.

---

[1] Reprinted with permission of Kenneth J. Withers, Federal Judicial Center.

## II. Preservation of Evidence

A. What steps have counsel taken to ensure that likely discovery material in their clients' possession (or in the possession of third parties) will be preserved until the discovery process is complete? If counsel have not yet identified all material that should be disclosed or may be discoverable, what steps have been taken to ensure that material will not be destroyed or changed before counsels' investigations are complete?

If more specific direction is needed:

B. Have counsel identified computer records relevant to the subject matter of the action? For example,

- Word processing documents, including drafts or versions not necessarily in paper form
- Databases or spreadsheets containing relevant information
- E-mail, voicemail, or other computer-mediated communications
- Relevant system records, such as logs, Internet use history files, and access records

C. Have counsel located the following computer records?

- Active computer files on network servers
- Computer files on desktop or local hard drives
- Backup tapes or disks, wherever located
- Archival tapes or disks, wherever located
- Laptop computers, home computers, and other satellite locations
- Media or hardware on which relevant records may have been "deleted" but are recoverable using reasonable efforts

D. Have counsel made sure all relevant computer records at all relevant locations are secure?

- Suspended all routine electronic document deletion and media recycling
- Segregated and secured backup and archival media
- Created "mirror" copies of all active network servers, desktop hard drives, laptops, and similar hardware

E. Have counsel considered entering into an agreement to preserve evidence?
F. Does either party plan to seek a preservation order from the court?

## III. Disclosure and Preliminary Discovery

A. Have counsel designated technical point-persons who know about their clients' computer systems to assist in managing computer records and answering discovery requests?

B. Have counsel prepared a description of their respective parties' computer systems for exchange? Does either party need to know more before discovery can proceed? If, after considering whether the hints in the following list may do more harm than good, the judge determines that the parties are unclear as to what they need to know at this stage and should get further guidance, the judge may suggest that they exchange information on the following points:

- Number, types, and locations of computers currently in use
- Number, types, and locations of computers no longer in use, but relevant to the facts of the case
- Operating system and application software currently in use
- Operating system and application software no longer in use, but relevant to the facts of the case
- Name and version of network operating system currently in use
- Names and versions of network operating systems no longer in use, but relevant to the facts of the case
- File-naming and location-saving conventions
- Disk or tape labeling conventions
- Backup and archival disk or tape inventories or schedules
- Most likely locations of records relevant to the subject matter of the action
- Backup rotation schedules and archiving procedures, including any backup programs in use at any relevant time
- Electronic records management policies and procedures
- Corporate policies regarding employee use of company computers and data
- Identities of all current and former personnel who had access to network administration, backup, archiving, or other system operations during any relevant time

C. Do counsel anticipate the need to notice any depositions or propound any interrogatories to obtain further information about the opposing party's computer systems or electronic records management procedures?

D. Have counsel explored with their clients (in appropriate situations) the procedures and costs involved to:

- Locate and isolate relevant files from e-mail, word processing, and other collections
- Recover relevant files generated on outdated or dormant computer systems (so-called legacy data)
- Recover deleted relevant files from hard drives, backup media, and other sources

E. Do counsel anticipate the need to conduct an on-site inspection of the opposing party's computer system?

- Consideration of an agreed-upon protocol
- Permission to use outside experts
- Agreement on neutral expert

## IV. Electronic Document Production

A. Will counsel use computerized litigation-support databases to organize and store documents and other discovery material?

B. Have counsel considered common formats for all electronic document exchange (e.g., TIFF images with OCR-generated text, e-mail in ASCII format, etc.)?

C. Have counsel (particularly in multiparty cases) considered a central electronic document repository?

D. Have counsel considered an attorney-client privilege nonwaiver agreement, to avoid the costs associated with intensive privilege screening before production?

E. Do counsel anticipate requesting data in nonroutine format, for example,

- Printing by respondent of electronic documents not normally in print form
- Creation by respondent of customized database reports
- Performance by respondent of customized searches or data mining

F. Have counsel agreed upon cost allocation outside the usual rule that parties absorb their own disclosure costs? For example,

- Requesting parties will pay nonroutine data retrieval and production costs
- Parties will negotiate data recovery and legacy data restoration costs

G. Does either party anticipate objecting to the production of computer records or software necessary to manipulate the records based on

- Trade secrets
- Licensing restrictions
- Copyright restrictions
- Statutory or regulatory privacy restrictions

## V. Testifying Experts

A. Will any testifying expert(s) rely on computer data provided by either party, or rely on his or her own data?

B. Will any testifying expert(s) use custom, proprietary, or publicly available software to process data, generate a report, or make a presentation?

C. Do counsel anticipate requesting discovery of either the underlying data or the software used by any testifying expert?

## VI. Anticipating Evidentiary Disputes

Have counsel considered discovery procedures designed to reduce or eliminate questions of authenticity, for example,

- ◆ Computer discovery supervised by neutral party
- ◆ Neutral, secure electronic document repository
- ◆ Exchange of read-only disks or CD-ROMs
- ◆ Chain-of-custody certifications

## Form 5.36
## Joint Stipulation and Order Regarding Meet and Confer Discussions

UNITED STATES DISTRICT COURT
FOR THE [Name District] OF [Name State]

| | | |
|---|---|---|
| [Name of Plaintiff], | ) | |
| | ) | |
| Plaintiff, | ) | |
| | ) | |
| v. | ) | Civil No. |
| | ) | |
| [Name of Defendant], | ) | |
| | ) | |
| Defendant. | ) | |

## Joint Stipulation and Order Regarding Meet and Confer Discussions

WHEREAS, the parties have reached agreement on a date for their first meet and confer discussions regarding the production of electronic documents, as well as certain ground rules, for such discussions generally;

NOW THEREFORE, the parties, through their respective counsel of record, hereby Stipulate as follows:

A. On __[date]__, the parties shall engage in meet and confer discussions regarding the production of electronic documents in this case. The meet and confer discussions will be attended by an electronic document consultant retained by __[party]__, who will have sufficient knowledge of __[party's]__ electronic documents to enable [party] to participate in a good faith effort to resolve all issues regarding the production of electronic documents without court action. The meet and confer discussions also will be attended by an electronic document consultant retained by the __[opposing party]__, who will have sufficient knowledge of the [opposing party]'s electronic documents to enable the __[opposing party]__ to participate in a good faith effort to resolve all issues regarding the production of electronic documents without court action.

B. Except as set forth in the next sentence, any electronic document consultant who personally attends any meet and confer regarding the production of electronic documents in this case shall not be subject to discovery requests, including requests for depositions, until such time as the parties otherwise agree or this Court orders that such discovery may be taken. If any such electronic document consultant provides testimony on an issue or issues in this case, whether by affidavit, declaration, deposition, or otherwise, he or she may be subject to discovery requests, including requests for depositions, limited to the issue or issues that are the subject of his or her testimony.

* * * *

[signatures of counsel]

PURSUANT TO STIPULATION, IT IS SO ORDERED.

Date: __[date]__                 _____

                                UNITED STATES MAGISTRATE JUDGE
                                United States District Court

**Form 5.37**
## Model Order Regarding Preservation

UNITED STATES DISTRICT COURT
FOR THE [Name District] OF [Name State]

| | |
|---|---|
| [Name of Plaintiff], | ) |
| | ) |
| Plaintiff, | ) |
| | ) |
| v. | ) Civil No. |
| | ) |
| [Name of Defendant], | ) |
| | ) |
| Defendant. | ) |

## Model Order Regarding Preservation

[The primary purpose of this model order is to have the parties to meet and confer to develop their own preservation plan. If the court determines that such a conference is unnecessary or undesirable, Section 3 may be modified to serve as stand-alone preservation order.]

### 1. Order to Meet and Confer

To further the just, speedy, and economical management of discovery, the parties are ORDERED to meet and confer as soon as practicable, no later than 30 days after the date of this Order, to develop a plan for the preservation of documents, data, and tangible things reasonably anticipated to be subject to discovery in this action. The parties may conduct this conference as part of the Rule 26(f) conference if it is scheduled to take place within 30 days of the date of this Order. The resulting preservation plan may be submitted to this Court as an Order under Rule 16(e).

### 2. Subjects for Consideration

The parties should attempt to reach agreement on all issues regarding the preservation of documents, data, and tangible things. These issues include, but are not necessarily limited to

    a. The extent of the preservation obligation, identifying the types of material to be preserved, the subject matter, time frame, the authors and addressees, and key words to be used in identifying responsive materials;

b. The form and method of providing notice of the duty to preserve to persons identified as custodians of documents, data, and tangible things;

c. The identification of persons responsible for carrying out preservation obligations on behalf of each party;

d. Mechanisms for monitoring, certifying, or auditing custodian compliance with preservation obligations;

e. Whether preservation will require suspending or modifying any routine business processes or procedures, with special attention to document management programs and the recycling of computer data storage media;

f. The methods to preserve any volatile but potentially discoverable material, such as voicemail, active data in databases, or electronic messages;

g. The anticipated costs of preservation and ways to reduce or share these costs; and

h. A mechanism to review and modify the preservation obligation as discovery proceeds, eliminating or adding particular categories of documents, data, and tangible things.

## 3. Duty to Preserve.

a. Until the parties reach agreement on a preservation plan, all parties and their counsel are reminded of their duty to preserve evidence that may be relevant to this action. The duty extends to documents, data, and tangible things in the possession, custody, and control of the parties to this action, and any employees, agents, contractors, carriers, bailees, or other nonparties who possess materials reasonably anticipated to be subject to discovery in this action. Counsel is under an obligation to exercise reasonable efforts to identify and notify such nonparties, including employees of corporate or institutional parties.

b. "Documents, data, and tangible things" is to be interpreted broadly, to include writings; records; files; correspondence; reports; memoranda; calendars; diaries; minutes; electronic messages; voicemail; e-mail; telephone message records or logs, computer and network activity logs; hard drives; backup data; removable computer storage media such as tapes, disks, and cards; printouts; document image files; web pages; databases; spreadsheets; software; books; ledgers; journals; orders; invoices; bills; vouchers; checks; statements; worksheets; summaries; compilations; computations; charts; diagrams; graphical presentations; drawings; films; charts; digital or chemical process photographs; video, phonographic, tape, or digital recordings or transcripts thereof; drafts, jottings, and notes. Information that serves to identify, locate, or link such material—such as file inventories, file folders, indices, and metadata—is also included in this definition.

c. "Preservation" is to be interpreted broadly to accomplish the goal of maintaining the integrity of all documents, data, and tangible things reasonably anticipated to be subject to discovery under Fed. R. Civ. P. 26, 45, and 56(e) in this action, preservation includes taking reasonable steps to prevent the partial or full destruction, alteration, testing, deletion, shredding, incineration, wiping, relocation, migration, theft, or mutation of such material, as well as negligent or intentional handling that would make material incomplete or inaccessible.

d. If the business practices of any party involve the routine destruction, recycling, relocation, or mutation of such materials, the party must, to the extent practicable for the pendency of this initial order, either

   i. Halt such business processes,

   ii. Sequester or remove such material from the business process, or

   iii. Arrange for the preservation of complete and accurate duplicates or copies of such material, suitable for later discovery if requested.

e. Before the conference to develop a preservation plan, a party may apply to the court for further instructions regarding the duty to preserve specific categories of documents, data, or tangible things. A party may seek permission to resume routine business processes relating to the storage or destruction of specific categories of documents, data, or tangible things, upon a showing of undue cost, burden, or overbreadth.

## 4. Procedure in the Event No Agreement Is Reached

If, after conferring to develop a preservation plan, counsel do not reach agreement on the subjects listed under Section 2 of this Order or on other material aspects of preservation, the parties are to submit to the court within three days of the conference a statement of the unresolved issues together with each party's proposal for their resolution of the issues. The court will consider the statements with any outstanding applications under Section 2e of this order in framing an order regarding the preservation of documents, data, and tangible things.

Entered this __[day]__ day of __[month]__, __[year]__.

_____
District Court Judge

The following Default Standard from the AdHoc Committee for Electronic Discovery used by the U.S. District Court for the District of Delaware, found at http://www.ded.uscourts.gov/Index.htm is also instructive.

## Form 5.38
## Default Standard for Discovery of Electronic Documents ("E-Discovery")

1. **Introduction.** It is expected that parties to a case will cooperatively reach agreement on how to conduct e-discovery. In the event that such agreement has not been reached by the Fed. R. Civ. P. 16 scheduling conference, however, the following default standards shall apply until such time, if ever, the parties conduct e-discovery on a consensual basis.

2. **Discovery conference.** Parties shall discuss the parameters of their anticipated e-discovery at the Fed. R. Civ. P. 26(f) conference, as well as at the Fed. R. Civ. P. 16 scheduling conference with the court, consistent with the concerns outlined below. More specifically, prior to the Rule 26(f) conference, the parties shall exchange the following information:

   - A list of the most likely custodians of relevant electronic materials, including a brief description of each person's title and responsibilities (see ¶ 6).
   - A list of each relevant electronic system that has been in place at all relevant times[1] and a general description of each system, including the nature, scope, character, organization, and formats employed in each system. The parties should also include other pertinent information about their electronic documents and whether those electronic documents are of limited accessibility. Electronic documents of limited accessibility may include those created or used by electronic media no longer in use, maintained in redundant electronic storage media, or for which retrieval involves substantial cost.
   - The name of the individual responsible for that party's electronic document retention policies ("the retention coordinator"), as well as a general description of the party's electronic document retention policies for the systems identified above (see ¶ 6).
   - The name of the individual who shall serve as that party's "e-discovery liaison" (see ¶ 2).

---

[1] For instance, in a patent case, the relevant times for a patent holder may be the date the patent(s) issued or the effective filing date of each patent in suit.

- Provide notice of any problems reasonably anticipated to arise in connection with e-discovery.

To the extent that the state of the pleadings does not permit a meaningful discussion of the above by the time of the Rule 26(f) conference, the parties shall either agree on a date by which this information will be mutually exchanged or submit the issue for resolution by the court at the Rule 16 scheduling conference.

3. **E-discovery liaison.** To promote communication and cooperation between the parties, each party to a case shall designate a single individual through which all e-discovery requests and responses are made ("the e-discovery liaison"). Regardless of whether the e-discovery liaison is an attorney (in-house or outside counsel), a third-party consultant, or an employee of the party, he or she must be:
   - Familiar with the party's electronic systems and capabilities in order to explain these systems and answer relevant questions;
   - Knowledgeable about the technical aspects of e-discovery, including electronic document storage, organization, and format issues; and
   - Prepared to participate in e-discovery dispute resolutions.

   The court notes that, at all times, the attorneys of record shall be responsible for compliance with e-discovery requests; however, the e-discovery liaisons shall be responsible for organizing each party's e-discovery efforts to ensure consistency and thoroughness and, generally, to facilitate the e-discovery process.

4. **Timing of e-discovery.** Discovery of electronic documents shall proceed in a sequenced fashion.
   - After receiving requests for document production, the parties shall search their documents, other than those identified as limited accessibility electronic documents, and produce responsive electronic documents in accordance with Fed. R. Civ. P. 26(b)(2).
   - Electronic searches of documents identified as of limited accessibility shall not be conducted until the initial electronic document search has been completed. Requests for information expected to be found in limited accessibility documents must be narrowly focused with some basis in fact supporting the request.
   - On-site inspections of electronic media under Fed. R. Civ. P. 34(b) shall not be permitted absent exceptional circumstances, where good cause and specific need have been demonstrated.

5. **Search methodology.** If the parties intend to employ an electronic search to locate relevant electronic documents, the parties shall disclose any restrictions as to scope and method that might affect their

ability to conduct a complete electronic search of the electronic documents. The parties shall reach agreement as to the method of searching and the words, terms, and phrases to be searched with the assistance of the respective e-discovery liaisons, who are charged with familiarity with the parties' respective systems. The parties also shall reach agreement as to the timing and conditions of any additional searches that may become necessary in the normal course of discovery. To minimize the expense, the parties may consider limiting the scope of the electronic search (e.g., time frames, fields, document types).

6. **Format.** If, during the course of the Rule 26(f) conference, the parties cannot agree to the format for document production, electronic documents shall be produced to the requesting party as image files (e.g., PDF or TIFF). When the image file is produced, the producing party must preserve the integrity of the electronic documents contents (i.e., the original formatting of the document, its metadata and, where applicable, its revision history). After initial production in image file format is complete, a party must demonstrate particularized need for production of electronic documents in their native format.

7. **Retention.** Within the first thirty (30) days of discovery, the parties should work toward an agreement (akin to the standard protective order) that outlines the steps each party shall take to segregate and preserve the integrity of all relevant electronic documents. To avoid later accusations of spoliation, a Fed. R. Civ. P. 30(b)(6) deposition of each party's retention coordinator may be appropriate.

   The retention coordinators shall:
   - Take steps to ensure that e-mail of identified custodians shall not be permanently deleted in the ordinary course of business and that electronic documents maintained by the individual custodians shall not be altered.
   - Provide notice as to the criteria used for spam and/or virus filtering of e-mail and attachments; e-mails and attachments filtered out by such systems shall be deemed nonresponsive so long as the criteria underlying the filtering are reasonable.
   - Within seven (7) days of identifying the relevant document custodians, the retention coordinators shall implement the above procedures and each party's counsel shall file a statement of compliance as such with the court.

8. **Privilege.** Electronic documents that contain privileged information or legal work product shall be immediately returned if the docu-

ments appear on their face to have been inadvertently produced or if there is notice of the inadvertent production within thirty (30) days of such.

9. **Costs.** In general, the costs of discovery shall be borne by each party. The court, however, will apportion the costs of electronic discovery upon a showing of good cause.

10. **Discovery disputes and trial presentation.** At this time, discovery disputes shall be resolved and trial presentations shall be conducted consistent with each individual judge's guidelines.

**Form 5.39**
## Consent Protective Order Governing Imaging, Inspection of _____ [insert company name] Computers and Protection of Confidential and Privileged Information

UNITED STATES DISTRICT COURT
FOR THE [Name District] OF [Name State]

| | | |
|---|---|---|
| [Name of Plaintiff], | ) | |
| | ) | |
| Plaintiff, | ) | |
| | ) | |
| v. | ) | Civil No. |
| | ) | |
| [Name of Defendant], | ) | |
| | ) | |
| Defendant. | ) | |

## Consent Protective Order Governing Imaging, Inspection of _____ [insert company name] Computers and Protection of Confidential and Privileged Information

IT IS STIPULATED AND AGREED by counsel for ___[insert party names]___, and hereby ORDERED that, pursuant to Rule 26 of the Federal Rules of Civil Procedure, the following procedure shall govern the inspection of ___[insert company name]___ computers during these proceedings.

Cloning Relevant Computers onto Evidentiary Hard Drives

- [Producing Party] will make all computers (hereinafter the "Relevant computers") that he or she owns, controls, and/or possesses available at a mutually convenient date and time, but not after the rescheduled date of [Producing Party's] deposition, to allow Defendant's/Plaintiff's expert or his representative to make a forensic copy of each of the hard drives installed in each of the Relevant Computers.

- Expert shall make a forensic bit-by-bit exact image clone of each of the hard drives (hereinafter the "Source drives") in the Relevant Computers.

- As Expert Company creates a clone of each Relevant Computer on its evidentiary hard drives, Expert Company will also create and embed a "digital fingerprint" (e.g., Cyclic Redundancy Check (CRC), SHA1 or an MD5 algorithm hash) verifying that the evidentiary hard drive contains an exact, precise, reliable, mirror image copy of the hard drive of each Relevant Computer.

♦ These "digital fingerprints" will also verify that no changes have been made to the evidentiary hard drives from the moment that the mirror images of each Relevant Computer were created.

♦ [Producing Party's] counsel, or his authorized representative, will be allowed to observe the removal of the Source Drive(s) and the creation of the clone of each Source Drive onto an Expert Company's Evidentiary Drive.

♦ The computer system clock setting shall be compared to actual time and documented.

♦ [Expert Name and/or Expert Company] and it representatives, will perform all work using Usual and Customary Practices and Industry Standards. Expert will create a forensic bit-by-bit exact image clone using a combination of one or more of the following techniques, depending upon the circumstances related to each computer:

## 1. Hanging an Evidentiary Drive onto Relevant Computers

a. Each of the Relevant Computers will be turned off. Special computers, such as servers, will be shut down by [Producing Party's] personnel, using normal shut-down procedures.

b. Each Relevant Computer case will be opened and the internal configuration of the computer noted.

c. Expert Company will attach a sanitized evidentiary hard drive (provided by Expert Company) to each of the Relevant Computers. The evidentiary hard drive will be attached to a ribbon connecting the evidentiary hard drive to the hard drive controller on the motherboard of each Relevant Computer.

d. Once the evidentiary hard drive is attached, a floppy disk (and/or CD where applicable) will be inserted into each of the Relevant Computers. A Disk Operating System ("DOS") version of the forensic acquisition software is written on the floppy disk or CD.

e. Each Relevant Computer will be turned on and booted up to DOS. This prevents any changes being made to the hard drive.

f. The forensic acquisition software will be launched, and a forensic copy of the Relevant Computer's hard drive will be created onto the evidentiary hard drive.

g. The evidentiary hard drive will be verified.

h. The Basic Input and Output System ("BIOS") clock accuracy will be noted.

i. Each Relevant Computer will be turned off.

## 2. Removing Relevant Computer Hard Drives, Attaching Write Protection and Making Copy

a. Each Relevant Computer will be turned off. Special computers, such as servers, will be shut down by [Producing Party] using normal shutdown procedure.

b. Each Relevant Computer case will be opened and the internal configuration of the computer noted.

c. Each Relevant Computer hard drive will be removed from its case, and a write-protection device attached to the Relevant Computer hard drive. The write-protection device prevents any data from being written to the Relevant Computer hard drive and prevents any changes from being made to any data on the Relevant Computer hard drive.

d. The write-protected Relevant Computer hard drive will be connected to an Expert Company field computer containing one or more evidentiary hard drives.

e. The Expert Company field computer will be booted up and the forensic acquisition software will be launched. An exact, mirror image copy of the Relevant Computer hard drive will then be made onto the Expert Company evidentiary hard drive.

f. The evidentiary hard drive will be verified.

g. The Expert Company field computer will be turned off, and the write-protected Relevant Computer hard drive will be returned to its case.

h. The Relevant Computer will be turned on and the BIOS clock accuracy will be noted.

## 3. Cable Acquisition Across Network Card or Parallel Port

a. Relevant computers will be connected to an Expert Company Field Computer via a crossover network cable or a parallel port lap-link cable.

b. Each relevant computer will be booted to DOS and placed into server mode.

c. An exact clone of each computer will be created on an evidentiary drive provided by Expert Company in a manner similar to that above.

## 4. Customized Acquisition

In exceptional circumstances, such as the inability to shut down the Relevant Computer, Expert Company will customize the acquisition of a forensic image so as to create a proper image with embedded digital fingerprints without disrupting the use of the Relevant Computer. These situations ought to be very rare, because almost all computer systems require downtime for many reasons, such as maintenance; and this downtime ought to be sufficient to create a forensic image.

## INTERROGATING CLONES: CONTEXTUAL AND CONCEPTUAL SEARCHES

- ◆ Expert Company, and/or its representative will search the entire hard drive, including in-use space (allocated areas), slack space, and unused space (unallocated areas), looking for evidence of the existence of information relating to issues in this lawsuit. Expert Company will simultaneously interrogate all of the evidentiary Hard Drives, containing forensic images of each Relevant Computer. Interrogation is accomplished electronically using a variety of electronic, software tools. No Expert Company personnel will "browse" the evidentiary Hard drives, hoping to find relevant data. Instead, Expert Company will use software tools to analyze the evidentiary Hard drives in two areas: Contextual Analysis designed to identify and extract relevant data and Conceptual Analysis designed to interpret artifacts and reach conclusions related to the manner in which the Relevant Computers were used.

- ◆ The interrogation and search of the evidential hard drive will take place at Expert Company. Because the evidential hard drive can be made in the presence of [Producing Party's] counsel, and subsequently verified via the MD5 hash checksum, the presence of [Producing Party's] personal counsel during the interrogation and search of the evidential hard drive(s) is unnecessary. Because much of the searching can be carried out in an automated, unattended fashion, if [Producing Party]'s personal counsel insists on attending the search, he or she agrees to pay Expert and/or Expert Company's fees for the time spent searching the evidential hard drive while it is being attended.

- ◆ Expert Company frequently agrees to protocols and procedures to protect privileged data. Expert Company will abide by the terms of any protocol or procedures ordered in this case, including the protocols contained in Plaintiff's Motion to Compel Electronic Discovery from Defendant.

- ◆ Expert Company shall report the results of its interrogation in the following manner:

1. Expert Company shall prepare a Report of Findings and an Executive Summary of the Report of Findings. The Executive Summary shall state the number of pages in the Report of Findings, the procedure and process used for all Contextual and Conceptual analysis of the

clone of the Source Drives, the number of relevant pieces of data extracted from the Source Drives, acquisition information related to the Source Drives, and a summary of significant findings.

2. Expert Company shall file the Executive Summary and shall file under seal the Report of Findings with this Court. Expert Company shall serve a copy of the Executive Summary on counsel for [Producing Party] and counsel for [Requesting Party].

3. Expert Company shall serve a copy of the Report of Findings on counsel for the Producing Party, who shall have ten (10) business days to redact the Report of Findings for privilege. Within ten (10) business days of receiving an electronic copy of the Report of Findings with Appendices and Exhibits, counsel for Producing Party will redact the Report for privilege, prepare a privilege log identifying the items in the Report of Findings redacted and the grounds therefore, and serve a copy of the Redacted Report of Findings on counsel for Requesting Party.

4. The Redacted Report of Findings will be served in the same format as it was created by Expert Company.

5. Service of the Executive Summary and Report of Findings shall be deemed complete for each when Expert Company places into the United States mail one or more CD-ROM containing an electronic copy of the Executive Summary and/or the Report of Findings, including all Appendices and Exhibits. The electronic copy shall be in PDF, Word format, or other format as required by the type of data in the opinion of Expert Company. The parties and Expert Company can agree to one or more formats for the production of the Executive Summary and Report of Findings, which shall be identified in the Expert Company's certificate of service to be filed upon completion of service as stated herein.

   ◆ Any information contained on [Producing Party]'s hard drive(s) that is not reported by Expert Company shall be considered Confidential Information and subject to the provisions of this Order. Any data reported by Expert Company that is claimed by Producing Party's counsel to be subject to attorney-client privilege shall be treated as Confidential Information. Expert Company and its representatives agree not to reveal to or discuss with Requesting Party's Counsel any Confidential Information.

   ◆ The inadvertent or intentional disclosure by Expert or any representative of Expert's Company of Confidential Information shall not be deemed a waiver in whole or in part of [Producing Party]'s claim of confidentiality of protection under this Order, either as to specific information disclosed or as to any other information relating thereto or on the same or related subject matter. Counsel for the parties, and [Producing Party]'s personal counsel, shall, in any event, upon discovery of inadvertent error, cooperate to restore the confidentiality and protection of the Confidential Information.

♦ Nothing in this Order shall prevent the parties from using relevant, nonconfidential information derived from the inspection of any Relevant Computer in connection with the trial, hearings, depositions, motions, memoranda, or other proceedings in this action.

Date: ___[date]___

APPROVED:

_____

Counsel for [Producing Party]

_____

Counsel for [Requesting Party]

IT IS SO ORDERED

_____

JUDGE [name]

# Sample Orders

## Form 5.40
## Order for Preservation of Records
## (Pharmaceutical Product Liability)

UNITED STATES DISTRICT COURT
FOR THE [Name District] OF [Name State]

| | | |
|---|---|---|
| [Name of Plaintiff], | ) | |
| | ) | |
| Plaintiff, | ) | |
| | ) | |
| v. | ) | Civil No. |
| | ) | |
| [Name of Defendant], | ) | |
| | ) | |
| Defendant. | ) | |

## Order for Preservation of Records
## (Pharmaceutical Product Liability)

It is ORDERED:

### 1. Preservation.

    a. During the pendency of this litigation, and for 60 days after entry of a final order closing all cases, each of the parties herein and their respective officers, agents, servants, employees, and attorneys, and all persons in active concert or participation with them who receive actual notice of this order by personal service or otherwise, are restrained and enjoined from altering, interlining, destroying, or permitting the destruction of any document in the actual or constructive care, custody, or control of such person, wherever such document is physically located.

    b. To facilitate preserving and collecting electronic documents related to __[insert name of pharmaceutical]__, which are created after entry of this Order, each Plaintiff and each corporate Defendant shall establish a dedicated electronic mailbox to receive copies, on a going-forward basis, of all electronic documents relating to __[insert name of pharmaceutical]   . The parties further agree to direct all of their employees to preserve   [insert name of pharmaceutical]   –related documents and to direct those employees (other than legal personnel) to send all future   [insert name of pharmaceutical]   –related electronic documents to the   [insert name of pharmaceutical]   mailbox.

c. The parties shall retain all existing "snap shots" of electronic servers and all existing backup tapes already archived and not used in the ordinary operation of the parties' electronic document management systems at   [insert names of manufacturer defendants]   facilities and any off-site storage facility housing documents created in these facilities. The parties shall secure the hard drives (or make mirror-image copies of the files on hard drives) of all computers (including laptop or desktop computers) used by the parties or their employees with   [insert name of pharmaceutical]   –related responsibilities that are not backed up in the ordinary course, before the reformatting, redeployment, or disposal of such hard drives. The parties may also continue routine erasures of computerized data pursuant to existing programs, but they shall (1) immediately notify opposing counsel about such programs and (2) preserve any printouts of such data. Notwithstanding any other provisions of this Order, as of the date of this Order, persons may generate documents in the future without preserving dictation, drafts, interim versions, or other temporary compilations of information if such documents would not have been preserved in the ordinary course of business.

## 2. Scope.

a. "Document" shall mean any writing, drawing, film, videotape, chart, photograph, phonograph record, tape record, mechanical or electronic sound recording, or transcript thereof, retrievable data (whether carded, taped, coded, electrostatically or electromagnetically recorded, or otherwise), or other data compilation from which information can be obtained, including (but not limited to) notices, memoranda, diaries, minutes, purchase records, purchase invoices, market data, correspondence, computer storage tapes, computer storage cards or disks, books, journals, ledgers, statements, reports, invoices, bills, vouchers, worksheets, jottings, notes, letters, abstracts, audits, charts, checks, diagrams, drafts, recordings, instructions, lists, logs, orders, recitals, telegram messages, telephone bills and logs, resumes, summaries, compilations, computations, and other formal and informal writings or tangible preservations of information.

b. This order pertains only to documents containing information that may be relevant to, or may lead to the discovery of information relevant to the __[insert name of pharmaceutical]__ litigation. Any __[insert name of pharmaceutical]__ –related document described or referred to in any discovery request or response made during this litigation shall, from the time of the request or response, be treated for purposes of this Order as containing such information unless and until the court rules such information to be irrelevant.

c. Counsel are directed to confer to resolve questions as to what documents are outside the scope of this Order or otherwise need not be preserved and as to an earlier date for permissible destruction of particular categories of documents. If counsel are unable to agree, any party may apply to the court for clarification or relief from this Order upon reasonable notice. A party failing, within 60 days after receiving written notice from another party that specified documents will be destroyed, lost, or otherwise altered pursuant to routine policies and programs, to indicate in writing its objection shall be deemed to have agreed to such destruction.

Dated: _____        BY THE COURT:

_____

Hon. __[name]__
United States District Court

## Form 5.41
## Order for Preservation of Documents
## (Multiparty, Complex Litigation)

UNITED STATES DISTRICT COURT
FOR THE [Name District] OF [Name State]

| | | |
|---|---|---|
| [Name of Plaintiff], | ) | |
| | ) | |
| Plaintiff, | ) | |
| | ) | |
| v. | ) | Civil No. |
| | ) | |
| [Name of Defendant], | ) | |
| | ) | |
| Defendant. | ) | |

## Order for Preservation of Documents
## (Multiparty, Complex Litigation)

IT IS HEREBY ORDERED:

## 1. Definitions

    a. "Document(s)" as used herein is synonymous in meaning and equal in scope to the usage of this term in Federal Rule of Civil Procedure 34(a), and as construed by the case law in this Circuit, including, without limitation, electronic or computerized records, files, and data.

    b. "Party" or "Parties" refers to each Plaintiff or Defendant of record or to all Plaintiffs and Defendants of record, respectively, in ___[insert case number]___.

    c. "Backup Systems" refers to computer systems that periodically store electronic information on tapes or comparable media to permit recovery of the information in the event of a disaster such as equipment failure.

    d. "Backup Tapes" refers to tapes onto which Backup Systems store such electronic information.

    e. "Identical copy" or "Identical copies" refers to

        i. Hard-copy Documents that are full and complete representations of the original Document. Full and complete representations do not include a copy of a hard copy Document that differs from the original of the hard-copy Document because of highlights, underlining, marginalia, total pages, attachments, markings, or other facial alterations.

ii. Electronic Documents that are exact duplicates of the same electronic Document. Exact duplicates do not include a copy of an electronic Document that differs from the original of the electronic Document because of the inclusion of highlights, underlining, marginalia, total pages, attachments, markings, revisions, the inclusion of tracked changes, or other facial alterations.

## 2. Scope

a. Covered Documents: This Order pertains to Documents in the possession, custody or control of a Party that are relevant to, or may lead to the discovery of information relevant to, any claim or defense at issue in any case transferred to or consolidated under __[insert case number]__ ("Covered Documents"). Covered Documents need not be admissible at trial if the Document appears reasonably calculated to lead to the discovery of admissible evidence. Any Document described or referred to in any discovery request or response made during this litigation shall, from the time of the request or response, be treated for purposes of this Order as containing such information unless and until the Court rules such information to be irrelevant.

b. Covered Persons: The persons subject to this Order shall be all persons who are in the possession, custody or control of Covered Documents and who are ultimately identified as "Covered Persons" after completion of the process set forth in the following paragraph. This Order, however, shall not apply to Covered Persons who are not in the possession, custody, or control of Covered Documents other than as recipients of duplicate copies.

c. List of Covered Persons or Noncovered Persons: Within forty-five (45) days of the entry of this Order, each party shall provide a list of its Covered Persons or a list of its Noncovered Persons to all other Parties. The list may identify Covered Persons or Noncovered Persons by individual name or by a grouping such as an agency, a division, a subdivision, a department or a group. Parties that elect to identify individual Covered Persons or Noncovered Persons shall specify the name, title, location, and job function for each individual identified on that Party's list. Parties that elect to identify Covered Persons or Noncovered Persons by grouping shall specify the name of and functions performed by each Covered or Noncovered agency, division, subdivision, department or group. The list of Covered Persons or Noncovered Persons, together with any additional information sufficiently detailed to enable an opposing Party to evaluate that Party's list of Covered Persons or Noncovered Persons, including a Party's current organizational charts to the extent they exist, shall be promptly served at the same time on all other Parties and, in any event, no later than forty-five (45) days after the effective date of this Order. Any other party may dispute such designations within forty-five (45) days of receipt of the above information.

d. Applicability: Beginning on the date of entry of this Order, and continuing during the time that a particular Plaintiff or Defendant is a party to one or more cases covered by this Order or to a pending appeal, such Plaintiff or Defendant is subject to this Order. This Order does not affect any Party's preexisting duty to preserve Documents under the Federal Rules of Civil Procedure or any other applicable law.

## 3. Preservation

a. All Covered Persons are restrained and enjoined from altering, destroying, or permitting the alteration or destruction of any Covered Document in the possession, custody or control of such person, wherever such Covered Document is physically or electronically located, except as provided under 3(b).

b. To the extent that a party has electronically stored Covered Documents as of the date of this Order, the party shall securely maintain the original Covered Documents or copies of the original Covered Documents. To the extent that a party has multiple identical copies of an electronically stored Covered Document, the party need only securely maintain the electronically stored original or a single electronically stored identical copy of the Covered Document.

   i. Backup Tapes: A party is not required to retain Backup Tapes currently in active use in the party's Backup System, which are scheduled to be recycled, erased, or reused in the ordinary course of business. Each party shall securely retain all other Backup Tapes that would not otherwise be recycled or reused in the ordinary course of business, pending further direction by the Court.

   ii. Existing Covered Documents: Parties must use a reasonable approach to preserve Covered Documents. In light of the number of parties and the wide range of approaches used by the parties to allow for the recovery of electronic information in the event of a disaster, it is not practical to attempt to define a single detailed process that all parties must follow in order to preserve Covered Documents. Instead, a party with one or more Backup Systems containing Covered Documents may use any reasonable method to preserve Covered Documents. Following are three nonexclusive examples of reasonable approaches that parties may use to preserve Covered Documents. A party using Backup Tapes may retain one set of Backup Tapes created in the ordinary course within thirty (30) days prior to the entry of the Order, provided that such day's Backup Tapes represent a complete backup of the Covered Documents contained on the servers as opposed to only an incremental backup of the data recently added to those servers. A party using an enterprise system may prepare a point-in-time restore for one day within thirty (30) days prior to the entry of this Order. Alternatively, if a party has the ability to segregate Covered Documents from other data contained on the backed-up servers, the party may segregate the covered Documents from the servers or the Backup Tapes and may retain those Covered Documents on tape or any other media capable of storing the Covered Documents in a retrievable format, including another server or servers dedicated to the purpose.

iii. Ongoing Creation of Covered Documents: Parties creating or receiving Covered Documents on an ongoing basis must use a reasonable approach to retain those Covered Documents. For example, and without limitation, a Party may designate a location on a shared server or other equipment and direct Covered Persons to copy Covered Documents created after the date of the entry of this Order to that location.

c. Current or legacy software and hardware necessary to access, manipulate, print, search, organize, collect, image, decrypt, decompress, etc. Covered Documents that either are "live" or have been archived or backed-up shall be securely retained, to the extent that they existed on the date of this Order. In addition, Documents (e.g., training manuals, instruction books, user guides, study guides, etc.) sufficient to describe or explain the installation, operation and use of all such current or legacy software or hardware shall be securely retained.

d. The Parties shall circulate to Covered Persons retention notices designed to ensure the preservation of Covered Documents.

e. By agreeing to preserve Covered Documents in accordance with the terms hereof, covered Parties do not waive any objection to the ultimate discoverability of such Covered Documents at such point when discovery is authorized in these actions.

f.   Nothing herein shall preclude any party from raising with counsel or the Court the limitation or modification of the foregoing in response to particular facts relevant to that Party.

## 4. Exemptions

a.   Multiple identical copies of a Covered Document are not covered by this Order so long as the original Document, or an identical copy of the original Document where identifying the original Document is unduly burdensome, remains in the possession, custody or control of a Party.

b.   Notwithstanding any other provision of this Order, Covered Persons may generate Covered Documents in the future without preserving dictation, drafts, interim versions, or other temporary compilations of information that would not be preserved in the ordinary course of business. Nothing herein prohibits the continued routine operation of each Party's computer systems, including systematic erasures and write-overs. All hard-copy drafts, hard-copy interim versions, or other hard-copy temporary compilations of Covered Documents generated prior to and existing as of the date of entry of this Order, however, must be preserved. If such material exists only in electronic format, it must also be preserved.

c.   Counsel are directed to confer to resolve any dispute concerning whether certain Documents are not covered by this Order. Until agreement is reached or an Order is issued on whether those Documents are covered by this Order, a party must preserve the Documents that are the subject of the dispute. If the parties cannot resolve such dispute, they may apply directly to the Special Master or the Court for clarification or relief from this Order upon reasonable notice. A party may continue to operate its routine document retention protocol, so long as such protocol was in existence at the outset of the litigation, and the party has in good faith instituted a litigation-hold targeted at information discoverable in these actions.

A party must disclose its document retention protocol to an adversary upon request by the adversary. If a party amends its protocol in a way that might materially affect document preservation in these actions, it must notify its adversaries. Finally, if a party intends to destroy specific information that may be discoverable in these actions other than by operation of its routine document retention program, it must provide to all adversaries written notice of its intention. Any party opposing destruction must provide its written objection within forty-five (45) days. If no written objection to this notice is received within forty-five (45) days, then such information may be destroyed; however, if a party's written objection is received within forty-five (45) days, the parties shall meet and confer promptly to try to resolve the dispute. If the parties cannot resolve the dispute within thirty (30) days after initiating the meet and confer, the party seeking to destroy documents shall have ten (10) days to affirmatively move for relief from the Order.

d. This Order shall not cover briefs, motions, legal or factual memoranda, notes, or other similar materials created by any attorney, law firm, or corporate legal department representing any party to any case in this proceeding in anticipation of or during the course of any litigation concerning __[insert nature of litigation]__. Scientific or medical studies, whether conducted in anticipation of litigation or not, shall not be subject to the exemption of this paragraph.

## 5. Implementation

a. Liaison counsel shall deliver a copy of this Order to counsel for all Parties. Thereupon, counsel for each Party shall provide written notice of this Order to each corporate or individual client whom counsel now or hereafter represents in any case that becomes part of these proceedings. Such notice shall include a copy of this Order.

b. Each Party shall, within thirty (30) days after receiving this Order, designate an individual who shall be responsible for monitoring and directing that Party's efforts to carry out the requirements of this Order.

## 6. Discoverability and Admissibility

Nothing in this Order shall be construed to affect the discoverability or admissibility of any Covered Document pursuant to the Federal Rules of Civil Procedure.

**Form 5.42**
**Sample State Court *Ex Parte* Order**

---

### *Ex Parte* Order Establishing Procedures for Examination, Copying, and Imaging of Computers, Hard Drives, or Other Electronic Storage Media

---

On __[date]__, the Court considered Respondent's motion for an *ex parte* order establishing procedures for the examination, copying and imaging of the Parties' computers, hard drives, or other electronic storage media pursuant to the Texas Rules of Civil Procedure and the Court's supervisory powers to preserve evidence. Upon due consideration, the Court is of the opinion that the following orders should be entered *instanter.*

IT IS, THEREFORE, ORDERED, ADJUDGED, AND DECREED that Petitioner immediately allow *Forensic Expert,* or its representatives or designees, access to all computers, hard drives, or other electronic storage media located at __[location]__ upon the following terms and conditions:

1. Petitioner shall immediately allow *Forensic Expert,* to access the computers, hard drives, and other electronic storage media, along with any peripherals or accessories, located at __[location]__, as may be necessary for them to perform their duties as set forth herein. Any action taken by Petitioner to interfere or obstruct *Forensic Expert* or its representatives or designees in or from the performance of their duties in connection with the examination, copying, or imaging shall be considered contempt of court. If *Forensic Expert,* or its representatives or designees is unable to perform their duties because of interference or obstruction, they are directed to take actual possession of the computers, hard drives and other electronic storage media, along with any peripherals or accessories, located at __[location]__, and remove them to a safe location pending further order of the Court

2. Respondent shall bear the initial costs associated with the examination copying or imaging of the data stored on the computers, hard drives, or other electronic storage media by *Forensic Expert.* To the extent Petitioner designates its own forensic expert in connection with this order, Petitioner shall initially bear the cost of such expert. The Court reserves the right to tax as costs, or to order the payment of any such expenses and fees, at the time of the final hearing or on the Court's own motion.

3. *Forensic Expert,* shall examine, copy and make images of all computers, hard drives, and other electronic storage media located at __ [location]__ for the purpose of preserving information relating to the books and records of the community estate of the parties, and to the separate estate of either party, and to obtain information relating to any Web sites accessed through the Internet. The procedure will be performed in a manner designed to ensure the integrity and continued ability to perform work on the computers, hard drives, and electronic storage media examined and will be performed in a completely nonintrusive manner consistent with thorough and accurate imaging and examination techniques.

4. To the maximum extent feasible under the circumstances, all computers, hard drives, and electronic storage media shall be examined and the copying and imaging performed without disturbing or harming the integrity of the original hard drives, including without limitation the copying and imaging of all existing files, all deleted files, all hidden files, all backup tapes, all renamed files, all slack space containing data or bits of data, the file allocation table (FAT), directory entry table (DET), and make file table (MFT) both active and deleted, and slack space on which deleted files or fragment files may exist. *Forensic Expert* shall keep a log of the hard drives and other media so accessed and imaged and label each imaged copy generated and file the log with the Court within 72 hours of completing the task. Petitioner may obtain copies thereof at his own expense.

5. To the extent that, either during the process of reviewing the files on hard drives, or at any time in the process in compliance with this order, Respondent or her counsel observe information otherwise privileged or confidential, such observation shall not be deemed a waiver of any otherwise valid privilege or right of confidentiality, and such party and counsel are hereby ORDERED to maintain such information in strictest confidence and not use the same except only in compliance and furtherance of this order.

6. *Forensic Expert* shall not disclose or reveal to anyone, including Respondent or her counsel, the nature or content of any documents or information observed during the process of examining the computers and hard drives, pending a ruling by the Court regarding the discovery of any such matter. The participants in the process of compliance with this order shall insure that such disclosure does not occur, except as described in paragraph 5 above.

7. The imaged disks or copies generated by *Forensic Expert* shall be individually stamped or numbered, and shall be maintained unaltered in a secure environment by them.

8. Any information that is contained on the computers, hard drives, or electronic storage media or otherwise viewed or accessed during the procedures contemplated herein shall remain and be treated by the parties and confidential and, if disclosed by the Court later, shall be used solely and exclusively for the purpose of this lawsuit. By treating these documents as confidential, neither party shall be deemed to have conceded or admitted that any such fact is confidential.

9. Nothing contained in this order shall affect the rights of any party with respect to its own documents or to information obtained or developed independently or documents, transcripts, or materials afforded confidential treatment pursuant to any order including, without limitation, the rights to information which is readily available or accessible in the public domain, readily available or accessible through any other lawful means. This order shall not be deemed to be a ruling concerning the permissible scope of discovery herein, or a ruling upon admissibility.

10. This order is without prejudice to the right of any party to seek modification or amendment of this order upon proper motion and notice.

IT IS SO ORDERED.


Date: _____          BY THE COURT:

                               _____
                               Hon. __[name]__
                               United States District Court

## Form 5.43
## *Ex Parte* Statutory Restraining Order Concerning Documents and Expedited Discovery

UNITED STATES DISTRICT COURT
FOR THE [Name District] OF [Name State]

| | | |
|---|---|---|
| [Name of Plaintiff], | ) | |
| | ) | |
| Plaintiff, | ) | |
| | ) | |
| v. | ) | Civil No. |
| | ) | |
| [Name of Defendant], | ) | |
| | ) | |
| Defendant. | ) | |

## *Ex Parte* Statutory Restraining Order Concerning Documents and Expedited Discovery

The plaintiff has filed a complaint for permanent injunction and other relief and moved *ex parte* for a statutory restraining order prohibiting the defendants from, among other things, destroying, altering, or disposing of or refusing to permit authorized representatives of the plaintiff to inspect and copy, when and as requested, any books, records, electronically stored data, including computers and computer data, or other documents wherever they may be. In addition, the plaintiff seeks leave to conduct expedited discovery.

The court has considered the pleadings, declarations, exhibits and memorandum filed in support of the plaintiff's motion. On the basis of the record provided by the plaintiffs, it appears that:

1. This court has jurisdiction over the subject matter of this case and is authorized to grant *ex parte* relief;
2. There is good cause to believe that the defendants have engaged in, are engaging in, or are about to engage in violations of (the applicable statutes); and
3. This is a proper case for granting an *ex parte* statutory restraining order to preserve the status quo, protect the public from loss and damage, and enable the plaintiff to fulfill its statutory duties.

Therefore the court orders as follows:

Definitions:

For the purpose of this order, the following definitions apply:

1. The term "document" is synonymous in meaning and equal in scope to the usage of the term in Federal Rule of Civil Procedure 34(a), and includes, but is not limited to, writings, drawings, graphs, charts, photographs, audio and video recordings, computer records (including, but not limited to floppy diskettes, hard disks, Zip disks, CD-ROMs, optical disks, backup tapes, printer buffers, smart cards, memory calculators, pagers, personal digital assistants such as Palm Pilot computers, as well as printouts or readouts from any magnetic storage device), and other data compilations from which information can be obtained and translated, if necessary, through detection devices into reasonably usable form. A draft or nonidentical copy is a separate document within the meaning of the term.
2. "Defendants" means   [insert party names]  , and any person insofar as he or she is acting in the capacity of their officer, agent, servant, employee, or attorney and any person who receives actual notice of this order by personal service or otherwise insofar as he or she is acting in concert or participating with them.

## *RELIEF GRANTED*

## I. Maintenance of Documents

IT IS HEREBY ORDERED that the defendants and all persons or entities who receive notice of this order by personal service or otherwise are restrained and enjoined from directly or indirectly destroying, mutilating, erasing, altering, concealing, or disposing of, in any manner, directly or indirectly, any books, records, or documents in the possession or control of the defendants, their agents, attorneys, partners, servants, representatives, employees, , any person(s) acting or purporting to act for or on their behalf, and/or acting for or on behalf of any corporation, partnership or any other type of entity in which defendants have an interest.

## II. Inspection and Copying of Documents

IT IS FURTHER ORDERED that representatives of the plaintiffs be immediately allowed to inspect the books, records, and other documents of the defendants, their agents, attorneys, partners, servants, representatives, employees, any person(s) acting or purporting to act for or on their behalf, and/or any corporate, partnership, or any other entity in which the defendants have an interest, wherever situated, including, but not limited to, paper documents, electronically stored data, tape recordings, and computer disks, wherever they may be situated, whether they are in the possession or control of the defendants, or the possession or control of others, and to copy said documents, data, and records, either on or off the premises.

## III. Expedited Discovery

IT IS FURTHER ORDERED that the parties are granted leave, at any time after service of this order, to take the deposition of and demand the production of documents from any person or entity for the purpose of discovering the nature and/or location of documents reflecting the business transactions of the defendants; forty-eight (48) hours notice shall be deemed sufficient for any such deposition and five (5) days notice shall be deemed sufficient for the production of any such documents.

IT IS FURTHER ORDERED that the limitations and conditions set forth in Federal Rule of Civil Procedure 30(a)(2)(B) regarding subsequent depositions of an individual shall not apply to depositions taken pursuant to this order. No depositions taken pursuant to this order shall count toward the ten-deposition limit set forth in Federal Rule of Civil Procedure 30(a)(2)(A).

## IV. Service of Order

IT IS FURTHER ORDERED that copies of this order may be served by any means, including facsimile transmission, upon any entity or person that may have possession, custody, or control of any documents of the defendants or that may be subject to any provision of this order and, additionally, that representatives of the plaintiffs are specially appointed by the court to effect service. Service of the summons, complaint, or other process may be effected in accordance with Federal Rule of Civil Procedure 4.

## V. Order to Show Cause

IT IS FURTHER ORDERED that each of the defendants shall appear before this court on the ___ day of _____, _____, at 9:00 A.M. before Magistrate _____ at the United States Courthouse for the District of _____, to show cause why this court should not enter a preliminary injunction enjoining the defendants from further violations of (the applicable statutes), and ordering any additional relief this court deems appropriate. Should any party wish to file a memorandum of law or other papers concerning the issuance of a preliminary injunction against the defendants, such materials shall be filed, served, and received by the parties on or before _____.

## VI. Force and Effect

IT IS FURTHER ORDERED that this order shall remain in full force and effect until further order of this court and that this court shall retain jurisdiction of this matter for all purposes.

SO ORDERED.

_____
United States District Judge


Date: _____

# Appendices

# *Glossary*[1]

THE SEDONA CONFERENCE® WORKING GROUP SERIES

The Sedona
Conference® Glossary
For E-Discovery And
Digital Information
Management

A Project of The Sedona Conference® Working Group on Electronic Document
Retention and Production (WG1) RFP+ Group

May, 2005 Version

---

[1] Reprinted with permission of the Sedona Conference.

The Sedona Conference® Glossary
for E-discovery and Digital Information Management

*Co-Editors:*
Conor R. Crowley, Esq.
Much Shelist Freed Denenberg
Ament & Rubenstein
Chicago, IL

Sherry B. Harris
Hunton & Williams
Richmond, VA

*Contributing Editors:*

Matthew I. Cohen, Esq.
Skadden, Arps, Slate,
Meagher & Flom
New York, NY

Anne Kershaw, Esq.
Anne Kershaw Attorneys
& Consultants, PC
Tarrytown, NY

Mark V. Reichenbach
Milberg Weiss
Bershad & Schulman
New York, NY

RFP+ Vendor Panel
(see http://www.thesedonaconference.org
for a listing of the RFP+ Vendor Panel)

Note to Users

The Sedona Conference® Glossary is published as a tool to assist in the
understanding and discussion of electronic discovery and electronic
information management issues; it is not intended to be an all-encompassing
replacement of existing technical glossaries published by ARMA International
(www.arma.org), American National Standards Institute (www.ansi.org),
International Organization for Standardization (www.iso.org), U.S.
National Archives & Records Administration (www.archives.gov) and
other professional organizations. As with all of our publications, your
comments are welcome. Please forward them to us at tsc@sedona.net.

Richard G. Braman
Executive Director
The Second Conference®
Sedona, AZ
USA
May, 2005

# Glossary

The Sedona Conference® Glossary of Commonly Used Terms for E-discovery and Digital Information Management[1]

30(b)(6): Under Federal Rule of Civil Procedure 30(b)(6), a corporation, partnership, association, or governmental agency is subject to the deposition process, and to provide one or more witnesses to "testify as to matters known or reasonably available to the organization" without compromising attorney-client privilege communications or work product. It is not unusual for the 30(b)(6) topics to be directed toward the discovery process, including procedures for preservation, collection, chain of custody, processing, review, and production. Early in the litigation, when developing a discovery plan, particularly with regard to electronic discovery, a party should be mindful of the obligation to provide one or more 30(b)(6) witnesses should the request be made by another party to the litigation, and include this contingency in the discovery plan.

**Ablate.** Describes the process by which laser-readable "pits" are burned into the recorded layer of optical disks, DVD-ROMs and CD-ROMs.

**Ablative.** Unalterable data. See *Ablate*.

**Acetate-base film.** A safety film (ANSI Standard) substrate used to produce microfilm.

**ACL (Access Control List).** A security type used by Lotus Notes developers to grant varying levels of access and user privileges within Lotus Notes databases.

**Active Data.** Active Data is information residing on the direct access storage media (disk drives or servers) of computer systems, which is readily visible to the operating system and/or application software with which it was created and immediately accessible to users without restoration or reconstruction.

**Active Records.** Active Records are those Records related to current, ongoing or in-process activities and are referred to on a regular basis to respond to day-to-day operational requirements. An active record resides in native application format and is accessible for purposes of business processing with no restrictions on alteration beyond normal business rules. See *Inactive Records*.

---

[1]Terms previously defined in *The Sedona Principles: Best Practices Recommendations & Principles for Addressing Electronic Document Production or The Sedona Guidelines: Best Practice Guidelines & Commentary for Managing Information & Records in the Electronic Age* are in bold.

**ADC.** Analog to Digital converter. Converts analog data to a digital format.

**Address.** Addresses using a number of different protocols are commonly used on the Internet. These addresses include e-mail addresses (Simple Mail Transfer Protocol or SMTP), IP (Internet Protocol) addresses and URLs (Uniform Resource Locators), commonly known as Web addresses.

**ADF.** Automatic Document Feeder. This is the means by which a scanner feeds the paper document.

**AIIM.** The Association for Information and Image Management—focused on electronic imaging.

**Algorithm.** A detailed formula or set of steps for solving a particular problem. To be an algorithm, a set of rules must be unambiguous and have a clear stopping point.

**Aliasing.** When computer graphics output has jagged edges or a stair-stepped, rather than a smooth, appearance when magnified. The graphics output can be smoothed using anti-aliasing algorithms.

**Alphanumeric.** Characters composed of letters, numbers (and sometimes punctuation marks). Excludes control characters.

**Ambient Data.** See *Residual Data.*

**Analog.** Data in an analog format is represented by continuously variable, measurable, physical quantities such as voltage, amplitude or frequency. Analog is the opposite of digital.

**Annotations.** The changes, additions, or editorial comments made or applicable to a document—usually an electronic image file—using electronic sticky notes, highlighter, or other electronic tools. Annotations should be overlaid and not change the original document.

**ANSI.** American National Standards Institute—a private, nonprofit organization that administers and coordinates the U.S. voluntary standardization and conformity assessment system.

**Aperture Card.** An IBM punch card with a window which holds a 35-mm frame of microfilm. Indexing information is punched in the card.

**Application.** An application is a collection of one or more related software programs that enable an end-user to enter, store, view, modify, or extract information from files or databases. The term is commonly used in place of "program," or "software." Applications may include word processors, Internet browsing tools, spreadsheets, e-mail clients, personal information managers (contact information and calendars), and other databases.

**Architecture.** The term architecture refers to the hardware, software or combination of hardware and software comprising a computer system or network. The term "open architecture" is used to describe computer and network components that are more readily interconnected and interoperable. Conversely, the term "closed architecture" describes components that are less readily interconnected and interoperable.

**Archival Data.** Archival Data is information an organization maintains for long-term storage and record keeping purposes, but which is not immediately accessible to the user of a computer system. Archival data may be written to removable media such as a CD, magneto-optical media, tape or other electronic storage device, or may be maintained on system hard drives. Some systems allow users to retrieve archival data directly while other systems require the intervention of an IT professional.

**Archive, Electronic Archive.** Archives are long-term repositories for the storage of records. Electronic archives preserve the content, prevent or track alterations, and control access to electronic records.

**ARMA International.** A not-for-profit association and recognized authority on managing records and information—paper and electronic—www.arma.org.

**Artificial Intelligence (AI).** The subfield of computer science concerned with the concepts and methods of symbolic inference by computer and symbolic knowledge representation for use in making inferences—an attempt to model aspects of human thought on computers. It is also sometimes defined as trying to solve by computer any problem once believed to be solvable only by humans. AI is the capability of a device to perform functions that are normally associated with human intelligence, such as reasoning and optimization through experience. It attempts to approximate the results of human reasoning by organizing and manipulating factual and heuristic knowledge. Areas of AI activity include expert systems, natural language understanding, speech recognition, vision, and robotics.

**ASCII (American Standard Code for Information Interchange).** Pronounced "ask-ee," ASCII is a nonproprietary text format built on a set of 128 (or 255 for *extended* ASCII) alphanumeric and control characters. Documents in ASCII format consist of only text with no formatting and can be read by most computer systems.

**Aspect Ratio.** The relationship of the height and width of any image. The aspect ratio of an image must be maintained to prevent distortion.

**Attachment.** An attachment is a record or file associated with another record for the purpose of retention or transfer. There may be multiple attachments associated with a single "parent" or "master" record. In many records and information management programs the attachments and associated record are managed and processed as a single unit. In common use, this term refers to a file (or files) associated with an e-mail for retention and storage as a single message unit.

**Attribute.** An attribute is a characteristic of data that sets it apart from other data, such as location, length, or type. The term attribute is sometimes used synonymously with "data element" or "property."

**Audit Trail.** In computer security systems, a chronological record of when users logged in, how long they were engaged in various activities, what they were doing, and whether any actual or attempted security violations occurred. An audit trail is an automated or manual set of chronological records of system activities that may enable the reconstruction and examination of a sequence of events and/or changes in an event.

**Author or Originator.** The author of a document is the person, office or designated position responsible for its creation or issuance. In the case of a document in the form of a letter, the author or originator is usually indicated on the letterhead or by signature. In some cases, the software application producing the document may capture the author's identity and associate it with the document. For records management purposes, the author or originator may be designated as a person, official title, office symbol, or code.

**AVI (Audio-Video Interleave).** A Microsoft standard for Windows animation files that interleaves audio and video to provide medium quality multimedia.

**Backbone.** The top level of a hierarchical network. It is the main channel along which data is transferred.

**Backfiles.** Existing paper or microfilm files.

**Backup.** To create a copy of data as a precaution against the loss or damage of the original data. Many users backup their files, and most computer networks use automatic backup software to make regular copies of some or all of the data on the network.

**Backup Data.** An exact copy of system data which serves as a source for recovery in the event of a system problem or disaster. Backup Data is generally stored separately from Active Data on portable media. Backup Data is distinct from Archival Data in that Backup Data may be a copy of Active Data, but the more meaningful difference is the method and structure of storage which impact its suitability for certain purposes.

**Backup Tape Recycling.** Backup Tape Recycling describes the process whereby an organization's backup tapes are overwritten with new data, usually on a fixed schedule determined jointly by records management, legal, and IT sources. For example, the use of nightly backup tapes for each day of the week with the daily backup tape for a particular day being overwritten on the same day the following week; weekly and monthly backups being stored offsite for a specific period of time before being placed back in the rotation.

**Backup Tapes.** Magnetic tapes used to store copies of data, for use when restoration or recovery of data is required. Data on backup tapes are generally recorded and stored sequentially, rather than randomly, meaning in order to locate and access a specific file or data set, all data on the tape preceding the target must first be read, a time-consuming and inefficient process. Backup tapes typically use data compression, which increases restoration time and expense, given the lack of uniform standards governing data compression.

**Bandwidth.** The amount of information or data that can be sent over a network connection in a given period of time. Bandwidth is usually stated in kilobits per second (kbps) or megabits per second (mps).

**Bar Code.** A small pattern of vertical lines that can be read by a laser or an optical scanner. In records management and electronic discovery, bar codes are often affixed to specific records for indexing, tracking and retrieval purposes.

**Batch Processing.** The processing of a large amount of data, or multiple records, in a single step.

**Bates Number.** Sequential numbering used to track documents and images in production data sets, where each page is identified by a unique production number. Often used in conjunction with a suffix or prefix to identify the producing party, the litigation, or other relevant information. See also *Production Number.*

**Baud Rate.** The number of times per second a communications channel changes the carrier signal it sends on a phone line. A 2400-baud modem changes the signal 2400 times a second.

**BBS (Bulletin Board System).** A computer system or service that users access to participate in electronic discussion groups, post messages and/or download files.

**BCS.** Boston Computer Society, one of the first associations of PC/Apple users and one of the largest and most active.

**Beginning Document Number or BegDoc#.** The Bates Number identifying the first page of a document or record.

**Bibliographical/Objective Coding.** Extracting objective information from electronic documents such as date created, author/recipient/copies, and associating the information with a specific electronic document.

**Binary.** The Base 2 numbering system used in digital computing which represents all numbers using combinations of zero and one.

**BIOS ( Basic Input Output System).** The set of user-independent computer instructions stored in a computer's ROM, immediately available to the computer when the computer is turned on. BIOS information provides the code necessary to control the keyboard, display screen, disk drives and communication ports in addition to handling certain miscellaneous functions.

**Bit Map.** A Bit Map provides information on the placement and color of individual bits and allows the creation of characters or images by creating a picture composed of individual bits (pixels).

**Bit Stream Backup.** A Bit Stream Backup is a sector-by-sector/bit-by-bit copy of a hard drive. A Bit Stream Backup is an exact copy of a hard drive, preserving all latent data in addition to the files and directory structures. Bit Stream Backup may be created using applications such as EnCase, SnapBack and Ghost. See *Forensic Copy.*

**Bit.** A bit (binary digit) is the smallest unit of computer data. A bit consists of either 0 or 1. There are eight bits in a byte.

**Bi-Tonal.** A bi-tonal image uses only black and white.

**BMP.** A Windows file format for storing bit map images.

**Bookmark.** A link to a Web site or page previously visited.

**Boolean Search.** Boolean Searches use the logical operators "and", "or" and "not" to include or exclude terms from a search.

**Boot Sector.** The very first sector on a hard drive which contains the computer code (boot strap loader) necessary for the computer to start up and the partition table describing the organization of the hard drive.

**Boot.** To start up or reset a computer.

**BPI (Bits Per Inch).** BPI measures data densities in disk and magnetic tape systems.

**Bps.** bits per second.

**Broadband.** Communications of high capacity and usually of multimedia content.

**Browser.** An application, such as Internet Explorer or Netscape Navigator, used to view and navigate the World Wide Web and other Internet resources.

**Bug.** A problem with computer software or hardware that causes it to malfunction or crash.

**Burn.** The process of a creating a copy of information onto a CD or DVD.

**Bus.** A parallel circuit that connects the major components of a computer, allowing the transfer of electric impulses from one connected component to any other.

**Business Process Outsourcing.** Business process outsourcing occurs when an organization turns over the management of a business function, such as accounts payable, purchasing, payroll or information technology to a third party.

**Byte (Binary Term).** A Byte is the basic measurement of most computer data and consists of 8 bits. Computer storage capacity is generally measured in bytes. Although characters are stored in bytes, a few bytes are of little use for storing a large amount of data. Therefore, storage is measured in larger increments of bytes. See *Kilobyte, Megabyte, Gigabyte, Terabyte, Petabyte,* and *Exabyte.*

**Cache.** A dedicated, high speed storage location which can be used for the temporary storage of frequently used data. As data may be retrieved more quickly from cache than the original storage location, cache allows applications to run more quickly. Web site contents often reside in cached storage locations on a hard drive.

**Caching.** The temporary storage of frequently used data to speed access. See also *Cache.*

**Case De-Duplication.** Eliminates duplicates to retain only one copy of each document per case. For example, if an identical document resides with three custodians, only the first custodian's copy will be saved. See *De-Duplication.*

**Catalog.** See *Index.*

**CCD (Charge Coupled Device).** A computer chip the output of which correlates with the light or color passed by it. Individual CCDs or arrays of these are used in scanners as a high-resolution, digital camera to read documents.

**CCITT Group 4.** A lossless compression technique/format that reduces the size of a file, generally about 5:1 over RLE and 40:1 over bitmap. CCITT Group 4 compression may only be used for bi-tonal images.

**CCITT.** Consultative Committee for International Telephone & Telegraphy. Sets standards for phones, faxes, modems etc. The standard exists primarily for fax documents.

**CDPD (Cellular Digital Packet Data).** A data communication standard using the unused capacity of cellular voice providers to transfer data.

**CD-R (Compact Disc Recordable).** A CD-ROM on which a user may permanently record data once using a CD Burner.

**CD-RW (Compact Disc Re-Writable).** A CD-ROM on which a user may record data multiple times.

**CD-ROM.** See *Compact Disc.*

**Centronics Interface.** A parallel interface standard for connecting printers and other devices to computers.

**Certificate.** Digital signature combining data verification and encryption key. See *PKI Digital Signature.*

**CGA (Color Graphics Adapter).** See *Video Graphics Adapter (VGA)*.

**Chaff/winnowing.** Advanced encryption technique involving data dispersal and mixing.

**Chain of Custody.** Documentation and testimony regarding the possession, movement, handling and location of evidence from the time it is obtained to the time it is presented in court; used to prove that evidence has not been altered or tampered with in any way; necessary both to assure admissibility and probative value.

**Character Treatment.** The use of all caps or another standard form of treating letters in a coding project.

**CIE (Commission International de l'Eclairage).** The international commission on color matching and illumination systems.

**Cine-Mode.** Data recorded on a film strip such that it can be read by a human when held vertically.

**Cinepak.** A compression algorithm; see *MPEG*.

**CITIS (Contractor Integrated Technical Information Service).** The Department Of Defense now requires contractors to have an integrated electronic document image and management system.

**Client/Server.** An architecture whereby a computer system consists of one or more server computers and numerous client computers (workstations). The system is functionally distributed across several nodes on a network and is typified by a high degree of parallel processing across distributed nodes. With client-server architecture, CPU intensive processes (such as searching and indexing) are completed on the server, while image viewing and OCR occur on the client. This dramatically reduces network data traffic and insulates the database from workstation interruptions.

**Client.** Any computer system that requests a service of another computer system. A workstation requesting the contents of a file from a file server is a client of the file server. See *Thin Client*.

**Clipboard.** A holding area that temporarily stores information copied or cut from a document.

**Cluster (File).** The smallest unit of storage space that can be allocated to store a file on operating systems that use a file allocation table (FAT) architecture. Windows and DOS organize hard disks based on Clusters (also known as allocation units), which consist of one or more contiguous sectors. Disks using smaller Cluster sizes waste less space and store information more efficiently.

**Cluster (System).** A collection of individual computers that appear as a single logical unit. Also referred to as matrix or grid systems.

**Cluster bitmaps.** Used in NTFS to keep track of the status (free or used) of clusters on the hard drive.

**CMYK.** Cyan, Magenta, Yellow and Black. A subtractive method used in four color printing and Desktop Publishing.

**Coding.** Automated or human process through which documents are examined and evaluated using pre-determined codes, and the results of those comparisons are logged. Coding usually identifies names, dates, and relevant terms or phrases. Coding may be structured (limited to the selection of one of a finite number of choices), or unstructured (a narrative comment about a document). Coding may be objective, i.e., the name of the sender or the date, or subjective, i.e., evaluation as to the relevancy or probative value of documents.

**COLD (Computer Output to Laser Disc).** A computer programming process that outputs electronic records and printed reports to laser disk instead of a printer.

**COM (Computer Output to Microfilm).** A process that outputs electronic records and computer-generated reports to microfilm.

**Comb.** A series of boxes with their top missing. Tick marks guide text entry. Used in forms processing rather than boxes.

**Comic Mode.** Human-readable data, recorded on a strip of film which can be read when the film is moved horizontally to the reader.

**Comma Separated Value (CSV).** A record layout that separates data fields/values with a comma and typically encloses data in quotation marks.

**Compact Disc (CD).** A type of optical disk storage media, compact discs come in a variety of formats. These formats include CD-ROMs ("CD Read-Only Memory") that are read-only; CD-Rs ("CD Recordable") that are write to once and are then read-only; and CD-RWs ("CD Re-Writable") that can be written to multiple times.

**Compliance Search.** The identification of relevant terms and/or parties in response to a discovery request.

**Component Video.** Separates video into luminosity and color signals that provide the highest possible signal quality.

**Composite Video.** Combines red, green, blue and synchronization signals into one video signal so that only one connector is required; used by most TVs and VCRs.

**Compression Ratio.** The ratio of the size of an uncompressed file to a compressed file, e.g., with a 10:1 compression ratio, a 1 MB file can be compressed to 100 KB.

**Compression.** Compression algorithms such as Zip and RLE reduce the size of files saving both storage space and reducing bandwidth required for access and transmission. Data compression is widely used in backup utilities, spreadsheet applications and data-base management systems. Compression generally eliminates redundant information and/or predicts where changes will occur. "Lossless" compression techniques such as Zip and RLE preserve the integrity of the input. Coding standards such as JPEG and MPEG employ "lossy" methods which do not preserve all of the original information, and are most commonly used for photographs, audio, and video.

**Computer Forensics.** Computer Forensics (in the context of this document, "forensic analysis") is the use of specialized techniques for recovery, authentication and analysis of electronic data when an investigation or litigation involves issues relating to reconstruction of computer usage, examination of residual data, authentication of data by technical analysis or explanation of technical features of data and computer usage. Computer forensics requires specialized expertise that goes beyond normal data collection and preservation techniques available to end-users or system support personnel, and generally requires strict adherence to chain-of-custody protocols. See also *Forensics* and *Forensic Copy.*

**Computer.** Includes but is not limited to network servers, desktops, laptops, notebook computers, mainframes and PDAs (personal digital assistants).

**Concept Search.** Searching electronic documents to determine relevance by analyzing the words and putting search requests in conceptual groupings so the true meaning of the request is considered. Concept searching considers both the word and the context in which it appears to differentiate between concepts such as diamond (baseball) and diamond (jewelry).

**Content Comparison.** A method of de-duplication that compares file content or output (to image or paper) and ignores metadata. See *De-Duplication.*

**Contextual Search.** The process of returning electronic evidence to its true context: when created, by whom, for what purpose, etc.

**Continuous Tone.** An image (e.g., a photograph) which has all the values of gray from white to black.

**Convergence.** Integration of computing, communications and broadcasting systems.

**Cookie.** A message given to a Web browser by a Web server. The browser stores the message in a text file. The message is then sent back to the server each time the browser requests a page from the server. The main purpose of cookies is to identify users and possibly prepare customized Web pages for them.

**Corrupted File.** A file damaged in some way, such as by a virus, or by software or hardware failure, so that it cannot be read by a computer.

**COTS (Commercial Off-the-Shelf).** Hardware or software products that are commercially manufactured, ready-made and available for use by the general public without the need for customization.

**CPI.** Characters Per Inch.

**CPU (Central Processing Unit).** The primary silicon chip that runs a computer's operating system and application software. It performs a computer's essential mathematical functions and controls essential operations.

**CRC (Cyclical Redundancy Checking).** Used in data communications to create a checksum character at the end of a data block to ensure integrity of data transmission and receipt.

**CRM (Customer Relationship Management).** Programs that help manage clients and contacts. Used in larger companies. Often a significant repository of sales, customer, and sometimes marketing data.

**Cross-Custodian De-Duplication.** Culls a document to the extent multiple copies of that document reside within different custodians' data sets. See *De-Duplication.*

**CRT (Cathode Ray Tube).** The picture tube of a computer monitor or television.

**Cryptography.** Technique to scramble data to preserve confidentiality or authenticity.

**Cull (verb).** To remove a document from the collection to be produced or reviewed. See *Data Filtering, Harvesting.*

**Custodian.** Person having control of a network, computer or specific electronic files.

**Custodian De-Duplication.** Culls a document to the extent multiple copies of that document reside within the same custodian's data set. See *De-Duplication.*

**Customer-Added metadata.** See *User-Added Metadata.*

**CYAN.** Cyan-colored ink reflects blue and green and absorbs red.

**Cylinder.** The set of tracks on both sides of each platter in the hard drive that is located at the same head position.

**DAC (Digital to Analog Converter).** Converts digital data to analog data.

**DAD (Digital Audio Disc).** Another term for compact disc.

**DAT (Digital Audio Tape).** A magnetic tape generally used to record audio but can hold up to 40 gigabytes (or 60 CDs) of data if used for data storage. Has the disadvantage of being a serial access device. Often used for backup.

**Data.** Any information stored on a computer. All software is divided into two general categories: data and programs. Programs are collections of instructions for manipulating data. In data-base management systems data files are the files that store the data-base information. Other files, such as index files and data dictionaries, store administrative information, known as metadata.

**Data Collection.** See *Harvesting.*

**Data Element.** A combination of characters or bytes referring to one separate piece of information, such as name, address, or age.

**Data Extraction.** The process of retrieving data from documents (hard copy or electronic). The process may be manual or electronic.

**Data Field.** See *Field.*

**Data Filtering.** The process of identifying for extraction specific databases on specified parameters.

**Data Formats.** The organization of information for display, storage or printing. Data is maintained in certain common formats so that it can be used by various programs, which may only work with data in a particular format, e.g., PDF, html.

**Data Harvesting.** See *Harvesting.*

**Data Mining.** Data mining generally refers to techniques for extracting summaries and reports from an organization's databases and data sets. In the context of electronic discovery, this term often refers to the processes used to cull through a collection of electronic data to extract evidence for production or presentation in an investigation or in litigation.

**Data Set.** A named or defined collection of data. See also *Production Data Set* and *Privilege Data Set.*

**Data Verification.** Assessment of data to ensure it has not been modified. The most common method of verification is hash coding by some method such as MD5. See also *Digital Fingerprint* and *File Level Binary Comparison* and *Hash Coding.*

**Database Management System (DBMS).** A software system used to access and retrieve data stored in a database.

**Database.** In electronic records a database is a set of data elements consisting of at least one file, or of a group of integrated files, usually stored in one location and made available to several users. In computing databases are sometimes classified according to their organizational approach with the most prevalent approach being the relational database—a tabular database in which data is defined so that it can be reorganized and accessed in a number of different ways. Another popular organizational structure is the distributed database which can be dispersed or replicated among different points in a network. Computer databases typically contain aggregations of data records or files, such as sales transactions, product catalogs and inventories, and customer profiles. SQL (Structured Query Language) is a standard computer language for making interactive queries from and updates to a database.

**Daubert (challenge).** *Daubert v. Merrell Dow Pharmaceuticals*, 509 U.S. 579 (1993), addresses the admission of scientific expert testimony to ensure that the testimony is reliable before considered for admission pursuant to Rule 702. The court assesses the testimony by analyzing the methodology and applicability of the expert's approach. Faced with a proffer of expert scientific testimony, the trial judge must determine first, pursuant to Rule 104(a), whether the expert is proposing to testify to (1) scientific knowledge that (2) will assist the trier of fact to understand or determine a fact at issue. This involves preliminary assessment of whether the reasoning or methodology is scientifically valid and whether it can be applied to the facts at issue. *Daubert* suggests a open approach and provides a list of four potential factors: (1) whether the theory can be or has been tested; (2) whether the theory has been subjected to peer review or publication; (3) known or potential rate of error of that particular technique and the existence and maintenance of standards controlling the technique's operation; and (4) consideration of general acceptance within the scientific community. 509 U.S. at 593-94.

**Decryption.** Transformation of encrypted (or scrambled) data back to original form.

**De-Duplication.** De-Duplication ("De-Duping") is the process of comparing electronic records based on their characteristics and removing or marking duplicate records within the data set. The definition of "duplicate records" should be agreed upon, i.e., whether an exact copy from a different location (such as a different mailbox, server tapes, etc.) is considered to be a duplicate. De-duplication can be selective, depending on the agreed-upon criteria. See also *Case De-Duplication, Content Comparison, Cross-Custodian De-Duplication, Custodian De-Duplication, Data Verification, Digital Fingerprint, File Level Binary Comparison, Hash Coding, Horizontal De-Duplication, Metadata Comparison,* and *Production De-Duplication.*

**De-Fragment ("de-frag").** Use of a computer utility to reorganize files so they are more contiguous on a hard drive or other storage medium, if the files or parts thereof have become fragmented and scattered in various locations within the storage medium in the course of normal computer operations. Used to optimize the operation of the computer, it will overwrite information in unallocated space. See *Fragmented.*

**Deleted Data.** Deleted Data is data that existed on the computer as live data and which have been deleted by the computer system or end-user activity. Deleted data may remain on storage media in whole or in part until they are overwritten or "wiped." Even after the data itself have been wiped, directory entries, pointers or other information relating to the deleted data may remain on the computer. "Soft deletions" are data marked as deleted (and not generally available to the end-user after such marking), but not yet physically removed or overwritten. Soft-deleted data can be restored with complete integrity.

**Deleted File.** A file with disk space that has been designated as available for reuse; the deleted file remains intact until it is overwritten.

**Deletion.** Deletion is the process whereby data is removed from active files and other data storage structures on computers and rendered inaccessible except through the use of special data recovery tools designed to recover deleted data. Deletion occurs on several levels in modern computer systems: (a) *File level deletion* renders the file inaccessible to the operating system and normal application programs and marks the storage space occupied by the file's directory entry and contents as free and available to re-use for data storage. (b) *Record level deletion* occurs when a record is rendered inaccessible to a data-base management system (DBMS) (usually marking the record storage space as available for re-use by the DBMS, although in some cases the space is never reused until the database is compacted) and is also characteristic of many e-mail systems (c) *Byte level deletion* occurs when text or other information is deleted from the file content (such as the deletion of text from a word processing file); such deletion may render the deleted data inaccessible to the application intended to be used in processing the file, but may not actually remove the data from the file's content until a process such as compaction or rewriting of the file causes the deleted data to be overwritten.

**Descenders.** The portion of a character which falls below the main part of the letter (e.g., g, p, q)

**De-shading.** Removing shaded areas to render images more easily recognizable by OCR. De-shading software typically searches for areas with a regular pattern of tiny dots.

**De-skewing.** The process of straightening skewed (tilted) images. De-skewing is one of the image enhancements that can improve OCR accuracy. Documents often become skewed when scanned or faxed.

**Desktop.** Generally refers to an individual PC.

**De-speckling.** Removing isolated speckles from an image file. Speckles often develop when a document is scanned or faxed.

**DIA/DCA (Document Interchange Architecture).** An IBM standard for transmission and storage of voice, text, or video over networks.

**Digital Certificate.** Electronic records that contain keys used to decrypt information, especially information sent over a public network like the Internet.

**Digital Fingerprint.** A fixed-length hash code that uniquely represents the binary content of a file. See also *Data Verification* and *File Level Binary Comparison* and *Hash Coding*.

**Digital.** Information stored as a string of ones and zeros. Opposite of analog.

**Digitize.** The process of converting an analog value into a digital (numeric) representation.

**Directory.** A simulated file folder or container used to organize files and directories in a hierarchical or tree-like structure. UNIX and DOS use the term "directory," while Mac and Windows use the term "folder."

**Disaster Recovery Tapes.** Portable media used to store data for backup purposes. See *Backup Data/Backup Tapes*.

**Disk mirroring.** A method of protecting data from a catastrophic hard disk failure or for long term data storage. As each file is stored on the hard disk, a "mirror" copy is made on a second hard disk or on a different part of the same disk. See also *Mirror*.

**Disk Partition.** A hard drive containing a set of consecutive cylinders.

**Disc/Disk.** Round, flat storage media with layers of material which enable the recording of data.

**Discovery.** Discovery is the process of identifying, locating, securing and producing information and materials for the purpose of obtaining evidence for use in the legal process. The term is also used to describe the process of reviewing all materials which may be potentially relevant to the issues at hand and/or which may need to be disclosed to other parties, and of evaluating evidence to prove or disprove facts, theories or allegations. There are several ways to conduct discovery, the most common of which are interrogatories, requests for production of documents and depositions.

**Discwipe.** Utility that overwrites existing data. Various utilities exist with varying degrees of efficiency—some wipe only named files or unallocated space of residual data, thus unsophisticated users who try to wipe evidence may leave behind files of which they are unaware.

**Disposition.** The final business action carried out on a record. This action generally is to destroy or archive the record. Electronic record disposition can include "soft deletions" (see *Deletion*), "hard deletions," "hard deletions with overwrites," "archive to long-term store," "forward to organization," and "copy to another media or format and delete (hard or soft)."

**Distributed Data.** Distributed Data is that information belonging to an organization which resides on portable media and nonlocal devices such as remote offices, home computers, laptop computers, personal digital assistants ("PDAs"), wireless communication devices (*e.g.*, Blackberry) and Internet repositories (including e-mail hosted by Internet service providers or portals and Web sites). Distributed data also includes data held by third parties such as application service providers and business partners. *Note*: Information Technology organizations may define distributed data differently (for example, in some organizations distributed data includes any nonserver-based data, including workstation disk drives).

**Dithering.** In printing, dithering is usually called *halftoning,* and shades of gray are called *halftones.* The more dither patterns that a device or program supports, the more shades of gray it can represent. Dithering is the process of converting grays to different densities of black dots, usually for the purposes of printing or storing color or grayscale images as black and white images.

**DLT (Digital Linear Tape).** A type of backup tape which can hold up to 80 GB depending on the data file format.

**Document.** A page, a collection of pages or any file produced manually or by a software application, that constitutes a logical single communication of information. Examples include a letter, a spreadsheet, or an e-mail.

**Document Date.** The original creation date of a document. For an e-mail the document date is indicated by the date-stamp of the e-mail.

**Document Imaging Programs.** Software used to store, manage, retrieve, and distribute documents quickly and easily on the computer.

**Document Metadata.** Data about the document stored in the document, as opposed to document content. Often this data is not immediately viewable in the software application used to create/edit the document but often can be accessed via a "Properties" view. Examples include document author and company, and create and revision dates. Contrast with *File System Metadata* and *E-mail Metadata.* See also *Metadata.*

**Document Type or Doc Type.** A typical field used in bibliographical coding. Typical doc type examples include letter, memo, report, article, and others.

**Domain.** A sub-network of servers and computers within a LAN. Domain information is useful when restoring backup tapes, particularly of e-mail.

**Domino Database.** Another name for Lotus Notes Database versions 5.0 or higher. See *NSF.*

**Dot Pitch.** Distance of one pixel in a CRT to the next pixel on the vertical plane. The smaller the number, the higher quality display.

**DPI (Dots Per Inch).** The measurement of the resolution of display in printing systems. A typical CRT screen provides 96 dpi, which provides 9,216 dots per square inch (96 x 96). When a paper document is scanned, the resolution, or level of detail, at which the scanning was performed is expressed in DPI. Typically, documents are scanned at 200 or 300 DPI.

**Draft Record.** A draft record is a preliminary version of a record before it has been completed, finalized, accepted, validated or filed. Such records include working files and notes. Records and information management policies may provide for the destruction of draft records upon finalization, acceptance, validation or filing of the final or official version of the record. However, draft records generally must be retained if (1) they are deemed to be subject to a legal hold; or (2) a specific law or regulation mandates their retention and policies should recognize such exceptions.

**Drag-and-Drop.** The movement of on-screen objects by dragging them with the mouse, and dropping them in another place.

**DRAM.** Dynamic Random Access Memory, a memory technology which is periodically "refreshed" or updated—as opposed to "static" RAM chips which do not require refreshing. The term is often used to refer to the memory chips themselves.

**Drive Geometry.** A computer hard drive is made up of a number of rapidly rotating platters that have a set of read/write heads on both sides of each platter. Each platter is divided into a series of concentric rings called tracks. Each track is further divided into sections called sectors, and each sector is subdivided into bytes. Drive geometry refers to the number and positions of each of these structures.

**Driver.** A driver is a computer program that controls various devices such as the keyboard, mouse, monitor, etc.

**DSP (Digital Signal Processor/Processing).** A special purpose computer (or technique) which digitally processes signals and electrical/analog waveforms.

**DTP (Desktop Publishing).** PC applications used to prepare direct print output or output suitable for printing presses.

**Duplex Scanners versus Double-Sided Scanning.** Duplex scanners automatically scan both sides of a double-sided page, producing two images at once. Double-sided scanning uses a single-sided scanner to scan double-sided pages, scanning one collated stack of paper, then flipping it over and scanning the other side.

**Duplex.** Two-sided page(s).

**DVD (Digital Video Disc or Digital Versatile Disc).** A plastic disk, like a CD, on which data can be written and read. DVDs are faster, can hold more information, and can support more data formats than CDs.

**ECM.** Enterprise content management.

**EDI (Electronic Data Interchange).** Eliminating forms altogether by encoding the data as close as possible to the point of the transaction; automated business information exchange.

**EDMS (Electronic Document Management System).** A system to electronically manage documents during all life cycles. See *Electronic Document Management.*

**EGA (Extended Graphics Adapter).** See *VGA.*

**EIA (Electronic Industries Association).**

**EIM (Electronic Image Management).**

**EISA (Extended Industry Standard Architecture).** One of the standard buses used for PCs.

**Electronic Discovery.** The process of collecting, preparing, reviewing, and producing electronic documents in the context of the legal process. See *Discovery.*

**Electronic Document Management.** For paper documents, involves imaging, indexing/coding and archiving of scanned documents/images, and thereafter electronically managing them during all life cycle phases. Electronic documents are likewise electronically managed from creation to archiving and all stages in between.

**Electronic File Processing.** Generally includes extraction of metadata from files, identification of duplicates/de-duplication and rendering of data into delimited format.

**Electronic Image.** An electronic or digital picture of a document (e.g., TIFF, PDF, etc.).

**Electronic Mail Message.** A document created or received via an electronic mail system, including brief notes, formal or substantive narrative documents, and any attachments, such as word processing and other electronic documents, which may be transmitted with the message.

**Electronic Mail/E-mail.** An electronic means for communicating information under specified conditions, generally in the form of text messages, through systems that will send, store, process, and receive information and in which messages are held in storage until the addressee accesses them.

**Electronic Record.** Information recorded in a form that requires a computer or other machine to process it and that otherwise satisfies the definition of a record.

**Electrostatic Printing.** Paper is exposed to electron charge. Toner sticks to the charged pixels.

**Em.** In any print, font or size equal to the width of the letter "M" in that font and size.

**E-mail address.** An electronic mail address. Internet e-mail addresses follow the formula: user-ID@domain-name; other e-mail protocols may use different address formats. In some e-mail systems, a user's e-mail address is "aliased" or represented by his or her natural name rather than a fully qualified e-mail address. For example, john.doe@abc.com might appear simply as John Doe.

**E-mail Metadata.** Data stored in the e-mail about the e-mail. Often this data is not even viewable in the e-mail client application used to create the e-mail. The amount of e-mail metadata available for a particular e-mail varies greatly depending on the e-mail system. Contrast with File System Metadata and Document Metadata.

**E-mail String.** A series of e-mails linked together by e-mail responses or forwards. The series of e-mail messages created through multiple responses and answers to an originating message. Also referred to as an e-mail "thread." Comments, revisions, attachments are all part of an e-mail string.

**Encryption.** A procedure that renders the contents of a message or file scrambled or unintelligible to anyone not authorized to read it. Encryption is used to protect information as it moves from one computer to another and is an increasingly common way of sending credit card numbers and other personal information over the Internet.

**Encryption Key.** A data value that is used to encrypt and decrypt data. The number of bits in the encryption key is a rough measure of the encryption strength; generally, the more bits in the encryption key, the more difficult it is to break.

**End Document Number or End Doc#.** The last single page image of a document.

**Endorser.** A small printer in a scanner that adds a document-control number or other endorsement to each scanned sheet.

**Enhanced Titles.** A meaningful/descriptive title for a document. The opposite of Verbatim Titles.

**Enterprise Architecture.** Framework for how software, computing, storage and networking systems should integrate and operate to meet the changing needs across an entire business

**EOF (End of File).** A distinctive code which uniquely marks the end of a data file.

**EPP (Enhanced Parallel Port).** Also known as Fast Mode Parallel Port. A new, industry standard parallel port, having higher transfer times competitive with SCSI.

**EPS (Encapsulated PostScript).** Uncompressed files for images, text and objects. Only print on PostScript printers.

**Erasable Optical Drive.** A type of optical drive that uses erasable optical disks.

**ESDI (Enhanced Small Device Interface).** A defined, common electronic interface for transferring data between computers and peripherals, particularly disk drives.

**ESI.** Electronically stored information.

**Ethernet.** A common way of networking PCs to create a Local Area Network (LAN).

**Evidentiary Image or Copy.** See *Forensic Copy.*

**Exabyte.** A unit of 1,000 petabytes. See *Byte.*

**Export.** Data extracted or taken out of one environment or application usually in a prescribed format, and usually for import into another environment or application.

**Extended Partitions.** If a computer hard drive has been divided into more than four partitions, extended partitions are created. Under such circumstances each extended partition contains a partition table in the first sector that describes how it is further subdivided.

**Extensible Markup Language (XML).** Short for Extensible Markup Language, a specification developed by the W3C (World Wide Web Consortium—the Web development standards board). XML is a pared-down version of SGML, designed especially for Web documents. It allows designers to create their own customized tag, enabling the definition, transmission, validation, and interpretation of data between applications and between organizations.

**Extranet.** An Internet based access method to a corporate intranet site by limited or total access through a security firewall. This type of access is often used in cases of joint defense, joint venture and vendor client relationships.

**False Positive/Negative.** A result that is not correct. This may be a result of performing a process incorrectly or using a process that is not accurate.

**FAT (File Allocation Table).** An internal data table on hard drives that keeps track of where the files are stored. If a FAT is corrupt, a drive may be unusable, yet the data may be retrievable with forensics. See *Cluster File.*

**FAX.** Short for facsimile. A process of transmitting documents by scanning them to digital, converting to analog, transmitting over phone lines and reversing the process at the other end and printing.

**Fiber Optics.** Transmitting information by sending light pulses over cables made from thin strands of glass.

**Field (or Data Field).** A name for an individual piece of standardized data, such as the author of a document, a recipient, the date of a document or any other piece of data common to most documents in an image collection, to be extracted from the collection.

**Field Separator.** A code that separates the fields in a record. For example, the CSV format uses a comma as the field separator.

**File Compression.** See *Compression.*

**File Extension.** Many systems, including DOS and UNIX, allow a filename extension that consists of one or more characters following the proper filename. For example, image files are usually stored as .bmp, .gif, .jpg or .tiff. Audio files are often stored as .aud or .wav. There are a multitude of file extensions identifying file formats. The filename extension should indicate what type of file it is; however, users may change filename extensions to evade firewall restrictions or for other reasons. Therefore, file types should be identified at a binary level rather than relying on file extensions. To research file types, see (http://www.filext.com). Different applications can often recognize only a predetermined selection of file types. See also *Format.*

**File Format.** The organization or characteristics of a file that determine with which software programs it can be used. See also *Format.*

**File Level Binary Comparison.** Method of de-duplication using the digital fingerprint (hash) of a file. File Level Binary comparison ignores metadata, and can determine that "SHOPPING LIST.DOC" and "TOP SECRET.DOC" are actually the same document. See *Data Verification, Digital Fingerprint,* and *Hash coding.* See *De-Duplication.*

**File Plan.** A document containing the identifying number, title, description, and disposition authority of files held or used in an office.

**File Server.** When several or many computers are networked together in a LAN situation, one computer may be used as a storage location for files for the group. File servers may be employed to store e-mail, financial data, word processing information or to backup the network. See *Server.*

**File Sharing.** Sharing files stored on the server among several users on a network.

**File Slack.** The unused space on a cluster that exists when the logical file space is less than the physical file space.

**File System Metadata.** Data that can be obtained or extracted about a file from the file system storing the file. Examples include file creation time, last modification time, and last access time.

**File System.** The engine that an operating system or program uses to organize and kept track of files. More specifically, the logical structures and software routines used to control access to the storage on a hard disk system and the overall structure in which the files are named, stored, and organized. The file system plays a critical role in computer forensics because the file system determines the logical structure of the hard drive, including its cluster size. The file system also determines what happens to data when the user deletes a file or subdirectory.

**File Transfer.** The process of moving or transmitting a file from one location to another, as between two programs or from one computer to another.

**File.** A collection of data or information stored under a specified name on a disk.

**Filename.** The name of a file, excluding root drive and directory path information. Different operating systems may impose different restrictions on filenames, for example, by prohibiting use of certain characters in a filename or imposing a limit on the length of a filename. The filename extension should indicate what type of file it is. However, users often change filename extensions to evade firewall restrictions or for other reasons. Therefore, file types must be identified at a binary level rather than relying on file extensions. See also *File Extension* and *Full Path.*

**FIPS.** Federal Information Processing Standards issued by the National Institute of Standards and Technology after approval by the Secretary of Commerce pursuant to Section 111(d) of the Federal Property and Administrative Services Act of 1949, as amended by the Computer Security Act of 1987, Public Law 100-235.

**Firewall.** A set of related programs, or hardware, that protect the resources of a private network from users from other networks. A firewall filters information to determine whether to forward the information toward its destination.

**Filter (verb).** See *Data Filtering.*

**Flatbed Scanner.** A flat-surface scanner that allows users to input books and other documents.

**Floppy Disc.** A thin magnetic film disk housed in a protective sleeve used to copy and transport relatively small amounts of data.

**Folder.** See *Directory.*

**Forensic Copy.** A forensic copy is an exact copy of an entire physical storage media (hard drive, CD-ROM, DVD-ROM, tape, etc.), including all active and residual data and unallocated space on the media. Compresses and encrypts to ensure authentication and protect chain of custody. Forensic copies are often called "image or imaged copies." See *Bit Stream Backup and Mirroring.*

**Forensics.** Computer forensics is the scientific examination and analysis of data held on, or retrieved from, computer storage media in such a way that the information can be used as evidence in a court of law. It may include the secure collection of computer data; the examination of suspect data to determine details such as origin and content; the presentation of computer based information to courts of law; and the application of a country's laws to computer practice. Forensics may involve recreating "deleted" or missing files from hard drives, validating dates and logged in authors/editors of documents, and certifying key elements of documents and/or hardware for legal purposes.

**Form of Production.** The manner in which requested documents are produced. Used to refer both to file format (native versus PDF or TIFF) and the media on which the documents are produced (paper versus electronic).

**Format (noun).** The internal structure of a file, which defines the way it is stored and used. Specific applications may define unique formats for their data (*e.g.*, "MS Word document file format"). Many files may only be viewed or printed using their originating application or an application designed to work with compatible formats. There are several common e-mail formats, such as Outlook and Lotus Notes. Computer storage systems commonly identify files by a naming convention that denotes the format (and therefore the probable originating application). For example, "DOC" for Microsoft Word document files; "XLS" for Microsoft Excel spreadsheet files; "TXT" for text files; "HTM" for Hypertext Markup Language (HTML) files such as web pages; "PPT" for Microsoft Powerpoint files; "TIF" for tiff images; "PDF" for Adobe images; etc. Users may choose alternate naming conventions, but this will likely affect how the files are treated by applications.

**Format (verb).** Makes a drive ready for first use. Erroneously thought to "wipe" drive. Typically, only overwrites FAT, but not files on the drive.

**Forms Processing.** A specialized imaging application designed for handling pre-printed forms. Forms processing systems often use high-end (or multiple) OCR engines and elaborate data validation routines to extract handwritten or poor quality print from forms that go into a database.

**Fragmented.** In the course of normal computer operations when files are saved, deleted or moved, the files or parts thereof may be broken into pieces, or fragmented, and scattered in various locations on the computer's hard drive or other storage medium, such as removable disks. Data saved in contiguous clusters may be larger than contiguous free space, and it is broken up and randomly placed throughout the available storage space. See *De-Fragment*.

**FTP (File Transfer Protocol).** An Internet protocol that enables the transfer of files between computers over a network or the Internet.

**Full Duplex.** Data communications devices which allow full speed transmission in both directions at the same time.

**Full Path.** A path name description that includes the drive, starting or root directory, all attached subdirectories and ending with the file or object name.

**Full-Text Search.** The ability to search a data file for specific words, numbers and/or combinations or patterns thereof.

**Full-Text Indexing and Search.** Every word in the document is indexed into a master word list with pointers to the documents and pages where each occurrence of the word appears.

**Fuzzy Search.** Subjective content searching (as compared to word searching of objective data). Fuzzy Searching lets the user find documents where word matching does not have to be exact, even if the words searched are misspelled due to optical character recognition (OCR) errors.

**GAL.** A Microsoft Outlook global address list—directory of all Microsoft Exchange users and distribution lists to whom messages can be addressed. The administrator creates and maintains this list. The global address list may also contain public folder names. Entries from this list can be added to a user's personal address book.

**Ghost.** See *Bit Stream Backup.*

**GIF (Graphics Interchange Format).** CompuServe's native file format for storing images. Limited to 256 colors.

**Gigabyte (GB).** A unit of consisting of either 1,000 or 1,024 megabytes. In terms of image storage capacity, one gigabyte equals approximately 17,000 81/2 inch x 11 inch pages scanned at 300 dpi, stored as TIFF Group IV images. See *Byte.*

**GMT Timestamp.** Identification of a file using Greenwich Mean Time as the central time authentication method.

**GPS Generated Timestamp.** Timestamp identifying time as a function of its relationship to Greenwich Mean Time.

**Gray Scale.** The use of many shades of gray to represent an image. *Continuoustone* images, such as black-and-white photographs, use an almost unlimited number of shades of gray. Conventional computer hardware and software, however, can only represent a limited number of shades of gray (typically 16 or 256).

**Groupware.** Software designed to operate on a network and allow several people to work together on the same documents and files.

**GUI (Graphical User Interface, pronounced "gooey").** Presenting an interface to the computer user comprised of pictures and icons, rather than words and numbers.

**Hacker.** Someone who breaks into computer systems in order to steal, change, or destroy information.

**Half Duplex.** Transmission systems which can send and receive, but not at the same time.

**Halftone.** See *Dithering*.

**Hard Disk Drive.** The primary storage unit on PCs, consisting of one or more magnetic media platters on which digital data can be written and erased magnetically.

**Harvesting.** The process of retrieving or collecting electronic data from storage media or devices; an e-discovery vendor "harvests" electronic data from computer hard drives, file servers, CDs, and backup tapes for processing and load to storage media or a database management system.

**Hash.** A mathematical algorithm that represents a unique value for a given set of data, similar to a digital fingerprint. Common hash algorithms include MD5 and SHA.

**Hash Coding.** To create a digital fingerprint that represents the binary content of a file unique to every electronically generated document; assists in subsequently ensuring that data has not been modified. See also *Data Verification* and *Digital Fingerprint* and *File Level Binary Comparison*.

**Hash Function.** A function used to create a hash value from binary input. The hash is substantially smaller than the text itself, and is generated by the hash function in such a way that it is extremely unlikely that some other input will produce the same hash value.

**HD (High Density).** A 5.25-inch HD Floppy Disk holds 1.2 MB and a 3.5-inch holds 1.4 MB.

**Head.** Each platter on a hard drive contains a head for each side of the platter. The heads are devices which ride very closely to the surface of the platter and allow information to be read from and written to the platter.

**Hexadecimal.** A number system with a base of 16. The digits are 0–9 and A–F, where F equals the decimal value of 15.

**Hidden Files or Data.** Files or data not visible in the file directory; cannot be accessed by unauthorized or unsophisticated users. Some operating system files are hidden, to prevent inexperienced users from inadvertently deleting or changing these essential files. See also *Steganography*.

**Hierarchical Storage Management (HSM).** Software that automatically migrates files from on-line to near-line storage media, usually on the basis of the age or frequency of use of the files.

**Hold.** See *Legal Hold*.

**Holorith.** Encoded data on aperture cards *or* old-style punch cards that contained encoded data.

**Horizontal De-duplication.** A way to identify documents that are duplicated across multiple custodians or other production data sets. See *De-Duplication.*

**Host.** In a network, the central computer which controls the remote computers and holds the central databases.

**HP-PCL & HPGL.** Hewlett-Packard graphics file formats.

**HTML.** HyperText Markup Language, developed by CERN of Geneva, Switzerland. The document standard of choice of Internet. (HTML+ adds support for multi-media.) The tag-based ASCII language used to create pages on the World Wide Web—uses tags to tell a web browser to display text and images.

**HTTP (HyperText Transfer Protocol).** The underlying protocol used by the World Wide Web. HTTP defines how messages are formatted and transmitted, and what actions Web servers and browsers should take in response to various commands. For example, when you enter a URL in your browser, this actually sends an HTTP command to the *Web server* directing it to fetch and transmit the requested Web page.

**Hub.** A network device that connects multiple computers/peripherals together and allows them to share data. A central unit that repeats and/or amplifies data signals being sent across a network.

**Hyperlink.** A link—usually appearing as a highlighted word or picture within a hypertext document—that when clicked changes the active view, possibly to another place within the same document or view, or to another document altogether, usually regardless of the application or environment in which the other document or view exists.

**HyperText.** Text that includes links or shortcuts to other documents or views, allowing the reader to easily jump from one view to a related view in a nonlinear fashion.

**Icon.** In a GUI, a picture or drawing which is activated by "clicking" a mouse to command the computer program to perform a predefined series of events.

**ICR (Intelligent Character Recognition).** The conversion of scanned images (bar codes or patterns of bits) to computer recognizable codes (ASCII characters and files) by means of software/programs which define the rules of and algorithms for conversion.

**IDE (Integrated Drive Electronics).** An engineering standard for interfacing PCs and hard disks.

**IEEE (Institute of Electrical and Electronic Engineers).** An international association which sponsors meetings, publishes a number of journals and establishes standards.

**ILM.** Information lifecycle management.

**Image.** To image a hard drive is to make an identical copy of the hard drive, including empty sectors. Also known as creating a "mirror image" or "mirroring" the drive.

**Image Copy, Imaged Copy.** See *Forensic Copy*.

**Image Enabling.** A software function that creates links between existing applications and stored images.

**Image File Format.** See *File Format and Format*.

**Image Key.** The name of a file created when a page is scanned in a collection.

**Image Processing Card (IPC).** A board mounted in the computer, scanner or printer that facilitates the acquisition and display of images. The primary function of most IPCs is the rapid compression and decompression of image files.

**Image Processing.** To capture an image or representation, usually from electronic data in native format, enter it in a computer system, and process and manipulate it. See also *Native Format*.

**Import.** Data brought into an environment or application which has been exported from another environment or application.

**Inactive Record.** Inactive records are those Records related to closed, completed, or concluded activities. Inactive Records are no longer routinely referenced, but must be retained in order to fulfill reporting requirements or for purposes of audit or analysis. Inactive records generally reside in a long-term storage format remaining accessible for purposes of business processing only with restrictions on alteration. In some business circumstances inactive records may be re-activated.

**Index/Coding Fields.** Data-base fields used to categorize and organize documents. Often user-defined, these fields can be used for searches.

**Index.** The searchable catalog of documents created by search engine software. Also called "catalog." Index is often used as a synonym for search engine.

**Indexing.** Universal term for Coding and Data Entry.

**Information.** For the purposes of this document, information is used to mean both documents and data.

**Input device.** Any peripheral that allows a user to communicate with a computer by entering information or issuing commands (e.g., keyboard).

**Instant Messaging ("IM").** A form of electronic communication involving immediate correspondence between two or more online users. Peer-to-peer IM communications may not be stored on servers after receipt; logging of peer-to-peer IM messages is typically done on the client computer, and may be optionally enabled or disabled on each client.

**Interlaced.** TV and CRT pictures must constantly be "refreshed." Interlace is to refresh *every other* line once/refresh cycle. Since only half the information displayed is updated each cycle, interlaced displays are less expensive than "noninterlaced." However, interlaced displays are subject to jitters. The human eye/brain can usually detect displayed images which are completely refreshed at less than 30 times per second.

**Interleave.** To arrange data in a noncontiguous way to increase performance. When used to describe disk drives, it refers to the way sectors on a disk are organized. In one-to-one interleaving, the sectors are placed sequentially around each track. In two-to-one interleaving, sectors are staggered so that consecutively numbered sectors are separated by an intervening sector. The purpose of interleaving is to make the disk drive more efficient. The disk drive can access only one sector at a time, and the disk is constantly spinning beneath.

**International Telecommunication Union (ITU).** An international organization under the UN headquartered in Geneva concerned with telecommunications that develops international data communications standards; known as CCITT prior to March 1, 1993. See http://www.itu.int.

**Internet Publishing.** Specialized imaging software that allows documents to be published on the Internet

**Internet.** A worldwide network of networks that all use the TCP/IP communications protocol and share a common address space. It supports services such as e-mail, the World Wide Web, file transfer, and Internet Relay Chat. Also known as "the net," "the information superhighway," and "cyberspace."

**Inter-Partition Space.** Unused sectors on a track located between the start of the partition and the partition boot record. This space is important because it is possible for a user to hide information here.

**Intranet.** A private network that uses Internet-related technologies to provide services within an organization.

**IP address (Internet Protocol address).** A string of four numbers separated by periods used to represent a computer on the Internet—a unique identifier for the physical location of the server containing the data. See *TCP/IP* (e.g., 206.143.200.1).

**IPX/SPX.** Communications protocol used by Novell networks.

**IS/IT Information Systems or Information Technology.** Usually refers to the people who make computers and computer systems run.

**ISA.** Industry Standard Architecture.

**ISDN (Integrated Services Digital Network).** An all digital network that can carry data, video and voice.

**ISIS and TWAIN Scanner Drivers.** Specialized applications used for communication between scanners and computers.

**ISO 9660 CD Format.** The International Standards Organization format for creating CD-ROMs that can be read worldwide.

**ISO.** International Standards Organization.

**ISP (Internet Service Provider).** A business that provides access to the Internet, usually for a monthly fee. ISPs may be a source of evidence through files (such as ISP e-mail) stored on ISP servers.

**IT (Information Technology) Infrastructure.** The overall makeup of business-wide technology operations, including mainframe operations, standalone systems, e-mail, networks (WAN and LAN), Internet access, customer databases, enterprise systems, application support, regardless of whether managed, used or provided locally, regionally, globally, etc., or whether performed or located internally or by outside providers (outsourced to vendors). The IT Infrastructure also includes applicable standard practices and procedures, such as backup procedures, versioning, resource sharing, retention practices, janitor program use, and the like.

**Janitor Program.** An application which runs at scheduled intervals to manage business information by deleting, transferring, or archiving on-line data (such as e-mail) which is at or past its scheduled active life. Janitor programs are sometimes referred to as "agents"—software that runs autonomously "behind the scenes" on user systems and servers to carry out business processes according to pre-defined rules. Janitor programs must include a facility to support disposition and process holds.

**Java.** Sun Microsystems' Java is a platform-independent, programming language for adding animation and other actions to Web sites.

**Jaz Drive.** A removable disk drive. A Jaz drive holds up to 2 GB of data. Commonly used for backup storage as well as everyday use.

**JMS.** Jukebox Management Software.

**Journal.** A chronological record of data processing operations that may be used to reconstruct a previous or an updated version of a file. In data-base-management systems, it is the record of all stored data items that have values changed as a result of processing and manipulation of the data.

**Journaling.** A function of e-mail systems (such as Microsoft Exchange and Lotus Notes) that copies sent and received items into a second information store for retention or preservation. Because Journaling takes place at the information store (server) level when the items are sent or received, rather than at the mailbox (client) level, some message-related metadata, such as user foldering (what folder the item is stored in within the recipient's mailbox) and the status of the "read" flag, is not retained in the journaled copy. The Journaling function stores items in the system's native format, unlike e-mail archiving solutions, which use proprietary storage formats that are designed to reduce the amount of storage space required. Journaling systems also lack the sophisticated search and retrieval capabilities contained in e-mail archiving solutions.

**JPEG (Joint Photographic Experts Group).** A compression algorithm for still images that is commonly used on the web.

**Jukebox.** A mass storage device that holds optical disks and loads them into a drive.

**Juke-Box.** Automated disk changer for high-performance, centralized storage for multifunction CD-ROMs and optical disks.

**Jump Drive.** See *Key Drive.*

**Kerning.** Adjusting the spacing between two letters.

**Key Drive.** A small removable data storage device that uses Flash memory and connects via a USB port. Keydrives are also known as keychain drive, thumb drive, jump drive, USB Flash drive. Can be imaged and may contain residual data.

**Key Field.** Data-base fields used for document searches and retrieval.

**Keyword Search.** A search of the text of documents in a data-base for documents containing one or more words that are specified by a user.

**Keywords.** Words designated by a user as important for searching purposes.

**Kilobyte (KB).** A unit of 1,024 bytes. See *Byte.*

**Kofax Board.** The generic term for a series of image processing boards manufactured by Kofax Imaging Processing. These are used between the scanner and the computer, and perform real-time image compression and decompression for faster image viewing, image enhancement, and corrections to the input to account for conditions such as document misalignment.

**LAN (Local Area Network).** A group of computers at a single location (usually an office or home) that are connected by phone lines or coaxial cable. See *Network.*

**Landscape Mode.** The image is represented on the page or monitor such that the width is greater than the height.

**Laser Disc.** Same as an optical CD, except 12 inches in diameter.

**Laser Printing.** A beam of light hits an electrically charged drum and causes a discharge at that point. Toner is then applied which sticks to the noncharged areas. Paper is pressed against the drum to form the image and is then heated to dry the toner. Used in laser printers and copying machines.

**Latency.** The time it takes to read a disk (or jukebox), including the time to physically position the media under the read/write head, seek the correct address and transfer it.

**Latent Data.** Latent or ambient data are deleted files and other data that are inaccessible without specialized forensic tools and techniques. Until over-written, these data reside on media such as a hard drive in unused space and other areas available for data storage.

**Leading/Ledding.** The amount of space between lines of printed text.

**Legacy Data, Legacy System.** Legacy Data is information the development of which an organization may have invested significant resources and has re-tained its importance, but has been created or stored by the use of software and/or hardware that has become obsolete or replaced ("legacy systems"). Legacy data may be costly to restore or reconstruct when required for in-vestigation or litigation analysis or discovery.

**Legal Hold.** A legal hold is a communication issued as a result of current or anticipated litigation, audit, government investigation or other such matter that suspends the normal disposition or processing of records. Legal holds can encompass business procedures affecting active data, including, but not limited to, backup tape recycling. The specific communication to busi-ness or IT organizations may also be called a "hold," "preservation order," "suspension order," "freeze notice," "hold order," or "hold notice."

**Level Coding.** Used in Bibliographical coding to facilitate different treatment, such as prioritization or more thorough extraction of data, for different cat-egories of documents, such as by type or source.

**LFP.** IPRO Tech's image cross reference file; an ASCII delimited text file re-quired for cross-reference of images to data.

**Lifecycle.** The records lifecycle is the life span of a record from its creation or receipt to its final disposition. It is usually described in three stages: cre-ation, maintenance and use, and archive to final disposition.

**Line Screen.** The number of half-tone dots that can be printed per inch. As a general rule, newspapers print at 65 to 85 lpi.

**Link.** See *Hyperlink*.

**Load file.** A file that relates to a set of scanned images and indicates where in-dividual pages belong together as documents. A load file may also contain data relevant to the individual documents, such as metadata, coded data and the like. Load files must be obtained and provided in prearranged for-mats to ensure transfer of accurate and usable images and data.

**Local Area Network (LAN).** See *Network*.

**Logical File Space.** The actual amount of space occupied by a file on a hard drive. The amount of logical file space differs from the physical file space because when a file is created on a computer, a sufficient number of clusters (physical file space) are assigned to contain the file. If the file (logical file space) is not large enough to completely fill the assigned clusters (physical file space) then some unused space will exist within the physical file space.

**Logical Volume.** An area on the hard drive that has been formatted for files storage. A hard drive may contain a single or multiple volumes.

**Lossless Compression.** Exact construction of image, bit-by-bit, with no loss of information.

**Lossy Compression.** Reduces storage size of image by reducing the resolution and color fidelity while maintaining minimum acceptable standard for general use.

**LTO (Linear Tape-Open).** A type of backup tape which can hold as much as 400 GB of data, or 600 CDs depending on the data file format.

**LZW (Lempel-Ziv & Welch).** A common, lossless compression standard for computer graphics, used for most TIFF files. Typical compression ratios are 4:1.

**Magenta.** Used in four color printing. Reflects blue and red and absorbs green.

**Magnetic/Optical Storage Media.** Includes, but is not limited to, hard drives, backup tapes, CD-ROMs, DVD-ROMs, Jaz and Zip drives.

**Magneto-Optical Drive.** A drive that combines laser and magnetic technology to create high-capacity erasable storage.

**Mailbox.** An area on a storage device where e-mail is placed. In e-mail systems, each user has a private mailbox. When the user receives e-mail, the mail system automatically puts it in the appropriate mailbox.

**Make-Available Production.** A process whereby what is usually a large universe of all potentially responsive documents are made available to the requestor; from this universe, the requestor then reviews and selects or tags the documents which they wish to obtain, and the producing party produces to the requestor only the selected documents. This is sometimes done under an agreement protecting against privilege and confidentiality waiver during the initial make available production; and the producing party, after the requestor has selected the documents they wish to obtain, reviews only the selected documents for privilege and confidentiality before the selected documents are physically produced to the requestor.

**MAPI (Mail Application Program Interface).** A Windows software standard that has become a popular e-mail interface used by MS Exchange, Group-Wise, and other e-mail packages.

**MAPI Mail Near-Line.** Documents stored on optical disks or compact discs that are housed in the jukebox or CD changer and can be retrieved without human intervention.

**Marginalia.** Handwritten notes in the margin of the page in documents.

**Master Boot Record.** See *Boot Sector.*

**Mastering.** Making many copies of a disk from a single master disk.

**MCA (Micro Channel Architecture).** An IBM bus standard.

**MDE (Magnetic Disk Emulation).** Software that makes a jukebox look and operate like a hard drive such that it will respond to all the I/O commands ordinarily sent to a hard drive.

**MD5.** Message-digest algorithm meant for digital signature applications where a large message has to be "compressed" in a secure manner before being signed with the private key

**Media.** An object or device, such as a disk, tape, or other device, on which data is stored

**Megabyte (M or MB).** A unit of approximately 1 million bytes or 1024 KB. See *Byte.*

**Memory.** Data storage in the form of chips, or the actual chips used to hold data; "storage" is used to describe memory that exists on tapes or disks. See RAM and ROM.

**Menu.** A list of options, each of which performs a desired action such as choosing a command or applying a particular format to a part of a document.

**Message Header.** Message headers generally contain the identities of the author and recipients, the subject of the message, and the date the message was sent.

**Metadata.** Metadata is information about a particular data set or document which describes how, when and by whom it was collected, created, accessed, and modified and how it is formatted. Can be altered intentionally or inadvertently. Can be extracted when native files are converted to image. Some metadata, such as file dates and sizes, can easily be seen by users; other metadata can be hidden or embedded and unavailable to computer users who are not technically adept. Metadata is generally not reproduced in full form when a document is printed. See also *Customer-Added Metadata, Document Metadata, E-mail Metadata, File System Metadata, User-Added Metadata,* and *Vendor-Added Metadata.* For a thorough discussion of Metadata, see *The Sedona Guidelines: Best Practice Guidelines & Commentary for Managing Information & Records in the Electronic Age,* Appendix D: *Technical Appendix.*

**Metadata Comparison.** A method of de-duplication that compares file metadata and ignores content. See *De-Duplication.*

**MFT (Master File Table).** Index to files on a computer. If corrupt, a drive may be unusable, yet data may be retrievable using forensic methods.

**MICR (Magnetic Ink Character Recognition).** The process used by banks to encode checks.

**Microfiche.** Sheet microfilm (4 inch by 6 inch) containing reduced images of 270 pages or more in a grid pattern.

**Migrated Data.** Migrated Data is information that has been moved from one database or format to another.

**Migration.** Moving files to another computer application or platform; may require conversion to a different format.

**Mirroring.** The duplication of data for purposes of backup or to distribute Internet or network traffic among several servers with identical data. See also *Disk Mirroring.*

**MIS.** Management Information Systems.

**MODEM.** Modulator/Demodulator. A device translates digital data from a computer into analog signals (modulates) and transmits the information over telephones lines. Another modem at the receiving computer will receive the information, translate it back from analog to digital (demodulate) and store it.

**Monochrome.** Displays capable of only two colors, usually black and white, or black and green.

**Mosaic.** A web browser popular before the introduction of Netscape and Internet Explorer.

**Mount, Mounting.** The process of making off-line data available for on-line processing. For example, placing a magnetic tape in a drive and setting up the software to recognize or read that tape. The terms "load" and "loading" are often used in conjunction with, or synonymously with, "mount" and "mounting" (as in "mount and load a tape"). "Load" may also refer to the process of transferring data from mounted media to another media or to an on-line system.

**MPEG-1 and -2.** Two different standards for full motion video to digital compression/decompression techniques advanced by the Moving Pictures Experts Group. MPEG-1 compresses 30 frames/second of full-motion video down to about 1.5 Mbits/sec from several hundred megabytes. MPEG-2 compresses the same files down to about 3.0 Mbits/sec and provides better image quality.

**MS-DOS.** Microsoft (MS)-Disk Operating System. Used in PCs as the control system.

**MTBF (Mean Time Between Failure).** Average time between failures. Used to compute the reliability of devices/equipment.

**MTTR (Mean Time To Repair).** Average time to repair. The higher the number, the more costly and difficult to fix.

**Multimedia.** The combined use of different media; integrated video, audio, text and data graphics in digital form.

**Multisynch.** Analog video monitors which can receive a wide range of display resolutions, usually including TV (NTSC). Color analog monitors accept separate red, green, and blue (RGB) signals.

**Native Format.** Electronic documents have an associated file structure defined by the original creating application. This file structure is referred to as the "native format" of the document. Because viewing or searching documents in the native format may require the original application (for example, viewing a Microsoft Word document may require the Microsoft Word application), documents are often converted to a vendor-neutral format as part of the record acquisition or archive process. "Static" formats (often called "imaged formats"), such as TIFF or PDF, are designed to retain an image of the document as it would look viewed in the original creating application but do not allow metadata to be viewed or the document information to be manipulated.

**Natural Language Search.** A manner of searching that permits the use of plain language without special connectors or precise terminology, such as "Where can I find information on William Shakespeare?" as opposed to formulating a search statement, such as "information" and "William Shakespeare."

**Near-Line Data.** A term used to refer to data or a robotic storage device (robotic library) that houses removable media, uses robotic arms to access the media, and uses multiple read/write devices to store and retrieve records. Examples include optical disks.

**Near-Line Data Storage.** Storage in a system that is not a direct part of the network in daily use, but that can be accessed through the network. There is usually a small time lag between the request for data stored in near-line media and its being made available to an application or end-user. Making near-line data available will not require human intervention (as opposed to "off-line" data which can only be made available through human actions).

**Network Gear.** Refers to the actual hardware used in the operation of networks—for example routers, switches, and hubs.

**Network.** A group of two or more computers and other devices connected together ("networked") for the exchange and sharing of data and resources. A local-area network (LAN) refers to connected computers and devices geographically close together (i.e., in the same building). A wide-area network (WAN) refers generally to a network of PCs or other devices, remote to each other, connected by telecommunications lines. Typically, a WAN may connect two or more LANs together.

**Neural Network.** Neural networks are made up of interconnected processing elements called units, which respond in parallel to a set of input signals given to each

**NIST (National Institute of Standards and Technology).** A federal technology agency that works with industry to develop and apply technology measurements and standards.

**Node.** Any device connected to a network. PCs, servers, and printers are all nodes on the network.

**Noninterlace.** When each line of a video image is scanned separately. Computer monitors use noninterlaced video.

**NOS (Network Operating System).** See *Operating System.*

**NSF.** Lotus Notes Format Database File (i.e., database.nsf) Can be either an e-mail database or the traditional type of fielded database.

**Objects.** In programming terminology, an object is a freestanding block of code that defines the properties of some thing. Objects are created and used in a high-level method of programming called object-oriented programming (OOP). OOP involves giving programming objects characteristics that can be transferred to, added to, and combined with other objects to make a complete program.

**OCR (Optical Character Recognition).** A technology process that translates and converts printed matter on an image into a format that a computer can manipulate (ASCII codes, for example) and, therefore, renders that matter text searchable. OCR software evaluates scanned data for shapes it recognizes as letters or numerals. All OCR systems include an optical scanner for reading text, and software for analyzing images. Most OCR systems use a combination of hardware (specialized circuit boards) and software to recognize characters, although some inexpensive systems operate entirely through software. Advanced OCR systems can read text in a large variety of fonts, but still have difficulty with handwritten text. OCR technology relies upon the quality of the imaged material, the conversion accuracy of the software, and the quality control process of the provider. The process is generally acknowledged to be only 80–85 percent accurate.

**Official Record Owner.** See *Record Owner.*

**Off-Line Data.** The storage of electronic data outside the network in daily use (e.g., on backup tapes) that is only accessible through the off-line storage system, not the network.

**Off-Line Storage.** Electronic records stored or archived on removable disk (optical, compact, etc.) or magnetic tape used for making disaster-recovery copies of records for which retrieval is unlikely. Accessibility to off-line media usually requires manual intervention and is much slower than on-line or near-line storage depending on the storage facility. The major difference between near-line data and offline data is that offline data lacks an intelligent disk subsystem, and is not connected to a computer, network, or any other readily accessible system.

**OLE.** Object Linking and Embedding. A feature in Microsoft's Windows which allows each section of a compound document to call up its own editing tools or special display features. This allows for combining diverse elements in compound documents.

**On-Line Review.** The culling process produces a data set of potentially responsive documents which are then reviewed for a final selection of relevant or responsive documents and assertion of privilege exception as appropriate. On-line Review enables the culled data set to be accessed via PC or other terminal device via a local network or remotely via the Internet. Often, the On-Line Review process is facilitated by specialized software which provides additional features and functions which may include: collaborative access of multiple reviewers, security, user logging, search and retrieval, document coding, redaction, and privilege logging.

**On-Line Storage.** The storage of electronic data as fully accessible information in daily use on the network or elsewhere.

**Online/On-Line.** Connected (to a network).

**Operating System (OS).** An Operating system provides the software platform which directs the overall activity of a computer, network or system, and on which all other software programs and applications can run. In many ways, choice of an operating system will effect which applications can be run. Operating systems perform basic tasks, such as recognizing input from the keyboard, sending output to the display screen, keeping track of files and directories on the disk and controlling peripheral devices such as disk drives and printers. For large systems, the operating system has even greater responsibilities and powers—becoming a traffic cop to makes sure different programs and users running at the same time do not interfere with each other. The operating system is also responsible for security, ensuring that unauthorized users do not access the system. Examples of operating systems are UNIX, DOS, Windows, LINUX, Macintosh, and IBM's VM. Operating systems can be classified in a number of ways, including: multiuser (allows two or more users to run programs at the same time—some operating systems permit hundreds or even thousands of concurrent users); multiprocessing (supports running a program on more than one CPU); multitasking (allows more than one program to run concurrently); multithreading (allows different parts of a single program to run concurrently); and real time (instantly responds to input—general-purpose operating systems, such as DOS and UNIX, are not real-time).

**Optical Disks.** Computer media similar to a compact disc that cannot be rewritten. An optical drive uses a laser to read the stored data.

**Optical Jukebox.** See "Jukebox."

**OST.** A Microsoft Outlook information store that is used to save folder information that can be accessed offline.

**Overwrite.** To record or copy new data over existing data, as in when a file or directory is updated. Data that is overwritten cannot be retrieved.

**PAB.** A Microsoft Outlook list of recipients created and maintained by an individual user for personal use. The personal address book is a subset of the global address list (GAL).

**PackBits.** A compression scheme which originated with the Macintosh. Suitable only for black and white.

**Packet.** A unit of data sent across a network that may contain identify and routing information. When a large block of data is to be sent over a network, it is broken up into several packets, sent, and then reassembled at the other end. The exact layout of an individual packet is determined by the protocol being used.

**Page File/Paging File.** A file used to temporarily store code and data for programs that are currently running. This information is left in the swap file after the programs are terminated, and may be retrieved using forensic techniques. Also referred to as a swap file.

**Page.** A single image of the equivalent of "one piece of paper." One or several pages make up a "Document."

**Parallel.** Transmission of all the bits (e.g., in a character) at the same time. If the character has eight bits, there are eight wires. Faster and more expensive than serial where the eight bits would be sent, "sideways," one at a time.

**Partition.** A partition is an individual section of computer storage media such as a hard drive. For example a single hard drive may be divided into several partitions. When a hard drive is divided into partitions, each partition is designated by a separate drive letter, i.e., C, D, etc.

**Partition Table.** The partition table indicates each logical volume contained on a disk and its location.

**Partition Waste Space.** After the boot sector of each volume or partition is written to a track, it is customary for the system to skip the rest of that track and begin the actual useable area of the volume on the next track. This results in unused or "wasted" space on that track where information can be hidden. This "wasted space" can only be viewed with a low level disk viewer. However, forensic techniques can be used to search these "wasted space" areas for hidden information.

**Password.** A secret code used, usually along with a user ID, in order to log on or gain access to a PC, network or other secure system, site or application.

**Path.** The hierarchical description of where a directory, folder, or file is located on a computer or network. In DOS and Windows systems, a path is a list of directories where the operating system looks for executable files if it is unable to find the file in the working directory. The list of directories can be specified with the PATH command. Path is also used to refer to a transmission channel, the path between two nodes of a network that a data communication follows, and the physical cabling that connects the nodes on a network.

**Pattern Matching.** A generic term that describes any process that compares one file's content with another file's content.

**Pattern Recognition.** Technology that searches data for like patterns and flags, and extracts the pertinent data, usually using an algorithm. For instance, in looking for addresses, alpha characters followed by a comma and a space, followed by two capital alpha characters, followed by a space, followed by five or more digits, are usually the city, state and zip code. By programming the application to look for a pattern, the information can be electronically identified, extracted, or otherwise used or manipulated.

**PCI.** Peripheral Component Interface (Interconnect). A high-speed interconnect local bus used to support multimedia devices.

**PCMCIA.** Personal Computer Memory Card International Association. Plug-in cards for computers (usually portables), which extend the storage and/or functionality.

**PDA (Personal Digital Assistant).** A small, usually hand-held, computer that "assists" business tasks.

**PDF (Portable Document Format).** An imaging file format technology developed by Adobe Systems. PDF captures formatting information from a variety of applications in such a way that they can be viewed and printed as they were intended in their original application by practically any computer, on multiple platforms, regardless of the specific application in which the original was created. PDF files may be text-searchable or image-only. Adobe® Reader, a free application distributed by Adobe Systems, is required to view a file in PDF format. Adobe® Acrobat, an application marketed by Adobe Systems, is required to edit, capture text, or otherwise manipulate a file in PDF format.

**Personal Computer (PC).** Computer based on a microprocessor and designed to be used by one person at a time

**Petabyte (PB).** A unit consisting of 1,000 or 1,024 terabytes. See *Byte*.

**Phase Change.** A method of storing information on rewritable optical disks.

**Physical Ddisc.** An actual piece of computer media, such as the hard disk or drive, floppy disks, CD-ROM disks, Zip disks, etc.

**Physical File Space.** When a file is created on a computer, a sufficient number of clusters (physical file space) are assigned to contain the file. If the file (logical file space) is not large enough to completely fill the assigned clusters (physical file space) then some unused space will exist within the physical file space. This unused space is referred to as file slack and can contain unused space, previously deleted/overwritten files or fragments thereof.

**PICA.** One sixth (1/6) of an inch. Used to measure graphics/fonts. There are 12 points per pica; 6 picas per inch; 72 points per inch.

**Picture Element.** The smallest addressable unit on a display screen. The higher the resolution (the more rows of columns), the more information can be displayed.

**Pitch.** Characters (or dots) per inch, measured horizontally.

**PKI Digital Signature.** A document or file may be digitally signed using a party's private signature key, creating a "digital signature" that is stored with the document. Anyone can validate the signature on the document using the public key from the digital certificate issued to the signer. Validating the digital signature confirms who signed it, and ensures that no alterations have been made to the document since it was signed. Similarly, an e-mail message may be digitally signed using commonly available client software that implements an open standard for this purpose, such as Secure Multipurpose Internet Mail Extensions (S/MIME). Validating the signature on the e-mail can help the recipient know with confidence who sent it, and that it was not altered during transmission. See *Certificate*.

**Plaintext.** The least formatted and therefore most portable form of text for computerized documents.

**Platter.** One of several components that make up a computer hard drive. Platters are thin, rapidly rotating disks that have a set of read/write heads on both sides of each platter. Each platter is divided into a series of concentric rings called tracks. Each track is further divided into sections called sectors, and each sector is subdivided into bytes.

**PMS (Pantone Matching System).** A color standard in printing.

**POD (Print on Demand).** Document images are stored in electronic format and are available to be quickly printed and in the exact quantity required, long or short runs.

**Pointer.** A pointer is an index entry in the directory of a disk (or other storage medium) that identifies the space on the disk in which an electronic document or piece of electronic data resides, thereby preventing that space from being overwritten by other data. In most cases, when an electronic document is "deleted," the pointer is deleted, which allows the document to be overwritten, but the document is not actually erased.

**Portable Volumes.** A feature that facilitates the moving of large volumes of documents without requiring copying multiple files. Portable volumes enable individual CDs to be easily regrouped, detached and reattached to different databases for a broader information exchange.

**Portrait Mode.** A display where the height exceeds the width.

**Preservation.** The process of ensuring retention and protection from destruction or deletion all potentially relevant evidence, including electronic metadata. See also *Spoliation*.

**Preservation Notice, Preservation Order.** See *Legal Hold*.

**Printout.** A printed version of text of data, another term for which is hard copy.

**Private Network.** A network that is connected to the Internet but is isolated from the Internet with security measures allowing use of the network only by persons within the private network.

**Privilege Data Set.** The universe of documents identified as responsive and/or relevant, but withheld from production on the grounds of attorney-client privilege or work product.

**Processing Data.** In the context of this document, synonymous with Image Processing.

**Production.** The process of delivering to another party, or making available for that party's review, documents deemed responsive to a discovery request.

**Production Data Set.** The universe of documents identified as responsive to document requests and not withheld on the grounds of attorney-client privilege or work product.

**Production De-Duplication.** Removal of a document if multiple copies of that document reside within the same production set. For example, if two identical documents are both marked responsive, nonprivileged, production de-duplication ensures that only one of those documents is produced. See *De-Duplication.*

**Production Number.** Often referred to as the BATES number. A sequential number assigned to every page of a production for tracking and reference purposes. Often used in conjunction with a suffix or prefix to identify the producing party, the litigation, or other relevant information. See also *Bates Number.*

**Program.** See *Application* and *Software.*

**Properties.** Fields of electronic information, or "metadata," associated with a record or document such as creation date, author, date modified, blind cc's and date received.

**Protocol.** Defines a common series of rules, signals and conventions that allow different kinds of computers and applications to communicate over a network. One of the most common protocols for networks is called TCP/IP.

**Proximity Search.** For text searches, the ability to look for words or phrases within a prescribed distance of another word or phrase, such as "accident" within 5 words of "tire."

**Public Network.** A network that is part of the public Internet.

**PST.** A Microsoft Outlook e-mail store. Multiple .pst files may exist and contain archived e-mail.

**QBIC (Query by Image Content).** An IBM search system for stored images which allows the user to sketch an image, and then search the image files to find those which most closely match. The user can specify color and texture—such as "sandy beaches" or "clouds."

**Quality Control (QC).** Steps taken to ensure that results of a given task, product or service are of sufficiently high quality; the operational techniques and activities that are used to fulfill requirements for quality. In document handling and management processes, this includes image quality (resolution, skew, speckle, legibility, etc.), and data quality (correct information in appropriate fields, validated data for dates, addresses, names/issues lists, etc.).

**Quarter Inch Cartridge (QIC).** Digital recording tape, 2000 feet long, with an uncompressed capacity of 5 GB.

**Query.** A request for specific information from a database or other data set.

**Queue.** A sequence of items such as packets or print jobs waiting to be processed. For example, a print queue holds files that are waiting to be printed.

**RAID (Redundant Array of Independent Disks).** A method of storing data on servers that usually combines multiple hard drives into one logical unit thereby increasing capacity, reliability and backup capability. RAID systems may vary in levels of redundancy, with no redundancy being a single, non-mirrored disk as level 0, two disks that mirror each other as level 1, on up, with level 5 being one of the most common. RAID systems are more complicated to copy and restore.

**RAM (Random Access Memory).** Hardware inside a computer that retains memory on a short-term basis and stores information while the computer is in use. It is the "working memory" of the computer into which the operating system, startup applications, and drivers are loaded when a computer is turned on, or where a program subsequently started up is loaded, and where thereafter, these applications are executed. RAM can be read or written in any section with one instruction sequence. It helps to have more of this "working space" installed when running advanced operating systems and applications. RAM content is erased each time a computer is turned off. See *Dynamic Random Access Memory—DRAM*.

**Raster/Rasterized (Raster or Bitmap Drawing).** A method of representing an image with a grid (or "map") of dots. Typical raster file formats are GIF, JPEG, TIFF, PCX, BMP, etc.

**Record.** Information created, received, and maintained as evidence and information by an organization or person, in pursuance of legal obligations or in the transaction of business (ISO 15489(1)).

**Record Custodian.** A records custodian is an individual responsible for the physical storage and protection of records throughout their retention period. In the context of electronic records custodianship may not be a direct part of the records management function in all organizations. For example, some organizations may place this responsibility within their Information Technology Department, or they may assign responsibility for retaining and preserving records with individual employees.

**Record Lifecycle.** The time period from which a record is created until it is disposed.

**Record Owner.** The records owner is the subject matter expert on the contents of the record and is responsible for the lifecycle management of the record. This may be, but is not necessarily, the author of the record.

**Record Series.** A description of a particular set of records within a file plan. Each category has retention and disposition data associated with it, applied to all record folders and records within the category. (DOD 5015)

**Record Submitter.** The Record Submitter is the person who enters a record in an application or system. This may be, but is not necessarily, the author or the record owner.

**Record.** Information, regardless of medium or format that has value to an organization. Collectively the term is used to describe both documents and recorded data.

**Records Hold.** See *Legal Hold.*

**Records Management.** Records Management is the planning, controlling, directing, organizing, training, promoting, and other managerial activities involving the life-cycle of information, including creation, maintenance (use, storage, retrieval), and disposition, regardless of media.

**Records Manager.** The records manager is responsible for the implementation of a records management program in keeping with the policies and procedures that govern that program, including the identification, classification, handling and disposition of the organization's records throughout their retention life. The physical storage and protection of records may be a component of this individual's functions, but it may also be delegated to someone else. See *Records Custodian.*

**Records Retention Period, Retention Period.** The length of time a given records series must be kept, expressed as either a time period (e.g., four years), an event or action (e.g., audit), or a combination (e.g., six months after audit).

**Records Retention Schedule.** A plan for the management of records listing types of records and how long they should be kept; the purpose is to provide continuing authority to dispose of or transfer records to historical archives.

**Records Store.** See *Repository for Electronic Records.*

**Recover, Recovery.** See *Restore.*

**Redaction.** A portion of an image or document is intentionally concealed to prevent disclosure of specific portions. Often done to avoid production of privileged or irrelevant materials.

**Refresh Rate.** The number of times per second a display (such as on a CRT or TV) is updated.

**Region (of an image).** An area of an image file that is selected for specialized processing. Also called a "zone."

**Registration.** Lining up a forms image to determine which fields are where. Also, entering pages into a scanner such that they are correctly read.

**Relative Path.** An implied path.

**Remote Access.** The ability to access and use digital information from a location off-site from where the information is physically located. For example, to use a computer, modem, and some remote access software to connect to a network from a distant location.

**Render Images.** To take a native format electronic file and convert it to an image that appears as the original format file as if printed to paper.

**Report.** Formatted output of a system providing specific information.

**Repository for Electronic Records.** Repository for Electronic Records is a direct access device on which the electronic records and associated metadata are stored. (DoD 5015) Sometimes called a "records store" or "records archive."

**Residual Data.** Residual Data (sometimes referred to as "Ambient Data") refers to data that is not active on a computer system. Residual data includes (1) data found on media free space; (2) data found in file slack space; and (3) data within files that has functionally been deleted in that it is not visible using the application with which the file was created, without use of undelete or special data recovery techniques. May contain copies of deleted files, Internet files and file fragments.

**Resolution.** See *DPI.*

**Restore.** To transfer data from a backup medium (such as tapes) to an on-line system, often for the purpose of recovery from a problem, failure, or disaster. Restoration of archival media is the transfer of data from an archival store to an on-line system for the purposes of processing (such as query, analysis, extraction, or disposition of that data). Archival restoration of systems may require not only data restoration but also replication of the original hardware and software operating environment. Restoration of systems is often called "recovery."

**Retention Schedule.** See *Records Retention Schedule.*

**Reverse Engineering.** The process of analyzing a system to identify its intricacies and their interrelationships, and create depictions of the system in another form or at a higher level. Reverse engineering is usually undertaken in order to redesign the system for better maintainability or to produce a copy of a system without using the design from which it was originally produced. For example, one might take the executable code of a computer program, run it to study how it behaved with different input, and then attempt to write a program that behaved the same or better.

**Review.** The culling process produces a data set of potentially responsive documents which are then examined and evaluated for a final selection of relevant or responsive documents and assertion of privilege exception as appropriate. Also see *On-Line Review.*

**Rewriteable Technology.** Storage devices where the data may be written more than once—typically hard drives, floppies and optical disks.

**RFC822.** Standard that specifies a syntax for text messages that are sent among computer users, within the framework of e-mail.

**RGB (Red, Green, and Blue).** The three primary colors in the additive color family that create all the computer color video signals for a computer's color terminal.

**RIP.** The procedures used to unbundle e-mail collections into individual e-mails during the e-discovery process while preserving authenticity and ownership.

**RIM.** Records and information management.

**RLE (Run Length Encoded).** Compressed image format; supports only 256 colors; most effective on images with large areas of black or white.

**ROM (Read Only Memory).** Random memory which can be read but not written or changed. Also, hardware, usually a chip, within a computer containing programming necessary for starting up the computer, and essential system programs that neither the user nor the computer can alter or erase. Information in the computer's ROM is permanently maintained even when the computer is turned off.

**Root Directory.** The top level in a hierarchical file system. For example on a PC, the root directory of your hard drive—usually C:—contains all the second-level subdirectories on that drive.

**Rotary Camera.** In microfilming, the papers are read "on the fly" with a camera that's synchronized to the motion.

**Router.** A device that forwards data packets along networks. A router is connected to at least two networks, commonly two LANs or WANs or a LAN and its ISP's network. Routers are located at gateways, the places where two or more networks connect.

**Sampling Rate.** The frequency at which analog signals are converted to digital values during digitization. The higher the rate, the more accurate the process.

**Sampling.** Sampling usually (but not always) refers to the process of testing a database for the existence or frequency of relevant information. It can be a useful technique in addressing a number of issues relating to litigation, including decisions about what repositories of data are appropriate to search in a particular litigation, and determinations of the validity and effectiveness of searches or other data extraction procedures.

**SAN (Storage Area Network).** A high-speed subnetwork of shared storage devices. A storage device is a machine that contains nothing but a disk or disks for storing data. A SAN's architecture works in a way that makes all storage devices available to all servers on a LAN or WAN. As more storage devices are added to a SAN, they too will be accessible from any server in the larger network. In this case, the server merely acts as a pathway between the end user and the stored data. Because stored data does not reside directly on any of a network's servers, server power is used for business applications, and network capacity is released to the end user. Also see *Network*.

**Scalability.** The capacity of a system to expand without requiring major re-configuration or re-entry of data. For example, multiple servers or additional storage can be easily added.

**Scale-to-Gray.** An option to display a black and white image file in an enhanced mode, making it easier to view. A scale-to-gray display uses gray shading to fill in gaps or jumps (known as aliasing) that occur when displaying an image file on a computer screen. Also known as *grayscale*.

**Scanner.** An input device commonly used to convert paper documents into images. Scanner devices are also available to scan microfilm and microfiche.

**Scanning Software.** Software that enables a scanner to deliver industry standard formats for images in a collection. Enables the use of OCR and coding of the images.

**Schema.** A set of rules or conceptual model for data structure and content, such as a description of the data content and relationships in a database.

**Scroll Bar.** The bar on the side or bottom of a window that allows the user to scroll up and down through the window's contents. Scroll bars have scroll arrows at both ends, and a scroll box, all of which can be used to scroll around the window.

**SCSI (Small Computer System Interface).** Pronounced "skuzzy." A common, industry standard, electronic interface (highway) between computers and peripherals, such as hard disks, CD-ROM drives and scanners. SCSI allows for up to 7 devices to be attached in a chain via cables. As of this writing, the current SCSI standard is "SCSI II," also known as "Fast SCSI."

**SDLT (Super DLT).** A type of backup tape which can hold up to 220 GB or 330 CDs, depending on the data file format. See *DLT.*

**Search.** See *Compliance Search, Concept Search, Contextual Search, Boolean Search, Full-Text Search, Fuzzy Search, Index, Keyword Search, Pattern Recognition, Proximity Search, QBIC, Sampling,* and *Search Engine.*

**Search Engine.** A program that enables search for keywords or phrases, such as on web pages throughout the World Wide Web.

**Sector.** A sector is normally the smallest individually addressable unit of information stored on a hard drive platter, and usually holds 512 bytes of information. Sectors are numbered sequentially starting with 1 on each individual track. Thus, Track 0, Sector 1 and Track 5, Sector 1 refer to different sectors on the same hard drive. The first PC hard disks typically held 17 sectors per track. Today, they can hold thousands of sectors per track.

**Serial Line Internet Protocol (SLIP).** A connection to the Internet in which the interface software runs in the local computer, rather than the Internet's.

**Serif.** The little cross bars or curls at the end of strokes on certain type fonts.

**Server.** Any central computer on a network that contains data or applications shared by multiple users of the network on their client PCs. A computer that provides information to client machines. For example, there are web servers that send out web pages, mail servers that deliver e-mail, list servers that administer mailing lists, FTP servers that hold FTP sites and deliver files to users who request them, and name servers that provide information about Internet host names. See *File Server.*

**Service-Level Agreement.** A service-level agreement is a contract that defines the technical support or business parameters that a service provider or outsourcing firm will provide its clients. The agreement typically spells out measures for performance and consequences for failure.

**SGML/HyTime.** A multimedia extension to SGML, sponsored by DOD.

**SHA-1.** Secure Hash Algorithm, for computing a condensed representation of a message or a data file specified by FIPS PUB 180-1.

**Signature.** See *Certificate.*

**SIMM (Single, In-Line Memory Module).** A mechanical package (with "legs") used to attach memory chips to printed circuit boards.

**Simplex.** One-sided page(s)

**Skewed.** Tilted images. See *De-skewing.*

**Slack/Slack Space.** The unused space on a cluster that exists when the logical file space is less than the physical file space. Also known as file slack. A form of residual data, the amount of on-disk file space from the end of the logical record information to the end of the physical disk record. Slack space can contain information soft-deleted from the record, information from prior records stored at the same physical location as current records, metadata fragments, and other information useful for forensic analysis of computer systems.

**Smart Card.** A credit card size device that contains a microprocessor, memory, and a battery.

**SMTP (Simple Mail Transfer Protocol).** The protocol widely implemented on the Internet for exchanging e-mail messages.

**Software application.** See *Application and Software.*

**Software.** Any set of coded instructions (programs) stored on computer-readable media that tells a computer what to do. Includes operating systems and software applications.

**Speckle.** Imperfections in an image as a result of scanning paper documents that do not appear on the original. See *De-speckling.*

**Splatter.** Data that should be kept on one disk of a jukebox goes instead to multiple platters.

**Spoliation.** Spoliation is the destruction of records which may be relevant to ongoing or anticipated litigation, government investigation or audit. Courts differ in their interpretation of the level of intent required before sanctions may be warranted. See *The Sedona Guidelines: Best Practice Guidelines & Commentary for Managing Information & Records in the Electronic Age, Guideline 3.*

**SPP (Standard Parallel Port).** See *Centronics.*

**SQL (Structured Query Language).** A standard fourth-generation programming language (4GL—a programming language that is closer to natural language and easier to work with than a high-level language). The popular standard for running database searches (queries) and reports.

**Stand-Alone Computer.** A personal computer that is not connected to any other computer or network, except possibly through a modem.

**Standard Generalized Markup Language (SGML).** An informal industry standard for open systems document management that specifies the data encoding of a document's format and content.

**Status Bar.** A bar at the bottom of a window that is used to indicate the status of a task. For example, when an e-mail message is sent, the status bar will fill with dots, indicating that a message is being sent.

**Steganography.** The hiding of information within a more obvious kind of communication. Although not widely used, digital steganography involves the hiding of data inside a sound or image file. Steganalysis is the process of detecting steganography by looking at variances between bit patterns and unusually large file sizes.

**Storage Device.** A device capable of storing data. The term usually refers to mass storage devices, such as disk and tape drives.

**Storage Media.** See *Magnetic or Optical Storage Media.*

**Subjective Coding.** The coding of a document using legal interpretation as the data that fills a field, versus objective data that is readily apparent from the face of the document, such as date, type, author, addresses, recipients and names mentioned. Usually performed by paralegals or other trained legal personnel.

**Subtractive Colors.** Since the colors of objects are white light *minus* the color absorbed by the object, they are called subtractive. This is how ink on paper works. The subtractive colors of process ink are CMYK (Cyan, Magenta, Yellow, and Black) and are specifically balanced to match additive colors (RGB).

**Suspension Notice, Suspension Order.** See *Legal Hold.*

**SVGA (Super Video Graphics Adapter).** A graphics adapter one which exceeds the minimum VGA standard of 640 by 480 by 16 colors. Can reach 1600 by 1280 by 256 colors.

**Swap File.** A file used to temporarily store code and data for programs that are currently running. This information is left in the swap file after the programs are terminated, and may be retrieved using forensic techniques. Also referred to as a page file or paging file.

**System Administrator (sysadmin, sysop).** The person in charge of keeping a network working.

**System.** A system is: (1) a collection of people, machines, and methods organized to perform specific functions; (2) an integrated whole composed of diverse, interacting, specialized structures and sub-functions; and/or (3) a group of subsystems united by some interaction or interdependence, performing many duties, but functioning as a single unit.

**T1.** A high-speed, high-bandwidth leased line connection to the Internet. T1 connections deliver information at 1.544 megabits per second.

**T3.** A high-speed, high-bandwidth leased line connection to the Internet. T3 connections deliver information at 44.746 megabits per second.

**Tape Drive.** A hardware device used to store or backup electronic data on a magnetic tape. Tape drives are usually used to back up large quantities of data, because of their large capacity and cheap cost relative to other data storage options.

**Taxonomy.** The science of categorization, or classification, of things based on a predetermined system. In reference to Web sites and portals, a site's taxonomy is the way it organizes its data into categories and subcategories, sometimes displayed in a site map.

**TCP/IP (Transmission Control Protocol/Internet Protocol).** A collection of protocols that define the basic workings of the features of the Internet.

**Telephony.** Converting sounds into electronic signals for transmission.

**Templates, Document.** Sets of index fields for documents, providing framework for preparation.

**Temporary File.** Temporary (or "temp") files are files stored on a computer for temporary use only, and are often created by Internet browsers. These temp files store information about Web sites that a user has visited and allow for more rapid display of the Web page when the user revisits the site. Forensic techniques can be used to track the history of a computer's Internet usage through the examination of these temporary files. Temp files are also created by common office applications, such as word process or spreadsheet applications.

**Terabyte.** A unit of 1,000 or 1,024 gigabytes, or approximately a trillion bytes.

**TGA.** Targa format. This is a "scanned format"—widely used for color-scanned materials (24-bit) as well as by various "paint" and desktop publishing packages.

**Thin Client.** A networked user computer that acts only as a terminal and stores no applications or user files. May have little or no hard drive space. See *Client.*

**Thread.** A series of postings on a particular topic. Threads can be a series of bulletin board messages (for example, when someone posts a question and others reply with answers or additional queries on the same topic). A thread can also apply to chats, where multiple conversation threads may exist simultaneously.

**Thumb Drive.** See *Key Drive.*

**Thumbnail.** A miniature representation of a page or item for quick overviews to provide a general idea of the structure, content and appearance of a document. A thumbnail program may be standalone or part of a desktop publishing or graphics program. Thumbnails take considerable time to generate, but provide a convenient way to browse through multiple images before retrieving the one needed. Programs often allow clicking on the thumbnail to retrieve it.

**TIFF (Tagged Image File Format).** One of the most widely used and supported graphical file formats for storing bit-mapped images, with many different compression formats and resolutions. File name has .TIF extension. Can be black and white, gray-scaled, or color. Images are stored in tagged fields, and programs use the tags to accept or ignore fields, depending on the application. The format originated in the early 1980s.

**TIFF Group III (compression).** A one-dimensional compression format for storing black and white images that is used by many fax machines. See *TIFF.*

**TIFF Group IV (compression).** A two-dimensional compression format for storing black and white images. Typically compresses at a 20-to-1 ratio for standard business documents. See *TIFF.*

**Toggle.** A switch that is either on or off, and reverses to the opposite when selected.

**Tool Kit Without An Interesting Name (TWAIN).** A universal toolkit with standard hardware/software drivers for multi-media peripheral devices.

**Toolbar.** The row of buttons right below the menu that perform special functions quickly and easily.

**Topology.** The geometric arrangement of a computer system. Common topologies include a bus (network topology in which nodes are connected to a single cable with terminators at each end), star (local area network designed in the shape of a star, where all end points are connected to one central switching device, or hub), and ring (network topology in which nodes are connected in a closed loop; no terminators are required because there are no unconnected ends). Star networks are easier to manage than ring topology.

**Track.** Each of the series of concentric rings contained on a hard drive platter.

**True Resolution.** The "true" optical resolution of a scanner is the number of pixels per inch (without any software enhancements).

**Typeface.** There are over 10,000 typefaces available for computers. The general categories are: oldstyle (faces have slanted serifs, gradual thick to thin strokes and a slanted stress—the "O" appears slanted), modern (faces have thin, horizontal serifs, radical thick to thin strokes and a vertical street—the "O" does not appear to slant); slab serif (faces have thick, horizontal serifs, little or no thick-to-thin in the strokes and a vertical stress—the "O" appears vertical); sans serif (faces have no serifs), script (from elaborate handwriting styles to casual, freeform, unconnected letter forms), decorative unusual fonts (designed to be very different and attention getting).

**Ultrafiche.** Microfiche that can hold 1,000 documents/sheet as opposed to the normal 270.

**UMS.** Universal messaging system.

**Unallocated Space.** The area of computer media, such as a hard drive, that does not contain *normally accessible* data. Unallocated space is usually the result of a file being deleted. When a file is deleted, it is not actually erased, but is simply no longer accessible through normal means. The space that it occupied becomes unallocated space, i.e., space on the drive that can be reused to store new information. Until portions of the unallocated space are used for new data storage, in most instances, the old data remains and can be retrieved using forensic techniques.

**Unitization—Physical and Logical.** The assembly of individually scanned pages into documents. Physical Unitization uses actual objects such as staples, paper clips and folders to determine pages that belong together as documents for archival and retrieval purposes. Logical unitization is the process of human review of each individual page in an image collection using logical cues to determine pages that belong together as documents. Such cues can be consecutive page numbering, report titles, similar headers and footers and other logical indicators. This process should also capture document relationships, such as parent and child attachments. See also *Attachment*.

**UNIX.** A software operating system.

**Upgrade.** New or better version of some hardware or software.

**Upload.** To send a file from one computer to another via modem, network, or serial cable. With a modem-based communications link, the process generally involves the requesting computer instructing the remote computer to prepare to receive the file on its disk and wait for the transmission to begin.

**URI (Uniform Resource Indicators).** A URL is a URI.

**URL (Uniform Resource Locators).** The addressing system used in the World Wide Web and other Internet resources. The URL contains information about the method of access, the server to be accessed and the path of any file to be accessed. A URL looks like this: http://thesedonaconference.org/publications_html.

**URL.** See *Address*.

**User-Added Metadata.** Data or work product created by a user while reviewing a document, including annotations and subjective coding information.

**V.32bis.** The ITU (see *ITU*) standard for 14.4 kbs modem communications.

**V.34.** The proposed ITU *(see ITU)* standard for 28.8 kbs modem communications.

**Validate.** In the context of this document, confirm or ensure well grounded logic, and true and accurate determinations.

**VAR/VAD/VASD.** Value-Added Reseller/Value-Added Dealer/Value-Added Specialty Distributor. Companies or people who sell computer hardware or software *and* "add-value" in the process. Usually, the value added is specific technical or marketing knowledge and/or experience.

**VDT (Video Display Terminal).** Generic name for all display terminals.

**Vector.** Representation of graphical images by mathematical formulas. For instance, a circle is defined by a specific position and radius.

**Vendor-Added Metadata.** Data created and maintained by the electronic discovery vendor as a result of processing the document. While some vendor-added metadata has direct value to customers, much of it is used for process reporting, chain of custody and data accountability. Contrast with Customer-Added Metadata.

**Verbatim Coding.** Extracting data from documents in a collection in a way that matches exactly as the information appears in the documents.

**Version, Record Version.** A particular form or variation of an earlier or original record. For electronic records the variations may include changes to file format, metadata or content.

**Vertical De-Duplication.** A process through which duplicate data are eliminated within a single custodial or production data set. See *Content Comparison, File level Binary Comparison Horizontal De-duplication,* and *Meta Data Comparison.*

**VGA (Video Graphics Adapter).** A PC industry standard, first introduced by IBM in 1987, for color video displays. The *minimum* dot (pixel) display is 640 by 480 by 16 colors. Then "Super VGA" was introduced at 800 x 600 x 16, then 256 colors. VGA can extend to 1024 x 768 x 256 colors. Replaces EGA, an earlier standard and the even older CGA. Newer standard displays can range up to 1600 x 1280.

**Video Electronics Standards Association (VESA).** Concentrates on computer video standards.

**Video Scanner Interface.** A type of device used to connect scanners with computers. Scanners with this interface require a scanner control board designed by Kofax, Xionics, or Dunord.

**Virus.** A self-replicating program that spreads by inserting copies of itself into other executable code or documents. A program into which a virus has inserted itself is said to be infected, and the infected file (or executable code that is not part of a file) is a host. Viruses are a kind of malware (malicious software). Viruses can be intentionally destructive, for example by destroying data, but many viruses are merely annoying. Some viruses have a delayed payload, sometimes referred to a bomb. The primary downside of viruses is uncontrolled self-reproduction, which desecrates or engulfs computer resources.

**Vital Record.** A record that is essential to the organization's operation or to the reestablishment of the organization after a disaster.

**VoIP (Voice over Internet Protocol).** Telephonic capability across an IP connection; increasingly used in place of standard telephone systems.

**Volume.** A volume is a specific amount of storage space on computer storage media such as hard drives, floppy disks, CD-ROM disks, etc. In some instances, computer media may contain more than one volume, while in others, one volume may be contained on more than one disk.

**Volume Boot Sector.** When a partition is formatted to create a volume, a volume boot sector is created to store information about the volume. One volume contains the operating system and its volume boot sector contains code used to load the operating system when the computer is booted up.

**VPN (Virtual Private Network).** A secure network that is constructed by using public wires to connect nodes. For example, there are a number of systems that enable creation of networks using the Internet as the medium for transporting data. These systems use encryption and other security mechanisms to ensure that only authorized users can access the network and that the data cannot be intercepted.

**WAV.** File extension name for Windows sound files. ".WAV" files can reach 5 Megabytes for one minute of audio.

**Web Site.** A collection of Uniform Resource Indicators (URIs), including Uniform Resource Locators (URLs), in the control of one administrative entity. May include different types of URIs (*e.g.*, file transfer protocol sites, telnet sites, as well as World Wide Web sites). See *URI* and *URL.*

**Workflow, Ad Hoc.** A simple manual process by which documents can be moved around a multi-user review system on an "as-needed" basis.

**Workflow, Rule-Based.** A programmed series of automated steps that route documents to various users on a multi-user review system.

**Workgroup.** A group of computer users connected to share individual talents and resources as well as computer hardware and software—often to accomplish a team goal.

**WORM Disks.** Write Once Read Many Disks. A popular archival storage media during the 1980s. Acknowledged as the first optical disks, they are primarily used to store archives of data that cannot be altered. WORM disks are created by standalone PCs and cannot be used on the network, unlike CD-ROM disks.

**WORM (Write-Once, Read-Many).** Data storage devices (e.g., CD-ROMs) where the space on the disks can *only* be written *once*. The data is *permanently* stored. This is often today's primary media for archival information. Common disk sizes run from 5.25 inches (1.3 gigabytes) to 12 inches (8 to 10 gigabytes) capacities. There is also a 14-inch disk (13 to 15 gigabytes), only manufactured by Kodak's optical storage group. WORMs can also be configured into jukeboxes. There are various technologies. The expected viable lifetime of a WORM is at least 50 years. Since it is impossible to change, the government treats it just like paper or microfilm and it is accepted in litigation and other record-keeping applications. On the negative side, there is no current standard for how WORMs are written. The only ISO standard is for the 14-inch version, manufactured only by one vendor. A 5.25-inch standard is emerging from the European Computer Manufacturing Association but is not yet accepted. Further, WORM disks are written on both sides, but there are currently no drives that read both sides at the same time. As for speed, WORM is faster than tape or CD-ROM, but slower than magnetic. Typical disk access times run between 40 and 150 milliseconds (compared with 11 milliseconds for fast magnetic disks and 300 ms for CD-ROM). Data transfer rates run between 1 and 2 MB/seconds (compared with 5 to 10 for magnetic disks and 600KB/seconds for CD-ROM).

**WWW (World Wide Web).** All of the computers on the Internet which use HTML-capable software (Netscape, Explorer, etc.) to exchange data. Data exchange on the WWW is characterized by easy-to-use graphical interfaces, hypertext links, images, and sound. Today the WWW has become synonymous with the Internet, although technically it is really just one component.

**WYSIWYG.** "What You See Is What You Get"—Display and software technology which shows on the computer screen exactly what will print. Often requires a large, high-density monitor.

**X.25.** A standard protocol for data communications.

**XML.** See *Extensible Markup Language*.

**Zip Drives.** A floppy disk drive that can hold a large amount of data, usually as much as 750 megabytes or more. Often used for backing up hard disks.

**ZIP.** A common file compression format that allows quick and easy storage for transport.

**Zone OCR.** An add-on feature of the imaging software that populates document templates by reading certain regions or zones of a document, and then placing the text into a document index.

# Electronic Evidence Case Digest[1]

## Case 1

---

United States District Court,
N.D. California.

ADVANTACARE HEALTH PARTNERS, LP and
Healthcare Pathways Management, Inc.,
Plaintiffs,

v.

ACCESS IV, Gary Dangerfield, and Gwen Porter, Defendants.

No. C 03-04496 JF.
August 17, 2004.

---

Jurisdiction: United States District Court, Northern District of California

Date: August 17, 2004

Keywords: Sanctions, Procedure, Preservation of Evidence/Spoliation, Discovery

During a lawsuit regarding misappropriation of proprietary information, the Plaintiffs filed a motion for sanctions, after the Defendants had failed to properly comply with a temporary restraining order to preserve electronic evidence and a preliminary injunction to destroy information. The Defendants responded, arguing that the Plaintiffs had failed to file the motion in a timely manner. The Court concluded that the Plaintiffs had filed the motion as soon as practicable, in view of the motion practice required by discovery disputes and attempts to resolve the issue short of litigation. The Court then heard arguments regarding the sanctions themselves.

---

[1]The authors would like to thank legal assistants Justin Brown and Ryan Buehler, both from American University's Washington College of Law, for their outstanding work in compiling this digest.

The Court considered a variety of sanctions, beginning with the most severe, which was a default judgment against the Defendants. The Court found that the Defendants had engaged in affirmative misconduct through the intentional destruction of files and passive refusal to act in failing to later delete the same files. Even though the Defendants had conceded that they had intentionally deleted files and the Court felt that these actions had clearly prejudiced the Plaintiffs, the Court held that lesser sanctions would be as effective as a default judgment.

The Court went on to state that the Defendants' had a duty to preserve the files and that they had destroyed said evidence in response to impending litigation. The Court felt that such behavior suggested that the evidence would have been threatening to the defense of the case. The Court held that a negative inference presuming that the Defendant had copied every file on the Plaintiffs' system, because of the erasure, would be an appropriate sanction. The Court also held that the Defendants needed to demonstrate that they were no longer using the Plaintiffs' property and therefore, had to allow examination of the hard drives by the Plaintiffs, though no special master was ordered to oversee the process. Lastly, while the Court was not inclined to award the Plaintiffs all of the monetary sanctions that they sought, the Court found that a $20,000 sanction was appropriate.

## Case 2

United States District Court,
N.D. Illinois, Eastern Division.

AERO PRODUCTS INTERNATIONAL, INC., a Florida corporation; and
Robert B. Chaffee, an individual, Plaintiffs,

v.

INTEX RECREATION CORPORATION, a California corporation;
Quality Trading, Inc.,
a California corporation; and Wal-Mart Stores, Inc., a Delaware corporation,
Defendants.

No. 02 C 2590.
January 30, 2004.

Jurisdiction: United States District Court, Northern District of Illinois, Eastern Division

Date: January 30, 2004

Keywords: Sanctions, Preservation of Evidence/Spoliation, Discovery

In a suit alleging patent infringement, the Plaintiffs filed a motion for discovery sanctions, seeking fees and costs for bringing the motion, deposing a witness, and investigating the Defendant's destruction of electronic evidence. In support of their motion the Plaintiffs argued that the Defendants had failed to comply with an earlier order regarding electronic discovery.

The previous order required the Defendant to make a full and complete undertaking to recover any and all deleted electronic documents. The Court found that the Defendants had attempted to comply with that order, but the Plaintiffs found the Defendants' submissions unacceptable and attempted to negotiate with the Defendants over the appointment of a computer forensics expert. The Court also found that at no time did the Plaintiffs file a petition, as was its right under the previous order, seeking the appointment of a computer forensics expert to assist in recovering electronic data. The Plaintiffs were also entitled to request that the Defendants bear the costs of the computer forensics expert. Instead, the Plaintiffs did nothing further before filing the motion for sanctions. Lastly, the Plaintiffs had waited more than seven months to bring the matter before the Court. Therefore, the Court held that it would also be unjust to award the sanctions so late in the game. Accordingly, the Court denied the Plaintiffs' motion seeking sanctions for the Defendants' alleged failure to comply with the order regarding electronic discovery.

## Case 3

United States Bankruptcy Appellate Panel
of the Ninth Circuit.

In re VEE VINHNEE, Debtor.
American Express Travel Related Services Company, Inc., Appellant,
v.
Vee Vinhnee, Appellee.

No. CC-04-1284-KMOP, LA 03-29549-SB, LA 03-02660-SB.
Argued and Submitted on January 20, 2005, at Pasadena, California.
Filed December 16, 2005.

Jurisdiction: United States Bankruptcy Appellate Panel of the Ninth Circuit

Date: December 16, 2005

Keywords: Admissibility, Procedure

After a trial in a bankruptcy proceeding, the Plaintiff appealed the trial court's decision not to admit the Plaintiff's computerized business records. The trial court determined that the business records were inadequately authenticated at trial and that the Plaintiff's post-trial submission to correct the foundational defects in the records was not satisfactory. At trial, an employee of the Plaintiff testified that he was the custodian of records and that the records appearing in the Plaintiff's exhibits were "duplicate copies" of electronic records. The trial court explained that because the records were maintained electronically it was necessary not only for the Plaintiff to establish the basic foundation for a business record, but also to establish an authentication foundation regarding the computer and software utilized in order to assure the accuracy of the records. The Plaintiff's employee could not provide this foundation, so the trial court deferred ruling on the admission of the exhibits. The trial court held the record open to allow the Plaintiff to file a post-trial declaration by a witness qualified to complete the foundation for admission of the electronic records. After the trial, the Plaintiff submitted this declaration. In the declaration, the witness asserted that he was employed by the Plaintiff and was familiar with the hardware, software, and record-keeping system used in the credit card industry. The trial court held this testimony was inadequate because it failed to inform the court about the witness' experience or training concerning the computers. The witness also identified the make and model of the equipment, named the software, and asserted that the hardware and software are regarded as reliable by industry standards. The trial court held this testimony inadequate because it did not speak to the accuracy of the computer in retention and retrieval of the electronic business records. The trial court refused to admit the electronic records.

The Court reviewed the trial court's evidentiary rulings of admissibility for abuse of discretion. The Plaintiff had to persuade the Court that there was a clear error by the trial court in rejecting the exhibits of the electronic business records. The Court found that all of the elements for introduction of business records under the hearsay exception for records of regularly conducted activity also apply to records maintained electronically. "These elements must either be established by the testimony of a custodian or other qualified witness or must meet prescribed certification requirements." The Court found also that these records would not be admitted unless a court is persuaded that the records are authentic. The Court reasoned that, for an electronic record to be authenticated, the proponent must show that the record retrieved from the electronic file is the same as the record that originally was created. The Court opined that when looking at authenticating these records, a court should look beyond the identification of the computer equipment and programs used. It held that a court should also look at the policies and procedures for use of and access to the equipment, databases, and programs. The Court determined the testimony at trial of the records custodian regarding the computer equipment and software involved in electronic record maintenance was vague and indicated a lack of knowledge concerning the accuracy of these tools. The Court also found that the post-trial declaration by the Plaintiff's witness lacked information concerning the reliability and accuracy of the record reproduced from the electronic record. It therefore perceived no error by the trial court in determining that the evidentiary foundation for the electronic records was inadequate. The Court held that the trial court did not abuse its discretion.

## Case 4

United States District Court,
D. Minnesota.

Nikki J. ANDERSON, Plaintiff,

v.

CROSSROADS CAPITAL PARTNERS, L.L.C., Crossroads, Inc.,
Video Update, Inc., and James A. Skelton, an individual, Defendants.

No. Civ.01-2000 ADM/SRN.
February 10, 2004.

Jurisdiction: United States District Court, District of Minnesota

Date: February 10, 2004

Keywords: Discovery, Sanctions, Preservation of Evidence/Spoliation

The Plaintiff brought a suit against her former employer, the Defendant, alleging sexual harassment and whistleblower claims. As the parties proceeded through discovery, the Defendants sought to recover the hard drive of the Plaintiff's personal computer because it allegedly contained a document that outlined the harassment. The Defendants wanted to know the exact date that the Plaintiff created the chronology and whether she had written different versions of the document. She claimed that she owned the same computer throughout the time frame applicable to the litigation, including the computer that she used to initially create the chronology, and that she could not recall altering the hard drive in any way. She also agreed on the record that she would not purge or delete that drive or delete any existing documents. After a protracted discovery battle, the Defendants initiated a motion to compel production of the Plaintiff's hard drive. A magistrate judge agreed that the hard drive contained discoverable material and ordered the Plaintiff to furnish the Defendants with a copy of all documents/files relevant to this litigation that existed on her personal computer as well as those that were deleted or otherwise altered. Pursuant to that order, the Defendants' computer expert examined the computer's hard drive. The expert discovered that the hard drive on the computer was manufactured a year later than the computer. In addition, he found that the hard drive contained a data wiping software application that had been used relatively recently. The Plaintiff claimed that she did not use the program to destroy evidence, and stated that she regularly used the program to protect her computer files. She also said that, in her view, she owned the same computer throughout the litigation despite changing the hard drive. The Defendants subsequently moved to dismiss the Plaintiff's complaint for discovery violations. The Court found that despite her actions and assertions regarding the discovery or her computer, the Plaintiff's behavior was not sufficiently egregious to warrant dismissal. Accordingly, the Court denied the Defendants' motion to dismiss; however, because she intentionally destroyed evidence and attempted to suppress the truth, the Court agreed to issue an adverse inference jury instruction at trial.

## Case 5

United States District Court,
D. Minnesota.

The ANTIOCH CO., Plaintiff,

v.

SCRAPBOOK BORDERS, INC., Lisa DeBonoPaula a/k/a Lisa dePaula, and
Luis DeBonoPaula d/b/a Solrac Enterprises, Defendants.

No. CIV. 02-100 (MJD/RLE).
April 29, 2002.

Jurisdiction: United States District Court, District of Minnesota

Date: April 29, 2002

Keywords: Experts, Discovery

In a copyright infringement action, the Court reviewed the Plaintiff's motions for an order for preservation of records, to expedite discovery, and to compel and appoint a neutral computer forensics expert, which were largely based on concern that the Defendant had or would destroy relevant documents and materials. The Plaintiff moved for an order for preservation of records, because the Defendant had made claims that it was going out of business, had only allowed the review of their paper documents, and had only maintained minimal paper records for their customers. The Defendant did not oppose the order and stated that they it not and would not destroy any records. Accordingly, the Court granted the motions and instructed all parties to preserve relevant documents and materials.

The Plaintiff moved to expedite discovery because of the same concerns. To prevent any loss of evidence, the Plaintiff wanted permission to conduct discovery prior to a discovery conference, which the Defendant opposed. The Defendant argued that it had not yet been afforded the chance to respond to the Plaintiff's document requests. In addition, the Defendant claimed that the parties were competitors and that discovery of the hard drives could reveal many irrelevant or privileged items that would harm the Defendant. The Court, however, concluded that the motion was appropriate, in order to ensure that the computer records would be preserved, and ruled accordingly.

Lastly, the Plaintiff sought an order compelling the Defendant to produce computer equipment for purposes of investigation, copying, imagining, and interrogation, by a Court-appointed computer forensics expert. The Plaintiff sought this order, asserting that data from a computer, which has been deleted, still remains on the hard drive, but is constantly being overwritten, irretrievably so, by the Defendant's continued use of that equipment. To ensure the recovery and preservation of such information, the Plaintiff suggested a neutral expert, which it would bear at its own expense, in addition to a discovery procedure that would prevent undue burden. The Court granted the motion with a slightly revised discovery procedure that more closely resembled past precedent.

## Case 6

United States District Court,
N.D. Georgia,

Atlanta Division.
APA EXCELSIOR III, L.P., et al., Plaintiffs,

v.

Rodney D. WINDLEY et al., Defendants.

No. CIV. 1:01-CV-3126-RWS.
July 27, 2004.

Jurisdiction: United States District Court, Northern District of Georgia, Atlanta Division

Date: July 27, 2004

Keywords: Experts, Computer Forensics, Evidence Alteration/Fabrication

The Plaintiffs, shareholders in one of the Defendant corporations, brought an action alleging that they were wrongfully frozen out in connection with a transfer and acquisition of corporate assets. The Plaintiffs filed a motion for permission to name expert witnesses. In doing so, the Plaintiffs claimed that certain documents revealed that the Defendants had cooked their books, giving rise to Plaintiffs' need for expert witnesses. The Plaintiffs argued that they needed an expert to evaluate the Defendants' computers and any backup documents in order to determine whether any files had been destroyed. Finally, the Plaintiffs asserted that the discrepancies that needed to be investigated did not become evident until after the close of discovery.

The Defendants responded that the Plaintiffs should not be able to obtain additional discovery through an expert who would search computer files. The Defendants argued that the Plaintiffs failed to name any experts during the discovery period and that the changes in numbers in any discovery documents simply reflected adjustments following a later audit. The Court concluded that the Plaintiffs were not entitled to name a computer expert witness at such a late date and that it would not allow the Plaintiffs to do indirectly what they could not do directly by attempting to obtain other financial records after the close of discovery. The Court found that the need for an expert should have been apparent during discovery, and that although the Defendants made certain productions following the close of discovery, the Plaintiffs had failed to show evidence of the blatant cooking of books that they alleged. Therefore, the Court held that the naming of experts was not justified and denied the Plaintiff's motion for permission to name expert witnesses.

# Case 7

United States District Court,
District of Columbia.

ARISTA RECORDS, INC., et al., Plaintiffs,

v.

SAKFIELD HOLDING COMPANY S.L. et al., Defendants.

No. CIV.A.03-1474(RCL).
April 22, 2004.

Jurisdiction: United States District Court, District of Columbia

Date: April 22, 2004

Keywords: Procedure, Spoliation, Experts, Computer Forensics

The Defendant moved for a second time to dismiss the Plaintiff's copyright infringement suit, claiming lack of personal jurisdiction and improper venue. In
denying the Defendant's first motion to dismiss, the Court had granted a period of jurisdictional discovery to aid in resolving the matter. The Plaintiff alleged that the Defendant owned and controlled a Web site, based in Spain,
that allowed persons to download the Plaintiff's copyrighted musical works
without authorization. The Court held that the Plaintiff had met the requirements for specific jurisdiction, by showing that, to download the music, users
in the District would have to fill out personal information, enter into a license
agreement, and download and install the Defendant's software and before
being able to download the music. In addition, if a user desired more than the
initial free allotment, a credit card transaction would occur as part of the
user's subscription. Such evidence of transacting business was corroborated
through the testimony of District residents and was available through credit
card statements.

The Plaintiffs also asserted that the Court had personal jurisdiction over
the Defendant, because it was doing business in the District. The Court stated
that it was not necessary for the residents to have subscribed to the paid
plans because the twenty-four-hour availability of downloadable files and
transfer of files to was exactly the sort of purposeful, active, systematic, and
continuous activity that constituted doing business. To determine whether
they were doing business, the court had compelled discovery of third party
computer servers that hosted the Web site; however, when the Plaintiffs' computer expert examined the servers, he found that the vast majority of information stored therein had been intentionally destroyed, after the Defendant
had been apprised of the impending lawsuit. The Defendant claimed that it

had deleted the files to prevent further transmission of any files, which the Court found to be ludicrous. The Court did not issue sanctions but did give the Plaintiff the opportunity to file for them. The expert was able to recover a small amount of information, though, that showed that at least 241 users were District residents and that they downloaded at least 20,000 files. While the Defendant attacked the expert's methods, the Court found that the data established that the Defendant had been doing business with the residents, and therefore, personal jurisdiction existed, making venue proper, as well. Accordingly, the Court denied the Defendant's second motion to dismiss.

# Case 8

Court of Appeals of North Carolina.

Donald ARNDT, Plaintiff,

v.

FIRST UNION NATIONAL BANK, First Union Corporation and Wachovia Corporation, Defendants.

No. COA04-807.

June 7, 2005.

Jurisdiction: Court of Appeals of North Carolina

Date: June 7, 2005

Keywords: Spoliation, Sanctions

The Plaintiff filed a complaint against the Defendants, alleging breach of contract, among other things, arising from an employment dispute. The Plaintiff won and was awarded damages. The Defendants appealed, claiming that the trial court erred in its instructions to the jury because the Plaintiff's evidence did not support an instruction to the jury on spoliation of evidence and that they were unfairly prejudiced by the instruction. The basis for the instruction concerned the Plaintiff's discovery request of profit and loss statements and the text of two e-mails.

The Court began its spoliation analysis by considering whether the Defendant had notice of the litigation. It found that the Plaintiff presented evidence that the Defendants' human resources partner was on notice and had detailed knowledge of the Plaintiff's claims. The Court stated that her notice specifically addressed the Defendants' notice of the Plaintiff's claims. Next, the Court considered whether the information claimed to have been lost was pertinent and supportive to the Plaintiff's case. The Court noted that the Plaintiff sought discovery of two e-mails, one concerning the Plaintiff's compensation and the other regarding how an employment structuring plan applied to the Plaintiff, in addition to annual profit and loss financial statements. The Court found that both e-mails were central to the issues at bar and that the profit and loss statements were relevant to the Plaintiff's damages, so the information sought was pertinent to the issues in dispute and supportive of the claims. The Court next addressed any additional evidence showing the Defendants' failure to preserve the documents. The Plaintiff offered testimony that the Defendants made no attempt to preserve the Plaintiff's computer and data and that the Defendants still maintained older profit and loss statements, to show that they intentionally let the documents be destroyed. The Court held that the Plaintiff proffered both direct and circumstantial evidence indicating that the Defendants allowed the destruction of pertinent documents while on notice of his claim, which supported the trial court's instruction on spoliation of evidence. Accordingly, the Court held that the trial court did not err in charging the jury on spoliation of the evidence and overruled that portion of the Defendants' assignment of error.

## Case 9

Court of Appeals of Arkansas,

Division IV.
Melvin Wayne AUTREY, Appellant

v.

STATE of Arkansas, Appellee.

No. CACR 04-561.
February 23, 2005.

Jurisdiction: Court of Appeals of Arkansas, Division IV

Date: February 23, 2005

Keywords: Spoliation, Sanctions

A jury convicted the Defendant of manufacturing and possessing drugs. He appealed, alleging that the trial court erred in refusing to instruct the jury regarding spoliation. At trial, the investigating police officer testified regarding his recollection of the events that culminated in the Defendant's arrest, including what he overheard while listening to a wire transmission of a confidential informant talking to the Defendant. He testified that he had a typewritten report as well, though it is not introduced into evidence. The Defendant questioned the officer about the report on re-cross-examination, and the officer testified that he made his typewritten report on a computer, based upon his handwritten notes and his memory, and that he no longer had the handwritten notes. The Court noted that, at trial, the Defendant did not object to the testimony or ask for any type of sanctions based upon the loss of the handwritten notes.

The Defendant asserted that the officer destroyed his handwritten notes and that the jury should have been instructed on spoliation, giving the jury the ability to infer that evidence destroyed was unfavorable to the party responsible for its spoliation. The Court noted that, although that may be true in civil cases, it was not the law in criminal cases. An instruction on spoliation is designed to remedy litigation misconduct and such an instruction in this case would have meant that the State had behaved improperly in failing to preserve the notes. The Court further stated, however, that the State was required only to preserve evidence that was expected to play a significant role in the defense, and then only if the evidence possessed both an exculpatory value that was apparent before it was destroyed and a nature such that the Defendant would be unable to obtain comparable evidence by other reasonably available means. The Court found that there was no showing that the handwritten notes would be exculpatory and that it was more likely that they would be inculpatory, as evidenced by the testimony and the typewritten report. In addition, the Court concluded that there was ample comparable evidence available in both the testimony and the typewritten report. Therefore, the Court held that the police were not required to preserve the evidence. Lastly, the Court held that the Defendant's claims of bad faith and best evidence were unsupported. The Court concluded that the Defendant's requested instruction regarding spoliation was an attempt to unfairly obtain an inference of misconduct on the part of the State when, in fact, the State had no obligation to preserve the handwritten notes and did not act in bad faith. As a result, the Court affirmed the trial court's ruling excluding the instruction.

# Case 10

Supreme Judicial Court of Massachusetts,
Middlesex.

BEAL BANK, SSB, Plaintiff,

v.

Richard R. EURICH, Defendant.

Argued May 3, 2005.
Decided August 3, 2005.

Jurisdiction: Supreme Judicial Court of Massachusetts, Middlesex

Date: August 3, 2005

Keywords: Admissibility

In an action brought to recover a deficiency on a mortgage note, the Plaintiff appealed the appellate court's ruling that it was error for the trial judge to allow into evidence two computer printouts showing the amount owed on the debt. The Plaintiff employed a company (EPS) to service the Defendant's loan. At the trial, the Plaintiff introduced two computer printouts created by EPS to prove the amount of deficiency on the loan. The two printouts contained the Defendant's payment and balance information. The trial judge admitted the printouts into evidence, finding that EPS had an obligation to report accurately to the Plaintiff and therefore the printouts could be considered the Plaintiff's business records. The appellate court reversed the trial judge's decision. The Plaintiff appealed and argued that the computer printouts should have been admitted as the Plaintiff's records under the business records exception to the hearsay rule.

The Defendant argued that the computer printouts were records of EPS and created by EPS, so the printouts should not be admissible as business records of the Plaintiff The Defendant also argued that the Plaintiff did not introduce testimony concerning EPS's business practices in maintaining such records, in order to establish accuracy. The Court found that a representative of EPS did not have to testify for the judge to admit the printouts as business records. The Court also noted that EPS had a business duty to report accurate information to the Plaintiff and that the Plaintiff routinely accessed and relied upon the accuracy of the information. The bank's (Plaintiff's) manager testified that the Plaintiff had a contract with EPS and had on-line access to the information at all times. The Court held that the testimony of the Plaintiff's manager provided sufficient evidence to support the admission of the printouts into evidence as business records. The Court held that the trial judge was correct in finding that the two printouts were made in good faith and in the regular course of business. The Court ruled that the trial judge did not err and that the printouts could be admitted as business records of the Plaintiff.

## Case 11

Court of Chancery of Delaware,

New Castle County.
Heinrich BECK, individually and on behalf of a class of similarly
situated individuals, Plaintiff,

v.

ATLANTIC COAST PLC, a Foreign Corp.; Digital Millennium, Inc.;
Salaman Zafar; and John Does A through L, Defendants.

C.A. No. 303-N.
Submitted: December 8, 2004.
Decided: February 11, 2005.

Jurisdiction: Court of Chancery of Delaware, New Castle County

Date: February 11, 2005

Keywords: Sanctions, Costs and Cost Shifting

The Plaintiff filed a complaint against the Defendant suggesting that, as an un-sophisticated computer user, he was duped into buying a software product that he thought would improve the operational efficiency of his computer, but that, in reality, did not. In his complaint, the Plaintiff specifically alleged to have purchased the product in question. In light of facts uncovered during discovery, the Defendant Atlantic moved to dismiss the complaint and sought an award of attorneys' fees on the grounds that the prosecution of the action had been in bad faith and frivolous. In the course of discovery and briefing, it became clear that, contrary to representations in the complaint, the Plaintiff had not been deceived and had never purchased the product in question. In actuality, the Plaintiff observed an Internet popup ad for the product, believed the product did not work, and initiated a lengthy series of e-mail communications with the software developer in which he made numerous misrepresentations that he could influence a school district's bulk purchase of the product, in order to elicit responses. The Plaintiff boasted about his triumph in duping the developer on his personal Internet Web page.

The Plaintiff received discovery requests from the Defendant that clearly required him to produce the content of the Internet Web page in its entirety. Instead of producing that material, he consciously chose to withhold much of it from production. Absent a diligent Internet search by the Defendant, the full content of the Web page, which was relevant to the litigation, would have gone unnoticed. The Court concluded that the Plaintiff had violated several rules of the court as well as prosecuting the action in bad faith. The Court found that the conduct was inexcusable and justified fee-shifting and sanctions. The Court then entered final judgment: (1) dismissing the action with prejudice as to the Plaintiff; (2) enjoining the Plaintiff's counsel from participating as counsel or plaintiff in any suit against the Defendant relating to the product; (3) requiring the Plaintiff and counsel to be jointly and severally liable for the Defendant and Court Atlantic Coast counsel fees; and (4) requiring counsel to submit a copy of the decision with any motion for pro hac vice filed by any of them. Lastly, the Court ordered the Plaintiff to bear each side's costs.

# Case 12

Court of Appeal, Second District, Division 2, California.

Shaileshkumar BHATT, Plaintiff and Appellant,

v.

The DEPARTMENT OF HEALTH SERVICES FOR the STATE of California, Defendant and Respondent.

No. B179321.
October 5, 2005.
As Modified October 27 and November 4, 2005.
Review Denied December 14, 2005

Jurisdiction: Court of Appeal, Second District, Division 2, California

Date: December 14, 2005

Keywords: Admissibility

A fiscal intermediary conducted an audit of the Plaintiff's records (CDRs) retrieved from a database and issued an audit report. Among other findings, the audit report found inadequate documentation for some billed services. The Plaintiff requested a formal hearing concerning the findings. During one administrative proceeding before an administrative law judge (ALJ), the Plaintiff objected to the admission of the CDRs into evidence, arguing that the CDRs did not qualify as business record exceptions to the hearsay rule. The ALJ, however, admitted the CDRs into evidence. The Chief ALJ reviewed this decision and rejected the decision. The Chief ALJ found that the CDRs did not qualify for the business record exception, but the CDRs did qualify for the official record exception to the hearsay rule. The Plaintiff filed a petition for writ of administrative mandamus in the superior court, arguing that the CDRs were inadmissible. The superior court denied his petition and found that the CDRs were admissible as official records. The Plaintiff appealed the superior court's denial of his petition.

The Plaintiff argued that the CDRs could not be admitted as official records because no testimony was provided to authenticate the CDRs; however, the Court noted that the official records exception to hearsay permits the court to admit an official record without requiring a witness to testify concerning the identity and mode of preparation of the record if the court takes judicial notice or sufficient evidence shows the records to be trustworthy. The Court found that the CDRs were created by public employees, because the fiscal intermediary regularly performed official duties required by statutes and regulations. The Court further found that the CDRs were made at or near the time of the act. The Court made the assumption that since the checks issued to the Plaintiff were generated by computer, it was reasonable to assume that the data was input into the computer between the time the fiscal intermediary received a claim and the time a check was issued. The Court found this assumption consistent with the statutory duties of the fiscal intermediary to maintain claim data in an electronic format. The Court held that there was a presumption that the CDRs' method of preparation was trustworthy because it was a regularly performed official duty. The Plaintiff failed to produce evidence of the CDRs' untrustworthiness. For these reasons, the Court held that the CDRs should be admitted under the official records exception to hearsay.

## Case 13

Supreme Court, Appellate Division, First Department, New York.

The BOARD OF MANAGERS OF the ATRIUM CONDOMINIUM,
Plaintiff-Respondent-Appellant,

v.

WEST 79TH STREET CORP., Defendant-Appellant-Respondent,
CVS Bleecker Street, LLC, etc., et al., Defendants.

April 5, 2005.

Jurisdiction: Supreme Court, Appellate Division, First Department, New York

Date: April 5, 2005

Keywords: Procedure, Discovery

The Court held that a default judgment regarding the Plaintiff's failure to timely serve a reply to counter claims should be denied, because the failure was not part of a demonstrable pattern of willful delay. The Court concluded that it appeared that the Plaintiff had reasonably believed that the matter was being held in abeyance pending then ongoing extensive negotiations and the Defendant was at all times aware of the Plaintiff's position and was not otherwise prejudiced by the delay. Therefore, the Court denied the Defendant's request for electronic discovery of the Plaintiff's attorneys' computers in order to find evidence of backdating and perjury.

## Case 14

Court of Appeals of Ohio, Tenth District, Franklin County.

Robbie A. BOGGS, Plaintiff-Appellant,

v.

THE SCOTTS COMPANY et al., Defendants-Appellees.

No. 04AP-425.
March 22, 2005.

Jurisdiction: Court of Appeals of Ohio, Tenth District, Franklin County

Date: March 22, 2005

Keywords: Procedure, Spoliation

The Plaintiff appealed from a judgment of the lower court that granted summary judgment in favor of the Defendants, in an employment action alleging age discrimination, retaliation, promissory estoppel, and spoliation of evidence. The Defendants had moved for summary judgment, claiming that the Plaintiff's evidence failed to raise a genuine issue of material fact supporting her claims, which the trial court agreed with. On appeal, the Plaintiff alleged that the trial court erred in granting the Defendants' motion for summary judgment on the Plaintiff's claim of spoliation of evidence. The Court stated that the elements of a cause of action for interference with or destruction of evidence are (1) pending or probable litigation involving the plaintiff, (2) knowledge on the part of the defendant that litigation exists or is probable, (3) willful destruction of evidence by defendant designed to disrupt the plaintiff's case, (4) disruption of the plaintiff's case, and (5) damages proximately caused by the defendant's acts. Furthermore, the state did not recognize a cause of action for negligent spoliation; therefore, in order to prove spoliation, the Plaintiff had to show willful or purposeful conduct by the Defendant designed to disrupt or deter litigation.

The Plaintiff complained about the Defendants' human resources department's destruction of relevant documents and e-mails. According to an employee's deposition, however, she did not shred documents that were considered significant to the Plaintiff. In addition, she asserted that the destruction of papers was a part of her effort to clean out her office in preparation for voluntarily leaving her employment. The Court found that the testimony did not support the Plaintiff's contention that the employee deliberately shredded documents in an effort to disrupt the Plaintiff's pending or probable litigation. Moreover, the Court held that the Plaintiff failed to produce convincing evidence that, at the time the documents were destroyed, she or the Defendants knew that litigation was likely. Finally, the Court concluded that the Plaintiff did not present any evidence that her case, in fact, had been disrupted by the loss of any documents or that any damage to her had proximately resulted. Thus, the Court agreed with the trial court that the Plaintiff failed to raise a genuine issue of fact on her spoliation claim, overruled her assignment of error, and affirmed the judgment of the lower court.

## Case 15

Commonwealth Court of Pennsylvania.

John M. BLICHA, Petitioner,

v.

UNEMPLOYMENT COMPENSATION BOARD OF REVIEW, Respondent.

Submitted on Briefs March 18, 2005.
Decided June 15, 2005.

Jurisdiction: Commonwealth Court of Pennsylvania

Date: June 15, 2005

Keywords: Computer Forensics, Experts

The Claimant petitioned for a review of the previous order that denied the Claimant unemployment benefits. He asserted that the Board erred in determining that his employer had met its burden of proof in demonstrating that the Claimant had been terminated for willful misconduct and that the Board erred by failing to afford the Claimant the opportunity to examine a computer and procure expert testimony.

Specifically, the Claimant challenged his Employer's computer expert, on the basis that he was not an on-site employee, that the firewall, which included a tracking function, was never activated, and that the expert testified that he lacked personal knowledge as to who actually accessed the computer in question. The Claimant also argued the possibility that other people had access to his computer and that someone else could have used the computer for an improper purpose. He further maintained that the record demonstrated that he unequivocally denied having viewed the pornographic material found on his computer and that such material was absolutely reprehensible.

The Court found that the record demonstrated that the Board had substantial evidence upon which to determine that the Employer had met its burden of demonstrating that the Claimant had committed willful misconduct. The record was clear that more than 150 pornographic images were found on the computer assigned to the Claimant and that such images were accessed during work hours using the assigned computer with the Claimant's own log-in and password. In addition, such access to pornographic material occurred on sixteen separate days over a ninety-day period. Furthermore, the fact that the Employer failed to present any witness to testify concerning a visual sighting of Claimant using the computer in a way that violated a work rule was of no consequence. The Court stated that where evidence demonstrated that files containing pornographic material were found in the computer used by the Claimant, such evidence may support the conclusion that the claimant was using the Employer's computer to download pornographic material in violation of the Employer's written policy and in disregard of the standard of behavior that the Employer has a right to expect of an employee. The Court found that the Board had substantial evidence to conclude that the Claimant was using the Employer's computer in violation of its policies and therefore, affirmed the order denying benefits.

## Case 16

United States District Court,
D. New Jersey.

In re BRISTOL-MYERS SQUIBB SECURITIES LITIGATION.

CIVIL ACTION NO. 00-1990 (GEB).
February 4, 2002.

Jurisdiction: United States District Court, District of New Jersey

Date: February 4, 2002

Keywords: Costs and Cost Shifting, Discovery

In a class action alleging violations of the Securities Exchange Act, the Defendants filed a motion to require the Plaintiffs to pay for costs resulting from production of documents in response to discovery requests. The Plaintiffs opposed the motion on two grounds, arguing that the Defendants had dumped unresponsive documents, thereby causing excessive reproduction costs, and that they had been fraudulently induced into an agreement to pay for photocopying. In addition, the Plaintiffs sought to have all the documents produced in electronic form, asserting that they should pay nothing.

The Court found it apparent that the Plaintiffs had had every opportunity to ask for electronic information but had failed to do so until after the bill for paper discovery became due. However, the Court held that the Plaintiffs correctly pointed out that parties are required to disclose computerized data and other electronically recorded information. The Plaintiffs then argued that the Defendants were required to advise that they had imaged or scanned all responsive documents. The Court, however, held that the requirement, by its plain language, only goes to data already in electronic form at the time mandatory disclosure is to be made. The Court further held that a party is not required to disclose to an adversary, absent an express request by the party or order of the court, any intention to prepare for trial by scanning documents into electronic form.

Ultimately, the Court granted in part and denied in part the Defendants' motion for an order requiring full reimbursement for paper copying costs. The Plaintiffs were ordered to pay for the paper production but were not ordered to pay one-half the costs of scanning documents into electronic form, as the Defendants had requested. Instead, the Plaintiffs were required to pay the nominal cost of duplicating compact discs.

## Case 17

United States District Court,
D. Maryland.

Dino BROCCOLI et al., Plaintiffs

v.

ECHOSTAR COMMUNICATIONS CORPORATION et al., Defendants

No. CIV. AMD 03-3447.
August 4, 2005.

Jurisdiction: United States District Court, District of Maryland

Date: August 4, 2005

Keywords: Spoliation, Sanctions,

After a jury trial in an employment discrimination case, the Plaintiff filed a motion for an award of attorneys' fees in respect to his wage payment claim. The Defendants filed a bill of costs based on their assertion that they were a prevailing party, to which the Plaintiff timely objected. In the Court's opinion, it articulated the reasoning for its earlier order granting in part the Plaintiff's motion for sanctions and determining the amount of fees and costs to be awarded to the Plaintiff. During discovery, the Plaintiff filed a motion for sanctions, alleging that the Defendants had culpably failed to preserve critical records and documents relevant to several claims and defenses in the case and were guilty of spoliation of evidence. In ruling on the motion for sanctions, the Court issued an order granting the motion in part, noting that it was clear beyond reasonable dispute that the Defendants had been guilty of gross spoliation of evidence. Consequently, at trial, the Court imposed certain limits on the Defendants' ability to present evidence and granted the Plaintiff's request for an adverse inference instruction based on spoliation of evidence.

The Court found that the Defendants' document retention policy was extraordinary and, although under normal circumstances such a policy could be a risky one, it could arguably be a defensible business practice undeserving of sanctions. The Court held that the Defendants were on actual notice of the need to preserve all documentation relevant to the Plaintiff, because of his verbal and e-mail complaints to supervisors. The Court found that the Plaintiff suffered palpable prejudice, owing to the absence of any kind of paper trail covering his interactions with his supervisors and co-workers. The Defendants plainly had a duty to preserve employment and termination documents when the management learned of the Plaintiff's potential claim. Yet, the discovery process revealed that none of the e-mails exchanged between the Plaintiff and his supervisors, regarding his complaints, were preserved. The Court held that the Defendants clearly acted in bad faith in their failure to suspend their e-mail and data destruction policy or preserve essential personnel documents in order to fulfill their duty to preserve the relevant documentation for purposes of potential litigation. Those bad faith actions prejudiced the Plaintiff in his attempts to litigate his claims and measurably increased the costs for him to do so. Therefore, the Court granted his motion for sanctions and included an adverse spoliation of evidence instruction in the jury instructions.

# Case 18

United States Bankruptcy Court,
N.D. California.

In re Case Terry BROWN, Debtor.

No. 03-56369 JRG.
June 30, 2005.

Jurisdiction: United States Bankruptcy Court, Northern District of California

Date: June 30, 2005

Keywords: Sanctions

A Chapter 13 Trustee moved for sanctions under bankruptcy laws against the debtor's attorney. After electronically filing the original version of an amended Chapter 13 plan that had been duly signed by the debtor, the debtor's attorney, realizing that a revision needed to be made, corrected the original hardcopy document and then modified the electronic document to match the hard copy, so that it too could be electronically filed. The debtor had approved the revision but had no knowledge of the attorney's actions, as he did not sign either version of the revised document. Because of the attorney's actions, she no longer had in her possession a copy of the original plan and also did not possess a signed copy of the revised plan, as the signature on it was not original and applied to the plan before it was revised. The Trustee was concerned about the integrity of the court's electronic filing system and argued that a document should be electronically filed only if a party has signed the original. According to the Trustee, electronic filing did not change the prior requirements that an attorney could not file a document on a client's behalf without an original signature. The debtor's attorney argued that she fell into an electronic filing trap and she inadvertently failed to maintain the original. She asserted that nothing she did constituted a rule violation that warranted the imposition of sanctions.

The Court stated that the electronic filing of a document purportedly signed by someone other than the registered participant shall be deemed a certification, by that person, that he or she has the document in question, bearing that someone's original signature, in his or her physical possession. The registered participant must produce the original signed document on request by the court. With respect to any document filed electronically that purports to be signed by someone other than the registered participant, the registered participant shall retain the document bearing the original signature until five years after the case or adversary proceeding in which the document was filed is closed. The Court found that even if the substance of the revised plans was the same, they did not represent the same document. The debtor's attorney argued that the electronically filed document would not be the same as the original unless the document filed with the court was scanned; however, the Court held that, if the original document is not scanned and is instead a converted word processing document, the only difference between the document filed and the original should be that the original bears an original signature and the filed document bears an "/s/" on the signature line, which was not the case here. By electronically filing a document, the debtor's attorney certified that she had the document in question, bearing the debtor's original signature, in her physical possession as required, which was not the case. The Court may impose sanctions if it determines that the statute has been violated. Here, the Court believed that sanctions in the amount of $250.00 to reimburse a portion of the Chapter 13 Trustee's attorneys' fees were warranted.

## Case 19

Court of Appeal, Fourth District, Division 3, California.

Peggie Jo BROWN et al., Plaintiffs and Appellants,

v.

ERIE INSURANCE EXCHANGE et al., Defendants and Respondents.

No. G031164.
(Super.Ct.No. 02CC00003).
February 20, 2004.

Jurisdiction: Court of Appeal, Fourth District, Division 3, California

Date: February 20, 2004

Keywords: Spyware, Procedure

The class-action consumer Plaintiffs sued the Defendant software manufacturer in California alleging various torts related to the operation of the software. The insurer refused to indemnify or defend the manufacturer because it was not a named insured on the policy. The settlement of the class-action lawsuit included an assignment to the Plaintiffs of the Defendant's rights against insurers who had refused tender of its defense. In the breach of contract action subsequently filed by the Plaintiffs against one of those insurers, the trial court granted the insurer's motion to quash service of summons because the Plaintiffs had failed to meet their burden to establish personal jurisdiction over the insurer.

The trial court concluded that because the Plaintiff failed to establish that either of the two former names under which the prior Defendant had operated were insureds under the Defendant's policy, the Plaintiff had failed to establish personal jurisdiction over the Defendant. The Court disagreed with the trial court. The Court found that the Plaintiff's complaint potentially encompassed injuries caused by the prior Defendant under an earlier name, while that entity was in existence and while the policy issued by the Defendant was in effect. The Plaintiff's first amended complaint named the entity's earlier name as the Defendant, alleging that it was a business entity of unknown form, headquartered in California, and that it delivered the offensive targeted advertising software to computer users. The only entity in existence during the time of the actions described used the same name that was insured under the policy. To the extent that the complaint encompassed injuries caused by the entity using later differing names, the Court found that those liabilities likely passed to the ultimately named prior Defendant by operation of law as the successor to the named insured under the policy. Accordingly, the Court held that there was sufficient showing of possible coverage, albeit for a very narrow window of time, to justify the California court's exertion of jurisdiction over this matter. The Defendant complained about the dearth of evidence regarding the true nature of the name changes and/or the mergers of the various entities. The Court, however, declined to address those substantive issues, as the Defendant and trial court had, and focused instead on jurisdiction. Therefore, the Court reversed the order granting the Plaintiff's motion to quash service of process and awarded the Plaintiff costs on appeal.

## Case 20

Court of Appeals of Georgia.

BRYAN

v.

The STATE.

No. A00A1967.
October 24, 2000.

Jurisdiction: Court of Appeals of Georgia

Date: October 24, 2000

Keywords: Admissibility

The Defendant was indicted for statutory rape, child molestation, aggravated child molestation, sodomy, and enticing a child for indecent purposes, based on acts committed against a fifteen-year-old girl. He appealed, claiming that the trial court erred in admitting into evidence twenty-six pornographic images that had been stored on computers retrieved from his home and workshop.

First, the Defendant argued that the images portrayed illegal acts similar to those for which he was convicted and, as such, were subject to the statute governing the admission of similar transaction evidence. The Court found that the images viewed by the jury did not depict the Defendant. They were not similar transactions or prior bad acts, as they would be if, for example, they depicted the Defendant engaging in sexual activity with a minor. Accordingly, the Court rejected the Defendant's argument that the State was required to comply with the statutory mandates, prior to the admission of the evidence in question.

Next, the Court considered Defendant's argument that the admission of the evidence contravened the rule that during a prosecution for a sexual offense, evidence of sexual paraphernalia found in the Defendant's possession is inadmissible unless it shows the Defendant's lustful disposition toward the sexual activity with which he is charged or his bent of mind to engage in that activity. Under the rule, the Court stated that sexually explicit material cannot be introduced merely to show a Defendant's interest in sexual activity. It can only be admitted if it can be linked to the crime charged. The Court found that the evidence at issue passed the stringent relevancy test, because the graphic images showed teenaged girls committing various sexual acts, which were relevant to show the Defendant's bent of mind to engage in sexual activity with the fifteen-year-old victim. Accordingly, the Court held that the trial court did not abuse its discretion in admitting the evidence, and therefore, it affirmed the Defendant's convictions.

## Case 21

United States District Court,
S.D. Texas, Houston Division.

Amanda K. BUCHANAN Plaintiff,

v.

HEEREMA MARINE CONTRACTORS U.S., INC. Defendant.

No. Civ.A. H-04-3885.
October 5, 2005.

Jurisdiction: United States District Court, Southern District of Texas, Houston Division

Date: October 5, 2005

Keywords: Admissibility, Experts, Sanctions, Spoliation, E-Evidence Alteration/Fabrication

The Plaintiff brought suit against her former employer, the Defendant, alleging negligence, intentional infliction of emotional distress, and sex discrimination. Specifically, the Plaintiff claimed that a former employee of the Defendant subjected her to repeated inappropriate sexual advances and comments. The Defendant submitted a motion for summary judgment.

During the time that the Plaintiff was employed by the Defendant, she claims inappropriate sexual advances were made by another employee of the Defendant. As evidence of this inappropriate behavior, the Plaintiff offered e-mails from her home computer. The e-mails were originally sent from the employee to the Plaintiff's office computer, and then the Plaintiff forwarded the messages off to her home computer. The Court ordered the Plaintiff to turn over her home computer to the Defendant's computer expert for inspection. Between the date the Court ordered the Plaintiff to turn over the computer and the date that the Plaintiff actually turned over the computer, 2,179 files were deleted from the Plaintiff's computer. The Court discovered that in several of the e-mails the Plaintiff forwarded to her home computer threatening and suggestive material was added after the e-mails were received in the Plaintiff's in-box. The Plaintiff denied altering the e-mails. The Court sanctioned the Plaintiff for deliberate spoliation of evidence by not allowing the Plaintiff to introduce the version of the e-mails from her home computer. Rather, the Court used the version of the e-mails retained on the Plaintiff's office computer.

## Case 22

United States District Court,
D. Delaware.

Corporal William BULLEN and, Corporal Jeffrey Giles, Plaintiffs,

v.

Colonel L. Aaron CHAFFINCH, individually and in his official capacity as Superintendent of the Delaware State Police; James L. Ford, Jr., individually and in his official capacity as Secretary of the Department of Safety and Homeland Security of the State of Delaware, and Division of State Police Department of Public Safety and Homeland Security, State of Delaware, Defendants.

No. CIV.A.02-1315-JJF.
September 17, 2004.

Jurisdiction: United States District Court, District of Delaware

Date: September 17, 2004

Keywords: Admissibility

In an employment discrimination suit, the Defendants moved for either a judgment as a matter of law or, in the alternative, for a new trial. On special interrogatories, the jury found that the Plaintiffs had proven their case by a preponderance of the evidence. In support of their motion, the Defendants argued that the Court erred with respect to the Court's evidentiary decision to admit a civilian e-mail describing the Defendants' recruiting process, claiming that the e-mail was irrelevant and unfairly prejudicial. The Court stated that a new trial was warranted based on a court's decision to admit or exclude evidence, if that ruling affects a substantial right of a party.

The Court concluded that the evidence was properly admitted, because the Court viewed it as relevant evidence. The Court noted that relevant evidence is evidence having any tendency to make the existence of any fact that is of consequent to the determination of the action more probable or less probable than it would be without the evidence. The Plaintiffs argued that the Governor's administration sought to be more aggressive than previous administrations with respect to minority hiring and promotions. Thus, the Court found that as the Plaintiffs contended at trial, the e-mail could have been viewed as the benchmark from which the Defendants' began efforts to secure a work force more reflective of the population of the state. In light of the e-mail author's civilian position of employment, with the Defendants, the Court was persuaded that allowing the jury to know and consider his views in the context of the factual issues that the jury was asked to decide was not error, because the author's discussion of the recruiting process was not evidence probative of the intent of the Defendants regarding the employment practices of the Defendants. In addition, the Court found that the e-mail was not unduly prejudicial to the Defendants, and, therefore, the Court concluded that the e-mail was properly admitted into evidence.

## Case 23

United States District Court,
E.D. California.

CABINETWARE INCORPORATED

v.

James W. SULLIVAN d.b.a. Starcode Software.

No. Civ. S. 90-313 LKK.
July 15, 1991.

Jurisdiction: United States District Court, Eastern District of California

Date: August 15, 1991

Keywords: Spoliation, Sanctions

In a copyright infringement suit, the matter came before the Court on the Defendant's objections to a magistrate's findings and recommendations regarding the Plaintiff's motion for sanctions. The Defendant objected to the magistrate's finding that the Defendant destroyed a hard copy of the source code after he had been served with a request for production in the action. While the Court upheld the magistrate's finding on that issue, it held that the Defendant's destruction of the electronic files, which remained uncontested, was more pertinent to the spoliation issue. The magistrate had held that, although fully aware of the request for production of the source codes and of their significance in copyright infringement actions, the Defendant purposefully destroyed the initial source codes in order to avoid having that code made available for comparison in the litigation. The Defendant's explanation that he destroyed the evidence by writing over the floppy disks because he needed more disks and did not want to bother to go out and buy additional disks simply could not wash. The Court noted that the magistrate's findings fully supported the conclusion that a discovery sanction was appropriate in the instant matter because of the Defendant's spoliation of evidence essential to the Plaintiff's case. The Court turned to the question of an appropriate sanction.

The magistrate recommended that a rebuttable presumption of copying be established, reasoning that it would put the Plaintiff in the same position as if the evidence had not been destroyed. The Court found that such a sanction would serve no deterrent or punitive function. As an alternative sanction that would be moderately punitive, the Court considered imposing a requirement on the Defendant that he rebut the presumption with clear and convincing evidence, which would put the Plaintiff in the position that he would have been in but for the Defendant's transgression. The Court concluded, however, that both sanctions were inadequate to protect the integrity of the court's process, because the Defendant's conduct in the action was an affront to the integrity of the judicial system. Accordingly, the Court held that nothing less than default judgment on the issue of liability would suffice to both punish the defendant and deter others similarly tempted.

## Case 24

United States District Court,
W.D. Pennsylvania.

CAPRICORN POWER COMPANY, INC., Capricorn Power Partners, L.P.,
CE Colver I, Inc., CE Colver Limited Partnership,
Inter-Power of Pennsylvania, Inc., and Inter-Power Resource Partners, L.P.
trading as Inter-Power/Ahlcon Partners, L.P., Plaintiffs,
v.
SIEMENS WESTINGHOUSE POWER CORPORATION, Defendant.

Civil Action No. 01-39J.
April 21, 2004.

Jurisdiction: United States District Court, Western District of Pennsylvania

Date: April 21, 2004

Keywords: Preservation of Evidence/Spoliation, Procedure

Both the Defendant and the Plaintiffs filed motions requesting orders of the Court directing the preservation of documents. The Court began its analysis by finding that it was apparent that the Plaintiff might be irreparably injured if the evidentiary documents necessary to prove its claim were destroyed or otherwise put beyond the reach of the court; however, the Court continued by stating that if the party who seeks an injunction shows potential irreparable injury, he has established merely one essential condition for relief. He must demonstrate in addition that there is real danger that the acts to be enjoined will occur, that there is no other remedy available, and that, under these circumstances, the court should exercise its discretion to afford the unusual relief provided by its injunction.

The Defendant testified that it had all of the original records in his possession and had no intention of destroying them, while the Plaintiff offered no proof that there was an imminent threat of destruction or concealment of the evidentiary documents before a satisfactory order could be obtained. The Court found that there was no adequate proof to meet the burden that rested upon the Plaintiff to demonstrate that the extraordinary remedy sought by it should be granted. The Court then went on to state that while it was true that the injunction sought would cause no hardship to the Defendant, a lack of hardship on the Defendant was not of itself sufficient reason to grant an injunction.

As a result, the Court concluded that the four-prong test typically applied to matters concerning injunctive relief was not a completely appropriate test to use when examining the need for a preservation order. The Court then established a three-part balancing test to be used when deciding a motion to preserve documents: (1) the level of concern the court has for the continuing existence and maintenance of the integrity of the evidence in question in the absence of an order directing preservation of the evidence; (2) any irreparable harm likely to result to the party seeking the preservation of evidence absent an order directing preservation; and (3) the capability of an individual, entity, or party to maintain the evidence sought to be preserved, not only as to the evidence's original form, condition, or contents, but also the physical, spatial, and financial burdens created by ordering evidence preservation. After applying the three-part test, the Court found that there was no need or justification to enter an order preserving evidence as requested by both parties.

## Case 25

United States District Court,
S.D. New York.

THE CARLTON GROUP, LTD., Carlton Advisory Services, Inc., and
Carlton Debt Advisors, Inc., Plaintiffs,

v.

William David TOBIN, Joseph A. Runk, Jr., John B. Guy, Jeffrey N. Phelps,
Kenneth Bauerenfreund, Mission Capital Advisors, Inc.,
Southshore Capital Co., Inc., Gulfstream Capital Partners, Inc.,
Prolific Solutions, Inc., Thomas P. Tobin, Giselle Handel, PDP Capital, LLC,
and Stacey Schurter, Defendants.

No. 02 Civ.5065 SAS.
July 31, 2003.

Jurisdiction: United States District Court, Southern District of New York

Date: July 31, 2003

Keywords: Sanctions, Costs and Cost Shifting

In a misappropriation of proprietary information suit, the Defendants sought sanctions against the Plaintiffs and their attorneys, claiming that they had filed a motion against the Defendants that lacked evidentiary support. The Plaintiffs maintained that their allegations, including that proprietary data had been misappropriated via computer, were factually supported, that the Defendants' motion should be denied, and that they should be sanctioned because of the meritless nature of their motion. In addition, the Plaintiffs argued that the Defendants should reimburse them for attorneys' fees and expenses incurred in defending the motion.

The Defendants claimed that the Plaintiffs' allegations against them were factually unsupported and therefore, insufficient to establish the Plaintiffs' theory of conspiracy. The Defendants argued that the Plaintiffs should have thoroughly investigated their claims before making them and that because they allegedly had not, they should be sanctioned. Furthermore, the Defendants argued that the Plaintiffs' attorneys should also be sanctioned, because they knew it was unreasonable not to investigate further before asserting claims. The Defendants further claimed that the Plaintiffs had a continuing duty to withdraw their claims when it became clear that they had no factual basis.

The Plaintiffs maintained that their allegations against the Defendants were objectively reasonable. The Court agreed, stating that the Plaintiffs' conclusions and suspicions regarding the Defendants were objectively reasonable and justified in light of all the circumstances surrounding the dispute. The Court also held that the Plaintiff was under no duty to withdraw its claims, which were well supported, after the Complaint was filed. Lastly, the Court found that the Defendants' requests for sanctions were not destined to fail or manifestly unreasonable, and therefore, the Plaintiffs' requests for sanctions and fees were denied, meaning both sides' motions were dismissed.

## Case 26

District Court of Appeal of Florida,
Second District.

CHANNEL COMPONENTS, INC., Canaan Ames, and Christopher T. Lowder,
Appellants,

v.

AMERICA II ELECTRONICS, INC., Appellee.

Nos. 2D04-5395, 2D05-16.
December 21, 2005.

Jurisdiction: District Court of Appeal Florida, Second District

Date: December 21, 2005

Keywords: Discovery, Procedure, Sanctions

In a suit alleging tortuous interference with business relationships and breach of employment contracts, the Appellants appealed a judgment entered against them as a sanction for their violation of discovery orders. The Appellants argued that the judgment amounted to a criminal sanction for discovery violations. They further argued that the sanction was entered without the procedural protections required and that the amount of the sanction was unrelated to the harm caused by their violation of the discovery orders.

The trial court entered orders compelling discovery twice. Prior to this, the trial court provided the Appellants notice and an opportunity to be heard. The Appellants continued not complying with the discovery orders. The trial court then allowed for another hearing with notice and an opportunity for the Appellants to be heard, followed by allowing the Appellants another week to provide the discovery. The Court held that civil contempt may be imposed in an ordinary civil proceeding upon notice and an opportunity to be heard. The trial court imposed a sanction fining the Appellants $2,500 per day for each day after that week that the Appellants did not comply with the discovery order. The Court explained that a contempt sanction is considered civil if it is remedial and for the benefit of the complainant. The Court ruled that the judgment represented a coercive civil contempt sanction. The Court explained that the most important safeguard in civil contempt cases is a finding by the trial court that "the contemnor has the ability to purge the contempt." The Court found that this sanction provided the Appellants with a purge provision, which allowed for them to avoid any fine, if they complied with the discovery order before the week was over. The Appellants still refused to comply. Before the trial court reduced the sanction to a final judgment, it had a hearing and determined that the Appellants always had the ability to comply because the Appellants finally produced the requested documents, *which consisted of, among other things, e-mails to customers and vendors.* The Court held that the trial court properly held the Appellants in contempt. The Court also held that, where a court imposes a coercive fine that can be avoided entirely by complying with an order, there is no requirement that the fine coincide with damages or losses caused by the noncompliance. The Court held that all of the procedural requirements for imposing the coercive sanction were met, and the Appellants were given every opportunity to avoid the sanction. The Court upheld the trial court's sanction of the Appellants.

## Case 27

United States District Court,
D. Massachusetts.

COGNEX CORPORATION, Plaintiff,

v.

ELECTRO SCIENTIFIC INDUSTRIES, INC., Defendant.

No. Civ.A. 01CV10287RCL.
Filed February 14, 2001.
July 2, 2002.

Jurisdiction: United States District Court, District of Massachusetts

Date: July 2, 2002

Keywords: Discovery, Procedure, Costs and Cost Shifting

In a patent infringement suit, the Plaintiff informally moved to compel a search, by the Defendant, of its electronic backup tapes for documents responsive to the Plaintiff's requests for production of documents. Although the Defendant conceded that it had not searched the subject backup tapes, it opposed the motion on the basis that it had already conducted an extensive, reasonable search for documents, that the cost and burden of the search sought by the Plaintiff was unreasonable, and that any responsive and nonprivileged documents uncovered would likely be duplicative.

The Court found that the Defendant's past search did not suggest that a search of backup files would be duplicative. The Court also felt that, in light of the sheer volume of data on the backup tapes, it was virtually inconceivable that the tapes did not contain additional relevant material, which would be appropriate for production. That said, however, the Court concluded that the Defendant's prior search had been reasonable and that the cost of the new search would likely be astronomical. The Plaintiff then suggested that the costs be shared, so the Court considered shifting the costs to the Plaintiff while attempting to protect the Defendant's privileged documents. In doing so, the Court mentioned the use of an independent electronic discovery consultant.

Ultimately, while the Discovery Master believed that the Plaintiff's willingness to pay for the search made the question of whether to compel the search a close call, the Discovery Master did not order the search sought by the Plaintiff. In reaching this conclusion, the Court considered the extensiveness of the prior search, the offer to fund the new search, the likelihood of new documents being produced, the lack of evidence of past document destruction, concerns regarding the deletion of e-mails, notions of fairness, and the Plaintiff's own retention policy. The Court then denied the Plaintiff's informal motion to compel the Defendant to search its backup tapes.

## Case 28

Massachusetts Superior Court.

COMMONWEALTH

v.

James N. ELLIS Jr., Nicholas J. Ellis, and James N. ELLIS, Sr., et al.

Nos. 97-192, 97-562, 98-355, 97-193, 97-561, 97-356, 97-563.
August 27, 1999.

Jurisdiction: Massachusetts Superior Court

Date: August 27, 1999

Keywords: Admissibility, Constitutionality

The Defendants filed a motion to suppress electronically stored evidence seized from two separate searches of their computer system, arguing that all of the computerized data from the first search should be suppressed because the search was illegal, improperly executed, and the Commonwealth did not promptly return seized items. The Defendants further argued that the evidence seized during second search should be suppressed because the affidavit filed in support of the application for the search warrant failed to set forth probable cause, contained false statements or material omissions, and was not sufficiently particular. Lastly, the Defendants argued that all of the evidence obtained as a result of both searches should be suppressed because the Commonwealth had destroyed evidence and because neither warrant provided for the protection of privileged documents. The Commonwealth opposed the Defendants' motion to suppress by arguing that the issuance of the warrants, the warrants themselves, and the execution of the warrants were proper in all respects.

The Court found that the execution of the search warrants was carefully planned and executed with caution. The Court also concluded that the Commonwealth took pains to limit the intrusiveness of the search, taking as little of the computer system as possible and returning what was no longer needed. Furthermore, the Court held that the Commonwealth was not obligated to return any of the original computer equipment or media it had retained for evidentiary purposes. Accordingly, the Court found that the on-site execution of the search warrants was reasonable in all respects. In regard to the off-site searches of the computer system, the Court held that they were not unreasonable under the circumstances of the case and that the Defendants had not been prejudiced by the length of time it took for the completion of the search because they had received copies of all hard drives, software programs, and other media and equipment necessary to the operation of their law practice within several days of the search. The Court then concluded that the warrants were supported by probable cause, were sufficiently particular, and provided adequate protection for privileged documents. Lastly, the Court denied the Defendants' motion.

## Case 29

United States District Court,
N.D. Illinois, Eastern Division.

COMPUTER ASSOCIATES INTERNATIONAL, INC., a Delaware corporation,
Plaintiff,

v.

QUEST SOFTWARE, INC., a California corporation, Michael J. Friel,
an Illinois resident, Deborah A. Jenson, an Illinois resident,
Robert M. MacKowiak, an Illinois resident, and Elizabeth W. Wahlgren,
an Illinois resident, Defendants.

No. 02 C 4721.
June 3, 2003.

Jurisdiction: United States District Court, Northern District of Illinois,
Eastern Division

Date: June 3, 2003

Keywords: Costs and Cost Shifting

In an action for copyright infringement and trade secret misappropriation, the Defendants filed a motion to require the Plaintiff to pay for the computer consultation that would be necessary to prepare hard drives for disclosure, after the Plaintiff had requested that the Defendants make certain computer hard drives available for electronic imaging. In determining whether the burden of the discovery request outweighed the likely benefit and whether to shift all or part of the cost of production to the requesting party, the Court used the seven-factor Rowe cost-shifting analysis.

The Court found that the Plaintiff's requests had been as specific as possible because the requests had sought only images of the hard drives that the Plaintiff reasonably believed had contained information relevant to the use of the source code in question. The Defendants did not dispute that they had had the source code in their possession, making it likely that a thorough search of the drives would lead to the discovery of some relevant information. The search would likely reveal what uses the Defendants had made of the source code and whether they had disclosed it to other parties. The Defendants were clearly in the best position to control the costs and scope of the consultation and had the incentive to do so. The review would largely be for the Defendants' protection and benefit, and shifting the costs of the consultation would remove all incentive for them to narrowly tailor the review of the drives. Lastly, the Defendants sought to recover the costs of their preventative measures undertaken before the actual disclosure of the information to the Plaintiff. The Court held that such costs were analogous to the review of documents for privileged information and should not be shifted to the requesting party. Therefore, the Court denied the Defendant's motion to require the Plaintiff to pay for its electronic discovery requests.

## Case 30

---

United States District Court,
E.D. Arkansas, Western Division.

CONCORD BOAT CORPORATION et al., Plaintiff,

v.

BRUNSWICK CORPORATION, a Delaware Corporation, Defendant.

No. LR-C-95-781.
December 23, 1996.

---

Jurisdiction: United States District Court, Eastern District of Arkansas, Western Division

Date: December 23, 1996

Keywords: Discovery, Preservation of Evidence/Spoliation, Procedure, Experts

During protracted litigation, the Plaintiffs filed two motions regarding the discovery of electronic materials. The first was to compel electronically stored information and to prevent further destruction of documents. The second was to compel compliance with a previous court order.

The Defendant claimed that it had sent teams to each location to search for responsive documents and that those teams had interviewed employees, using the checklist during their efforts, which produced a large number of responsive documents. The Plaintiffs, however, felt that the search was not broad enough. They requested volumes of additional electronic documentation, in order to determine, for themselves, whether more relevant material exists. The Defendant asserted that the search had been reasonable and that a great deal of expense and trouble had been incurred because of it. It further maintained that complying with the Plaintiffs' demands would result in unbearable expense and interruption in conducting its business. In addition, it claimed that the recovery of earlier e-mail would be impossible because of software and hardware changes. The Plaintiffs argued that they were unable to evaluate the truth of the affidavits or to rebut them because the Defendant had refused to allow the Plaintiffs' experts to talk with Defendant's experts or to study the Defendant's computer systems.

The Court found that there was merit to both sides' positions and that part of the problem in resolving the electronic discovery issues was based on the Defendant's apparent refusal to have meaningful discussions to explore solutions. Therefore, the Court ordered the parties to have a meeting with counsel and computer experts, for both sides, to conduct a good faith discussion to see whether an agreement could be reached, on some of the outstanding issues, and to exchange information on what types of computer information was available, so that the Plaintiffs could more narrowly tailor their discovery demands. The Court expected the parties to be prepared to discuss issues, such as the choice of an expert, the procedure for specifying the expert's responsibilities, and allocation of the costs.

## Case 31

United States District Court,
S.D. New York.

CONVOLVE, INC., and Massachusetts Institute of Technology, Plaintiffs,

v.

COMPAQ COMPUTER CORP. and Seagate Technology, Inc., Defendants.

No. 00CIV.5141(GBD)(JCF).
August 17, 2004.

Jurisdiction: United States District Court, Southern District of New York

Date: August 17, 2004

Keywords: Discovery, Spoliation, Sanctions, Production of Evidence

The Plaintiffs asserted claims of patent infringement and theft of trade secrets against the Defendants, alleging that the Defendants breached an agreement by misappropriating technology and incorporating it into their own products. Among nine different discovery motions were those filed by the Plaintiffs to compel the Defendants to produce procurement documents and to impose sanctions for the Defendants' alleged discovery abuse.

In the motion to compel, the Court found the threshold question to be whether discovery was limited to specific disk drive models that the Plaintiffs accused of being infringing, or, alternatively, encompassed any computer system that included drives that could be switched between quiet mode and performance modes. The Plaintiffs complained that the Defendants had failed to produce requested documents, including those related to special mode drives. The Court found that requiring the Defendants to disclose all bills of materials for every computer system that might have incorporated either an accused drive or one that, while not accused, was special mode supportable, would require an expenditure of time and resources far out of proportion to the marginal value of the materials to this litigation. The Court noted that the documents did not indicate the specific instances when a relevant drive was actually installed in a system. Moreover, even if it were possible to obtain such information by linking each bill of materials to other data in the procurement system, there had been no showing that it would go beyond the information already provided by the Defendants in summary form. Lastly, the Court concluded that the Plaintiff had not presented evidence that would suggest that such summaries were either incomplete or inaccurate. Therefore, the Court held that there was no basis for requiring production of the bills of materials. In addition, the Plaintiff asked that the Defendants be sanctioned for failing to preserve certain information, consisting of e-mails, that came to light during a deposition. The Court found that, although the Defendants were obligated to preserve anything that they may have generated or received that was relevant to the claims or defenses, sanctions were not warranted, on the basis of the record, because the Plaintiff made no effort to determine the substance of the communications or the circumstances of their destruction. Accordingly, the Court held that the Plaintiff had not justified an adverse inference or any sanction.

## Case 32

United States District Court,
S.D. New York.

Louis COOK, Plaintiff,

v.

DELOITTE & TOUCHE, LLP, et ano., Defendants.

No. 03 Civ. 3926LAKFM.
September 30, 2005.

Jurisdiction: United States District Court, Southern District of New York

Date: September 30, 2005

Keywords: Discovery, Procedure, Sanctions

The Plaintiff brought an employment discrimination suit against his former employer, the Defendant, alleging that he was terminated on the basis of an actual or perceived disability. Following discovery, the Defendant moved for summary judgment. The Plaintiff opposed that motion and requested a continuance to take further discovery pursuant to Rule 56(f) of the Federal Rules of Civil Procedure.

Two months after the discovery deadline and one month after the Defendants' motion for summary judgment, the Plaintiff requested the continuance for further discovery under Rule 56(f). The Plaintiff claimed that the Defendants' responses to discovery were inadequate and therefore a continuance was necessary. The Court found that, if the Plaintiff had problems with the adequacy of the discovery material the Defendant provided, the Plaintiff should have raised the complaints before discovery ended and before the Defendant prepared its summary judgment papers. The Plaintiff contends that there were several instances where the Defendant's witnesses indicated that they made certain electronic entries in the course of their work, but the electronic entries had not been produced by the Defendant during discovery. The Plaintiff sought further electronic discovery on that basis. The Court found no showing that critical electronic entries were kept from the Plaintiff. The Court held that it was therefore uncontested that the Defendant produced all of the relevant electronic entries. There was also an e-mail produced by the Defendant indicating that the Defendant wanted to replace the Plaintiff at an earlier date. The Plaintiff contended that other e-mails concerning this existed in the Defendant's computer archives, but were never produced. The

Court found that, even if such e-mails did exist, the Plaintiff did not make a "showing necessary to warrant their retrieval at this late date" at the Defendant's expense, nor did the Plaintiff volunteer to pay for the cost of retrieving these e-mails. The Court determined that the Plaintiff was not entitled to a continuance for further discovery. The Court granted the Defendant's motion for summary judgment.

## Case 33

United States District Court,
E.D. Michigan, Southern Division.

DAIMLERCHRYSLER MOTORS, Plaintiff,

v.

BILL DAVIS RACING, INC. Defendant.

No. Civ.A. 03-72265.
December 22, 2005.

Jurisdiction: United States District Court, Eastern District of Michigan, Southern Division

Date: December 22, 2005

Keywords: Sanctions, Spoliation

In a case involving a dispute over a written agreement, the Plaintiff moved for sanctions for destruction of evidence. The Plaintiff terminated the agreement between it and the Defendant and instituted the lawsuit against the Defendant. The Court found that the Defendant's obligation to preserve relevant records and communication concerning the business relationship flowing from the agreement began when it received the summons and complaint.

The Defendant argued that its copies of e-mail messages were lost because its computer system was set up to delete internal and external e-mails automatically, unless an affirmative action was taken to preserve them. The Court found that the procedure of destroying documents should have been suspended, because the Defendant was on notice of the pending litigation. The Court found no evidence to suggest that the Defendant even attempted to retain computer data. The Court found that the Defendant failed to prevent spoliation. The Court, however, did not find that the Defendant's failure to preserve these communications was a result of bad faith. The Court held that a sanction proportionate to the circumstances should be imposed upon the Defendant. The Court recommended that a special instruction advising the jury that the destroyed evidence could be presumed to be unfavorable to the Defendant was appropriate.

## Case 34

Court of Appeal, Fourth District, Division 2, California.

DODGE, WARREN & PETERS INSURANCE SERVICES, INC.,
Plaintiff and Respondent,

v.

James W. RILEY et al., Defendants and Appellants.

No. E031719.
February 5, 2003.

Jurisdiction: Court of Appeal, Fourth District, Division 2, California

Date: February 5, 2003

Keywords: Procedure, Preservation of Evidence/Spoliation

In a case involving misappropriation of trade secrets and similar causes of action regarding the termination of the Defendants' employment, the Defendants appealed an order issuing a preliminary injunction against them, which required the preservation of electronic evidence by prohibiting the Defendants from destroying, deleting, or secreting from discovery any of their electronic storage media and by requiring them to allow a court-appointed expert to copy all of their media, to recover lost or deleted files, and to perform automated searches for evidence. The Defendants claimed that the trial court had erred in issuing the injunction because an adequate remedy at law had already existed and because the Plaintiff provided no evidence in support of its issuance.

The Court first set out to determine whether it had been appropriate for the trial court to issue an injunction to prevent the potential destruction of evidence pending discovery. The Court could not conceive, as a matter of policy, in light of the broad discretion possessed by the trial court to ensure the effective administration of justice, why injunctive relief should not have been available under the circumstances. The Defendants claimed that the injunction was not properly issued because the Civil Discovery Act of 1998 provided the Plaintiff with an adequate remedy at law. The Court held that the Defendants provided no authority for their proposition and that they failed to establish that the Discovery Act provided any protection such as that sought by the Plaintiffs. In addition, the Court was unconvinced that the availability of sanctions for misuse of the discovery statutes established an adequate remedy at law for the preservation of evidence.

Next, the Defendants claimed that the injunction had not been properly issued because the Plaintiff had not made the showing necessary to obtain it. The Court did not find that the trial court had abused its discretion in determining that Defendants' media contained information that the Plaintiff would have a right to discover. In addition, the Court did not find that the trial court had abused its discretion in determining that the Plaintiff would suffer greater harm should the injunction not be issued than the Defendants would suffer if it were. Therefore, the Court affirmed the order issuing the injunction.

## Case 35

United States District Court,
S.D. New York.

John DOE; American Civil Liberties Union; and American Civil Liberties
Union Foundation, Plaintiffs,

v.

John ASHCROFT, in his official capacity as Attorney General of the
United States; Robert Mueller, in his official capacity as Director of the
Federal Bureau of Investigation; and Marion Bowman, in his official capacity
as Senior Counsel to the Federal Bureau of Investigation, Defendants.

No. 04 Civ. 2614(VM).
September 28, 2004.

Jurisdiction: United States District Court, Southern District of New York

Date: September 28, 2004

Keywords: Discovery, Constitutionality

The Plaintiffs challenged the constitutionality of 18 U.S.C. § 2709, the statute that authorizes the Federal Bureau of Investigation to compel communications firms, such as Internet service providers or telephone companies, to produce certain customer records whenever the FBI certifies that those records are relevant to an authorized investigation to protect against international terrorism or clandestine intelligence activities. The lead Plaintiff was described in the complaint as an Internet access firm that received a National Security Letter. The Plaintiffs asserted that the statute's broad subpoena power violated the First, Fourth, and Fifth Amendments of the United States Constitution, and that the nondisclosure provision violated the First Amendment. They argued that the statute was unconstitutional on its face and as applied to the facts of the case. The Plaintiffs' main complaints were that, first, the statute gave the FBI extraordinary and unchecked power to obtain private information without any form of judicial process, and, second, that the statute's nondisclosure provision burdened speech categorically and perpetually, without any case-by-case judicial consideration of whether that speech burden was justified. The parties cross-moved for summary judgment on all claims.

The Court granted Plaintiffs' motion in concluding that the statute violated the Fourth Amendment because, at least as it was applied, it effectively barred or substantially deterred any judicial challenge to the propriety of an

NSL request. In the Court's view, ready availability of judicial process to pursue such a challenge was necessary to vindicate important rights guaranteed by the Constitution or by statute. On separate grounds, the Court also concluded that the permanent ban on disclosure, which the Court was unable to sever from the remainder of the statute, operated as an unconstitutional prior restraint on speech in violation of the First Amendment. In the Court's final analysis, it deemed it unnecessary to rule upon Plaintiff's Fourth Amendment facial challenge. The Court also declined the Plaintiffs' invitation to decide the measure of Fourth Amendment protection demanded when the Government made NSL requests generally or in any particular case. The Court decided only that those rights, as well as other rights attaching to protected speech content that may be revealed to the Government as a result of an NSL, are implicated to some extent when an individual receives an NSL, thus necessitating the practical availability of some form of access to the judicial system to challenge the NSL. On the record before it, the Court found that in practice those rights were substantially curtailed by the manner in which the FBI administered the statute. The Court agrees with the Plaintiffs that the nondisclosure provision was unconstitutional, as it failed to pass muster under the exacting First Amendment standards because it was so broad and open-ended. Because the Court could not sever the provision from the remainder of the statute, the Court granted the remedy the Plaintiffs requested enjoining the Government from using the statute in any case as a means of gathering information from the sources specified in the statute.

The Court concluded that the compulsory, secret, and unreviewable production of information required by the FBI's application of 18 U.S.C. § 2709 violated the Fourth Amendment and that the nondisclosure provision violated the First Amendment. The Court held that the Government was therefore enjoined from issuing NSLs or from enforcing the nondisclosure provision.

## Case 36

Superior Court of New Jersey,
Appellate Division.

Jane DOE individually and as g/a/l for Jill Doe, a minor, Plaintiff-Appellant,

v.

XYC CORPORATION, Defendant-Respondent.

Argued September 28, 2005.
Decided December 27, 2005.

Jurisdiction: Superior Court of New Jersey, Appellate Division

Date: December 27, 2005

Keywords: Constitutionality, Procedure

The Plaintiff brought a claim to hold the Defendant responsible for transmission of pornographic photos of the Plaintiff's daughter to the Internet by the Defendant's employee, using the Defendant's computer. The Plaintiff appealed a summary judgment dismissing her complaint against the Defendant.

The Plaintiff argued that the Defendant knew or should have known the employee was using the computer to view and download child pornography, had a duty to report the activity to the authorities, breached its duty, and a direct and proximate cause of this breach of duty was the employee's ability to continue photographing and molesting the Plaintiff's daughter, resulting in her suffering permanent harm. Through evidence gathered by accessing the employee's work computer and the employee's server logs, the Defendant was aware that the employee visited pornographic Web sites from the computer. The employee's supervisors asked the employee on several occasions to refrain from this activity. The employee stored pornographic pictures of the Plaintiff's minor daughter on the Defendant's computer and transmitted pornographic photos of the Plaintiff's minor daughter to an Internet site from the Defendant's computer. The Court found that the Defendant possessed and could have implemented software that would have allowed the Defendant to monitor the employee's activities. The Court found that the Defendant was aware that it had the right to monitor the Web sites accessed by employees and monitor its employees' e-mails. The Court further found that the Defendant was on notice that the employee was viewing child pornography on the computer. The Court also found that with this knowledge came the duty of the Defendant to prevent the employee from intentionally harming others or creating a risk of bodily harm to others. The Court held that determining whether the breach of duty proximately caused harm to the Plaintiff's daughter is an issue for the trier of fact. The Court reversed the summary judgment.

## Case 37

Superior Court of New Jersey,
Appellate Division.

Victor EISENBERG, Plaintiff-Appellant,

v.

FORT LEE BOARD OF EDUCATION, John C. Richardson, Robert Taglieri &
Joan Voss, Defendants-Respondents.

Submitted October 18, 2005.
Decided November 3, 2005.

Jurisdiction: Superior Court of New Jersey, Appellate Division

Date: November 3, 2005

Keywords: Discovery, Experts, Spoliation

The Plaintiff appealed the summary judgment dismissing his claims of breach of contract, breach of covenant of good faith and fair dealing, and discrimination. Among other things, the Plaintiff argues that the Defendant's spoliation of critical evidence warranted a denial of summary judgment. The Plaintiff argued that the trial judge misconstrued his argument about the spoliation of evidence.

The issue of spoliation concerned a memorandum written by the Defendant. The memorandum was referred to in other discovery documents, but the Defendant was unable to produce it. The Defendant, in cooperation with the Plaintiff, hired a forensic electronic retrieval firm to search all of the hard drives in the school to try to find the document, but that was not successful. This document discussed the Plaintiff, along with other teachers in similar positions, who were under consideration for nonrenewal of their teaching contracts. The Court found that there was no evidence that the content of the document was critical to the Plaintiff's case. The Court determined that the trial judge understood the Plaintiff's spoliation argument, even though she denied it as a basis for denial of summary judgment. The Court held that there was no basis for a spoliation inference in this case because the Defendant went to great lengths to retrieve the document and provided as much information about the document as possible.

# Case 38

Court of Appeals, Fourth District, Division 3, California.

ELECTRONIC FUNDS SOLUTIONS et al., Plaintiffs and Respondents,

v.

Michael MURPHY et al., Defendants and Appellants.

No. G031778.
December 14, 2005.

Jurisdiction: Court of Appeals, Fourth District, Division 3, California

Date: December 14, 2005

Keywords: Spoliation, Sanctions, Discovery

The Plaintiffs asserted business tort claims against the Defendants. The Plaintiffs filed a motion for terminating sanctions against the Defendants, after the Defendants repeatedly did not comply with discovery orders and requests. After entering an order striking the Defendant's answer as a discovery sanction, the trial court entered a default judgment in favor of the Plaintiffs. The Defendants appealed the judgment contending among other things that the sanction striking the Defendants' answer violated their due process rights.

The Defendants objected to the Plaintiff's first set of document inspection demands, but stipulated to producing all responsive documents not covered by the attorney-client and work product privileges. The trial court entered this stipulation as a court order expressly requiring production of all electronic data. The Defendants then served a supplemental statement affirming they had produced all documents covered by the order; however, they claimed a computer virus destroyed responsive e-mails on one of the Defendants' computers. The trial court held that this did not comply with the court order. The trial court imposed $1,000 sanctions against each Defendant and ordered the Defendants to submit a revised supplemental statement and to produce all responsive documents per the stipulated order within seven days. The Defendants then provided a revised supplemental statement and additional documents. The Defendants did not turn over any electronic data. The Plaintiffs moved for sanctions and to compel production on their second document inspection demands seeking to inspect the Defendants' computers. Upon inspection, the Plaintiffs' computer forensic consultant concluded that four of the computers had their hard drives "wiped" by "Data Eraser" software between the time the court ordered the inspection and the inspection of the forensic consultant. A fifth computer had some of the information "wiped" from it, but through forensic techniques some data could be recovered. The Defendants, however, asserted under oath that they had fully complied with the demands and mentioned no removal of data from the computers. The Court held that the trial court did not violate the Defendants' rights to due process by issuing the terminating sanctions. The Court held that there is ample evidence to support the trial court's issuance of a terminating sanction. The Court found that, despite the Defendants' agreement to turn over documents and the court's order that the Defendants produce the responsive materials in their entirety, Defendants ran a "Data Eraser" program on the hard drives in an apparent attempt to destroy the e-mails responsive to the previous document request. The Court determined that, in light of the Defendants' violation of the discovery order in the face of an express warning that terminating sanctions would be issued, the trial court could have concluded that a lesser sanction would not have been sufficient to compel compliance and the terminating sanctions were necessary to provide the Plaintiffs with the due process they deserved.

## Case 39

Supreme Court, Nassau County, New York

Deborah ETZION, Plaintiff,

v.

Rafael ETZION, Defendant.

February 17, 2005.
7 Misc.3d 940, 2005 WL 689468

Jurisdiction: Supreme Court, Nassau County, New York

Date: February 17, 2005

Keywords: Procedure, Discovery, Experts, Costs and Cost Shifting

In a matrimonial action, the Court delineated means to limit disclosure of nondiscoverable communications, after the Plaintiff made an all-encompassing request for computer data, to which the Defendant objected. The Court appointed an Attorney Referee to supervise the discovery. The Plaintiff's expert, the Defendant's expert, and the attorney referee were ordered to physically be present at all of the locations that the Defendant designated as sources of computer data. The Plaintiff's expert was then ordered to clone or copy the hard drives of the computers. The resultant hard drives were to be immediately turned over to the Referee.

After all of the cloned drives had been handed over to the Referee, the hard drives were to be examined by the experts and the Referee at a location jointly selected by all three. Hard copies of business records only found on the hard drives were to be made and distributed to the attorneys for both parties. Nothing else was to be transmitted to the attorneys. After reviewing the cloned hard drives, the Referee was ordered to maintain control of the clones until the conclusion of the matter, at which time the cloned hard drives were to be returned to the Defendant for disposal. Any questions that arose as to the appropriate review of a particular document were ultimately subject to the Referee's determination.

Lastly, the Court ordered the Plaintiff to temporarily bear the production costs, while both parties had to pay for their own expert fees. The Defendant's application for a reimbursement bond for any potential damage to his computer system or business interests was denied, as the Defendant's computer expert and the Referee were intended to protect the Defendant from such damages during discovery.

## Case 40

Appellate Court of Connecticut.

FEDERAL DEPOSIT INSURANCE CORPORATION

v.

Ralph CARABETTA.

Federal Deposit Insurance Corporation

v.

Salvatore P. Carabetta.

Federal Deposit Insurance Corporation

v.

Evelyn M. Carabetta.

Federal Deposit Insurance Corporation

v.

Salvatore R. Carabetta.

No. 17923.
Argued April 28, 1999.
Decided October 19, 1999.

Jurisdiction: Appellate Court of Connecticut

Date: October 19, 1999

Keywords: Admissibility, Procedure

On appeal, the Defendants raised evidentiary challenges, maintaining that the trial court had improperly admitted testimonial and documentary evidence to establish the amount of their debts, after the trial court had awarded damages to the Plaintiff against the Defendants. The Defendants' claimed that the trial court improperly admitted testimonial evidence regarding the interest due, arguing that the information relied upon to calculate the interest due purportedly came from the records of the bank, and therefore, it was hearsay within hearsay. The Court found, however, that the witness had had personal knowledge of the manner in which the computer records were kept and of how the documents she had relied on had been admitted into evidence. The Court held that the trial court had properly admitted the testimony of the witness.

The Defendants also claimed that the trial court had improperly admitted documentary evidence, specifically an exhibit as proof of the principal balance on the promissory notes. The Court, however, did not agree in concluding that the keeping of a report in the failed bank's data bank that served as the basis of whether the Plaintiff had been owed money under a note and loan agreement satisfied the statutory requirement of record and that such a record could reasonably be found to have been made in the course of the Plaintiff's business, that it was the regular course of such business to make such a record and that it was made at the time of the act described in the report or within a reasonable time thereafter. Accordingly, the Court affirmed the damages awarded to the Plaintiff.

## Case 41

United States District Court,
E.D. Washington.

FEDERAL TRADE COMMISSION, Plaintiff,

v.

MAXTHEATER, INC., a Washington corporation, and Thomas L. Delanoy,
individually and as an officer of MaxTheater, Inc., Defendants.

No. 05-CV-0069-LRS.
March 31, 2005.

Jurisdiction: United States District Court, Eastern District of Washington

Date: March 31, 2005

Keywords: Spyware

The Plaintiff, the Federal Trade Commission, filed a complaint for injunctive and other equitable relief, pursuant to Section 13(b) of the Federal Trade Commission Act and moved ex parte for a temporary restraining order. The Court granted the FTC's motion and entered a temporary restraining order. The parties then stipulated to the entry of a stipulated order for preliminary injunction and other equitable relief and requested the Court to enter them. In the Order, the Defendants defined spyware as programs that secretly install on a computer without a user's permission or knowledge and may cause pop ups, banner advertisements, and other extraneous ads, send spam e-mail messages, hijack search engine links or home pages, track online activity, allow others to remotely access a computer, record private information, or steal passwords. They also indicated that spyware includes adware, keyloggers, trojans, hijackers, dialers, viruses, spam, and general ad serving. The Defendants defined an antispyward product as any product, however denominated, including, but not limited to, "SpywareAssassin," that does or purports to identify, monitor, remove, block, or otherwise prevent spyware from residing on a computer.

Pursuant to the stipulation, the Court ordered that the Defendants were restrained and enjoined from engaging, participating, or assisting others in any capacity whatsoever, in the advertising, promoting, marketing, offering, providing, selling or offering for sale of any antispyware product or service. Furthermore, in connection with advertising, promoting, marketing, offering, providing, selling, or offering for sale any product or service, the Defendants were restrained and enjoined from making, or assisting others in making, directly or indirectly, expressly or by implication, any representation of material fact that it would be false or misleading. The Court then ordered the Defendants to deposit $76,000.00, an amount approximating the total expenditures made by purchasers of the Defendants' antispyware product, into a trust account. Lastly, the Court ordered that Defendants preserve all documents and business records, regardless of media storage, and that they be prevented from exercising control over any business ventures.

## Case 42

United States District Court,
D. New Hampshire.

FEDERAL TRADE COMMISSION

v.

SEISMIC ENTERTAINMENT PRODUCTIONS, INC., SmartBot.Net, Inc., and
Sanford Wallace

No. Civ. 04-377-JD.
October 21, 2004.

Jurisdiction: United States District Court, District of New Hampshire

Date: October 21, 2004

Keywords: Spyware, Procedure

The Federal Trade Commission brought an action against the Defendants, under the Federal Trade Commission Act, seeking an injunction to stop the Defendants from engaging in certain Internet marketing practices. The FTC claimed that the Defendants' marketing practices were unfair because they affected commerce. The FTC then filed a motion for a temporary restraining order and other equitable relief, to which the Defendants filed an objection.

The Court stated that when the FTC seeks temporary injunctive relief pending further proceedings on the complaint for a permanent injunction, the court does not use the traditional temporary restraining order standard but instead applies the more lenient public interest standard. Under the public interest standard, the FTC need not prove irreparable harm, but instead the court considers the likelihood that the FTC will succeed on the merits and balances the equities implicated by the challenged activities. The Court found that the FTC was likely to succeed in showing that the Defendants' activities were unfair and deceptive practices within the meaning of the FTCA. The Court also concluded that those activities caused and would continue to cause substantial injury to consumers by negatively affecting the performance of their computers and requiring significant time and expense to remedy the problems the defendants caused. Consumers were not able to avoid the problems because the Defendants accessed their computers, installed software and programs, and made changes without the user's knowledge or consent. Because the Defendants offered no countervailing benefit from their activities the Court held that the FTC appeared likely to succeed on the merits of the claim.

For similar reasons, the Court also held that the balance of the equities favored granting temporary injunctive relief. The Defendants challenged the proposed prohibition against using Web browser security vulnerabilities to download software or other content. They argued that the prohibition could include legitimate and accepted marketing practices. The Court found that the public interest in curtailing the Defendants' unauthorized access to consumers' computers was amply demonstrated. Therefore, the balance of the equities favored granting the protection requested by the FTC. The Court then granted temporary injunctive relief, in which the Defendants were ordered to curtail all of their business activities and preserve all relevant records.

## Case 43

United States District Court,
S.D. Texas.

FEDERAL TRADE COMMISSION, Plaintiff,

v.

TRUSTSOFT, INC. d/b/a Swanksoft and Spykiller, Danilo Ladendorf,
individually and as an officer of Trustsoft, Inc., Defendants

No. Civ. H05-1905.
June 14, 2005.

Jurisdiction: United States District Court, Southern District of Texas

Date: June 14, 2005

Keywords: Spyware, Procedure

The Plaintiff, the Federal Trade Commission, pursuant to sections of the Federal Trade Commission Act and the Controlling the Assault of Non-Solicited Pornography and Marketing Act ("CAN-SPAM Act") et seq., filed, against the Defendants, a complaint for injunctive and other equitable relief, including consumer redress, and applied ex parte for a temporary restraining order. After consideration and in response, the Court issued a temporary restraining order with an asset freeze and granted other equitable ancillary relief. Both parties then stipulated to the entry of a stipulated preliminary injunction order and requested the Court to enter it.

The Plaintiff claimed that there was good cause to believe that the Defendants engaged in deceptive acts or practices in violation of Section 5 of the FTC Act, by making numerous materially deceptive representations in their marketing, selling, and distribution via the Internet of their spyware-removal product, "SpyKiller." These misrepresentations included false reports of scans of consumers' computers for spyware, false reports of spyware found on consumers' computers, and false statements about the removal capabilities of SpyKiller. In addition, the Plaintiff asserted that the Defendants had initiated commercial e-mail that failed to comply with the requirements of the CAN-SPAM Act. The Plaintiff further maintained that there was good cause to believe that the Defendants would continue with such illegal actions, if not restrained from doing so by order of the Court, and that there was good cause to believe that immediate and irreparable damage would result from the Defendants' ongoing violations, unless the Defendants were restrained and enjoined by order of the Court. Lastly, the Plaintiff argued that there was good cause to believe that immediate and irreparable damage to the Court's ability to grant effective final relief for consumers in the form of monetary restitution would result from the sale, transfer, or other disposition or concealment by the Defendants of their assets or business records, unless the Defendants were immediately restrained and enjoined by order of the Court. The Defendants disputed and denied the contentions of the Plaintiff, but agreed to the stipulated preliminary injunction to expedite a resolution of the matter. The Court then ordered, until further order from the Court, that the Defendants halt their current activities, that their assets be frozen, that they provide the Plaintiff with a full financial reporting and accounting, that they retain all assets and records thereof, that they produce and preserve all records, and that they identify their affiliates and customers.

## Case 44

United States District Court,
S.D. Indiana, Indianapolis Division.

FERMAGLICH, Eric, Fermaglich, Marcia, Southern Response Inc, Plaintiffs,

v.

STATE of Indiana

No. IP-01-1859-T/K.
September 29, 2004.

Jurisdiction: United States District Court, Southern District of Indiana, Indianapolis Division

Date: September 29, 2004

Keywords: Constitutionality

The Plaintiffs brought an action alleging violations of their rights to be free from unreasonable searches and seizures under the Fourth Amendment. The cause came before the Court on summary judgment and related motions filed by the Defendants.

The Plaintiffs alleged that four computers, as well as computer equipment, were seized from them and that the terms of the warrant did not explicitly include computers or computer equipment. The Court noted, however, that the warrant permitted the seizure of any and all records pertaining to the purchase of, use, and destruction of drugs used by the company. The Court concluded that it could reasonably be inferred that such records would be stored and maintained by a computer. Because there was no Seventh Circuit case precedent on the issue, the Court relied on district and state court opinions to resolve whether the seizure of computers was permissible under a warrant that authorized seizure of information that a police officer could reasonably infer to be contained within a computer. In reviewing the opinions, the Court held that the seizure of the computers and computer equipment did not exceed the scope of the warrant and thus, did not violate Plaintiffs' Fourth Amendment rights.

## Case 45

United States Court of Appeals,
Federal Circuit.

FIRST USA BANK, N.A., Plaintiff-Appellee,

v.

PAYPAL, INC., Defendant,

v.

Peter A. Thiel, Subpoenaed Party-Appellant.

No. 03-1558.
DECIDED: August 21, 2003.

Jurisdiction: United States Court of Appeals, Federal Circuit

Date: August 21, 2003

Keywords: Procedure

In a patent infringement suit, the Defendant moved for a stay, pending appeal, of a previous order directing him to produce his laptop computer, for forensic inspection, and to appear for a deposition. The Plaintiff opposed his motion and argued that the Defendant's appeal should be dismissed.

The Defendant had used the laptop while he was the CEO of the allegedly infringing company and had subsequently purchased it when he left. The Plaintiff had sought discovery from the Defendant pursuant to a subpoena, to which he had objected. The Defendant had been ordered to be available for a deposition and to create a privilege log, should any relevant documents be found on his computer. The district court affirmed the magistrate's order, and the Defendant appealed.

The Plaintiff argued that the Defendant's appeal should be dismissed, because he had appealed from a nonfinal interlocutory order and that the Perlman doctrine that had been asserted by the Defendant was inapplicable. The Court agreed, stating that orders requiring the production of evidence in a subpoena proceeding are generally not immediately appealable by the subpoenaed party and that the subpoenaed party must refuse to comply and appeal any subsequent contempt order. The Court found that the Defendant, who was the subpoenaed party, had appealed and, that because his appeal did not fall within the Perlman doctrine, the interlocutory appeal had to be dismissed. Accordingly, the Court dismissed the Defendant's appeal and held that his motion to stay was moot.

## Case 46

Court of Appeals of Minnesota.

Jeffrey L. FOUST et al., Respondents,
v.
John R. McFARLAND et al., Appellants.

Nos. A04-760, A04-1956.
June 14, 2005.

Jurisdiction: Court of Appeals of Minnesota

Date: June 14, 2005

Keywords: Spoliation, Sanctions, Procedure

In a personal injury case where a jury found the Defendants liable for millions of dollars in damages, the Defendants appealed from the denial of their motion for judgment notwithstanding the verdict. They asserted that an abuse-of-discretion standard of review is inappropriate in spoliation cases where a party intentionally and in bad faith destroys evidence. They also argued that a de novo standard of review should be applied. The Court disagreed, holding that there was no authority limiting an abuse-of-discretion standard to cases involving only negligent or unintentional destruction of electronic evidence. It found that the standard of review applies to any case where critical evidence has been destroyed and that regardless of intent, disposal of evidence is spoliation when a party knows or should know that the evidence should be preserved for pending or future litigation.

The Defendants also challenged the sanction for spoliation of evidence, arguing that the adverse instruction sanction given was not harsh enough. The Court found, however, that the sanction was appropriate, because the district court had recognized the seriousness of the Plaintiff's conduct, weighed the record, and made a determination that an unfavorable inference instruction was appropriate, as it was a sanction permitted by the state courts in spoliation of evidence claims. The Court held that the district court had not erred by no granting a JNOV and affirmed the ruling.

## Case 47

United States District Court,
N.D. Texas, Fort Worth Division.

Wayne A. FOWLER

v.

BELL HELICOPTER TEXTRON, INC.

No. Civ.A. 4:03-CV-842Y.
March 9, 2005.

Jurisdiction: United States District Court, Northern District of Texas,
Fort Worth Division

Date: March 9, 2005

Keywords: Computer Forensics, Metadata, Procedure

In a suit based on claims or copyright infringement, breach of contract, promissory estoppel, theft of trade secrets, and several others, the Defendant moved for partial summary judgment declaring that the Defendant was the exclusive owner of software that had been written by the Plaintiff. The Defendant argued that the program had been developed by the Plaintiff, during his employment with the Defendant, using their information and capabilities, thereby making the program their proprietary information pursuant to a confidentiality agreement. The Plaintiff claimed that he had created the program at home on his personal computer before his employment with the Defendant and that the only work performed on the program while he was employed with them was to configure the program for use with the Defendants' specifications.

To support his position, the Plaintiff offered an affidavit from a computer-forensic expert who indicated that it would be an enormous task to reset the clock on the floppy disks containing the original code and that, in his opinion, the Defendant authored the code in question at the time reported by the disks. The Defendants also offered their own expert, who reached the opposite conclusion. The Court found that there was a genuine issue of material fact, because a rational trier of fact could find that the Plaintiff had developed the software prior to his employment. Therefore, the Court denied the Defendants' motion for partial summary judgment.

## Case 48

United States District Court,
E.D. New York.

FOX INDUSTRIES, INCORPORATED, Plaintiff,

v.

Leonid GUROVICH, a/k/a Leo Gore, Defendant.

No. CV-03-5166.
August 25, 2004.

Jurisdiction: United States District Court, Eastern District of New York

Date: August 25, 2004

Keywords: Discovery, Procedure, Experts, Computer Forensics

The Defendant, who had previously been found in contempt of prior orders of the court, objected to the magistrate judge's report and recommendation granting the Plaintiff lost profits and attorney's fees and costs relating to the Defendant's contemptuous conduct. Specifically, the Defendant objected to the Court's appointment of a forensic computer expert to examine his computer, unless the Defendant's attorney was present through the examination and did not let the expert look at privileged or personal documents or e-mails.

The Court held that the Defendant could certainly propose a protective discovery order to the judge concerning the modus operandi of the search of his computer and that his attorney could be present, if he wished, at any forensic examination of the Defendant's computer while a tamper-proof mirror image of the computer's files was made. In addition the Court stated that the Defendant's attorney may also subsequently identify any documents or e-mails as being, in his view, personal or privileged. The Court warned that mere assertions that a document or e-mail was personal or privileged would not suffice to prevent its discovery and that such matters would be decided by the judge, in accordance with his procedures. Therefore, the Court affirmed the report and adopted it as an order of the court.

## Case 49

Superior Court of Pennsylvania.

In the Interest of: F.P., A Minor
Appeal of: F.P., A Minor, Appellant

No. 1126 W.D.A.2004.
June 15, 2005.

Jurisdiction: Superior Court of Pennsylvania

Date: June 15, 2005

Keywords: Admissibility

The Defendant appealed his conviction of one count of aggravated assault. The Defendant argued that the trial court erred in having permitted the introduction of a computerized instant message into evidence, because the instant message was inadmissible as not being properly authenticated. He claimed that the instant message should not have been admitted because it had not been proven that he was the author. He further asserted that, in view of the inherent unreliability of e-mail and instant messages, it had been incumbent upon the Commonwealth to authenticate the documents by introducing evidence of their source, from the Internet service provider, or presenting the testimony of a computer forensic expert.

The Court found that there was clearly sufficient evidence that the Defendant had been the author and sent the threatening messages. The Court noted that he referred to himself by his first name. He had repeatedly accused the victim of stealing from him, which had mirrored testimony that the Defendant had been angry about a stolen DVD. The Defendant referenced the fact that the victim had approached high school authorities about the instant messages. The Defendant had repeatedly called the victim vile names and threatened to beat him up. The Court held that all of this evidence, taken together, had been clearly sufficient to authenticate the instant message transcripts, as having originated from the Defendant, and it found no abuse of discretion in the admission of the messages. The Court concluded its findings by stating that the Defendant sought the Court to create a whole new body of law just to deal with e-mails and instant messages. The Court was unwilling to do so, explaining that similar uncertainties exist with traditional written documents, as they do for electronic forms of communication. A signature can be forged; a letter can be typed on another's typewriter; distinct letterhead stationary can be copied or stolen. In affirming the Defendant's conviction, the Court ruled that the documents were admissible and had been properly authenticated through the use of circumstantial evidence.

## Case 50

Court of Appeals of Texas,
Beaumont.

Jerry FRIDELL, Appellant

v.

The STATE of Texas, Appellee.

Nos. 09-04-200 CR, 09-04-201 CR.
Submitted November 23, 2004.
Delivered December 22, 2004.

Jurisdiction: Court of Appeals of Texas, Beaumont

Date: December 22, 2004

Keywords: Experts, Computer Forensics

The Defendant, who had been found guilty of charges stemming from the possession of child pornography, appealed his conviction, challenging the sufficiency of the evidence. The Defendant contested that there had been no clear link between himself and the alleged pornographic images and that others had had access to the computer from which the images had been acquired. He supported this contention by citing testimony from a computer forensic expert. The expert had testified that he had not found anything on the recovered photographs, such as the Defendant's name, that had specifically linked them to the Defendant or had shown that the Defendant had created them.

Regarding the Defendant's argument that others had had access to the computer, the Court found that the Defendant had failed to provide any reference to a record, showing that others had such access. In addition, while the Defendant maintained that he did not use certain search terms in his Web browser, he also stated that he did not know who at his home might have done so or even had an interest in such matters. Moreover, when attacking his possession conviction, the Defendant never argued that the computer was not his or that the images that had been obtained from his computer were not child pornography. The Court deferred to the fact finder's determination of the weight and credibility to be given to Defendant's testimony and did not substitute its judgment for that of the fact finders.

The Court held that the numerous photographs that had been recovered, the extensive use of Defendant's computer in searching for child pornography, and the Defendant's attempts to erase material from the computer all showed that Defendant's possession of child pornography had been knowing or intentional. Therefore, the Court found that the evidence had been legally sufficient to support the Defendant's conviction. Likewise, the Court held that the evidence had also been factually sufficient and that the convictions had been neither clearly wrong nor manifestly unjust. The Court affirmed the trial court's judgment.

# Case 51

United States District Court,
E.D. Virginia, Alexandria Division.

GALAXY COMPUTER SERVICES, INC., Plaintiff,

v.

Lara BAKER et al., Defendants.

No. 1:04CV1036 (JCC).
May 27, 2005.

Jurisdiction: United States District Court, Eastern District of Virginia, Alexandria Division

Date: May 27, 2005

Keywords: Procedure, Admissibility, Experts

In a bankruptcy case, both parties filed motions in limine to exclude testimony from witnesses and experts on both sides. The Plaintiff had sought to introduce the opinion testimony of a computer forensic expert, to establish that the Defendants had deleted certain files of the Plaintiff, and the Defendants filed a motion in limine, to exclude that expert's testimony. The Plaintiff had offered the expert's testimony for the purposes of authenticating the recovered documents and seeking jury instructions on spoliation of evidence and consciousness of wrongdoing. In attempting to exclude the testimony, the Defendants argued that the expert opinion was irrelevant to the issues that had been set for trial, that the expert was not qualified to give expert testimony, that the expert did not follow proper procedures, and that he could not opine about altered or deleted data. Consequently, the Defendants asserted that the expert's proposed testimony had been irrelevant and not helpful to the jury.

The Court disagreed holding that the interactions between the Plaintiff's officers and directors and the Defendant's agents, including intentional file deletions, were highly relevant to the Plaintiff's claims in its complaint and supported jury instructions on consciousness of guilt and spoliation of evidence. The Defendants also argued that the expert had not been qualified to testify as a computer expert because of his educational background and lack of certifications. The Court, however, found that he had been qualified as an expert on the basis of his knowledge, skill, experience, training, and education, stating that the field of computer forensics does not require a background in computer programming or reading and writing code. The Defendants also argued that the expert had failed to follow his employer's own internal chain-of-custody procedures, when he had examined the Plaintiff's hard drives, and thus could not ensure that the recovery and analysis of the data had been accurate and untainted. The Court, however, stated that the possibility of a break in the chain of custody goes only to the weight of the evidence. The Court then denied the Defendant's motion, allowing the expert to testify, subject to the Defendants' cross-examination regarding chain of custody and other issues.

## Case 52

Superior Court of Massachusetts.

William Francis GALVIN, Secretary of the Commonwealth of Massachusetts
v.
The GILLETTE COMPANY.

Nos. 051453BLS, 051543BLS.
May 19, 2005.

Jurisdiction: Superior Court of Massachusetts

Date: May 19, 2005

Keywords: Procedure, Discovery

In a case involving fraud, the Court heard arguments during a Rule 16 confer-ence regarding what, if anything, remained to be litigated. The Secretary of the Commonwealth sought wide-ranging orders regarding compliance with a sub-poena and other matters occurring after the latest memorandum order in the case. The Defendant claimed that nothing remained to be litigated and that it had complied properly with all outstanding requests from the Secretary. In one of the proposed orders, the Secretary sought to have the Defendant, at its own expense, permit an electronic discovery company to have access to and the opportunity to search all of the Defendant's e-mail, servers, archives, disks, backup tapes, hard drives, and all backup systems thereof, and all other databases, necessary to investigate and accomplish retrieval, preservation, and copying of documents.

The Court found that, in view of the size of the Defendant and its huge number of employees, any request to examine the kinds of electronic and com-puterized devices listed in the proposed order was nearly impossible to com-ply with. An affidavit from the Defendant reported that there were 18,500 active users on the Defendant's e-mail system and that the total volume of e-mail traf-fic on the system was approximately fourteen million messages per month, of which approximately seven million were internal. Further, the Defendant stated that in view of the tremendous volume of e-mail and in an effort to conserve system resources and assure functionality, the Defendant encouraged users not to retain unneeded e-mail. The Court concluded that the sheer magnitude of any effort to recover the materials sought was daunting. The Court observed that it was other parties that were being investigated for fraud committed on the Defendant, and possibly its shareholders, and not the other way around. The Court was not convinced that the issuance of an order to compel compli-ance should be granted, and therefore it denied the Secretary's motion.

## Case 53

United States District Court,
N.D. Illinois, Eastern Division.

In re: GENERAL INSTRUMENT CORPORATION SECURITIES LITIGATION

No. 96 C 1129.
November 18, 1999.

Jurisdiction: United States District Court, Northern District of Illinois, Eastern Division

Date: November 18, 1999

Keywords: Discovery

In a class-action shareholder lawsuit, the Plaintiffs moved to compel the Defendants to produce e-mail and other computer-generated documents. The Plaintiffs argued that the Defendant improperly limited its document search, that many e-mail documents had been retrieved and given to defense counsel but had not been produced to the Plaintiffs, and that retrieving the e-mail from the backup tapes would not be unduly burdensome. In response, the Defendants argued that the production of more documents would be of little value to the Plaintiffs, in light of the enormous number of documents already in their possession, that the Plaintiffs' counsel had indicated to the court that they were done with discovery, and that the document review required to produce the additional documents would impose an undue burden.

The Court found that the likely benefit of the requested discovery was minimal and that, although the requested documents could be retrieved from backup tapes without undue expense, the burden on the Defendants would be significant. In weighing the burden of the requested discovery against its likely benefit, the Court held that the burden outweighed the benefit and that the Plaintiffs' motion should therefore be denied.

# Case 54

Court of Appeals of North Dakota.

John J. GOSBEE, Plaintiff and Appellant

v.

Rob MARTINSON; Eskrawl, Inc.; Mailwiper, Inc.; Spy Deleter, Inc.; Defendants and Appellees and John and Mary Does 001 through 100; and Doe & Doe, Inc. 101-200, Defendants.

No. 20050056CA.
July 6, 2005.

Jurisdiction: Court of Appeals of North Dakota

Date: July 6, 2005

Keywords: Spyware, Costs and Cost Shifting, Procedure

The Plaintiff appealed from a judgment dismissing his RICO action against the Defendants. The Plaintiff alleged that the Defendants intentionally highjacked his computers in a fraudulent scheme to create sales of their "Spy Wiper" program. The Plaintiff sued the Defendants alleging RICO violations and sought damages, treble damages, and attorneys' fees. In addition, the Plaintiff sought certification of the lawsuit as a class action. The Defendants moved for dismissal of the complaint for failure to state a claim, or alternatively, for summary judgment. The Defendants alleged that any highjacking of the Plaintiff's computers was caused by one of the Defendants' marketing affiliates and that they were not responsible for the actions of the affiliate. The trial court granted the Defendants' motion for dismissal, and judgment was entered dismissing the action and awarding costs and disbursements to the Defendants. The Plaintiff filed written objections to the award of costs and disbursements and filed a separate motion for reconsideration and to amend his complaint. The trial court, without holding a hearing, summarily denied his objections and motion. The Defendant appealed, alleging that the trial court erred in failing to hold a hearing on his objections and motion and that the trial court erred in denying his motion to amend the complaint.

The Court stated that, if objections are filed, the clerk shall promptly submit them to the judge who ordered the judgment and the court by ex parte order shall fix a time for hearing the objections. The Court further proclaimed that the parties may waive the right to a hearing. The Court found that the Plaintiff filed timely objections to the costs and disbursements, did not waive his right to a hearing, and in fact, requested that a hearing be set. The Court held that the rule is mandatory and affords no discretion to the trial court to dispense with the required hearing, unless expressly waived by the parties. Accordingly, the Court concluded that the trial court erred in failing to hold a hearing on the Plaintiff's objections to costs and disbursements.

The Plaintiff's motion for reconsideration and to amend the judgment was submitted, included an express request for a hearing. The Court stated that when any party who has timely served and filed a brief requests oral argument, the request must be granted. The Defendants argued that the Plaintiff's request for a hearing was incomplete because he did not secure a time for the hearing. The Court, however, concluded that he did all that he was required to do. Accordingly, the Court held that the trial court's failure to provide a hearing was error. The Defendants then claimed that, if the trial court's failure to provide a hearing on the Plaintiff's objections and motion was erroneous, the error was harmless. The Court held that, at every stage of the proceeding, it must disregard any error or defect in the proceeding that does not affect the substantial rights of the parties. Therefore, the Court concluded that the trial court's erroneous failures affected the Plaintiff's substantial rights and were not harmless error. Lastly, the Court stated that when a trial court has erroneously failed to provide a required hearing, the appropriate remedy is a remand for a hearing. Accordingly, the Court reversed the judgment and remanded for a hearing on the objections to costs and disbursements and on the motion for reconsideration and to amend the complaint.

## Case 55

United States Bankruptcy Court,
D. New Jersey.

In the matter of TRI-STATE ARMORED SERVICES, INC., Debtor.
Great American Insurance Companies, Plaintiff,

v.

Thomas J. Subranni, Esquire, Trustee for the Estate of
Tri-State Armored Services, Inc., Defendant.

Bankruptcy No. 01-11917/JHW.
Adversary No. 01-1132.
October 3, 2005.

Jurisdiction: United States Bankruptcy Court, District of New Jersey

Date: October 3, 2005

Keywords: Spoliation

In a bankruptcy proceeding, the Plaintiff sought a declaratory judgment determining that the Defendant was not entitled to insurance coverage under the crime insurance policies the Plaintiff issued to the Defendant prior to the Defendant filing for Chapter 7 bankruptcy. The Plaintiff sought rescission of policies issued to the Defendant on the ground of equitable fraud. The Defendant asserted counterclaims that the Plaintiff participated in intentional spoliation and/or negligently failed to preserve evidence that proved insurance coverage.

The Defendant alleged that the Plaintiff fraudulently concealed e-mails that the trustee believed supported a finding of coverage under the insurance policies. The Defendant contended that the Plaintiff destroyed evidence of these e-mails after the litigation began and after requests for discovery were made by the Defendant. The Court looked at five elements the Defendant must show to establish the cause of action of intentional spoliation. First, the Court found that the Plaintiff had a legal obligation to disclose evidence in connection with the litigation. Second, the Court found that evidence concerning the manner in which the claim was adjudicated was material to the litigation. Third, the Court found that the Defendant could not reasonably have obtained access to the evidence from another source. Fourth, the Court found one could surmise from supporting evidence that the Plaintiff intentionally withheld or destroyed the evidence. The Court found, however, that the Defendant failed to demonstrate it had been damaged in the underlying action by the

Plaintiff's concealment of the evidence. The Court held that a showing of damage in the underlying action is necessary in order for intentional spoliation to be found. The Court held that the Defendant did not prove this element. The Defendant also alleged that the Plaintiff negligently concealed evidence of the e-mails. The Court held that a cause of action based on negligence required the Defendant to show injury caused by the Plaintiff's breach of duty, and in the instant case the Defendant failed to show the requisite injury caused by the Plaintiff. The Court dismissed the Defendant counterclaims against the Plaintiff.

## Case 56

United States District Court,
C.D. California.

W.E. GREEN, Plaintiff,

v.

Leroy BACA et al., Defendant.

No. CV02-04744 MMM(MANX).
January 25, 2005.

Jurisdiction: United States District Court, Central District of California

Date: January 25, 2005

Keywords: Discovery, Sanctions, Costs and Cost Shifting

Before the Court was the question of whether an award of reasonable fees and costs should be issued against the Defendant, Los Angeles County. In the case, the Plaintiff's efforts to obtain discovery regarding the overdetention of inmates in the Los Angeles County jail system were unduly complicated and extraordinarily delayed by the failure of the County and/or its counsel to investigate promptly and effectively the records available, both in hard-copy and computer-based formats, regarding such overdetentions. In addition, the Court and the Plaintiff's counsel were never specifically apprised of the availability of computer-based records regarding over-detentions, despite extensive questioning by the Court and Court orders that declarations be provided regarding the availability of such documents and the burden associated with their production. Notwithstanding the extensive proceedings, the Court first became aware of the availability of highly relevant, computer-based records regarding overdetentions in reviewing documents produced for in camera review, because four computer-generated documents were scattered among the 11,704 documents delivered to the Court. The Court then raised the issue of whether sanctions should be assessed against the County and/or its counsel based on the failure to reveal the availability of, and to produce, computer-generated records regarding overdetentions.

In view of the history of the Court's efforts to resolve the discovery dispute, the Court found it clear that, even if the Plaintiff's counsel had acted entirely reasonably and in the utmost good faith, the production of relevant documents would not have occurred without court intervention. In addition, the Court concluded that the County's failure to provide relevant information and/or documents was not substantially justified. Accordingly, the Court held that it was appropriate to require the County to pay the Plaintiff the reasonable expenses incurred in making the motion, including attorneys' fees. After reviewing the Plaintiff's alleged expenses, the Court reduced the total billable hours, in connection with the discovery dispute, by 42, to 181.25 and reduced the counsel's requested hourly rate from $550 to $300, which calculated to a reasonable fee award of $54,375. The Court entered the award of that amount for the Plaintiff.

# Case 57

United States District Court,
D. New Jersey.

Christopher GRENDYSA, Plaintiff,

v.

EVESHAM TOWNSHIP BOARD OF EDUCATION et al., Defendants.

No. Civ.A. 02-1493(FLW).
September 27, 2005.

Jurisdiction: United States District Court, District of New Jersey

Date: September 27, 2005

Keywords: Computer Forensics

Prior to this suit, the Plaintiff was arrested and charged with four counts of endangering the welfare of a child and one count of official misconduct. Following this, the Plaintiff made a plea agreement with prosecutors and plead guilty to the Unauthorized Use of a Computer. The Plaintiff brought suit for, among other claims, malicious prosecution against a detective and school officials. The Defendants moved for summary judgments.

For purposes of the claim of malicious prosecution against the detective, the Court had to determine whether objective facts available to the detective at the time he arrested the Plaintiff were sufficient to justify a reasonable belief that the Plaintiff committed the crimes of endangering children and official misconduct. The Plaintiff admitted that Web logs showed that a computer in his classroom accessed Web sites inappropriate for children on days that the Plaintiff was present at the school and in the classroom. He also admitted that students interviewed by the detective reported viewing inappropriate Web sites with Plaintiff. The Plaintiff, however, argued that the detective should have seized the computer at issue and examined its content. The Plaintiff claims that the detective's failure to seize the computer and examine its content violated policies and procedures published by the State. The Court found that these policies and procedures cited by the Plaintiff were published after the investigation at issue commenced. The Court held that, although the detective's investigation could have been more complete, that alone did not preclude a finding of probable cause. The Court held that the evidence of the Web logs, the Plaintiff's attendance record, and the corroborative interview statements of the students could lead the Detective to reasonably believe that the Plaintiff committed the charged crimes. The Court further held for the same reasons the school officials could have reasonably believed the Plaintiff committed the charged crimes. The Court granted summary judgments for the detective and for the school board.

## Case 58

United States District Court,
S.D. New York.

GTFM, INC., Nautica Apparel, and PRL U.S.A. Holdings, Inc., Plaintiffs,

v.

WAL-MART STORES, INC., Defendant.

No. 98CIV.7724(RPP).
November 9, 2000.

Jurisdiction: United States District Court, Southern District of New York

Date: November 9, 2000

Keywords: Costs and Cost Shifting, Sanctions

In an earlier opinion, the Court granted the Plaintiffs' motion for sanctions in the form of reimbursement of all of the Plaintiffs' expenses and legal fees unnecessarily expended, because of the Defendant's failure to make an accurate disclosure of its computer capabilities. The Plaintiffs submitted an application for reimbursement of their legal fees and expenses. The Defendant responded to the Plaintiffs' application for reimbursement arguing that several categories of legal fees and expenses should be subtracted from the Plaintiffs' calculation, either because the Plaintiff would have incurred those expenses even if Defendant had disclosed the information about its computer capability in a timely manner or because the expenses were too vague to be attributed to activities relating to the inaccurate information provided by the Defendant.

The Court held that the Defendant's computerized information would have enabled the Plaintiffs to establish the relevant information in a prompt and efficient fashion, without the painstaking review of the inventory and transactional documents, and that the review of such documents was necessitated by the Defendant's failure to disclose its computer's capability. Accordingly, the Court awarded the Plaintiffs various fees and expenses caused by the Defendant's failure to provide accurate discovery information in response to valid discovery requests.

## Case 59

United States District Court,
E.D. Wisconsin.

HAGEMEYER NORTH AMERICA, INC., n/k/a Hagemeyer (N.A.) Holdings, Inc.,
Plaintiff,

v.

GATEWAY DATA SCIENCES CORPORATION a/k/a Brownshire Holdings, Inc.,
Defendant.
Gateway Data Sciences Corporation a/k/a Brownshire Holdings, Inc.,
Counterclaimant,

v.

Hagemeyer North America, Inc., n/k/a Hagemeyer (N.A.) Holdings, Inc.,
Counterdefendant.

No. 97-C-635.
August 12, 2004.

Jurisdiction: United States District Court, Eastern District of Wisconsin

Date: August 12, 2004

Keywords: Procedure, Discovery, Costs and Cost Shifting

In a corporate discovery dispute, the Plaintiff filed a motion to compel production of e-mails, financial statements, employee billing statements, computer backup tapes, and other documents from the Defendant. The Plaintiff asserted that the Defendant had a duty to segregate the material that had been requested from nonresponsive documents. Lastly, it asked the Court to order the Defendant to search the Defendant's tapes for responsive e-mails, at its own cost.

The Court stated that a responding party cannot attempt to hide a needle in a haystack by mingling responsive documents with large numbers of nonresponsive documents when producing documents; however, a responding party has no duty to organize and label the documents, if it has produced them as they are kept in the usual course of business. The Court found that the Defendant's materials had been kept in the usual course of business and that no attempt had been made to hide responsive documents among nonresponsive documents. The Court denied the Plaintiff's motion to compel production because the Defendant had discharged its duty to produce the documents as they were kept in the usual course of business. The Plaintiff also sought to compel production of a full backup of the Defendant's e-mails. The

Court, however, found that the Plaintiff had failed to establish the existence of such backup tapes, and therefore, it did not grant the Plaintiff's motion to compel production of e-mail backup tapes.

Lastly, the Plaintiff had asked that the Defendant search its backup tapes for e-mails containing certain search terms, which the Defendant had refused to do, citing the undue burden and expense that would be involved in restoring and then searching the documents. The Plaintiff had then offered to search the tapes at its own expense, which the Defendant had also refused. Finally, the Plaintiff moved to compel the Defendant to restore and search the backup tapes, while the Defendant demanded that the Plaintiff defray the costs for doing so, because they would be too burdensome. After considering the several tests for cost shifting, the Court followed *McPeek* and *Zubulake* and required the Defendant to restore a sample of backup tapes and required the parties to make additional submissions addressing whether the burden or expense of satisfying the entire request was proportionate to the likely benefit. The Court would then address the search of the backup tapes at a later hearing

## Case 60

United States Court of Appeals,
Eleventh Circuit.

Bonnie HARBUCK, Plaintiff-Appellant,

v.

Peter B. TEETS, Acting Secretary of the Air Force, Defendant-Appellee.

No. 05-10594.

October 12, 2005. (Unpublished)

Jurisdiction: United States Court of Appeals, Eleventh Circuit

Date: October 12, 3005

Keywords: Discovery, Procedure

In this Title VII action, the Plaintiff alleged that the Defendant retaliated against her for past EEOC activities and subjected her to a hostile work environment. The Plaintiff filed a motion to compel discovery claiming that the Defendant deliberately deleted e-mails and destroyed evidence in order to frustrate the Plaintiff's discovery. The district court had two telephone conferences and two discovery hearings regarding these discovery issues. The district court ordered both parties to submit their copies of data to the district court's Information Technology personnel to see if the material could be retrieved. The court's personnel could retrieve the material from the data without any problems. The district court closed discovery and did not require the Defendant to do anything further regarding discovery. In granting summary judgment for the Defendant, the district court found no reason to believe the Defendant was hiding information or attempting to harass the Plaintiff in the discovery process. The Plaintiff appealed the district court's grant of summary judgment for the Defendant and asserts the district court erred when it (1) allowed the district court's own personnel to evaluate electronic data, (2) found the Defendant fully produced electronic discovery, and (3) failed to impose an adverse inference against the Defendant for not producing all discoverable evidence.

The circuit court noted that it will not overturn discovery rulings unless it is shown that the district court's ruling resulted in substantial harm to the case. The Plaintiff failed to present prima facie cases for either discrimination or a hostile working environment, so the district court's ruling on discovery could not have caused substantial harm to the Plaintiff's case. The circuit court also ruled that the district court is a neutral party in the case and did not abuse its discretion in having its personnel evaluate the data. The circuit court also agreed with the district court that there was no reason to believe that the Defendant was hiding information or attempting to harass the Plaintiff during the discovery process. The circuit court upheld the Defendant's motion for summary judgment.

## Case 61

United States District Court,
E.D. Louisiana.

Martin HARRISON et al.

v.

JONES, WALKER, WAECHTER, POITEVENT, CARRERE & DENEGRE, L.L.P.
d/b/a/ Jones Walker et al.

No. Civ.A. 04-1651.
February 24, 2005.

Jurisdiction: United States District Court, Eastern District of Louisiana

Date: February 24, 2005

Keywords: Procedure

In a case involving alleged breach of contract, after originally bringing suit against the Plaintiffs, the Defendants were granted an expedited discovery order to preserve evidence, after the Defendants discovered an e-mail written by the Plaintiffs evidencing their intent to destroy discoverable evidence pertinent to the Defendants' claims. The discovery order authorized the Defendants, with the aid of an independent computer expert and through the sheriff, to preserve evidence by imaging computers at the Plaintiffs' address, which the Defendants carried out. The Plaintiffs then filed the present action alleging that the state court's expedited discovery order and its execution were invalid, that the Defendants violated the Plaintiffs' Fourth and Fourteenth Amendment rights and that the Defendants were liable for trespass, invasion of privacy, and abuse of rights. The Plaintiffs alleged that they were deprived of the right to be secure in their persons, houses, papers, and effects from unreasonable searches and seizures. The Court stated that assuming, arguendo, that the Defendants' actions constituted an unreasonable search and/or seizure, the Plaintiffs must also allege that the Defendants acted under color of law (i.e., that the deprivation of a federal right was fairly attributable to the State). The Defendants responded by filing a motion to dismiss the claims.

The Plaintiffs' complaint alleged that the Defendants conspired to effect the search and seizure and that one or more of the Defendants reached an understanding with the deputy to cause the search and seizure. The Court found that the Plaintiffs did not allege that the Defendants conspired with the judge who issued the discovery order. Nor did the Plaintiffs set forth any specific factual allegations with respect to a conspiracy or an understanding between the deputy and of the Defendants. The Court held that the complaint did not identify any facts or evidence that would support the findings sought by the Plaintiffs, because they made merely conclusory allegations of a conspiracy. The Court concluded that without any evidence of willful participation or some concerted effort or plan between the Defendants and the deputy, there was no genuine issue of material fact with respect to the Plaintiffs' claims. Accordingly, the Court granted the Defendants' motion to dismiss the Plaintiffs' claims and did so without prejudice.

## Case 62

United States District Court,
N.D. Ohio, Eastern Division.

In re: TELXON CORPORATION SECURITIES LITIGATION
WILLIAM S. HAYMAN et al., Plaintiffs,

v.

PRICEWATERHOUSECOOPERS, LLP, Defendant.

No. 5:98CV2876, 1:01CV1078.
July 16, 2004.

Jurisdiction: United States District Court, Northern District of Ohio, Eastern Division

Date: July 16, 2004

Keywords: Metadata, Preservation of Evidence/Spoliation, Procedure, Discovery

In a case involving alleged violations of the Securities and Exchange Act, the SEC had requested documents from the Defendant relating to its financial audit of the Plaintiff, who in turn sought sanctions against the Defendant claiming that it had committed fraud, misrepresentation, and breach of contract in relation to the Plaintiff's financial statements. The Plaintiff also argued that the Defendant had failed to produce all relevant versions of documents and databases and to preserve said documents from alteration or destruction. Lastly, the Plaintiff claimed that the Defendant had produced hard-copy versions of documents that had differed from the electronic versions and had failed to produce certain e-mails, metadata, and other documents.

The Court found that the absence of the e-mails suggested spoliation for the time period after the Defendant had been put on notice to preserve them. The Court also concluded that the Defendant had to have known that multiple database versions had existed and that the hard-copy production had failed to capture all of the relevant components of the database, such as metadata. Lastly, the Court held that no reasonable person could have believed that the Defendant's discovery response to the Plaintiff was a good faith production. Accordingly, the Court ruled that the Defendant would have to bear the burden created by its own conduct, when ordering a default judgment against the Defendant.

## Case 63

United States District Court,
W.D. Michigan, Southern Division.

Steven HOLT, M.D., Plaintiff,

v.

THE NORTHWESTERN MUTUAL LIFE INSURANCE COMPANY, Defendant.

No. 1:04-CV-280.
November 30, 2005.

Jurisdiction: United States District Court, Western District of Michigan, Southern Division

Date: November 30, 2005

Keywords: Discovery, Sanctions, Spoliation

In a case alleging entitlement to payment under disability insurance policies, the Plaintiff moved to compel discovery and award sanctions for perceived discovery violations by the Defendant. Specifically, the Plaintiff argued that the Defendant produced documents one year after initial disclosure and that one of the Defendant's representatives destroyed documents subject to discovery. The Plaintiff sought summary judgment, attorneys' fees and costs, an order prohibiting the use of any of the documents not properly disclosed, and an order providing the jury with an adverse inference instruction concerning the spoliation of evidence.

The Court found that the documents at issue were not fraudulently created, but that the failure to timely produce them was the result of confusion concerning the operation of a new electronic claims database which replaced the Defendant's paper filing system. The Court, however, found that this did not excuse the untimely production of documents. The Court held that, because the delay in the production of the documents was neither harmless nor justified, it should impose a sanction upon the Defendant. The Court found that the accuracy of the information of the documents could be verified by questioning individuals involved with the documents, so the Court found no reason to exclude the documents. The Court granted the Plaintiff an additional 30-day period to conduct discovery reasonably necessary as a result of the delay in document production. The sanction the Court imposed on the Defendant was the payment of the Plaintiff's costs incurred from this extra discovery. The Plaintiff also alleged that the Defendant's representative deleted e-mails concerning the Defendant's investigation into the Plaintiff's claims.

The Court found that the Defendant is not obligated to preserve every e-mail, electronic document, and backupbackup tape. The Court held that the Defendant was obligated only to preserve relevant material. The Court found no evidence that the content of the e-mails was substantive or was favorable to the Plaintiff. For this reason, the Court held that the sanction of adverse inference jury instruction did not apply to this case. The Court also held that the Plaintiff was not entitled to summary judgment or attorneys' fees or costs.

## Case 64

Superior Court of Pennsylvania.

Mary Jo HOOD-O'HARA, Appellee
v.
Robert W. WILLS, Appellant.

Argued February 16, 2005.
Filed April 22, 2005.

Jurisdiction: Superior Court of Pennsylvania

Date: April 22, 2005

Keywords: Admissibility

The Defendant appealed from a Protection from Abuse order entered against him, arguing that the trial judge abused her discretion in not admitting evidence offered by him in the form of e-mails purported to be from the Plaintiff's mother. At a previous hearing, the Defendant attempted to offer into evidence e-mails, purportedly authored by the Plaintiff's mother and containing references to the Plaintiff's drinking problem. The Defendant claimed that the exclusion of the e-mails rendered the hearing incomplete and prejudiced the trial judge's credibility determinations. The trial judge stated dual reasons for her exclusion of the e-mails, which the Court held that it must agree with.

The Court stated that, under the rules of evidence, an out of court statement that is offered for the truth of the matter asserted is excluded as hearsay. Although there are several exceptions to the hearsay rule, the Court found that none were applicable here, because the Defendant was offering the e-mail, and specifically the portion regarding the Plaintiff's drinking habits, as proof of the Plaintiff's problems with alcohol. Therefore, the Court held that the e-mails were properly excluded. In addition, as pointed out by the trial judge, there were also authentication problems regarding the e-mails. The Court noted that although testimony revealed that the e-mail address did in fact belong to the Plaintiff's mother, it was denied by her that she was the author of the e-mails. Again, the Court held that the e-mails were properly excluded. Because it found no merit to the Defendant's arguments, the Court affirmed the order of the trial court.

## Case 65

United States District Court,
D. Maryland.

Louis H. HOPSON et al., Plaintiffs,

v.

The MAYOR AND CITY COUNCIL OF BALTIMORE, A Municipal Corporation of
the State of Maryland, and the Baltimore City Police Department,
Defendants.

No. CIV.A. AMD-04-3842.
November 22, 2005.

Jurisdiction: United States District Court, District of Maryland

Date: November 22, 2005

Keywords: Costs and Cost Shifting, Discovery, Procedure, Production of
Evidence

The Plaintiffs brought disparate impact and disparate treatment claims
against the Defendants, in an employment action alleging racial discrimination. The Plaintiffs served extensive interrogatories and document production
requests on the Defendants. The document production requests focused on
electronically stored records and data. The interrogatories were designed to
discover information about electronically stored records, the information
technology capabilities, the nature of archived data, e-mail, and records-retention policies of the Defendants. The Defendants answered with objections
to much of the discovery on the grounds of burdensomeness and expense to
produce the documents. The Defendants, however, did not provide an estimate of the number of hours required to comply with the requests, nor did
they show how compliance with the requests would adversely impact the "fiscal and operational capabilities" of the Defendants. The Court found that the
Defendants' answers failed to particularize the unreasonable burden the discovery would cause and failed to provide suggested alternatives which would
reasonably satisfied the Plaintiff's discovery needs. At a hearing, the Defendants expressed concern about the cost and burden of performing prepro-
duction privilege review of the records. The Plaintiffs moved to compel production of documents and interrogatories. The Court ordered the Defendants
to meet with the Plaintiffs and their information technology representative in
order to informally discover information about the Defendants' information
technology systems and electronic records. The Court also ordered the par-

ties to discuss the factors involved with the procedures the Defendants should take to perform a review for privilege and work product claims. The Court ordered the parties to formulate a discovery plan and submit it to the Court for review and approval. The Court advised the parties that, at follow-up hearings, it would issue orders compelling the production of electronic records based on the amount of electronic discovery the Court permits. The Court stated that counsel for the parties had "a duty to take the initiative in meeting and conferring to plan appropriate discovery of electronically stored information at the commencement of any case in which electronic records will be sought."

## Case 66

Supreme Court of Wisconsin.

In the Matter of a JOHN DOE PROCEEDING Commenced by Affidavit Dated July 25, 2001: Custodian of Records for the Legislative Technology Services Bureau, Petitioner,

v.

State of Wisconsin and the Honorable Sarah B. O'Brien, presiding, Respondents.

No. 02-3063-W.
Argued November 4, 2003.
Decided June 9, 2004.

Jurisdiction: Supreme Court of Wisconsin

Date: June 9, 2004

Keywords: Constitutionality

During a John Doe investigation of certain state legislators and legislative employees, for what was suspected to be criminal conduct, the Director of the Legislative Technology Service Bureau (LTSB) filed a writ of assistance asking that the John Doe judge's subpoena, which had authorized the search and seizure of backup tapes for fifty-four servers, be quashed, asserting issues of privilege, violations of the state constitution, and that the subpoena had been overly broad and therefore unreasonable.

The Director first argued that the LTSB was statutorily obligated to treat all information within its possession as confidential and, therefore, that he was not required to comply with the subpoena. However, the Court agreed with the State in concluding that the confidentiality requirement did not create a privilege for the Director to refuse to comply with the subpoena. After finding that the legislators had had a reasonable expectation of privacy in the data sought, the Court evaluated the subpoena to determine whether it was overbroad. The Court found that the subpoena had requested all of the data from the computer system of an entire branch of state government, in order to investigate whether a crime had been committed. It had not specified the topics or the types of documents in which evidence of a crime might be found. The subpoena also did not specify any time period for which it sought records. The Court held that an open-ended time span during which the records had been produced or received was unacceptable and accordingly, quashed the subpoena because it had been overly broad and could not pass Fourth Amendment muster. The Court granted the Director's writ.

## Case 67

United States District Court,
S.D. New York.

David JONES, Issac Nelson, Kevin Martin, William Meachem, Clarence Suber,
Tobias Walls, Henry Moreno, James White, Ramon Blas, Angelo Caravaggio,
Roy Davis, Luciano Ortiz, Rory Dolan, Liberato Bermudez, Gregory Smith,
Fruitquan Bailey, Todd Brockington, Renaldo Rivera, James Dixon,
Juan Perdomo, Herbert Junior, Hector Lopez, Juan Rivera, Dwayne Faust,
and all others similarly situated, Plaintiffs,

v.

Glenn S. GOORD, Acting Commissioner of the New York State Department of
Correctional Services, Edmund Wutzer, Chairperson of the New York State
Commission of Correction, Thomas J. Goldrick, Commissioner of the
State Commission of Correction, Floyd Bennett, Superintendent of Elmira
Correctional Facility, Hans Walker, Superintendent of Auburn Correctional
Facility, Robert H. Kuhlmann, Superintendent of Sullivan Correctional
Facility, David Miller, Superintendent of Eastern Correctional Facility and
Christopher Artuz, Superintendent of Green Haven Correctional Facility,
Defendants.

No. 95 CIV. 8026(GEL).
May 16, 2002.

Jurisdiction: United States District Court, Southern District of New York

Date: May 16, 2002

Keywords: Discovery

In a class-action lawsuit brought by inmates against the New York State Department of Correctional Services challenging a program for double-celling in
maximum-security prisons, the Plaintiffs filed a motion seeking access to various electronic databases maintained by state correctional authorities.

   The Plaintiffs sought the production of electronic records and databases,
arguing that the electronic data they sought was properly within the scope of
discovery demands for inmate data, served years before. The Court found
that the factual findings regarding the motion were largely uncontested. It
noted that the Defendants had compiled an impressive record, documenting
the technical issues involved in assessing the burdens and risks and the ob-
stacles to securing the hoped-for benefits of ordering the discovery sought.
The Plaintiffs, on the other hand, blithely declined to respond to that presentation, relying on the facially plausible generalities put forth in their initial mo-

tion papers. Nevertheless, the Court carefully and skeptically reviewed the papers submitted by the Defendants, only to find them ultimately persuasive and accurate.

Assuming that the databases sought by the Plaintiffs were relevant and not privileged, the Court found that discovery should be denied because the Defendants made a compelling showing that the burden of the proposed discovery far outweighed its likely benefit for resolving the issue, particularly in light of the failure of the Plaintiffs to seek such discovery, despite ample opportunity to do so in a more timely manner, and the vast amount of material largely duplicating the contents of the databases sought, which had already been provided by the Defendants. The Court was not willing to impose additional burden, expense, and risk of harm to the parties, especially the Defendants, so far into the lawsuit, after the expenditure of so much effort and expense, on the undocumented hope of obtaining such speculative benefits. The Court then denied the Plaintiffs' motion to compel.

## Case 68

United States District Court,
M.D. Tennessee, Nashville Division.

Lowell KATT, On Behalf of Himself and All Others Similarly Situated,
Plaintiffs,

v.

TITAN ACQUISITIONS, INC.; United Technologies Corporation;
William Trachsel, Ari Bousbib, Angelo Messina, Gilles Renaud, and
David Fitzpatrick, Defendants.

No. 99-CV-655.
January 10, 2003.

Jurisdiction: United States District Court, Middle District of Tennessee

Date: January 10, 2003

Keywords: Sanctions, Procedure

In a class-action lawsuit alleging the creation of golden parachutes for corporate executives and violations of the Best Price Rule, the Defendants moved for summary judgment, which the Court granted. The Plaintiffs, however, moved to sanction the Defendants for spoliation of electronic evidence. The Court reserved ruling on the Plaintiffs' motion for sanctions and expressly reserved ancillary jurisdiction over that motion. The Court noted that a federal court may consider collateral matters such as sanctions after an action has been terminated, and it may assert ancillary jurisdiction to manage its proceedings, vindicate its authority, and effectuate its decrees. The Court found that the Plaintiffs' motion for sanctions clearly dealt with a collateral matter that was incidental to the underlying securities claims of this action, as was required to maintain ancillary jurisdiction. The Court held that it was well within its discretion to deal with the sanctions issue after granting summary judgment. Therefore, despite the dismissal of all of the Plaintiffs' claims and entry of final judgment on the merits, the Court retained jurisdiction for the purpose of holding a hearing on the Plaintiffs' motion for sanctions.

## Case 69

United States District Court,
D. Kansas.

Joedy KLEINER, Plaintiff,

v.

Becky BURNS et al., Defendants.

No. 00-2160-JWL.
December 15, 2000.

Jurisdiction: United States District Court, District of Kansas

Date: December 15, 2000

Keywords: Procedure, Sanctions

In a copyright infringement action, the Defendant moved to compel the Plaintiff to provide computations and supporting evidence of her claimed damages, and the Plaintiff moved to compel the Defendant to disclose all voice mails, electronic mail, Web sites, Web pages, and other electronic data relevant to the action. The Plaintiff also sought discovery sanctions against the Defendant.

The Defendant sought evidence upon which the Plaintiff had relied in claiming statutory damages for the alleged posting of eighteen of her copyrighted photographs. The Defendant noted that, in support of the Plaintiff's claim for damages, she had only produced evidence of two of her copyrighted photographs that had been posted on the Defendant's Web site. The Plaintiff claimed that she had produced more than 600 pages of documents evidencing her damage claims. The Court found that an affirmation from the Plaintiff, declaring that she possessed no more documents or evidentiary materials in support of her claims, had been conspicuously missing, and therefore the Court granted the Defendant's motion to compel and ordered the Plaintiff to produce all evidence supporting her claim for damages in each of the eighteen claims of infringement. The Plaintiff also maintained that she was not required to disclose a computation of damages because she had sought statutory damages rather than actual damages. After reviewing the legislative history, the Court also granted the Defendant's motion to compel the production of a computation of the Plaintiff's actual damages.

In support of the Plaintiff's motion to compel, she stated that she had been able to independently retrieve two pieces of electronic data relevant to disputed facts, alleged with particularity, in the pleadings, but that such data had not been produced by the Defendant in the initial disclosures. The Defendant responded by stating that it had complied with its obligations and that it was diligently attempting to locate backup copies regarding the data accompanying the Plaintiff's motion. The Court found it implausible that the Defendant did not have the data in its possession, and therefore it granted the Plaintiff's motion and ordered the Defendant to disclose all data in its possession that was relevant to the claims. Lastly, the Court took the Plaintiff's motion for sanction under advisement, to allow an opportunity for further review of the Defendant's actions.

## Case 70

Court of Appeal, Second District, Division 3, California.

KRAUSZ PUENTE LLC, Plaintiff and Respondent,

v.

Frank WESTALL et al., Defendants and Appellants.

No. B164989.
(Los Angeles County Super. Ct. No. BC213129).
January 25, 2005.

Jurisdiction: Court of Appeal, Second District, Division 3, California

Date: January 25, 2005

Keywords: Sanctions, Experts, Preservation of Evidence/Spoliation

After a trial alleging breach of contract, the Defendants appealed a judgment in favor of the Plaintiff, claiming that the trial court erred in imposing discovery sanctions. Following a discovery motion by the Plaintiff, the trial court ordered the Defendants to immediately make available to Plaintiff's designated expert all computers, including hard drives, and all other electronic storage media in their possession, custody, and/or control.

The Defendants delayed compliance for six days and, in the meantime, deleted numerous files and folders, including materials relating to the case. The Plaintiff then moved for evidence sanctions, as well as monetary sanctions in the amount of $16,330, on the ground that the Defendants had deliberately destroyed more than 5,300 relevant computer files in direct violation of the trial court's discovery order. They, in turn, argued that the files were personal in nature and had little, if anything, to do with the substance of the litigation. The trial court found that the Defendants willfully destroyed relevant evidence, subject to a prior court order, and that they deleted the files for the malicious purpose of depriving the Plaintiff of evidence that would be helpful to it in the prosecution of its case. In determining the appropriate sanction, the trial court selected an evidence sanction, which prohibited the Defendants from testifying on behalf of themselves about their books, records, relationships to one another, or their financial histories. Although the evidence sanction was slightly modified, a previously ordered monetary sanction remained.

The Court reviewed the trial court's imposition of discovery sanctions for an abuse of discretion. The Defendants claimed that the evidence sanction was overbroad, was unworkable, and that monetary sanctions would have been sufficient. The Court found their arguments to be meritless. The trial court found that, in view of the nature of the discovery violation, namely, a willful destruction of computer records subject to a prior court order, monetary sanctions would have been insufficient to remedy the harm to the Plaintiff, which the Court agreed with. As for the evidence sanction being overbroad and unworkable, the Court held that the Defendants had no cause to complain, as it had been modified on their behalf. The Court concluded that the trial court acted judiciously in seeking to tailor the sanction to the egregious discovery abuse committed by the Defendant and accordingly held that there was no prejudicial abuse of discretion in the trial court's ruling. Therefore, the Court affirmed the trial court's judgment.

## Case 71

Court of Appeals of Virginia.

Ray KROMER

v.

COMMONWEALTH of Virginia.

Record No. 1900-04-2.
June 14, 2005.

Jurisdiction: Court of Appeals of Virginia

Date: June 14, 2005

Keywords: Procedure

The Defendant appealed his conviction of fifteen counts of misdemeanor possession of child pornography, arguing that the evidence had been insufficient to sustain his convictions. Specifically, he maintained that the Commonwealth had failed to prove that he knowingly possessed the images that had been contained within the computer.

The Court found that it was clear that someone had acquired the offensive images and had brought them into the Defendant's home, via the Internet. The Court's inquiry focused on who had possessed the images after they had already been procured. The Court then analyzed whether the evidence had sufficiently connected the Defendant to the computer and the images. In doing so, the Court stated that it did not need to determine whether the Defendant was the person who had downloaded the pornographic images but, rather, whether the Defendant had known that the images had existed and, if so, had he exercised dominion and control over them, after they had been downloaded.

The Defendant maintained that he was innocent by arguing that others, including family members or friends, could have used the computer and downloaded the images. The Court reiterated that the determinative issue was not who had downloaded the images, but whether the Defendant had knowingly possessed the images after they had previously been downloaded into the computer. After reviewing the record, the Court concluded that the evidence had sufficiently supported the trial court's findings that the Defendant had exclusive control of the residence and the computer. In doing so, the Court held that it was not suggesting that anyone who uses a computer containing child pornography is guilty of possessing it, but rather that, in the case, the record supported the reasonable inference that the Defendant used the computer and had knowledge and control over its contents. The Court then affirmed the decision of the trial court.

## Case 72

Court of Appeals of Texas,
Dallas.

Kyle Dewayne KUPPER, Appellant
v.
The STATE of Texas, Appellee.

No. 05-03-00486-CR.
January 14, 2004.

Jurisdiction: Court of Appeals of Texas, Dallas

Date: January 14, 2004

Keywords: Admissibility

The Defendant had been convicted of four counts of aggravated sexual assault, and he challenged the admissibility of certain evidence at trial, consisting of e-mails, a photograph, and a story, all retrieved from either his work or home computer.

The Defendant objected to their admissibility on grounds of lack of proper predicate as to chain of custody and authentication, based on the testimony of the computer forensic officer. The Defendant argued that the State failed to show that the evidence came from a computer that he actually used. The Court rejected this contention. The Defendant then claimed that some of the contents had been obtained from deleted files, and therefore the hard drive had been altered or tampered with, by the State. The Court did not reach this conclusion, however, explaining that the Defendant offered no evidence of alteration or deletion in or on the documents themselves. The Defendant also argued that several documents were offered into evidence as e-mails, though they had never been sent as e-mails. In rejecting the Defendant's argument, the Court found that the issue was whether the documents were authenticated as documents from the computers and not whether they were e-mails that had been sent or received. Although the Defendant had raised the issue of chain of custody, the Court declared there was no evidence to support a chain-of-custody issue.

Having resolved the Defendant's issues against him, the Court affirmed the trial court's judgment.

## Case 73

Court of Appeals of Maryland.

William LeJEUNE

v.

COIN ACCEPTORS, INC.

No. 111, September Term, 2003.
May 13, 2004.

Jurisdiction: Court of Appeals of Maryland

Date: May 13, 2004

Keywords: Computer Forensics, Experts

In a case involving misappropriation of trade secrets, the Plaintiff appealed from a preliminary injunction, enjoining him from working for a competitor of the Defendant. The circuit court found that the Plaintiff had misappropriated trade secrets that would give the competitor an unfair competitive advantage.

To obtain injunctive relief, the Defendant first needed to establish that the Plaintiff had indeed misappropriated its trade secrets, which included software, business plans, pricing and cost lists, and hardware specifications, among other things. The Plaintiff argued that a finding of actual or threatened misappropriation is the only basis for granting an injunction and that the evidence admitted at the hearing did not establish this. The Plaintiff maintained that he had not acquired any information improperly, because the Defendant had voluntarily provided it to him, without requesting its return until the start of litigation. In addition, the Plaintiff argued that the Defendant had not presented any evidence that he had used or disclosed the trade secrets or even intended to do so.

In response, the Defendant urged that the evidence did support a finding for misappropriation of trade secrets. The evidence purported to show that the Plaintiff had copied information from his laptop onto a CD and retained hard copies of documents, after allegedly telling the Defendants that he had returned everything. The Court determined that several of the documents at issue were indeed trade secrets and that the Defendants had not given him permission transfer trade secrets from the company laptop to a CD. The Plaintiff attempted to justify his actions by explaining that he had done so only to retain personal documents and had inadvertently captured the other documents in the process. An expert had testified, however, that the Plaintiff had specifically selected the files to be transferred, outside of his personal documents, including the trade secrets. The Court did not believe the Plaintiff's version, because his actions suggested that he was attempting to hide his conduct and was aware that transferring the files was improper. Therefore, the Court held that evidence in the case was sufficient to support the circuit court's finding that the trade secrets had been acquired by improper means and were thereby misappropriated.

## Case 74

United States District Court,
D. Minnesota.

LEXIS-NEXIS, a division of Reed Elsevier Inc., Plaintiff,

v.

David BEER, Defendant.

No. Civ. 98-2517 (DSD/JMM).
March 22, 1999.

Jurisdiction: United States District Court, District of Minnesota

Date: March 22, 1999

Keywords: Sanctions, Preservation of Evidence/Spoliation

In a suit alleging misappropriation of trade secrets and unfair competition, among other things, the Plaintiff filed a motion for sanctions, claiming that the Defendant destroyed evidence critical to its noncompete and trade secret claims and violated several pretrial orders, including a prior temporary restraining order. To remedy the alleged abuses, the Plaintiff asked the Court to draw from the destroyed material evidentiary inferences adverse to the Defendant and award the Plaintiff the costs and attorneys' fees that the Defendant's alleged misconduct caused.

The Court stated that sanctions are appropriate when a party destroys discoverable material that the party knew or should have known was relevant to pending, imminent, or reasonably foreseeable litigation. The Court found that the Plaintiff established the last three elements of the destruction of evidence claim, because from the moment the Defendant decided to go to work for the Plaintiff's competitor, he either knew or should have known that the Plaintiff's material that he possessed was relevant to reasonably foreseeable litigation. However, the Court was not convinced that the Plaintiff could show that relevant evidence was actually destroyed, which was the first and most important element. First, the Court found that the documents that the Plaintiff initially believed were deleted were, in fact, still present in undeleted form on the Defendant's laptop hard drive. Second, while the Defendant conceded that he discarded the Zip disk that he used in transferring the Plaintiff's materials to his laptop, the vast majority of the information on that disk, if not all of it, was preserved on a disk that he produced for the temporary restraining order and on the laptop computer. Third, while the Defendant conceded that he inadvertently overwrote some inactive data when making an image copy of the laptop hard drive, the Court found that the Plaintiff had not demonstrated that any of this lost data would have contained evidence pertinent to the litigation. Moreover, the Court concluded that even if it did find some relevant information had been overwritten, the Plaintiff had not demonstrated that the loss of evidence would prejudice its case. The Court was unwilling to presume that any lost data contained information any more sensitive or damning than what the Plaintiff expected to find in the first place.

Accordingly, the Court held that it would not draw any adverse evidentiary inferences. Regardless, the Court did conclude that the Defendant's delay in revealing electronic evidence set off a high-tech wild goose chase that needlessly multiplied the time and expense of the litigation. Therefore, the Court held that monetary sanctions were appropriate, but was unwilling to establish the size of the sanction, at that time, because it was still early in the litigation. The Court then denied in part and continued in part the Plaintiff's motions.

## Case 75

Appellate Court of Illinois,
First District, Second Division.

LIEBERT CORPORATION, an Ohio corporation, and Zonatherm Products,
Inc., an Illinois corporation, Plaintiffs-Appellants,

v.

John MAZUR, an individual, Gregory N. Schwabe, an individual,
Jerome Mazur, an individual, Mario Belluomini, an individual,
Laurence Bergfalk, an individual, Aerico, Inc., an Illinois limited corporation,
and American Power Conversion Corporation, a Massachusetts corporation,
Defendants-Appellees.

No. 1-04-2794.
April 5, 2005.

Jurisdiction: Appellate Court of Illinois, First District, Second Division

Date: April 5, 2005

Keywords: Computer Forensics, Experts

During litigation regarding misappropriation of trade secrets, the Plaintiffs
had sought to enjoin the Defendants from using alleged trade secrets in their
new competing business. The Plaintiffs alleged that the Defendants had misappropriated confidential customer lists, historical bids, quotations, sales history, and price books. The trial court had denied the Plaintiffs' motion for a
preliminary injunction, and the Plaintiffs appealed.

At trial, the Plaintiffs' allegations of trade secret misappropriation had
hinged on the Defendants' computer activities, before and after resigning from
employment with the Plaintiff. Most of the Plaintiffs' evidence had been presented through the testimony of the Plaintiffs' expert witness, an expert in
computer forensics. He had testified that the Defendants' had accessed the
Plaintiffs' Web site and downloaded price book files from it. The Defendants'
then moved the files into a Zip file embedded in another Zip file, which also
contained other Zip files that contained documents, including quote histories
and budgets. The all inclusive Zip file was moved to a folder that was automatically created by the computer for burning files to a CD. The original Zip
files were deleted, however, and most of the information was irrecoverable,
though the expert believed that the files had been successfully burned to a
CD.

The trial court had held that, although the Plaintiffs had shown that the Defendants had downloaded price books, they had also erased all of the information and there had been no showing, from the evidence presented, that the price books still existed or that anyone else took price books. The Court had further found that there was no real chance of succeeding on the question of whether the Defendants used the price books before they had been destroyed.

## Case 76

United States District Court,
E.D. Virginia.

William D. LIGGETT, Plaintiff,

v.

Donald RUMSFELD, Secretary U.S. Department of Defense, Defendant.

No. Civ.A. 04-1363(GBL).
August 29, 2005.

Jurisdiction: United States District Court, Eastern District of Virginia

Date: August 29, 2005

Keywords: Sanctions, Spoliation, E-Evidence Alteration/Fabrication

The Plaintiff brought a suit against his former employer, the Defendant, alleging that he was discriminated against on the basis of race and was subjected to a hostile work environment and that the Defendant retaliated against the Plaintiff in violation of Title VII and the Civil Rights Act of 1964. The Defendant moved for a Judgment on the Pleadings and a Summary Judgment.

During a review of the Defendant's firewall, it was revealed that the Plaintiff allegedly accessed several sexually explicit Internet sites from his work computer. As a result, the Plaintiff's computer was examined, and sexually explicit materials were found on the hard drive, along with evidence that sexually explicit Web sites had been accessed from that computer. The Defendant suspended the Plaintiff for 10 days for the misuse of government property. The Defendant used the investigative reports concerning the Plaintiff's misuse of the computer to support its burden of showing that there was a nondiscriminatory reason for an adverse employment action against the Plaintiff. The Defendant, however, did not preserve the hard drive. The Plaintiff requested an adverse inference against the Defendant based on the fact that Defendant failed to preserve the hard drive of the Plaintiff's computer. The Court found that the Defendant should have preserved the hard drive, but its failure to preserve the hard drive did not in and of itself suggest fraud or fabrication of evidence. In its reasoning, the Court looked at the fact that the investigation of the computer was not initiated by any of the Plaintiff's supervisors and none of the supervisors performed the investigation. The Court also found that the Plaintiff raised no genuine fact for trial regarding whether the investigation of the Plaintiff's misuse of the computer and the Defendant's failure to preserve the hard drive was based on race or retaliation for EEOC activity. The Court granted the Defendant's request for Summary Judgment.

## Case 77

Supreme Court, Nassau County.

LIPCO ELECTRICAL CORP. and Action Electrical Contracting Co., Inc., J.V.,
Plaintiffs,

v.

ASG CONSULTING CORPORATION, Anthony Cardillo,
Tap Electrical Contracting Service, Inc. And Philip P. Gulizio, Defendants.
Action # 2 ASG Consulting Corp., Tap Electrical Contracting Service, Inc.,
Anthony Cardillo and Philip P. Gulizio, Plaintiffs,

v.

Action Electrical Cont. Co. Inc. a/k/a Action Electrical Contracting Lipco
Electrical Corp., Lipco Electrical Corp. and Action Electrical Contracting Co.
Inc., J.V. Gaspare "Sal" Lipari and Anthony Spina, Defendants.
ASG Consulting Corp., Tap Electrical Contracting Service, Inc.,
Anthony Cardillo and Philip P. Gulizio, Plaintiffs,

v.

Action Electrical Cont. Co. Inc. a/k/a Action Electrical Contracting Company,
Inc., Lipco Electrical Corp., Lipco Electrical Corp. and Action Electrical
Contracting Co. Inc., J.V. Gaspare "Sal" Lipari and Anthony Spina.

No. 8775/01.
August 18, 2004.

Jurisdiction: Supreme Court of New York, Nassau County

Date: August 18, 2004

Keywords: Discovery, Costs and Cost Shifting

In a dispute regarding billing agreements, the Defendant claimed that the parties had agreed to a flat monthly rate as their billing scheme that was not dependent upon the hours expended, and the Plaintiffs disagreed, asserting that they had agreed to a monthly scheme that was subject to revision and adjustment at the conclusion of the projects. The Plaintiffs brought suit to recover alleged overcharges.

Although the Plaintiffs had been provided with a hard-copy printout of various records sought, they asserted that the only way that they could confirm that the hard-copy data were true and accurate was by obtaining the raw data in computerized form. The Defendant contested the Plaintiffs' electronic discovery request because it had already provided them with a hard copy of the material and because extracting the information from its systems would be extremely difficult, time consuming, and expensive. Having concluded that the material was discoverable, the Court set out to determine the procedure for its production and who would bear the cost of the discovery.

The Court noted that cost shifting of electronic discovery was not an issue in the state, because the courts had held that, under state statutes, the party seeking discovery should incur the costs incurred in the production of discovery material. Therefore, the Court held that the analysis of whether electronic discovery should be permitted in the state was much simpler than in the federal courts. The Court concluded that it needed only to determine whether the material was discoverable and whether the party seeking the discovery was willing to bear the cost of production of the electronic material. The Court found that it was unable to determine if the materials should be produced because the parties had failed to establish the costs, procedures, and willingness of each party to bear costs involved in the production. The Court ordered the parties to submit further briefs in support of their positions so that it could rule on compelled production and cost shifting.

## Case 78

United States District Court,
District of Columbia.

In re LORAZEPAM & CLORAZEPATE ANTITRUST LITIGATION
This document relates to: Health Care Service Corporation, Plaintiff,

v.

Mylan Laboratories, Inc., et al., Defendants,

and

Blue Cross Blue Shield of Minnesota et al., Plaintiffs,

v.

Mylan Laboratories, Inc., et al., Defendants.

No. MDL NO. 1290.
Nos. MISC.NO.99-276(TFH/JMF), 01-2646(TFH/JMF).
January 16, 2004.

Jurisdiction: United States District Court, District of Columbia

Date: January 16, 2004

Keywords: Discovery, Computer Forensics, Experts

In an antitrust case alleging illegal agreements to monopolize portions of the pharmaceuticals industry, the Defendant claimed that the Plaintiffs had already been provided with all of the discovery materials that had been produced for previous plaintiffs. The Plaintiffs asserted that, although they had finally received an index to the volumes of paper documents and CDs produced, the index was utterly insufficient and that the Defendant owed them a meaningful and detailed document index. The Defendant argued that the Plaintiffs had to do their own work and look diligently at what they had been provided and that the Defendant owed no further obligation, because it had provided everything that could possibly be responsive to the Plaintiffs' discovery demands.

In response to the Plaintiffs' complaints that they had been unable to locate certain documents, the Defendant maintained that everything that was responsive to the discovery request was in the response provided to the Plaintiffs, and, if they could not find it, it did not exist. The Plaintiffs protested that an unindexed, document dump did not meet the Defendant's obligation to match documents with discovery requests as specifically as possible. Although the Court seemed extremely frustrated by the parties' inability to prevent and resolve the situation, the Court found that, through the Plaintiffs own actions of searching through boxes and requesting certain documents, it appeared as though the Plaintiffs did not need an index to the documents. In regard to the CDs, the Plaintiff's claimed that they could not read the information. The Court stated that if the information could be made readable and thereby searchable, there would be no need for an index. The issue of CD readability and indexing, however, was left to be determined by the Plaintiff and experts, to then be reviewed by the Court.

## Case 79

Court of Appeals of Texas,
Houston (14th Dist.).

Lanny LOWN, Appellant,

v.

The STATE of Texas, Appellee.

No. 14-04-00147-CR.
August 25, 2005.

Jurisdiction: Court of Appeals of Texas, Houston (14th District)

Date: August 25, 2005

Keywords: Admissibility, Computer Forensics, Constitutionality, Procedure

The Appellant appealed his conviction for theft of property. On appeal, the Appellant claimed the trial court erred in admitting into evidence computer data disks allegedly obtained in violation of the Fourth Amendment. The Appellant also claimed the trial court erred in admitting into evidence testimony regarding the content of the disks. The Appellant engaged in a Ponzi scheme via an entity known as One West Financial Services (One West). An assistant to the Appellant requested that a witness back up the data on One West's computer system. The witness made two sets of disks when he backed up the system and kept one set of disks with the knowledge of the Appellant's assistant. The witness turned the disks over to the District Attorney's office when the prosecutor requested the disks from the witness. The backup disks were not seized pursuant to any search warrant or subpoena.

The Court held that the Appellant had the burden to prove facts establishing a legitimate expectation of privacy in the information contained in his computer files, in order to show a violation of the Fourth Amendment. The Court held that the Appellant could meet this burden if he proved "that by his conduct, he exhibited an actual subjective expectation of privacy . . . and that circumstances existed under which society was prepared to recognize his subjective expectation as objectively reasonable." The Court found that there was no evidence that any of the files were the subject to a confidentiality agreement. Further, the Court found no evidence to suggest that the Appellant took steps to protect his privacy in the information contained on the computer system. The Court also found that there was no evidence indicating that the Appellant's assistant lacked authority either to tell the witness to back up the system or to give him permission to take copies of the backup disks. The

Court found that even if the Appellant did show that he had a subjective expectation of privacy in the information stored on the computer system, he did not show that he had an expectation of privacy in the computer files which society accepts as objectively reasonable. The Appellant did not satisfy the burden. The Court held that the trial court did not abuse its discretion in admitting the backup disks into evidence. It concluded that the Appellant did not have standing to challenge the State's acquisition of the backup disks.

## Case 80

United States District Court,
S.D. New York.

LYONDELL-CITGO REFINING, LP, Plaintiff,

v.

PETROLEOS DE VENEZUELA, S.A. and PDVSA-Petroleo, S.A., Defendants.

No. 02 Civ. 0795(CBM).
August 30, 2004.

Jurisdiction: United States District Court, Southern District of New York

Date: August 30, 2004

Keywords: Discovery, Sanctions

In a lawsuit regarding breach of contract, the Plaintiff filed a motion for default judgment against the Defendants, alleging failure to comply with a discovery order. For several months the parties had been engaged in a discovery dispute. The Plaintiff sought the production of electronic documents relevant to its claims, and the Defendants asserted that they were unable to produce said documents as had been ordered by the attorney general of their country. After many hearings and deadline extensions, the Court had finally ordered that the Plaintiff would have a prepared default judgment that would become effective in sixty days from that conference, if the Defendants had not produced the documents. Before the sixty days had commenced, the Plaintiff filed the motion, claiming that the Defendants had failed to produce the electronic documents. The Defendants responded, countering that the motion was premature and unwarranted. Soon thereafter, the Defendants produced discovery materials, which the Plaintiffs then claimed were incomplete, stating that the Defendants still had not completely fulfilled their court ordered duty. The Defendants denied this contention and said that they had produced everything and that, if anything was missing, it had been inadvertent. During yet another meeting, the Court asked the Defendants to produce a comprehensive sales summary, which was the document most keenly sought by the Plaintiffs. The Defendants refused and had not produced the document before the instant hearing had commenced.

The Court, however, found that the entry of a default judgment was unwarranted. The Court held that the possible entry of a default judgment had been conditioned upon the Defendants' failure to produce particular documents involved with their attorney general's directive. The Court found that the sales summary did not fall into this group, and therefore, its production was not subject to the agreed upon possibility of default judgment. The Court went on to state that sanctions can only be imposed for violation of a specific, previously entered court order and that there was no sufficient justification for the extreme measure of entering a default judgment, because the Defendants had taken steps to remedy the alleged gaps in production. Accordingly, the Court denied the Plaintiff's motion for default judgment.

## Case 81

United States District Court,
D. Maine.

Dale W. MARTIN Petitioner

v.

STATE of Maine Respondent

No. Civ.04-126-B-W.
November 24, 2004.

Jurisdiction: United State District Court, District of Maine

Date: November 24, 2004

Keywords: Procedure

The Defendant, who conditionally pleaded guilty to twelve counts of dissemi-nating sexually explicit images of minors, filed a petition seeking federal relief from his state sentence. In his petition, he argued that the rejection of his claim that his guilty plea was involuntary was wrong. The Defendant claimed that his guilty plea was not knowing and intelligent because he was not fully aware of each offense that he was pleading guilty to and was not properly in-formed about the nature of the charges brought against him. The factual basis for his claim was that he did not understand what the prosecution would have to prove had he gone to trial, because he believed that he could be convicted under the state statute for possessing images of pornography that involved only artificially created or computer-generated minors engaging in sexually explicit conduct.

The Court held, however, that the problem with the Defendant's argu-ment was that he was not subject to prosecution for disseminating images that were not of actual children. The portion of the order on the motion to dis-miss pertaining to the issue reflected the State's concession that the state statute in question prohibited dissemination and possession only of visual material depicting real children. Thus, the Court concluded that his prosecu-tion was in full compliance with the federal principles. The evidence before the postconviction court was that the issue of the State's burden apropos the images was raised early on in the proceeding, resolved favorably toward the Defendant, and he was given a copy of the decision stating as much by coun-sel. The Court found that despite his self-serving protestations at the postconviction hearing, he would not have pled guilty if he had known that the State had to prove that the images involved actual children, he had testified that he had no reason to believe that they were not actual children. The Court denied the Defendant relief, because it concluded that the Defendant's claims were either unexhausted or without merit.

## Case 82

United States Court of Appeals,
Sixth Circuit.

Carol MCDANIEL, Plaintiff-Appellant,

v.

TRANSCENDER, LLC, and Aneel Pandey, Defendants-Appellees.

No. 03-5599.
January 31, 2005.

Jurisdiction: United States Court of Appeals, Sixth Circuit

Date: January 31, 2005

Keywords: Spoliation, Sanctions

In an employment discrimination case, the Plaintiff appealed the district court's grant of a summary judgment in favor of the Defendants. In her complaint, the Plaintiff alleged claims of retaliatory discharge under the Fair Labor Standards Act and of age discrimination under the Age Discrimination in Employment Act. On appeal, the Plaintiff also challenged the district court's refusal to grant her a default judgment or to impose sanctions upon the Defendants for their allegedly willful spoliation of relevant evidence.

During its spoliation analysis, the Court noted that the Plaintiff served the Defendants with a request for inspection and copying of their computers. The Plaintiff alleged that the Defendants destroyed the external creation date of a memorandum, which the Defendants asserted was prepared by an employee on a specific date. The document outlined many of the reasons for the Defendants' dissatisfaction with the Plaintiff's work. In her appeal, the Plaintiff argued that the employee testified, among other things, that he did not believe she should have been terminated, never recommended her termination, and did not recall preparing the memorandum, which ostensibly supported her termination. The Court concluded that the district court did not abuse its discretion in denying the Plaintiff a default judgment and sanctions. The Court stated that, assuming that the allegedly spoiled evidence would have shown, as the Defendant claimed, that the employee did not write the contested memorandum, that information would not have established a sufficient evidentiary basis upon which the Court could determine that the district court's denial of a default judgment or sanctions constituted an abuse of its discretion. Accordingly, the Court affirmed the district court's denial of default judgment and sanctions against the Defendants.

## Case 83

United States District Court,
District of Columbia.

Steven McPEEK, Plaintiff,

v.

John D. ASHCROFT et al., Defendants.

Civ.A. No. 00-201(RCL/JMF).
January 9, 2003.

Jurisdiction: United States District Court, District of Columbia

Date: January 9, 2003

Keywords: Production of Evidence, Constitutionality

In a sexual harassment suit, at the Plaintiff's urging, the Court had previously permitted the search of certain backup tapes of the Defendant to ascertain whether that search would justify any additional searches. After the search had been performed, the parties vehemently disagreed as to what the search revealed. The Plaintiff claimed that it had produced useful, relevant information that justified a second search of backup tapes for certain periods. He provided an affidavit from a computer forensics technician who insisted that a second search would not be that difficult or expensive, in light of what the first search had accomplished. The Defendant disagreed and insisted that the first search had produced only documents that were cumulative of what the Plaintiff had already possessed and that a second search would be expensive and time consuming and therefore completely unjustified. The Defendant then ascertained that only certain backup tapes were still available and that the question presented narrowed substantially to whether another search of the available backup tapes would be appropriate.

Whether a search of the backup tapes would be appropriate involved an assessment of the likelihood that they would contain data that would produce information relevant to the lawsuit. The Court found that, with the exception of searching the backup tape for one particular employee on one particular date, it need not order any additional searches of the available backup tapes for other employees. The Court found that the likelihood of relevant documents being found was either so small or impossible that additional searches were unjustified, because the tapes to be searched were backups of dates occurring either before the events in question or years later. In only one instance was the Court able to reason that the date of the backup sufficiently coincided with an event at issue, thereby warranting a search of that tape for relevant documents only. Otherwise, additional searches of the backup tapes were denied.

## Case 84

United States District Court,
W.D. Tennessee,
Western Division.
MEDTRONIC SOFAMOR DANEK, INC., Plaintiff/Counterclaim Defendant,
v.
Gary Karlin MICHELSON, M.D. and Karlin Technology, Inc.,
Defendants/Counterclaimants,
and
Gary K. Michelson, M.D., Third Party Plaintiff,
v.
Sofamor Danek Holdings, Inc., Third Party Defendant.
No. 01-2373-M1V.
May 13, 2003.

Jurisdiction: United States District Court, Western District of Tennessee, Western Division

Date: May 13, 2003

Keywords: Discovery, Costs and Cost Shifting, Experts

In a case involving trade secrets, patents, and trade information in the field of spinal fusion medical technology, the parties had not been able to agree on a discovery protocol for production, on the scope of production, or, most importantly, on who should bear the cost of production. The Defendant filed a motion to compel the Plaintiff to produce approximately 996 network backup tapes containing, among other things, e-mail and an estimated 300 gigabytes of electronic data that was not in a backup format, all of which contained items potentially responsive to discovery requests that had been propounded by the Defendant. The Plaintiff responded, claiming that the discovery requests were unduly burdensome because extracting the data from backup tapes and reviewing it for relevance and privilege would be astronomically costly. The Defendant countered that the Plaintiff, as the producing party, should bear the cost of disclosure and requested that the court appoint a special master to help the parties establish a discovery protocol.

In light of the volume of data at issue, the Court agreed that the process, as a whole, would be burdensome. The Court therefore set out to determine whether the burden on the Plaintiff, as the producing party, was undue, and, if so, whether it should be shifted in whole or in part to the Defendant, as the requesting party. Using the seven-factor Rowe cost-shifting analysis, the Court found it appropriate to shift some of the electronic discovery cost to the Defendant. The parties were instructed to agree on a neutral computer expert or to provide the Court with names of candidates to serve as a special master, to oversee discovery. The Court ordered the parties to equally bear the cost of the special master, to both bear portions of the electronic discovery costs, and to commence an electronic discovery plan, which the Court outlined.

## Case 85

United States District Court,
W.D. Tennessee, Western Division.

MEDTRONIC SOFAMOR DANEK, INC., Plaintiffs/Counterclaim Defendant

v.

Gary K. MICHELSON, M.D., and Karlin Technology, Inc.,
Defendants/Counterclaimants,
MEDTRONIC SOFAMOR DANEK, INC., and Medtronic, Inc., Plaintiffs,

v.

Gary K. MICHELSON, M.D., and Karlin Technology, Inc., Defendants.

No. 01-2373-MLV, 03-2055-MLV.
May 3, 2004.

Jurisdiction: United States District Court, Western District Tennessee, Western Division

Date: May 3, 2004

Keywords: Discovery, Preservation of Evidence/Spoliation

The Defendants filed a motion objecting to a Special Master's order regarding the Plaintiff's production of electronic deleted files and requesting expedited resolution of the matter. The Defendants argued that the Plaintiff had failed to produce its deleted files, as required by the order, and asserted that the Plaintiff should be required to do so, despite the Special Master's ruling to the contrary. The Defendants also requested that the Plaintiff be ordered to bear all costs associated with the production of deleted files responsive to their discovery requests. The Court found that the Special Master had never been assigned the duty of making determinations as to whether the Plaintiff could be compelled to produce deleted electronic files and e-mails and that the Special Master's order went beyond the scope of his authority to make such a ruling. Therefore, the Court reviewed the Special Master's order de novo.

The Court found that the issue was essentially a motion to compel and that the Defendants' maintained that they were entitled to the production of deleted electronic files and e-mails because those files were included within the scope of the court's order directing the Plaintiff to produce electronic data. The Court then raised two questions: whether the scope of the court's order had included the production of all of the Plaintiff's responsive deleted files and, if so, whether the production of responsive deleted files could be compelled at such a late stage of litigation. During its analysis, the Court found that the Defendants had been dilatory in their efforts to compel the production of the deleted files. The Court then held that the Defendants' request was untimely and that the process of recovering deleted files so late in litigation would be an undue burden on the Plaintiff, because there was mere speculation that relevant deleted files could be recovered. Accordingly, the Court overruled the Defendants' objections to the Special Master's ruling and denied their request for the production of deleted documents.

## Case 86

District Court of Appeals of Florida,
Fourth District.

David MENKE, Petitioner,

v.

BROWARD COUNTY SCHOOL BOARD, Respondent.

No. 4D05-978.
September 28, 2005.

Jurisdiction: District Court of Appeals of Florida

Date: September 28, 2005

Keywords: Discovery, Expert, Constitutionality

In a disciplinary action brought against the Petitioner, a high school teacher accused of exchanging sexually explicit e-mails with students and making derogatory comments regarding school officials, an administrative law judge ("ALJ") entered an order compelling production of all computers in the Petitioner's household for examination by the Respondent's expert. The ALJ's order allowed for the expert to inspect the hard drives of all of the home computers to discover whether they contained various categories of information. The order allowed for the Petitioner to have his own expert present during the inspection. The ALJ ordered the Respondent's expert not to retain, provide, or discuss with Respondent's counsel any communication discovered on the computer that might be considered privileged. The order provided that if Petitioner's expert believed a privileged communication was discovered, the ALJ would perform an in camera inspection of the document before it was delivered to the Respondent. The Petitioner petitioned for a writ of certiorari contending that the production of the computers and their contents would violate his Fifth Amendment right against self-incrimination and privacy and would disclose privileged communications.

The Court held "intrusive searching of the entire computer by an opposing party should not be the first means of obtaining relevant information." The Court further held that, where electronically stored information is demanded during discovery, searching for relevant information should first be done by the Defendant to protect confidential information, unless there is evidence of data destruction designed to prevent the discovery of relevant information. The Court found no evidence that the Petitioner destroyed or attempted to destroy evidence. The Court also looked at the fact that the Respondent requested no other method of discovery of relevant information, nor presented evidence that there is no less intrusive method of obtaining the information. The Court found the order at issue did not allow the Petitioner to assert privilege as to information on the computer in advance of its disclosure to the Respondent's expert. The order prevented the Petitioner from exercising his right to assert privilege, his Fifth Amendment right against self-incrimination, and his and others in his household's right to privacy. The Court granted the writ and quashed the discovery order.

## Case 87

United States District Court,
S.D. New York.

In re MERRILL LYNCH & CO., INC. RESEARCH REPORTS
SECURITIES LITIGATION
In re: MERRILL LYNCH INFOSPACE ANALYST REPORTS
SECURITIES LITIGATION

No. 02 MDL 1484(MP), 01 CV 6881(MP).
February 18, 2004.

Jurisdiction: United States District Court, Southern District of New York

Date: February 18, 2004

Keywords: Discovery, Preservation of Evidence/Spoliation

During litigation involving securities claims, the Plaintiffs moved for an order lifting a previous automatic stay of discovery. The Plaintiffs' essential claim was that discovery was necessary to preserve and restore e-mails that the Defendant had deleted. The Court stated that the Private Securities Litigation Reform Act mandated that all discovery shall be stayed during the pendency of a motion to dismiss. Furthermore, that provision was balanced by imposing a contemporaneous duty on parties to preserve all relevant evidence as if they were the subject of a continuing request for production of documents. Because the Court had been asked to consider, but had not yet ruled on, the legal sufficiency of the complaint, it found that discovery could be permitted only if exceptional circumstances, such as the necessity to preserve evidence or to prevent undue prejudice to a party, existed.

In the Defendants' opposition to the Plaintiffs' motion, they avowed that they were aware of their obligations and had taken and continued to take all necessary steps to preserve all potentially relevant electronic evidence. On the basis of that declaration, the Court concluded that there was nothing that it could order the Defendants to do to preserve the relevant evidence that they had not already done or represented to the Court that they would do. Therefore, the Court held that an order lifting the mandatory, automatic stay of discovery was not warranted, as there was no imminent risk established that any deleted data would be overwritten and rendered irretrievable. Accordingly, the Court denied the Plaintiffs' motion.

# Case 88

United States District Court,
N.D. Indiana, Fort Wayne Division.

Kevin D. MILLER, Plaintiff,

v.

JAVITCH, BLOCK & RATHBONE, LLP, and Melville Acquisitions Group, LLC,
Defendants.

No. 1:05-CV-211-TS.
October 26, 2005.

Jurisdiction: United States District Court, Northern District of Indiana,
Fort Wayne Division

Date: October 26, 2005

Keywords: Admissibility

The Plaintiff brought a suit against the Defendants alleging malicious prosecution, invasion of privacy, and breach of the Fair Debt Collections Practices
Act. The Plaintiff moved to exclude or strike certain evidence. Specifically, the
Plaintiff argued that the declaration of an employee of the Defendant contained inadmissible hearsay.

The Defendant MAG was law firm JB & R's client in the collection of debt
that the Plaintiff purportedly owed MAG. Track America was the company
that managed MAG's debt portfolio. The declaration at issue was that of an attorney at JB & R. The declaration had attached to it as exhibits an electronic
file submitted to MAG by Track America and an electronic database created
by JB & R using the information contained in Track America's electronic file.
The Plaintiff argued that these files were inadmissible as hearsay because
they contained the statements of Track America and not JB & R or MAG. In the
attorney's declaration, he stated that the electronic file and the database were
true, authentic, and accurate copies of records JB & R kept in the ordinary
course of business. He also stated that he was familiar with the record-keeping system associated with these records. The Court held that the electronic
file and database were admissible and could be considered under the business records exception to the hearsay rule. The Court denied the Plaintiff's
motion to exclude or strike this evidence.

## Case 89

Supreme Court, Westchester County, New York.

MIRIAM OSBORN MEMORIAL HOME ASSOCIATION, Petitioner,

v.

ASSESSOR OF the CITY OF RYE, the Board of Assessment Review of the
City of Rye, and the City of Rye, Respondents,

and

Rye City School District, Intervenor-Respondent.

August 29, 2005.

Jurisdiction: Supreme Court, Westchester County, New York

Date: August 29, 2005

Keywords: Admissibility, Procedure

In a case involving real property tax issues, the Petitioner sought to admit into
evidence the compilation of an electronic printout of data maintained by the
state office of real property services and downloaded by a Petitioner's witness
from the state office of real property services' Web site.

The Petitioner asserted that the electronic printout of the data was admissible because it was a public record. The Petitioner further argued that
the compilation was prepared by the state office using certified state forms,
which were a matter of public record, so it is a compilation of public records.
The Respondent argued that the compilation on the Web site makes no warranties concerning the accuracy, completeness, reliability, or suitability for
the use of the information contained therein. The Court held that it would not
take judicial notice of the compilation because the possibility of inaccuracy
and unreliability existed. The Court further found that the Petitioner could
not demonstrate that the forms, upon which the compilation was based,
were mandated by the law to be filed as public records. Therefore, the Court
held that the compilation from the Web site is inadmissible under the statutory hearsay exception for certain public records; however, the Court held
that the common law public hearsay exception was not superseded by the
statutory hearsay exceptions. Under the common law hearsay exception, the
Court held that there is a presumed reliability to documents maintained by
public employees and such documents are admissible. Here, the Court found
that the compilation on the Web site fell under this common law hearsay exception and was admissible, so long as it was authenticated. The Court did
not opine on whether it thought the exhibit was authenticated, instead it

moved on to the issue of whether the exhibit fell under the electronic record umbrella. Under state law, electronic records were admissible in an exhibit that is a true and accurate representation of the record. The Court noted that the Petitioner's witness testified as to the manner in which she downloaded, printed, and copied the electronic record on the Web site and turned it into a tangible exhibit. The Court found that the compilation satisfied the requirements for an electronic record under state law and therefore was admissible as an exhibit.

## Case 90

United States District Court,
D. Maryland.

MMI PRODUCTS, INC., Plaintiff,

v.

Henry F. LONG, Jr., et al., Defendants.

No. CIV PJM 03-2711.
August 15, 2005.

Jurisdiction: United States District Court, District of Maryland.

Date: August 15, 2005

Keywords: Expert, Sanctions

In a suit alleging misappropriation of a laptop computer, the Plaintiff objected to the magistrate judge's proposed sanction. The sanction ordered the Plaintiff and Plaintiff's counsel to pay the fees of the Defendant's expert because the Plaintiff and Plaintiff's counsel failed to make reasonable inquiries into the reliability of their own expert's report, which was incorporated into the Plaintiff's answers to interrogatories.

    After the Defendant returned the laptop to the Plaintiff, Plaintiff employed a computer expert to preserve the contents of the hard drive, recover deleted files, and analyze the contents of the hard drive. The expert found evidence that there was an attempt to overwrite data. The expert's conclusion was submitted to the Defendant. Following this, the Defendant retained its own computer expert. The Defendant's expert concluded that any evidence of an attempt to overwrite data was the result of normal processes, not an effort by the Defendant to delete information. Following this, the Plaintiff announced it was withdrawing its expert's report and that the expert would not be called at trial. The Defendant requested that the magistrate judge award him expert and attorneys' fees incurred in refuting the Plaintiff's expert's report. In particular, the Defendant argued that there was no substantial justification for the allegations in the Plaintiff's expert's report. The magistrate judge held that because the Plaintiff's counsel certified and incorporated the report into the answer, it was liable for sanctions, in this case the Defendant's expert's fees. The Court found that the counsel's certification of the answer and report certifies only that "the lawyer has made a reasonable effort to assure that the client has provided all of the information and documents available to him that are responsive to the discovery demand." The Court found further that the typical sanctions for expert reports because of untimeliness or incompleteness have been exclusion of the reports in whole or in part or dismissal of the case. The Court found no cases where the counsel or the client had been sanctioned monetarily for errors or mistakes in an expert's report, even where the report is incorporated into an answer to interrogatories. The Court held that sanctioning a litigant for the deficient or erroneous report of its expert would be highly undesirable. The Court reversed the magistrate judge's order and found for the Plaintiff, removing the sanction.

## Case 91

United States District Court,
D. Maryland.

MMI PRODUCTS, INC.

v.

LONG et al.

No. PJM-03-CV-2711.
April 1, 2005.
2005 WL 757073

Jurisdiction: United States District Court, District of Maryland

Date: April 1, 2005

Keywords: Computer Forensics, Costs and Cost Shifting, Experts

In a case regarding the alleged misappropriation of a work issued laptop, the Defendant moved for fees and costs related to a computer forensic expert's examination of the laptop at issue. The Plaintiff claimed that the Defendant, sua sponte, elected to retain a computer expert to address peripheral issues, as the Plaintiff's complaint alleged that the Defendant only misappropriated tangible property and not the information stored within. It was clear to the Court that the Plaintiff speculated that the Defendant had misappropriated information from the laptop and that is why the Plaintiff had retained its computer forensic expert. The Court also presumed that the Defendant retained a computer expert to refute the Plaintiff's expert's report, especially those conclusions suggesting that the Defendant had deliberately deleted or overwrote data.

The Court noted that an expert report is not a discovery request, response, or objection. In addition, the Plaintiff's expert report at issue was not certified by the Plaintiff's counsel. Therefore, because FRCP 26(g)(2) does not govern expert reports, sanctions typically could not be imposed under Rule 26(g)(3). The Court, however, found that, by incorporating the Plaintiff's expert's report in its Answers, which Plaintiff's counsel signed, the report fell within the scope of Rule 26(g)(2). Because the Plaintiff's counsel failed to make reasonable inquiries upon receiving the Plaintiff's expert's report, in light of the Defendant's discovery requests, and included the report in the Defendant's signed response to the requests, without substantial justification, the Court found an award of the expert's costs, but not attorneys' fees, was reasonable under Rule 26(g)(3).

## Case 92

United States District Court,
D. New Jersey.

MOSAID TECHNOLOGIES INCORPORATED, Plaintiff,

v.

SAMSUNG ELECTRONICS CO., LTD., Samsung Electronics America, Inc.,
Samsung Semiconductor, Inc., and Samsung Austin Semiconductor, L.P.,
Defendants.

No. 01-CV-4340 (WJM).
December 7, 2004.

Jurisdiction: United States District Court, District of New Jersey

Date: December 7, 2004

Keywords: Preservation of Evidence/Spoliation, Sanctions, Costs and
Cost Shifting

During a discovery dispute, the Defendant appealed sanctions handed down
in a previous order, regarding a spoliation inference jury instruction, concerning the Defendant's destruction of e-mails, and monetary sanctions, constituting attorneys' fees and costs associated with the Plaintiff's motion for
sanctions and attempts to obtain discovery.

The Court stated that the duty to preserve potentially relevant evidence
is an affirmative obligation that a party may not shirk. When the duty to preserve is triggered, it cannot be a defense to a spoliation claim that the party
inadvertently failed to place a litigation hold or off switch on its document retention policy to stop the destruction of that evidence. As discoverable information becomes progressively digital, e-discovery, including e-mails and
other electronic documents, plays a larger, more crucial role in litigation. The
Court found that counsel are required to investigate how a client's computers
store digital information, to review with the client potentially discoverable evidence, and to raise the topic of e-discovery at the discovery conference, including preservation and production of digital information. Unless and until
parties agree not to pursue e-discovery, the parties have an obligation to preserve potentially relevant digital information. Parties who fail to comply with
that obligation do so at the risk of facing spoliation sanctions.

The Court concluded that the Defendant was aware that it had a duty to
preserve potentially discoverable evidence. It knew that its technical e-mails
were potentially relevant to the claims and defenses existing in the lawsuit,

and it chose to do nothing about the spoliation of those e-mails. The Court found that, as a result, the Plaintiff had suffered prejudice from the nonproduction of countless e-mails because its ability to prove infringement, and other issues, had been potentially hindered. Therefore, the Court affirmed the spoliation inference jury instruction and monetary sanctions that had previously been imposed. Lastly, the Court noted that those were the least burdensome sanctions it could impose while still attempting to level what had become an uneven playing field.

## Case 93

Superior Court of Massachusetts.

Suni MUNSHANI,

v.

SIGNAL LAKE VENTURE FUND II, LP et al.

No. 005529BLS.
October 9, 2001.

Jurisdiction: Superior Court of Massachusetts

Date: October 9, 2001

Keywords: Computer Forensics, Sanctions, Experts

In a prior opinion in a breach of contract case, the Court had appointed a computer forensics expert to determine whether a certain e-mail purportedly sent to the Plaintiff was authentic. The expert concluded that the questioned message was clearly not authentic. The Court accepted the expert report in its entirety and directed that it be docketed with the pleadings in the case. The Plaintiff responded to the report stating that he had decided to invoke his Fifth Amendment privileges and declined to testify about or respond to the report. The Court noted that this was a civil action and, consequently, the invocation of the privilege could result in sanctions against the litigant asserting it, including an adverse inference, dismissal of the complaint, and an award of legal fees and costs. The question before the Court then became what action it should take in light of the expert report, as there had clearly been a fraud on the Court.

The Court found that the evidence was material to the case and that had the Plaintiff succeeded with his fraud, he could have dramatically changed the face of the case before the Court, to the serious detriment of the Defendants and the Court. The Court also concluded that the Plaintiff had been shown to have acted knowingly in his submission and defense of the fabricated e-mail. The expert report made it quite clear that the Plaintiff had intentionally fabricated the disputed e-mail and then attempted to hide that fabrication. Then, when discovered, the Plaintiff persisted in protesting his innocence and insisting that the document that he had altered was authentic. This Court held that the Defendants and the Court had both been grossly abused by the fraud and that the Plaintiff had, thereby, forfeited the privilege of using the system and manipulating it any further. The Court then dismissed the Plaintiff's complaint and ordered the Plaintiff to reimburse the Defendants for their contribution to the expert's costs and for the fees and expenses reasonably charged by counsel for the Defendants relating to the discovery of the fraud, such that the entire cost thereof should be borne by the perpetrator.

## Case 94

United States District Court,
C.D. California.

NEW.NET, INC., Plaintiff,

v.

LAVASOFT, an entity of unknown form; Nicolas Stark Computing AB,
an entity of unknown form, and Does 1-25, inclusive, Defendants.

No. CV 03-3180GAFCWX.
November 6, 2003.

Jurisdiction: United States District Court, Central District of California

Date: November 6, 2003

Keywords: Spyware

The Plaintiff, whose business ultimately depends on its ability to distribute as many copies of its software as possible, sought an order that the Defendants cease distributing their software or delete the Plaintiff's software from its target list. The Plaintiff complained that the Defendant has unfairly targeted and mislabeled its software, inaccurately associated its software with the worst of the worst Internet downloaders, and recommended to computer users that its program be uninstalled. This activity, according to the Plaintiff, constituted false advertising, unfair competition, common law trade libel, and tortious interference with prospective economic advantage. The Plaintiff sought a preliminary injunction barring the distribution of the Defendants' program unless it deleted or changed what it said about the Plaintiff's software.

The Plaintiff was a company that downloaded software to individual computers through the Internet, often without the knowledge or request of the computer user, and the Defendants, which produced and distributed software that located programs like the Plaintiff's, notified computer users of their presence, and, if requested, removed the programs from the user's hard drive. The Defendants argued that the distribution of its software constituted speech and that the Plaintiff sought an impermissible prior restraint, even if the Plaintiff's allegations were found to be true. The Defendants, however, maintained that their program did not mislabel the Plaintiff's software, that its inclusion on the target list was not unreasonable, and that they did not recommend deletion of the software, but rather left that decision to the computer user. They also noted that they distribute their free program only to individuals who request it because of their desire to identify programs that have found their way onto users' computers without their knowledge or consent. Thus, from the Defendants' perspective, the case impacts on the right of computer users to control what resides on their hard drives and the uses to which their computers are put.

The Court concluded that the Plaintiff's motion was not meritorious and that it brought the suit to protect its ability to surreptitiously download its software by silencing a company whose computer program, at the request of a computer owner, called attention to the software's presence on the user's hard drive. The Court held that the Plaintiff's case required the Court to determine whether it may grant the requested injunction without running afoul of the First Amendment prohibition against prior restraints. The Court found that, whether or not the speech was viewed as less-protected commercial speech, it fell within the scope of First Amendment protections because it addressed a matter of public interest. Thus, on First Amendment principles, the Court denied the Plaintiff's motion for preliminary injunction.

## Case 95

United States District Court,
C.D. California.

NEW.NET, INC., Plaintiff,

v.

LAVASOFT; Nicolas Stark Computing AB, Defendant.

No. CV 03-3180 GAF.
May 20, 2004.

Jurisdiction: United States District Court, Central District of California

Date: May 20, 2004

Keywords: Spyware

The case involved a dispute between two downloadable software providers, the Plaintiff, whose software was downloaded onto individual computers often without the knowledge or request of the computer owner, and the Defendants, whose software was purposefully downloaded by the computer user to detect and remove programs like the one written by the Plaintiff. The Plaintiff complained that the injuries caused by the Defendants' inclusion of the Plaintiff's software in their database were actionable under both state and federal law. The Court had previously denied the Plaintiff's motion for a preliminary injunction, concluding that the Defendants, through their software, were engaging in First Amendment protected speech. The Defendants then moved to dismiss the state claims in their entirety under California's anti-SLAPP statute, which provided an expedited procedure for dismissing lawsuits designed to stifle speech on issues of public importance. The Court concluded that the motion was well taken and should be granted. In addition, the Court held that the remaining federal question claims should also be dismissed. Because of the Plaintiff's persistence in the litigation, the Defendants finally moved to strike the Plaintiff's causes of action for, unfair competition, trade libel, and tortious interference with prospective economic advantage. The Defendant also sought judgment on the pleadings as to the Plaintiff's federal Lanham Act false advertising claim.

The Court stated that the contest in the case was between computer users, who acquire software precisely to determine what programs they may have unsuspectingly downloaded onto their hard drives, and the Plaintiff, which apparently needs the ability to deliver its program to as many unwitting users as possible to further its business plan.

During its lengthy analysis, the Court found that the Defendant's motion was not improper under the state statutes, because the Defendants were not primarily engaged in the business of selling goods, neither they nor the Plaintiff were not making statements about their own products, and lastly the Defendants' purported statements were not made in the course of delivering goods. In addition, the Court held that the Defendants' speech addressed a matter of public interest and that it did so in a public forum. Regarding the Plaintiff's unfair competition claims, the Court concluded that the Defendants' speech was not commercial but was speech afforded full First Amendment protection, that the Defendants were not engaged in an unlawful practice, and that the speech was not fraudulent and did not involve false advertising. Lastly, the Court held that the Plaintiff's Lanham Act claim did not state a claim for relief because it could not prove the elements of false advertising. Accordingly, the Court granted the Defendants' motion in its entirety, ordered the lawsuit dismissed with prejudice, and awarded the Defendants attorneys' fees and costs.

## Case 96

United States District Court,
S.D. New York.

NEXANS WIRES S.A. and Lacroix & Kress GmbH, Plaintiffs,

v.

SARK-USA, INC. and Sarkuysan Elektrolitik Bakir Sanayii Ve Ticaret A.S.,
Defendants.

No. 03 CIV. 2291(MGC).
May 25, 2004.

Jurisdiction: United States District Court, Southern District of New York

Date: May 25, 2004

Keywords: Procedure

The Plaintiffs filed an action for unfair competition, and the Defendants moved to dismiss the action, claiming that the Plaintiffs lacked standing to sue under the Computer Fraud and Abuse Act. By a previous order, the Defendants' motion to dismiss was converted into a motion for summary judgment. The Plaintiffs asserted that in order to maintain a business relationship with another entity, it was necessary to store their confidential propriety information, consisting of pricing schedules and manufacturing information, on the computers of the other entity. The information was stored in a secure centralized computer system at both of the companies' offices and was segregated from other files and password protected to insure confidentiality. The Plaintiffs alleged that the Defendants, former employees of the other entity, left their former employment to create the Defendant corporation, which is a direct competitor of the Plaintiffs and that the new corporation served as a repository of the Plaintiffs' stolen and misappropriated confidential, proprietary information. Specifically, the Plaintiffs claimed that other employees of the Plaintiff, who had full access to the information, stole the information by downloading it via a personal e-mail account and then sending it to the Defendants, at their urging.

The Court noted that the CFAA is a criminal statute but that it also provides for a civil right of action, which may only be brought if the conduct involves one of the factors set forth in the statute. The only applicable one for the case was the loss to one or more persons during any one-year period, aggregating at least $5,000 in value, which the Plaintiffs asserted. They maintained that their losses were travel expenses resulting from meetings occurring in response to the Defendant's actions, but the Court found that nothing in the case law or the legislative history suggested that something as far removed from a computer as the travel expenses of senior executives constituted a loss. Therefore, the Court held that the international travel expenses, in which no computers were said to have been examined and no computer consultant was said to have been present could not satisfy the $5,000 loss requirement of the statute. The Plaintiffs then argued that the revenue they lost as a result of the Defendants' use of their information to unfairly compete for business constituted a loss; however, the Plaintiffs later stated that they were not arguing that the revenue that they lost as a result of the alleged unfair competition alone satisfied the loss requirement, and the Court found their argument unpersuasive. Accordingly, the Court granted the Defendants' motion for summary judgment dismissing the Plaintiffs' claims under the CFAA.

## Case 97

District Court of Appeal of Florida,
Fifth District.

Beverly Ann O'BRIEN, Appellant,
v.
James Kevin O'BRIEN, Appellee.

No. 5D03-3484.
February 11, 2005.

Jurisdiction: District Court of Appeal of Florida, Fifth District

Date: February 11, 2005

Keywords: Spyware, Admissibility

During a contentious divorce proceeding, the Husband discovered the Wife's clandestine attempt to monitor and record his conversations with an online chat partner and uninstalled the "Spector" software the wife had installed. He then filed a motion for a temporary injunction, which was subsequently granted, to prevent the Wife from disclosing the communications. Thereafter, the Husband requested and received a permanent injunction to prevent the Wife's disclosure of the communications and to prevent her from engaging in similar activity in the future. That motion also requested that the trial court preclude introduction of the communications into evidence in the divorce proceeding, which was also granted. The trial court, without considering the communications, entered a final judgment for dissolution of the marriage. The Wife moved for a rehearing, which was subsequently denied. The Wife appealed the order granting the permanent injunction, the final judgment, and the order denying the Wife's motion for rehearing on the narrow issue of whether the trial court erred in refusing to admit evidence of the Husband's computer activities obtained through the spyware the Wife secretly installed on the computer. The Wife argued that the electronic communications did not fall under the umbra of the Security of Communications Act because the communications were retrieved from storage and, therefore, were not intercepted communications as defined by the Act. In opposition, the Husband asserted that the Spector spyware, installed on the computer, acquired his electronic communications real-time as they were in transmission and, therefore, were intercepts illegally obtained under the Act.

The Court concluded that, because the spyware installed by the Wife intercepted the electronic communication contemporaneously with transmission, copied it, and routed the copy to a file in the computer's hard drive, the electronic communications were intercepted in violation of the Florida Act. The Court also found that the intercepted electronic communications in the case were not excludable under the Act. However, because the evidence was illegally obtained, the Court held that the trial court did not abuse its discretion in refusing to admit it. Accordingly, the Court affirmed the judgment of the lower court. The Wife's motion for rehearing, regarding an implicit assertion that the Court had convicted the Wife of a crime, was also denied.

# Case 98

United States District Court,
S.D. New York.

Therese Patricia OKOUMOU, Plaintiff,

v.

SAFE HORIZON and Carol Weinman, as Director of the Staten Island
Community Office, Defendants.

No. 03 Civ.1606 LAK HBP.
September 30, 2005.

Jurisdiction: United States District Court, Southern District of New York

Date: September 30, 2005

Keywords: Costs and Cost Shifting, Discovery, Sanctions

In an employment suit, the Plaintiff alleged wrongful termination. The Plaintiff moved for sanctions against the Defendant, alleging that the Defendant improperly failed to produce documents as required by the Court's discovery order.

The discovery order at issue directed the Defendant to produce the Plaintiff's employment records and job description for a particular position, nonprivileged correspondence and e-mails concerning the Plaintiff, and any of the Plaintiff's written work supporting the argument that the Plaintiff was terminated for cause. The Plaintiff produced to the Court many documents she claimed should have been produced by the Defendant in compliance with this discovery order. The Plaintiff, however, refused to disclose how she came into possession of these documents. The author of these documents, a Defendant, submitted an affidavit identifying the documents as her "personal supervision file" and claiming that she did not turn over these documents because the documents were missing from her files when she checked her files for the requested discovery documents. The Court found that the Defendant should not be sanctioned because it appeared that the Defendants' failure to produce these documents was due to the fact that the documents had been misappropriated by someone and given to the Plaintiff and were not in the Defendants' possession at the time of discovery. The Plaintiff also argued that sanctions should have been imposed for the Defendants' failure to produce e-mails. The Defendants countered, claiming that they had produced all relevant e-mails that could be readily retrieved, but that there may have been relevant e-mails on an obsolete, archived e-mail system, which was no longer readily accessible. The Court found no evidence of bad faith on the part of the Defendants in producing documents. The Court further directed the Plaintiff that if she wanted to pursue discovery on the archived e-mail system she could do so and advise the Court in writing of this request. The Court held that the extent to which those e-mails were discoverable and the allocation of the costs of restoring those e-mails required further analysis by the Court. The Court held that the Defendant should not receive sanctions for its actions in response to the discovery order.

## Case 99

United States District Court,
N.D. Illinois, Eastern Division.

In re OLD BANC ONE SHAREHOLDERS SECURITIES LITIGATION

No. 00 C 2100.
December 8, 2005.

Jurisdiction: United States District Court, Northern District of Illinois,
Eastern Division

Date: December 8, 2005

Keywords: Discovery, Sanctions, Spoliation

In a suit alleging misrepresentation, the Plaintiffs filed a motion for sanctions due to spoliation of evidence. In the motion, the Plaintiffs argued that the appropriate remedy was a default judgment for the Plaintiffs. In the alternative, the Plaintiffs requested a negative inference jury instruction against the Defendant. The magistrate judge recommended that the Plaintiffs' motion for sanctions be granted, and that as a sanction, Defendant would be precluded from cross-examining Plaintiffs' financial expert. The Plaintiffs objected to the report and recommendations of the magistrate judge.

During discovery, the Plaintiffs requested documents concerning the Defendant's methodology and calculations concerning the economic impact of a payment processing problem. The Defendant could not produce many of the documents because the documents could not be found. The Defendant argued that they preserved documents relating to the litigation, produced enough information for the Plaintiffs to adequately challenge estimates and methodology, and the information requested was unnecessary to the case. The Defendant admitted many of the documents were not been produced despite the Defendant's best efforts to find them. The Court found that the Defendant could have reasonably foreseen the relevance of certain documents because of a pending lawsuit and the filing of a complaint. The Court found that the Defendant was on notice and had a duty to preserve relevant documents. The Court held that for the Defendants to meet their obligations, it should have created a comprehensive document retention policy and disseminated it to the company. The Court found that the Defendant had notice of the categories of relevant documents and therefore had a duty to retain them. The Court found that because the Defendant was unable to produce the documents, it breached its duty to preserve the documents. The Court found no evidence that the Defendant willfully destroyed the documents. The Court held that "to suffer substantive prejudice due to spoliation of evidence, the lost evidence must prevent the aggrieved party from using evidence essential to the underlying claim." The Court found that the documents which could not be produced went to the Plaintiffs' expert's estimation of the economic impact, which went to the heart of whether the Defendants misstated financial well-being. The Court, however, held that the sanction of default judgment was not warranted in this case and upheld the magistrate judge's recommendation.

# Case 100

United States District Court,
E.D. Pennsylvania.

PARAMOUNT PICTURES CORP.

v.

John DAVIS

No. Civ.A. 05-0316.
December 2, 2005.

Jurisdiction: United States District Court, E.D. Pennsylvania

Date: December 2, 2005

Keywords: Preservation of Evidence/Spoliation, Sanctions, Procedure

In a suit alleging copyright infringement, the Plaintiff and Defendant filed cross-motions for summary judgment. The Plaintiff claimed the Defendant violated its exclusive rights to reproduce and distribute a motion picture, by willfully and knowingly obtaining a digital copy of the motion picture and making it available for digital distribution through an Internet distribution center.

The Plaintiff hired an antipiracy technology specialist to identify copyright infringers on the Internet. This specialist identified an infringer's IP address. The Plaintiff then commenced a John Doe lawsuit against the unidentified infringer and filed a motion to obtain the infringer's true identity from his Internet service provider (ISP). The ISP checked its subscriber logs and determined the infringer's identification was that of the Plaintiff. The ISP notified the Defendant of the lawsuit and provided the Plaintiff with the Defendant's identification. The Plaintiff requested access to the Defendant's computer to investigate the hard drive of the computer. A third-party forensic specialist determined that the Defendant wiped his hard drive clean of all data and reinstalled an operating system on his computer 16 days after receiving notification of the lawsuit. The cleaning of the hard drive and reinstallation of the operating system made it impossible to determine whether a digital copy of the motion picture or the Internet distribution software were present on the computer prior to the cleaning of the hard drive. The Plaintiff alleged that the Defendant's actions were intended to prevent the detection of infringing activities. The Defendant claimed he cleaned the hard drive and installed a new operating system to prepare the computer to be sold to another individual. For a judge to issue summary judgment, there must exist no issue of material facts and the moving party must be entitled to the motion as a matter of law.

The Plaintiff argued that the lack of evidence on the Defendant's computer did not create genuine issues of material fact, because the Defendant is subject to spoliation sanctions for intentionally cleaning the hard drive of all data to make it impossible to determine whether the motion picture or Internet distribution software existed on the computer at the time of the infringing activity. In determining spoliation sanctions, the Court looked at the following factors in exercising its discretion: "(1) the degree of fault of the party who altered or destroyed the evidence; (2) the degree of prejudice suffered by the opposing party; and (3) whether there is a lesser sanction that will avoid substantial unfairness to the opposing party and, where the offending party is seriously at fault, will serve to deter such conduct by others in the future." The Court determined that, once the Plaintiff knew of the lawsuit pending against him, he either knew or should have known that the computer's memory was a crucial piece of evidence in the action. The Court also determined that the Plaintiff was prejudiced by the destruction of the evidence because it was impossible for the Plaintiff to determine whether the motion picture or distribution center software was stored on the computer at the time of the infringement. The Court found that a spoliation inference sanction jury instruction would be appropriate in this case; however, both parties waived the right to a jury trial, so the Plaintiff wished for the Court to use the spoliation inference to determine that the Defendant's computer contained the motion picture and the Internet distribution software at the time of the infringement. The Court held that a spoliation inference sanction against a defendant is not appropriate at the summary judgment stage of the case. The Court denied both motions for summary judgment. The Court determined that the Defendant's willful destruction of evidence would be taken into consideration at the time of trial.

## Case 101

United States District Court,
S.D. Texas, Houston Division.

In re APPLICATION FOR PEN REGISTER AND TRAP/TRACE DEVICE WITH
CELL SITE LOCATION AUTHORITY

No. H-05-557M.
October 14, 2005.

Jurisdiction: United States District Court, Southern District of Texas

Date: October 14, 2005

Keywords: Constitutionality, Procedure

During an ongoing criminal investigation, the government sought a court order compelling a cell phone company to disclose records of a customer's cell phone use. Among the records sought was "cell site data." Cell site data reveals the user's physical location when the phone is turned on. Cell site data allows for continuous tracking of actual movement, similar to a tracking device. The government combined its request for subscriber records with an application to install a pen register and trap-and-trace device on the target phone. A pen register records the numbers of outgoing calls, while a trap-and-trace device captures the numbers of incoming calls. These, coupled with "cell site data," may provide investigators with the general geographic location of a target device and may allow for investigators to determine a suspect's location. Subscriber records may be obtained by a court order upon proof of "specific and articulable facts . . . showing reasonable grounds to believe that . . . the records or other information sought, are relevant and material to the ongoing criminal investigation." To use pen register and/or trap-and-trace surveillance, a law enforcement officer need only show that information likely to be obtained by the pen register or trap-and-trace device "is relevant to an on-going criminal investigation." The Court looked at the legal standard the government must satisfy to compel the disclosure of "prospective" or real-time cell site data.

The Court held that, because the government could not demonstrate that cell site data tracking would never under any circumstances implicate Fourth Amendment privacy rights, there is no reason to treat cell site data tracking differently than other forms of tracking, which routinely require probable cause. The Court concluded that cell site data is properly categorized as tracking device information under 18 U.S.C. §3117. The Court denied the government's request for prospective cell site data. The Court held, however, that this type of surveillance is available to the government upon a showing of traditional probable cause. The Court concluded that converting a cell phone in to a tracking device without probable cause would raise serious Fourth Amendment concerns.

## Case 102

Court of Appeal, Third District, California.

The PEOPLE, Plaintiff and Respondent,

v.

Randy William BAKER, Defendant and Appellant.

No. C043459.
(Super.Ct.No. 00F10550).
October 29, 2004.

Jurisdiction: Court of Appeal, Third District, California

Date: October 29, 2004

Keywords: Admissibility

The Defendant appealed his conviction of seventy-three counts of sexual offenses against three minors, arguing, among other things, that evidence of pornography on the Defendant's computer should have been excluded because the Defendant did not have sole access to the computer and that the Defendant was denied effective assistance of counsel by his attorney's decision to use the Defendant as an expert witness on computers.

The Defendant asserted that there was a lack of foundation to admit the contents of his computer, because he did not have sole access to the computer. The Court stated that the Defendant was not charged with possession of pornography, and therefore his possession of the images was not an element of any crime for which he was charged that needed to be proven beyond a reasonable doubt. Rather, the evidence was offered both as evidence of the crimes the Defendant committed at the time he showed pornographic images to the victim and also as evidence of the Defendant's deviant sexual intent and interest in young girls. The Court held that the preliminary fact required to establish the relevance of the computer files was the connection between the Defendant and the images. The Court concluded that the evidence was sufficient for the jury to conclude that the Defendant accessed these images on the Internet, downloaded them to his computer, and showed the victim images similar to the ones presented to the jury. Accordingly, the Court held that the trial court did not abuse its discretion in admitting the evidence.

The Defendant also argued that his counsel was constitutionally deficient for using the Defendant as his own expert witness on the subject of computers. According to the Defendant, the key point was the significance of thumbnail images found on Defendant's hard drive. The police department's computer expert testified that the thumbnails had been actively sought out on the Internet, downloaded, accessed, and intentionally deleted. In his own defense, the Defendant claimed that all the files were found in his Internet cache, which he cleared on a weekly basis, that because the images were thumbnails they were not viewable, that the images were automatically downloaded from pornographic sites by a software program, and that the deletion was the result of a different software program. After hearing both sides, the Court found that nothing in the record showed why the Defendant's counsel decided to rely upon the cross-examination of the police computer expert and use the Defendant's own computer knowledge in this case. As such, the Court held that the claim was not cognizable on appeal. On the merits, the Defendant failed to demonstrate that the counsel's conduct fell below an objective standard of reasonableness, because the Defendant argued nothing more than that the use of the Defendant had drawbacks and that the reliance on the cross-examination of the Prosecution's witness was flawed, which was not enough. Therefore, the Court rejected the Defendant's arguments and affirmed the remaining convictions.

# Case 103

Court of Appeals of Michigan.

PEOPLE of the State of Michigan, Plaintiff-Appellee,

v.

Robert Babur BASAT, Defendant-Appellant.

No. 252518.
May 10, 2005.

Jurisdiction: Court of Appeals of Michigan

Date: May 10, 2005

Keywords: Admissibility

The Defendant was convicted of counts related to sexual misconduct, based in part on evidence obtained from his computer. The Defendant appealed his conviction, arguing that he was entitled to a new trial because the trial court failed to exclude testimony about nonpornographic items recovered from his computer, specifically bits of data and photographs and names of bulletin boards and Web sites, which were accessed by the Defendant. The Defendant's sole argument on appeal was that the bulk of information served only to confuse the jury, which was called upon to determine whether the photographs admitted at trial constituted child sexually abusive material. The Court held that the Defendant's vague argument was insufficient to properly present the issue for its review. The Court stated that a defendant may not announce a position and leave it to the Court to explain or rationalize that position, nor may he provide only cursory treatment with little or no citation to authority. The Court noted that the Defendant never objected to the testimony or evidence challenged on appeal. So, it reviewed the unpreserved issues for plain error affecting the Defendant's substantial rights.

The Defendant was charged with possession of child sexually abusive material. He maintained that he was accessing information and frequently visiting message boards, involving relationships with children, to assist the FBI in fighting child pornography. Two agents from the FBI disputed that the Defendant worked for the FBI as an informant or provided verifiable or reliable information. The Court found that the Defendant's computer activities, including the timing of his access to message boards and the downloading of images of children, were relevant to rebut the Defendant's claim that he was accessing pornography to assist law enforcement. The Court held that they were also relevant to demonstrate his intent with respect to his possession of child sexually abusive material. The Court concluded that the Defendant had not demonstrated that the admission of the challenged evidence of his computer activities constituted plain error. Accordingly, the Court affirmed the Defendant's convictions.

# Case 104

Supreme Court, Nassau County, New York.

PEOPLE of the State of New York,
v.
Robert CARRATU, Defendant.

January 22, 2003.

Jurisdiction: Supreme Court, Nassau County, New York

Date: January 22, 2003

Keywords: Admissibility, Constitutionality

The Defendant moved to suppress statements, identification testimony, and physical evidence. The motions raised the novel issue of whether a warrant authorizing a search of the text files of a computer, for documentary evidence pertaining to a specific crime, will authorize a search of image files that appear to contain evidence of other criminal activity. The Court concluded that the officers had ample probable cause that the Defendant had criminally possessed forgery devices, in regard to illegal cable boxes, and that the warrantless arrest of the Defendant was valid.

The Court held that the Defendant had standing to challenge the search of his computer, because placing data in files on the hard drive of his computer manifested a reasonable expectation of privacy in the contents of those files. The substance of the Defendant's argument was that the search exceeded the scope of the warrant. Specifically, the Defendant claimed that the officer conducting the search of his computer made no effort to first examine the files or directories that, by their name or nature, might indicate some type of record or list, nor did he check whether the nature of the file was graphic, database, spread sheet, or word processing. The Court stated that a warrant authorizing a search of the text files of a computer, for documentary evidence pertaining to a specific crime, will not authorize a search of image files containing evidence of other criminal activity. The Court then concluded that an examination of the supporting affidavit and the warrants had made it clear that the search warrants had been issued to authorize a search of the Defendant's computers for documentary evidence relating to his illegal cable box operation. Because none of the image files containing false identification documents were inadvertently discovered, the Court held that the People could not rely on the plain view doctrine to justify the search for those image files. Therefore, the Defendant's motion to suppress was granted as to all computer files containing images of false identification documents, but the motion to suppress physical evidence in all other respects was denied.

## Case 105

Court of Appeal, Fourth District, Division 1, California.

The PEOPLE, Plaintiff and Respondent,

v.

James David DOMINGUEZ, Defendant and Appellant.

No. D041946.

(Super.Ct.No. SCE217892).

May 13, 2004.

Jurisdiction: Court of Appeal, Fourth District, Division 1, California

Date: May 13, 2004

Keywords: Admissibililty

The Defendant was found guilty of the continuous sexual abuse of a child and possession of child pornography, and he appealed, arguing that the trial court erred in the admission and exclusion of evidence, in refusing to sever counts for trial, and in failing to instruct concerning the requirement of jury unanimity with regard to both charges. He additionally argued that the evidence was insufficient to support a conviction on the possession of child pornography offense and that the prosecutor committed misconduct.

As to the possession of child pornography charge, the Government conceded that the trial court erred prejudicially when it failed to instruct that the jury was required to agree unanimously that at least one of the images found on appellant's computer was child pornography, and the Court agreed with the Government's position. Therefore, the Court reversed the Defendant's conviction for that offense. The Court noted that, because the Defendant also claimed that the evidence was insufficient to support the child pornography charge, it still needed to deal with the issue, because, if the Court agreed, he could not be retried on that offense.

The Court rejected the Government's argument that the evidence had been admitted as evidence of a propensity to commit child related sex crimes, because the trial court had denied admission on that basis. The Government suggested that it could admit the evidence to show a common scheme or plan or else to prove the specific intent of the elements of the molestation and sexual misconduct charges. But the Court found that the first argument was meritless and that the second theory was troubling. Therefore, the Court held that the trial court had allowed highly inflammatory evidence to be admitted to prove an issue about which there was no meaningful dispute. Because the computer evidence was clearly more prejudicial than probative, the Court concluded that it was an abuse of discretion to admit it. Lastly, the Defendant argued that for a variety of reasons the evidence was insufficient to support his conviction for possession of child pornography. The Court noted that there was no evidence concerning when the images were accessed, downloaded, or placed in the computer's inactive memory and that the offense has a one-year statute of limitations. Therefore, the Court stated that the Government had to prove that the possession occurred within one year of the commencement of the prosecution. After reviewing the evidence, the Court concluded that the evidence was sufficient to find that the possession offense was not time barred. Accordingly, the Court reversed the Defendant's conviction.

## Case 106

Appellate Court of Illinois,
First District, Third Division.

The PEOPLE of the State of Illinois, Plaintiff-Appellee,

v.

Howard DONATH, Defendant-Appellant.

No. 1-04-0458.
April 13, 2005.

Jurisdiction: Appellate Court of Illinois, First District, Third Division

Date: April 13, 2005

Keywords: Admissibility, Constitutionality

The Defendant, who had been convicted of thirty-three counts related to child pornography, appealed his conviction, arguing that the trial court had erred in denying his motion to suppress evidence. The issue before the Court was whether uploading child pornography on one occasion, five months prior to obtaining a warrant, had provided probable cause for that warrant. The Defendant argued that the single act of uploading 304 child pornographic photographs had not constituted a continuing course of conduct on which probable cause for a search warrant could be properly based. He also claimed that the affidavit supporting the search warrant had failed to establish probable cause, because it merely alleged that the Defendant was a collector of child pornography, without actually having established that fact.

The Court held that there was evidence from which it could have been concluded that the Defendant had possessed child pornography in his home shortly before the warrant had been executed. The Court was confident that the number of images that had been uploaded indicated that the Defendant had been a collector of such images, especially considering that the Defendant had uploaded the images as opposed to downloading them. The Court found that this distinction had made it reasonable to infer that the Defendant had possessed child pornography somewhere in his home. The Court then reasoned that the information in the affidavit and application for a search warrant had been sufficient to establish a probability of criminal activity and that the trial court had properly denied the Defendant's motion to suppress evidence. The Defendant further maintained that the warrant had sought items for which probable cause had not existed and that it had called for a blanket search of his home without meaningful particularity. This argument was based on the seizure of an eight-millimeter tape. The Court, however, held that the seizure of the tape was not unreasonable as it was in a box where electronic media would likely be found. Lastly, the Defendant asserted that the seizure of the tape was outside the scope of the warrant because it was not readily apparent that it contained child pornography. The Court, however, held that the off-site viewing of the tape was justified, because one cannot ascertain the contents of such a tape without playing it. The Court then affirmed the Defendant's conviction.

## Case 107

Court of Appeal, Sixth District, California.

The PEOPLE, Plaintiff and Respondent,
v.
Weibin JIANG, Defendant and Appellant.

No. H026546.
June 16, 2005.

Jurisdiction: Court of Appeal, Sixth District, California

Date: June 16, 2005

Keywords: Admissibility, Privilege

On appeal, the Defendant, who was convicted by jury trial for committing sexual offenses against an acquaintance, alleged that the trial court prejudicially erred in denying his suppression motion and in finding that the information in documents on his laptop were not protected by the attorney-client privilege. The trial court found that these documents were not subject to the privilege because the Defendant had no reasonable expectation of privacy in documents on an employer-issued laptop computer. The Attorney General maintained that the information in the documents on the Defendant's second work-issued laptop computer was not privileged because the Employee Proprietary Information and Inventions Agreement, signed by the Defendant, eliminated any reasonable expectation of privacy in any documents on that laptop. He also argued that the Defendant waived any privilege by failing to object when the prosecutor stated that she was going to open some documents.

The Court found that the password-protected electronic documents on the Defendant's second work-issued laptop computer indisputably contained information that the Defendant prepared at the direction of his attorney for his attorney and transmitted to his attorney. By proffering evidence that the electronic documents were password-protected and placed in a folder called Attorney for the explicit purpose of protecting them from disclosure, the Court concluded that the Defendant satisfied the initial evidentiary burden imposed on privilege claimants. In attempting to satisfy the burden to prove that the documents were not confidential, the prosecutor relied on the simple fact that the Defendant had signed the Employee Agreement, which gave his employer the right to inspect the laptop. She claimed that the Agreement established that the documents on the laptop were not confidential. The Court held that even if it assumed that the trial court properly used an objective standard to evaluate the confidentiality of the Defendant's information, it was convinced that the Defendant's belief in the confidentiality of his information was an objectively reasonable one, because nothing in the Agreement would have suggested that the employer would make any effort to gain access to information in documents on an employee's computer that were clearly segregated as personal and password-protected. The Court concluded that, under the circumstances of the case, it was objectively reasonable for the Defendant to expect that attorney-client information would remain confidential. The Attorney General argued that, even if the documents were originally privileged, the privilege was waived by the Defendant when he failed to object after the prosecutor said that she was going to open the documents; however, the Court found that the Defendant did not waive his privilege, because the prosecutor produced no evidence that the Defendant had consented to waiving the privilege and did not prove that the Defendant failed to claim the privilege when he had an opportunity to do so. Accordingly, the Court held that suppression of the privileged documents was obviously necessary. Lastly, the Court noted that should the DA's office elect to retry the case, the trial court should hold a hearing to consider whether recusal of the prosecutor or the DA's office would be merited because of the prosecutor's exposure to the privileged attorney-client information. The Court reversed the judgment and remanded for possible retrial.

## Case 108

Court of Appeal, Second District, Division 6, California.

The PEOPLE, Plaintiff and Respondent,
v.
Frank MARZEC, Defendant and Appellant.

2d Crim. No. B171884.
(Los Angeles County Super.Ct. No. VA073656-01).
February 2, 2005.

Jurisdiction: Court of Appeals, Second District, Division 6, California

Date: February 2, 2005

Keywords: Admissibility, Computer Forensics, Experts

The Defendant appealed his conviction of several sexual offenses, arguing that the trial court abused its discretion by admitting evidence of child pornography that was discovered on his computer and was not the basis for any of the charges. Over the Defendant's objection, the Prosecution's forensic computer expert testified that one of the Defendant's computers contained three pornographic videos. The videos were not shown to the jury, but the expert explained what they depicted. The Defendant argued that the evidence was irrelevant and was inadmissible. The Court found that Defendant's possession of the pornographic videotapes was a specific instance of conduct that tended to show his bad character. The Court held that it was relevant and admissible because it tended to show that the appellant had a sexual interest in children and that he acted with the requisite specific intent to give or obtain sexual gratification. The Court also held that the evidence was also admissible, because it tended to prove the Defendant's disposition to commit sexual acts with children.

The Defendant maintained that, notwithstanding the arguable relevancy of the evidence, the trial court should have excluded testimony about the videos as unduly prejudicial. The Court concluded that there was no abuse of discretion. The expert's testimony about the videos was relatively brief and the information he conveyed was not particularly inflammatory compared with the other evidence supporting the charges against the Defendant. The jury was not shown the actual videos, further reducing the likelihood that the jury would be unfairly influenced. Lastly, the Defendant noted that visitors to his home had access to his computers and complained that the prosecution did not establish that he was the person who had downloaded the videos. The

Court found that the Defendant had been free to make that argument to the jury but that, for the purposes of admissibility, the evidence supported the inference that the videos belonged to the Defendant. The Court noted that he was the owner of the computer on which the videos were found and was the person with the greatest access to that computer. The Court then affirmed the judgment.

## Case 109

Appellate Court of Illinois,
First District, Second Division.

The PEOPLE of the State of Illinois, Plaintiff-Appellee,

v.

Jose RIVERA, Defendant-Appellant.

No. 87-2951.
April 4, 1989.

Jurisdiction: Appellate Court of Illinois, First District, Second Division

Date: April 4, 1989

Keywords: Admissibility

The Defendant appealed his conviction of two counts of possession of a controlled substance with intent to deliver, arguing that various errors in the admission of evidence required a new trial. During the Court's analysis of the sufficiency of the foundation proof, it noted that the basis for the admissibility of the records is that the circumstantial probability of their trustworthiness is a practical substitute for cross-examination of the individual making the entries. The Court then held that the standards of admissibility of computer records include that it be shown that the electronic computing equipment is recognized as standard, that the entries are made in the ordinary course of business at or reasonably near the time of the happening of the event recorded, and that the testimony satisfies the court that the sources of information, the method, and the time of preparation were such as to indicate its trustworthiness and justify its admission. The Defendant argued that in order for a computer program to be admissible it needs to be shown that it is standard, unmodified, and operates according to its instructions, which the Court did not agree with.

The Court found that the computer was standard and reliable and that the judge correctly held that he could take judicial notice that IBM was a standard, reliable computer. The court also found that the procedures followed were in the regular course of business, so the first two tests had been met. The Court then had to determine whether the third prong had been met, which dealt with the material that was put into the computer. On that point, the Defendant argued the State would not be able to establish that the information that went into the computer was put in contemporaneously with the event. The Court found that testimony that the entries were made contemporaneously with the event refuted the Defendant's argument. The Court then concluded that the trial judge had not abused his discretion in admitting the records, because he could properly consider that the information retrieved from the computer had been consistent with the other circumstances disclosed by the evidence. According, the Court affirmed the Defendant's convictions.

# Case 110

Court of Appeal, Fourth District, Division 2, California.

The PEOPLE, Plaintiff and Respondent,

v.

Kenneth Wayne SELF, Defendant and Appellant.
In re Kenneth Wayne SELF, on Habeas Corpus.

Nos. E031553, E033364.
(Super.Ct.No. RIF93923).
November 24, 2003.

Jurisdiction: Court of Appeal, Fourth District, Division 2, California

Date: November 24, 2003

Keywords: Admissibility, Computer Forensics, Experts

The Defendant appealed from the judgment entered after a jury found him guilty as charged of the first-degree murders of two victims, raising claims of error in his appeal. First, he claimed that the trial court committed reversible error by admitting into evidence one of the victim's calendar and computer records. The Defendant objected to the admissibility of that evidence on the ground that it was hearsay and not relevant to any issue at trial. The Defendant next challenged the sufficiency of the evidence to prove murder.

In regard to the admission into evidence of the victim's calendar and computer records, the Defendant asserted that the victim's state of mind was not relevant to any issue at trial and, therefore, the trial court erred in admitting the evidence in question. The Court agreed with this argument, but found that the most damning evidence in its view was the ballistics test results. In view of that evidence, the Court had no reasonable doubt that the error in admitting the calendar and computer files into evidence did not contribute to the verdict in the case. The Defendant next argued that the evidence was insufficient to support the verdicts finding him guilty of the murders. Specifically, the Defendant claimed that the circumstantial evidence in this case was reasonably susceptible of two interpretations, and, therefore, the jury was required to accept the inference pointing to innocence and acquit Defendant. The Court found that there were significant defects in the Defendant's argument. The Defendant's claim was predicated on the view that the circumstantial evidence in this case supported a reasonable interpretation pointing to the Defendant's innocence. The Court held that it did not. Therefore, the Court rejected the Defendant's challenge to the sufficiency of the evidence.

Lastly, the Defendant complained that the trial counsel should have hired a forensic computer analyst to show that the victim did not input the data recovered from his computer and to show that the evidence otherwise was unreliable. The Court merely reiterated that the information recovered from the computer was not relevant and therefore should not have been admitted at trial but that the error was not prejudicial. Accordingly, the Court concluded that it was not reasonably probable that the jury would have reached a result more favorable to the Defendant if the trial counsel had retained a forensic computer analyst and that person had been able to undermine the validity or source of the data retrieved from the victim's computer. The Court then affirmed the judgment.

## Case 111

Court of Appeal, Sixth District, California.

The PEOPLE, Plaintiff and Respondent,

v.

Michael Benjamin TENORE, Defendant and Appellant.

No. H025173.
(Santa Clara County Super. Ct. No. 210574).
January 29, 2004.

Jurisdiction: Court of Appeal, Sixth District, California

Date: January 29, 2004

Keywords: Experts, Preservation of Evidence/Spoliation

Following a court trial, the Defendant was convicted of several counts related to sexual misconduct involving minors and one count of attempted destruction of evidence. On appeal, the Defendant alleged that there was insufficient evidence to support a conviction for attempted destruction of evidence. During the investigation of the sexual misconduct charges, the police searched the Defendant's townhouse and seized a laptop computer, a Zip drive, a Zip disk, and a digital camera from his bedroom. A police computer expert examined the computer, Zip drive, and memory module of the digital camera. He discovered that more than 2,000 files had been deleted, including files of pictures of young girls in various stages of undress. Two groups of photos, from consecutive nights, appeared to have been deleted very recently. The police also recovered a history of Internet sites visited by the Defendant and pictures downloaded from them, finding thousands of images of juvenile girls engaging in sexual acts.

   The Defendant argued that there was insufficient evidence to support the conviction for attempted destruction of evidence. The evidence that was the subject of the charge was the computer files on the hard drive, Zip drive, and digital camera, representing photographs, which the Defendant deleted from his computer, before he was arrested. The act was charged as an attempt because, despite the Defendant's best efforts, the photographs were recoverable. The Defendant argued that the evidence was insufficient because he attempted to remove the computer files in question before he knew that a police investigation had begun and certainly before a case was pending in court. The Court stated that the statute requires that the actor know that the object is about to be produced in evidence. The Court found that the evidence supported the conclusion that at the time he deleted the pictures from the digital camera, he knew that they were about to be produced for a police investigation, because he was a former police officer and had testified that he was aware of some allegations being made against him. The Court concluded that although the Defendant may, as he testified, have deleted the pictures following a wave of self-revulsion for having taken them, the evidence fully supported the trial court's implicit conclusion that he deleted the photographs to prevent them from being produced as evidence in an imminent police investigation of the events of the previous night. Accordingly, the Court affirmed his conviction.

## Case 112

Court of Appeal, Second District, Division 3, California.

The PEOPLE, Plaintiff and Respondent,

v.

James Henry TIMBERLAKE, Defendant and Appellant.

No. B163233.

(Los Angeles County Super. Ct. No. GA047502).

April 30, 2004.

Jurisdiction: Court of Appeal, Second District, Division 3, California

Date: April 30, 2004

Keywords: Admissibility

The Defendant appealed his convictions, following a jury trial, for committing a lewd act upon a child, continuous sexual abuse, forcible rape, and possession or control of child pornography. On appeal, he argued that the trial court erred by admitting evidence regarding nonchild pornography found on his computer. At trial, he objected to the admission of evidence of the total number of sexual and pornographic images found on his hard drive as unduly prejudicial. He argued that the fact that more than 30,000 images were discovered was inflammatory, that much of the material was legal, and that the evidence should have been limited to images containing child pornography. He also asserted that the file name listing was overly inclusive in that it referenced files downloaded before the period that he was charged with possession. Lastly, he claimed that several of the file names were unduly inflammatory because they contained references to bestiality. The Prosecutor countered that the number of pornographic images was relevant because it demonstrated Timberlake's obsession and his intent to sexually arouse himself or the children during the molestations. Further, at the preliminary hearing, the Defense had elicited from an expert that items may be surreptitiously downloaded from the Internet onto a computer without the user's knowledge; therefore, the number of images was evidence that the child pornography had not been loaded by accident or by a remote Web site without the Defendant's knowledge. The trial court denied his motion to exclude.

The Court found that the trial court did not abuse its discretion, because the large number of images was highly relevant to prove that the Defendant knew the images were on the computer and had not been placed there by someone else or by accident. The Court also found that the trial court's comments indicated it weighed the probative value of the evidence and understood and fulfilled its responsibilities. The Court then held that, for the same reasons, the filename listing was properly admitted. Next, the Court concluded that the fact that the Defendant was charged with possession during a particular time frame did not necessarily make evidence of events occurring outside that time frame inadmissible and that the list was relevant to show the person who placed the images on the computer had been doing so for an extended period, therefore leading to an inference that the possession was knowing and intentional during the relevant time period. The Defendant also argued that the possession of pornography in general did not tend to establish that he molested the victims or possessed child pornography. The Court, however, held that the evidence of the images found was highly probative to prove intent and knowledge in the possession of child pornography charges. Lastly, the Court concluded that faced with all of the evidence of molestation, it was highly improbable that the jury would have come to a more favorable verdict on any count had the evidence of the extensive computer library been excluded. There was therefore no reversible error. Accordingly, the Court affirmed the convictions that were based on the images.

## Case 113

Court of Appeals of Michigan.

PEOPLE of the State of Michigan, Plaintiff-Appellee,

v.

Russell Douglas TOMBS, Defendant-Appellant.

Docket No. 236858.
Submitted June 4, 2003, at Detroit.
Decided December 30, 2003, at 9:00 a.m.

Jurisdiction: Court of Appeals of Michigan

Date: December 30, 2003

Keywords: Procedure

A jury convicted the Defendant of distributing or promoting child sexually abusive material, and other charges stemming from the possession of child pornography. On appeal, the Defendant argued whether he could be found to have distributed child sexually abusive material, on the basis that he returned to his employer a laptop computer that contained, within it, child sexually abusive material.

The Court stated that the statute required an intent to disseminate child sexually abusive material to others. Therefore, the Court resolved the ambiguity of the word "distributes" by giving effect to the Legislature's intention to prevent the dissemination of child sexually related material by requiring an intent to disseminate child sexually abusive material to others. In applying the Court's construction to the case, it concluded that the Prosecution failed to present evidence that the Defendant intended for anyone to see or receive child sexually abusive material when returning the computer to his employer. Therefore, the Court held that insufficient evidence was presented that the Defendant distributed child sexually abusive material in violation of the statute and reversed the Defendant's conviction on that charge.

## Case 114

Court of Appeal, Fourth District, Division 2, California.

The PEOPLE, Plaintiff and Respondent,

v.

David Leroy TURNER, Defendant and Appellant.

No. E029256.
(Super.Ct.No. INF 035845).
June 21, 2002.

Jurisdiction: Court of Appeal, Fourth District, Division 2, California

Date: June 21, 2002

Keywords: Computer Forensics, Experts

The Defendant appealed the judgment entered against him following jury convictions for multiple counts stemming from check fraud. The Defendant argued that there was insufficient evidence that he possessed or issued the checks upon which his convictions were based. The Defendant also complained that an expert witness improperly testified that the Defendant was guilty of check cashing fraud and that his trial attorney had committed ineffective assistance of counsel by not objecting to the error.

The Defendant argued that there was insufficient evidence to support the convictions because circumstantial evidence pointed to his innocence. The Defendant claimed that there was evidence that his accomplices might also have produced checks on the computer and that there was no direct evidence that the Defendant produced any of the checks. The Defendant argued that, although the evidence showed that he predominantly used the computer found in the bedroom, references to his accomplices were also found on the computer, indicating they also used it; however, the Court concluded that, despite the evidence of the accomplices' involvement in the check fraud scheme, there was ample evidence supporting the trial court's finding that the Defendant was the producer in question. The Court further stated that the evidence was more than sufficient to sustain the Defendant's convictions. The information found on the Defendant's computer hard drive tied the Defendant to the checks in question and the testimony established that the Defendant was not only the mastermind behind the scheme, but also the one who produced the checks. Based on the abundance of evidence, the Court concluded there was sufficient evidence to convict the Defendant of the charges.

The Defendant also maintained that his trial attorney was guilty of ineffective assistance of counsel by failing to object to the computer expert's improper expert opinion testimony that the Defendant was guilty of check fraud, which the Defendant complained embraced the ultimate issue of guilt. The Defendant argued that his counsel's failure to object was prejudicial because the jury likely placed great weight on the expert testimony, and it invited the jury to speculate that his opinion was based not only on factors mentioned during his testimony, but also on other unstated, inadmissible information. The Court concluded that the Defense counsel's failure to object was not prejudicial, because, due to overwhelming evidence of the Defendant's guilt, there was not a reasonable probability that, but for counsel's failure to object, the result of the proceeding would have been different. There was an abundance of evidence that the Defendant was the mastermind behind the fraudulent check cashing scheme. Therefore, the Court affirmed the Defendant's conviction.

## Case 115

Court of Appeal, Sixth District, California.

The PEOPLE, Plaintiff and Respondent,
v.
Andrew Thomas UPTON, Defendant and Appellant.

No. H026092.
(Santa Clara County Super. Ct. No. CC241825).
September 17, 2004.

Jurisdiction: Court of Appeal, Sixth District, California

Date: September 17, 2004

Keywords: Admissibility

The Defendant appealed his conviction of four counts of committing a lewd or lascivious act on a child under fourteen, asserting that the trial court had erred by admitting evidence of child erotica recovered from his computers, because the evidence had been more prejudicial than probative.

The Court found that the erotic images were relevant and admissible to prove intent. The Defendant's denial of the charged crimes had placed his intent of arousing, appealing to, or gratifying the lust, passions, or sexual desires, of himself or the victim at issue. The Court held that evidence that the Defendant's computers had contained pornographic images of preteen girls, about the same age as the victim, and that the Defendant had visited Web sites, with teen names in their titles was probative of the Defendant's intent to commit a lewd or lascivious act on the victim. Moreover, the evidence of the photographs was probative to show the Defendant's sexual attraction to young girls about the same age as the victim. The Court concluded that the jury could infer from the images on the Defendant's computer that the Defendant had a prurient interest in adolescent girls and that he had intended to act on that interest. Therefore, the Court held that the erotic images were admissible to prove intent. The Court affirmed the Defendant's conviction.

## Case 116

Court of Appeal, Fifth District, California.

The PEOPLE, Plaintiff and Respondent,

v.

Timothy Ray WARD, Defendant and Appellant.

No. F037718.
(Super.Ct.No. CRF0057946).
August 12, 2002.

Jurisdiction: Court of Appeal, Fifth District, California

Date: August 12, 2002

Keywords: Admissibility

The Defendant appealed his conviction of four counts of lewd and lascivious acts upon two of his stepchildren who were under the age of fourteen years. He argued that evidence of child pornography that was found on his home computer was erroneously and prejudicially admitted, because there was not sufficient evidence that he possessed child pornography or that the images actually were child pornography and that the admission of the images was more prejudicial than probative because possession of child pornography was not sufficiently similar to the charged offense to be probative of his propensity to commit lewd acts on children.

The Court found that whether the images were, in fact, child pornography was properly a matter for jury consideration because they are elements of the alleged prior sexual misconduct. The Court held that it would not assign error to the trial court's decision to submit the evidence to the jury unless the evidence was more prejudicial than probative or consumed undue judicial resources or resulted in confusion of the issues, or unless the evidence presented to the jury was legally insufficient to establish the truth of the alleged prior misconduct by a preponderance of the evidence. Because the vast bulk of the computer-related questioning related to the single issue of possession, the Court concluded that there was little possibility that the jury was confused by the presentation of the testimonial evidence. The Court also found that the evidence of the Defendant's prior sexual misconduct was admitted to show his intent in inappropriately touching and photographing the victims. The Court then held that the time expended to establish the evidence of the Defendant's prior sexual misconduct was not wasteful or unduly prolonged. Therefore, the Court concluded that the presentation of the evidence of the alleged possession of computer-based child pornography neither misled the jury nor consumed undue time and that the Defendant's contentions were without merit. Accordingly, the Court held that the trial court did not abuse its discretion in presenting this evidence to the jury for its consideration.

Lastly, the Defendant argued that the evidence of the child pornography was unduly prejudicial because there was not sufficient similarity between possession of child pornography and the charged offenses, which the Court found to be without merit. The Court concluded that possessing pornographic images of nude children in sexual contexts and taking photographs of the nude genital area of a child for no apparent legitimate reason bore a close enough similarity to each other to be admissible. Because the relevance of, and similarity between, the alleged prior sexual misconduct and the acts that comprised the substantive counts was sufficient to justify the admission of the prior misconduct, the Court concluded that the trial court did not err in admitting the computer-based evidence of possession of child pornography. The Court affirmed the Defendant's conviction.

## Case 117

Court of Appeal, Third District, California.

The PEOPLE, Plaintiff and Respondent,

v.

Heath Daniel WOODWARD, Defendant and Appellant.

No. C041318.
March 8, 2004.

Jurisdiction: Court of Appeal, Third District, California

Date: March 8, 2004

Keywords: Procedure

The Defendant appealed his conviction for lewd conduct and possessing child pornography, arguing that the trial court's erroneous instruction on the affirmative defense to child pornography possession violated due process principles. The Defendant claimed that the Prosecution's special instruction defining the statutory affirmative defense to child pornography possession was fundamentally unfair, violated the due process clause, and had a substantial and injurious influence. The Defendant further argued that the trial court should have instructed the jury with the simple statutory language, rather than including dicta from a case that predated the adoption of the statute.

The Court agreed that the instruction was erroneous but concluded that the error was not prejudicial. It held that the erroneous inclusion of factors from an earlier case did not deprive the Defendant of a defense, because the challenged portion of the instruction used the questions as optional factors, which may or may not be considered in determining whether the defense applied and not as elements of the defense. Contrary to the Defendant's claim, the Court found that the error did not deprive the Defendant of due process, as he had received the statutory affirmative defense instruction. The Court noted that the jury had witnessed a wealth of pornographic evidence and that the Defendant's stockpiles of material were augmented by his admitted actual participation in child-centered online sexual activity. Therefore, the Court held that had the jury been given the instruction without the nonstatutory factors, it would not be reasonably probable that an outcome more favorable to the Defendant would have resulted. Accordingly, the Court concluded that no miscarriage of justice occurred, and it affirmed the Defendant's conviction.

## Case 118

United States District Court,
N.D. Illinois, Eastern Division.

PETER ROSENBAUM PHOTOGRAPHY CORPORATION, an Illinois corporation,
Plaintiff,

v.

OTTO DOOSAN MAIL ORDER LTD., a Korean corporation, Otto Sumisho Inc.,
a Japanese corporation, Otto Gmbh, a German corporation, and
Bradford Matson, an individual, Defendants.

No. 04 C 0767.
November 30, 2004.

Jurisdiction: United States District Court, Northern District of Illinois,
Eastern Division

Date: November 30, 2004

Keywords: Procedure

In a case alleging violations arising out of the Defendants' use of at least 150 photographs that the Plaintiff had created and furnished to a third party solely for limited uses, the Plaintiff moved to compel the third party to comply with outstanding subpoenas. The Plaintiff had served the third party, who had sought protection under bankruptcy laws, with subpoenas seeking documents and information relating to the third party's relationship with the Defendant. The third party had objected to the subpoenas on the basis that they were overbroad and unduly costly, particularly the potential costs involved in searching its computer system for responsive documents, including e-mail communications, and then reviewing those documents and communications for privileged material. The third party refused to produce documents and would not reach an agreement on how to handle the electronic discovery. The Plaintiff then brought a motion for rule to show cause for the third party's failure to comply with the subpoenas, to which the third party attempted to seek protection under the bankruptcy automatic stay.

The Plaintiff moved to compel the third party to comply with the subpoenas. In response, the third party argued that no debtor that had filed for protection under the bankruptcy laws was subject to any discovery in a civil action, absent a lifting of the automatic stay by the bankruptcy court. The Court found, however, that there were no cases that supported that contention, while the Plaintiff offered authority that quite clearly held just the opposite. On the basis of precedent, the Court found that the Plaintiff was entitled to serve and proceed with discovery against the third party, because the automatic was inapplicable as the third party was not a defendant, but simply an interested nonlitigant. Accordingly, the Court granted the Plaintiff's motion to compel the third party's response to its subpoenas.

## Case 119

United States District Court,
D. Massachusetts.

In re PHARMATRAK, INC. PRIVACY LITIGATION

No. CIV.A.00-11672-JLT.
August 13, 2002.

Jurisdiction: United States District Court, District of Massachusetts

Date: August 13, 2002

Keywords: Procedure, Spyware

The Plaintiffs brought a consolidated amended class-action complaint alleging that the Defendants, various pharmaceutical companies, secretly intercepted and accessed the Plaintiffs' personal information and Web browsing habits through the use of cookies and other devices, in violation of state and federal law. The Plaintiffs argued that technology employed by the Defendants permitted them to collect extensive, detailed information about the Plaintiffs regarding Web sites the Internet users were at prior to the time they went to the Defendants' Web sites, questions they asked and typed in at those prior sites, information they entered while at the Defendants' Web sites, and the types of computers they were using. The parties sought summary judgment against each other.

In the first count, which came from the Wiretap Act, the Plaintiffs argued that the Defendants intentionally intercepted the Plaintiffs' electronic communications with the Web sites they visited without their knowledge, authorization, or consent. The Court held that, because the Plaintiffs were unable to present any evidence whatsoever of a tortious intent, the Defendants were entitled to summary judgment on Count I. In Count II, coming from the Stored Communications Act, the Plaintiffs argued that the Defendants' conduct of accessing data in the Plaintiffs' computers constituted electronic trespassing and fell within the ambit of the statute. The Court found that, if the Defendants did not consent to the alleged interceptions, as the Plaintiffs persistently asserted, they could not have intentionally accessed without authorization any electronic communications. The Court concluded that without the necessary intent under the statute, the Defendants could not be held liable and were therefore entitle to summary judgment on Count II. In the Final Count, the Plaintiffs argued that their sensible interpretation of the CFAA allowed recovery for a cognizable loss, as distinct from economic damage, for the invasion of their privacy and the concomitant loss of control over the dissemination of their private information, stressing that they alleged both loss and damages, and that the statutory damage threshold of $5,000 could be met by aggregating the claims among individuals and over a one-year period. The Court, however, found that the Plaintiffs had not shown any evidence whatsoever that the Defendants had caused them at least $5,000 of damage or loss, for any single act of the Defendants. Accordingly, the Court granted summary judgment for the Defendants on Count III and dismissed all Counts.

## Case 120

United States District Court,
E.D. Virginia.

PHYSICIANS INTERACTIVE (a division of Allscripts, LLC) Plaintiff,

v.

LATHIAN SYSTEMS INC., Stephan Martinez and John Doe(s) 1-10,
Defendants.

No. CA 03-1193-A.
December 5, 2003.

Jurisdiction: United States District Court, Eastern District of Virginia

Date: December 5, 2003

Keywords: Procedure, Computer Forensics, Experts

In a civil suit alleging that the Defendants had hacked the Plaintiff's Web site by sending electronic robots to steal its customer list, computer code, and confidential data, the Plaintiff filed motions for a temporary restraining order and preliminary injunction and for limited expedited discovery. The question presented to the Court was whether an injunction should issue where the Plaintiff had shown probable cause to believe that the Defendant's information technology employee used both a work computer and his home computer to hack into the Plaintiff's Web site, using computer software to secretly collect customer lists and proprietary software.

The Court concluded that the Plaintiff had made a preliminary showing of an invasion of its computer system, unauthorized copying of its customer list, and theft of its trade secrets. Accordingly, the Court held that the Plaintiff had demonstrated a likelihood of irreparable harm if the Court denied injunctive relief and that the likelihood of irreparable harm to the Defendant, if the court did grant the relief, was nonexistent by comparison. The Court further held that the Plaintiff had sufficiently shown a likelihood of success on the merits of all of its seven claims.

Therefore, the Court granted both of the Plaintiff's motions. The Court enjoined the Defendant from engaging in any activity beyond the scope of a normal user or guest to the Plaintiff's Web site, from using any information obtained in violation thereof, and from using or disclosing any information that the Defendant might have obtained in connection with the computer attacks that the Plaintiff alleged in its pleadings. In addition, in granting the Plaintiff's motion for expedited discovery, the Court allowed the Plaintiff to enter the Defendant's computer server, work and home computers, and any sites where the computers used in the alleged attacks would be located, in order to obtain a mirror image of the computer equipment containing electronic data relating to the attack. Lastly, the Court ordered that the discovery must be done with the assistance of a computer forensic expert.

## Case 121

United States District Court,
S.D. California.

PLAYBOY ENTERPRISES, INC., Plaintiff,

v.

Terri WELLES et al, Defendants.

No. Civ. 98-0413-K (JFS).
August 2, 1999.

Jurisdiction: United States District Court, Southern District of California

Date: August 2, 1999

Keywords: Discovery

The parties had attended a discovery conference conducted before a magistrate judge. The Plaintiff had requested the discovery hearing in order to address four issues, one of them being whether the Plaintiff could have access to the Defendant's hard drive, in order to recover deleted files, including e-mails, which may have been relevant for discovery.

The Defendant first argued that any request to compel information from the hard drive was procedurally defective, because the Plaintiff had never made a request for information specifically relating to the hard drive. The Plaintiff argued that the Defendant's interrogatories, in response to the Plaintiff's discovery requests, had contained very few e-mails or hard copies of computer files. The Court found that, by requesting documents, the Plaintiff had also effectively requested production of information stored in electronic form. The Court went on to state that, if the Defendant had printed any relevant e-mails, such e-mails would have been produced as a document. The Court found that the Plaintiff needed to access the hard drive of the Defendant's computer, only because the Defendant's actions in deleting those e-mails had made it impossible to produce the information as a document. The Court held that the Plaintiff's prior discovery request had satisfied any procedural requirements.

The Court also found that it was likely that relevant information had been stored on the hard drive of the Defendant's personal computer, because the Defendant had used her e-mail system for both business and personal communications. The Court noted that the only restriction, for this type of discovery, was that the producing party be protected against undue burden and expense and/or invasion of privileged matter. The Plaintiff asserted that the e-mails might provide evidence in support of its claims, as well as a defense to the Defendant's counter claim. The Defendant argued that her business would suffer financial losses because of the approximate shut-down time required to recover information from the hard drive and that privileged e-mail might be recovered. The Court determined that the need for the requested information outweighed the burden to the Defendant and that only responsive and relevant information would be discoverable, after imaging the drive during the Defendant's computer down time.

## Case 122

Court of Appeals of Texas,
Houston (14th Dist.).

Timothy Dennis PORATH, Appellant

v.

The STATE of Texas, Appellee.

No. 14-02-01026-CR.
July 27, 2004.

Jurisdiction: Court of Appeals of Texas, Houston (14th District)

Date: July 27, 2004

Keywords: Admissibility, Constitutionality

The Defendant had been convicted of felony possession of child pornography. In twelve issues, he argued that the trial court had erred in denying his motion to suppress evidence, his motion to declare the state statute unconstitutional, and his motion for pretrial determination of admissibility. The Court affirmed the Defendant's conviction.

The Defendant argued that the affidavit in support of the search warrant had not set forth sufficient facts to establish probable cause that the specifically described property or items to be searched for or seized constituted evidence of the offense. The Court, however, disagreed and noted that, because the Defendant had used Internet chat rooms, it was not unreasonable for the magistrate to have inferred that the Defendant would use his home computer for the purpose of enticing children. The Defendant also claimed that the trial court erred in denying his motion to suppress because the warrant sought seizure of protected speech and was a general warrant, which violated the Fourth Amendment; however, the Court found that the warrant did not authorize the seizure of literary material because of the ideas contained in the material but rather because of the suspected child pornography.

The Defendant also challenged the constitutionality of the relevant state child pornography statute on the basis that it was overly broad, vague, and violated the First Amendment, because it drew no distinction between possession of actual child pornography and child pornography created by digital or computer imaging. The Court held that, because that statute prohibited only pornography depicting actual children, the statute is not vague or overbroad. Further, the Court noted that, because pornography produced with actual children is not a category of speech protected by the First Amendment, the statute's prohibition of these materials does not violate the First Amendment. Lastly, the Defendant argued that the State was required to present expert testimony that the images seized were actual images of children and not computer-generated images of virtual children. The Court noted that several courts had determined that the presentation of pictures alone constituted sufficient evidence for determining that an actual child was depicted in the pornographic image. Thus, the Court held that the trial court was capable of reviewing the evidence without the benefit of expert testimony.

## Case 123

United States District Court,
N.D. Illinois, Eastern Division.

Ronald PORTIS, Madric Lance, and Emmett Lynch, individually and on
behalf of a class, Plaintiffs,
v.
CITY OF CHICAGO et al. Defendants.

No. 02 C 3139.
December 7, 2004.

Jurisdiction: United States District Court, North District of Illinois,
Eastern Division

Date: December 7, 2004

Keywords: Costs and Cost Shifting

In a class-action civil rights lawsuit filed against the City of Chicago, the Plaintiffs sought an order to determine how the expenses from a previous motion were to be calculated. The ruling had ordered the Defendants to split the costs with the Plaintiffs of producing a database that both sides wanted to use during discovery. The Plaintiffs had originally approached the Defendants about cooperatively creating a database regarding thousands of arrests in the City of Chicago. After the Defendants declined to help, the Plaintiffs sought the necessary data from the Defendants through discovery requests and created the database of their own expense. After completion, the Defendants felt that the database was crucial to the litigation and successfully moved to compel the Plaintiffs to supply it to them, though the Defendants were ordered to split the expense of producing the database.

At issue in the motion was how to determine the expense. The Defendants argued that the costs associated with the use of paralegals should be commensurate with their salaries, while the Plaintiffs successfully argued to the court that the costs should be associated with the paralegals' billing rate that the Plaintiff was denied from collecting during the database creation. Although the Court sided with the Plaintiff, it held that the Defendants share of the cost should be measured at the Defendant's lower billing rate for paralegals.

## Case 124

United States District Court,
N.D. Texas, Dallas Division.

POSITIVE SOFTWARE SOLUTIONS INC., Plaintiff,

v.

NEW CENTURY MORTGAGE CORP. et al., Defendants.

No. CIV.A. 303CV0257N.
May 2, 2003.

Jurisdiction: United States District Court, Northern District of Texas, Dallas Division

Date: May 2, 2003

Keywords: Preservation of Evidence/Spoliation

The Plaintiff, concerned about possible spoliation, brought several motions regarding an earlier opinion and order to compel arbitration. The Court stated that it took spoliation very seriously and that it was confident that an arbitrator would also take spoliation very seriously. To ensure that no other potentially relevant information was deleted before the arbitration commenced, the Court ordered the Defendants to preserve all extant backups or images of all servers or personal computers, to refrain from deleting files still resident on any servers or personal computers, and to preserve all extant backups or images of all e-mail servers, pending further order of the Court or directive of the arbitrator.

The Plaintiff also complained that its request to image servers had not been overbroad. The Court acknowledged that one of the Plaintiff's motions had somewhat limited the universe of servers to be imaged but that it nonetheless still sought imaging of all of Defendants' media potentially containing any of the software and electronic evidence relevant to the claims in this suit and all images of the Defendants' computer storage facilities, drives, and servers taken to date. The Court found that imaging would include not only the files at issue but also anything else that happened to be on a server containing one of those files, which could include irrelevant or privileged information not otherwise discoverable, possibly even including deleted files. The Court remained of the opinion that the scope of the proposed imaging was substantially overbroad and affirmed its order to compel arbitration.

## Case 125

United States District Court,
N.D. Texas, Dallas Division.

POSITIVE SOFTWARE SOLUTIONS, INC. Plaintiff,

v.

NEW CENTURY MORTGAGE CORPORATION et al., Defendants.

No. Civ.A. 303CV0257N.
September 28, 2004.

Jurisdiction: United States District Court, Northern District of Texas, Dallas Division

Date: September 28, 2004

Keywords: Procedure, Privilege

In a copyright infringement suit, the Plaintiff filed a motion to hold the Defendants in contempt for violation of the Court's preliminary injunction and protective order. After the Defendants failed to pay the Plaintiff licensing fees for its software, the Plaintiff investigated the Defendants' use of the software and determined that it had been making improper uses of the Plaintiff's intellectual property rights. Litigation soon followed. To protect the parties' confidential information during the pendency of the action, the Court had entered a protective order that had expressly provided that no confidential information should be disclosed to nonattorney employees during discovery responses. The Defendants had represented that the backup tapes and forensic copies of the software would be kept securely in the custody and control of the Defendants' counsel. Notwithstanding those representations, the Defendants had continued to make use of the software, which was discovered by the Plaintiff.

Following the foregoing revelations, the Court authorized discovery into the use of the software and held that the attorney-client privilege and work product immunity had been waived under the crime-fraud exception. Contrary to the Defendants' representations, it became apparent that they had maintained numerous copies of the software in backup tapes that were easily restorable by the Defendants. The Court then addressed whether the Defendants' conduct had actually violated the protective order. The Defendants argued that their conduct had been proper under two provisions of the order. The Court found that neither of the provisions had authorized the Defendants' conduct. Furthermore, the Court held that the Defendants' interpretation would have resulted in the order having no practical effect, which the Court was reluctant to support, especially considering that there was an alternative construction that gave life and effect to the order that did not need to be implied into the words of the order. The Court also ruled that the order should be read in the context of the litigation and that the order required less specificity when written for lawyers. Lastly, the Defendants argued that the order could not be enforced by a contempt finding because the order was not sufficiently definite. The Court believed that, although the order had a definite meaning, there were characteristics of the language that perhaps did not specifically prohibit the Defendants' actions. Therefore, the Court, with considerable reluctance, held that the protective order was not sufficiently clear and definite to be enforced by contempt, even though the Defendants' conduct was not appropriate. Accordingly, the Court denied the Plaintiff's motion for contempt.

## Case 126

United States District Court,
D. Massachusetts.

PREMIER HOMES AND LAND CORPORATION, Plaintiff

v.

CHESWELL, INC., Defendant

No. CIV.A. 02-30118-KPN.
December 19, 2002.

Jurisdiction: United States District Court, District of Massachusetts

Date: December 19, 2002

Keywords: E-Evidence Alteration/Fabrication, Sanctions, Costs and
Cost Shifting

In a case regarding the unlawful occupancy of premises, the Defendant requested fees and costs totaling $31,255.99, as it had been discovered that the Plaintiff had fabricated a portion of the lease at issue. In response, the Plaintiff acknowledged the Defendant's right to fees and costs, but disputed the amount requested, suggesting instead that the Defendant should receive $21,095.99.

The Court found that it was quite clear that the Plaintiff had abused the judicial process, because it willfully had engaged in a scheme to deceive the lower court. The Plaintiff's asserted right to evict the Defendant from the property had been grounded in fabricated evidence attached to the Plaintiff's complaint. Moreover, the Court held that the disputed evidence had been central to the Plaintiff's cause of action. Finally, the Court concluded that the Plaintiff had been both persistent and intentional in its actions, first by knowingly filing the fabricated evidence in court and then by attempting to use that evidence. The Defendant's claim for fees and costs was comprised of $13,118.64 for its computer consultants' fees and costs and $18,137.35 in attorneys' fees. In seeking to reduce the amount to $21,095.99, the Plaintiff raised a number of objections.

With respect to the consultants' fees and costs, the Plaintiff raised five objections, only one of which the Court agreed with. The Plaintiff argued that the consultants' $200 hourly rate was too high. The Court agreed with the Plaintiff that an hourly rate of $100 was appropriate and reduced the consultants' total by one half. Regarding attorneys' fees, the only objection that the Plaintiff had concerned $760 charged to attend the mirror imaging process, during which time the Plaintiff asserted that the attorney brought a substantial amount of work relating to other cases. Without further investigating this claim, the Court held that an eight-hour reduction would be appropriate, because there appeared to be no reason why all of the time was reasonable or necessary. Accordingly, the court reduced the attorneys' fees claimed by $760. Lastly, the court allowed the Defendant's request for fees and costs in the total amount of $24,845.99.

## Case 127

In re: PRICELINE.COM INC. SECURITIES LITIGATION
This document relates to: All Actions

No. 3:00CV01884(DJS).
December 8, 2005.

Jurisdiction: United States District Court, District of Connecticut

Date: December 8, 2005

Keywords: Cost and Cost Shifting, Discovery, Metadata

In a suit alleging violation of securities regulations, the Plaintiffs filed a motion to compel production of electronic discovery from the Defendant. The Defendant did not object to producing responsive information, but there was disagreement about how the responsive information would be produced.

The Plaintiffs sought information found within computer files; however, this information was difficult to find. The data at issue was stored as "snapshots," which is the same as a full backup of what was located on the Defendant's corporate file server on a specific date, or it was stored on backup tapes, which had to be restored to their native format in order to view. The data files stored as "snapshots" are reproduced in the same way that the information is stored in a computer system, so the files are generally organized in a random configuration. The files had to be searched to find responsive information. The data files stored on backup tapes had to first be returned to native form using the software program the files were created on, then had to be searched for responsive information in the same manner used on the "snapshot" files. The Court ordered the Defendants to retain possession of the original data with the opportunity to review the material for responsiveness and privilege, before producing the information in discovery. The Court reasoned that, because of the expense and time involved in restoring backup tapes, before the Court ordered the backup tapes to be restored, there had to be some indication that the information contained on the backup tape might be relevant. The Court ordered the parties to meet and confer regarding which backup tapes should be restored. The Court acknowledged that, if the parties disagreed, the parties should proceed to motion the Court for guidance. The Court stated that when it looked at these disagreements it would focus on the justification for restoring the tape and which party should pay for the restoration of the tape. The Court directed the Defendants to file a motion to shift the cost of restoration either once restoration was completed or once the cost of restoration had been determined. The Court also ordered the Defendants to "produce responsive information from stored data files to [P]laintiffs in TIFF or PDF form with Bates numbering and appropriate confidentiality designations." The Court further ordered the Defendants to produce searchable metadata databases and maintain the original data in native form for the duration of the litigation. The Court directed the Defendants to submit monthly status reports to the Court concerning the status of review and production of the backup tapes and "snapshot" files. The Court further noted that it was not making any cost-shifting decisions at that time, but if cost-shifting issues arose it would use the analysis set forth by the Civil Rules Advisory Committee to determine the propriety of cost shifting.

## Case 128

United States Court of Appeals,
Tenth Circuit.

THE PROCTER & GAMBLE COMPANY, and the Procter &
Gamble Distributing Company, Plaintiffs-Appellants,

v.

Randy L. HAUGEN, Freedom Tools Incorporated, Freedom Associates, Inc.,
Steven E. Brady, Stephen L. Bybee, Eagle Business Development, Inc.,
Ted Randall Walker, and Walker International Network, Defendants-
Appellees. Microsoft Corporation, Exxonmobil Corporation, Nike, Inc., and
Lawyers for Civil Justice, Amici Curiae.

No. 03-4234.
October 19, 2005.

Jurisdiction: United States Court of Appeals, Tenth Circuit

Date: October 19, 2005

Keywords: Discovery, Sanctions

The Plaintiff appealed the district court's order dismissing claims brought against the Defendants. The district court dismissed the Plaintiff's claims under the Lanham Act as a sanction for the Plaintiff's failure to preserve "relevant electronic data."

The Plaintiff argued that before the district court imposed dismissal as a sanction, it had to address on the record: "the degree of actual prejudice to the other party; the amount of interference with the judicial process; the culpability of the litigant; whether the court warned the party in advance that dismissal of the action would be a likely sanction for noncompliance; and the efficacy of lesser sanctions." The Court agreed with the Plaintiff and held that the failure to address these issues on the record was sufficient to reverse the district court's dismissal. The Plaintiff went on to argue that it did not act willfully, in bad faith, or with culpability in not preserving or producing the electronic data. The Court found that the Plaintiff did not possess or own the electronic data requested, but only had access to that data for a fee paid to the company that owned the data. The Court also found that the computer capacity and expenses the Plaintiff would have incurred in archiving the data would have been overwhelming to the Plaintiff. The Court further found that the district court and magistrate judge never defined "relevant data" and never suggested steps to preserve the data. The Court found that all of the discovery orders from the magistrate judge and district court were framed around the data the Plaintiff "possessed," and in this case the Plaintiff did not actually possess this electronic data. The Court found that it was unclear what the district court believed the Plaintiff's duties were regarding the preservation and production of the electronic evidence. For these reasons, the Court held that the Plaintiff did not act with the requisite culpability to justify the sanction of dismissal. The Court further found that it was not clear from the record that the electronic data was necessary to rebut the Plaintiff's expert. The Court held that issues of material fact were still present as to whether the Defendants were prejudiced by their lack of access to the electronic data. The Court also found no evidence in the record that the magistrate judge or the district court warned the Plaintiff that if the electronic data was not produced, the sanction of dismissal would be ordered. There was also no indication that the magistrate judge or district court considered lesser sanctions. The Court held that the sanction of dismissal for failure to preserve electronic data was improper.

## Case 129

United States District Court,
D. New Jersey.

In re the PRUDENTIAL INSURANCE COMPANY OF
AMERICA SALES PRACTICES LITIGATION.

MDL No. 1061.
Civil Action No. 95-4704.
January 6, 1997.

Jurisdiction: United States District Court, District of New Jersey

Date: January 6, 1997

Keywords: Preservation of Evidence/Spoiation, Sanctions

The Defendant's policyholders commenced class actions against the Defendant, alleging that it engaged in a scheme to sell life insurance through deceptive sales practices. Shortly thereafter, the Court entered its first order, requiring that all parties preserve all documents and other records containing information potentially relevant to the subject matter of the litigation. Subsequently, the Defendant's preservation of documents became a pervasive issue. The Plaintiffs then obtained an order to show cause why sanctions should not be imposed in connection to the document destruction. By order of the Court, the Plaintiffs then conducted a massive investigation into the alleged destruction, in order to ascertain whether the Defendant's notification of destruction of documents was satisfactory. The Court found that, although there was no proof that the Defendant, through its employees, engaged in conduct intended to thwart discovery through the purposeful destruction of documents, its haphazard and uncoordinated approach to document retention indisputably denied its party opponents potential evidence to establish facts in dispute. The Court held that because some of the destroyed records were permanently lost, the Court would draw the inference that the destroyed materials were relevant and, if available, would have led to the proof of a claim.

In determining the appropriate inference, the Court found that the Defendant's consistent pattern of failing to prevent unauthorized document destruction warranted the imposition of substantial sanctions. Although the Court did not find that there was willful misconduct, it did find that the document destruction, including the cleansing of more than 9,000 files, was substantial and caused prejudicial harm to party opponents. The Court was also satisfied that the destruction of document issue hindered and burdened the administration of justice and that there were no mitigating factors for the senior management's failure to comply with the order of the Court. The Court noted that it considered the range of sanctions available and determined that each of the sanctions to be imposed befitted the Defendant's conduct and were absolutely necessary to remedy the waste of judicial resources protect the authority of the Court. The Court imposed seven sanctions in total, the most severe being a $1,000,000 fine to the Court and the payment of the Plaintiffs' attorneys' fees and costs related to the Defendant's destruction of documents.

## Case 130

United States Court of Federal Claims.

The PUEBLO OF LAGUNA, Plaintiff,

v.

The UNITED STATES, Defendant.

No. 02-24 L.
March 19, 2004.

Jurisdiction: United States Court of Federal Claims

Date: March 19, 2004

Keywords: Preservation of Evidence/Spoliation

In a case seeking an accounting and recovery of monetary loss and damages relating to the Government's alleged mismanagement of the tribe's trust funds and other properties, the Plaintiff moved for a document preservation order directing various government agencies to take steps to ensure the preservation and availability of documents, in various media, potentially relating to its claims against the Government. The Plaintiff argued that, without the order, the destruction or loss of relevant documentation would result, as evidenced by the government's mishandling of Indian records in cases pending before the other courts. The Defendant argued that the Court lacked jurisdiction to enter such an order and also claimed that the proposed order was unnecessary and would be overly burdensome.

At the outset, the Court addressed the authority issue, whereby the Defendant argued that because the Court was an Article I tribunal, it lacked the inherent powers afforded Article III courts to order the preservation of relevant evidence. The Court, however, concluded that it did in fact have the power to preserve evidence and issue orders in furtherance thereof. Regarding the second issue of the order requested, in order to support its position, the Plaintiff relied heavily on what had transpired in similar cases where there were numerous instances of the Government mishandling Indian records, including but not limited to the destruction of documents, including electronic records, containing, or possibly containing, Indian-related information. The Court viewed the failures evidenced in the other cases as being so pervasive and systematic that they provided ample support for the issuance of a document preservation order in instant case. Despite concerns that the benefits of the Plaintiff's proposed protocols would be outweighed by the costs and burdens that they would impose, the Court saw no reason not to adopt them, with minor modifications. The Court felt that the looming specter of sanctions, which could include the entry of a default judgment, provided the best incentive to effectuate the preservation plan. Accordingly, the Court ordered a general obligation to preserve, document inspection and indexing protocols, mechanisms for monitoring compliance, and the continued threat of sanctions, should the order not be fully complied with.

## Case 131

United States District Court,
S.D. New York.

Claudia QUINBY, Plaintiff,

v.

WESTLB AG, Defendant.

No. 04Civ.7406(WHP)(HBP).
December 15, 2005.

Jurisdiction: United States District Court, Southern District of New York

Date: December 15, 2005

Keywords: Costs and Cost Shifting, Discovery, Experts, Sanctions

In a suit alleging gender discrimination, the Plaintiff moved for sanctions, including reasonable attorneys' fees, against the Defendant and Defendant's counsel. During discovery, the Plaintiff requested that the e-mail accounts of seventeen of the Defendant's employees be searched for certain terms. The Defendant objected to many of the requests, claiming that they were overly broad and would result in an undue burden. The Court ordered the Defendant to provide the Plaintiff's counsel with an affidavit discussing the technical issues raised by the discovery requests for e-mails and other electronic communications. The Defendant submitted an affidavit detailing the high cost and lengthy time involved in restoring the backupbackup tapes on which the e-mails were saved. The Plaintiff claimed that, after deposing two witnesses, she learned that many of the e-mails she requested were already readable and accessible on databases, a Lotus server, and archive tapes. All of these were "faster and less costly" to access.

The Plaintiff claimed the affidavit from the Defendant was incomplete and misleading because it focused only on the more expensive and lengthy process of retrieving the e-mails from the backupbackup tapes. The Plaintiff also claimed the Defendant made misleading statements before the Court. The Defendant argued that it did not make any misrepresentation regarding e-mail discovery or violate the Court's order, because most of the e-mails the Plaintiff wanted to search were available only on the backupbackup tapes and backupbackup tapes were the most complete source of e-mails. The Defendant claimed that, because the backupbackup tapes were the most complete source, they would have been searched in any event. The Court found that while the other storage systems covered a narrow time frame and a limited number of users, the backupbackup tapes were the most complete source. The Court held that the Defendant acted appropriately in focusing on the backupbackup tapes as the most complete source for the e-mails, because the backupbackup tapes included all of the relevant e-mail accounts and most if not all of the time periods requested. The Court also found that the Defendants did not mislead the Court or the Plaintiff regarding other available storage systems, because those other systems contained far less data. The Court also found the fact that the Defendant was producing e-mails from the most expensive source, prior to any decision shifting the cost of producing the e-mails to the Plaintiff, was compelling evidence of the Defendant's honesty and good faith. The Court denied the motion for sanctions against the Defendant and its counsel.

## Case 132

Court of Appeals of South Carolina.

QZO, INC., d/b/a Palmetto Ambulance Service, Respondent,

v.

· Darrin MOYER, Jerry Benenhaley, Alice Childers, of whom Darrin Moyer is Appellant.

No. 3759.
Heard February 11, 2004.
Decided March 15, 2004.

Jurisdiction: Court of Appeals of South Carolina

Date: March 15, 2004

Keywords: Sanctions

In a suit alleging violations of the state trade secrets act, the Defendant appealed several rulings from the lower court in favor of the Plaintiff, specifically the imposition of sanctions for violating that order. The Plaintiff's original complaint claimed that the Plaintiff had reason to believe that a computer belonging to it was in the Defendant's possession and contained evidence of the Defendant's wrongful acts. The complaint sought to enjoin the Defendant from using any proprietary information and order the Defendant to surrender the computer either to the Plaintiff or a neutral third party. The lower court determined that the information in the Plaintiff's computer was in danger and therefore, issued the temporary restraining order, which immediately ordered the Defendant to surrender the computer. The Plaintiff's computer expert discovered that the hard drive had been reformatted a day before the computer was turned over, effectively erasing any information the computer may have contained. The Plaintiff then moved for sanctions based on the Defendant's alleged willful violation of the order, which the lower court granted by entering a judgment in favor of the Plaintiff.

On appeal, the Defendant argued that the trial court erred by granting sanctions. The Court stated that the decision of whether or not to award sanctions is generally entrusted to the discretion of the trial court and that it is the burden of the Defendant to show that the trial court abused its discretion in imposing sanctions for failing to comply with a discovery order. The Defendant essentially argued that there was no evidence to suggest that he intentionally violated the order. The Court disagreed, citing the record, which contained evidence that the Defendant's testimony lacked credibility and that the

Defendant did not turn the computer over until seven days after the order's issuance. When the computer was eventually turned over, it became clear that the hard drive had been formatted the day before, effectively erasing any information contained therein. The Court concluded that there was evidence to support the trial court's finding that the Defendant willfully violated the temporary restraining order. Lastly, the Defendant argued that the trial court had not considered the severity of the sanction, though the Court found otherwise, citing the lower court's own words. Accordingly, the Court held that the trial court did not abuse its discretion in awarding sanctions and affirmed its ruling.

## Case 133

Superior Court of Connecticut,
Judicial District of Stamford-Norwalk.

Mary RANTA

v.

Jeffrey RANTA.

No. FA980195304S.
February 25, 2004.

Jurisdiction: Superior Court of Connecticut, Judicial District of Stamford-Norwalk

Date: February 25, 2004

Keywords: Experts, Electronic Evidence Protocols

In a divorce proceeding, the wife, who was the Plaintiff, was ordered to immediately stop using, accessing, turning on, powering, copying, deleting, removing or uninstalling any programs, files and or folders, or booting up her laptop computer located in her home. She was ordered to immediately deposit the laptop computer with the chief clerk of the court, so that it could be marked as a court exhibit and stored in the evidence vault of the court. The order extended to any and all floppy disks, CDs, Zip files, or any other similar type of computer storage device. Both parties and anyone acting on their behalf were barred from editing, accessing, or otherwise tampering with the laptop and/or any computer storage device marked as an exhibit. The laptop and the storage devices were only to be accessed in open court by a recognized testifying computer expert. The Plaintiff was to prepare a privilege log of any privileged item therein, to be submitted to the Defendant. The presiding judge was given authority to continue the computer expert examination in camera if there were any privilege objections during a hearing. Any request by the Defendant to access any document in the privilege log would be heard in such a hearing. The parties were instructed to pay equally all costs and expenses associated with the computer expert, unless otherwise ordered by the court. The computer expert was to sign a confidentiality agreement that the results of the search of the laptop and storage devices would be kept confidential and not disclosed to anyone. The parties were both instructed to mutually select the computer expert, and if they could not agree, they were to submit the names and addresses of two computer experts each, for the court to select one. The Defendant was ordered to purchase a comparable replacement laptop with similar programs and storage devices, to be installed in the Plaintiff's home at the Defendant's expense, when the old laptop was placed into evidence. In order to effectuate that order, the Plaintiff would provide a list to the Defendant of all of the programs, files, and folders currently used on the laptop, which would be transferred at the Plaintiff's expense if they were not readily available to the Defendant's installer. The laptop and all devices were then to become the sole property of the Plaintiff. After their use as evidence, the trial judge would enter orders to dispose of the old laptop and storage devices.

## Case 134

United States Court of Federal Claims.

RENDA MARINE, INC., Plaintiff,

v.

The UNITED STATES, Defendant.

No. 02-306 C.

August 29, 2003.

Jurisdiction: United States Court of Federal Claims

Date: August 29, 2003

Keywords: Discovery, Privilege, Preservation of Evidence/Spoliation

In a government contract dispute, the Plaintiff, a marine dredging contractor, had filed suit against the United States, alleging that it had encountered differing site conditions during the course of its contract performance of a project. During discovery, several disputes had arisen about the parties' responsibilities to preserve and produce evidence. The Plaintiff filed a motion to compel access to hard drives and e-mail systems, while the Defendant filed its own motion to compel.

The Plaintiff asserted that, based on the Defendant's own admission, the Defendant had not searched any hard drives or backup tapes in preparing its response to the Plaintiff's document production requests, which had specifically asked for backup tapes. The Defendant objected that the request was overly broad, but the Plaintiff countered by arguing that it had been narrowly tailored to cover communications specific to the project at issue. The Defendant also claimed that it had produced copies of relevant e-mails that had been retrieved from backup tapes, while the Plaintiff raised concerns of spoliation. The Court found that the Defendant's policy on record management seemed to be inconsistent with its admitted legal obligation to preserve evidence. The Court did not believe that such a policy, when inconsistent with a party's obligations, excused the party's failure to respond to discovery. The Court then held that the Defendant not only had a duty to preserve but that it also reasonably should have known of a potential litigation claim and that the deletion of relevant e-mail documents that continued, even after the filing of the action, violated the Defendant's duties. Accordingly, the Court directed the Defendant to produce, at its expense, backup tapes and hard drives.

The Defendant moved to compel the Plaintiff to produce a privilege log and documents responsive to its requests. The Court found that the pivotal consideration in deciding discovery challenges, where a large number of documents have been produced as they are kept in the usual course of business election, is whether the filing system for the produced documents is so disorganized that it is unreasonable for the requesting party to make its own review. The Defendant did not allege that the filing system was disorganized, though, but rather that the large volume of production made the response burdensome. Therefore, the Court denied the Defendant's motion for relief.

## Case 135

United States Court of Appeals,
Second Circuit.

RESIDENTIAL FUNDING CORPORATION, Plaintiff-Appellee,

v.

DeGEORGE FINANCIAL CORP., DeGeorge Home Alliance, Inc. and
DeGeorge Capital Corp, Defendants-Appellants.

No. 01-9282.
Argued: August 8, 2002.
Decided: September 26, 2002.

Jurisdiction: United States Court of Appeals, Second Circuit

Date: September 26, 2002

Keywords: Discovery, Sanctions

In a case regarding breach of contract, the Defendants appealed a final judg-ment in favor of the Plaintiff. On appeal, the Defendants challenged the denial of their motion for sanctions, in the form of an adverse inference instruction, for the Plaintiff's failure to produce certain e-mails in time for trial.

The Court held that where the nature of the alleged breach of a discov-ery obligation is the nonproduction of evidence, a District Court has broad discretion in fashioning an appropriate sanction, including the discretion to delay the start of a trial (at the expense of the party that breached its obliga-tion), to declare a mistrial if trial has already commenced, or to proceed with a trial with an adverse inference instruction. The Court also held that discov-ery sanctions, including an adverse inference instruction, may be imposed where a party has breached a discovery obligation not only through bad faith or gross negligence, but also through ordinary negligence. Next, the Court found that a judge's finding that a party acted with gross negligence or in bad faith with respect to discovery obligations is ordinarily sufficient to support a finding that the missing or destroyed evidence would have been harmful to that party, even if the destruction or unavailability of the evidence was not caused by the acts constituting bad faith or gross negligence. Lastly, the Court concluded that the District Court had applied the wrong standard in deciding the Defendant's motion for sanctions. Accordingly, the Court vacated the order of the District Court and remand with instructions for a renewed hear-ing on discovery sanctions.

## Case 136

Court of Appeals of Ohio, Tenth District, Franklin County.

RFC CAPITAL CORPORATION, Plaintiff-Appellee,

v.

EARTHLINK, INC., Defendant-Appellant.

No. 03AP-735.
December 23, 2004.

Jurisdiction: Court of Appeals of Ohio, Tenth District, Franklin County

Date: December 23, 2004

Keywords: Preservation of Evidence/Spoliation

The Defendant appealed the denial of its motion for directed verdict and grant of judgment in favor of the Plaintiff. The Plaintiff filed suit alleging conversion, tortious interference with a contractual relationship, unjust enrichment, impairment of security interest, and a right to an accounting. Prior to the parties trying the case to a jury, the Defendant moved for a directed verdict, which was denied and, at the conclusion of the trial, the jury found the Defendant liable and awarded the Plaintiff $6 million. On appeal, the Defendant claimed that the trial court erred in three different respects, when it gave a special jury instruction on spoliation.

During the deposition of an employee of the Defendant, the employee admitted that he destroyed documents, and upon this admission, the Plaintiff filed a motion for sanctions restricting the Defendant's future admission of evidence and instructing the jury to assume that the evidence destroyed was favorable to the Plaintiff. In response, the Defendant asserted that the only document possibly destroyed that was not already disclosed was a report, which it then obtained and delivered to the Plaintiff. However, before the start of the trial, the trial court delivered an adverse jury instruction. The Court concluded that, because discovery regarding the documents had been served almost eight months prior and because the Defendant offered no explanation as to why it did not attempt to collect the documents, there was no abuse of discretion for the trial court to conclude that the failure to preserve amounted to malfeasance or gross neglect. However, through testimony and proffering the deleted document, the Court found that the purge of the documents did not deprive the Plaintiff of favorable evidence relevant to the issues. Therefore, the Court concluded that the Defendant rebutted the presumption of prejudice, and thus, the trial court abused its discretion in giving a spoliation instruction to the jury. Further, even if some kind of spoliation instruction was warranted, the Court held that it was error to instruct the jury to make the specific presumptions included in the instant instruction. Thus, it was also an abuse of discretion to instruct the jury to presume facts in the Plaintiff's favor. Accordingly, the Court sustained the Defendant's assignments of error and concluded that a reversal of the trial court's judgment was warranted and that a new trial was necessary.

## Case 137

United States District Court,
N.D. Illinois, Eastern Division.

RKI, INC., d/b/a ROLL-KRAFT, Plaintiff,

v.

Steven GRIMES and Chicago Roll Co., Inc., Defendants.

No. 01 C 8542.
May 3, 2002.

Jurisdiction: United States District Court, Northern District of Illinois, Eastern Division

Date: May 3, 2002

Keywords: Preservation of Evidence/Spoliation

In a trade secret violation trial, the Court had entered a finding in favor of the Plaintiffs. The Defendants filed motions for a new trial or to alter or amend the judgment, raising questions regarding the liability and damages components of the earlier decision. The Defendant asserted that the finding of misappropriation against him had been based solely on his access to the Plaintiff's computers and the defragmentation of his computer four times. The Court, however, disagreed citing the Defendant's other actions as well, which had involved deleting 60 megabytes of data, equaling 29,297 pages of text, from his home computer while his computer was being inspected by a computer forensics expert. The forensic expert explained that finding no deletions coupled with defragmentation raises a red flag of eliminating data or concealing electronic data. Furthermore, the expert found data belonging to the Plaintiff on the Defendant's home computer. In finding that the corporate Defendant was also liable for misappropriation of the Plaintiff's trade secrets, the Court relied on similar actions, such as defragmentation of the hard drive and deletion of data from the computer of the vice president of sales, when no deletions had occurred prior to the threat of litigation.

In upholding its prior judgment, the Court stated that because direct evidence of misappropriation of trade secrets is typically not available, a plaintiff can rely on circumstantial evidence to prove misappropriation. The Court held that, in this case, the Plaintiff had constructed a web of circumstantial evidence. The Court drew inferences from this evidence and was convinced that it was more probable than not that what the Plaintiff had alleged did in fact take place. Therefore, the Court upheld the ruling that the Defendants had violated the Illinois Trade Secrets Act by misappropriating the Plaintiff's trade secrets.

# Case 138

United States District Court,
S.D. New York.

ROWE ENTERTAINMENT, INC., Leonard Rowe, Bab Productions, Inc.,
Bernard Bailey,
Sun Song Productions, Inc., Jesse Boseman, Summit Management
Corporation, Fred Jones, Jr., Lee King Productions, Inc., and Lee King,
Plaintiffs,
v.
THE WILLIAM MORRIS AGENCY, INC., Creative Artists Agency, LLC,
Agency for the Performing Arts, Inc., Monterey Peninsula Artists,
QBQ Entertainment, Howard Rose Agency Ltd., Renaissance Entertainment
Inc., Variety Artists International, Inc., Beaver Productions Inc.,
Belkin Productions, Inc., Bill Graham Enterprises, Inc., the Cellar Door
Companies, Inc., Cellar Door Concerts of Carolinas Inc., Cellar Door Concerts
of Florida Inc., Cellar Door Productions of Michigan Inc., Cellar Door North
Central, Inc., Cellar Door Productions Inc., Cellar Door Productions of D.C.,
Inc., Cellar Door (Southern) Corporation, Cellar Door Entertainment, Inc.,
Concert/Southern Promotions, Inc., Contemporary Productions Inc.,
Delsener/Slater Enterprises, Ltd., Decesare-Engler, Inc., Don Law Company,
Inc., Electric Factory Concerts Inc., Evening Star Productions, Inc., Fantasma
Productions of Florida, Inc., Jam Productions Ltd., Magicworks Concerts,
Inc., Pace Concerts, Inc., SFX Entertainment Inc., Sunshine Promotions Inc.,
and WJS III, Inc., Defendants.

No. 98 Civ. 8272 RPP JCF.
January 16, 2002.

Jurisdiction: United States District Court, Southern District of New York

Date: January 16, 2002

Keywords: Costs and Cost Shifting

The Plaintiffs had filed suit contending that they were frozen out of the market for promoting events with white bands by the discriminatory and anticompetitive practices of the Defendants, who were all involved in the concert promotion industry. During discovery, the Defendants had responded to the Plaintiffs' requests by permitting inspection of their concert files, which contained documents relating to the promotion of concerts. Some of the Defendants, however, moved for a protective order relieving them of the obligation of producing electronic mail that might be responsive to the Plaintiffs' discovery requests.

The moving Defendants argued that they should be relieved of their discovery obligations because the burden and expense involved would far outweigh any possible benefit in terms of discovery of additional information. If production would be nevertheless required, the Defendants asked that the Plaintiffs bear the cost. The Plaintiffs first argued that the discovery of e-mail was critical to their case. Furthermore, the Plaintiffs maintained that the Defendants' cost estimates were wildly inflated and that they would be willing to forego certain responsive documents in order to help hedge the discovery costs.

The Court held that the Plaintiffs had successfully demonstrated that the discovery they sought was generally relevant and that there was no justification for a blanket order precluding discovery of the Defendants' e-mails on the ground that such discovery was unlikely to provide relevant information or would invade the privacy of nonparties. The Court then stated that the more difficult issue was the extent to which each party should pay the costs of production. The Court found that the expense of locating and extracting the responsive e-mails would be substantial, and therefore, it would be appropriate to determine which, if any, of these costs, were undue, thus justifying allocation of those expenses to the Plaintiffs.

The Court then adopted a balancing approach for its analysis based on the following factors: (1) the specificity of the discovery requests; (2) the likelihood of discovering critical information; (3) the availability of such information from other sources; (4) the purposes for which the responding party maintains the requested data (5) the relative benefit to the parties of obtaining the information; (6) the total cost associated with production; (7) the relative ability of each party to control costs and its incentive to do so; and (8) the resources available to each party. The Court held that factors 1, 2, 4, 5, 6, and 7 supported cost shifting, while 3 and 8 did not. Accordingly, the Court concluded that the relevant factors tipped heavily in favor of shifting to the Plaintiffs the costs of obtaining discovery of e-mails. It then outlined a discovery protocol to be followed regarding the use of computer forensic experts. Lastly, the Court denied the Defendants' motion for a protective order as the Plaintiffs would bear the costs of production, while the Defendants would still continue to be responsible for the expense of any review of privileged or confidential material.

## Case 139

United States District Court,
N.D. Illinois, Eastern Division.

In the Matter of the Search of: 3817 W. WEST END, FIRST FLOOR CHICAGO, ILLINOIS 60621.

No. 04 M 108.
May 27, 2004.

Jurisdiction: United States District Court, Northern District of Illinois, Eastern Division

Date: May 27, 2004

Keywords: Constitutionality

The Court had issued a warrant that authorized the search of a home and the seizure of any computers that might be found but that conditioned the search of the computer's contents upon the Government providing the Court with a search protocol describing both the information the Government sought to seize from the computer and the methods the Government planned to use to locate that information without generally reviewing information on the computers that was unrelated to the alleged criminal activity. After the warrant had been executed and a computer and computer disks had been seized, the Government orally requested that the Court allow the government to commence its search of the computer hard drive and disks without providing a protocol.

The Court began by stating that the Government's motion raised a serious question, whether, when deciding to issue a warrant that would involve the seizure and subsequent search of a home computer, a magistrate judge had the authority to require the government to set forth a search protocol that attempted to ensure that the search would not exceed constitutional bounds. The Court concluded that the answer to the question was yes. In requiring a protocol, the Court emphasized that it did not seek to dictate the specific criteria that the Government may employ to supply particularity to its search and seizure of contents of the computers. The Court also did not envision that a set of criteria initially approved would be forever set in stone and did not foreclose the possibility that those criteria might need to be adjusted in response to what was found once the computer search had commenced. The Court concluded that the Government had sought a license to roam through everything in the computer without limitation and without standards. The Court held that such a request failed to satisfy the particularity requirement of the Fourth Amendment, and the Court therefore would not approve it.

Accordingly, the Court denied the government's motion to reconsider.

## Case 140

United States District Court,
M.D. Florida.

Edgar SEARCY, Plaintiff,

v.

MICROSOFT CORPORATION et al. and America Online Corporation et al.,
Defendants.

No. 5:04CV5700C-10GRJ.
May 4, 2005.

Jurisdiction: United States District Court, Middle District of Florida

Date: May 4, 2005

Keywords: Spyware

The Plaintiff filed a pro se motion, apparently alleging that the Defendants had engaged in a wholesale violation of federal law prohibiting wire and electronic communications interception by manufacturing, distributing, and using a device that surreptitiously intercepts activity that occurs through the Internet, telephone, cable, and air. The Plaintiff further complained that, for nearly a decade, the Defendants illegally intercepted the Plaintiff's e-mail and use of the Internet, while he used computers located in public libraries. Requesting to proceed as a class action because the unnamed and unidentified illegal devices were placed on a large class of individuals computers', the Plaintiff demanded a jury trial, with damages in the amount of $10,000.00 per class member, declaratory judgment, and injunctive relief.

The Court stated that it had the authority to review the complaint to determine whether it should be dismissed. After such review, the Court dismissed the Plaintiff's complaint with prejudice because it failed to state a claim upon which relief could be granted and because the action was frivolous. The Court found that, although a complaint submitted by a pro se plaintiff is held to a less stringent standard than that submitted by a licensed attorney and is construed as alleging all fairly and reasonably inferred claims, a pro se litigant must allege the essential elements of a claim for relief. Here, the Court could only speculate as to whether the Plaintiff had alleged essential elements of a claim, because it was unclear what that claim was. Beyond those problems, to the extent that Plaintiff's allegations could be construed as a violation of his privacy rights by the Defendants vis-à-vis their distribution of software, which ultimately subjects the Plaintiff to the threat of online hackers, the Defendants could not be held liable as a matter of law. Likewise, they could not be held liable for the manufacture and distribution of software, which, while making Internet access possible, also presented the threat of virus or spyware infiltration. In view of the foregoing, the Court respectfully recommended that the Plaintiff's complaint be dismissed with prejudice and that the clerk be directed to close the file and terminate all other pending motions in the matter.

## Case 141

United States District Court,
S.D. Indiana, Indianapolis Division.

SIMON PROPERTY GROUP L.P., a Delaware limited partnership, Plaintiff,

v.

mySIMON, INC., a California corporation, Defendant.

No. IP 99-1195-C H/G.
June 7, 2000.

Jurisdiction: United States District Court, Southern District of Indiana, Indianapolis Division

Date: June 7, 2000

Keywords: Discovery

In a trademark dispute, the Plaintiff had moved to compel the Defendant to produce documents and make computers available for inspection and access, for the purpose of attempting to recover deleted files. In part, because the Plaintiff had shown in its motion papers some troubling discrepancies with respect to the Defendant's document production, the Court concluded that the Plaintiff was entitled to attempt to recover deleted computer files from certain computers, at the Plaintiff's own expense. The Court then faced the challenge of arranging the recovery effort so that it would not be an undue burden to the Defendant, by disrupting or interfering with the Defendant's business.

The Court stated that the central focus of the disputed discovery was the effort by the Plaintiff to develop evidence supporting the Plaintiff's contention that the Defendant acted in bad faith, in selecting the mySimon name and creating the Simon character. Bad faith and/or intent to palm off is a relevant factor in assessing the likelihood of confusion in a trademark case. However, mere awareness of another entity's similar trademark would not necessarily show bad faith, at least if the Defendant reasonably believed its use of a similar mark would not infringe the first mark. The Court believed that the Plaintiff was entitled to look for such materials, but the Court was not entirely convinced that the subject of this very expensive discovery lay at the very heart of the case. Therefore the Court granted the motion to compel and outlined a discovery protocol that would minimize the expenses and burdens of the Defendant.

## Case 142

Court of Appeals of Virginia,
Chesapeake.

James Osias SIMONE, Jr.

v.

COMMONWEALTH of Virginia.

Record No. 0551-04-1.
March 15, 2005.

Jurisdiction: Court of Appeals of Virginia, Chesapeake.

Date: March 15, 2005

Keywords: Procedure

The Defendant appealed his conviction of four counts of possession of child pornography. He argued that the trial court had erred in finding that he had knowingly possessed three images located in the temporary Internet file cache of a computer, along with one image displayed as the wallpaper, in finding that the images that had been found in the computer had constituted four separate offenses, and in finding that he had not abandoned the computer and the items that had been contained therein.

The Defendant maintained that because he had previously abandoned the computer, he was not in possession of the computer or its contents, when pornography was discovered on it. The Commonwealth responded that there was no evidence to suggest that the Defendant had intended to abandon the property. The Court found that there was nothing in the record to suggest that the Defendant had exercised any control over the computer images on the date in question. Nor was there evidence that the Defendant, after having vacated the premises, had returned to exercise dominion and control over the computer or any other property left there. There was also no evidence that he had made any effort to retrieve the computer or even retained a key to the apartment.

Therefore, the Court held that the Defendant, as a prior tenant, did not have sufficient dominion and control over the computer, on the date in question, to conclude that he possessed the images contained therein on that date. Accordingly, the Court reversed, dismissed, and remanded the conviction.

# Case 143

United States District Court,
N.D. Illinois, Eastern Division.

Stephen SOTELO, individually and on behalf of all persons similarly situated,
Plaintiff,

v.

DIRECTREVENUE, LLC; Directrevenue Holdings, LLC; Betterinternet, LLC;
Byron Udell & Associates, Inc., d/b/a Accuquote; Aquantive, Inc. and
John Does 1-100, Defendants.

No. 05 C 2562.
August 29, 2005.

Jurisdiction: United States District Court, Northern District of Illinois,
Eastern Division

Date: August 29, 2005

Keywords: Spyware

The Plaintiff brought a class-action complaint alleging that the Defendants
caused "spyware" to be downloaded onto his personal computer without his
consent. The Plaintiff alleged that the "spyware" tracked his Internet use, invaded his privacy, and damaged his computer. The Plaintiff asserted various
claims under Illinois law and sought injunctive relief and compensatory damages. Several Defendants filed motions to dismiss pursuant to certain Federal
Rules of Civil Procedure. The Court granted one Defendant's motion to dismiss
for lack of personal jurisdiction. Several Defendants filed motions to stay litigation in favor of arbitration pursuant to the Federal Arbitration Act. The Court
denied the Defendants' motion to stay the litigation in favor of arbitration.

In the first count, the Plaintiff brought a claim for trespass to personal
property against the Defendants. The Court held that trespass to personal
property may be asserted by a computer user who alleges unauthorized,
harmful electronic contact with his computer system. The Court found that
the Plaintiff sufficiently alleged that: the "spyware" damaged his personal
property; the Defendants intentionally placed advertisements through "spyware" that interfered with the Plaintiff's use of his computer; and he was damaged by trespasses onto his computer. The Court denied the Defendants' motion to dismiss Count I. In Count II, the Plaintiff argued that the Defendants
violated the Illinois Consumer Fraud and Deceptive Practices Act through misleading advertisements for "free" software downloads, when the software was

bundled with "spyware." The Defendants argued that this count was not pled with the "sufficient particularity" required of fraud claims. The Court held that claims brought under the Deceptive Trade Practices Act are not subject to the "sufficient particularity" pleading standard of fraud claims. The Court denied the Defendants' motion to dismiss Count II. In Count III, the Plaintiff argued that the Defendants were unjustly enriched to his detriment through advertising fees and revenues from an increase in business. The Court held that the Defendants' "wrongful conduct" alone did not support a claim for unjust enrichment, where the Plaintiff had no claim or entitlement. The Court found that the Plaintiff failed to allege that he paid any money to the Defendants, or that he had claim or entitlement to the advertising fees paid or the revenue earned by the Defendants from the "spyware." The Court granted the Defendants' motion to dismiss Count III. In Count IV, the Plaintiff argued that the Defendants breached their duty not to harm his computer and their duty to monitor "spyware" distributors to ensure they received user consent prior to installing the "spyware." The Court denied the Defendants' motion to dismiss Count IV, because it found the Plaintiff expressly defined the Defendants' duty and sufficiently alleged that "spyware" was the cause of damage to his computer. In Count V, which came from the Illinois' Computer Crime Prevention Law, the Plaintiff argued that the Defendants knowingly and without authorization from the Plaintiff inserted "spyware" onto the Plaintiff's computer knowing that the "spyware" might damage the computer. The Court denied the Defendants' motion to dismiss Count V, because it found the Plaintiff sufficiently alleged the installation of the "spyware" was unauthorized. Accordingly, the Court denied the motions to dismiss Count I, Count II, Count IV, and Count V, and granted the motion to dismiss Count III.

# Case 144

United States District Court,
D. South Carolina, Charleston Division.

SOUTHEAST BOOKSELLERS ASSOCIATION et al., Plaintiffs,

v.

Henry D. McMASTER, Attorney General of South Carolina, et al., Defendants.

No. C.A. 2:02-3747-23.
May 23, 2005.

Jurisdiction: United States District Court, District of South Carolina, Charleston Division

Date: May 23, 2005

Keywords: Constitutionality, Procedure

The Plaintiffs brought a pre-enforcement constitutional challenge to permanently enjoin the operation of S.C.Code § 16-15-385, which provided criminal sanctions for disseminating harmful material to minors as applied to digital electronic files that are sent or received via the Internet. The parties came before the Court upon cross-motions for summary judgment. The controversy in the case centered primarily around an amendment to the Act, signed by the former Governor, which added the following definition of "material" Material means pictures, drawings, video recordings, films, digital electronic files, or other visual depictions or representations but not material consisting entirely of written words. Pursuant to the amendment, the Act proscribed the dissemination to minors of obscene digital electronic files. The Plaintiffs alleged that the proscription violated the First Amendment and the Commerce Clause because it prohibited adults, and even older minors, from viewing and sending constitutionally protected images over the Internet and had the effect of prohibiting constitutionally protected communications nationwide. With respect to their First Amendment claim, the Plaintiffs argued that the Act, as a content-based restriction on speech, could not survive strict scrutiny and was unconstitutionally overbroad because it substantially infringed on protected speech of adults. As for their Commerce Clause arguments, the Plaintiffs maintained that the proscription constituted an unreasonable and undue burden on interstate and foreign commerce and subjected interstate use of the Internet to inconsistent state regulation.

After a lengthy constitutional analysis of the statute, the Court ordered that the Plaintiffs' motion for summary judgment be granted and the Defendants' motion for summary judgment be denied. The Court there by, permanently enjoined the Defendants and prohibited them from enforcing S.C.Code Ann. § 16-15-385 as applied to digital electronic files that were sent or received via the Internet.

## Case 145

United States District Court,
S.D. Texas, Galveston Division.

Teddy ST. CLAIR, Plaintiff,
v.
JOHNNY'S OYSTER & SHRIMP, INC., Defendant.

No. Civ.A. G-99-594.
December 17, 1999.

Jurisdiction: United States District Court, Southern District of Texas, Galveston Division

Date: December 17, 1999

Keywords: Admissibility

The Plaintiff had brought claims for personal injuries allegedly sustained while he had been employed as a seaman aboard a vessel for the Defendant. The Defendant filed a motion to dismiss. The basis for the Defendant's motion to dismiss surrounded the ownership of the vessel at the time of Plaintiff's accident. The Defendant alleged that it did not own or operate the vessel at the time the alleged incident. The Defendant noted that two months prior to the incident, the ownership had been transferred to a third party and that ownership had again been transferred to another party at the beginning of the month of the incident. Therefore, the Defendant sought dismissal because it was not the owner of the vessel.

The Plaintiff responded that he had discovered evidence, taken from the Internet, nearly four months after the incident, revealing that the Defendant had in fact owned the vessel in question. The Court found that the Plaintiff's electronic evidence was totally insufficient to withstand the Defendant's motion. The Court was wary that there was no way of verifying the authenticity of the alleged evidence that the Plaintiff wished to rely upon. The Court stated that there was no way that the Plaintiff could overcome the presumption that the information that he had discovered on the Internet was inherently untrustworthy. For those reasons, the Court held that any evidence procured from the Internet was adequate for almost nothing, even under the most liberal interpretation of the hearsay exception rules. The Court then gave the Plaintiff two months to produce hard-copy backup documentation in admissible form from the United States Coast Guard or to discover alternative information verifying what the Plaintiff alleged. If the Plaintiff could not provide the Court with credible, legitimate information supporting his position, the Court concluded that it would be inclined to grant the Defendant dispositive relief.

## Case 146

United States District Court,
N.D. Illinois, Eastern Division.

Shirley STALLINGS-DANIEL Plaintiff,

v.

THE NORTHERN TRUST COMPANY, Defendant.

No. 01 C 2290.
March 12, 2002.

Jurisdiction: United States District Court, Northern District of Illinois, Eastern Division

Date: March 12, 2002

Keywords: Discovery, Experts

The Plaintiff, in an employment discrimination suit, filed a motion seeking the Court to reconsider its order, denying her use of an expert to conduct electronic discovery of the Defendant's e-mail system. The Plaintiff had originally argued that some of the e-mails that the Defendant had produced to her, in hard copy, in response to her document requests, had appeared incomplete, either because they had not shown the entire chain of recipients or because they had referred to other e-mails that she did not think she had been given. The Court had denied her request because it had been supported with nothing more than speculation.

In support of her motion for reconsideration, the Plaintiff argued that she had recently become aware of new information that added weight to her speculation that the Defendant had altered some of its e-mail documentation, before producing it. The new information was her discovery that in a previous, separate, and entirely independent employment discrimination case, the Defendant had redacted several documents it had produced and had not identified them as redacted. The Plaintiff argued that, because the individual who had redacted documents in the previous case had also produced documents in this case, certain suspicious e-mails that had been produced to the Plaintiff very possibly might have been altered before production.

The Plaintiff wished to conduct electronic discovery on several specific documents. The Court found that none of the Plaintiff's evidence supported her speculations about the documents she wished to have examined. The Court held that absent any court decision detailing and discussing the Defendant's actions, in the previous case, it would decline to form any opinion on the alleged activity. After examining the documents and evidence in question, the Court was not convinced that the Defendant had provided misleading information, stating that nothing in the documents produced justified an intrusive and wholly speculative electronic investigation into the Defendant's e-mail files. Thus, the Court denied the Plaintiff's motion for reconsideration.

## Case 147

Supreme Court of Connecticut.

STATE of Connecticut
v.
Alfred SWINTON.

No. 16548.
Argued September 26, 2003.
Decided May 11, 2004.

Jurisdiction: Supreme Court of Connecticut

Date: May 11, 2004

Keywords: Admissibility, Experts

The Defendant appealed his conviction, rendered after a jury trial, of one count of murder, claiming that the trial court improperly admitted into evidence computer enhanced photographs and computer-generated exhibits without a proper foundation. At trial, the State presented several images of bite marks that were computer enhancements of a photograph taken at the victim's autopsy. The enhancements were created through the use of a software program. The State introduced the enhancements through the overseer of the division of scientific services in the state department of public safety, who had a master's degree in forensic science and extensive experience in the forensic field but who was not qualified to testify as an expert in computer software or programming.

The Defendant objected to the admission of the enhanced photographs arguing that the testimony laid an inadequate foundation, which the trial court overruled. On appeal, the Defendant argued that the evidence at issue resembled composite photographs and, therefore, should be governed under a similar standard. The Defendant also claimed that, because the evidence actually was created by and through the use of a computer, it was computer-generated evidence and thus entailed additional foundational requirements. The State argued that the enhanced photographs were mere reproductions of the photograph of the bite mark and that their admissibility therefore should be governed by the foundational standard for photographs. The State argued that the enhancements had met that standard because the authenticity of the original photographs was never questioned and the testimony at trial was that the enhancements accurately reflected the content of the originals. The State further argued that a photographer's in-court testimony was not required for the admission of a photograph and therefore a computer programmer's testimony was not required in this case. The Court determined that the evidence was more than a mere enlargement of a photograph, as the State argued. The Court stated that enlargement simply involved making the details of an image larger, whereas the enhancement process revealed parts of an image that previously were unviewable, as in this case. The Court held that because it could not be sure to what extent the difference between presenting evidence and creating evidence had been blurred in the case, caution should guide the decision. Ultimately, the Court did not agree with the State's proposition that the enhanced photographs were like any other photographs admitted into evidence and concluded that, to the extent that a computer was both the process and the tool used to enable the enhanced photographs to be admitted as evidence, they were computer generated. After going through the factors of the standard for authentication, the Court held that the State laid an adequate foundation for the enhancements of the bite mark photograph. Accordingly, the Court rejected the Defendant's claims and affirmed the judgment of the trial court.

## Case 148

Superior Court of Connecticut,
Judicial District of Windham.

STATE of Connecticut,

v.

Lennard TOCCALINE.

No. CR000109519.
July 18, 2003.

Jurisdiction: Superior Court of Connecticut, Judicial District of Windham

Date: July 18, 2003

Keywords: Constitutionality

The Defendant moved to suppress contraband and pornographic images obtained from his home as a result of a search-and-seizure warrant. The Defendant also sought the return of his seized property, arguing that the warrant was facially invalid and that no probable cause had existed for the issuance of the warrant. The Defendant asserted that, without any allegation that usa-lolita.com offered illegal child pornography or that the Defendant downloaded illegal pornography, probable cause could not be found in the application for the warrant. The State did not contest the Defendant's contentions regarding the lack of allegations; however, it did argue that because the Defendant's name was in Site-key's database and this list allegedly contained exclusively the names of people who used the service to purchase child pornography, it was reasonable to infer that usa-lolita.com was a child pornography Web site. The state further argued that the magistrate could reasonably infer, based upon the use of the term lolita in usa-lolita.com and the fact that several of the listed Web sites containing child pornography were similarly named, that usa-lolita.com was a child pornography site.

The Court rejected the State's argument that the issuing judge could have drawn inferences supporting a finding that the defendant had committed the offense of attempted possession. The Court also held that the inferential chain that the issuing judge would have had to follow in order to find probable cause was that the defendant had used two credit cards to purchase access to a Web site from an adult online verification service and the service was known to provide online verification to other Web sites, which contained illegal child pornography. Without any averment or factual basis to demonstrate that the Web site, which the Defendant bought access to, contained child pornography, the Court founds that the inferential leap that the issuing judge would have to make to determine that the Defendant possessed child pornography was simply too great. The Court also found that the averments that the Web site's domain name and description contained the word "lolita" and that the defendant was a convicted sex offender, were insufficient to bridge the gap.

Because of the nature of the crime as the sort that evidence could reasonably be expected to be kept for long periods of time, the court found that the facts set out in the affidavit were not stale at the time that the warrant was issued, despite the exceedingly long span of time between when the Defendant had allegedly accessed the Web site and when the warrant was issued, as well as the fact that the Defendant was incarcerated during a substantial portion of this time span. Accordingly, the court found that the warrant was not facially defective on the ground of staleness but that the affidavit had failed to present a substantial factual basis for the magistrate's conclusion that probable cause existed. Therefore, the Court granted the Defendant's motion to suppress all of the contraband and pornographic images obtained as a result of the search-and-seizure warrant.

## Case 149

Superior Court of Delaware.

STATE of Delaware

v.

Henry A. DUHADAWAY

June 7, 2002.

Jurisdiction: Superior Court of Delaware

Date: June 7, 2002

Keywords: Computer Forensics, Experts

The Defendant moved for postconviction relief after being convicted on numerous charges, some of which were based on evidence of child pornography found on the Defendant's computer. The Defendant claimed that he had received ineffective assistance of counsel. The Court stated that to prove this, the Defendant must meet the criteria of a two-prong test. First, the Defendant must show that the counsel's representation fell below an objective standard of reasonableness and second, that the counsel's actions were so prejudicial that there was a reasonable probability that, but for counsel's errors, the Defendant would not have pled guilty and would have insisted on going to trial.

In support of his claim, the Defendant argued that his attorney was a close friend of a detective who served on the Defendant's case. His counsel acknowledged as much, but stated that it did not affect his representation of the Defendant. The Detective was going to be called as an expert witness, regarding the forensic computer examination that was performed on the Defendant's computer. The Defendant believed that the Detective had tampered with his computer. His counsel believed that the Detective had no motive to do such a thing and in order to disprove it, he advised the Defendant to retain a forensic computer expert. Despite this concern, the Defendant declined. The Court found that if he genuinely believed that the Detective was going to tamper with the computer, then he would have retained his own expert to check it. Since he did not, the Court held that his allegations were unfounded. Accordingly, the Court denied the Defendant's motion for postconviction relief.

## Case 150

Superior Court of Delaware.

STATE

v.

John WHITE

Submitted February 28, 2002.
Decided March 1, 2002.

Jurisdiction: Superior Court of Delaware

Date: March 1, 2002

Keywords: Discovery, Experts

The Defendant was charged with three counts of unlawful sexual intercourse in the first degree, three counts of unlawful sexual penetration in the third degree, sexual exploitation of a child, using a computer to unlawfully depict a child engaging in a prohibited sexual act, and possession of child pornography. The Court had previously denied the Defendant's motion to compel the delivery of a computer hard drive, certain computer disks, and a digital camera, to the defense investigator for transport to a forensic laboratory in Virginia. Because child pornography is illegal contraband, the Court required that the authorized inspection must take place in Delaware on the premises of a Delaware State Police facility or such other location as the parties agreed.

The Defendant then moved for an order compelling the State to make redacted copies of the hard drive for analysis in Virginia. The State opposed the motion and argued that, because of the nature of the computer media, it could not guarantee that all pornography could in fact be redacted. The Court requested an affidavit from the defense explaining why any analysis must be done in Virginia. The affidavit filed provided that the process at the private laboratory could proceed around the clock with a minimal amount of hours expended and that it would allow the Defendant's computer forensic examiner to more effectively use the Defendant's limited resources to conduct the examination. Essentially, they were rearguments of the original defense motion to compel, which the Court had addressed. The Court held that it had not been assured that the media still would not contain child pornography, which is considered contraband and may not be transported across state lines. The Court affirmed the conditions previously imposed on discovery and ordered that they be continued.

## Case 151

Supreme Court of Kansas.

STATE of Kansas, Appellee,

v.

Joseph "Zeke" Rupnick, Appellant

No. 92, 193.
December 16, 2005.

Jurisdiction: Supreme Court of Kansas

Date: December 16, 2005

Keywords: Procedure, Admissibility, Constitutionality

The Defendant appealed convictions of a felony computer crime and two mis-demeanors, claiming among other things that the trial judge erred in refusing to suppress evidence regarding data on his laptop, because the laptop was seized without a warrant and without the Defendant's consent. The Defendant formerly worked at Harrah's North Kansas City Casino. After leaving that casino, the Defendant began working at Sac & Fox Casino. Shortly after begin-ning work at Sac & Fox, the Defendant asked two computer technicians to download two disks onto his computer. The technicians saw proprietary in-formation from Harrah's on the disks, refused to download the disks, and no-tified their supervisors who notified the State Gaming Agency.

A warrantless seizure is per se unreasonable and a violation of the Fourth Amendment unless it falls within a recognized exception. One recog-nized exception is probable cause plus exigent circumstances. For the proba-ble cause plus exigent circumstances exception, the Court listed the following circumstances as issues to look at when determining whether exigent cir-cumstances exist: (1) the gravity or violent nature of the offense; (2) whether the suspect is reasonably believed to be armed; (3) a clear showing of proba-ble cause; (4) strong reasons to believe the suspect is in the premises; (5) a likelihood that the suspect will escape if not apprehended; and (6) the peace-ful circumstances of the entry. The Court held that loss or destruction of evi-dence is also to be considered when determining whether exigent circum-stances existed at the time of the seizure or search. The Court held that, because of the Defendant's admission to an agent of the State Gaming Agency that the Defendant's laptop had proprietary information on it belonging to a previous employer, this satisfied the exigent circumstance of a clear showing of probable cause to seize the laptop without a warrant. The Court also held that the fact that a key stroke or two could have destroyed the evidence supported the warrantless seizure of the laptop by the State Gaming Agent. Prior to searching the computer's hard drive, the Gaming Agency obtained a search warrant from a district magistrate judge. The Court held that a valid warrant is necessary to search the hard drive of a suspect's personal computer, unless there is probable cause plus exigent circumstances. The Court determined that the warrant was invalid and could not support the search of the Defendant's computer because the warrant was executed outside of the jurisdiction of the district magistrate judge who issued the warrant. The Court held that the evidence from the laptop should be suppressed.

## Case 152

Court of Appeals of Minnesota.

STATE of Minnesota, Appellant,

v.

Steven James KANDEL, Respondent.

No. A04-266.
August 10, 2004.

Jurisdiction: Court of Appeals of Minnesota

Date: August 10, 2004

Keywords: Sanctions

The State challenged the district court's pretrial order granting the Defendant's motion to suppress all evidence and dismiss the possession of child pornography case against him as a sanction for discovery violations. The State contended that its discovery violations were justified, did not prejudice the Defendant, and could have been properly rectified by a continuance rather than dismissal. The State first argued that its failure to allow access to the computer was justified because the Defendant initially requested only a forensically sound image copy of the hard drive of the computer and only later requested physical access to the actual computer. The Court stated that, without a court order and before the scheduled omnibus hearing, the prosecuting attorney should allow access to all matters within the prosecuting attorney's possession or control that relate to the case. The Court found that the State did not do so, that the district court continued the matter to give it more time to do so, and that it never complied with the Defendant's request for a copy of the hard drive. The State countered, arguing that it did not provide access because, if the computer was turned on, it would lose all forensic value as a piece of evidence. The Court found that the computer had been turned on at least three times, however, that the State did not attempt to explain why the evidence was not harmed in those instances, and that the State must have corrupted the evidence by the terms of its own argument.

The State next asserted that it was denied the opportunity present expert testimony, but the Court held that the State made no effort to do so. The State then argued that it was prohibited from disseminating copies of pornographic images of children to anyone, including defense counsel, by operation of federal law. The Court held that the State's argument was misplaced because the State could have made the evidence available for the defense's inspection, which it failed to do, and because the law does not apply to possession during the performance of official duties by peace officers, court personnel, or attorneys. If not, the State itself would have been in violation of the law. The State then argued that it had made sufficient disclosure when it provided photocopies of images retrieved and a list of cookies. The Court held that the images represented only a fraction of the evidence the state allegedly possessed and that the list of cookies was undated and its origin was impossible to establish without examining the materials the Defendant had requested. Therefore, the Court concluded that the State's partial compliance was insufficient. Finally, the State argued that it made an effort to facilitate discovery when it requested the name of the Defendant's expert. The Court found that the Defendant had provided his expert's name in a letter months earlier and that the Defendant's failure to answer did not indicate an intent to obstruct discovery. The Court held that the State's failure to comply with the discovery requests effectively prevented the Defendant from preparing a defense, though the state argued that there was no prejudice because the evidence remained unchanged. The Court still concluded that the Defendant was prejudiced. Despite the State's arguments that any prejudice could have been rectified by a continuance, the Court found that the dismissal of the charge against the Defendant was a proper exercise of the district court's discretion. Accordingly, the Court affirmed the district court's suppression and dismissal.

## Case 153

Missouri Court of Appeals,
Western District.

STATE of Missouri, Respondent,

v.

Zacheriah TRIPP, Appellant.

No. WD 63005.
June 7, 2005.

Jurisdiction: Missouri Court of Appeals, Western District

Date: June 7, 2005

Keywords: Admissibility

The Defendant appealed his convictions of first-degree murder, kidnapping, and forcible rape, arguing that the trial court had plainly erred in permitting testimony regarding the contents of his laptop, claiming that the testimony was legally irrelevant, because its prejudicial effect outweighed any probative value that it may have had. The Defendant's argument was based on the fact that the State had been permitted to argue that a wipe utility had been used on the computer, raising an inference of consciousness of guilt, when in fact, there had been no evidence showing that there had been anything incriminating on the laptop.

The evidence that had been presented at trial established that the Defendant had once had the Microsoft Office suite installed on his computer, had used the computer for word processing, and had deleted the Office suite on the night of the victim's disappearance. There had also been evidence of a substantial amount of empty space on the computer and a reference to wipeinfo.exe in the computer's swap file. The Court found that the testimony regarding the use of the wipe utility had stopped short of any indication that the primary use of such a utility would be to conceal information and that it did not appear that such a conclusion could be inferred from the testimony in the record. Regardless, the Court held that the evidence had not been significantly relied upon by the State in its argument. The first mention of the laptop during argument had been made by the Defendant's counsel. The State had briefly touched upon that testimony during its rebuttal. The State had not made an argument that the Defendant wiped files from the system concerning the crime nor had the State expressed an argument that the jury should consider the activity on the hard drive of the computer as raising an inference of consciousness of guilt. Instead, the only argument by the State had been a passing reference to the free space on the computer and that there had been evidence that a wiping utility had been used on portions of the hard drive. The Court was unconvinced that the testimony or the arguments of counsel on the issue had had a decisive effect on the jury's verdict. The Court then affirmed the trial court's judgment.

## Case 154

Superior Court of New Hampshire.

THE STATE of New Hampshire

v.

Shannon WALTERS

THE STATE of New Hampshire

v.

Erin WYLIE

Nos. 04-S-2103-2107, 2117-2121.
June 23, 2005.

Jurisdiction: Superior Court of New Hampshire

Date: June 23, 2005

Keywords: Admissibility

The Defendants were charged with theft by receiving stolen property, conspiracy to commit burglary, conspiracy to commit theft, and cruelty to animals, which arose in connection with the drowning of a miniature dachshund dog. The Defendants moved to suppress all of the evidence that the police obtained after their vehicles were stopped, alleging that the police were prohibited from relying on information contained in certain e-mails to effectuate the stops. Specifically, they claimed the e-mails were obtained in violation of the wiretap statute and thus, any evidence derived from the e-mails must be suppressed, to which the State objected.

The Court found that one of the Defendants' neighbors installed a key-logger program onto the Defendants' computer, surreptitiously obtained the Defendants' password, logged on to the Defendants' e-mail account, and read a series of e-mail exchanges between the Defendants, which revealed the Defendants involvement in the dog's death. The defendants challenged the admissibility of the evidence, including the dog and their statements, claiming that use of any evidence derived in contravention of the wiretap statute would violate due process under both the State and Federal constitutions and therefore, the evidence had to be suppressed. The Defendants argued that, because their neighbor violated the wiretap statute by illegally intercepting the Defendants' password and using it to read her e-mails, the police were prohibited from relying on information contained in the e-mails to stop the Defendants. As a result, the Defendants claimed that all of the evidence derived from the e-mails, including the dog and their subsequent statements, should be suppressed. In contrast, the State argued that the neighbors did not intercept the e-mail password and, thus, the wiretap statute did not apply. The State also claimed that even if the e-mails were improperly intercepted, the evidence should not be suppressed because the police did not participate in the intercept and were unaware that the e-mails were improperly intercepted at the time of the stop. The Court found that the e-mails had been illegally obtained and declined to adopt a clean hands exception, based on the language of the statutory exclusionary provision. Accordingly, the Court held that the dog and the statements the Defendants made at the scene of the stop were dependent upon the illegal intercept and should therefore be suppressed. The Court, however, found that the statements made at the police station were sufficiently attenuated from the initial intercept, were not derived from the illegal interception, and were therefore admissible. The Court granted in part and denied in part the Defendants' motion to suppress.

## Case 155

Superior Court of New Jersey,
Appellate Division.

STATE of New Jersey, Plaintiff-Respondent,

v.

Allen MAY, Defendant-Appellant.

Argued May 21, 2003.
Decided August 18, 2003.

Jurisdiction: Superior Court of New Jersey, Appellate Division

Date: August 18, 2003

Keywords: Constitutionality, Experts

The Defendant had been convicted of two counts of endangering the welfare of a child, for his alleged receipt, possession, and subsequent distribution of child pornography. After a jury trial, the Defendant was convicted of both charges. The Defendant appealed his conviction arguing that the state statute was unconstitutionally overbroad, that that he was entitled to an acquittal because the State's own experts could not prove whether the images were of real people and, even if they were, whether they were children.

The Court found that there was much merit in the Defendant's argument that the trial court had erred when it had declined to instruct the jury regarding the sufficiency of the evidence relating to whether the images were of real people. The Defendant asserted that, in light of the court's instruction, the jury could have viewed his virtual-image defense as irrelevant under the law or even agreed with it but nevertheless felt compelled to find him guilty. The Court held that the conviction had to be reversed on that basis and remanded the matter for retrial with more comprehensive jury instructions reflecting the State's proof obligations, in the face of the Defendant's virtual-image defense.

In doing so, however, the Court declined to hold that the instructions that were given shifted the burden of proof on the issue of age from the State to the Defendant. In addition, the Court emphasized that, irrespective of how the State chooses to prove the age element, the trial judge must charge the jury that speculation about age is not permitted and that the jury must be persuaded by the evidence that, in each instance, the sixteen-year age threshold had been proven.

# Case 156

Court of Appeals of Ohio,
Fourth District, Washington County.

The STATE of Ohio, Plaintiff-Appellee,

v.

Eugene R. ANDERSON, Defendant-Appellant.

No. 03CA3.
Decided March 2, 2004.

Jurisdiction: Court of Appeals of Ohio, Fourth District, Washington County

Date: March 2, 2004

Keywords: Admissibility

The Defendant appealed his conviction on charges stemming from the possession of child pornography, asserting that the evidence was insufficient to support his convictions and that his convictions were against the manifest weight of the evidence. The Defendant argued that in three separate instances, the State did not produce evidence showing that he had accessed images on media or that he had knowledge of the materials on that media as required under the statutes. Each time, the Court found that, after viewing the circumstantial evidence in a light most favorable to the prosecution, any rational trier of fact could have found the essential elements of each of the proven charges beyond a reasonable doubt. Hence, the Court held that the convictions were supported by sufficient evidence. In all three instances, the Defendant also argued that jury verdicts were against the manifest weight of the evidence. The Defendant pointed to places in the record that supported his version of the facts, while the State did the same to support its version of the facts. The Court found that the State introduced substantial circumstantial evidence to show that the Defendant accessed the images on the various media with knowledge of the nature of the material. Hence, the Court held that the convictions were not against the manifest weight of the evidence. Accordingly, the Court affirmed the Defendant's convictions.

## Case 157

Court of Appeals of Ohio,
Second District, Montgomery County.

STATE of Ohio, Plaintiff-Appellee

v.

Douglas J. BOLDEN, Defendant-Appellant.

No. 19943.
Decided May 7, 2004.

Jurisdiction: Court of Appeals of Ohio, Second District, Montgomery County

Date: May 7, 2004

Keywords: Constitutionality

The Defendant was found guilty upon a plea of no contest to one count of importuning, regarding solicitation, by means of a telecommunication device, to engage in sexual activity with another, whom the offender believed was a minor. The Defendant filed several motions to dismiss and a motion to compel, all of which were denied by the lower court, which the Defendant appealed.

The Defendant claimed that the police officers engaged in outrageous government conduct, thus warranting the dismissal of the charge against him. The Defendant argued that there was no ongoing criminal activity and that the police lurked in adult chat rooms targeting unsuspecting individuals to enter so they might strike up improper conversations. Second, he stated that the police consistently offered overwhelming encouragement to commit importuning. Third, he argued that it was clear that he did not want to break the law. Lastly, he asserted that the State was not acting to protect a victim, because he had flatly stated that he did not want to have sex or meet with the alleged victim. Considering the totality of the circumstances, the Court found no outrageous government conduct, stating that the police did no more than to make the fictitious victim available to the Defendant on a cyberspace street corner and that the detective did not initiate the sexual nature of the conversations. The Defendant also claimed that the state statute violated the Commerce Clause of the United States Constitution, arguing that the state legislature was attempting to regulate a system that, because of its vast nature, invoked national control and that it was imposing the laws of the state upon others. The Court held that the statute did not violate the Commerce Clause because it was narrowly tailored to serve the interest of the state in promoting the welfare of children, without interfering with interstate commerce, because it regulated the conduct of adults who sought to solicit minors to engage in sexual activity in conversations by means of the Internet or other telecommunications devices, which was not protected by the First Amendment. The Defendant also argued that the trial court erred in failing to compel the production of certain transcripts of three chat logs, allegedly missing from the state's records. Even assuming that the allegedly missing chat logs existed as described, the Court concluded that they were either not exculpatory or were irrelevant because the charge related to solicitation, to which there is no defense of "I didn't mean it." Accordingly, the Court affirmed the Defendant's conviction after overruling each of his assignments of error.

## Case 158

Court of Appeals of Ohio,
Second District, Montgomery County.

The STATE of Ohio, Appellee,

v.

COOK, Appellant.

No. 19061.
Decided September 13, 2002.

Jurisdiction: Court of Appeals of Ohio, Second District, Montgomery County

Date: September 13, 2002

Keywords: Computer Forensics, Admissibility, Constitutionality

The Defendant appealed his conviction on 20 counts of possessing or viewing material showing a minor in a state of nudity. On appeal, the Defendant raised several assignments of error, two of which involved the search of his residence and the admission of materials that had been generated from a mirror image that had been made of the hard drive of his computer.

The Defendant argued that where the probable cause for a search warrant is based in part on a prior warrantless search and seizure of personal property by a private citizen at the instigation of the police, the evidence seized as a result of the search must be suppressed.

The Court held, however, that the officers needed only sufficiently reliable information that criminal activity was being conducted on the premises and that they had it through the pictures and the statement that had been provided by the Defendant's guest. The Court then found that even if the guest had acted as an agent of the state, his actions were irrelevant to the issue of probable cause. Since the officers had had sufficient information justifying a search of the Defendant's home, the first assignment of error was without merit.

In the second assignment of error, the Defendant argued that the trial court erred in overruling his objection to admission of exhibits concerning the computer hard drive as well as evidence, such as mirror images, that had been generated by the hard drive. His argument was founded on the lack of reliability of computer forensics processes used to create two mirror images of the hard drive. However, the Court found, through the testimony of both sides' experts, that there was no doubt that the mirror image was an authentic copy of what was present on the computer's hard drive. Therefore, the Court found that neither of the assignments of error had merit, and it affirmed the judgment of the trial court.

**Case 159**

Court of Appeals of Ohio,
Twelfth District, Butler County.

The STATE of Ohio, Appellee,
v.
GANN, Appellant.

No. CA2002-05-110.
Decided July 28, 2003.

Jurisdiction: Court of Appeals of Ohio, Twelfth District, Butler County

Date: July 28, 2003

Keywords: Experts

The Defendant appealed his conviction of charges related to sexual misconduct involving a minor, specifically several charges involving the illegal use of a minor in a nudity-oriented material or performance. The charges arose from allegations that the Defendant contacted several teenage girls via the Internet and, among other things, offered them money for sexual acts. On appeal, the Defendant alleged several assignments of error.

First, the Defendant challenged the sufficiency of the evidence upon which his conviction was based. He argued that the State failed to prove that the individuals depicted in images and movies found on his computer were actual persons or minors. The Court found that the materials in question all depicted young girls in various stages of sexual congress and that they were all substantially younger than 18. The Defendant attempted to argue that modern technology made it almost impossible to determine from looking if an image was true or somehow altered by a computer. Because the Defendant presented no evidence to show that the persons depicted were not actual persons or minors, the Court found that the images spoke for themselves and that the trial court had not committed error on that point. He also asserted that the State failed to prove that he recklessly possessed the material that formed the basis for the same charges, because it failed to prove that he accessed the files or had knowledge or notice of their contents. However, the Court found that the State presented ample evidence to demonstrate that Gann was on notice of the nature and character of the files he downloaded, as presented by his computer expert, and upheld the sufficiency of the evidence. The Defendant next questioned the effectiveness of his counsel, arguing that his counsel failed to call an expert witness on computers to contradict the testimony of the State's expert. The Court concluded that the Defendant was unable to show what such an expert's testimony would have been helpful but also that any such expert witness could have been called to willingly testify on his behalf. The Court stated that the Defendant could not demonstrate that his counsel's decision not to call an expert witness on his behalf fell below an objective standard of reasonableness or that there was a reasonable probability of a different outcome had he done so. Accordingly, the Court denied this assignment of error as well.

# Case 160

Court of Appeals of Ohio,
Tenth District, Franklin County.

STATE of Ohio, Plaintiff-Appellee,

v.

Peter M. SCHMITZ, Defendant-Appellant.

No. 05AP-200.
Decided December 13, 2005.

Jurisdiction: Court of Appeals of Ohio, Tenth District, Franklin County

Date: December 13, 2005

Keywords: Computer Forensics, Experts, Preservation of Evidence/Spoliation

The Defendant was convicted of gross sexual imposition and tampering with evidence. The Defendant appealed his conviction of tampering with evidence, arguing that the evidence had been insufficient to support the conviction. The Defendant argued that he was unaware that an official proceeding or investigation was about to be or likely would be instituted. The Defendant also argued that the state failed to demonstrate that the Defendant deleted the photographs.

The Court held that "when an offender commits an unmistakable crime the offender has constructive knowledge of an impending investigation of the crime committed." The Court looked at the record in a light most favorable to the prosecution and construed the facts to show that the Defendant molested BD. The Court further held that it could be reasonably determined that after the Defendant molested BD, the Defendant knew an official proceeding or investigation was likely to be instituted. The Court found that the Defendant was constructively informed of an impending investigation. The Court found that the state relied solely on the testimony of a forensic computer examiner regarding the image files deleted from a disk the Defendant gave to BD's "uncle." The forensic computer examiner testified that images of BD were deleted from a disk Defendant possessed, but he could not determine whether the image files were deleted purposefully by manually telling the operating system to delete them, or inadvertently by transferring or downloading the files to a computer. The Court found that the forensic examiner's testimony neither directly nor circumstantially proved the Defendant purposefully deleted the image files in order to make them unavailable as evidence. The Court found that the state forced the jury to speculate that the reason the disk was blank when the police received it was because the Defendant deleted the images. The Court also found that the state asked the jury to find that the Defendant purposefully deleted the files based solely on the testimony of the forensic examiner, who said the files could have been deleted purposefully or inadvertently. The Court held that there was insufficient evidence to support the jury's verdict convicting the Defendant of tampering with evidence.

## Case 161

Court of Appeals of Ohio,
Fifth District, Licking County.

STATE of Ohio, Plaintiff-Appellee

v.

Scott WAGNER, Defendant-Appellant.

No. 03 CA 82.
Decided July 26, 2004.

Jurisdiction: Court of Appeals of Ohio, Fifth District, Licking County

Date: July 26, 2004

Keywords: Admissibility

The Defendant appealed the decision of the lower court that found him guilty of multiple counts regarding a variety of sexual misconduct. The Defendant argued that the trial court committed error when it admitted into evidence irrelevant and inadmissible evidence concerning pornography. He asserted that the State's repeated references to the items in question were irrelevant and served only to inflame the passions of the jury. The Court noted that the admission or exclusion of evidence rests within the sound discretion of the trial court. Therefore, the Court stated that it would not reverse a trial court's evidentiary ruling unless it found an abuse of discretion.

During the trial, the Defendant did not object to the admission of the evidence and therefore the Court concluded that the Defendant waived the issue for the purposes of appeal. The Court went on to hold that even if it were to address the issue, it would conclude that the pornography found on the Defendant's computer was admissible to show the Defendant's motive, intent, scheme, or plan in committing the sexual abuse, because the evidence established that it was gathered and viewed by someone interested in child pornography. Therefore, the Court denied that portion of the Defendant's appeal.

## Case 162

Supreme Court of South Dakota.

STATE of South Dakota, Plaintiff and Appellee,

v.

William Boyd GUTHRIE, Defendant and Appellant.

No. 22311.
Considered on Briefs October 8, 2002.
Decided November 20, 2002.

Jurisdiction: Supreme Court of South Dakota

Date: November 20, 2002

Keywords: Sanctions, Discovery, Experts

This appeal arose from a remand hearing in which the circuit court determined that the sanctions that had been levied against the Defendant's attorney for violating a discovery order had been reasonable. The only issue that the Court needed to address in the remand hearing was whether the sanctions had been reasonable.

The attorney argued that the trial court erred in finding that the Government's computer forensic expert's rebuttal testimony would not have been necessary if the pretrial discovery order had not been violated. The Court found that if the note had been properly given to the State during the discovery period, evidence concerning the note's creation date and its incriminating nature would have presumably deterred the defense from introducing it at trial. Therefore, the further costs were directly and totally caused by the violation of the discovery order.

The attorney next argued that the expert's fees were unreasonable and that the State made little effort to find a local expert. The trial court found that Robbins' fee of $350 per hour was reasonable because he is a highly qualified expert, and the Court held that it could not say that the trial court was clearly erroneous when it reached its conclusion.

Lastly, the attorney argued that the equities of the case did not support a sanction of $8,866 because he did not act in bad faith. Yet, the trial court had found that he tried to ambush the State with this purported suicide note, hoping the State would not have time to refute the evidence and therefore, that his actions had amounted to a high degree of bad faith. This Court held that there was sufficient evidence to support the trial court's finding that the attorney acted in bad faith.

The Court did, however, note that the attorney was court-appointed at the time of the violation. Though the Court reiterated that all attorneys have the same high ethical obligations to the court, it felt that a sanction of $8,866 would be devastating to the attorney at issue and therefore reduced the sanctions to $5,500.

## Case 163

Supreme Court of South Dakota.

STATE of South Dakota, Plaintiff and Appellant,

v.

Charles Edwin HELLAND, Defendant and Appellee.

No. 23705.

Considered on Briefs October 3, 2005.

Decided December 7, 2005.

Jurisdiction: Supreme Court of South Dakota

Date: December 7, 2005

Keywords: Admissibility, Constitutionality, Procedure

In a suit alleging twenty counts of child pornography, Appellant appealed the order of the circuit court to suppress evidence obtained in search of Appellee's computer at his employer's place of business. The Appellant argued, among other things, that the circuit court erred when it held that the issuing court had insufficient probable cause to issue a search warrant.

The circuit court held that the search warrant lacked sufficient evidence to support it because the affidavit supporting it did not explain the nature of temporary Internet files and did not explain that all of the pornographic files viewed by the witness were temporary Internet files. The Court determined that the correct standard to use when reviewing the circuit court's decision is whether the information contained in the affidavit was sufficient for the judge to come to a "common sense" conclusion that there was a "fair probability" that a crime had been committed and that evidence in the affidavit would be found at the place to be searched. The Court found that the issuing court had been presented with evidence that a witness viewed several files with suspicious names in the temporary Internet file folders and saw several photographic images of nude young males contained in files on the computer. The Court found further that the affidavit was clear that the witness made some of these observations while looking at the temporary Internet file folder, but it did not specify that all of the images observed existed in temporary Internet files. The Court held that the affidavit did not have to state how the pornography became stored on the computer in order to support probable cause. The Court further held that the issuance of the search warrant did not necessitate identifying who placed the child pornography in the temporary Internet files to support probable cause. The Court held that the issuing court had all of the facts necessary to establish reasonable probability that someone committed the crime of possession of child pornography and that evidence of the crime would be found on the computer. The Court held that the search warrant was supported by probable cause. The Court overturned the order to suppress the evidence.

## Case 164

Court of Criminal Appeals of Tennessee,
at Nashville.

STATE of Tennessee,

v.

Michael E. BIKREV.

No. M2001-02910-CCA-R3-CD.
Assigned on Briefs November 5, 2002.
June 24, 2003.

Jurisdiction: Court of Criminal Appeals of Tennessee, at Nashville

Date: June 24, 2003

Keywords: Admissibility

The Defendant had been charged with and convicted of burglary. He appealed, arguing that the State had not established a proper chain of custody concerning the stolen property (a computer) in the case. He claimed that the chain of custody had been broken when the Sheriff's Department had allowed the victims to take the recovered property home overnight. The Court stated that it is well-established that as a condition precedent to the introduction of tangible evidence, a witness must be able to identify the evidence or establish an unbroken chain of custody, as is required by Rule of Evidence 901(a). Evidence may be admitted when the circumstances surrounding the evidence reasonably establish the identity of the evidence and its integrity.

The Court concluded that the State had established a sufficient chain of custody of the recovered stolen property to justify its admission into evidence. It had presented testimony by each witness who had had possession of the property, from the time of its recovery until the time of trial. Although the victims had possessed the recovered property for approximately twenty-four hours, there had been no indication of tampering, loss, substitution, or mistake regarding the recovered property. Therefore the Court found that the trial court did not err by allowing the property into evidence and that legally sufficient evidence had been presented at the Defendant's trial to support his conviction. The Court affirmed the judgment of the trial court.

## Case 165

Court of Criminal Appeals of Tennessee,
at Nashville.

STATE of Tennessee, Plaintiff and Respondent,
v.
Kelly Michael PICKETT, Defendant and Appellant.

No. M2004-00732-CCA-R3-CD.
March 9, 2005 Session.
October 3, 2005.

Jurisdiction: Court of Criminal Appeals of Tennessee, at Nashville.

Date: October 3, 2005

Keywords: Computer Forensics

The Defendant appealed his conviction on eleven counts of exploitation of a minor. The Defendant claimed, among other things, that the evidence was insufficient to support the convictions because the State failed to prove that he "possessed" pornographic images. Police searched the Defendant's computer and discovered numerous pornographic images of children in the temporary Internet folder and unallocated spaces.

The Defendant argued that he did not knowingly possess the pictures because the pictures were automatically saved to his computer when he visited child pornography Web sites. The Defendant claims he did not actively download and save the pictures to the hard drive of his computer. The Court found, that according to the computer's Internet history, the Defendant voluntarily visited a large number of child pornography Web sites and visited these Web sites to access the images that ended up being stored in his computer's temporary Internet folder. The Court cited a case stating the notion that repeatedly visiting a Web site that is clearly labeled child pornography is circumstantial evidence of knowing possession. The Court found that the Defendant had control over the images he viewed and deleted some of the images from his temporary Internet file, resulting in the images being stored in the computer's unallocated space. The Court held that the ability to destroy images by deleting them from the hard drive demonstrates ultimate control and dominion over the images." The Court held that the Defendant knowingly possessed the images.

# Case 166

Supreme Court of Vermont.

STATE of Vermont

v.

Patrick VOORHEIS.

No. 02-478.
February 13, 2004.

Jurisdiction: Supreme Court of Vermont

Date: February 13, 2004

Keywords: Electronic Evidence Fabrication/Alteration

The Defendant appealed a jury conviction for attempting to promote a lewd performance by a child. The Defendant claimed that the trial court had erred in denying his motion for a judgment of acquittal. He first argued that the trial court had abused its discretion by not dismissing the charges of incitement and attempt, for lack of sufficient evidence. According to the Defendant, the only evidence presented was the instant message text, which was retrieved from another's computer and which the owner claimed to have edited.

The Court found that the captured instant messaging text had offered substantial evidence of the Defendant's requests to pose the child and take additional pictures for his own viewing. The text also contained ample evidence, in the form of the electronic conversations together with witness testimony, that he had solicited consent to carry on his own lewd photo session. The Court held that this evidence had been sufficient for a jury to reasonably conclude that the Defendant had incited another to use her daughter in a sexual performance and/or to consent to her daughter's participation in a sexual performance, both of which are felonies.

Lastly, the Defendant argued that the electronic text was meager evidence of guilt, because the text was admittedly doctored and edited. The Court found, however, that the jury could find this recovered correspondence reliable and choose to disbelieve claims of manipulation of the content. The Court then remarked that it was not a question of sufficiency of the evidence but rather of its credibility, which falls entirely within the jury's province. The Court ruled that the evidence was sufficient and upheld both verdicts.

# Case 167

Court of Appeals of Washington,
Division 2.

STATE of Washington, Respondent,

v.

James Patrick DeGROFF, Appellant.

No. 30758-8-II.
June 29, 2005.

Jurisdiction: Court of Appeals of Washington, Division 2

Date: June 29, 2005

Keywords: Constitutionality

The Defendant appealed his convictions related to the possession of child pornography, raising several issues but primarily challenging the search warrants for his home. The Defendant asserted that the first warrant was invalid because the police lacked probable cause to believe that his home or computer contained business records. The Court disagreed, finding that, in view of the information provided in the affidavit, an issuing magistrate could reasonably infer that the Defendant might maintain business records in his home and computer. The Court concluded that probable cause developed from such inferences when a detective saw what appeared to be an office with computer and files in the Defendant's home. Therefore, the Court held that his challenge to the first warrant on that basis failed. The Defendant also challenged the first warrant on a claim that it was overbroad, because it did not set forth a sufficiently specific search methodology for locating business records on his computer. He argued that the search should have been limited to computer files identifiable as text or spreadsheet topics, but the Court found that his proposition was unreasonable, because text documents can be hidden in all manner of files, even graphic or image files, and there was no way to know what was in a file without examining its contents. The Court found that the opening of image and graphic files was part of a proper search for business records, and therefore, the challenge on that basis was without merit.

The Defendant then argued that the second warrant only authorized the seizure of the physical computer, not a search of its contents. The Court found that it did not need to address that issue for other reasons, but stated that it would fail anyway, if the warrant was read in a commonsense manner. Therefore, that challenge failed, as did the next claim that the second warrant was overbroad. In response, the Court held that the warrant specifically indicated that evidence of child pornography was to be diligently obtained. Lastly, the Defendant challenged the sufficiency of the evidence supporting his convictions. The Court stated that the charge required proof that an individual knowingly possessed the materials. The Defendant did not dispute that the computer was his, that it was located in his home, and that he routinely used it. However, he asserted the issue of possession, claiming that others had access to his computer and that nothing more tied him to the images. The State presented evidence that refuted the Defendant's claims and the jury rejected them, finding that he was responsible for the images on his computer. Accordingly, the Court held that the evidence was sufficient to support the jury findings that the Defendant knowingly possessed child pornography. The Court rejected the Defendant's warrant challenges.

# Case 168

Court of Appeals of Washington,
Division 1.

STATE of Washington, Respondent,

v.

Ronald Joseph LUTHER, Appellant.

No. 52391-1-I.
January 10, 2005.

Jurisdiction: Court of Appeals of Washington, Division 1

Date: January 10, 2005

Keywords: Constitutionality

The Defendant had been charged with seven separate counts of possessing depictions of minors engaged in sexually explicit conduct, was found guilty of one count of attempted possession of depictions of minors engaged in sexually explicit conduct, and appealed his conviction. On appeal, the Defendant claimed that the offense of attempted possession of depictions of minors engaged in sexually explicit conduct was constitutionally overbroad. The Defendant also asserted that the evidence, presented at trial, was insufficient to convict him of attempted possession of depictions of minors engaged in sexually explicit conduct.

The Court disagreed with the Defendant on his first point. The Court found that the Defendant presented no persuasive argument or authority that the First Amendment or state counterpart prevented a trier of fact from basing a defendant's conviction for attempted possession of child pornography, upon the defendant's possession of materials that appear to be child pornography but that may in fact not depict actual minors engaging in sexually explicit conduct. The Court also disagreed with the Defendant's argument that the offense of attempted possession was constitutionally overbroad, holding that the state statute did not expand the crime of possession of child pornography to images that appeared to depict minors, as the federal statute did. The Defendant also asserted that the crime of attempted possession was overbroad because it criminalized possession involving adults or materials that are not proven to feature an actual child and that an attempt offense would criminalize the behavior of those who are trying to obtain pictures of people who only appear to be minors rather than actual child pornography. The Court ruled that the argument was without merit because a criminal attempt requires that a person have the intent to commit a particular crime. Lastly, regarding the Defendant's second point, the Court found that, based on images and on-line chats, the Defendant's intent was to possess depictions of minors engaged in sexually explicit conduct.

The Court then affirmed the Defendant's conviction of attempted possession of depictions of minors engaged in sexually explicit conduct.

# Case 169

Court of Appeals of Wisconsin.

STATE of Wisconsin, Plaintiff-Respondent,

v.

Jack P. LINDGREN, Defendant-Appellant.

Nos. 03-1868-CR, 03-1869-CR.
Submitted on Briefs February 23, 2004.
Opinion Filed July 21, 2004.

Jurisdiction: Court of Appeals of Wisconsin

Date: July 21, 2004

Keywords: Constitutionality

The Defendant appealed from his conviction for five counts of possession of child pornography. On appeal, he argued that the search warrant allowing the police to search his home lacked probable cause because there was an insufficient nexus between the conduct complained of and the location searched, and, therefore, the evidence discovered and used against him as a result of the illegal search should have been suppressed. He further claimed that the evidence against him was insufficient to support a charge of possession of child pornography.

The Defendant asserted that the affidavit did not demonstrate probable cause for searching his home because all of the conduct complained of occurred at his business. Specifically, he argued that the investigating officer did not present any grounds for believing that a crime was committed at the Defendant's residence. The Court noted that the affidavit stated an expectation that the detectives would find photographic material of underage children of sexually explicit nature and a computer with associated devices for storage and duplication of photographic material. The Court found that the officer had placed a plausible scenario, based on facts and experience, before the court. The officer had alleged that it was reasonable to expect that the perpetrator of this sort of crime would go to great lengths to conceal the objects sought and might have kept a record of the illegal activity on a home computer. Although the Court found that the officer could have presented a more complete foundation for the search of the Defendant's residence, it held that the issuance of the search warrant was a practical, commonsense decision, based on the circumstances set forth in the affidavit. The Defendant then challenged the court's finding that he possessed child pornography. At trial, the

State presented eleven exhibits obtained from the Defendant's computer, specifically five thumbnail images and six corresponding enlarged pictures. The State's computer expert testified that, for the photographs to be stored as they were, the person would have had to go to a Web site and click on the small thumbnail pictures to enlarge the images. Upon clicking to enlarge the image, it would be stored on the hard drive and such an action reflected an attempt to control or manipulate the images. The Court found that, despite the Defendant's attempts to paint himself as the victim of computer viruses and unwanted pop-up ads, there was sufficient evidence in the record to demonstrate that he knowingly possessed the child pornography on his computer. Accordingly, the Court affirmed the Defendant's convictions.

# Case 170

Court of Appeals of Virginia,
Alexandria.

Michael Joseph STATON,
v.
COMMONWEALTH of Virginia.

Record No. 1362-01-4.
August 6, 2002.

Jurisdiction: Court of Appeal, Fifth District, California

Date: August 6, 2002

Keywords: Admissibility

The Defendant was convicted in a jury trial of charges relating to sexual misconduct involving a minor and appealed, arguing that the trial court erred in admitting into evidence references to child pornography found on the his family computer, because the prejudicial effect of the evidence outweighed any probative value. The Court noted that, as a general rule, evidence that shows or tends to show that the accused is guilty of the commission of other crimes and offenses at other times, even though they are of the same nature as the one charged in the indictment, is incompetent and inadmissible for the purpose of showing the commission of the particular crime charged. Furthermore, it was also well established that evidence of other offenses should be excluded if offered merely for the purpose of showing that the accused was likely to commit the crime charged in the indictment. The general rule was subject to certain exceptions, including that the evidence of prior bad acts could be properly be admitted, for certain reasons.

The Commonwealth argued that the existence of child pornography on the Defendant's computer and the Defendant's false statement concerning it are probative of his mental state, his intent to commit the crimes on trial, and his attitude toward the victim. The Court found those arguments to be unpersuasive, because the case involved no genuine issue of intent. The Court concluded that the case turned solely on whether the alleged acts actually occurred. The Court found that the Defendant had never suggested that he committed the alleged acts innocently, accidentally, or without lascivious intent and that he had steadfastly maintained that the acts never occurred. Moreover, the acts alleged themselves bespeak lascivious intent. Consequently, his intent was not an issue on trial and the evidence of child pornography was, in that regard, irrelevant. Because the issue on trial was whether the acts were committed, rather than the Defendant's intent in committing the acts, the Court held that the intent exception did not support introduction of evidence of other crimes. Therefore, the Court concluded that, because his possession of child pornography was collateral and irrelevant to the issues on trial, the trial court should not have permitted the Commonwealth to explore that possession. Lastly, the Court found that the admission denied him a fair trial on the issues. Accordingly, the Court reversed the judgment of the trial court.

# Case 171

Court of Appeals of Texas,
Texarkana.

In the Matter of the ESTATE OF Gene E. STEED, Deceased.

No. 06-03-00115-CV.
Submitted October 13, 2004.
Decided December 17, 2004.

Jurisdiction: Court of Appeals of Texas, Texarkana

Date: December 17, 2004

Keywords: Procedure

At the death of a lawyer, who had prepared his own will several times, competing applications were filed to probate three different wills. The lawyer's sons filed a will, which was the most recent, that they had found on their father's computer. A jury determined that the computer will was never executed. The sons appealed, raising the question of whether there was legally and factually sufficient evidence to support the jury finding that the computer will was not executed. The sons argued that they proved as a matter of law that the will, which was found after their father's death, was executed or that the jury answer finding that it was not executed was made against the great weight and preponderance of the evidence. The will was found on the father's office computer and was labeled as a final draft of his will, though no signed copy was ever produced. The jury had found that the father had not executed an instrument that purported be his last will and testament on the particular date in question of the computer will.

The Court first looked to see whether there was any evidence to support the jury finding that no will was executed by the father on that date. The Court noted that it was important to understand that the jury did not answer any questions concerning the validity of the execution of the will. The Court found that the evidence directly supporting the jury finding that the father had not executed the will was that the will produced to the jury was not executed. There was also evidence that the sons took the computer hard drives from the office and that the drives were not recovered until several months later. A document examiner, who admittedly was not an expert in the computer field, testified that, in her opinion, the will was not reliable because it was computer generated and the dates shown for the creation of the will could be easily changed. She did not, however, examine the computer for a determination of whether such a date change had in fact occurred. Therefore, the Court found some evidence existed to support the jury finding. The Court then reviewed whether the evidence of no execution was factually sufficient to support the verdict. The sons relied on the testimony of two subscribing witnesses and a notary public to establish that the will was executed by their father. They all corroborated that they witnessed the father execute a will on the day in question, though only one of them had read its contents and could identify it as the will in question, and his veracity was questionable. A computer specialist from the police department, however, testified that it would be very simple to detect if a computer date had been manipulated and that he had found no such manipulation. In light of the testimony and evidence proffered, the Court concluded that the jury answer was not factually supported by the evidence and that the finding was so against the great weight and preponderance of the evidence as to be clearly wrong and unjust. Accordingly, the Court reversed the judgment of the district court and remanded the case for a new trial consistent with the opinion.

## Case 172

United States District Court,
D. Kansas.

SUPER FILM OF AMERICA, INC., Plaintiff,

v.

UCB FILMS, INC., Defendant,

v.

Super Film Sanayi Ve Ticaret A.S., Counterclaim-Defendant.

No. 02-4146-SAC.
February 9, 2004.

Jurisdiction: United States District Court, District of Kansas

Date: February 9, 2004

Keywords: Discovery

In a case regarding breach of contract for the sale of goods, the Defendant filed a motion to compel discovery responses from the Plaintiff, including documents and electronic versions of various documents within the Plaintiff's possession and control. The Plaintiff opposed the motion on the grounds that it had produced all of the documents that it could or would be required to produce.

The Plaintiff asserted that it had produced all of the requested documents and that it had nothing further in its possession, custody, or control which was responsive to the requests. The Court found that the documents in question appeared, at least at one point, to have been in the possession of the Plaintiff. The Court then held that some of the documents that had been identified in the Defendant's motion to compel were relevant to the claims and defenses and, therefore, had to be produced by the Plaintiff. To the extent that the documents in question were no longer in the Plaintiff's possession, the Court directed the Plaintiff to explain to the Defendant in detail and in writing, the disposition of those documents.

The Defendant next argued that the Court should order the production of documents from the Plaintiff that were in the possession of a third party. The Plaintiff opposed such production, claiming that it did not have the control over the documents that was required by statute and, therefore, could not be compelled to produce them. The Court found that the Defendant had sufficiently demonstrated a commonality of interest between the Plaintiff and the third party to impute the control necessary to compel production of additional documents. Accordingly, the Court ordered the third party to produce certain documents in question that may not have been in the possession of the Plaintiff but were under the control of the third party. Lastly, despite the Plaintiff and third party's objections that the third party was incapable of producing electronic discovery responses, the Court held that the third party had to produce electronic versions of documents requested by the Defendant.

## Case 173

United States District Court,
E.D. Pennsylvania.

SYNTHES SPINE COMPANY, L.P., Plaintiff,

v.

Robert WALDEN et al., Defendants.

No. CIV.A. 04-CV-4140.
December 21, 2005.

Jurisdiction: United States District Court, Eastern District of Pennsylvania

Date: December 21, 2005

Keywords: Discovery, Experts, Procedure

The Defendants filed a motion to compel discovery and require disclosure. The Plaintiff cross-motioned for a limited protective order. The Defendants sought production of all information, regardless of its privileged status, "considered" by the Plaintiff's damages expert in developing his conclusion. The Plaintiff agreed to produce various categories of documents but refused to produce the expert's notes from a meeting with Plaintiff and Plaintiff's counsel; the content of a conversation between the expert, the Plaintiff, and Plaintiff's counsel; and unredacted versions of documents reviewed by the expert, *including e-mails, summary spreadsheets, sales charts, and time analysis.* The Plaintiff contended that this information is protected from disclosure by work product privilege and/or the attorney-client privilege.

The Court required the disclosure of all information, including privileged information, that a testifying expert used in connection with fashioning his opinions, even if the testifying expert rejected the information. The Court found that the Plaintiff had to disclose all materials that the Plaintiff's expert generated, reviewed, reflected upon, read, and/or used in connection with the formulation of his opinions, even if the testifying expert ultimately rejected the information. The Court further found that the Plaintiff had to produce the notes the expert created in his role as testifying expert at the meeting with the Plaintiff and Plaintiff's counsel, regardless of whether the notes contained information that falls under the protection of work product privilege or attorney-client privilege. But, the Court held that the Defendants were not entitled to notes regarding conversations unrelated to the instant case. The Court also held that the Defendants were not entitled to notes that had no relation to the expert's role as a testifying expert on the issue of damages. Following the above reasoning, the Court held that the Plaintiff's expert had to disclose the content of all oral communications the expert considered in preparing his opinion as a testifying expert in the case, regardless of whether the communication came from the Plaintiff or the Plaintiff's counsel. The Court granted some of the Plaintiff's limited protective order. The protective order prohibited disclosure to nonparties of the produced documents, prohibited attendance by nonparties at the expert's deposition, and prohibits the Defendant from asking the Plaintiff's expert questions about the content of conversations between the Plaintiff and Plaintiff's counsel that the expert did not consider in formulating his opinions concerning damages in the case.

# Case 174

United States District Court,
E.D. Texas, Marshall Division.

TANTIVY COMMUNICATIONS, INC., Plaintiff,

v.

LUCENT TECHNOLOGIES INC., Defendant.

No. Civ.A.2:04CV79 (TJW).
November 1, 2005.

Jurisdiction: United States District Court, Eastern District of Texas,
Marshall Division

Date: November 1, 2005

Keywords: Discovery, Sanctions, Spoliation

In a patent infringement suit, the Plaintiff brought a motion to exclude based on alleged discovery abuses by the Defendant. Specifically, the Plaintiff claimed the Defendant withheld interoperability testing data and documents, misrepresented the existence of interoperability testing data and documents, allowed the destruction of documents, and produced documents for the first time in a report that the Defendant never provided to the Plaintiff. During discovery, the Plaintiff requested all documents relating to the alleged infringing product located on or available for download from any Web site, including customer Web sites. The Plaintiff also requested documents related to interoperability testing of the alleged infringing product. Also, a discovery order from the Court required the Defendant to produce all documents, data compilations, and tangible things in the Defendant's possession that were relevant to the claims or defenses of the case. Throughout the discovery process, the Defendant repeatedly ignored requests for interoperability testing or denied the existence of documents related to interoperability testing. The Court found that these interoperability testing documents related directly to the issue of whether the Defendant infringed on a patent of the Plaintiff and were at all times relevant to the case. During a deposition of a representative of the Defendant, the representative admitted that documents related to interoperability existed and that the Defendant had allowed for many of those documents to be destroyed through normal document destruction practices. Also, near the date of the trial, the Defendant produced a report of noninfringement by one of its experts. The report contained four documents heavily relied upon by the expert, but those documents had never been produced during discovery to the Plaintiff. The Court held that the failure by one party to re-tain relevant records during litigation allows for an adverse inference to be drawn against that party. The Court also held that a party involved in litiga-tion must suspend its document destruction policy to ensure that relevant documents are preserved. The Court determined that the Plaintiff had been prejudiced by the Defendant's actions, but to grant a continuance would award the Defendant for ambushing the Plaintiff. The Court decided that it would issue an appropriate remedy after it considered the evidence in the case, the materiality of the information withheld by the Defendant, and the prejudice caused by the late production.

## Case 175

United States District Court,
N.D. Illinois, Eastern Division.

TELEWIZJA POLSKA USA, INC. a Delaware Corporation, Plaintiff,

v.

ECHOSTAR SATELLITE CORPORATION, a Colorado corporation, Defendant.

No. 02 C 3293.
October 15, 2004.

Jurisdiction: United States District Court, Northern District of Illinois, Eastern Division

Date: October 15, 2004

Keywords: Admissibility

In a breach of sales contract dispute, both the Plaintiff and the Defendant filed multiple motions in limine. The Court stated that a motion in limine should be granted only if the evidence clearly is not admissible for any purpose. In one of its motions, the Plaintiff moved to preclude the Defendant from introducing any exhibits that it produced as translations, performed by a company specializing in translation services. The exhibits purported to transcribe e-mails from unidentified individuals to the Plaintiff's officers, in both the original Polish text and English translations. The Plaintiff attacked the admissibility of the exhibits on numerous fronts, the most persuasive being the accuracy of the translations, which the Court held were obviously inaccurate on their face. The exhibits consisted of e-mail communications between two alleged consumers and the Plaintiff's president, who offered both individuals identical responses, which were translated quite differently, although the e-mails were verbatim. The Defendant offered no explanation for the obvious differences between the translations, and the Court held that the differences were significant, because one of the translations strongly supported the Plaintiff's claim. The Plaintiff, however, did not offer a competing translation of the e-mails, though the Defendant had substantially eased the Plaintiff's burden in attacking the accuracy of the Defendant's translations.

The Plaintiff also stated that the inaccurate translations were evidence of sanctionable conduct on the Defendant's part; however, the Court disagreed that the translations alone were sufficient evidence of sanctionable conduct, because there simply was not enough evidence before the Court to sanction the Defendant at the time. Lastly, the Court held that the decision to strike the translations as being inherently unreliable, and therefore excluding them, was better left to the trial judge and denied the Plaintiff's motion. The Plaintiff also sought to bar the Defendant from introducing an exhibit to prove what its Web site looked like after the expiration of the contract period. The Plaintiff claimed that the exhibit constituted double hearsay and, therefore, the Defendant should not be permitted to present it at trial. The Court disagreed, stating that the images and text were not statements and fell outside of the hearsay rule. The Plaintiff then argued that the exhibit had not been properly authenticated. The Court found that the Plaintiff presented no evidence that the Internet Archive that was used to authenticate the exhibit was unreliable or biased. Under the circumstances, the Court stated that the Internet Archive affidavit was sufficient to satisfy the threshold requirement for admissibility. The Plaintiff also asserted that the Internet Archive witness was an undisclosed expert witness and that her affidavit authenticating the exhibits should be barred. The Court rejected the Plaintiff's assertion that she was offering an opinion, expert or otherwise, rejected Plaintiff's argument, denied the Plaintiff's Motion in limine. Lastly, the Plaintiff sought to bar the introduction of a redacted e-mail. The Plaintiff claimed that the document should not be admitted because it had not been authenticated, among other reasons. The Defendant countered that the alleged creator of the e-mail authenticated it by identifying it in his deposition, though he had only acknowledged that the e-mail contained his e-mail address and little more. The Court held that, because he neither recognized the e-mail nor remembered sending it, it had not been authenticated. Accordingly, the Court granted that motion in limine, while it denied the other two.

## Case 176

United States District Court,
N.D. Illinois, Eastern Division.

TEMPCO ELECTRIC HEATER CORPORATION, Plaintiff,

v.

TEMPERATURE ENGINEERING COMPANY, d/b/a Prime Industries, Defendant.

No. 02 C 3572.
June 3, 2004.

Jurisdiction: United States District Court, Northern District of Illinois, Eastern Division

Date: June 3, 2004

Keywords: Computer Forensics, Experts

The Plaintiff brought suit against one of its former distributors, alleging, among other things, misappropriation of trade secrets regarding a pricing database. The Defendant moved for partial summary judgment on the grounds that the Plaintiff had not presented any evidence that the Defendant had ever misused the database. The Plaintiff claimed that the Defendant had used the database to benefit the Plaintiff's competitors, asserting that there existed both direct evidence and a web of circumstantial facts that led to the inference of misuse of the database.

The Court found that the Plaintiff presented no direct evidence but a fair amount of circumstantial evidence, which it could rely on to prove misappropriation. The Court, however, stated that the nonmoving party must present circumstantial evidence of a quantity and quality sufficient to allow a reasonable jury to draw legal inferences that would permit it to find for the nonmoving party by a preponderance of the evidence in consideration both of any direct evidence submitted by the nonmoving party, and also all evidence, both direct and circumstantial, presented by the moving party.

The Defendant responded to the Plaintiff's allegations and evidence by retaining a computer forensic company to inspect its computers and report whether any remnants of the database existed on them. Further, the Defendant noted that, although the Plaintiff could have paid for its own inspection of the computers during discovery, it elected not to do so. The Court found that the test conducted was only a minimalist inspection of the computers, but it found the Defendant's facts and argument to be persuasive and held that the Defendant could have sought and potentially found rebuttal evidence that the database had secretly remained installed. As such the Court held that the Defendant's inspection met the Defendant's initial summary judgment burden of showing an absence of material fact by showing that the database did not exist on the computers. The Court stated that, to rebut, the Plaintiff needed to produce actual evidence that the database remained in the Defendant's possession, rather than producing mere speculation and conjecture through circumstantial facts. Accordingly, the Court granted partial summary judgment for the Defendant.

## Case 177

United States District Court,
D. Maryland.

Carmen THOMPSON et al., Plaintiffs,

v.

UNITED STATES DEPARTMENT OF HOUSING AND URBAN DEVELOPMENT et al.,
Defendants.

No. CIV.A. MJG-95-309.
December 12, 2003.

Jurisdiction: United States District Court, District of Maryland

Date: December 12, 2003

Keywords: Discovery, Sanctions

The Plaintiffs filed a motion in limine to bar the Defendants from calling certain witnesses, based on the Defendants' failure to produce employee e-mails. Originally, the Plaintiffs served a series of Rule 34 document production requests on the Defendants, on several occasions. Despite some confusion by the Defendants regarding whether e-mail records were sought in the requests, the Court had previously ruled that the requests for production clearly sought electronic records, including e-mail. When the Defendants failed fully to produce e-mail records, after the Court ruled that they were discoverable, the Plaintiffs filed a motion seeking sanctions. The Plaintiffs were granted relief in an order ruling that the Defendants could not call as witnesses at trial former or present employees of the Defendants, unless they were able to demonstrate by a preponderance of evidence that there were no e-mail records generated or received by the witness that were responsive to the Plaintiffs' Rule 34 requests or, if such records did exist, that they had been produced to the Plaintiffs by a certain date.

The Plaintiffs asserted that the Defendants were proposing to call witnesses in violation of that order and filed the motion in limine, to prevent those witnesses from testifying. Specifically, the Plaintiffs asked that the Defendants be precluded from calling three particular witnesses. The basis for the requested relief was the failure of the Defendants to produce e-mail records of the witnesses as ordered, as well as the belated production of e-mail records, long after the deadlines identified in the order. Intertwined with the issues was the Plaintiffs' contention that sanctions were appropriate for the unexpected discovery by the Defendants of approximately 80,000 e-mail records responsive to Plaintiffs' Rule 34 requests. The discovery of the records, and therefore their production, was long after the discovery cutoff for fact discovery and long after the deadlines imposed by the order. The court concluded that the Defendants had violated the earlier orders of the court to produce electronic records, and that Rule 37(b) sanctions were justified because the noncompliance by the Defendants was not substantially justified and also was prejudicial to the Plaintiffs. Accordingly, the Court modified the existing Rule 37(b)(2) sanctions by (1) precluding the Defendants from introducing into evidence in their case any of the 80,000 e-mail records that were discovered during the last minute; (2) ordering that counsel for the Defendants were forbidden to use any of these e-mail records to prepare any of their witnesses for testimony at trial, and that at trial, counsel for the Defendants were forbidden from attempting to refresh the recollection of any of their witnesses by using any of the 80,000 undisclosed e-mail records; (3) ordering that the Plaintiffs were permitted to use any of the 80,000 e-mail records during their case and in cross-examining any of the Defendants witnesses, (4) ordering that, if the Plaintiffs incurred any additional expense and attorneys' fees in connection with reviewing the 80,000 records and analyzing them for possible use at trial, this could be recovered from the Defendants upon further motion to the court; and finally (5) ordering that if, at trial, the evidence revealed additional information regarding the nonproduction of the e-mail records to clear up the many uncertainties that existed as of the current resolution of this issue, that the Plaintiffs were free to make a motion to the court that the failure to produce e-mail records as ordered by the Court constituted a contempt of court, under Rule 37(b)(2)(D). Lastly, the Court held that an adverse inference instruction was not appropriate for the simple fact that it was a bench trial and that the judge would be aware of the proceedings and certainly would be able to draw reasonable inferences from the Defendants' failure to preserve and produce e-mail records as ordered.

## Case 178

United States District Court,
S.D. New York.

Natalie TILBERG (a/k/a Tasha Tilberg), Plaintiff,

v.

NEXT MANAGEMENT CO. et al., Defendants.

No. 04CIV7373 (RJH RLE).
October 24, 2005.

Jurisdiction: United States District Court, Southern District of New York

Date: October 24, 2005

Keywords: Discovery, Experts

Discovery in this case involved a forensic search of the Defendants' computer files. The Court ordered the Defendants to make their e-mail servers available to the Plaintiff's forensic specialist. When the forensic specialist went to the Defendants' place of business, he could not access one of the two servers and the system crashed several times. The Plaintiff requested that the Defendants set a new date for the specialist to access the second server, but the Defendants refused.

The Plaintiff requested that the Court order the Defendants to make the second server available. The Plaintiff also requested that the Court allow for expansion of the computer forensic searching by allowing the specialist to search the Defendants' central server for non-e-mail documents and allow the specialist to search the desktop computers of two of the Defendants. The Defendants requested that the Court not allow for further discovery because the discovery deadline had passed and the partial forensic search failed to produce any relevant e-mails. The Court found that the limited scope of the original search was based on erroneous statements by the Defendants indicating that their search had produced no relevant documents. The Court determined that relevant documents did exist on the Defendants' e-mail servers, central server, and individual workstations. The Court held that because the Defendants failed to produce these relevant documents the Plaintiff would be allowed to perform a complete search of the Defendants' computer system. The Court further held that, because the Defendants either inadvertently or deliberately delayed or obstructed discovery in this case, claims that a document was irrelevant do not justify nonproduction of that document.

## Case 179

Court of Appeal, Sixth District, California.

TOSHIBA AMERICA ELECTRONIC COMPONENTS, INC., Petitioner,

v.

The SUPERIOR COURT of Santa Clara County, Respondent;
Lexar Media, Inc., Real Party in Interest.

No. H027029.
December 3, 2004.

Jurisdiction: Court of Appeal, Sixth District, California

Date: December 3, 2004

Keywords: Costs and Cost Shifting

In a case involving alleged misappropriation of trade secrets and unfair competition, the parties disagreed about whether the demanding or responding party should pay the electronic discovery costs. At issue were the Defendant's more than 800 backup tapes, which the Plaintiff wanted to be searched for responsive documents. After consulting an expert, the Defendant had determined that processing all of the tapes would cost several million dollars and that processing just a sample selection would still cost several hundred thousand. The Defendant then asked the Plaintiff to shoulder at least some of the cost, and the Plaintiff refused, proceeding to move to compel production of all responsive documents contained in the tapes. After arguments by both sides, the trial court granted the Plaintiff's motion without comment or explanation, ordering full production at the Defendant's expense.

In addressing the matter, the Court referred to the state statute regarding expenses involved in the production of data compilations. At that point, the only dispute between the parties was whether the phrase "at the reasonable expense of the demanding party" was a mandatory cost-shifting provision or whether it merely permitted the trial court to shift the cost to the demanding party when the responding party objected. After hearing both sides, the Court found that by enacting the state statute, the state legislature had identified the expense of translating data compilations into usable form, as one that should be placed upon the demanding party. The Court then held that the trial court's decision, which was based upon the general rule that the responding party bears that expense, was based upon a faulty legal analysis and was, therefore, an abuse of discretion, because the trial court had never been asked to decide whether and to what extent the reasonable subdivision of expense applied to the production in dispute. The Court pointed out that its conclusion did not mean that the demanding party must always pay all of the costs associated with retrieving usable data from backup tapes; rather that it was clear that the demanding party was expected to pay only its reasonable expense for a necessary translation, which begs purely factual issues that are to be at the discretion of the trial court. Finally, the Court vacated the Plaintiff's earlier motion to compel and permitted further proceedings to determine how the statute applied to the Plaintiff's demand for electronic documents.

## Case 180

United States District Court,
S.D. Indiana, Indianapolis Division.

Justin TRACY, Plaintiff,

v.

FINANCIAL INSURANCE MANAGEMENT CORPORATION, Defendant.

No. 1:04-CV-00619-TABDFH.
August 22, 2005.

Jurisdiction: United States District Court, Southern District of Indiana, Indianapolis Division

Date: August 22, 2005

Keywords: Discovery, Procedure, Sanctions

In an employment suit, the Plaintiff moved for sanctions against the Defendant for violations of the discovery process. Specifically, the Plaintiff contended that the Defendant hindered and prejudiced the discovery process when it produced requested e-mails extremely late in the discovery process and after depositions of key witnesses had concluded.

In the discovery request at issue, the Plaintiff requested "all e-mails written by or about Plaintiff." The parties did engage in ongoing discussions regarding the Defendant's production, resulting in several supplemental responses by the Defendant. In February 2004, the Defendant informed the Plaintiff that it had no additional responsive e-mails. In April 2004, however, on the last day the Plaintiff was conducting intrastate depositions, the Defendant supplemented its responses again and produced additional responsive e-mails. The Defendant claims that, because of a physical upgrade to its computer systems subsequent to the Plaintiff's termination, discovery of e-mails and other electronic data stored on its computers was delayed until April 2004. The Defendant claims this delay was inadvertent and an unforeseen consequence of upgrades to its computer systems. The Defendant argued that the Plaintiff was not prejudiced by this late production. The Plaintiff argued that it was prejudiced when it relied on the February 2004 statements of the Defendant claiming that all responsive e-mails had been produced. The Plaintiff also argued that the Defendant did not demonstrate a substantial justification for the late production and therefore a sanction was appropriate. The Court found no evidence that the Defendant failed to retain and preserve electronic data; however, the Court did find that the tardiness of the production of the e-mails in April 2004 was not substantially justified. The Court looked at the fact that the Defendant was aware of the physical upgrades to its computer system and should have been aware that possible responsive electronic data existed somewhere other than the new computer system. The Defendant was aware of all of this in February 2004 when it led the Plaintiff to believe that all responsive electronic data had been produced. The Court found that the Defendant's actions warranted some amount of sanction. The Court denied the Plaintiff's motion to order further investigation by the Plaintiff for missing electronic data. The Court granted the Plaintiff's motion seeking an opportunity to redepose the Defendant's witnesses which were the subjects of the intrastate deposition. The Court ordered the Defendant to pay all costs associated with telephonic depositions of these witnesses. The Court also ordered that costs of any in-person depositions of these witnesses should be divided equally between the Plaintiff and Defendant.

## Case 181

United States District Court,
D. Oregon.

Dawn TRAVERS, Plaintiff,

v.

MCKINSTRY COMPANY, a Washington corporation; et al., Defendants.

No. Civ.01-1206-JO.
November 16, 2001.

Jurisdiction: United States District Court, District of Oregon

Date: November 16, 2001

Keywords: Electronic Evidence Protocols, Procedure, Preservation of Evidence/Spoliationo

The Court issued the following order in response to the Defendants' expedited motion to compel and preserve evidence. "The Defendants shall select a computer forensics expert and inform the Court and the Plaintiff of the identity of the chosen expert within ten days of this order. Assuming there are no objections to the selected expert, the expert and assistants he or she designates shall sign an appropriate protective order and be appointed as officers of the Court. From that time forward, all communications between the designated expert and the Defendant shall take place either in the presence of the Plaintiff, or if by written or electronic communication, with copies sent to the Plaintiff. The Plaintiff shall produce her home computer(s) to the designated expert, who will create a forensic copy of the hard drive on the computer(s) produced. The expert will then provide the recovered information to the Court for in camera review. After its review, the Court will provide copies of any and all discoverable information to all parties, and all remaining information will be returned to the Plaintiff. Discovery will be limited to information relevant to the Defendants' counterclaims, relating to the Plaintiff's alleged improper use of the Defendants' confidential information, and the Defendants' request for information regarding the Plaintiff's personal Internet activities, relating to her claims for sexual harassment and battery, is denied."

## Case 182

United States District Court,
E.D. Virginia, Richmond Division.

TRIGON INSURANCE COMPANY (Formerly Blue Cross and
Blue Shield of Virginia), Plaintiff,

v.

UNITED STATES of America, Defendant.

No. CIV. 3:00CV365.
December 17, 2002.

Jurisdiction: United States District Court, Eastern District of Virginia, Richmond Division

Date: December 17, 2002

Keywords: Costs and Cost Shifting, Sanctions

The Plaintiff had petitioned for attorneys' fees and costs that had arisen as a consequence of the spoliation of evidence by the United States that was heard in an earlier opinion. The Court had concluded that remedies, including the requested attorneys' fees and costs, were appropriate for the offense of spoliation. The Plaintiff sought $179,725.70 for expenses and fees incurred in its efforts to discern the scope, magnitude, and direction of the spoliation of evidence, to participate in the recovery process, and to follow up with depositions to help prepare its own case and to meet the defense of the United States.

The United States opposed the award sought for several reasons. First, the United States opposed an award of any fees incurred before the date upon which the Plaintiff filed its motion seeking a declaration of spoliation and a remedy therefore. Although the United States was correct that the remedy chosen was largely as compensation for fees and expenses incurred as a consequence of the spoliation, the Court held that that did not foreclose a claim for the fees and expenses associated with documenting the spoliation and seeking judicial redress therefrom, which was quite modest. The United States then argued that the record did not permit an accurate analysis of the fees and expenses incurred, but the Court disagreed, finding that the claimed expenses and fees were lower than one would have expected, in light of the extent of the spoliation, the nature of the recovery effort, and the necessary follow-up discovery. Third, the United States protested that the claim for fees and costs was excessive, which the Court rejected as without merit. Lastly, the United States argued that recovery of postmotion fees should not be permitted because the Plaintiff had not made extensive use at trial of the expert reports that had been billed. The Court held that it was not essential that the recovered evidence be used at trial. The value of having disclosed the spoliation and having recovered some of that evidence transcended the use of the evidence to cross-examine the experts at trial. The Court then affirmed the award of fees and expenses for $179,725.70.

## Case 183

United States District Court,
E.D. Texas, Texarkana Division.

In re: TRITON ENERGY LIMITED SECURITIES LITIGATION

No. 5:98CV256.
March 7, 2002.

Jurisdiction: United States District Court, Eastern District of Texas, Texarkana Division

Date: March 7, 2002

Keywords: Spoliation, Privilege, Costs and Cost Shifting, Computer Forensics, Experts, Preservation of Evidence/Spoliation

During securities litigation, the Plaintiffs filed a motion for a log of withheld documents and for certification of preservation and retention of documents and production of the Defendants' computer storage systems. The Plaintiffs filed their motion, complaining that documents that bore significantly on the lawsuit had just recently been produced as opposed to when disclosures were made initially. Specifically, the Plaintiffs asserted that recent events discovered in the deposition phase of the case raised a serious concern that documents had been destroyed in violation of the Court's previous document preservation order, in addition to the local rules. As an example of this concern, the Plaintiffs stated that the Defendants failed to include in their initial disclosures basic information and correspondence that supported the Plaintiffs' allegations that a pipeline transaction was not a sale, but rather an off-balance sheet transaction virtually identical to the transactions used by Enron to hide debt, mislead shareholders, and falsely inflate the Defendants' earnings. The Plaintiffs further asserted they did not receive the documents until six months after the Defendants' initial disclosures were due. In addition, the Plaintiffs asserted that the Defendants only produced the documents after the Plaintiffs specifically demanded them and threatened to file a motion to compel.

In light of the evidence, the Court ordered that the Defendants produce a log of all documents withheld by a claim of privilege, including a description of the documents and electronic data, as well as the reason why it was being withheld. The Court also ordered the Defendants to produce any additional document that bore significantly on the claims and defenses of the lawsuit to continue to supplement their production. The Court placed upon the Defendants the burden of paying the costs for any additional deposition that the Plaintiffs might need to take because they did not have the documents timely. Lastly, the Court ordered that the parties meet, confer, and submit to the Court mutually agreeable names of an outside forensic computer specialist. At that time the Court would appoint a computer specialist to retrieve information from the Defendants' computer storage systems, including servers and hard drives. The computer specialist would conduct nondestructive testing of these systems to determine what documents and e-mails, if any, had been deleted. Accordingly, the Court granted the Plaintiffs' motion in part.

# Case 184

United States Court of Appeals,
Fourth Circuit.

Notra TRULOCK, III; Linda Conrad, Plaintiffs-Appellants,

v.

Louis J. FREEH, in his personal capacity; Neil Gallagher, in his personal capacity; Steve Dillard, in his personal capacity; Brian Halpin, in his personal capacity; Steven Carr, in his personal capacity; Jane Doe, I, in her personal capacity, Defendants-Appellees.

No. 00-2260.
Argued May 7, 2001.
Decided December 28, 2001.

Jurisdiction: United States Court of Appeals, Fourth Circuit

Date: December 28, 2001

Keywords: Constitutionality

The Plaintiffs, former government officials, filed a Bivens suit alleging that their constitutional rights had been violated during a law enforcement interview and later during a search of their home and computer. Prior to discovery, the Defendants, also government officials, had moved to dismiss the complaint, arguing that it failed to state a constitutional violation either for unlawful search and seizure or for retaliation. Each Defendant also argued that he was entitled to qualified immunity on both counts. The district court granted the Defendants' motion to dismiss, holding that the Defendants, having violated no clearly established law, were entitled to qualified immunity. On appeal, the Court was required to determine whether the Plaintiffs' complaint had alleged sufficient facts to proceed to discovery.

The Plaintiffs argued that the search of the password-protected files violated their Fourth Amendment rights. They asserted that the search was improper because, there had been no warrant, no voluntary consent to the search, and no authority to consent to a search of the files regardless. The Court concluded that the consent to search had been involuntary, and that even if it had been voluntary, it would not have authorized a search of the private, password-protected files, because the Defendants had not had the authority to consent because of the password protecting of personal files and therefore limited access to them. Nevertheless, the Court found that the Defendants were entitled to immunity because a reasonable officer in their position would not have known that the search would violate clearly established law. Therefore, the Court agreed that the Fourth Amendment claims, alleging an illegal interrogation and search of a townhouse and a computer, had been properly dismissed, primarily on the basis of qualified immunity.

# Case 185

United States District Court,
D. Massachusetts.

UNITED STATES of America, Plaintiff,

v.

Christopher ALBERT, Defendant.

No. CR.A. 01-40001-NMG.
January 18, 2002.

Jurisdiction: United States District Court, District of Massachusetts

Date: January 18, 2002

Keywords: Experts

The Defendant was indicted for possession and distribution of child pornography, as well as criminal forfeiture. Among other motions, the Defendant filed an ex parte motion for funds for employment of a forensic computer expert. The Defendant sought $15,000 for the employment of a computer forensics expert, to undertake a complete defensive assessment and analysis of the alleged contents of any and all computer disks, computer hard drives, and computer files seized by the Government. The Defendant was indigent and asserted that such analysis was necessary in order to prepare an adequate defense.

The Court noted that an attorney for an indigent defendant may request expert services in an ex parte application, and payment may be authorized by the Court in an amount not to exceed $1,000. The Defendant bears the burden of demonstrating the necessity of expert services for an adequate defense. The Court found that the Defendant had met this burden, because he was indigent and unable to afford the services of an expert, as evidenced by the court's appointment of counsel, and because his defense of the case depended largely on the analysis of the evidence contained on the Defendant's computer and computer equipment. While the Court held that funds in excess of $1,000 were warranted, because no sufficient showing had been made to justify the full $15,000 requested, the Court authorized $5,000.

## Case 186

United States District Court,
N.D. Illinois.

UNITED STATES of America, State of Illinois, ex rel., and Cleveland Tyson,
Plaintiffs,

v.

AMERIGROUP ILLINOIS, INC., and Magistrate Judge Cole Amerigroup
Corporation, Defendants.

No. 02 C 6074.
October 21, 2005.

Jurisdiction: United States District Court, Northern District of Illinois

Date: October 21, 2005

Keywords: Discovery

This qui tam suit was filed under the False Claims Act and Illinois Whistle-blower Reward and Protection Act. These cases were brought by a relator try-ing to redress fraud upon the government. If the claim was proven, the relator receive a percentage of the recovery. The Defendants served a subpoena on the Illinois Department of Healthcare and Family Services ("HFS") asking for production of e-mails of three named HFS employees. HFS moved to quash the subpoena served on it by the Defendants on the ground that compliance with the subpoena would be unduly burdensome, especially since HFS was not a party to the case.

As the party objecting to the document request, HFS must show by af-firmative and compelling proof that the burden of producing the one year's worth of e-mails was undue. The Court found that HFS provided such evi-dence through the affidavit of a testimonially competent HFS employee. The employee was the chief of HFS's bureau of information systems and was fa-miliar with HFS's e-mail system, as well as the procedure for backing up e-mail files and restoring old files. The employee testified that a review of one year's worth of employee e-mails would take approximately six weeks, during which time backup tapes would be used to restore the e-mail data from the past year. The Court found that cases have supported the notion that restor-ing e-mails through the use of backup tape is a "unique burden." The Court found that the backup tapes were stored off-site and were therefore more dif-ficult to access. The Defendants did not cite a single case in which a nonparty was subjected to the significant burden of restoring electronic data from backup tapes. The Court also held that "nonparty status" is a significant factor to be considered in determining whether the burden imposed by a subpoena is undue. The Court held that the burden on HFS to produce the requested e-mails was substantial and undue and precluded production. The Court quashed the subpoena.

## Case 187

United States District Court,
D. Nebraska.

UNITED STATES of America, Plaintiff,

v.

Thomas Edward BAILEY, Defendant.

No. 4:02CR3040.
May 12, 2005.

Jurisdiction: United States District Court, District of Nebraska

Date: May 12, 2005

Keywords: Experts

During the Defendant's sentencing for convictions of charges related to the possession of child pornography, the Defendant asked the Court to impose a nonprison sentence, to assists the Defendant's young daughter recover from previous sexual abuses. The Defendant came to the attention of the FBI during the course of a child pornography investigation. Following the execution of a search warrant, subscriber lists to various e-groups were obtained, and the Defendant's name was found. Thereafter, the FBI served a search warrant at the offices of his employer. Located on the Defendant's work computer were about forty pictures of child pornography that the Defendant obtained through the e-groups. Accordingly, he was charged with possession of child pornography, to which he ultimately pled guilty. The government advised the probation officer that the case was unique, as compared to other cases involving the possession of child pornography. Although he had obtained the pictures by accessing the e-group several times, he had not permanently stored them; they remained only in the temporary Internet cache in his computer. Therefore, it was determined that the Defendant did not take steps that had been normally associated with possessing child pornography for the purpose of keeping it for long periods of time, which distinguished his case from many others. The Defendant also provided a detailed report from a computer expert who concluded that the majority of the images charged in the Defendant's indictment were temporary Internet files and thus not downloaded to the his computer by his conscious choice but rather, by the default settings in his operating system. One of the files was of a woman of legal age, and the remaining three found in the recycle bin appeared to have actually been downloaded but were immediately deleted into the recycle bin.

In regard to the Defendant's sentence, the Court heard evidence of the Defendant's daughter, who had been sexually abused on multiple occasions, while staying with the Defendant's ex-wife. The Court found that the one person in the daughter's life that she consistently expressed trust in was the Defendant. A highly regarded forensic psychologist and expert in children and sex abuse created a report detailing the impact on this nine-year-old girl of sending her father to prison. The expert concluded that he had significant concern for the girl should she be separated from her father because the child suffered from many symptoms and the Defendant was critical to her continued recovery.

Applying the foregoing to the facts of this case, the Court found that the Defendant's presence was critical to the child's continued recovery and that the defendant's presence could not reasonably be duplicated by using other providers. Therefore, the Court granted the Defendant's motion for departure in part, holding that an eight-level departure to offense level 8, criminal history category I, providing for a probationary sentence, was reasonable, despite the Defendant's conviction.

## Case 188

United States District Court,
W.D. Texas, Midland/Odessa Division.

UNITED STATES of America, Plaintiff,

v.

Michael J. BARTH, Defendant.

No. MO-98-CR-33.
September 21, 1998.

Jurisdiction: United States District Court, Western District of Texas

Date: September 21, 1998

Keywords: Constitutionality

In a case involving child pornography, the Defendant filed a motion to suppress evidence. The Defendant argued that the searches of the contents of his hard drive and of his office violated his right to be free of unreasonable searches and seizures. The Court found that the computer technician's (an FBI informant) initial discovery of an image of child pornography did not violate the Fourth Amendment, because he was not a government actor and because there was no evidence that he intended to assist law enforcement officers when he initially viewed the image. The Court found the technician's subsequent viewing of other files more troublesome, because he was no longer opening private files in an effort to repair the machine but did so for the purpose of assisting law enforcement officials. The Court also held that the Defendant did have a reasonable expectation of privacy in his computer hard drive. The Court then found that the police officers' viewing and copying of the hard drive's entire contents exceeded the scope of the technician's initial searches. Furthermore, the Court concluded that the police could not have reasonably believed that the technician had apparent authority to consent to a search of the hard drive. The Court held that, because no exceptions applied to the case, the warrantless viewing and copying of the hard drive violated the Defendant's Fourth Amendment rights.

The Court went on to find that the federal warrant to search the office was based on the evidence discovered on the hard drive and, therefore, the independent source doctrine did not apply to the warrant or the evidence obtained during that search. The Court also held that the inevitable discovery doctrine did not apply because the Government had not shown an independent investigative channel that would have yielded the evidence. Because the

Defendant was informed that a search warrant had already issued, the Court concluded that the Defendant was aware that his right to refuse consent was meaningless, thereby his consent to search meaningless. The Court held that, considering the temporal proximity, intervening circumstances, and purpose and flagrancy of the official actions, the taint of the prior Fourth Amendment violations had not dissipated at the time the Defendant made his oral and recorded statements and, therefore, should be suppressed. As such, Defendant's oral and written statements should be suppressed. Lastly, the Court concluded that the good faith exception did not apply to the case. The Court held that, under the circumstances, all evidence seized from the search of the Defendant's computer hard drive and from the search of his office was to be suppressed and that the Defendant's motion to suppress in regard to each search and seizure was therefore granted.

## Case 189

United States Court of Appeals,
Tenth Circuit.

UNITED STATES of America, Plaintiff-Appellee,

v.

Brian BASS, Defendant-Appellant.

No. 04-6049.
June 29, 2005.

Jurisdiction: United States Court of Appeals, Tenth Circuit

Date: June 29, 2005

Keywords: Procedure

The Defendant appealed his conviction of five counts of knowing possession of child pornography, arguing that there had been insufficient evidence to support the convictions, and that the indictment had been deficient.

For the first issue, the Court needed to determine whether there had been sufficient evidence presented for the jury to have concluded beyond a reasonable doubt that the Defendant had knowingly possessed the pornographic images that had been found on the computer hard drive. The Defendant claimed that the case also begged the question of whether an individual could be found guilty of knowing possession of child pornography, for viewing such images over the Internet, while ignorant of the fact that the images are automatically stored on the computer. The Court found, however, that the jury reasonably could have inferred that the Defendant knew that the child pornography was automatically saved to the computer, based on the evidence that he had attempted to remove the images by using two different software programs. In light of such evidence, the Court held that there had been sufficient evidence of knowing possession of child pornography.

The Defendant also argued that several counts of his indictment had been deficient because they had identified images as .bmp files rather than .jpeg files, as they had existed on the computer. Using a practical analysis, the Court ruled that the indictment had been sufficient to put the Defendant on notice of the charges against him. The Court then upheld the Defendant's convictions.

# Case 190

United States Court of Appeals,
Eighth Circuit.

UNITED STATES of America, Plaintiff-Appellee,

v.

Jason Albert BECHT, Defendant-Appellant.

No. 00-3690.
Submitted: August 21, 2001.
Filed: October 3, 2001.

Jurisdiction: United States Court of Appeals, Eighth Circuit

Date: October 3, 2001

Keywords: Procedure

The Defendant appealed his conviction for knowingly possessing and disseminating, through interstate commerce, child pornography. The Defendant argued that the Government offered insufficient evidence for the jury to find him guilty beyond a reasonable doubt. The Defendant had conceded that the only element at issue was his knowledge that his Web site contained child pornography and not whether the images constituted child pornography or whether they had been transported through interstate commerce.

The Government offered thirty-nine images, of the hundreds found, to prove the Defendant's actual knowledge or deliberate ignorance. The images were supported by expert testimony that the proprietor of a pornographic Web site likely would have accessed his Web site to assess its appearance and functionality. The Government also showed that the most cursory check of the Young subdirectory would have revealed child pornography. In addition, the Government offered evidence that child pornography had been successfully sorted by hand into the Young subdirectory. As part of its proof in that respect, the Government asked the jurors to infer that the Defendant must have seen the images in the course of this sorting process. The Government also asked the jurors, to infer from the appearance of the images, that the Defendant would have known that the images were child pornography, as they involved children as young as four. Ultimately the Court found no prejudicial grounds for error and therefore affirmed the Defendant's conviction.

## Case 191

UNITED STATES OF AMERICA, Appellant,

v.

BRADFORD C. COUNCILMAN, Defendant, Appellee.

No. 03-1383
United States Court of Appeals, First Circuit.
August 11, 2005

Jurisdiction: United States Court of Appeals, First Circuit

Date: August 11, 2005

Keywords: Spyware, Constitutionality

During an en banc hearing, the issue in the case was whether the interception of an e-mail message in temporary, transient electronic storage constituted an offense under the Wiretap Act, as amended by the Electronic Communications Privacy Act of 1986. The Court noted that the Act made it an offense to intentionally intercept, endeavor to intercept, or procure any other person to intercept or endeavor to intercept, any wire, oral, or electronic communication. The two terms at issue were "electronic communication" and "intercept." The Defendant alleged that the e-mail messages that he obtained were not electronic communications when his modified software program copied them, and moreover, the method by which they were copied was not an interception under the Act. While the Government argued that the term electronic communication should be understood as it was defined in the statute, the Defendant asserted that Congress intended to exclude any communication that was in electronic storage, even if momentarily. The Court found that the statute's text did not clearly state whether a communication was still an electronic communication within the scope of the Act, when it was in electronic storage during transmission. On the basis of the legislative history, the Court concluded that the term "electronic communication" included transient electronic storage that was intrinsic to the communication process for such communications and rejected the Defendant's proposed distinction between in transit and in storage. In regard to the issue of interception, the Court stated that the Defendant's argument relied on his definition of electronic communication, which they had just rejected. Therefore, the Court concluded that the Defendant's interpretation of the Act was inconsistent with Congress' intent.

The Defendant then argued that the acquisition of electronic communications in temporary electronic storage was regulated by the Stored Communications Act and not the Wiretap Act, which he was charged under. From this he inferred that such acquisition was not regulated by the Wiretap Act, or that, at a minimum, the potential overlap implicated the rule of lenity or other doctrines of fair warning. He argued that he could be exempted from the SCA, so the same conduct should also be exempted from the other statute. The Court found the argument unpersuasive, because if two statutes cover the same conduct, the Government may charge a violation of either and because the exceptions from the SCA, by their terms, did not apply to the Act. Next, the Defendant argued that the acts were sufficiently confusing that principles of fair warning required the dismissal of the indictment. However, the Court found that, although the statute contained some textual ambiguity, it was not grievous and, because the Court had construed the text using traditional tools of construction, lenity was inapplicable. The Court also held that the Wiretap Act was not unconstitutionally vague in its application in the case, because, from the text, a person of average intelligence would, at the very least, be on notice that, unless explicitly provided otherwise, electronic communications could not be intercepted. In addition, the Court noted that the Act put service providers on notice of both the prohibited conduct and the narrow provider exception. Therefore, notice was considered adequate. Lastly, the Court concluded that its interpretation was not a novel construction beyond prior fairly disclosed scope. Accordingly, the Court held that the district court erred in dismissing the indictment and vacated the judgment, remanding for further proceedings consistent with the opinion.

## Case 192

United States Court of Appeals,
Tenth Circuit.

UNITED STATES of America, Plaintiff-Appellee,
v.
Brent Ray BROOKS, Defendant-Appellant.

No. 04-4255.
October 26, 2005.

Jurisdiction: United States Court of Appeals, Tenth Circuit.

Date: October 26, 2005

Keywords: Constitutionality, Computer Forensics, Admissibility

The Defendant moved to suppress images of child pornography found during an officer's manual search of the Defendant's computer and the police laboratory's forensic search of Defendant's computers, compact disks and diskettes. The district court denied these motions. The Defendant appealed the denial of his motion to suppress evidence. Law enforcement officers obtained and executed a search warrant to search the Defendant's home, including computer equipment, for child pornography. One officer requested consent from the Defendant to use a "pre-search" disk on the Defendant's computer to search for image files. The Defendant signed a search consent form stating that the Defendant authorized a "complete search" including a "pre-search for child pornography" of his computer; had been advised of his right to refuse consent; gave consent voluntarily; and authorized agents to take any items they determined were related to their investigation. The "pre-search" disk did not function correctly on the computer, so the officer did a manual search of the computer's image files. The officer found several images of adolescent boys engaged in sexual activity. After the officers viewed the images, they seized the computer. They subsequently obtained a third warrant authorizing a search of three computers, twelve compact disks, and seven diskettes at the Defendant's residence. This forensic search was carried out at a police laboratory.

The Defendant argued that officers exceeded their scope of consent when they searched his computer by means other than those explained to him in the course of obtaining written consent and the warrant for the computer search was not adequately specific. The Court found that the Defendant understood the officer was going to search the computer for pornographic images and voluntarily consented to the search. The Court found that the officer's manual search on the computer was the functional equivalent of running the "pre-search disk." The Court determined that the Defendant was unable to supply a reason why the officer's manual search process exceeded the permission granted. The Court held that the search did not exceed an objectively reasonable interpretation of the Defendant's consent. The Court also held that the government is not required to describe its specific search methodology to satisfy the particularity requirement of the Fourth Amendment.

## Case 193

United States Court of Appeals,
Seventh Circuit.

UNITED STATES of America, Plaintiff-Appellee,

v.

William CONEY, Defendant-Appellant.

No. 02-3361.
Argued February 25, 2005.
Decided May 11, 2005.

Jurisdiction: United States Court of Appeals, Seventh Circuit

Date: May 11, 2005

Keywords: Admissibility

The Defendant, who was convicted of federal drug offenses, appealed his conviction, challenging the admissibility of tapes made pursuant to a wiretap intercept order. The Court stated that, as laid out in the Wiretap Act, the contents of an intercept shall if possible be recorded, and immediately upon the expiration of the period covered by the intercept order, such recordings shall be made available to the judge issuing such order and sealed under his direction. The presence of the seal or a satisfactory explanation for the absence thereof shall be a prerequisite for the use or disclosure of the contents of the intercept. The Court noted that the purpose of the provisions was to prevent the Government from editing or otherwise tampering with the recordings.

In the case, the intercept order in question had expired and the tapes made pursuant to it were not submitted to the chief judge and sealed until ten days later. The Government pointed out that only five days of the ten-day period were business days, but the Court immediately found that irrelevant, because the prosecutors had access to their offices even when the building in which their offices were located was closed. During the ten days, the tapes were sitting in an evidence bag, readily accessible to anyone in the office in which the bag was stored. The bag was closed, but it was not locked or sealed, or in a safe or, so far as appeared, in any other locked container. The Court held that ten days was too long to be thought of as immediate and that the term "immediately" meant that the tapes should be sealed either as soon as practical after the surveillance ended or as soon as practical after the final extension order expired. Therefore, the tapes were admissible only if the Government provided a satisfactory explanation for the delay in submitting the tapes to the chief judge for sealing. The Defendant argued that an explanation for a delay in sealing that did not establish a good reason for the delay that instead revealed carelessness could never be deemed satisfactory. The Court found that, although such a rule would increase due diligence, it would be too strict. The Court held that an explanation is satisfactory if, in the circumstances, it dispels any reasonable suspicion of tampering. The believability of the explanation is critical, and depends in part simply on its plausibility: the more plausible, the more believable. The length of the delay is relevant as well, and also the nature of the crime, including its notoriety or the notoriety of the defendant, and thus the pressure on the government to obtain a conviction; and also the importance of the tapes to the government's case. The Court concluded that the explanation offered for the lapse was satisfactory and so the district judge was correct to deny the motion to suppress.

## Case 194

United States Court of Appeals,
First Circuit.

UNITED STATES of America, Appellant,

v.

Bradford C. COUNCILMAN, Defendant, Appellee.

No. 03-1383.
Heard December 8, 2004.
Decided August 11, 2005.

Jurisdiction: United States Court of Appeals, First Circuit.

Date: August 11, 2005

Keywords: Computer Forensics, Procedure

In a case alleging conspiracy to violate the Wiretap Act, the Defendant moved to dismiss the indictment, arguing that the interception of e-mails in temporary electronic storage is not covered by the Wiretap Act. The Court reviewed the case de novo, assuming the truth of the facts as alleged in the indictment. The Defendant was Vice President at an on-line rare and out-of-print book listing service, which also acted as an e-mail provider for customers. The Defendant managed the e-mail service and customer subscriptions. The Defendant directed employees to intercept and copy all incoming e-mails to subscribers from Amazon.com. Before delivering any message from Amazon.com to a recipient's electronic mailbox, a copy of the message was made and placed in the Defendant's mailbox. This copying and delivery occurred within the Defendant's company's computer, either in the random access memory or in hard disks.

The Defendant argued that the e-mail messages were not "electronic communications" when they were copied and sent to his mailbox, because the messages were not traveling between computers but rather were in the electronic storage of a computer when the message was copied and delivered to the Defendant's mailbox. The Court found that the text of the Wiretap Act, as amended, is not clear on whether a communication is still an "electronic communication" when it is in electronic storage during transmission. The Court looked to the legislative history of the Wiretap Act to determine legislative intent. Using legislative history, the Court found that "the term 'electronic communication' includes transient electronic storage that is intrinsic to the communication process" involved in the transmission of e-mails. The

Defendant also argued that the method of retrieving the messages was not an interception under the Wiretap Act, because the messages were in electronic storage when acquired and were not "electronic communications." The Court found that this second argument was subsumed by the Defendant's first argument. Because the Court already decided that the e-mail messages in electronic storage were electronic communication, the Defendant's second argument failed as well. The Court held that interception of an e-mail message in electronic storage is an offense under the Wiretap Act.

## Case 195

United States District Court,
N.D. New York.

UNITED STATES of America, Plaintiff,

v.

James B. COX, Defendant.

No. 01-CR-481.
March 11, 2002.

Jurisdiction: United States District Court, Northern District of New York

Date: March 11, 2002

Keywords: Experts, Constitutionality

The Defendant was charged with receipt, distribution, and possession of child pornography via the Internet. He presented an omnibus motion seeking relief in the form of suppression of all physical evidence seized directly or indirectly from the Defendant, a protective order permitting the Defendant to possess the contraband material at issue during the pendency of the criminal proceedings, and an order directing the Government to provide expert witness disclosure.

    The Defendant sought suppression of the evidence seized at his home and from his computer on the basis that the search warrants issued in this case were not supported by probable cause. The Defendant averred that the Defendant's America Online subscriber information was private and that there was no probable cause to support the warrant, which allowed the police to obtain his billing address from AOL. The Court found, however, that the Defendant provided no factual declarations or legal authority to support his contention. The Defendant next asserted that the warrant, which allowed the FBI to search the Defendant's home and seize his personal computer, was not supported by probable cause since the allegations in the warrant application were stale and did not establish probable cause that the computer activity was actually occurring at the residence. The Court, however, disagreed, because the warrant affidavit averred that the user of the AOL account in question, which had received numerous images of child erotica and child pornography over an almost three-year period, would likely retain the images collected and that these images could be retrieved by a forensic computer analysis. Moreover, the affidavit, which detailed the daily AOL account activity, amply set forth probable cause to suggest that the computer activity was occurring at the residence. Therefore, the Court denied the Defendant's motion for suppression of the physical evidence.

The Defendant next claimed that he was entitled to a return of the contraband material at issue in this case during the pendency of these criminal proceedings. The Court held that he was mistaken, because the Government had indicated that it would make any and all evidence seized from the Defendant's home and computer available to him for inspection but not copying upon reasonable notice. The Defendant provided no factual basis for his assertion that physical possession of the Government's evidence was necessary to adequately prepare his defense, nor did he cite legal authority that suggested he was entitled to return of illegal materials seized in the course of a criminal investigation. Therefore, the Court denied the Defendant's motion for a protective order requiring the Government to provide him with copies of its physical evidence.

Lastly, the Defendant sought an order requiring the Government to provide an expert witness disclosure. The Government did not state whether it had retained any experts who would testify at the Defendant's trial, but the Court held that it must so advise the Defendant prior to trial. Since the Government acknowledged its discovery obligations under the Court's pretrial order, the Court denied the Defendant's motion on the issue.

## Case 196

United States Court of Appeals,
Tenth Circuit.

UNITED STATES of America, Plaintiff-Appellee,

v.

Robert Wayne FISCUS, Defendant-Appellant.

No. 02-4172.
April 29, 2003.

Jurisdiction: United States Court of Appeals, Tenth Circuit

Date: April 29, 2003

Keywords: Admissibility, Constitutionality

The Defendant appealed the district court's denial of his motion to suppress evidence that had been obtained from the search of his home and the seizure of his computer hard drive and diskettes, in addition to later statements that he had made to law enforcement agents. The Defendant argued that all of the evidence taken from his home should be suppressed because it was an invalid parole search, as it was not based upon reasonable suspicion, and the purpose of the search was not reasonably related to the parole officer's duties. The Defendant claimed that the officers lacked reasonable suspicion to search his home because the tip from a computer repairman, which they relied on, was unreliable and stale. The Court found that the repairman viewed the images while repairing the Defendant's computer and that his personal knowledge was the basis of his tip. Moreover, the repairman had provided detailed information to the police, regarding the images he had observed on the computer, the Defendant's Internet capabilities, and his criminal history, and therefore the Court held that the tip was reliable.

The Defendant argued, however, that the tip was stale when his home had been searched because the tip had been provided more than two months before the search had been conducted. The repairman had informed the police that he believed the Defendant obtained the images from the Internet, that he had continued to have Internet access, and that he had asked the repairman not to look at the files or images. The Court concluded that this information, in addition to the Defendant's criminal past, established a reasonable suspicion that he had violated the terms of his parole. The Defendant further claimed that the officers' had lacked justification to seize his diskettes and that the incriminating nature of the disks was not immediately apparent to the officers. The Court held that the seizing officers had a reasonable suspicion that the Defendant was in violation of his parole agreement by possessing child pornography on his computer, so they were thus entitled to search his residence, and because the officers had arrived in the place where his diskettes had been plainly apparent, the seizure was justified under the plain view doctrine. The Court also found that the incriminating character of the computer and diskettes had been immediately apparent to the officers searching the Defendant's residence and that the officers had a lawful right of access to the disks, because the parole agreement had authorized the officers to search all of the Defendant's property. Lastly, the Defendant argued that the search of the diskettes was illegal because the officers were required to obtain a search warrant prior to conducting the search. The Court ruled that because the evidence actually obtained in the search of the diskettes had been consistent with the original justification for the seizure the search was permissible. The Court then affirmed the district court's denial of the Defendant's motion to suppress.

## Case 197

United States Court of Appeals,
Sixth Circuit.

UNITED STATES of America, Plaintiff-Appellee,
v.
James Stanley FULLER, Defendant-Appellant.

No. 02-3303.
October 9, 2003.

Jurisdiction: United States Court of Appeals, Sixth Circuit

Date: October 9, 2003

Keywords: Constitutionality

The Defendant appealed his conviction of four counts related to child pornography on the grounds that the district court had failed to make adequate factual findings and that the Defendant's convictions for three of the counts must be vacated because the Government had failed to prove that the depictions in the computer files were of actual human beings. He also challenged the search and seizure of evidence, arguing that the warrant lacked particularity and that the validity of the consent to search was also lacking. The Court did not accept the distinction made in the Defendant's particularity argument and held that the warrant was sufficiently particularized. Nor did the Court agree with the consent argument, finding that the lessee had authority to consent to the search of the spare bedroom and its contents—namely, the Defendant's computer.

The Defendant then went on to claim that the Government offered no proof that the victim was in fact a minor, that any sexual activity occurred, or that there was the necessary nexus to interstate or foreign commerce. He also asserted that both the minor age of the victim and the occurrence of a sexual act are elements of the charged offense, which the Court ruled was meritless because the statute criminalized both the enticement and attempted enticement and not the actual performance of the sexual activity. The Court also found that a defendant may be charged with knowingly attempting to persuade, induce, entice, or coerce a minor to engage in sexual activity, even though he is mistaken as to the true age of the person with whom he admittedly communicated. The Defendant then attempted to argue that there was insufficient evidence to support a finding that he believed he was communicating with a minor. The Court held that transcripts of IM sessions and telephone calls more than satisfied the need for sufficient evidence from which a rational trier of fact could find that the Defendant believed he was communicating with a minor. Lastly, the Defendant also attempted to argue that phone calls made to a local ISP phone number did not constitute interstate commerce, though the Court rejected that argument because of indisputable evidence that the Defendant had used both the Internet and the telephone in committing the offense.

Regarding the Defendant's computer-generated images argument, the Court found that it was clear that there had been sufficient evidence that actual minors were involved in the production of the images and went on to uphold the district court's findings and sentencing.

## Case 198

U.S. Court of Appeals for the Armed Forces.

UNITED STATES, Appellee,

v.

Gino J. GALLO, Airman First Class, U.S. Air Force, Appellant.

No. 00-0560.
Crim.App. No. 33303.
Argued April 20, 2001.
Decided September 20, 2001.

Jurisdiction: United States Court of Appeals for the Armed Forces

Date: April 20, 2001

Keywords: Constitutionality

The Defendant had been convicted of advertising, transporting, receiving, and placing on the Internet, child pornography. The Court granted review as to whether or not the Defendant had been subjected to an unreasonable search and seizure, based on a warrant, whose affidavit, among other things, alleged that the Defendant had child pornography on his work site computer.

In discussing the sufficiency of the probable cause required in an affidavit, the Court stated that several factors had bolstered the opinion as to where the child pornography might be found in the Defendant's home. There were 262 pictures found, the Defendant fit the pedophile profile, he had advertised for child pornography, solicited child pornography, and downloaded and uploaded child pornography from his work computer. On the basis of those factors, the Court found that it was reasonably probable that the Defendant would keep and work on this material in a place which he had substantial control. Therefore, it was reasonable to infer that the additional materials would be secreted in a place other than his office, such as the Defendant's home. In addition, the Court also held that the breadth of the supporting factors justified application of the good faith exception. The Court then affirmed the Defendant's conviction.

## Case 199

United States District Court,
D. Oregon.

UNITED STATES of America, Plaintiff,

v.

Robert Ian GREATHOUSE, Defendant.

No.CR 02-476.
October 20, 2003.

Jurisdiction: United States District Court, District of Oregon.

Date: October 20, 2003

Keywords: Admissibility, Constitutionality

The Defendant was charged with the unlawful possession of child pornography and criminal forfeiture of his computer equipment. The Defendant moved to suppress all of the evidence that had been seized from his computer claiming that the search warrant had lacked probable cause and that, even if there was probable cause for the warrant, there had been no probable cause to seize his computer and the officers' execution of the warrant had been overly broad.

The Defendant argued that the affidavit submitted in support of the search warrant contained insufficient information to believe that anyone at the residence had committed any crime, because the information was simply too thin and the incriminating information was too stale to support probable cause. The Court found that it was entirely reasonable for the agents to have presumed, based upon the evidence available, that they had been investigating a single computer located in a single family residence, and that there had been sufficient information to give rise to probable cause to believe that evidence of child pornography would be found on a computer at the residence. The Court, however, found the Defendant's claim that the information that had been obtained from the German police had been stale was more problematic. The Court held that the thirteen-month delay in the case was simply too long. The Court stated that one year, absent evidence of ongoing or continuous criminal activity, is the line that should be drawn for child pornography cases, especially when no explanation or justification for such a significant delay was ever offered. Accordingly, the Court granted the Defendant's motion to suppress the evidence on this basis.

In addition, the Court also granted the motion to suppress, based on the Defendant's room serving as a separate residence, which the search warrant had not specifically addressed as a place to be searched. Lastly, the Court rejected the Defendant's claim that the seizure of all eight computers was overly broad, following precedent that authorities can seize computers when the authorities have no way of knowing that they will encounter more computers than were anticipated. Because the Court found that the warrant had lacked probable cause, the motion to suppress was granted.

## Case 200

U.S. Navy-Marine Corps Court of Criminal Appeals.

UNITED STATES, Appellant,

v.

Travis D. GREENE, Aircraft Electrician's Mate Airman (E-3), Appellee.

NMCM 200102232.
Decided 25 March 2002.

Jurisdiction: U.S. Navy–Marine Corps Court of Criminal Appeals

Date: March 25, 2002

Keywords: Constitutionality

On an appeal, the general issue in the case was whether the military judge had erred in suppressing evidence that had been seized during a consent search of the Defendant's barracks room. More specifically, the Government argued that the military judge erred in ruling that investigators exceeded the scope of the Defendant's consent to search for child pornography.

On the day in question, the Defendant had consented to a Naval Criminal Investigative Service (NCIS) search of his barracks room and personal property therein, specifically including his computer. He had also consented to NCIS seizure and retention of any property found during the search that was desired for investigative purposes. The Court held that the totality of the circumstances clearly showed the voluntariness of that consent. NCIS had found nothing of investigative value in the room search, which left the Defendant's computer as the remaining object of the search. Considering the plain language of the consent search form and the technical difficulties of an on-site computer search, the Court concluded that the NCIS acted reasonably and did not exceed the scope of the Defendant's consent. The Court held that the military judge had erred in his application of the law and reversed his ruling.

## Case 201

United States District Court, D. Massachusetts.

UNITED STATES of America, Plaintiff,

v.

Kevin L. HABERSHAW, Defendant.

No. CR. 01-10195-PBS.
May 13, 2001.

Jurisdiction: United States District Court, District of Massachusetts

Date: May 13, 2001

Keywords: Admissibility, Constitutionality

The Defendant, who was charged with possession of child pornography, moved to suppress the fruits of an initial warrantless search and of a later search of his computer, pursuant to a warrant. The Defendant first argued that both the search of his apartment and computer and the seizure of that computer were unconstitutional and that even if the Defendant had given verbal consent, it was not voluntary. The Defendant also claimed that the warrant that had been issued was overbroad and failed to particularize what was to be searched and seized from the hard drive of the Defendant's computer. Lastly, the Defendant argued that the warrant to search the computer had not been supported by probable cause, because the pornographic image of the child had not been presented to the Magistrate.

The Court denied the Defendant's motion to suppress the evidence. The Court found that that Defendant's decisions to allow the officers to enter, to lead them around the apartment, to show them certain computer files, and to allow them to operate the computer were each the products of an essentially free and unconstrained choice. With regard to both the seizure of the computer and disks and the method of searching those items, the Court held that the warrant had complied with the strictures of the warrant clause. Lastly, the Court ruled that, even if the picture had not been attached to the warrant application, the search of the computer would still be supported by probable cause or valid under the good faith exception.

# Case 202

United States Court of Appeals,
Eleventh Circuit.

UNITED STATES of America, Plaintiff-Appellee, Cross-Appellant,

v.

Frederick Stanley HALL, Jr., Defendant-Appellant, Cross-Appellee.

No. 01-16626.
November 20, 2002.

Jurisdiction: United States Court of Appeals, Eleventh Circuit

Date: November 20, 2002

Keywords: Procedure

The Defendant appealed his convictions for distribution and receipt of child pornography by computer through interstate or foreign commerce. The Defendant argued that that the district court's jury instructions were erroneous. The Court noted that at the time of the Defendant's indictment and trial, the definition of child pornography included both images made using actual minors, as well as virtual child pornography, as added by the Child Pornography Prevention Act of 1996. Thus, in charging the jury, the district court defined child pornography using the words "such visual depiction is, or appears to be." Subsequent to the Defendant's trial, the Supreme Court struck down, as unconstitutional, the words "or appears to be" from the definition of child pornography, contained in the statute, and left intact a ban on actual child pornography. On appeal, the Defendant challenged his conviction in light of the Supreme Court's decision, arguing that the district court erred in its jury charge, rendering it impossible to determine from the record whether the jury relied on the unconstitutional definitions of child pornography in convicting him.

The Court noted that the Government properly conceded that the jury instruction was erroneous because it included the words "or appears to be" and that the error was plain. The Government submitted, however, that the error did not affect the Defendant's substantial rights and, alternatively, that affirming his convictions would not seriously affect the fairness, integrity, or public reputation of judicial proceedings. The Court found that the Defendant had not carried his burden of plain error review. The Court reached its conclusion because the evidence established that the children depicted in the pictures, introduced at trial, were actual children and because no one had ever claimed, or even hinted that the images were of virtual children. After examining the pictures sent out to the jury during the Defendant's trial, the Court concluded that the evidence showed that the children depicted in the images were real and that no reasonable jury could have found that the images were virtual children created by computer technology as opposed to actual children. Accordingly, the Court affirmed the Defendant's convictions on all counts.

## Case 203

United States District Court,
C.D. California.

UNITED STATES of America, Plaintiff,

v.

Justin Barrett HILL, Defendant.

No. CR 02-01289 AK.
June 17, 2004.

Jurisdiction: United States District Court, Central District of California

Date: June 17, 2004

Keywords: Computer Forensics, Experts, Constitutionality

The Defendant was indicted on one count of possession of child pornography and brought a series of pretrial motions. The Defendant anticipated that, at trial, the Government would likely offer into evidence files from two Zip diskettes recovered in a search of the Defendant's home. The Defendant sought to suppress the evidence on two grounds. He argued that the affidavit on which the warrant was based did not establish probable cause to believe that he was in possession of child pornography and that the warrant was overbroad because it allowed seizure of all computer disks belonging to the Defendant regardless of whether they contained child pornography, and because it placed no limitations on the forensic examination of the disks that were seized. The Defendant had also filed a motion for discovery, requesting mirror image copies of the computer media seized from him that were in the Government's possession.

A computer technician was repairing the Defendant's computer when she discovered what she believed to be child pornography. She called the police, who, based on the computer technician's affidavit describing two images of child pornography, got a warrant to search the Defendant's home. The Court stated that not all nude pictures of children are child pornography and that only images containing lascivious exhibition of the genital or pubic area qualify. The Court further noted that, to support issuance of the warrant, the affidavit had to establish probable cause that the images on defendant's computer were lascivious. The Court found that the test for determining such was not particularly helpful, and it therefore adopted a test that, if an image of a minor displays the minor's naked genital area, there was probable cause to believe that the image was lascivious unless there were strong indicators that it was not lascivious. The Court held that there were no such indicators and that the judge had a substantial basis for concluding that there was probable cause for a warrant authorizing the search of defendant's home and seizure of evidence of child pornography.

The Defendant also argued that the warrant was overbroad because it allowed the seizure of all computer media without requiring inspection at the scene, even though the affidavit did not explain why such an inspection would not be feasible, and it placed no limits or controls on the search methodology police used to analyze the seized media. The Court concluded that the warrant authorized precisely such a seizure of intermingled materials that are difficult and time consuming to separate on-site and that the difficulties of examining and separating electronic media at the scene are well known. It was doubtless with these considerations in mind that the state court judge authorized seizure of all of defendant's storage media, not merely those containing contraband or evidence of crime.

The Defendant then argued that the warrant was overbroad because it did not define a search methodology. He claimed that the search should have been limited to certain files that are more likely to be associated with child pornography. The Court found that the Defendant's proposed search methodology was unreasonable, because computer records are extremely susceptible to tampering, hiding, or destruction, whether deliberate or inadvertent.

In addition, the Government intended to introduce into evidence more than 1,000 images of child pornography and/or child erotica, which it discovered on two 100-megabyte Zip diskettes taken from Defendant's home. The Defendant wished to obtain two mirror image copies of the computer media analyzed by the Government's expert to allow his own expert to conduct a forensic analysis and his counsel to prepare his defense. The Government opposed producing the items, offering instead to permit the Defense to view the media in an FBI office and to conduct its analysis in the government's lab. The Court held that there was no indication that the Defendant's counsel or expert could not be trusted with the material. The parties then presented a stipulation setting forth procedures to be employed by the Defense counsel and his expert in the handling of these materials, and the Court has adopted it, because the Court believed that the safeguards provided a useful framework for how the materials could be handled.

Lastly, the Court held that the facts alleged in the affidavit were sufficient for the state court judge to conclude that there was probable cause and that the warrant she issued was not overbroad. Accordingly, the Defendant's motion to suppress was therefore denied and the Defendant's motion for discovery was granted.

## Case 204

United States Court of Appeals,
First Circuit.

UNITED STATES of America, Respondent, Appellant,

v.

David HILTON, Petitioner, Appellee.

No. 03-1741.
Heard September 13, 2003.
Decided September 27, 2004.

Jurisdiction: United States Court of Appeals, First Circuit

Date: September 27, 2004

Keywords: Constitutionality

The Defendant had been convicted of a one-count violation of the Child Pornography Prevention Act. The Defendant had sought and was granted postconviction relief, in light of a Supreme Court decision holding that the Government may not criminalize possession of nonobscene sexually explicit images that appear to, but do not in fact, depict actual children. The Government appealed.

The Court stated that, after the Supreme Court decision, the Government must prove that an image depicts actual children to sustain a conviction. The Court then reiterated that the Government is not released from its burden of proof by a defendant's failure to argue, or by an absence of evidence otherwise suggesting, the artificiality of the children portrayed. The Government must prove that the children in the images are real, as it amounts to an element of the crime, and the burden of this proof should not be displaced to the Defendant as an affirmative defense. The Court found that the Defendant had a right to have the fact finder decide whether the children in the images were real.

The Government argued that expert findings at trial, as to the young age of those represented in the images, based on the Tanner Scale, had satisfied the element of actuality. The Court did not endorse this view, holding that the trial court had found the Defendant guilty of possessing images that appeared to be children engaged in sexually explicit conduct. Because the trial court had not made a finding of fact as to an essential element of the crime, which was the reality of the children represented in the images, the Court affirmed the grant of habeas relief.

## Case 205

United States District Court,
D. Utah, Central Division.

UNITED STATES of America, Plaintiff,

v.

Bryan Vance JONES, Defendant.

No. 2:04CR00510PGC.
April 12, 2005.

Jurisdiction: United States District Court, District of Utah, Central Division

Date: April 12, 2005

Keywords: Admissibility

During a previous hearing, the Defendant moved to suppress evidence in connection with an authorized search warrant. The Court denied that motion on Fourth Amendment grounds but left open the possibility that the evidence might be suppressed under the Federal Wiretap Act. Based on printed e-mail messages from the Defendant's e-mail accounts provided by a confidential informant, FBI Agents obtained a warrant to search the Defendant's e-mail accounts and computer. The Defendant claimed that the confidential witness may have violated the Federal Wiretap Act by accessing his personal e-mail accounts and urged the Court to suppress any evidence obtained in violation of the Act, as well as any other derivative evidence. To support his motion to suppress, the Defendant moved to compel discovery of the identity of the informant witness and the means by which the informant accessed his private e-mail communications. To protect the safety of that informant, this court refused to order disclosure and articulated a hypothetical containing the relevant facts to provide the Defendant a sufficient basis for presenting his claim about the Wiretap Act. The Defendant argued that the scenario presented in the hypothetical constituted a violation of the Wiretap Act that should lead to the suppression of evidence.

The Court noted that in order to prove a violation of the Act, the Defendant would have to prove that the informant acted intentionally and that his e-mail messages were intercepted contemporaneous to their transmission. Although unauthorized interception of electronic communications is unlawful, there is no provision for the suppression of intercepted electronic communications under the Act. Even though § 2511 prohibits the interception and disclosure of any wire, oral, or electronic communication, the suppression remedy in § 2515 applies only to intercepted wire and oral communications. The Defendant argued nonetheless that the statute, by negative implication, provided for the suppression of electronic communications, asserting that the provision suggested that any wire, oral, or electronic communication that was illegally intercepted could not be used in a court proceeding. The Court found that his interpretation was flawed. Finally, the Defendant raised the possibility that the informant accessed his e-mail accounts after intercepting his password by means of an unlawful wire or oral interception, but the Government filed a pleading under seal, which proved that the informant did not obtain information to access to the e-mail account by intercepting any wire or oral communications through the use of a mechanical, or other device. Accordingly, the Court denied the Defendant's motion to suppress evidence pursuant to the Wiretap Act.

## Case 206

United States District Court,
D. Kansas.

UNITED STATES of America, Plaintiff,

v.

Arlan Dean KAUFMAN and Linda Joyce Kaufman, Defendants.

No. CRIM.A.04-40141-01, CRIM.A.04-40141-02.
September 21, 2005.

Jurisdiction: United States District Court, District of Kansas

Date: September 21, 2005

Keywords: Admissibility, Constitutionality

In a suit alleging Medicare fraud, civil rights violations, and subjecting victims to involuntary servitude, the Defendants moved to suppress evidence and for the return of property, arguing that search warrants issued for their property and home were overly broad for purposes of a lawful Fourth Amendment search. Specifically, the Defendants asked the Court to suppress all data and information obtained from the search of a computer seized in 2001.

The Defendants argued that the entire computer search was illegal because law enforcement officers failed to take appropriate steps in the search, when they discovered relevant files intermingled with irrelevant files. The Court, however, found no evidence presented by the Defendants that showed the computer files were intermingled. The Court further found that the Defendants' representations in their brief were misleading. The Defendants claimed a specific agent unlawfully searched the computer files, however the evidence at the hearing showed that that particular agent had no role in searching the Defendants' computer. The Court held that, based on the Defendants' failure to produce evidence that relevant and irrelevant files were intermingled, along with the Defendants' misrepresentations concerning the search in their brief, the search method the employed by the agents was proper. The Court held that the evidence obtained from the computer in this search was admissible.

## Case 207

United States Court of Appeals,
Tenth Circuit.

UNITED STATES of America, Plaintiff-Appellee,

v.

Randy C. KIMLER, Defendant-Appellant.

No. 02-3097.
July 7, 2003.

Jurisdiction: United States Court of Appeals, Tenth Circuit

Date: July 7, 2003

Keywords: Experts

The Defendant had been convicted of one count of receiving or distributing, by computer, images of minors engaged in sexually explicit conduct, one count of possession of such images, and four counts of distribution of such images. The Defendant appealed on multiple issues.

First, he argued that his activities were solely intrastate as there had been no showing of a substantial effect on interstate commerce and because merely having a connection to the Internet does not by itself establish the interstate commerce element of the statute. The Court held that there had been sufficient direct evidence that the Defendant had received and transmitted proscribed images over the Internet across state lines via telephone wires and his computer and that those computer images were the ones stored on his computer's hard drive.

Next, the Defendant argued that the evidence had been insufficient to support the jury's conclusion that he had been the one receiving, distributing, and possessing the images of child pornography, since others had had access to his computer; however, the Court found that there had been evidence presented at trial that had supported the plausible inference that the Defendant was the one committing said acts.

The Defendant then claimed that either direct evidence of the identity of the children in the proscribed images or expert testimony that the images depicted were of real children rather than computer-generated virtual children, was required. The Court ruled that a broad, categorical requirement that, in every case on the subject, absent direct evidence of identity, an expert must testify that the unlawful image is of a real child.

Lastly, the Defendant opposed the sentencing enhancements arguing that experts were needed to determine whether the images involved prepubescent children or sadistic acts and that such acts were already contemplated by the statute. The Court disagreed on all three arguments in affirming the Defendant's convictions and sentence.

## Case 208

United States District Court, D. New Hampshire.

UNITED STATES of America, Plaintiff,

v.

Sean LAINE, Defendant.

No. CR. 99-075-JD.
November 18, 1999.

Jurisdiction: United States District Court, District of New Hampshire

Date: November 18, 1999

Keywords: Admissibility, Constitutionality

The Defendant, who had been charged with possession of child pornography, moved to suppress all evidence, gathered as a result of a search of his home, including certain evidence that was seized from his residence. He argued that the search and seizure violated his Fourth Amendment rights, because they were conducted without a search warrant, and his consent to the search was involuntary, as a result of coercion.

On the basis of the testimony, affidavits, and other evidence submitted, looking at the totality of the circumstances, the Court concluded that the Government had met its burden of showing that the Defendant voluntarily gave consent to the search of his home and voluntarily signed the written consent form to permit a further search of the contents of his computer and the diskettes. Therefore, the Court denied the Defendant's motion.

## Case 209

U.S. Navy-Marine Corps Court of Criminal Appeals.

UNITED STATES of America, Plaintiff,

v.

Jennifer N. LONG, Lance Corporal (E-3), U.S. Marine Corps., Defendant.

NMCCA 200201660.
Sentence Adjudged October 3, 2001.
Decided May 11, 2005.

Jurisdiction: U.S. Navy-Marine Corps Court of Criminal Appeals

Date: May 11, 2005

Keywords: Admissibility, Constitutionality

The Defendant, who was convicted for use of ecstasy, ketamine, and marijuana, appealed her conviction, claiming that the military judge erred by denying the defense motion to suppress e-mails sent and received by the Defendant on her Government computer. The appellant argued that the e-mails were seized from the Government network domain server at the behest of law enforcement officials, without the appellant's consent, and without a lawful search authorization based on probable cause.

The Court stated that answering the question of whether the actions passed constitutional muster had to begin with the question of whether the Defendant had standing under the Fourth Amendment to challenge the validity of the search and that the Defendant could challenge the validity of the search for evidence only if she could assert a subjective expectation of privacy and that such an expectation was objectively reasonable. The Court found that the Defendant's use of the password system provided precautions necessary to safeguard her privacy in her e-mails, as well as her ability to exclude others from her e-mail account. In addition, the Court found that nowhere did the network logon banner mention search and seizure of evidence of crimes unrelated to unauthorized use of a Government computer. Therefore, the Court concluded that the Defendant held a subjective expectation of privacy in her e-mail account as to all others but the network administrator. The Court also found that it was reasonable, under the circumstances presented in the case, for an authorized user of the Government computer network to have a limited expectation of privacy in their e-mail communications sent and received via the Government network server. Specifically, although the e-mails may have been monitored for purposes of maintaining and protecting the system from malfunction or abuse, they were subject to seizure by law enforcement personnel only by disclosure as a result of monitoring or when a search was conducted in accordance with the principles enunciated in the Fourth Amendment. Therefore, the Court concluded that the military judge erred in denying the motion to suppress the e-mails at trial, but, on the basis of the overwhelming evidence of guilt provided by the Government witnesses, the Court held that the erroneous admission of the e-mails did not contribute to the conviction and denied her relief.

# Case 210

United States District Court,
M.D. Florida, Orlando Division.

UNITED STATES of America, Plaintiff,
v.
Jesse Issa MAALI, M. Saleem Khanani, Big Bargain World, Inc., SS Mart, Inc.,
Jeans Unlimited, Inc., Denim Unlimited, Inc., Barakat Corporation,
Barakat International, Inc., David Portlock, Defendants.

No. 6:02-CR-171-ORL28KRS.
August 8, 2004.

Jurisdiction: United States District Court, Middle District of Florida,
Orlando Division

Date: May 27, 2004

Keywords: Constitutionality

The Defendants, charged with seventy-one counts related to employing and harboring aliens and tax evasion, sought motions to suppress evidence seized during a wide-scale search-and-seizure operation. The Defendants challenged both the search warrants themselves and the manner in which the searches and seizures were carried out. They argued that the search warrants were facially invalid because they were unconstitutionally overbroad and lacking in particularity, and they asserted that the agents who executed the warrants seized items that were beyond the scope of even the overbroad warrants. The Defendants also argued that the invalidity of the warrants was not cured by good-faith reliance on the warrants, and the Defendants maintained that the manner in which the search was conducted and the seizure of numerous items mandated wholesale suppression of all evidence seized, even evidence admittedly within the terms of the warrants.

The Court held that the provisions of the Master Affidavit were sufficient to support probable cause that evidence of the alleged crimes would be found on computers at the search locations. Furthermore, the Court found that the lack of a detailed computer search strategy did not render the warrant deficient as to the search and seizure of computers. The Court also held that the Defendants' argument regarding the execution of the computer searches was without merit as the search was without constitutional infirmity, because the seizure of superfluous computer files is virtually inevitable and the agents had limited their searches to text strings that were credible. Therefore, the Court found that no abuse of the Fourth Amendment had been shown as to the computer search and seizure and that such evidence would not be suppressed.

## Case 211

United States District Court,
E.D. Pennsylvania.

UNITED STATES of America, Plaintiff,

v.

James E. MACEWAN, Defendant.

No. CRIM.A.04-262.
December 29, 2004.

Jurisdiction: United States District Court, Eastern District of Pennsylvania

Date: December 29, 2004

Keywords: Procedure

The Defendant had been charged with three counts for the receipt of child pornography. The Defendant had pled guilty, without any plea agreement with the Government, for the third count, and had agreed to a trial on the remaining first two. Following the Government's evidence, the Defendant moved for a directed verdict and rested. The Government argued that the facts proven were sufficient to show that the offenses were committed within the statute of limitations for the first count. The Defendant disputed that and also asserted that the Government had not proven the interstate commerce nexus for the second count.

The Court found that the Government had not proven, beyond a reasonable doubt, that the offense charged in the first count had been committed within the period of the statute of limitations. There was no evidence as to when the material had been received, and no evidence from which the Court could make an inference. Thus, the Court granted the Defendant's motion for judgment of acquittal, as to the first count.

With regard to interstate commerce, the Court held that the evidence, which the Government had presented, that the images on the Defendant's computers had been received through the use of the Internet, was sufficient to carry its burden of proof as to interstate commerce, and that it was not necessary to prove that the specific images had been received from a source outside of the state. The Court granted a directed verdict in favor of the Defendant as to the first count and found the Defendant guilty under the second.

# Case 212

U.S. Air Force Court of Criminal Appeals.

UNITED STATES of America

v.

Senior Master Sergeant Jose A. MANTILLA,
FR134-42-8540 United States Air Force

No. ACM 31778.
September 12, 1996.

Jurisdiction: United States Air Force Court of Criminal Appeals

Date: September 12, 1996

Keywords: Computer Forensics, Experts

The Defendant was convicted of wrongfully possessing, reproducing, distributing, and communicating the contents of controlled test materials, as well as providing access to test material and illegal study materials and soliciting another to violate the same. The Defendant appealed, arguing that the evidence was factually insufficient to sustain his convictions and that his counsel was ineffective.

In regard to his claim of factual insufficiency, the Defendant claimed that his conviction rested solely on the testimony of one person, whose testimony was unbelievable, self-contradicting, and unreliable. He noted that the home computers were not examined and that the computer forensics expert was not able to determine who created the test document or tie the test documents to the Defendant. In addition, he argued that there was no fingerprint analysis of the disks. The Court stated that the test for factual sufficiency was whether, after weighing the evidence in the record of trial and making allowances for not having personally observed the witnesses, the members of the Court are themselves convinced of the Defendant's guilt beyond a reasonable doubt. The Court further noted that the evidence need not be free of conflict for the fact finder to convict and that the Court is entitled to believe the testimony of Government witnesses against those testifying for the accused. The Court found that the essential elements of the testimony were credible and that it was convinced, beyond a reasonable doubt, that the Defendant committed the offenses described. In analyzing the diskettes, the forensic expert concluded that someone put a disk into the drive, pulled up the document, put in a new disk, and then saved that document to that diskette. The Court held that that process was consistent with and corroborated the recitation of events, as testified to. Accordingly, the Court rejected the Defendant's assignment of error.

Lastly, the Defendant asserted that his counsel was ineffective during the pretrial and findings phase of his trial because counsel did not request a computer investigator to assist in examining the Government's case. Without elaborating, the Court concluded that the Defendant's contention was without merit and rejected the assignment of error. Therefore, the Court affirmed the Defendant's convictions.

# Case 213

United States District Court,
D. New Jersey.

UNITED STATES of America, Plaintiff,

v.

Anthony MARCHAND, Defendant.

No. CRIM. 02-813.
March 5, 2004.

Jurisdiction: United States District Court, District of New Jersey

Date: March 5, 2004

Keywords: Experts

The Defendant, accused of possessing child pornography, contested whether the images that the he possessed depicted real minors and whether he knew that the images he possessed depicted real minors. The Court noted that the possession of virtual images of minors engaged in sexually explicit conduct was not a crime under the statute charged. The Defendant maintained that technology existed to create realistic virtual images of child pornography that are indistinguishable from real images of child pornography and that nothing in the bit structure of the digitized computer image would inform a diligent observer that the image was real rather than virtual. The Government presented evidence that eleven of the images were taken from magazines created prior to the invention of such computer technology, that varying law enforcement agents could positively identify the children in several pictures, and that an expert determined the images to be of children based on their development. The Court found that the evidence left no reasonable doubt that the images depicted real children.

In regard to whether he knowingly possessed pictures of actual children, the Defendant argued that the application of willful blindness was not appropriate because a computer could create virtual images of children that appeared realistic. Because the Court already found that the evidence was clear that the children were real, the crux of the issue was whether the Government's evidence proved beyond a reasonable doubt that the Defendant knew that the pictures were of real children. After viewing the images, the Court concluded that all of the children in the images looked utterly real and that the multiplicity of the images and the fact that the Defendant downloaded them from different Web sites supported a finding that the Defendant knew that at least one of the images depicted a real child. In addition, the Government presented the Defendant's own testimony, in which he referred to the images as child pornography, as evidence of his state of mind. To rebut that evidence, the Defendant attempted to argue that his labeling some disks "Yoda" demonstrated that he knew that the images were fake, though the Court didn't agree. Lastly, the Court stated that although the Defendant proved that software to create virtual images existed, no images created by it looked as real as those possessed by the Defendant, which the Defendant's computer expert thought were real. The Court concluded that, if the Defendant did not have actual knowledge that real children were portrayed, he deliberately avoided knowing the truth. Accordingly, the Court held that the Government proved each element of the crime, beyond a reasonable doubt, and convicted the Defendant.

## Case 214

United States District Court,
E.D. Pennsylvania.

UNITED STATES of America et al., Plaintiffs,

v.

MERCK-MEDCO MANAGED CARE, L.L.C., et al., Defendants.

No. 00-737, 99-2332.
February 2, 2005.

Jurisdiction: United State District Court, Eastern District Pennsylvania

Date: February 2, 2005

Keywords: Discovery

The Plaintiff filed an expedited motion to modify a case management order and establish certain discovery deadlines. After the Court had issued an earlier case management order, the Defendant filed a notice with the Court of its failure to comply with that order. Furthermore, the Defendant failed to inform the Court of when it would complete discovery and what documents still needed to be produced. At the time of the instant hearing, the Defendant still had not produced electronic data that had been requested over four months earlier; however, the Defendant claimed that its production was complete, with three exceptions, one of those being corrupted data that was being restored. The Plaintiff cited technical defects in data already produced, when asserting that the Defendant's production was still incomplete. The Defendant argued that it had not been made aware of any defects in its electronic document production, which the Court found disingenuous. The Court then held that the Defendant had to correct any technical problems arising under the electronic document production, correct any hard drive disk errors, explain any files containing questionable or missing data, and resolve other technical file related issues in regard to documents that had yet to be produced.

This Court also found that the Defendant had been dilatory in its disclosure of the defective files, costing the Plaintiff unnecessary time and expense. Consequently, the Court admonished the Defendant for its discovery practices and reminded the Defendant of its obligations to the Court regarding diligent discovery. The Court also held that any further violations of the Court's orders could result in sanctions. As a result of the Defendant's conduct and its resulting prejudice to the Plaintiff, the Court granted several extensions to the discovery schedule and established additional safeguards to protect against further dilatory discovery production. Lastly, the Plaintiff sought the appointment of a special master or neutral consultant, which the Court ruled would not expedite the resolution of the technology issues. The Court then amended the case management order pursuant to its findings.

## Case 215

United States Court of Appeals,
Seventh Circuit.

UNITED STATES of America, Plaintiff-Appellee,

v.

Albert J. MUICK, Defendant-Appellant.

No. 98-1315.
Argued December 2, 1998.
Decided February 8, 1999.

Jurisdiction: United States Court of Appeals, Seventh District

Date: February 8, 1999

Keywords: Procedure

The Court of Appeals affirmed the Defendant's conviction of receiving and possessing sexually explicit photos of minors on his computer. He had challenged the conviction and his sentence on the grounds that there was insufficient evidence to support his conviction and that the district court improperly imposed a sentence enhancement for distribution of child pornography.

This Court held that the evidence presented, including a statement signed by the Defendant, twenty-four computer files depicting actual persons who were under the age of fourteen, a computer directory labeled "Kiddie Porn," and evidence of downloads from a Mexican computer system, were more than sufficient to support the jury's conviction and permit them to find the Defendant guilty beyond a reasonable doubt. The Court also held that the sentencing enhancement was similarly warranted by the evidence, which showed that the Defendant had received money and computer files in exchange for providing child pornography and established that he had intentionally distributed child pornography for pecuniary gain. The Sentencing Guidelines mandated at least a five-point sentence enhancement if the offense involved distribution of child pornography. The Court went on to state that distribution can mean distribution for pecuniary gain and that pecuniary gain is a broad concept.

## Case 216

United States Court of Appeals,
Eighth Circuit.

UNITED STATES of America, Appellee,

v.

Thomas Eli RAY, Appellant.

No. 05-1655.
Submitted: November 15, 2005.
Filed: November 22, 2005.

Jurisdiction: United States Court of Appeals, Eighth Circuit

Date: November 22, 2005

Keywords: Experts, Computer Forensics

The Appellant was charged with attempting to extort $2.5 million from Best Buy by sending the company e-mails threatening to exploit a breach in its computer security. The FBI traced the e-mails back to three different accounts, one belonging to Appellant. Portions of three of the extortion letters were found on the Appellant's computer. The Appellant appealed the jury's conviction and contended that the evidence was insufficient to show that he sent the e-mails.

The Appellant admitted that he used his computer and logged onto the Internet several times a day. The Appellant admitted that three of the e-mails sent to Best Buy traced back to the Internet address he was using on the given day and times the extortion e-mails were sent. A FBI computer forensic expert found three of the e-mails and other incriminating evidence on the Appellant's hard drive. The expert also testified that the e-mails were typed by someone on that computer and that someone had logged onto the Internet from that computer using the screen name and password used to send the e-mails. The expert also testified that there was no evidence of hacking or remote access found on the computer. The Court affirmed the conviction based on the above evidence.

## Case 217

United States District Court,
S.D. New York.

UNITED STATES of America, Plaintiff,

v.

John J. RIGAS, Timothy J. Rigas, Michael J. Rigas, and Michael C. Mulcahey,
Defendants.

No. 02 Cr. 1236(LBS).
September 22, 2003.

Jurisdiction: United States District Court, Southern District of New York

Date: September 22, 2003

Keywords: Privilege

The Defendants, who were charged with conspiracy and multiple fraud charges in connection with the management of a large telecommunications corporation, applied for an order authorizing them to retain certain privileged documents contained on a computer hard drive that was produced to the Defendants by the Government during discovery. On the same day that the Government learned of the inadvertent disclosure of files, it sent a letter to the Defendants asserting the work product privilege with respect to those files and requesting their prompt return. They declined to return the documents to the Government but did agree to provide them to the Court pending resolution of whether the Defendants could retain the privileged materials produced by the Government.

The Defendants argued that the Government waived its work product privilege when it voluntarily permitted them to copy the hard drive containing the files. The Government, in contrast, asserted that the disclosure was inadvertent and therefore did not constitute a waiver of privilege. The Court stated that, as a general rule, the voluntary production of a privileged document waives any claim of privilege with respect to that document. Courts, however, are divided among three schools of thought when it comes to waiver through inadvertent disclosure, and the Court had adopted the middle-of-the-road approach. Under this flexible test, the Court balanced four relevant factors: (1) the reasonableness of the precautions taken by the producing party to prevent inadvertent disclosure of privileged documents; (2) the volume of discovery versus the extent of the specific disclosure at issue; (3) the length of time taken by the producing party to rectify the disclosure; and (4) the overarching issue of fairness. The Court found in favor of the Government on all four factors and denied the Defendants' application.

## Case 218

U.S. Army Court of Criminal Appeals.

UNITED STATES, Appellant,

v.

Sergeant Josh R. RITTENHOUSE, United States Army, Appellee.

ARMY MISC 20050411.
October 13, 2005.

Jurisdiction: U.S. Army Court of Criminal Appeals

Date: October 13, 2005

Keywords: Admissibility, Computer Forensics, Constitutionality

The Defendant was charged with violating the Child Pornography Prevention Act and engaging in "conduct that was prejudicial to good order and discipline or service discrediting by possessing, in the barracks, images of minors engaged in sexually explicit conduct." At arraignment, the Defendant moved to suppress evidence found during a search of his computer and computer disks seized from the Defendant's barracks. The military judge found that a consent form signed by the Defendant did not authorize the seizure and removal of these items and also that the evidence was not admissible pursuant to inevitable discovery. The government appealed the military judge's ruling.

The charges arose after another soldier reported that he saw sexually explicit pictures of children on the Defendant's computer. During questioning by a special agent, the Defendant signed a consent form granting the government consent to search his room, "computers, hard disk drives, removable data storage media, portable data storage devices, cameras." The consent form authorized the search for text, graphics, electronic mail message, and other data related to the sexual exploitation of minors. The Court found that the Defendant voluntarily consented to the search of his room. The Court further found that, because a reasonable person reading the consent form would have understood that the computer and disks could be seized, the Defendant's consent to search the computer and data storage devices included "inherent authorization" for those items to be removed from the room so the government could conduct a forensic search on them. The Court also found that, even if the search of the computer and disks exceeded the scope of the Defendant's consent, the evidence inevitably would have been discovered through routine practices of law enforcement. The Court based this inevitable discovery finding on the Defendant's admissions to the special agent that, among other things, he looked at pictures of naked children on his computer, searched for these pictures on the Internet, and saved the photos onto DVDs. The Court found that these factors would have established probable cause for the government to seize the computer and disks. The Court held that the seizure of the computer and disks was admissible and the evidence should not be suppressed.

**Case 219**

United States District Court,
S.D. Texas, Houston Division.

UNITED STATES of America, Plaintiff,

v.

William Douglas ROBERTS, Defendant.

No. H-99-471.
February 24, 2000.

Jurisdiction: United States District Court, Southern District of Texas

Date: February 24, 2000

Keywords: Admissibility

The Defendant, who was charged with two counts of possession of child pornography, moved to suppress the evidence seized and the statements that he made during the search of his person and personal effects. He argued that customs officials may not use the border search exception as a pretext to conduct a warrantless export search, seeking evidence of criminal activity unrelated to any export control law. The Government argued that the border search exception applies regardless of the customs officials' motives for conducting the export search. The Court likened the search of the Defendant's computer and diskettes to the opening of a closed container, such as luggage, in concluding that the search would clearly be nondestructive and fall within a routine border search. The Court then noted that, even if the officers had been motivated by the desire to uncover violations of laws other than currency reporting and export control laws, that fact would not make the export search, if otherwise valid, unconstitutional.

The Government then argued that the subsequent searches of the Defendant's computer and diskettes could not have violated the Fourth Amendment because the Defendant consented to those searches. The Defendant argued that the Government had induced his consent. On the basis of the totality of the circumstances, the Court held that the Defendant voluntarily gave his consent and that the later searches of his computer, diskettes, or other effects were constitutional in light of the consent. The Court ruled that the customs agents' well-founded threats that they intended to search the Defendant's computer and Zip diskettes, even absent his consent, did not vitiate the Defendant's consent to that search, because they were not threats to conduct a search that they could not lawfully have made without consent. Therefore, the Court denied the Defendant's motion to suppress the evidence.

## Case 220

United States District Court,
S.D. New York.

UNITED STATES of America, Plaintiff,

v.

Ahmed Abdel SATTAR, a/k/a "Abu Omar," a/k/a "Dr. Ahmed," Yassir Al-Sirri,
a/k/a "Abu Ammar," Lynne Stewart, and Mohammed Yousry, Defendants.

No. 02 CR. 395(JGK).
November 5, 2003.

Jurisdiction: United States District Court, Southern District of New York

Date: November 5, 2003

Keywords: Admissibility, Discovery

The Defendant moved for an evidentiary hearing on both government non-compliance with discovery obligations, principally concerning electronic surveillance evidence, and the admissibility of electronic surveillance evidence. The Defendant claimed that the motion was warranted, because the Government had acknowledged that it was unable to retrieve roughly 2 percent of certain voice calls recorded and because the FBI's procedures for handling electronic evidence allegedly raised doubts about the admissibility of the electronic surveillance evidence.

The Defendant requested a pretrial hearing on the admissibility of the electronic surveillance evidence obtained, but the Court held that there was no reason at that point to believe that the issues relating to the admissibility of this evidence could not be resolved efficiently at trial and, therefore, denied her motion for a pretrial hearing. She also asserted that the Government had failed to comply with its discovery obligations to preserve evidence because the FBI was unable to retrieve the audio files for certain intercepted telephone calls, which warranted sanctions. The Court, however, found that her motion was without any merit because she could show neither materiality nor bad faith, and she provided no support for her conclusory allegations that the irretrievable evidence was exculpatory.

The Court held that the Defendant's motion to sanction the Government for failure to preserve all of the audio files also failed for the independent reason that she had not shown any bad faith on the part of the Government. She maintained that the Government's bad faith was evident in the FBI's alleged track record for sloppiness in storing and retrieving electronic evidence, and the Court responded that there was simply no showing by the Defendant that the FBI's failure to retrieve some of the recorded voice calls was the result of bad faith on the part of the Government. Finally, she argued that the Government's bad faith could be inferred from timing of the transition between new and old recording systems. The Court concluded that there was no reason to believe that transition was detrimental to the Defendant or that it occurred in bad faith. Accordingly, the Court denied her motion.

# Case 221

United States District Court,
N.D. Illinois, Eastern Division.

UNITED STATES of America, Plaintiff,
v.
Michael SEGAL, Daniel Watkins, and Near North Insurance Brokerage, Inc.,
Defendants.

No. 02-CR-112.
March 31, 2004.

Jurisdiction: United States District Court, Northern District of Illinois, Eastern Division

Date: March 31, 2004

Keywords: Privilege, Admissibility

During prosecution for mail and wire fraud, the Defendants requested that the Court order the Government not to review or use any of the Defendants' attorney-client privileged communications, including seized electronic communications, for any purpose and that the Court suppress such materials.

The Defendants first requested that the Court order the Government not to review or use the Defendants' attorney-client privileged communications for any purpose. The Court declined to issue such a broad order because the attorney-client privilege was a narrowly construed evidentiary rule designed to encourage full disclosure and to facilitate open communication between attorneys and their clients. Instead, the Court issued a narrower order to protect the Defendants' attorney-client privileged communications requiring the Government not to review the documents on Defendants' privilege log and not to use those documents as evidence at trial unless and until the Court determined that the Defendants' claim of privilege was unfounded.

The Defendants then claimed that the Government should also be barred, under the fruit of the poisonous tree doctrine, from introducing at trial any evidence derived from its violation of the Defendants' attorney-client privilege. The Court held that the attorney-client privilege is an evidentiary privilege and not a constitutional right and that the violation of their privilege did not require suppression of derivative evidence. The Defendants also asserted that the suppression of derivative evidence was warranted because the Government's disregard for their attorney-client privilege violated their constitutional right to due process. The Defendants identified the Government's disregard of their attorney-client privilege when it reviewed the seized electronic communications by failing to screen its agents from the seized privileged communications as an action that allegedly justified the suppression of derivative evidence. The Court held, however, that the Government's ill-advised failure to use the screening procedures identified by the Defendants proactivelydid not violate Defendants' due process rights. Therefore, the Court partially granted and partially denied the Defendants' motion.

## Case 222

United States District Court,
D. Minnesota.

UNITED STATES of America, Plaintiff,
v.
Susan Anne SEIFERT, Defendant.

No. 04-CR-113 JMR.
January 7, 2005.

Jurisdiction: United States District Court, District of Minnesota

Date: January 7, 2005

Keywords: Admissibility

The Defendant, who was charged with arson in connection with a building, objected to the government's proposed exhibit of a digitally enhanced surveillance videotape as not being the best evidence and untrustworthy. The Defendant claimed that the enhanced video no longer accurately recorded the surveillance images and, as such, was no longer an admissible original recording. The Court did not agree and held that the proffered tape might be admitted. The Court found that the Government had laid adequate foundation showing that the enhanced tape accurately reproduced the scenes that took place, and was even more accurate, authentic, and trustworthy than the original. The Court found the enhanced version to be a fair and accurate depiction of the original videotaped image, because the enhancements more readily revealed, but remained true to, the recorded events. As such, the Court held that they could be entered into evidence before the jury.

The Court also found that because the first image transfer, from analog to digital format, changed the image only in a metaphysical sense, the viewer's perceived image is identical. In addition, the transition had no effect on the accuracy of the image, so the Court viewed it is an equivalent duplication technique that accurately reproduced the original. Beyond that, the Court found that the adjustments to brightness or contrast, or enlargement of the image, while arguably a manipulation, were in fact no more manipulative than the recording process itself. The Court concluded that the evidence showed that the technician adjusted the digital image's brightness and contrast, but maintained the relationships between the light and dark areas of the image. As a result, the Court held that the enhanced tape accurately presented a true and accurate replica of the image recorded by the security camera. Accordingly, the Court found the enhanced videotape was a duplicate admissible under the best evidence rule, and therefore, the Court denied the Defendant's motion to exclude it.

# Case 223

United States District Court,
D. Maryland.

UNITED STATES of America
v.
Jay Dana SHERR

No. CRIM. CCB-03-0477.
November 16, 2005.

Jurisdiction: United States District Court, District of Maryland

Date: November 16, 2005

Keywords: Constitutionality, Procedure

The Defendant, who was indicted on charges stemming from possession of child pornography, moved to suppress evidence and dismiss the case.

While investigating a suspect under suspicion of trafficking child pornography, the government discovered the suspect transmitted images of child pornography to the Defendant's America Online screen name. The government used an administrative summons to obtain the biographical information of the Defendant's screen name from America Online. The Court found that the Defendant's constitutional rights were not violated when America Online divulged his subscriber information to the government because individuals have no Fourth Amendment privacy interests in subscriber information given to an Internet service provider. The government executed a search warrant on the Defendant's home and seized the Defendant's computer. The government discovered 147 still images and eight videos of minors engaged in explicit conduct on the Defendant's hard drive. The Court found that the evidence of three transmissions, by the Defendant, of images of minors engaged in sexual activity, along with the Defendant's on-line communication indicating interest in exchanging pornographic pictures of minors supported the conclusion that there was probable cause to search the Defendant's computer. The Court further found that, based on the testimony and documents provided by the agent who searched the computer's hard drive, the qualifications of the agent, and the focused nature of the search on the Defendant's computer, the government did not perform a "general search" on the Defendant's computer. The Court denied the Defendant's motion to suppress the government's search and seizure. The Court also denied the Defendant's motion to dismiss.

## Case 224

United States Court of Appeals,
Tenth Circuit.

UNITED STATES of America, Plaintiff-Appellee/Cross-Appellant,

v.

Stanley Howard SIMS, Defendant-Appellant/Cross-Appellee.

Nos. 03-2151, 03-2177.
November 9, 2005.

Jurisdiction: United States Court of Appeals, Tenth Circuit

Date: November 9, 2005

Keywords: Admissibility, Constitutionality, Procedure

The Defendant appealed his conviction for attempting to entice a minor to engage in sexual acts, traveling in interstate commerce for engaging in sexual acts with a minor, and transporting child pornography by interactive computer system. Among other things, the Defendant argued that his Fourth Amendment rights were violated and that the government failed to prove beyond a reasonable doubt that the pornographic images were images of "actual children."

This case stemmed from the Defendant's actions of communicating with what he believed was a sixteen-year-old girl and a twelve-year-old girl in Internet chat rooms. During this communication, the Defendant participated in sexually explicit conversations with the "girls" and sent sexually explicit images of children to the "girls." Authorities were notified of the Defendant's actions by the recipient of these communications, who was actually a middle-aged man posing as the girls. The first search of the Defendant's computer occurred when law enforcement had an information systems security manager at the Defendant's employer's search the Defendant's work computer remotely through the use of a server. The district court suppressed the evidence obtained during that warrantless search, holding it violated the Defendant's Fourth Amendment rights. The Defendant argued that the arrest warrant and the warrants to search the Defendant's office, home computer, and disks seized from the Defendant's luggage all relied in part upon this illegal warrantless search. Therefore, the Defendant argued that the evidence obtained from these warrants should be thrown out. The Court noted that where unconstitutionally obtained information taints a warrant, the warrant can still be upheld if there was probable cause absent the unconstitutionally gathered information. The Court looked at the affidavit submitted for the search warrant. The affidavit detailed the Defendant's contact with the man posing as the children. It also contained information about the images sent to the man, as well as detailed plans for the Defendant to go to Missouri to meet with the "girls." The Court found that the specific information the affidavit contained was sufficient to warrant suspicion and gave reasonable ground to believe relevant evidence would be found. The Court held that the warrants were based on probable cause even without the information gathered from the warrantless search. The Defendant further argued that the search warrant issued for his office and computer was executed one day after the date printed on the warrant, so the actual search was warrantless because the warrant had expired. The Court held that, because the mistake was nonprejudicial and unintentional and also that it was executed within the 10-day requirement, the evidence obtained should not be suppressed. The Defendant further argued that the government failed to prove beyond a reasonable doubt that the images depicted actual minors. He argued that the government had to do this either by identifying actual children in the image or prove that the images were not computer generated. The Court held that, while the government did have the burden to prove beyond a reasonable doubt that the images depict actual minors, it was not necessary to require the government to produce expert testimony that the images were not computer generated nor identify the actual children in the images. The Court held that a jury could distinguish these facts for itself and that the Defendant presented no evidence casting any doubt on the authenticity of the images.

## Case 225

United States District Court,
D. Connecticut.

UNITED STATES of America

v.

Charles SPADONI

No. 3:00-CR-217 (EBB).
September 16, 2005.

Jurisdiction: United States District Court, District of Connecticut

Date: September 16, 2005

Keywords: Computer Forensics, Experts, Preservation and Spoliation

After a jury convicted the Defendant of racketeering charges, the Defendant filed a Motion for a New Trial or acquittal on multiple charges. Specifically, the Defendant asked that the Court grant him a new trial or acquit him on his conviction for obstruction of justice. The Defendant argued that the government did not produce evidence that he disobeyed a subpoena, destroyed documents that were subject to a subpoena, or destroyed documents he knew would likely be ordered by a grand jury. The Court looked at the evidence produced by the government at trial to determine whether "the Defendant, with knowledge, or at least anticipation, of a pending judicial proceeding, committed an act with the intent to impede that proceeding."

On May 22, 1999, a grand jury subpoena was issued to a member of the alleged racketeering enterprise requesting any records regarding dealings with employees of the State. A witness at trial testified that the Defendant was aware of this subpoena prior to Memorial Day. The witness also testified that the Defendant said that an attorney advised the Defendant to get rid of documents on his computer that the subpoena did not ask for or that he did not need for business. According to the witness's testimony, the attorney recommended the Defendant use a computer program called "Destroy-It" to assist in the destruction of documents. Another witness testified that the Defendant recommended the "Destroy-It" program for use in hiding documents. An FBI Agent testified that he examined the Defendant's laptop and found that the "Destroy-It" program was installed on the laptop less than one month after issuance of the subpoena. The agent also testified that the program had been run on several directories in the laptop, which had names associated with other individuals involved in the racketeering allegations. The agent further testified that data that had been on the laptop prior to May 31, 1999 was no longer on the computer when the agent obtained it by subpoena in April 2000. The Court held that all of this evidence was sufficient for a reasonable jury to conclude that the Defendant knew his actions were likely to affect the grand jury proceedings and to obstruct the administration of justice. The Court denied the Defendant's motion for a new trial or acquittal on his obstruction of justice conviction.

## Case 226

United States Court of Appeals,
Eleventh Circuit.

UNITED STATES of America, Plaintiff-Appellee,

v.

Bradley Joseph STEIGER, Defendant-Appellant.

Nos. 01-15788, 01-16100 and 01-16269.
January 14, 2003.

Jurisdiction: United States Court of Appeals, Eleventh Circuit

Date: January 14, 2003

Keywords: Constitutionality

The Defendant appealed his convictions related to the possession a computer containing child pornography, challenging the district court's conclusion that neither the Fourth Amendment nor the Wiretap Act warranted suppression of the evidence used to convict him. The Defendant claimed that the search warrant had been obtained in violation of his Fourth Amendment right against unreasonable searches and seizures because it was based in part on information from an anonymous source who hacked into his computer; however, the Court found that the district court had correctly held that suppression was not warranted on this ground, because a search by a private person does not implicate the Fourth Amendment unless he acts as an instrument or agent of the government. The Court held that the probable cause for the search warrant had been based on information provided in the anonymous source's first and second e-mails, which the source had acquired before making any contact with the MPD. The Court also rejected the Defendant's argument for suppression based on the agent's failure to advise the judge issuing the warrant that the information had been obtained from a source that had hacked into the Defendant's computer. The Defendant asserted that no judge would have found probable cause knowing that the source had hacked into his computer, which the Court disagreed with.

The Defendant then argued that the district court should have granted his motion to suppress pursuant to the Wiretap Act. The Court addressed the two questions raised by his contention: whether the anonymous source had intercepted any electronic communications in violation of the Wiretap Act, and if so, whether any of the Act's provisions require suppression. The Court found that the anonymous source had not intercepted electronic communications in violation of the Wiretap Act, and that while the Wiretap Act clearly provided criminal and civil sanctions for the unlawful interception of electronic communications, the Act provided no basis for moving to suppress such communications. Therefore, the Court affirmed the judgment of the district court.

## Case 227

United States Court of Appeals,
Tenth Circuit.

UNITED STATES of America, Plaintiff-Appellee,

v.

Russell Lane WALSER, Defendant-Appellant.

No. 01-8019.
December 28, 2001.

Jurisdiction: United States Court of Appeals, Tenth Circuit

Date: December 28, 2001

Keywords: Admissibility, Procedure

The Defendant appealed the denial of his motion to suppress evidence that had been garnered in two searches of his personal computer. He also appealed the imposition of a special condition of supervised release that prohibited him from using the Internet. The Defendant maintained that the officer had lacked probable cause to seize the computer at the time of the original search. The Defendant also argued that the officer had exceeded the scope of the warrant by opening an AVI (Audio-Video Interleave) file while searching for records of drug transactions. Lastly, the Defendant contended that the district court had erred when it had imposed a special condition of supervised release that barred his use of or access to the Internet, without the prior permission of a United States Probation officer.

The Court found that the size of the computer's hard drive—more than 22 gigabytes—combined with the importance that the search take place in a controlled laboratory setting, where proper forensic expertise and equipment would be available, satisfied the requisite probable cause for the seizure. The Court also held that the officer had used a clear search methodology while searching for relevant records in places where such records might logically be found. It was during the search of a logical folder that the officer came across the AVI file, which appeared to consist of child pornography. He then suspended his search and got a new warrant. The Defendant argued that the AVI file, as an audiovisual or video file, could not possibly have contained the type of drug transaction evidence that the officer had been authorized to search for. The Government countered that officers should be able to examine any file because computer files can be relabeled to disguise their contents. The

Court avoided this argument by simply agreeing that the file access did not constitute an impermissible broadening of the warrant. Lastly, the Court stated that because the Defendant had not been completely banned from using the Internet, as he just had to obtain permission from the probation office, the special condition was not unreasonable. The Court denied the Defendant's motion and affirmed the district court rulings.

## Case 228

United States District Court,
D. Kansas.

UNITED STATES of America, Plaintiff,

v.

Douglas WELCH, Defendant.

No. 05-20033 JWL.
November 18, 2005.

Jurisdiction: United States District Court, District of Kansas

Date: November 18, 2005

Keywords: Experts, Computer Forensics, Admissibility

The Defendant submitted a motion to suppress child pornography evidence seized during a warranted search of his house and computers. The Defendant challenged the scope of the search and the computer search methodology. The original search warrant authorized a search for "MDMA, methamphetamine, precursor chemicals, glassware, any and all chemicals and apparatus that either have been or could be used to manufacture a controlled substance, drug records, U.S. Currency, firearms that may facilitate the possession, protection or distribution of MDMA or methamphetamine, formulas containing methods to manufacture MDMA or methamphetamine, and computers."

The Defendant argued that this search warrant was not sufficiently particular because the warrant failed to state a particular description of what the agents could search. The Court held that although the description of drug-related items in the warrant was not limited to a specific computer at the Defendant's residence, the description allowed the searcher to ascertain and identify the things authorized to be searched and seized. The Court determined that the computer forensic specialist searching the computers knew that this was a drug case and limited his search to items relating to methamphetamine and MDMA. The specialist searched two or three computer hard drives for images related to the design of drug labs, the manufacturing of methamphetamine or MDMA, glassware, and drug formulas. While conducting this search, the specialist searched the unallocated portion of the hard drive, where he accessed more than 100 images, many of which were not descriptively named. He discovered eleven images he believed could be child pornography. He stopped the search and contacted a detective in order to get a search warrant directed at child pornography. The Court held that because the officer sought a second warrant after finding a minimal number of images of child pornography, he did not exceed the scope of the search warrant. The Court also held that the government was not required to employ a specific search methodology in searching for drug evidence on the computers. It only requires "that officers must describe with particularity the objects of their search." The Court opined that in this case it would be impossible and impracticable for a warrant to state a particular description of what computer files were to be searched. The Court denied the Defendant's motion to suppress the search of his computer for evidence of drugs, which resulted in an additional warrant for child pornography.

## Case 229

United States Court of Appeals,
Ninth Circuit.

UNITED STATES of America, Plaintiff-Appellee,

v.

Raymond WONG, Defendant-Appellant.

No. 02-10070.
Argued and Submitted December 6, 2002.
Filed June 26, 2003.

Jurisdiction: United States Court of Appeals, Ninth Circuit

Date: June 26, 2003

Keywords: Admissibility, Procedure

The Defendant had pleaded nolo contendere to charges of receiving and possessing child pornography and appealed the denial of his motion to suppress evidence retrieved pursuant to the three search warrants. The Defendant claimed that the first warrant lacked probable cause that evidence of criminal activity would be found on the computers and specificity and that the second warrant was overbroad.

The Court found that because of the Defendant's behavior, threats made to the victim, and the fact that the victim had lived in the place to be searched, the magistrate judge had had a substantial basis for believing that the items listed in the warrant, including those items that could reasonably be located on a computer, could be found in the Defendant's house or cars. Therefore, the determination that probable cause existed, for the search of his computers for the other items listed in the warrant, was not clearly erroneous. The Court also held that the first warrant had been sufficiently specific and had satisfied the particularity requirement. Probable cause had existed for the search. The officers had been provided with objective standards that had alerted them to the items that could be seized, and they had been on notice that they could only search the computer for the items that had been listed in the warrant, all of which were detailed and specific. Lastly, the items were particularly described in the warrant. Therefore, the first search warrant had neither lacked probable cause nor had been overbroad. Because the warrant had sought evidence related to murder, the Court stated that the child pornography that had been seized must have been in plain view during the search for evidence of the murder. The Court found that because the police had been lawfully searching for evidence of murder in the graphics files, which they had legitimately accessed and where the incriminating child pornography was located, the evidence had been properly admitted under the plain view doctrine.

Lastly, since the Court held that the first warrant had been sufficiently specific, it also found that the second warrant had been more than sufficiently specific to satisfy the particularity requirement, because it had included all of the information from the first warrant in addition to further information. Therefore, the Court found that the second warrant had been supported by probable cause, had provided objective standards for what could be seized from the computers, and had been described with sufficient particularity. The Court then affirmed the constitutionality of the warrants.

## Case 230

United States Court of Appeals,
Sixth Circuit.

UNITED STATES of America, Plaintiff-Appellee,

v.

Howard ZIMMERMAN, Defendant-Appellant.

No. 04-5544, 04-6385.
November 15, 2005.

Jurisdiction: United States Court of Appeals, Sixth Circuit

Date: November 15, 2005

Keywords: Computer Forensics, Discovery, Experts, Procedure

The Defendant appealed a decision by the district court convicting him of six counts of child pornography and sentencing him to forty-one months imprisonment. He also appealed the decision by the district court denying his motions for a new trial, for an evidentiary hearing, and for an order compelling the government to produce evidence. The Defendant claimed he discovered new evidence of his innocence that could not have been previously recovered and would likely produce his acquittal.

The first piece of evidence was shipping records from the computer company, stating that the computer was delivered to the Defendant after the date of some of the images on the computer. The Court determined this was cumulative evidence and did not justify a new trial, because the Defendant's ex-wife testified to the same month and year of delivery of the computer in the Defendant's cross-examination of her. After the trial, the Defendant hired a computer expert, who looked at the computer's directory listings and log files. The expert found that many of the pornographic images on the computer could only have been downloaded using a Zip file, CD-ROM, or another computer's hard drive on a date that the Defendant did not have access to the computer. The Court found that the expert could have reached this conclusion with due diligence prior to the trial, because the expert analyzed printouts of directory listings and logs available to the Defendant prior to the trial. The third piece of evidence was one of the Defendant's former employee's Web site, which purported to admit to placing "goodies" on the Defendant's computer for the authorities to find. The Court found that the statements on this Web site would not likely produce reasonable doubt on the reliability of the evidence supporting the Defendant's guilt because the Web site mixed "grotesque fantasy" with reality. The Court held that the Defendant was not entitled to a new trial because the evidence he offered was cumulative, could have been produced prior to the trial with due diligence, or was not likely to produce an acquittal. The Court further held that the Defendant was not entitled to an evidentiary hearing because the shipment date of the computer and directory listing and log files could have been discovered previously with due diligence, and the statements on the Web site failed to raise a "clear-cut" issue of fact. Finally, the Court denied the Defendant's motion to compel the government to produce evidence because all he wanted was an exact copy of the computer's hard drive, which he had an opportunity to examine previously.

## Case 231

United States District Court,
N.D. California.

In re VERISIGN, INC. SECURITIES LITIGATION

No. C 02-02270 JW.
March 10, 2004.

Jurisdiction: United States District Court, Northern District of California

Date: March 10, 2004

Keywords: Discovery

In a class-action securities case, the Defendants objected to a discovery order that compelled the Defendants to produce to the Plaintiffs a copy of the responsive electronic data in the original format, as it was kept in the usual course of business. That order was based on a previous order, compelling the Defendants to produce responsive documents in electronic form and requiring the parties to meet and confer about how to proceed with the production process, as production of a TIFF version alone would not be sufficient and the electronic versions had to be searchable and include metadata. The Defendants had objected to the previous order, arguing that they could not be required to produce documents in electronic form and that they had been preparing documents in TIFF and that converting them back to their original .pst format would be too burdensome. The Court understood the newer order to mean that the Defendants were required to produce responsive electronic documents in their native .pst format if that is how they were stored in the Defendants' usual course of business.

The Defendants claimed that an order directing them to produce responsive electronic documents in their native format is contrary to law and clearly erroneous. The Court found that such a request was not contrary to law because the text of the Federal Rules of Civil Procedure clearly anticipated that a Defendant may be directed to produce electronic documents in electronic format and that a party who produces documents for inspection shall produce them as they are kept in the usual course of business or shall organize and label them to correspond with the categories in the request. The Defendants also argued that it was clearly erroneous to require the production of documents in their original .pst format because producing them in that format, with corresponding Bates numbers and privilege redactions, would be overly burdensome and prejudicial, because the Defendants had been preparing to produce the responsive documents in TIFF format and converting them back to .pst format would be extremely time consuming and expensive. The Court, however, was not convinced that a mistake had been made, stating that the expectation of electronic production was reasonable, given that the documents need only be produced in their native format, even though it may be difficult for the Defendants to incorporate their redactions and bates numbers into the .pst format. Therefore, the Court denied the Defendants' objections to the discovery orders.

## Case 232

United States District Court,
M.D. Florida.
Orlando Division.

In Re: Search WARRANT

No. 03-1130-01JGG.
December 16, 2003.

Jurisdiction: United States District Court, Middle District of Florida,
Orlando Division

Date: December 16, 2003

Keywords: Constitutionality

The Government asked the Court to issue a search warrant to seize electronic data, including the contents of electronic communications, maintained by a Web site in the Northern District of California. Among other things, the Government sought to learn the names of all Web site users who had accessed certain pornographic images of children posted on the Web site.

The Court concluded that it did not have statutory authority to issue an out-of-district warrant for electronic evidence of a crime other than for domestic or international terrorism. In doing so, the Court stated that according to a logical extension of the Government's argument, a court in Florida would have the statutory authority to seize the names and computer addresses of everyone in the world who viewed an adult pornographic image posted on a Web site in California, as well as e-mails and other electronic data that are evidence of any federal or state felony or misdemeanor. Because the Court held that it did not have the requisite statutory authority to issue the out-of-district warrant requested, the Court found it unnecessary to assess whether the application and affidavit established probable cause to seize the full scope of the data that the Government sought.

Accordingly, the Court declined to issue the requested search warrant to seize electronic data maintained by a dot-com Web site in the Northern District of California in an investigation concerning child pornography. Lastly, the Court reiterated that Congress had not authorized it to seize out-of-district property except in cases of domestic terrorism or international terrorism.

## Case 233

Supreme Court, New York County, New York.

Jeffrey A. WEILLER, individually and on behalf of all others similarly situated, Plaintiff,

v.

NEW YORK LIFE INSURANCE COMPANY, Unumprovident Corporation and the Paul Revere Insurance Company, Defendants.

No. 604285/04.
March 16, 2005.

Jurisdiction: Supreme Court, New York County, New York

Date: March 16, 2005

Keywords: Preservation of Evidence/Spoliation

In a class action alleging improper claims handling by disability insurance carriers, the Plaintiff moved for an order compelling the Defendants to preserve certain material as evidence. At the time of the filing, two other preservation orders had already existed, in addition to the statutory preservation duties imposed by the Private Securities Litigation Reform Act. The Court found that the Plaintiff's requested preservation order did not directly add to the protections already afforded under the PSLRA because the PSLRA provided for the possibility of court-ordered sanctions in response to a party's "willful failure" to comply with the duty to preserve relevant evidence. The Court, however, then held that the federal protections were not directly binding, because, unlike a federal court, the Court could not independently enforce a breach of the obligations to preserve.

The Plaintiff urged that the requested preservation order was necessary because of alleged destruction of e-mail messages by the Defendants in the past. The Court was not convinced by this argument, however, concluding that the Plaintiff may have been exaggerating the situation and that the prior loss of e-mail, caused by the overwriting of backup tapes, was not deliberate, but inadvertent. The Court expressed concerns for scenarios in which the existing preservation orders might not be sufficient protection for the Plaintiff, such as the federal court not requiring the production of certain materials or documents. To prevent such a scenario, the Court granted the motion for a preservation order. The Defendants then objected to the proposed preservation order on grounds of overbreadth, including the request that e-mail backup tapes, computer hard drives, and disks containing communications be protected. The Defendants attested that the previous preservation of computer hard drives had cost the Defendants more than $1,000,000.00. Responding to the Defendants' monetary concerns, the Court stated that it was not insensitive to the cost entailed in electronic discovery and would, at the appropriate juncture, entertain an application by the Defendants to obligate the Plaintiff, as the requesting party, to absorb all or a part of the cost of the e-discovery that it would seek but that it would not constrain the production of possibly relevant evidence on account of the later need to allocate the cost.

## Case 234

United States District Court,
E.D. Michigan, Southern Division.

WELLS FARGO & CO., et. al., Plaintiffs,

v.

WHENU.COM, INC., Defendant

No. 03-71906.
November 19, 2003.

Jurisdiction: United States District Court, Eastern District Michigan, Southern Division

Date: November 19, 2003

Keywords: Procedure

The question before the Court was whether pop-up advertisements violated trademark or copyright law. The Plaintiffs asked the Court for a preliminary injunction against the Defendant, whose business was Internet contextual advertising.

In regard to the Plaintiffs' trademark claims, the Court found that they had not demonstrated a strong likelihood of success on the merits. The Court held that the Defendant did not use the Plaintiffs' marks in commerce, because the Defendant did not hinder access to the Plaintiffs' sites. In addition, the Court concluded that some advertisements appearing on a computer screen, at the same time that the Plaintiffs' Web pages were visible, did not constitute a use in commerce of the Plaintiffs' marks for three reasons. First, the positioning of the Defendant's advertisements did not constitute framing. Second, the Defendant was engaged in legitimate comparative advertising. Third, the inclusion of URLS that included portions of the Plaintiffs' trademarked names in the Defendant's scrambled directory was not a use in commerce. In addition, the Court held that the Plaintiffs had not demonstrated a likelihood of confusion, finding that the Plaintiffs' survey evidence was unpersuasive for several reasons. First, the surveys lacked probative value because they did not remotely approximate actual market conditions and did not survey the appropriate population. Next, the Court held that the survey questionnaires were unclear and leading. Lastly, the Court found that the survey was not properly administered, contained no control questions to generate an error rate, and employed a design that rendered the results uninterpretable. In addition, in regard to the Plaintiffs' copyright claims, the Court concluded that they again had not shown a likelihood of success on the merits, this time because they had not shown any infringement of their right to prepare derivative works.

The Court also held that the Plaintiffs had not sufferable irreparable harm because their delay in asserting their rights rebutted such a claim and because the Defendant posed threat to the Plaintiffs' relationship with their banking regulators. Lastly, the Court concluded that an issuance of a preliminary injunction would harm the Defendant, its clients, and the general public while denying the motion would not damage the Plaintiffs other than in a manner compensable by an award of monetary damages in the event that the Plaintiffs eventually prevailed on the merits. Accordingly, the Court found that the balance of the equities weighed against granting the Plaintiffs' motion. Therefore, the Court denied the Plaintiffs' motion for a preliminary injunction.

## Case 235

United States District Court,
N.D. Illinois, Eastern Division.

Amy WIGINTON, Kristine Moran, Norma Plank Fethler, Andrea Corey and
Olivia Knapp, individually and on behalf of all persons similarly situated,
Plaintiffs,

v.

CB RICHARD ELLIS, INC., Defendant.

No. 02 C 6832.
Filed September 25, 2002.
August 10, 2004.

Jurisdiction: United States District Court, Northern District of Illinois,
Eastern Division

Date: August 10, 2004

Keywords: Costs and Cost Shifting, Production of Evidence Discovery

In a class-action complaint alleging a nationwide pattern and practice of sexual harassment at the Defendant's offices, the Plaintiffs filed a motion for costs related to electronic discovery. They argued that the Defendant should bear the costs of searching its own e-mail backup tapes to find documents containing pornographic terms and images, as well as documents relating to its workplace environment generally, because of the large number of these types of documents that had been found in a controlled sampling. The Defendant responded, claiming that only a small fraction of the e-mails that had been found had contained arguably relevant material and that it should not be forced to pay for the search or production.

In beginning its cost-shifting analysis, the Court stated that of the available tests, it agreed with prior precedent that the marginal utility test was the most important factor for consideration. Therefore, the Court modified the *Zubulake* rules by adding a factor to consider the importance of the requested discovery in resolving the issues of the litigation. The Court's altered test considered the following factors: (1) the likelihood of discovering critical information; (2) the availability of such information from other sources; (3) the amount in controversy as compared to the total cost of production; (4) the parties' resources as compared to the total cost of production; (5) the relative ability of each party to control costs and its incentive to do so; (6) the importance of the issues at stake in the litigation; (7) the importance of the requested discovery in resolving the issues at stake in the litigation; and (8) the relative benefits to the parties of obtaining the information.

At all times the Court kept in mind that because the presumption was that the responding party pays for discovery requests, the burden remained with the Defendant to demonstrate that costs should be shifted to Plaintiffs. That said, the Court found the following:

> Factors 1 and 2, the most important factors, weighed slightly in favor of cost shifting to the Plaintiffs. For the cost factors: factor 3 weighed in favor of cost shifting; factor 4 weighed against cost shifting; and factor 5 weighed slightly in favor of cost shifting. Factor 6 was neutral; factor 7 weighed slightly in favor of cost shifting; and factor 8 was neutral. Therefore, because the factors favored cost shifting, but the presumption was that the responding party pays for discovery costs, the Court held that the Defendant should bear 25 percent and the Plaintiffs 75 percent of the discovery costs of restoring the tapes, searching the data, and transferring it to an electronic data viewer. Each party was ordered to bear their own costs of reviewing the data and printing documents, where necessary.

## Case 236

United States District Court,
N.D. Illinois, Eastern Division.

Amy WIGINTON, individually and on behalf of all persons similarly situated,
Plaintiff,

v.

CB Richard ELLIS, Defendant.

No. 02 C 6832.
October 27, 2003.

Jurisdiction: United States District Court, Northern District of Illinois,
Eastern Division

Date: October 27, 2003

Keywords: Preservation of Evidence/Spoliation, Sanctions

In a class-action lawsuit alleging sexual harassment, the Plaintiff had requested that the Defendant retain all electronic materials and records relevant to the lawsuit. The Defendant followed its normal document retention and destruction policies, and the Plaintiff then filed motions to prevent the further destruction of evidence and to sanction the Defendant for spoliation of evidence.

The Court found the Defendant's argument that preserving relevant data would be too cost prohibitive not entirely persuasive, because it had the duty to preserve only relevant information, not every electronic record. The Court also did not find the Defendant's claims that it would require thousands and thousands of hours to search through electronic data for relevant documents credible, because spam could be filtered out, nonspam could be searched using particular sexual key words, and certain file types likely to contain pornographic images could be searched, as well. The Court then held that the Defendant had the duty to preserve relevant electronic documents that were likely to be the subject of discovery requests, that it had knowledge of this duty, and that it willfully and intentionally did not fulfill this duty.

After an extensive thorough sanctions analysis, the Court concluded that in this particular case, unlike most cases in which documents have been destroyed, there was a way to determine the effect that the Defendant's actions had on the Plaintiff's case. While the entire scope and extent of the lost documents was not known, the backup tapes for the lost three months that had been produced by the Plaintiff could provide some indication as to what had been destroyed. For that reason, the Court recommended that the Plaintiff's motion for sanctions be denied without prejudice. Lastly, the Court held that, if the Plaintiff's expert was able to discover relevant documents on the backup tapes, the Plaintiff should be allowed to renew its motion for appropriate sanctions on the basis of the destroyed evidence.

# Case 237

Supreme Court of Kentucky.

John WILLIAMS, Appellant,

v.

COMMONWEALTH of Kentucky, Appellee.

No. 2003-SC-1024-MR.
November 23, 2005.

Jurisdiction: Supreme Court of Kentucky

Date: November 23, 2005

Keywords: Admissibility, Procedure

The Defendant appealed his conviction of four counts of use of a minor in a sexual performance. The Defendant argued, among other things, that the trial judge erroneously permitted the Commonwealth to introduce extraneous evidence of other pornographic images found on the Defendant's computer. Specifically, he argued the testimony of a detective regarding the existence of other pornographic material on the Defendant's computer was inadmissible.

The Court determined that the objections by the Defendant's counsel in the initial trial focused on the introduction of pornographic images, not the mentioning of the images. The jury was only informed about the other pornographic images on the Defendant's computer. There were no descriptions or visual presentations of those images. The Court held that the introduction of this testimony was admissible to show the Defendant's intent or knowledge. The Court also held that the reference to these images was relevant and probative of the issue of whether the photographs taken by the Defendant constituted a sexual performance. The Court held the testimony of the detective about other pornographic images on the Defendant's computer was admissible.

## Case 238

United States District Court,
D. Massachusetts.

Isaac WILLIAMS, Jr., Plaintiff,

v.

MASSACHUSETTS MUTUAL LIFE INSURANCE COMPANY
(a/k/a Massmutual Financial Group)
and David L. Babson & Company, Inc. (a/k/a David L. Babson and Company),
Defendants

Civ.A. No. 03-11470-MAP.
February 2, 2005.

Jurisdiction: United States District Court, District of Massachusetts

Date: February 2, 2005

Keywords: Preservation of Evidence/Spoliation, Computer Forensics, Experts

In an employment discrimination suit, the Plaintiff moved to compel discovery and appoint a neutral expert in computer forensics. The Plaintiff claimed that the Defendants should produce a document that allegedly reflected a practice and policy of the Defendants' to use its performance review and progressive discipline policies for purposes of discriminating against African-American employees.

The Court was not inclined to appoint a neutral expert in computer forensics to help the Plaintiff confirm highly speculative conjecture that an e-mail existed that was something other than what the Defendants had reproduced. The Court found that the Plaintiff had presented no credible evidence that the Defendants were or had been unwilling to produce computer-generated documents or that they had withheld relevant information. The Court was similarly disinclined to allow the Plaintiff to conduct the forensic study at his own expense. The Court stated that an inquiring party must present at least some reliable information that the opposing party's representations are misleading or substantively inaccurate and that the Plaintiff had provided no such evidence. The Court, however, did order the Defendants to preserve all documents, hard drives, and e-mail boxes that were searched by their forensic expert in response to the Plaintiff's motion. The Court denied the Plaintiff's motion in all respects but one, the retention of certain data relevant to the present dispute.

## Case 239

United States District Court,
D. Kansas

Shirely WILLIAMS et al., Plaintiffs,

v.

SPRINT/United Management Company, Defendant

No.CIV.A.03-2200-JWLDJW

Jurisdiction: United States District Court, District of Kansas

Date: September 29, 2005

Keywords: Data Preservation, Discovery, Metadata, Spoliation

Plaintiffs filed a suit claiming that age was a determining factor in the Defendant's decision to terminate them during a reduction in force (RIF). During discovery, the court ordered the Defendant to provide the Plaintiffs with Microsoft Excel Spreadsheets containing information regarding the RIF and RIF-related materials. The Defendant turned over 3,083 electronic spreadsheets. Prior to turning over the spreadsheets, however, the Defendant used software to scrub the metadata from the spreadsheets and also locked certain cells on the spreadsheets so the Plaintiff could not access the locked cells. The Court ordered the Defendant to show cause why it should not produce electronic spreadsheets in the manner in which they were maintained and why it should not be sanctioned for scrubbing metadata and locking cells prior to producing these spreadsheets.

The Defendant first argued that it scrubbed the metadata from the spreadsheets to preclude the possibility that the Plaintiffs could recover privileged and protected information properly deleted from the spreadsheets and to limit the information contained on the spreadsheets to the information from which it made the RIF decisions. The Defendant claimed that there is a presumption against the production of metadata unless it is specifically requested or relevant. The Court found insufficient guidance in the federal rules and in case law regarding metadata, so the Court looked to the Sedona Conference Principles for guidance. The Court held that "when a party is ordered to produce electronic documents as they are maintained in the ordinary course of business, the producing party should produce the electronic documents with their metadata intact, unless the party timely objects to the production of metadata, the parties agree that the metadata should not be produced, or the producing party requests a protective order." The burden with regard to the initial disclosure of metadata is placed on the party to whom the request or order to produce is directed. The Court further found that some of the metadata scrubbed from the spreadsheets was relevant, particularly the metadata concerning changes to the spreadsheet. The Court also found that if the Defendant was concerned with privileged information being produced in the metadata, the Defendant should have raised this issue prior to unilaterally deciding to scrub the information from the spreadsheets. The Defendant next argued that the Plaintiff never sought production of the metadata. The Court held that, although the metadata was not mentioned during discovery meetings, the Defendant should have reasonably been aware that the metadata was encompassed in the Court's order to produce the spreadsheets. Finally, the Defendant argued that the removal of the metadata was consistent with the judge's previous orders. The Court did not find the removal of the metadata consistent with the judge's previous orders but held that, if the Defendant believed the removal of the metadata was consistent, it should have either objected or requested a protective order before it produced the spreadsheets without the metadata.

The Defendant argued that it locked cells within the spreadsheets to ensure the integrity of the information in order to avoid inadvertent or accidental alterations of the data. The Court found that the Defendant did not show cause for unilaterally locking cells and data on these spreadsheets. The Court held that the Defendant should have reasonably been aware that locking these cells did not comply with the spirit of the Court's order to produce the spreadsheets as they were kept in the ordinary course of business.

The Court ordered that "unlocked" spreadsheets, including metadata not concerning adverse impact analyses and social security numbers, be produced by the Defendant at the next discovery conference. It further found that the Defendant should not be sanctioned due to the lack of clarity of the law concerning metadata and ambiguity in previous court rulings concerning metadata.

## Case 240

Court of Appeals of Texas,
Eastland.

Anthony Finley WILLIFORD, Appellant,

v.

STATE of Texas, Appellee.

No. 11-02-00074-CR.
January 15, 2004.

Jurisdiction: Court of Appeals of Texas, Eastland

Date: January 15, 2004

Keywords: Experts, Admissibility, Constitutionality

The Defendant had been convicted of thirty-four counts of third-degree felony possession of child pornography, and he presented three issues for review. First, the Defendant asserted that the trial court erred in failing to exclude certain testimony regarding the scientific technique used to reproduce pictures, because the detective was not qualified to testify as an expert witness. Thus, the Defendant argued that the State did not establish the proper predicate for admission of the pictures. Second, he claimed that the seizure of his computer was illegal because there had been no search warrant and no exception to the requirement for a warrant. Third, the Defendant asserted that his consent to search the computer had been involuntary because of the unlawful seizure of his computer, which had occurred immediately prior to the request for consent.

The Court addressed the Defendant's first issue, using the three Kelly criteria for reliable evidence derived from a scientific theory and the seven factors that can affect the proper determination of those criteria. After reviewing the facts under this standard, the Court held that the trial court had not abused its discretion in admitting the testimony. Regarding the Defendant's second issue, the Court reasoned that the facts available to the officer at the time of the seizure of the computer would warrant a man of reasonable caution in the belief that the computer had contained contraband or evidence of a crime, and, therefore, the seizure of the computer was proper. The Defendant's final argument that his consent to the search had been involuntary was based on the premise that the seizure had been illegal. Because it was not, the Court ruled against the Defendant and affirmed the judgment of the trial court.

## Case 241

United States District Court,
D. Connecticut.

Susan E. WOOD, Plaintiff,

v.

SEMPRA ENERGY TRADING CORPORATION, Defendant.

No. 3:03-CV-986 (JCH).
December 9, 2005.

Jurisdiction: United States District Court, District of Connecticut

Date: December 9, 2005

Keywords: Discovery, Procedure, Sanctions, Spoliation

The Plaintiff brought a suit against her former employer, the Defendant. In a Motion in Limine, the Plaintiff sought a ruling to preclude certain evidence or granting of an adverse inference against the Defendant. Specifically, the Plaintiff complained of the Defendant's failure to search for and produce e-mails and other documents relating to the Plaintiff, failure to produce a notebook referred to by a witness, and failure to deliver financial statements in a timely fashion.

The Court held that where an alleged breach of discovery is the nonproduction of evidence, a district court has broad discretion in determining an appropriate sanction. The Plaintiff moved to exclude evidence of e-mails without specifically identifying the e-mails she wanted excluded. Instead, she vaguely referred to e-mails that the Defendant would rely on at trial but not produce during discovery. She also asked the Court to infer that the e-mails not produced by the Defendant would have provided evidence against the Defendant. A party seeking an adverse inference instruction because evidence was not produced in time for trial must establish "that the party having control of the evidence had an obligation to timely produce it; that the party that failed to produce the evidence had a culpable state of mind; and that the destroyed evidence is relevant to the party's claim or defense such that a reasonable trier of fact could find that it would support the claim or defense." The Court held that the Plaintiff's failure to timely file the motion was reason enough to decline the Plaintiff's motion for an adverse inference. The Plaintiff filed this motion more than a year after the document production, on which she based her motion, took place. The Court then moved on to look at whether the motion would be granted even if it was filed in a timely manner.

The Plaintiff claimed she made requests for production of documents that related to her termination and communication among other employees about her. She claimed she did not receive these documents. She also cited the testimony of the Defendant's witnesses as support for her conclusion that the Defendant did not do an adequate search for these documents in its files. The Court looked at the content of the depositions along with a memorandum submitted by the Defendant's counsel to determine whether the Defendant complied with discovery requests. The memorandum submitted by the Defendant's counsel represented that a freeze was put on document destruction after it was learned that the Plaintiff filed a complaint against the Defendant. It also stated that backup tapes of the Defendant's computer system were searched in compliance with the discovery request. The Court found that the Defendant did comply with the discovery requests of the Plaintiff and did not purposefully withhold any documents from the Plaintiff. The Court also rejected the Plaintiff's other argument that, because she wrote many e-mails, others in the office must have written many e-mails, none of which were produced. The Court found this to be a speculative claim. The Court held that the Plaintiff failed to establish a record of the Defendant's noncompliance with discovery and therefore did not grant the Plaintiff's motion for adverse inference.

## Case 242

United States District Court,
N.D. Illinois, Eastern Division.

YCA, LLC, Plaintiff,

v.

Kevin J. BERRY, Defendant.

No. 03 C 3116.
May 7, 2004.

Jurisdiction: United States District Court, Northern District of Illinois, Eastern Division

Date: May 7, 2004

Keywords: Sanctions, Computer Forensics, Costs and Cost Shifting

The Plaintiff filed a seven-count complaint against one of its former employees, alleging that he breached duties of nonsolicitation, nonrecruitment, and nondisclosure that he agreed to as part of a restrictive covenant he signed when he commenced work as a consultant for the Plaintiff. In response, the Defendant moved to strike the testimony of the Plaintiff's computer forensics expert, who recovered a plethora of deleted documents from the Defendant's old work computer. He argued that the Plaintiff failed to disclose the expert by the required discovery cut-off deadline and that it deliberately withheld the expert's name from its interrogatory and document production responses, which was filed after the close of discovery by agreement of the parties. The Defendant claimed that he was prejudiced as he prepared his summary judgment motion, because he did so without full knowledge of the Plaintiff's case against him. As a sanction, the Defendant asked the Court to strike the expert's declaration and the documents he recovered from the computer.

The Court concluded that any such delay by the Plaintiff was justified, because it submitted the discovery responses in light of the Defendant's deposition testimony, in which he stated that he had no contact with another employee regarding the formation of another business, other than an e-mail exchange regarding a projected cash-flow statement. The Defendant originally asserted that the exchange took place on either his AOL or Yahoo account, and, therefore, the Plaintiff had no reason to suspect that the Defendant's work computer would contain discoverable information. Later, the Defendant augmented his testimony with a sworn affidavit admitting to printing and creating documents, which the Court held justified the late-found interest in the computer and did not prejudice the Defendant. The Plaintiff also alleged that documents recovered by the expert proved that the Defendant perjured himself. The Court concluded that the documents and communications had revealed perjury but that it did not warrant a default judgment, as the perjury ultimately only hurt the Defendant. The Court did, however, feel that a sanction was appropriate as a punishment for his misleading and dishonest testimony and awarded the Plaintiff all of its attorneys' fees and costs stemming from the perjury, including retaining the computer expert's services. Lastly, the Defendant moved for summary judgment against disclosure of confidential information claim, arguing that much of the information taken from the Plaintiff was not confidential information. The Court agreed, finding that, although metatags embedded in the Plaintiff's templates indicated their source and could be construed as information, customers would have no interest in this information that provided no useful content. Accordingly, the Court granted the Defendant summary judgment as to any claims arising out of disclosure of the information divulged by the metatags, denied the Defendant's motion to strike the expert's testimony, and entered sanctions against the Defendant.

## Case 243

United States District Court,
N.D. Illinois, Eastern Division.

ZENITH ELECTRONICS CORPORATION, Plaintiff/Counter-Defendant,

v.

WH-TV BROADCASTING CORPORATION, Defendant/Counter-Plaintiff.

No. 01 C 4366.
July 19, 2004.

Jurisdiction: United States District Court, North District of Illinois,
Eastern Division

Date: July 19, 2004

Keywords: Costs and Cost Shifting, Discovery, Experts

During a breach of contract dispute, Zenith and WH-TV motioned to review costs that had been taxed in favor of GI and Motorola. Because the claims against the two parties were different and the defenses against those claims and the costs associated with the defenses would have differed, the Court found that the Zenith's motion should be granted to segregate the costs. WH-TV went on to object to GI and Motorola's bill of costs, most notably costs associated with the production of documents stored in electronic format.

The Court then held that costs incurred from printing documents stored on computer disks were not recoverable because the printing was done merely for GI and Motorola's convenience. In addition, the Court did not grant costs for computer time, as it is not statutorily provided for. In regard to computer consultant costs related to compiling, searching, and printing the electronic compiling, the Court found that the cost of a computer consultant is not a statutorily recoverable expense and that a consultant's review for responsive documents cannot be considered part of the cost of reproducing documents. In addition, as before, the costs associated with printing and numbering were merely for GI and Motorola's convenience and therefore, were not recoverable. The Court affirmed all of the objections related to the production of electronic evidence.

# Case 244

United States District Court,
D. Kansas.

Wei-Kang ZHOU, Plaintiff,

v.

PITTSBURG STATE UNIVERSITY, Defendant.

No. 01-2493-KHV.
February 5, 2003.

Jurisdiction: United States District Court, District of Kansas

Date: February 5, 2003

Keywords: Discovery

In an employment discrimination suit, the Plaintiff filed a motion to compel the Defendant to produce computer-generated documents, instead of type-written documents that had been compiled by hand and had already been produced, reflecting the salaries of certain faculty members, who had been employed by the Defendant.

The Court stated that the inclusive description of documents was re-vised to accord with changing technology. The term "documents," for eviden-tiary purposes, applies to electronic data compilations, from which informa-tion can be obtained only with the use of detection devices, and that, when that data can, as a practical matter, be made usable by the discovering party only through the respondent's devices, the respondent may be required to use its devices to translate the data into usable form. In many instances, that means that the respondent will have to supply a printout of computer data. Similarly, if the discovering party needed to check the electronic source itself, the court could protect the respondent with respect to the preservation of its records, confidentiality of nondiscoverable matters, and costs. Simply put, the disclosing party must take reasonable steps to ensure that it discloses any backup copies of files or archival tapes that will provide information about any deleted electronic data.

The Court granted the Plaintiff's motion to compel to the extent that the Defendant had to disclose all data compilations, computerized data, and other electronically recorded information that reflected the salaries of the particular faculty employed by the Defendant, including but not limited to the computerized data and other electronically recorded information used by the

Defendant to compile the salary table and handwritten salary adjustment recommendations that had both previously been provided to the Plaintiff. Furthermore, the Court ordered that the parties preserve the evidence that they knew or should have known, was relevant to the ongoing litigation, including the preservation of all data compilations, computerized data, and other electronically recorded information.

## Case 245

United States District Court,
S.D. New York.

Laura ZUBULAKE, Plaintiff,

v.

UBS WARBURG LLC, UBS Warburg, and UBS AG, Defendants.

No. 02 Civ. 1243(SAS).
July 24, 2003.
216 F.R.D. 280, 92 Fair Empl.Prac.Cas. (BNA) 684, 56 Fed.R.Serv.3d 326

Jurisdiction: United States District Court, Southern District of New York

Date: July 24, 2003

Keywords: Cost and Cost Shifting, Discovery

In the first opinion handed down in the Zubulake case (*Zubulake I*), the Court had ordered the Defendant to perform a sample restoration and search of a few tape backups that contained potentially responsive e-mails to the Plaintiff's discovery request. This sample was performed, at the Defendant's expense, in order to determine that there were relevant e-mails on the backups, prior to then using the seven-part cost-shifting analysis. After the sample search was performed, both parties moved to have the other side bear the full expense of the full search and restoration of the tape backups.

Before beginning the analysis, the Court reiterated that cost shifting is only potentially appropriate when inaccessible data is being sought. After reviewing each of the seven factors, as applied to the facts of the case, the Court held that the first four factors cut against cost shifting, that factors five and six were neutral, and that factor seven cut in favor of cost shifting. The Court then held that, in light of the determination, some cost shifting would be appropriate, but that the Defendant would still pay for the majority of the restoration, as they would split the cost 75 percent to the Defendant and 25 percent to the Plaintiff.

Finally, the Court held that, when cost shifting is appropriate, it is only appropriate for the costs related to the restoration and searching the data to be shifted. Other costs, such as the review and production of the electronic data, once it has been restored, should always be borne by the responding party, because they have the means of controlling the review of the data, cost shifting is only appropriate for inaccessible data, and once the data has been restored, it is no longer inaccessible and should be produced at the responding party's expense, just as any other accessible data would be. Therefore, the Court ordered the Defendant to bear the full expense of any and all costs beyond the restoration and searching of the data from the backup tapes.

## Case 246

United States District Court,
S.D. New York.

Laura ZUBULAKE, Plaintiff,

v.

UBS WARBURG LLC, UBS Warburg, and UBS AG, Defendants.

No. 02 Civ. 1243(SAS).
October 22, 2003.
216 F.R.D. 280, 92 Fair Empl.Prac.Cas. (BNA) 684, 56 Fed.R.Serv.3d 326

Jurisdiction: United States District Court, Southern District of New York

Date: October 22, 2003

Keywords: Preservation of Evidence/Spoliation, Sanctions

In a continuing gender discrimination case fraught with electronic discovery issues, the question before the Court, in the latest motion, was how to determine an appropriate penalty for the party that caused the loss of documents, the Defendant, and conversely, how to determine an appropriate remedy for the party that was injured by the loss of the data, the Plaintiff. After ordering the restoration of backup tapes containing e-mails relevant to the Plaintiff's claims, the parties discovered that certain backup tapes were missing and that specific active e-mails had been deleted after the Defendant's document retention policy should have been in place.

The Plaintiff sought an order requiring the Defendant to pay, in full, the costs of restoring the remainder of the monthly backup tapes, an adverse inference instruction against the Defendant with respect to the backup tapes that were missing, and an order directing the Defendant to bear the costs of redeposing certain individuals concerning the issues raised in newly produced e-mails. The Court stated that the determination of an appropriate sanction for spoliation of evidence was confined to the sound discretion of the trial judge.

In making this determination, the Court noted that a party can only be sanctioned for destroying evidence, if it had a duty to preserve the evidence. This obligation arises when the party has notice that the evidence is relevant to litigation or when a party should have known that the evidence might be relevant to future litigation. The duty to preserve evidence concerns not only when it attaches but also what evidence it attaches to. Here, the duty to preserve began when relevant employees of the Defendant anticipated litigation.

A potential litigant is under the duty to preserve what it knows or reasonably should know is relevant in the pending action, including that which is reasonably calculated to lead to the discovery of admissible evidence or is reasonably likely to be requested during discovery, in addition to that which is the subject of a pending discovery request. The duty to preserve applies to all relevant documents that exist at the time the duty attaches and to any relevant documents created thereafter. The Defendant did not adequately preserve all of its evidence as was previously mentioned. In light of the Defendant's failed duty, the Court considered all three of the Plaintiff's motions, initially holding that reconsideration of the cost shifting order from *Zubulake III* would be inappropriate, because the evidence to be reconsidered had already been considered in the original cost shifting analysis.

The Court then held that an adverse inference jury instruction against the Defendant would also not be appropriate. The Court used a three-part sanction test for spoliation of evidence in considering whether or not to issue the adverse inference instruction. The party seeking a sanction must demonstrate that: (1) the party having control over the evidence had an obligation to preserve it at the time it was destroyed; (2) the records were destroyed with a "culpable state of mind"; and (3) the destroyed evidence was "relevant" to the party's claim or defense, such that a reasonable trier of fact could find that it would support that claim or defense. Destruction of evidence in bad faith is sufficient in and of itself to demonstrate relevance.

The Court had previously determined that the Defendant had a duty to preserve the evidence at the time it was destroyed. The Court found that the Defendant was merely negligent because, although the duty to preserve existed, the issue of preserving tape backups was still a gray area, and, therefore, it was understandable that a company might believe it could continue recycling its tape backups. Because the Defendant was merely negligent in the destruction, the Plaintiff still needed to prove that a reasonable trier of fact could find that the missing e-mails were not only relevant but that they also supported her claim. The Court held that the e-mails were relevant as they dealt with the issues of the litigation but that there was no evidence that the lost e-mails would be more likely to support the Plaintiff's claims. Therefore, the Court ruled that it would be inappropriate to give an adverse inference instruction to the jury.

Finally, although the Court found that the Defendant should not be sanctioned through an adverse inference instruction, it did hold that the Defendant should bear the costs for the Plaintiff to redepose certain witnesses for the limited purpose of inquiring into issues raised by the destruction of the evidence and any newly discovered e-mails.

## Case 247

United States District Court,
S.D. New York.

Laura ZUBULAKE, Plaintiff,

v.

UBS WARBURG LLC, UBS Warburg, and UBS AG, Defendants.

No. 02 Civ. 1243(SAS).
May 13, 2003.
217 F.R.D. 309, 91 Fair Empl.Prac.Cas. (BNA) 1574

Jurisdiction: United States District Court, Southern District of New York

Date: May 13, 2003

Keywords: Costs and Cost Shifting, Discovery

In hearing a gender discrimination case, the district judge established a seven-part multifactor cost-shifting analysis, to determine if and when cost shifting of discovery costs is proper. The Plaintiff's discovery request included responsive e-mails that could only be obtained by restoring tape backups from the Defendant. The Defendant sought the protection of the court, arguing that the process of restoring and producing the backups would be an undue burden and expense. The Court stated that cost shifting does not need to be considered in every case involving the discovery of electronic data because the presumption stands that the responding party will bear the expense of complying with discovery requests. Therefore, cost shifting should be considered only when electronic discovery imposes an undue burden or expense on the responding party. For electronic evidence, this burden can depend largely on the accessibility of the data requested. The Court then examined five categories of data accessibility, finding that the responsive data at issue in the case was of the second-most-inaccessible type, that found on a tape backup. It went on to state that the Defendant would have to engage in the costly and time-consuming process of backup restoration, in order to search for responsive e-mails on the backups. Therefore, the court determined that consideration of cost shifting was appropriate.

The Court and both parties addressed the existing Rowe eight-factor cost shifting test; however, the Court ruled that the Rowe factors too greatly favored cost shifting, because cost shifting was the outcome in every case that previously used this analysis. The Court stated that in order to maintain the presumption that the responding party should bear the costs of discovery, a cost-shifting analysis must be neutral. The Court then modified the Rowe test to create a seven-part test, as listed in descending order of importance:

1. The extent to which the request is specifically tailored to discover relevant information;
2. The availability of such information from other sources;
3. The total cost of production, compared to the amount in controversy;
4. The total cost of production, compared to the resources available to each party;
5. The relative ability of each party to control costs and its incentive to do so;
6. The importance of the issues at stake in the litigation; and
7. The relative benefits to the parties of obtaining the information.

The Court went on to order that a *McPeek* sample search be performed, to ensure that relevant e-mails would be located during a search of the backups, before actually applying a cost-shifting analysis.

## Case 248

United States District Court,
S.D. New York.

Laura ZUBULAKE, Plaintiff,

v.

UBS WARBURG LLC, UBS Warburg, and UBS AG, Defendants.

No. 02 Civ. 1243(SAS).

July 20, 2004.

2004 WL 1620866 (S.D.N.Y), 94 Fair Empl.Prac.Cas. (BNA) 1, 85 Empl. Prac.
December P 41,728

Jurisdiction: United States District Court, Southern District of New York

Date: July 20, 2004

Keywords: Sanctions, Preservation of Evidence/Spoliation

In the fifth opinion from the Court, the Plaintiff again moved to sanction the Defendant for failure to produce relevant information and for tardy production of such material. The Court was charged with answering whether the Defendant was responsible for said claims, and if so, did it act negligently, recklessly, or willfully in doing so? The issue raised addressed counsel's obligation to ensure that relevant information is preserved by giving clear instructions to the client to preserve such information and, perhaps more importantly, a client's obligation to heed those instructions. The dispute stemmed from many discoverable e-mails that were not produced to the Plaintiff for nearly two years, despite being responsive to an early document request, whereas other responsive e-mails were deleted and lost altogether. In addition, the Defendant's counsel played a role in these failures, as they failed to properly obtain certain information and safeguard other information. The central question that the Court considered was whether the Defendant's counsel took all of the necessary steps to guarantee that relevant data was both preserved and produced. If they did not, then the next question was whether the Defendant acted willfully in its failures. If it did, the Defendant was not only mentally culpable, but the material was inferentially relevant. If not, the Plaintiff had to show that the information was relevant. The Court noted that once a party reasonably anticipates litigation, it must suspend its routine document retention/destruction policy and put in place a litigation hold to ensure the preservation of relevant documents. Counsel must oversee compliance with the litigation hold, monitoring the party's efforts to retain and produce the relevant documents. Although there are no definitive requirements as to what must be done to satisfy the counsel's duty, it is not sufficient to notify all employees of a litigation hold and expect that the party will then retain and produce all relevant information. The Court found that, although counsel failed in its duties to enforce the litigation hold, the duty to preserve and produce documents primarily rests on the party.

Although more diligent action on the part of counsel would have mitigated some of the damage caused by the Defendant's actions and inactions, it was the Defendant itself who took such actions in defiance of counsel's explicit instructions. Therefore, the Defendant acted willfully in destroying potentially relevant information, which resulted either in the absence of such information or its tardy production. The Court held that the lost information would then be presumed relevant because the Defendant's spoliation had been deemed willful. As a result, the Court ordered that an adverse inference instruction be given to the jury in regard to the e-mails that were either deleted or irretrievably lost through recycling of the Defendant's backup tapes. Secondly, the Defendant was ordered to pay the costs for redeposing those involved with the e-mails that were produced late. Lastly, the Defendant was ordered to pay the costs of the motion.

## Case 249

United States District Court,
S.D. New York.

Laura ZUBULAKE, Plaintiff,

v.

UBS WARBURG LLC, UBS Warburg, and UBS AG, Defendants.

No. 02 Civ. 1243(SAS).
March 16, 2005.
2005 WL 627638 (S.D.N.Y), 95 Fair Empl.Prac.Cas. (BNA) 1194, 66 Fed. R. Evid. Serv. 969

Jurisdiction: United States District Court, Southern District of New York

Date: March 16, 2005

Keywords: Preservation of Evidence/Spoliation, Sanctions

The Defendants argued that the Court's previous decisions in the case, including the imposition of sanctions on the Defendant, were irrelevant to the Plaintiff's discrimination claims and would unfairly prejudice the Defendant. The Court agreed and remarked that placing the five previous decisions in the case before the jury would serve no legitimate purpose. The Court ordered that the Plaintiff could introduce correspondence between counsel on discovery matters if the Defendants opened the door by introducing evidence as to whether their failure to produce was reasonable. If the Defendant did not offer to prove that its failure to produce e-mails was justified, the Plaintiff would not be permitted to introduce any of the correspondence between counsel, in her case in chief.

# Table of Cases

**727**

# Index

# About the Authors

**Sharon D. Nelson** is the President of Sensei Enterprises, Inc., a computer forensics and legal technology firm located in Fairfax, Virginia. Ms. Nelson graduated from Georgetown University Law Center in 1978 and has been in private practice ever since. Her primary practice areas include technology and electronic evidence law. Ms. Nelson frequently writes and speaks on electronic evidence and legal information technology subjects. She is co-editor of the Internet newsletter *Bytes in Brief*® and co-author and co-editor of the book *Information Security for Lawyers and Law Firms* (ABA, 2006).

Ms. Nelson is the Past President of the Fairfax Bar Association, a Director of the Fairfax Law Foundation, and currently serves as Chair of the American Bar Association TECHSHOW® 2006 Board and on ARMA's e-Discovery Advisory Board. She is also a graduate of Leadership Fairfax and serves on the Virginia State Bar Mandatory Continuing Legal Education Board and the Virginia State Bar Special Committee on Law and Technology, and as the Chair of its Court Technology Subcommittee. She is a member of the Virginia Bar, the American Bar Association, the Virginia Bar Association, and the Fairfax Bar Association.

Ms. Nelson's contact information:

Sharon D. Nelson, Esq.
President, Sensei Enterprises, Inc.
3975 University Dr., Suite 225
Fairfax, VA. 22030
703-359-0700 (phone)
703-359-8434 (fax)
snelson@senseient.com (e-mail)

**Bruce A. Olson** is a shareholder in the Milwaukee-based law firm of Davis & Kuelthau, S.C., working from its Milwaukee and Green Bay offices. He is a trial lawyer concentrating his trial practice in the areas of commercial litigation, employment litigation, personal injury litigation, product liability litigation, environmental litigation, and insurance defense. Mr. Olson is AV rated in Martindale-Hubbell, and is a Board-Certified Civil Trial Specialist, having been certified by the National Board of Trial Advocates in 1997 and re-certified in 2002. He has tried more than sixty jury trials to verdict in either the Federal District Courts or the Circuit Courts of Wisconsin, and has handled appeals, including oral argument, at the Wisconsin Court of Appeals, the Wisconsin Supreme Court, and the 7th Circuit Court of Appeals.

Mr. Olson is also a nationally recognized legal technologist, focusing primarily on the areas of e-Discovery and litigation technology. He was the recipient of the prestigious "TechnoLawyer of the Year" in 2002, awarded by the TechnoLawyer Community. He is a Past-Chair of the American Bar Association TECHSHOW® Board, and has been a frequent speaker at the ABA TECHSHOW, and at various LegalTech presentations and State Bar-sponsored presentations throughout the United States. He has published articles in *Law Office Computing, Law Technology News, Law Firm Governance,* and other national publications. Mr. Olson is also a member of the newly established e-Discovery Advisory Group (EDAG) of the ARMA International. Prior to joining Davis & Kuelthau, S.C., Mr. Olson was President of ONLAW Trial Technologies, LLC, a legal technology consulting service, and he was the managing member of Olson Law Group, LLC.

Mr. Olson's contact information:

In Milwaukee, Wisconsin:

Bruce A. Olson
Davis & Kuelthau, S.C.
111 E. Kilbourn Ave., Suite 1400
Milwaukee, WI 53202-6613
414-276-0200
bolson@dkattorneys.com

In Green Bay, Wisconsin:

Bruce A. Olson
Davis & Kuelthau, S.C.,
318 South Washington St.
Green Bay, WI 54301
920-435-9378
bolson@dkattorneys.com

**John W. Simek** is the Vice President of Sensei Enterprises, Inc. He is an EnCase Certified forensic Examiner (EnCE). Mr. Simek has a national reputation as a computer forensics technologist and has testified as an expert witness throughout the United State.

Mr. Simek regularly writes and speaks on electronic evidence and legal information technology subjects. He is co-editor of the Internet newsletter *Bytes in Brief*® and co-author and co-editor of the book *Information Security for Lawyers and Law Firms* (ABA, 2006).

Mr. Simek holds a degree in engineering from the United States Merchant Marine Academy and an MBA in finance from Saint Joseph's University. After forming Sensei, he ended his 20+ year affiliation with Mobil Oil Corporation, where he served as a senior technologist troubleshooting Mobil's networks throughout the western hemisphere. Mr. Simek has in-depth experience with network troubleshooting, hardware and software implementations, systems integration, and logistical and financial expertise in a wide range of computer engineering designs and solutions. He has an extensive knowledge of multi-protocol environments and a diverse range of networking technologies.

In addition to his EnCase Certification (EnCE), Mr. Simek is a Certified Novell Engineer, Microsoft Certified Professional + Internet, Microsoft Certified Systems Engineer, NT Certified Independent Professional, a Certified Internetwork Professional and a Certified Trial Technologist. He is also a member of the High Tech Crime Network and of the International Information Systems Forensics Association as well as the American Bar Association. Mr. Simek is a member of the ABA TECHSHOW® Board. He currently provides information technology support to over 150 Northern Virginia law firms, legal entities, and corporations.

Mr. Simek's contact information:

John W. Simek
Vice President, Sensei Enterprises, Inc.
3975 University Dr., Suite 225
Fairfax, VA. 22030
703-359-0700 (phone)
703-359-8434 (fax)
jsimek@senseient.com

## The Lawyer's Guide to Effective Yellow Pages Advertising, Second Edition

*By Kerry Randall and Andru J. Johnson*

Although Yellow Pages advertising should be a major profit-building business marketing strategy for many law firms, the harsh reality is that most ads simply don't work. This book will provide you with the information you need to create effective, powerful Yellow Pages ads and drive your client development programs forward. You'll find information on identifying and focusing on your target market, as well as how to plan and design the perfect ad that not only reaches potential clients, but motivates them to call.

## The Lawyer's Guide to Balancing Life and Work, Second Edition

*By George W. Kaufman*

Updated and revised, this Second Edition is written specifically to help lawyers achieve professional and personal satisfaction in their career. Writing with warmth and seasoned wisdom, George Kaufman examines the roots of stress, including how the profession has changed over the last five years (what's better and what's worse), then offers philosophical approaches, practical examples, and valuable exercises to help lawyers reconcile their goals and expectations with the realities and demands of the legal profession. You'll find information on empowering yourself to take charge of your environment and how to achieve your plan for personal growth. Interactive exercises are provided throughout the text and on the accompanying CD, to help you discover how stress is affecting you. New lawyers, seasoned veterans, and those who have personal relationships to lawyers will all benefit from this insightful book.

## Compensation Plans for Law Firms, Fourth Edition

*Edited by James D. Cotterman, Altman Weil, Inc.*

In this newly revised and updated fourth edition, you'll find complete and systematic guidance on how to establish workable plans for compensating partners and associates, as well as other contributors to the firm. Discover how to align your firm's compensation plans with your culture, business objectives, and market realities. The book features valuable data from leading legal consulting firm Altman Weil's annual and triennial surveys on law firm performance and compensation, retirement, and withdrawal and compensation systems. You'll see where your firm stands on salaries and bonuses, as well as benefit from detailed analyses of compensation plans for everyone in your firm.

## Paralegals, Profitability, and the Future of Your Law Practice

*By Arthur G. Greene and Therese A. Cannon*

This is your essential guide to effectively integrating paralegals into your practice and expanding their roles to ensure your firm is successful in the next decade. If you're not currently using paralegals in your firm, you'll learn why you need paralegals and how to create a paralegal model for use in your firm—no matter what the size or structure. You'll learn how to recruit and hire top-notch paralegals the first time. If you are currently using paralegals, you'll learn how to make sure your paralegal program is structured properly, runs effectively, and continually contributes to your bottom line. Finally, eight valuable appendices provide resources, job descriptions, model guidelines, sample confidentiality agreements, sample performance evaluations, and performance appraisals. In addition, all the forms and guidelines contained the appendix are included on a CD-ROM for ease in implementation!

## The Lawyer's Guide to Marketing Your Practice, Second Edition

*Edited by James A. Durham and Deborah McMurray*

This book is packed with practical ideas, innovative strategies, useful checklists, and sample marketing and action plans to help you implement a successful, multi-faceted, and profit-enhancing marketing plan for your firm. Organized into four sections, this illuminating resource covers: Developing Your Approach; Enhancing Your Image; Implementing Marketing Strategies and Maintaining Your Program. Appendix materials include an instructive primer on market research to inform you on research methodologies that support the marketing of legal services. The accompanying CD-ROM contains a wealth of checklists, plans, and other sample reports, questionnaires, and templates—all designed to make implementing your marketing strategy as easy as possible!

## The Complete Guide to Designing Your Law Office

*By Suzette S. Schultz and Jon S. Schultz*

Here's the information you need to create an impressive, efficient law office that meets your business requirements. Learn the best approaches for designing every area in the law office, including offices and work stations, conference rooms and reception areas, and more. You'll be guided through every step of the process, from determining your optimal square footage, to selecting the right security systems and technology, to hiring and working with movers. In addition, helpful checklists, schedules, forms, and letters are included on an accompanying CD-ROM to make your renovation or relocation as easy as possible. For anyone contemplating a new or redesigned office, this is the book that covers all the details.

# 30-Day Risk-Free Order Form
## Call Today! 1-800-285-2221
### Monday–Friday, 7:30 AM – 5:30 PM, Central Time

| Qty | Title | LPM Price | Regular Price | Total |
|---|---|---|---|---|
| _____ | Compensation Plans for Law Firms, Fourth Edition (5110507) | $ 79.95 | $ 94.95 | $_____ |
| _____ | The Complete Guide to Designing Your Law Office (5110537) | 99.95 | 129.95 | $_____ |
| _____ | The Lawyer's Guide to Adobe® Acrobat®, Second Edition (5110529) | 49.95 | 59.95 | $_____ |
| _____ | The Lawyer's Guide to Balancing Life and Work, Second Edition (5110566) | 29.95 | 39.95 | $_____ |
| _____ | The Lawyer's Guide to Creating Persuasive Computer Presentations, Second Edition (5110530) | 79.95 | 99.95 | $_____ |
| _____ | The Lawyer's Guide to Effective Yellow Pages Advertising, Second Edition (5110538) | 54.95 | 69.95 | $_____ |
| _____ | The Lawyer's Guide to Extranets (5110494) | 59.95 | 69.95 | $_____ |
| _____ | The Lawyer's Guide to Fact Finding on the Internet, Third Edition (5110568) | 84.95 | 99.95 | $_____ |
| _____ | The Lawyer's Guide to Marketing on the Internet, Second Edition (5110484) | 69.95 | 79.95 | $_____ |
| _____ | The Lawyer's Guide to Summation (5110510) | 29.95 | 34.95 | $_____ |
| _____ | Paralegals, Profitability, and the Future of Your Law Practice (5110491) | 59.95 | 69.95 | $_____ |
| _____ | The Lawyer's Guide to Marketing Your Practice, Second Edition (5110500) | 79.95 | 89.95 | $_____ |

| *Postage and Handling | |
|---|---|
| $10.00 to $24.99 | $5.95 |
| $25.00 to $49.99 | $9.95 |
| $50.00 to $99.99 | $12.95 |
| $100.00 to $349.99 | $17.95 |
| $350 to $499.99 | $24.95 |

**\*\*Tax**
DC residents add 5.75%
IL residents add 9.00%

| | |
|---|---|
| *Postage and Handling | $_____ |
| **Tax | $_____ |
| TOTAL | $_____ |

## PAYMENT

❏ Check enclosed (to the ABA)

❏ Visa    ❏ MasterCard    ❏ American Express

Account Number    Exp. Date    Signature

Name _____ Firm _____
Address _____
City _____ State _____ Zip _____
Phone Number _____ E-Mail Address _____

## Guarantee
If—for any reason—you are not satisfied with your purchase, you may return it within 30 days of receipt for a complete refund of the price of the book(s). No questions asked!

**Mail: ABA Publication Orders, P.O. Box 10892, Chicago, Illinois 60610-0892**
**♦ Phone: 1-800-285-2221 ♦ FAX: 312-988-5568**

**E-Mail: abasvcctr@abanet.org ♦ Internet: http://www.lawpractice.org/catalog**